MUSLIM COMMUNITIES IN NORTH AMERICA

SUNY Series in Middle Eastern Studies
Shahrough Akhavi, Editor

MUSLIM COMMUNITIES IN NORTH AMERICA

edited by

YVONNE YAZBECK HADDAD

and

JANE IDLEMAN SMITH

State University
of New York
Press

Published by
State University of New York Press, Albany

© 1994 State University of New York

Production by Susan Geraghty
Marketing by Bernadette LaManna

Printed in the United States of America

For information, address State University of New York
Press, State University Plaza, Albany, N.Y., 12246

Library of Congress Cataloging-in-Publication Data

Muslim communities in North America / edited by Yvonne Yazbeck Haddad
    and Jane Idleman Smith.
        p.   cm. — (SUNY series in Middle Eastern studies)
    Includes bibliographical references (p.   ) and index.
    ISBN 0-7914-2019-1 (alk paper). — ISBN 0-7914-2020-5 (pbk. : alk
paper)
        1. Islam—United States. I. Haddad, Yvonne Yazbeck, 1935–
II. Smith, Jane Idleman, 1937–   . III. Series.
BP67.U6M86   1994
297'.0973—dc20   93-36564
                                                                         CIP

10   9   8   7   6   5   4   3   2

CONTENTS

CONTRIBUTORS

Miriam Adeney is an associate professor at Seattle Pacific University and adjunct professor at Regent College. She is the author of three books and numerous articles. Her research interests include Islam, women, ethnicity, oral media genres, and small-scale economic development.

Barbara C. Aswad is a professor of anthropology at Wayne State University in Detroit. She is the author of two books, *Property Control and Social Strategies: Settlers on a Middle Eastern Plain*, and *Arabic Speaking Communities in American Cities*, and numerous articles. She is a past president of the Middle East Studies Association of North America.

Barbara J. Bilgé is a lecturer in anthropology, sociology, and women's studies at Eastern Michigan University in Yspilanti, Michigan. Her published work includes "Toward a Theory of Ethnicity and Ethnic Groups," "Class, Ethnicity, and the Family in Contemporary Society," and "Islam in the Americas." She is coeditor of *American Muslim Families* (forthcoming).

Mehdi Bozorgmehr is currently a lecturer in the Department of Sociology and a postdoctoral fellow at the Institute for Social Science Research, University of California, Los Angeles. He has written numerous articles and book chapters on Middle Eastern immigrants in the United States, including Arabs, Armenians, and Iranians.

R. M. Mukhtar Curtis is a chaplain for the Muslim inmates at the Federal Correctional Institution in Milan, MI. He has a Ph.D. from the University of Michigan and is a researcher on African American Muslims in the United States.

Kathryn Teigen DeMaster has a degree in cross-cultural ministries and English from Seattle Pacific University. She has traveled extensively in Muslim countries and has collaborated on various projects with Miriam Adeney.

Marc Ferris was an instructor in history at the City College of New York and at Pace University. He is the author of "The Workingman's Party of Hampshire County, 1811–1835," has contributed to the forthcoming *Columbia Encyclopedia*, and is an assistant editor of the *Encyclopedia of New York City* (forthcoming).

Jonathan Friedlander is the assistant director of the UCLA Center for Near Eastern Studies. He is the writer and producer of the television documentary *Arabs in America*, the editor of *Sojourners and Settlers: The Yemeni Immigrant Experience*, and the associate editor of *Irangeles: Iranians in Los Angeles*. His current work deals with religion and identity in Brazil, India, Israel, and the United States.

Mattias Gardell is a researcher and lecturer at the Institute of Comparative Religion at the University of Stockholm. He has written extensively on Islam in the African American community including "Behold, I Make all Things New! Black Militant Islam and the American Apocalypse."

Marcia Hermansen is professor of Islamic studies and world religions at San Diego State University. Her research interests include Islamic thought in the premodern period, Islam in South Asia, women in Islam and Muslims in America.

Asad Husain is professor of political science and director of the Summer Institute of Islamic Studies at Northeastern Illinois University in Chicago. He is also president of the American Islamic College, founder of the Consultative Committee of Indian Muslims, Muslim community, Chicago, and of the Institute of Muslim Minority Affairs, King Abdul Aziz University, in Jeddah, Saudi Arabia.

Steve A. Johnson is an instructor of English and philosophy at Indiana University in Indianapolis. He is also adjunct instructor of Islamic studies at Christian Theological Seminary and of religion at the College of St. Francis. A former editor of *Islamic Horizons*, he is the author of numerous articles and a contributor to the book *Muslims in America*.

Ron Kelley holds a degree in anthropology from Michigan State University and an MFA in photography from the Department of Art at UCLA. He is the recent recipient of an Artist Grant from the Cultural Affairs Department of the City of Los Angeles and a Fulbright research grant for continued work on immigration to and from the Middle East. His works include *Irangeles: Iranians in Los Angeles* (1993). He is currently concluding a volume of his photographs and interviews of Muslims in Southern California.

Christine Kolars is currently working as a consultant in the field of international health care. She received a Master of Arts degree in Middle Eastern and North African Studies as well as a Master of Public Health degree in international health from the University of Michigan.

Mary Lahaj is an American Muslim of Lebanese descent, whose grandparents were founding members of the Islamic Center of New England, in Quincy, Massachusetts. She has a masters degree in Islam and Christian-Muslim relations from the Hartford Seminary, Hartford, Connecticut. She is currently a consultant and lecturer at universities and churches in New England.

Sheila McDonough is a professor of religion at Concordia University in Montreal. A graduate of the McGill Institute of Islamic Studies, she has taught for three years in a women's university in Pakistan. Her publications include *Muslim Ethics and Modernity: Jinnah Maker of Modern Pakistan*, and *The Authority of the Past*.

Yusuf Nuruddin is a faculty member in the Department of Social and Behavior Sciences at Medgar Evers College of the City University of New York. Born in the Bedford-Stuyvesant section of Brooklyn and educated at Columbia, Harvard, and Princeton Universities, he has been a practicing Sunni Muslim for nearly twenty years. He is the editor of *Timbuktu: A Journal of Contemporary African American Muslim Thought* (forthcoming).

Fariyal Ross-Sherif is professor of social work at Howard University in Washington, D.C. She has worked extensively with the Ismaili community in the United States.

Georges Sabagh is professor of sociology and director of the University of California Los Angeles Center for Near Eastern Studies. He has written extensively on the immigration of Middle Easterners to the United States and was coprincipal investigator of a National Science Foundation–funded study of Iranians in Los Angeles.

Abdulaziz Sachedina is a professor of religious studies at the University of Virginia. He is the author of *Islamic Messianism: The Idea of the Mahdi in Twelver Shi'ism* and *The Just Ruler in Shi'ite Islam: The Comprehensive Authority of the Jurist in Imamite Jurisprudence*.

Tamara Sonn is associate professor and director of International Studies at St. John Fisher University in Rochester, New York. She is the author of *Qu'ran and Crown*.

Frances Trix is assistant professor of anthropology at Wayne State University in Detroit. She has worked in Muslim communities in the Detroit area for many years and has recently seen published *Spiritual Discourse: Learning with an Islamic Master*, an analysis of a murshid-talib relationship, based on her twenty years of study with Albanian Muslim leader, Baba Rexhep.

Harold Vogelaar is a consultant on Christian-Muslim relations. He is scholar in residence at the Lutheran School of Theology in Chicago. He is working with the Reformed Church in America and with the Evangelical Lutheran Church in America.

Linda Walbridge holds a Ph.D. in anthropology from Wayne State University. She has conducted research among the Lebanese Shi'i community of Dearborn, Michigan, and the Ahmadiyya community in New York. She is currently an adjunct professor at Columbia University and assistant director of its Middle East Institute.

Gisela Webb is assistant professor in the Department of Religious Studies at Seton Hall University in South Orange, New Jersey, teaching in the areas of comparative religion and Islamic Studies. Her doctoral work was in classical Islamic philosophy and mysticism, and she has written in the areas of both medieval and contemporary Islamic spirituality. She is also author of *Readings in World Religions*.

PREFACE

Interest in the growth and development of a range of religious communities in America is currently very high, particularly in those that have their roots in non-Western cultures. The diversity of American culture is increasingly apparent in the wide variety of religious groupings and institutions that are flourishing in this country. Prominent among these is the community of Muslims, which is present on the American scene in a wide range of institutional and cultural manifestations as well as theological perspectives. The recent growth of the Muslim population in the United States and the ongoing efforts to organize religious communities to service members of the faith are drawing the attention of historians of religion, sociologists and others interested in the phenomenon of religion in America.

This volume of essays is not intended to be a comprehensive study of the different Muslim groups in America, but rather a sampling of the range and variety present among immigrants, African Americans and white converts to Islam. The volume is organized into three parts, each illustrating a different way in which community is understood. The first presents material about religious communities organized around specific doctrines or charismatic leadership. Community is thus defined by particularity of theology and practice. Here groups are treated such as the Shi'a, the Sufis, the sectarian movements of Louis Farrakhan and the Five Percenters and the Sunni Dar ul-Islam. The second part attempts to provide a general overview of the variety of groups that are located in a number of the major metropolitan areas of America. The third section provides descriptions of specific ethnic mosques and the way people from different parts of the world are faring in America. Included are such groups as Albanians, Turks, Pakistanis, Yemenis, Iranians, Lebanese, and African Americans. Community for these groups becomes equated with a mosque or center characterized by one particular ethnic or national identity.

Two major themes run through many of the essays in each of these sections. One is the issue of acculturation and the tensions communities experience as they try to accommodate to life in the American context. The other is the question of how to respond to the pressures currently being exerted by Islamists to conform to the concept of *umma*, community, as a unifying ideal over against the particularities of local ethnic and national identity.

The majority of Muslims in America do not identify in a regular way with any of these understandings of community, and are not active participants in the organized religious life of any mosque or Islamic center. Nonetheless they continue to identify themselves as Muslim, are responsive to the examples of prejudice against Islam that they experience in the American context, and may come together with fellow Muslims or compatriots for special occasions such as the celebration of *eids*, Muslim festivals. To this extent many of them in fact may be in contact on an occasional basis with the members of the particular groups and communities dealt with in this volume.

All of the essays contained here were solicited specifically for this volume, with the exceptions of those by Sachedina, Bilgé, and Nuruddin, which were delivered at the University of Massachusetts conference, The Muslims of America, in April 1989 at Amherst, Massachusetts.[1] The conference was funded by the National Endowment for the Humanities, the Department of Education, the Arabian American Oil Company, Mobiloil Corporation, and Five College Incorporated. The viewpoints and beliefs expressed by the papers presented at that meeting are those of the individual authors and do not necessarily reflect the opinions of the endowment.

Special gratitute is expressed to David Sawan and Alice Izer of the History Department at The University of Massachusetts and to Sylvia Roebuck of Iliff School of Theology for their technical assistance.

NOTE

1.   The proceedings of that conference, not including the three papers in this volume, were published as *The Muslims of America*, ed. Yvonne Y. Haddad (New York: Oxford University Press, 1991).

MUSLIM COMMUNITIES IN NORTH AMERICA: INTRODUCTION

Muslim communities in America have experienced a slowly emerging sense of identity framed by the cultural claims of the United States as well as by the growing awareness of, and identification with, the religion of Islam itself. Their history encompasses the experiences of a range of immigrant peoples over the past century as well as the different ways in which a large number of African Americans have chosen to identify as Muslim. This volume introduces readers to a variety of Islamic communities in America, immigrant and indigenous, Sunni and Shi'i, mainline and sectarian, some of whose members are prosperous and well-educated whereas others struggle to survive in economically marginal circumstances. The essays contained in it provide analyses of the ways in which both immigrant and African American Muslims are attempting to maintain their cultural, ethnic and religious identity in the context of a society in which such forms of identification are often extremely difficult and in which prejudice and misunderstanding in relation to Islam are longstanding and vibrant.

Early Muslim immigrants to this country began to come in the late 1800s, primarily from the Middle East. Usually young men with no intention of settling in America, they hoped to earn enough money in this country to be able to return to their countries of origin to establish homes and families. Opportunities for employment in America were hard to come by, however, and they found themselves working as migrant laborers, peddlers, and petty traders. Some decided to homestead in places such as Ross, North Dakota, home of one of the earliest Muslim settlements. Others ended up serving as cheap labor on work gangs, such as those in the Seattle area who were employed on the railroads. For many their dreams of returning home were as futile as their hopes of earning a fortune in the new land.

As Muslims settled in various parts of the country they began to establish permanent businesses such as small groceries, coffee houses, and restaurants. Some stayed for the explicit purpose of working in American factories and plants, like those employed by the Ford Motor Company in Dearborn, Michigan, and in the shipbuilding industry in Quincy, Massachusetts. Not surprisingly they looked to each other for comradeship in the context of American culture. They began to organize themselves for social interchange and for the maintenance of a sense of ethnic identity, enjoying cultural events such as folk dancing, religious festivals, and rites of passage rooted in the Middle East. For some, an important dimension of this attempt to maintain their identity came through corporate meetings to observe some of the basic elements of the Islamic faith. Even though this early generation of immigrants for the most part had not been mosque attenders in the Middle East and often were religiously illiterate, they nonetheless found in the common acknowledgment of their Islamic identity in America a bond for social cohesion.

Muslims who wanted to come together for religious observance in the early part of the century often found themselves at a loss for trained leadership. They looked to the few educated members of their communities for guidance, and many times had to rely on the volunteer services of persons untrained in the Islamic sciences to act as teachers or leaders of the prayer. In time even some of those who initially were uninterested in participating in any Islamic activities found their ideas changing as they settled, started families, and began to be concerned for the religious education of their children.

Soon the interest in providing a context for the observance and perpetuation of Islam became serious enough that a number of communities began to consider the importance of establishing a mosque in their area. To a significant degree this movement toward "institutionalization" also represented an attempt to legitimate their religion in the American context, particularly to Jews and Christians who locate themselves in churches and synagogues, as well as to form institutions parallel to those of their sister religious communities. They were able to incorporate some American practices within what they called a mosque setting. It was not that they were deliberately "Westernizing" the religion of Islam or creating a context of emancipation for its attendees, but that they had no models with which to work except what was already available in this culture. The construction of buildings to serve as mosques or Islamic centers began in the 1920s and 1930s; by 1952 there were over twenty mosques that joined in the formation of the Federation of Islamic Associations of America.

At the same time, during the early part of the century, that immigrants were finding ways in which to affirm their identity, a number of African Americans began to be attracted to one or more of the sectarian or separatist groups in this country claiming an identification with the religion of Islam. Moving from the cotton fields of the South to the ghettos of the North, they were motivated primarily by reasons of economics (many groups that claimed some kind of Muslim identity maintained platforms of economic advancement for blacks); of justice (reacting to continuing racism in America they found the egalitarian teachings of Islam particularly attractive); of identity and rootedness in a history, culture, and people from which they had been severed by the experience of slavery; and of rejection of Christianity, which they believed not only had provided the ideological justification for their enslavement but centered on the worship of Jesus depicted as a blue-eyed, fair-haired Caucasian man.

Movements such as the Moorish American Science Temple of Noble Drew Ali and the Nation of Islam of Elijah Muhammad provided Americans of African descent the means for affirmation of black identity and advancement in the face of white oppression under a loose rubric of what were claimed to be Islamically oriented beliefs and practices. From these movements grew a range of other African American groups professing affiliation with Islam, some sectarian such as the Ansaar Allah and the Five Percenters, and others Sunni groups such as the Dar ul-Islam, the Islamic Party of North America, the Islamic Brotherhood, Inc., and the Hanafi Movement. The relationship of these groups to communities of immigrant Muslims has been minimal, although more recently increased efforts have been made at conversation and cooperation. After 1975 Warith Deen gradually changed the sectarian, racist, and separatist teachings of his father Elijah Muhammad in the Nation of Islam to parallel the orthodoxy and orthopraxy of Sunni Muslims. Relations have been cordial between the followers of Warith Deen and Sunni Muslims, although full integration has not yet been realized.

After the middle of this century there were significant changes in the numbers of immigrant Muslims coming to America as well as in the circumstances under which they emigrated. Those arriving in the 1950s and 1960s from the Middle East were primarily committed to Arab socialism and nationalism and were basically secular in orientation. The organizations that they formed here tended to emphasize Arab culture and the politics of the Middle East rather than the religion of Islam. With the changes in immigration laws that altered the quota system and allowed for the admission of immigrants from Asia during the administration of President Lyndon Johnson, the situation changed dramatically. Qualified people came from many areas of the world, especially Southeast Asia, contributing heavily to what has become known as the brain drain in that area.

With the influx of this new group of educated and professionally oriented immigrant Muslims, and with the availability of funds from Arab states interested in the growth of Islam in America, a second wave of mosque building flourished in the 1970s, which has continued to the present and shows every sign of increasing despite the cessation of overseas support. Muslims seek an outward and visible symbol of their faith such as that provided in the structure of the mosque, which is both a formal context for worship and a center for the communal gathering of its members. A variety of issues are involved in building a mosque. What are the appropriate functions of the building? How should it be financed if borrowing from a bank involves the Islamically prohibited paying of interest? What is appropriate dress for men and women when attending the mosque? How can the administration of the mosque be organized so as to accommodate different racial and ethnic communities and their distinctive cultural preferences? These and other issues are addressed in the essays that follow. Despite these concerns both the construction of Islamic buildings and the formation of new organizations has continued apace; by 1992 there were over 2300 Islamic institutions in North America including mosques, schools, community centers, publishing houses, and media programming units.

Because early immigrants to this country had very limited skills in English and because of the chain migration that followed bringing members of ethnic groups to be with their compatriots in America, the early mosque communities tended to be ethnically oriented—Arab, Albanian, Tartar Russian, Turkish, Circasian, Yugoslav, and many others. With changes in the immigration laws of the 1960s, new immigrants have been coming from many more places in the world, representing much more diversity. This has further complicated the difficult task of finding some way in which to determine a basis of unity and Islamic identity in an already very diverse American Muslim community.

In the latter half of this century several factors have been influential in determining the character of Muslim life in America. In the 1960s there was a significant influx of Muslim students committed to the new Islamist ideologies of Egypt and Pakistan. These students had a significant impact on the "Islamization" of Muslim communities. Representing organizations such as the Muslim Brotherhood of Egypt and the Jamaati Islami of the Indo-Pakistani subcontinent, they brought with them a very different concept of community than had developed among the immigrants in America, namely, the idea of the *umma* as articulated by Sayyid Qutb and Mawlana Mawdudi.[1] With a prescriptive definition of what community means, they were often shocked and dismayed by what they found happening in mosques and Muslim groups in this country. In addition, and probably more important, their ideology was a reaction not only to what they saw going on in the American scene but also to what was taking place across the Islamic world as a result of the "modernization" (liberalization, secularization, Westernization) of Muslim society. They therefore set about trying to experiment in forming idealistic communities, at times attempting to impose their response to Western influences in Islamic countries on Muslims in America.

Local communities here, on the one hand, were eager to learn from these educated and Islamically articulate students. On the other hand, they found that some of the things being told to them, at times forced upon them, were too extreme for their liking and unnecessary or even counterproductive in the American context. These tensions have continued both between student and local groups, and between some of the more recent immigrants who are advocates of the conservative Islamist ideology and those who have been longer in this country and are more comfortable with the general acculturation that has taken place.

Another reality that has impinged on the lives of American Muslims has been the interest of oil-rich countries as well as wealthy Muslim individuals in the welfare of Muslims living as minorities in various areas of the world. This has resulted in the donation of considerable funds for the construction of mosques and Islamic centers in this country since the early 1970s, inevitably bringing the influence of the donors to bear on the thinking and directions taken by the recipients.

A number of factors come to play in the decision of some Islamic groups to forego the ideal of an integrated community in favor of continuing, or establishing anew, what are clearly ethnic mosques or centers. One obviously is numbers. When the group is small and living in proximity it is necessary to find ways in which to worship together without distinctions. When there are enough Arabs or Pakistanis or Slavs or whatever, one has a critical mass representing a specific language and cultural group. Another factor is generational. When there is a kind of chain migration with the parents and relatives of Muslims already in this country coming without facility in English, there is a strong demand for a unit in which they can feel comfortable speaking their own tongue and enjoying their own customs. It is also the case that there are clear cultural and even theological differences among groups from different parts of the world; many of these play themselves out especially in the ways in which holidays are celebrated as well as in consideration of appropriate functions of the mosque. Issues such as whether or not a man should wear a hat during prayer or whether women can be elected to mosque executive committees have inevitable consequences for the sense of unity among ethnically diverse peoples.

The tensions that exist around acculturation continue to engage Muslims in America. What is the heritage that is going to be passed on to the children? Are they going to be taught to live as Muslims in an alien society, or are they going to be integrated as Americans who happen to be Muslim? These and other issues to be examined in this book come to bear on decisions whether to put the ideal unity of Islam above sectarian or ethnic differences or whether to acknowledge that Islam is made up of different peoples, groups, and ideologies that must be allowed to maintain their individuality.

The relationship of immigrant and African American Muslims continues to be a significant issue in this country. Over the course of this century Muslims from overseas have made a few notable efforts to reach African Americans. The Ahmadiyya missionary movement of Pakistan has actively recruited Americans of African descent into its fold since the early 1900s. W. D. Fard, whose exact ethnic identity remains unknown (he was probably either Turkish or Iranian), served as the inspiration for the beginning of the Nation of Islam under Elijah Muhammad. A number of articles in this volume reflect the initial as well as the continuing impact of the ideology of the Nation of Islam on African American Muslim groups. More recently the Pakistan-based Tableeghi Jamaat has had extensive operations in some urban areas of America.

The African American Muslim community for its part has proved to be influential in several ways on the immigrant Muslims. African Americans have challenged immigrants both to be stricter in their observance of Islamic laws and practices, such as abstention from alcohol and pork products, and to abide by the Islamic ideal of genuine racial equality. Many times African Americans initially have been attracted to Islam because of that ideal and then deeply disappointed that it is not always realized. African Americans also have insisted on adopting and keeping Islamic names. Students coming from overseas in the 1960s expressed their horror that many immigrant Muslims had chosen to anglicize their names or simply discard them for something more American sounding. African Americans, on the other hand, have been diligent in their insistence that to be Muslim means to accept the identity that comes with a new name, that to be American does not mean one has to look and sound like members of the Judeo-Christian majority.

In some cases immigrants have exhibited great curiosity about African American Muslims, particularly in the ghetto areas of the cities. In places such as Rochester and Los Angeles that has taken the form of concrete efforts to reach out to the African American community. Rarely are African American and immigrant communities integrated, although several mosques in this country serve both groups. On the whole, however, there has been and continues to be minimal social contact between immigrants and African American Muslims, even for worship or sharing in holidays and celebrations. As Christine Kolars remarks in relation to the two groups in the Hudson Valley of New York, on the one hand, first- and second-generation immigrants are struggling with what it means to be American; on the other hand, African Americans are adjusting to a new identity as first- or second-generation Muslims. Many of the latter continue to wonder if the inclusiveness of Islam really means that their immigrant sisters and brothers welcome them into the fold. They question why some of the immigrants seem to be less concerned with matters of dress and other outward symbols of Islamic identification than they feel themselves to be, at the same time that they resent being excluded from community participation for reasons of not knowing Arabic or not having access to culturally defined practices. Many immigrant Muslims, on the other hand, question whether some of the African American groups, especially sectarian movements or the Nation of Islam under Farrakhan, are Islamic at all. Several of the studies in this volume point to the resentment African Americans feel if they are not recognized by immigrants as "real" Muslims or when they perceive immigrant organizations such as the Islamic Society of North America (ISNA) to be dictating to them while restricting their participation.

One of the issues that has faced immigrant Muslims in America is that of relating as a community of orthodoxy, however that might be defined, to groups that claim Islamic identity but have developed in ways that depart from what is understood as the essence of that orthodoxy and in some cases make little reference to Islam except to use certain Islamic terminology. In some African American groups, for example the Nation of Islam and the Five Percenters, racism is an acknowledged part of their doctrine. This is difficult for Muslims who believe in the egalitarian principles of Islam to accept. Some of these African American groups are dealing with problems and issues that are different from the concerns of immigrants. Indigenous Muslims are often driven to formulate their ideologies to address the socioeconomic problems that they have experienced in America, while those with ties overseas may be more interested in international political concerns and developments in places like Palestine, Kashmir, Bosnia, and the like. African American sectarian movements often emphasize their distinctiveness as defined over against American culture as part of their long-standing efforts to achieve parity in a country that has consistently relegated them to second-class status. Immigrant communities, on the other hand, tend to stress the similarities between the dominant teachings of Islam and those of Christianity and Judaism. Generally eager to be accepted as full citizens, they try to acknowledge those elements of their faith that underscore commonality and help open doors to full participation in American society.

It is clear from this study of different Muslim communities in America that the goal of an Islamic unity, regardless of the strength of that ideology, is subject to enormous strains. Most students of religion, and especially sociologists, acknowledge that culture is indeed a component of religion. For many communities in this country the primary concern today is how not to compromise the ideal of unity in Islam while still maintaining some degree of ethnic identity and cultural affiliation. They struggle with ways in which to create an Islamic culture that is not necessarily "local", that is, determined by the cultural trappings of any particular geographical area of the world (Arab, Pakistani, Iranian, or whatever). "The extraordinary ethnic, cultural, and racial diversity of Muslims in Los Angeles," says Ron Kelley by way of example, "poses critical challenges to the desired model of dedicated communal unity." The task as some see it is to allow for a culturally pluralistic Islam that is not at the same time an ideologically pluralistic Islam. In general Muslims agree on ideological issues, with the exception in some cases of the Shi'a. But Islam is primarily a religion of orthopraxy, in which minor differences of practice have developed along cultural lines in different geographic areas according to the teachings of the four schools of law. Some Muslims in America are raising the question of what a deculturalized Islam might actually be, and whether or not it is a goal important enough to warrant the sacrifice of different ethnic and cultural interpretations.

Concerns over matters of acculturation, then, are among the most commonly raised in the studies represented in this volume. How does a second- and third-generation Muslim community that has adapted in significant ways to American culture respond to the challenges offered by the presence of newer immigrants representing a more conservative ideology or by the addition of an Islamically trained and often more legalistic Imam? The lack of an American-raised, American-oriented Muslim leadership, necessitating the use of untrained lay leaders, has led some to feel that it is essential to bring to this country more Imams trained overseas. The tensions between a leadership that affirms an Islam incubated in a different country and the growing community that has adjusted to American realities can be severe.

Some of the Imams from overseas are financed by and thus accountable to foreign countries and tend to preach according to those interests. Muslim communities in America often find it difficult to express to foreign Imams that they are American Muslims with a special understanding of Islam that is different from that fostered by Saudi Arabia or other Islamic countries. This brings to the forefront the issue of having to choose between conformity to a single interpretation of Islam, that which some would want to say is Arab Islam, or acknowledging and honoring the pluralism that indeed seems to be a reality in this country. If it is the latter that is most highly valued, to what extent is that an impediment to the cohesion of the Muslim community? The difficulties some overseas Imams have understanding the real issues and problems of American Muslims are raised in a number of the essays to follow.

One of the problem areas in community building identified by several of these authors is the reality of class and economic differences. To a certain extent this pertains among the immigrants themselves. A substantial number of the earlier immigrants tended to be from rural areas, less well-educated and economically less well-off than is generally the case with the more recent immigrants who are often highly educated and occupy high-level professional positions. Economic and class distinctions are even more obvious between immigrants and African Americans, which in some cases serves to underscore the frustration of blacks who look to Islam as an answer to the continuing experience of economic (as well as social) marginalization that they experience in the American context.

The matter of Sunni-Shi'i relations is the focus of a number of essays, as well as the role that Shi'is sometimes see themselves to be playing as a "minority within a minority," as Abdulaziz Sachedina describes it. Only fairly recently have Shi'i communities experienced a sense of their own separate identity in the context of Islam in America as well as an awareness on the part of the American public of their distinctiveness, primarily because of events in Iran and Lebanon. This, of course, is painful insofar as they become identified in the American mind with extremism and violence. One of the interesting recent developments within the Shi'i community is the increase in the numbers of African Americans who are converting to Shi'i Islam and joining these communities, to which several authors in this volume make reference.

Living in America has brought many changes to immigrant groups. Some of those changes occur through the involvement of women in the community. In the Middle East women seldom even attend the mosque, let alone take a prominent role in its activities. Although their emergence as involved participants in mosque organizations in this country varies according to country of origin, in some cases it has been real and crucial for the formation and maintenance of the organization. In some communities they function much as women have functioned for generations in Christian churches, preparing bake sales, running bazaars, and holding luncheons and dinners. Like their Christian sisters, however, some are also venturing into roles of leadership within the mosque organizations and are active in forming groups specifically for Muslim women. Others on university campuses are contributing to the effort of helping non-Muslim Americans better understand the religion of Islam. Still others are involved in providing Islamic education for the young or debating issues of dress for women.

A number of other themes emerge in the studies presented here, among them the attempts made by a number of Muslim leaders to initiate and foster interfaith communication and dialogue; the relation of Sufi communities to other Islamic groups in America; political differences determined by ideologies, events, and sources of funding coming from other parts of the Islamic world; and the strains of trying to keep Muslim youth involved in the community and responsive to its values and of providing a context in which the elderly can feel wanted in the American environment that tends to foster loneliness, depression and alienation. Virtually all of these studies underscore the fact that one of the significant motivating factors in the communities under consideration is the necessity of understanding their identity and role within American society and culture in the context of a long-standing and continuing atmosphere of prejudice and misunderstanding. From such obvious things as continuing government surveillance of the Nation of Islam and Arab Americans, and the recent verbal and physical assaults on mosques and groups as a result of international events, to the more subtle but continuing "micro-moments of racism" experienced in their daily lives, Muslims see evidence of the realities that face them as they struggle to live as persons of faith and integrity in what is an alien and often hostile environment.

Muslims in America are increasingly aware of the fact that they are in the business of building community. Originally they were content simply to find other Muslims with whom to share the concerns they had about being Muslim in the American context. Those associations have served to provide a haven against the hostility they often experienced. But they have come to realize that the fact that people have in common an identity as Muslim does not automatically ensure community. The current effort to determine what, if anything, binds Muslims together in a whole may be unique to this country and is an experiment that is multifaceted. The key to understanding how to come to terms with it is in the recognition that diversity runs in a number of different directions. There is diversity between the recently arrived and the third- and fourth-generation immigrants, between immigrants and American-born Muslims, between rural and urban people, between members of the working and the professional classes. There are differences between student communities and those who have decided to settle permanently in America. This is seen especially when the children of those who have settled grow older and their focus is more specifically on America whereas that of the students and recent immigrants is still on overseas concerns. And of course there are the vast cultural differences already noted among those who come from a variety of different countries and areas of the world.

Given all of these distinctions how are Muslims today organizing to create community and underscore the things they do hold in common? One way is through a strong emphasis on maintaining Islamic values and ideals through the educational system, both in Sunday schools and in day schools. Many Muslims feel that they should organize and even build their own schools so that their children can be Islamically educated as well as protected from the influences and possible dangers of American society. Even when there is consensus on the importance of such schools, however, it is often difficult to achieve agreement as to what constitutes an appropriate Islamic education. In many cases it is African American rather than immigrant Muslims who opt for parochial school education for their children.

Other ways are also underscored as opportunities for creating Islamic community. Considerable literature is being developed in the English language that supports a de-ethnicized Islam with a universal creed and base. Annual conventions are held to provide a special sense of participation in a large group sharing ideas and experiences. This kind of group experience has proved to be empowering in the sense of communal identity with its emphasis on unity despite the variety of individual participants. Many areas are making special efforts to hold common meals and celebrations around Islamic holidays to try to replicate the sense of community experienced in countries where there is little ethnic diversity. Sharing a common meal brings a feeling of participating in an extended family within the context of American society. This is seen as particularly important for Muslim children as they experience their own sense of belonging to a community clearly defined by its Islamic identity.

In general the new mosque and center communities have attempted to reconstitute themselves into self-consciously more Islamic and less ethnically stylized organizations. That such an effort can be made is due to the fact that more recent immigrants to this country are educated in English and can communicate with Muslims from other areas. (There are, of course, significant exceptions to this, such as the Yemenis and Shi'ite Lebanese in Dearborn, Michigan, discussed later.) These attempts at more pluralistic Islamic centers also have reflected the ideology that became dominant in the 1970s and 1980s in which the bond of the brotherhood of Islam is seen to transcend all racial, ethnic and color differences. That this idea of a pluralistic rather than an ethnic mosque community is a major challenge, however, will be well illustrated in the articles to follow.

It is perhaps inevitable that Muslim communities in America to some degree will adapt, accommodate, and acculturate to the realities of existence in the American context. What seems evident from the studies in this volume is that Muslims are, in fact, both understanding of the need for this kind of adaptation and creative in finding ways in which to make it happen while still remaining true to their understanding of what it means to be Muslim. As Sheila McDonough writes of the Muslims in Montreal, "There seems every reason to suppose that the vitality the Muslim people of this city exhibit and express will give birth to new forms of Muslim existence in this distinctive setting." That the Muslim presence in America is real, vibrant, and growing is now quite apparent. How that presence is acknowledged by the rest of America's citizens will undoubtedly color the ways in which Muslims themselves understand their role as members of American society as well as of the larger community of Islam. The extent to which the racial-ethnic, cultural, and socioeconomic distinctions that exist within and among the Muslim communities in this country will be seen either as divisive in the task of identifying an overall unity or healthy, natural, and creative to the life of the whole will be the agenda for the ongoing deliberations of Muslims as they continue to forge their identity in the American context.

NOTE

1. The idea that there is an Islamic identity that is the central bond for the *umma* or community has been a major theme in the development of Islamic revivalism. The late Ismail Al-Faruqi was prominent in the call of the Islamic Society of North America for an emphasis on what he termed the *ummatic* ideal. Revivalist Muslims today are calling for a community that transcends language and geographical units in the common bond of belief.

PART 1

Religious Communities

CHAPTER 1

A Minority Within a Minority:
The Case of the Shi'a in North America

Abdulaziz A. Sachedina

Within the context of the general study of Muslim communities the question of the "minority within a minority" in North America is of particular importance. Immigrant Muslims have been preoccupied with ensuring the survival of the Islamic population as a whole insofar as they perceive it to be threatened by the non-Muslim majority in this country. Therefore they have tended to avoid such issues as might suggest "dissensions" among Muslims in the Western context. Sunni sensitivity to the matter of division within the community derives from the effort they have always made to demonstrate to their host countries that Muslims are a community united under the teachings of Islam, particularly as preserved by the majority of the community who identify with Sunni Islam.

Perhaps in part as a result of these efforts, Islam and Muslims in the Western context in general and in the North American setting in particular tend to be viewed quite monolithically. In fact, however, diversity among Muslims is evident in a variety of ways, from different national and cultural groupings—even among Arabs—to the various schools of thought to which Muslims belong. Nationality, culture and sectarian affiliation in turn influence the religious practices of both Sunnis and Shi'is (also designated Shi'a).[1] Moreover, the complexity of theological and practical religious differences among the immigrant Muslim community has been virtually incomprehensible not only to outside observers but also to many Muslims, who in their native countries have belonged

3

to and thus been familiar with one particular school of thought. Only in fairly unusual cases—such as in Iraq, Lebanon, Pakistan and India—have Muslims acknowledged the existence of other minority Muslim groups within the majority. In some areas, such as Saudi Arabia, it has been in the interest of the government to deny the existence of the Shi'i minority within its borders to give an impression of a factionless Muslim society.

In many cases the governments of Middle East countries have exercised considerable influence in the United States over the immigrant Sunni community by providing members with badly needed financial assistance to set up Islamic centers and other such organizations, with the aim of preserving the Islamic characteristics of the minority in North America. These very efforts, however, many times have tended to obscure adequate recognition of the vibrant Shi'i Muslim minority that is equally engaged in providing religious centers and facilitating systems of organization to protect the Islamic identity of its members. Even the academic enterprise has been remiss; until recently little acknowledgment was made of Shi'i realities or information provided about Shi'i communities in this country in conferences and studies on Islam in the American context.[2]

Only in the last decade or so have Shi'is in North America been accorded significant recognition. The obvious reason for this, of course, is the success of the Islamic revolution in Iran, followed by Shi'i activism in Lebanon in the aftermath of the Israeli invasion of 1983 and the death of the 241 Marines in Beirut at the hands of a Shi'i group. These events in Iran and Lebanon, in addition to the Iran-Iraq war which was reduced by both the Western press and the Arab nationalists to a Sunni-Shi'i and Arab-Persian struggle, fostered a negative image of the Shi'is and a lack of understanding or appreciation of their demands for justice in the context of Islamic ideals and aspirations.

The largest subdivision of the Shi'i community is known as the Ithna 'Ashariyya or Twelvers. They believe that there were twelve successive Imams from among the male descendents of the Prophet Muhammad (d. 632 A.D.) who provided legitimate leadership to the Islamic community. The last of these twelve Imams, according to Shi'i belief, disappeared in the tenth century. Shi'is expect that he will return at the end of time as their messianic deliverer, the Mahdi, who will create a rule of justice and equity on earth. In the meantime they acknowledge the religious leadership of their scholars (*mujtahids*, also known as ayatollahs) who continue to guide the community in mundane as well as spiritual affairs. It is with this group, also known as the Imamiyya or simply Shi'a, that this essay is concerned.[3]

We are not sure exactly when the early Shi'i immigrants began to settle in North America, nor do we know much about the life of those who did come. Immigration records are unhelpful as they fail to designate sectarian affiliation, and we have no written sources compiled or maintained by the Shi'i families in North America to give us definite word on the background of the community. Their history on this continent still needs to be written.

It seems reasonable to assume, considering the numbers of Muslims who emigrated in the late nineteenth and early twentieth centuries, that some Shi'i families from India and Lebanon settled here well before the middle of this century, although the appearance on the American scene of a significant well-educated and professional Shi'i middle class is a comparatively recent phenomenon.[4] We know, for example, through oral history transmitted by second- and third-generation families from Hyderabad, India, now residing in Toronto, that there was in this period an annual commemoration of the martyrdom of Hussein b. 'Ali, grandson of the Prophet Muhammad and third Imam of the Shi'a.[5] This clearly points to the existence of some kind of Shi'a community; it seems highly likely that any members able to do so would have made every effort to come together for these annual devotional meetings. (We should note in this connection, however, the research of Abdolmaboud Ansari indicating that a sense of religious cohesiveness and identity among Iranian immigrants in the United States is a recent phenomenon, dating specifically from the time of the Iranian revolution of 1978–1979.)[6]

The Muslim Student Association, Persian Speaking Group (MSA/PSG) came into existence at the time of the Iranian revolution. Since then other student groups have been formed, including those of Shi'i Arabs from Iraq, Lebanon, and the Persian Gulf region. Their organizations, like the MSA/PSG, are located in the context of university student administration. They cater mainly to the religious interests of Shi'i students and their immediate families, with only marginal concern for immigrant Shi'i families. A number of these students have chosen for personal or political reasons to reside permanently in the United States. Both the Iranian revolution and the deterioration of the economic situation in the aftermath of the Iran-Iraq war have discouraged a number of highly qualified and conscientious students from returning to Iran. Some of them, especially members of the PSG, have married American women who would find it difficult to go to Iran and follow the strict moral codes introduced under the "Islamization" program there with regard to the role of a Muslim woman in modern society. The circumstances of Shi'i student bodies are varied and interesting, but it is more with immigrant Shi'i communities in the North American context that this study is concerned.

It is certain that by the 1950s there were small clusters of Shi'i families in some of the major cities of Canada and the United States. We know through the memoires of community religious leaders of the existence of certain families who participated in the annual religious observances during the month of Muharram. It is probably the case that other Shi'is were also present although they did not participate in these annual commemorations. If one takes into account what we know about these immigrants and their families, plus statistics on newly arriving Iranians and (in smaller numbers) Iraqi and Lebanese Shi'is, it is reasonable to estimate that today Shi'is make up at least 30 percent of the total Muslim population of North America.

The traditional religious structure of the community plays an important role in the functioning of Shi'i life in this country. As was indicated, the Imams from among the descendents of the Prophet are regarded as the sole leaders of the Muslim community. In the absence of the twelfth Imam al-Mahdi, religious scholar-jurists, known as *mujtahids*, are acknowledged as his deputies and spokesmen in directing the spiritual and social activities of their followers. Since the nineteenth century the Twelver Shi'a community around the world has recognized the centralized leadership of *mujtahids* centered mainly in the Shi'i holy cities of Iraq and Iran.[7] This institution of religious leadership has developed into a powerful, highly centralized authority called the *marja' al-taqlid*, or *marja'iyya*. Technically this means "the most learned juridical authority in the Imamiyya community whose rulings on the Shari'a are followed by those who acknowledge him as such and commit themselves to base their religious practice in accordance with his judicial opinions." It has provided a sense of unity as well as of direction in all matters pertaining to the living of a religio-moral life for the Shi'a since the time of the twelfth Imam's occultation. The institution of *marja'iyya* has remained independent of any government control because it depends solely on revenues derived from the religious tax of *al-khums* (the fifth) paid by Shi'is for the maintenance of religious institutions administered by the *marja' al-taqlid*. The latter authorizes the manner in which *khums* contributions are to be allocated to various religious projects in the Shi'a community.

In North America, *khums* revenues provide for the construction of Islamic centers as well as for the salaries of religious preachers and teachers who cannot be supported by other community-generated revenues such as annual dues. The *khums* in the Shi'i community therefore has been important for the independence of Shi'i centers from outside interference. Moreover, the preachers supported by this fund have found themselves in a better position to exert their autonomy in relation to the communities they serve in their capacity as religious guides and teachers.

It is especially important for the Shi'is in North America that the independent nature of the *marji' al-taqlid* and the self-generated and self-managed financial structure of the Shi'i religious organization has made it possible for the community to organize its affairs independent of the control of Muslim governments in the Middle East or anywhere else. Thus the political or religious problems of some of the Islamic centers funded by such countries as Saudi Arabia or Libya do not exist for the Shi'i community. Much of this independence is a direct result of the pioneer immigrants and their attachment to their religious heritage. Their desire to transmit this legacy to succeeding generations has been the driving force in their efforts to maintain institutions necessary for the preservation of their identity in an alien environment. The appointment by the *marja' al-taqlid* of financial and religious deputies (*wukala'*) among the trusted community members has inspired the necessary confidence among individual members to contribute toward their spiritual well-being and has generated the incentive to engage in major projects such as the construction of Islamic centers and facilities for religious education considered necessary for the continued prosperity of the Shi'a community in North America.

Thus far it has not been possible for the various Shi'a groups from around the world to come together as a single community in

North America, however, and problems of cultural diversity have been significant in affecting fundamental religious attitudes. The uniting factor within individual groups often seems to be a common language and national ties rather than religious affiliation as such, making efforts to create a federation of Shi'a communities under a single leadership marginal or largely ineffective. One such attempt to unite the Shi'a immigrants of Asian origin, mainly from East Africa, has resulted in the formation of what is called the North American Shi'a Ithna-Asheri Muslim Communities (NASIMCO). Some seventeen communities (*Jama'*at), approximately 6000 individuals, are members. This organization, whose secretariat is located in Toronto, is responsible for providing necessary religious guidance through regular contact with Shi'i centers of learning in Iran and Iraq, as well as financial support for capital projects undertaken by individual member communities. Primary sources of funding for NASIMCO supported projects are individual donations and a portion of the religious tax of the *khums* authorized by the *marja' al-taqlid*. In recent years some non-East African Shi'i groups have also joined NASIMCO in order to benefit from its financial and religious resources.

Evidence of cultural regionalism can also be seen in the celebrations of the commemoration of Muharram, with devotions carried out in local vernacular rather than in English, the language common to Muslims living in the North American context. Cultural differences have made it difficult for the leadership committed to the vision of a new North American Islamic community to create a common agenda for directing the lives of its members. Diverse linguistic and cultural backgrounds increasingly seem to have assumed importance, and the universal message of the Islamic creed to have given way to "regionalism" and "exclusivism" among the Shi'is.

Ironically, one of the main obstacles to the creation of a primary allegiance to universal Islam has been the religious leadership of preachers imported from abroad who, because they do not know English sufficiently well, teach and preach in their local tongues. Iranian Shi'a listen to Persian-speaking preachers, while those from the subcontinent of India and Pakistan have their worship led in Urdu. Although community leaders have adopted English as the administrative language of their respective groups, the use of other tongues for preaching and teaching has given rise to dual communal leadership with clear conflicts of interest. Such conflicts jeopardize the welfare of these Islamic communities in the Western sociopolitical environment.

There are great differences, for example, in the attitudes taken toward the Western way of life. Community leaders who have been raised in the North American environment understand well the problems of adjustment that Muslim immigrants face. Generally, however, they have little grounding in the sources of Islamic tradition that can provide solutions to these problems. On the other hand, religious leaders imported from other countries generally are thoroughly versed in the religious tradition, but often have little understanding of the problems faced by believers in the North American context. This situation has made it extremely difficult for members of the Shi'a community to keep the younger generation interested in the Islamic faith. Thus far the solutions offered by community leaders have been temporary, failing to effect the resolution necessary for the future religious loyalty and spiritual well-being of the members. The lack of religious leaders who are both locally trained and fully instructed in Islamic tradition has been identified as the most urgent concern facing the future survival of the community in the secular Western environment.

International political events have clear implications for the religious outlook of activist Shi'ism today. Particularly important, of course, has been the Islamic revolution in Iran. Viewed as an Islamic response to Western-American cultural imperialism, it has served to awaken religious sentiment and pride in the Shi'a community in general, and also has been influential in some Sunni areas where the revolution is interpreted in nonsectarian terms.[8] It has been of immeasurable and unprecedented influence in the Shi'a community in North America insofar as it has been interpreted as a kind of neutralization of the "cultural colonization"[9] of Western forces. Despite propaganda generated through the concerted efforts of several Arab Middle East governments to discredit both the Imam and Shi'ism in North America, the image of a successful Imam Khomeini has given Muslims a renewed confidence in preserving their identity in a secular-atheistic culture. This confidence is reflected in the enormous rise in religious awareness and the emergence of a "reborn" attitude among younger generations of Shi'a and Sunnis alike. A number of young men and women in Shi'a organizations have adopted Islamic codes of behavior and have challenged Sunni authorities to view them as authentic Muslims following a leader whom they consider to be a true Muslim in comparison with other Islamic leaders around the world. Dissatisfaction with the Sunni Arab interpretation of Islam, which tends to legitimate and support Arab Muslim governments, along with an attraction to the kind of activist leadership that the Ayatollah gave Shi'ism, has caused a number of African Americans in North America to change their affiliation in the last ten years. Exact figures are unavailable, but the growing number of African American Shi'a centers indicates that converts are steadily increasing.

However, enthusiastic support for Iran among North American Shi'is has been tempered by the Iran-Iraq war and by the reality of clear differences of opinion among the various *maraji' al-taqlid* who have followers in Canada and the United States. For the most part these differences concern the matter of Shi'a leadership and whether or not that leadership should assume political authority in a Shi'a state pending the return of the messianic Imam Mahdi. Some Shi'a scholars, such as the late *marji'* Ayatollah Khu'i living under the prevailing unfavorable sociopolitical conditions in Iraq, have regarded the political involvement of a learned religious scholar as harmful to the spiritual well-being of the Muslim community and have opposed Khomeini's idea of "Guardianship of the Jurist" (*wilayat al-faqih*) in a modern state. The fact that this "guardianship" has actually been institutionalized in the constitution of the modern state of Iran has complicated its acceptance by Shi'is in other parts of the world and caused it to be questioned even by those leading Shi'a religious authorities sympathetic to the Ayatollah's notion of a new kind of activist religious leadership among the Shi'is. The nationalist overtones of the Iranian revolution have given rise to the recognition of several other *maraji'* among Arabic-speaking Shi'is who prefer their Arab *marja' al-taqlid* over the demand for unity seemingly necessitated by the acceptance of the Ayatollah Khomeini as the one *marja'*. The institution of the *marja' al-taqlid* therefore has suffered from a kind of decentralization, resulting in factionalism among Shi'a groups in North America. Nonetheless, almost all Shi'is, whomever they accept as their *marja' al-taqlid*, are united in their support for the Islamic revolution in Iran.

It is important to note, however briefly, that Shi'a communities in the United States and Canada have created some important institutions for the well-being of their members. In conjunction with the Islamic centers that have been built in major cities such as New York, Washington, Los Angeles, Chicago, Vancouver, Edmonton and Toronto, Shi'is have created a highly efficient educational weekend religious school system. This school system is regarded as second only to the weekly and annual gatherings to commemorate Imam Husayn b. 'Ali's martyrdom as a guarantee of the continuation of Islamic moral-religious education.

The commemorative gatherings, of course, have been the best platform for the spread of religious education to adults. But their traditional outlook and conservative spirit have meant that neither the role of Muslim women in the West nor the concerns of Shi'a youth who have grown up in the American environment have received the attention that they deserve. Some in the Shi'a community are calling for a reformation of traditional practices that are really the products of a particular culture rather than Islamic per se and a reappropriation of the essential teachings of Islam. These teachings they understand to include the encouragement of women and youth to participate in and contribute more actively to the religious organization and ultimately to the future of the community.

Occasionally the guidance of the *marja' al-taqlid* is sought in working out these reform measures. The *marja'*, fully informed about the essential teachings of the Qur'an and the spirit of Islamic religious-moral law, actually have been far more progressive than many of their followers in the West in helping to determine solutions to problems. For example, some Shi'a centers in North America were opposed to the idea of using closed circuit television to allow women, who usually sit separately in the mosque behind a partition, to watch the male speaker during religious lectures. The religious ruling of the *marja'* was sought, and with the interpretation that such a device is religiously commendable permission was given for its use.

It is clear that one of the most serious concerns facing the Shi'a community in North America is that of the nonparticipation of Muslim youth in adult gatherings. A solution that has repeatedly been proposed is the use of English rather than another language usually spoken only by the adults or used by the preacher. One of the problems, of course, is the reluctance of adults to give up the use of a language familiar from birth. Another is the lack of preachers able to function sufficiently well in English.

As a move toward the solution of this latter problem a new generation of local preachers is being trained in a seminary type of institution recently established in Medina, New York. The seminary has two parts, the *jami'a wali al-'asr* for male students and the *madrasa al-khadija al-kubra* for female students. Students begin a four-year training after the completion of high school. Those responsible for teaching the Islamic sciences have been trained in Shi'a centers of learning such as Qum in Iran and Najaf in Iraq by prominent Shi'a scholars. As such they are equipped to train their students in the traditional sources, including Arabic and Islamic theological-juridical studies as taught in Shi'a Islamic seminaries in Iran and Iraq. The most remarkable feature of this seminary is the inclusion of female students, who receive training that traditionally has been reserved for male students. Upon completion of their studies in this seminary these graduates will be qualified to become prayer leaders and preachers in Islamic centers and teachers in the community school system. Some may choose to continue their education by doing further study in Iran or Iraq, after which they would qualify to be teachers in the seminary. The creation of this institution is an important step toward the preservation of Shi'a teachings and identity in the North American context, although it is too soon to evaluate the success of its program and its implications for the future religious leadership of the Shi'a community.

Despite the problems identified here, the Shi'a minority within the larger Muslim minority in North America has been remarkably successful in maintaining its identity. Among the reasons for this success two have been particularly important. One is the independence of Shi'a communities in the United States and Canada from any control of foreign Muslim governments or their agencies. Another is the strong tradition of dynamic rituals connected with the annual commemoration of the martyrdom of Imam Hussein, as well as the fundamental Islamic practices such as salat, fasting, and pilgrimage. These religious practices have functioned as regular and successful means for bringing together members of the Shi'a community for worship and religious discourse. They also have provided the leaders with an important instrument by which to effect necessary changes and to generate positive attitudes as this religious minority struggles to assert and preserve its identity in the midst of the challenges of the pluralistic society in which it finds itself.

NOTES

1. Within the Sunni community one can speak about the Wahhabi generated "conservative" beliefs and strict adherence to the letter of the Shari'a, or mystically oriented Sufi beliefs and practices. Among the Shi'is there is non-Shar'i esoterically oriented Nizari Isma'ilism, Shari'a oriented Musta'li Isma'ilism, etc.

2. One can note, for example, from the proceedings of the symposium on Islam in North America held at the University of Alberta in Edmonton, Canada, May 17–21, 1980, the conspicuous absence of any information on the main group of Shi'is (the "Twelvers") of North America at the time when they had become part of the international political discourse, due to the Iranian revolution.

3. Other subdivisions of the Shi'i community such as the Isma-'iliyya, both the Nizari (followers of the Aga Khan [for information on this group see Azim Nanji, "The Nizari Ismaili Muslim Community in North America: Background and Development," in *The Muslim Community in North America*, ed. Earle H. Waugh, Baha Abu-Laban, and Ragula B. Qureshi (Edmonton: University of Alberta Press, 1983), pp. 149–164]) and the Musta'li (Bohra) branches, and the Zaydiyya will not be discussed in this chapter.

4. Abdolmaboud Ansari, *Iranian Immigrants in the United States: A Case Study of Dual Marginality* (Millwood, N.Y.: Associated Faculty Press, 1988) discusses patterns of Iranian immigration that generally hold true for other educated middle-class emigrants from Third World countries to Canada and the United States.

5. For the significance of the martyrdom of Imam Hussein and the religious practices that grew out of this commemoration, see Mahmoud Ayoub, *Redemptive Suffering in Islam. A Study of the Devotional Aspects of "Ashura" in Twelver Shi'ism* (The Hague: Mouton Publishers, 1978).

6. Ansari, *Iranian Immigrants*, pp. 116–21.

7. For the doctrinal basis of the deputyship of the Shi'i religious scholars, see my *Islamic Messianism: The Idea of the Mahdi in Twelver Shi'ism* (Albany: State University of New York Press, 1981). For the leadership of the deputies and their powers, see my *The Just Ruler in Shi'ite Islam: The Comprehensive Authority of the Jurist in Imamite Jurisprudence* (New York: Oxford University Press, 1988).

8. For the impact of the Iranian revolution on the Syrian Sunni Muslims see Yvonne Haddad, "The Impact of the Islamic Revolution in Iran on the Syrian Muslims of Montreal," in *The Muslim Community in North America*, pp. 165–181.

9. The phrase has been employed by Nikki R. Keddie, "Islamic Revival as Third Worldism," in *Le Cuisier et le philosophe: hommage a*

Maxime Rodinson. Etudes d'ethnographie historique du Proche-Orient, reunies par J. P. Digard, pp. 275–281, in her discussion about the social classes to whom "Third Worldism" appeals. Islamic revivalism is also, in her opinion, a form of "Third Worldism" that appeals to the militantly oriented classes who have a poorer place on the socioeconomic ladder.

CHAPTER 2

The Sun of Islam Will Rise in the West: Minister Farrakhan and the Nation of Islam in the Latter Days

Mattias Gardell

Few American religions have been so completely surrounded by a mist of misunderstanding and disinformation as the Nation of Islam (NOI).[1] This is in part due to its mingling of ethnic and religious standards, in itself representing a double opposition to Anglo-American culture, being both *black* and *Islamic*. The present leader, Minister Louis Farrakhan Muhammad, is presented as a demagogue, a hate monger, an inverted racist, an anti-Semite, and a black Hitler. The news media wallow in the controversial positions of the NOI, reporting that its members supported Saddam Hussein in the Gulf War, receive financial support from Libya, and loudly proclaim the imminent destruction of white America. With a few notable exceptions,[2] the academic studies published on the NOI refer mainly to secondhand sources, including media articles based on information produced or channeled by the FBI. This essay takes this confusion as a point of departure. Its purpose is to provide an introductory presentation of the Nation of Islam. After a brief historical description it deals with the NOI under the leadership of Minister Farrakhan and includes a discussion of some of the aforementioned controversial aspects. The intention is to provide the reader with means for a fuller understanding and to facilitate an interpretation of the headlines that are sure to come in the future.

BEHOLD, I SEE THE PROPHET ELIJAH

Detroit 1931. The city had experienced a dramatic influx of southern blacks that within a single decade multiplied its African American population by 611 percent. Among these new city dwellers was the young family Poole, Elijah and Clara and the first five of eight children.[3] Son of a Georgia farmer and Baptist preacher, Elijah had come to seek a prosperous future in the industrial North. Unemployed in the first year of the Big Depression, Elijah heard of a Prophet of God who was delivering a message specifically for the black community. Variously known as W. D. Fard or Master Farad Muhammad, the prophet used to tell his audience that they were no so-called Negroes, on the bottom of society, but the Original people and the former rulers of the earth. They had been stolen by "the Caucasian cave man" and brought to a life of slavery in "the Wilderness of North America."[4] God, whose proper name is Allah, had finally found His lost people and decided to transfer them back home to Paradise in two steps. The first, preparatory phase was cultural. The African Americans had to return to their original way of life. They should relearn their original language, Arabic, and reconvert to their original religion, Islam. They should stop eating unhealthy soul-food and go back to their original diet, eating only once a day. They should return their surnames to the former slave owners and retake their original Islamic names as a manifest symbol of their mental emancipation.[5] At the end of this reculturalization, Allah would bless them by the physical phase in which they would be transferred back to Mecca.

Elijah Poole became interested enough to attend a sermon in a temple hall. According to the historiography of the Nation of Islam, Elijah directly realized who the mysterious person was in reality. When speaking to the prophet after the meeting, Elijah Poole said, "I know who you are, you're God Himself." W. D. Fard answered whispering, "That's right, but don't tell it now! It is not yet time for it to be known."[6] From that moment on, the two men developed a unique relationship. For a period of nine months, Fard daily visited Elijah to teach him the mysteries of the universe and to infuse him with divine wisdom, thus building a character strong enough to guide the Original People through the Latter Days. In highest secrecy, Fard entrusted his disciple to be his Messenger, and gave him back his original name: Elijah Muhammad.

When the prophet of God disappeared in 1933–1934, as mysteriously as he had arrived, his Apostle was prepared to reveal the hidden truth:[7] Master Farad was not a prophet, but God Himself, a black man. The African Americans are part of the Original Nation, the true owners of the earth. All that exists in the universe is a creation of the black intellect. This includes the white man, who is neither truly human nor a direct creation of God. The Caucasians are human-made, grafted by a black scientist named Mr. Yakub. He was a man of incredible learning, and dissatisfied with the God-given, Islamic conditions then prevailing in Asia, as the planet was originally called. Poisoned by jealousy, he set about to produce an exclusively evil race, thereby introducing a destructive force to ruin the original harmony. With his followers he withdrew to the island of Patmos, where by means of a complicated system of gene-manipulation he managed to gradually drain the divine substance out of the original people. In 200-year intervals he produced the brown, red, and yellow races, before the proclaimed target became reality: a white race of devils, unable to do right, think of goodness, act decently, or obey the laws of Islam. God in His omniscience gave the white devil 6000 years to rule the earth and the Original People were put to sleep. This period of time is the most recently experienced period of world history, and the regime of evil is the cause of its distinctive features: poverty, oppression, slavery, colonialism, war, epidemics, ghetto life, unemployment, and injustice. White Christian fundamentalists argue that creation was but 6000 years ago. Their minds are as limited as the period predestined for white supremacy. *They* were grafted 6000 years ago, which means that their time now has come to an end.

The countdown for the era of evil started in 1555, when the devil John Hawkins arrived at the shore of Africa piloting the slave ship *Jesus*. He kidnapped members of the twelfth tribe, headed by Imam Shabazz—scripturally known as Abraham—and brought them as chattel to a life of slavery in the Wilderness of North America. They had been strengthened for their divine task as Trojans and brought into the fortress of evil. As God explained to Imam Shabazz in Genesis 15:13–14: "Thy seed shall be a stranger in a land that is not theirs, and they shall serve them; and they shall afflict them for four hundred years; and also that nation, whom they will serve, will I judge: and afterward shall they come out with great substance." The 400 years of slavery has expired. God came to His nation in the person of Master Farad Muhammad and raised from among them a Messenger. His task is to proclaim the mental resurrection. When the dry bones receive the breath of the Lord they will become alive. Realizing their true divine ontology, the black race will walk out of Babylon, leaving her to be destroyed by the wrath of God. This is the necessary prelude to the coming Final Battle. Allah will in the immediate future erase the devils from the earth. He will thereby retransform the universe to a black paradise, in which freedom, justice, and equality, that is, Islam, again will prevail.

The message represents a positive solution to the problem of identity, so central for the postemancipation black community. They were Africans but not Africans, Americans but not Americans. Who were they? Black nationalists have suggested various secular concepts for the perceived identity, none of which so far has been met with universal agreement. The heat in the debate of whether or not they should be called Negroes, Colored, or Blacks, Negro-Saxons, Anglo-Africans, Euro-Africans, Afro-Americans, African-Americans, or most recently African Americans highlights the emotional significance of the dilemma. Black religious nationalists have added the crucial question: *why?* Why did they have to go through the cataclysm of slavery? Was there a *meaning* to this incomparable suffering? The answers given differ in detail and elaboration but have a certain structure, a specific and basic theme in common. The African American nation is the chosen people. They belong to the aboriginal humanity that in prehistoric times was governed directly by God, with whom they have a covenant. The blacks are the originators of civilization. They were masters of art and science of which the pyramids stand forth as the prime symbol. For some reason, usually said to be the sin or unfaithfulness of their forefathers, they lost world hegemony. But time moves in circles. What has been will be again. White supremacy is a vicious but necessary lesson to learn before the pale-skinned tools of God have served their purpose. Thereafter—in the "hereafter," which is a concretely and earthly interpreted concept in this context—the wheel of history will turn and the black nation will regain its original position. Slavery is thus but a baptism of fire, strengthening the leaders to be. Based on this theme—by some scholars christocentrically termed *Ethiopianism*—black religious nationalists have created their own concepts of identity, normally replacing the secular bipolar concepts with a unitarian one that reflects the perceived divine meaning of the nation. Thus, we find religious groups asserting that blacks in reality are Ethiopians,[8] Jews,[9] Moors,[10] or Bilalians.[11] The teaching of the Honorable Elijah Muhammad, arguing the African American adherence to an original, black, "Asiatic," Islamic nation, belongs to this tradition.

When considering the NOI teachings on the borderline between myth and legend, explaining the origin of races and the course of history, the reader should realize the nature of the religious narratives. It is not necessary to believe every detail in the highly elaborated descriptions. The inner kernel and the consequences are matters of belief, not the exact wording. The Brothers and sisters believe it to be true that the blacks were the first to have their origin in God. They believe the Caucasians to be an historically young people, deriving from the blacks. They believe white supremacy is opposed to the long-term will of God, who is to replace the present world order with a regime of justice. In much of the preaching on this theme, an epic elaboration is made that is not to be interpreted literally. In one sermon Minister Farrakhan spoke of the origin of the white man, how he crawled on all fours, making love with dogs. "Who is the [white] man's best friend?" Farrakhan asked, "You? No—the dog. He and the dog had a love affair."[12] The message is given in an entertaining form, using humor to make a serious point.

The Nation of Islam never confined itself to metaphysical escapism, but advocated an active piety. The interim program established was at the same time seen as a practical way of surviving in the devil's society, and as a necessary prelude to the coming divine destruction of that society. America was identified as the Babylon that inevitably would meet her doom. In this context, any call for integration in the city of evil stands forth as a program of dangerous insanity. The only rational course of action is clearly specified in Revelation 18:4: "Come out of her, my people, that ye be not partakers of her sins, and that ye receive not of her plagues." The program envisioned can be summarily described as a process of separation, believed to liberate gradually the African American in a quest for independence. As compensation for centuries of unpaid slave labor the NOI demanded a "separate state" on an area "fertile and minerally rich."[13] Economically, Elijah Muhammad urged the African American to "pool your resources" and create a separate black infrastructure.[14] Through the establishment of enterprises in various sections, the NOI over the years succeeded in becoming "the most potent organized economic force in the black community."[15] Singling out the need for "reeducation" as an important key to black progress, the NOI established schools of its own known as "universities of Islam."[16] Disliking racial intermixture, the NOI advocated racial endogamy and provided opportunities for study, work, and recreation within its confines. Rejecting the Stars and Stripes as being the banner of slavery, cruelty, and death,[17] the Muslims hailed "the Flag of Islam" that resembles the Turkish flag, red with a white star and crescent.[18] Most independent nations have a uniformed army, and the NOI established the male cadre, the *Fruit of Islam* (FOI), as defenders against internal corruption and external enemies.[19] As indicated by the name, they were seen as the fruit of the teaching, in themselves carrying the seed of the future transformation of the African American.

The theory and practice just described attracted attention outside the black community, not the least from agents employed to defend America against its dissident citizens. From World War II, when the NOI was believed to be pro-Japanese,[20] the FBI kept a permanent eye on the believers. In 1959 the routine of passive surveillance changed to active counterintelligence. That year, the media interest exploded with articles in leading magazines, such as *Time, U.S. News and World Report, Saturday Evening Post,* and in various newspapers. The sudden outburst is commented on by NOI apologist Bernard Cushmeer: "Back in 1959, the white press, as if on signal, launched a furious attack on Messenger Muhammad and the Nation of Islam . . . white America spewed forth a flood of articles, both superficial, spurious and poisoness (sic) in nature. . . . They conspired to deceive the public. . . . Members of a large orchestra do not accidentally play the same tune."[21]

He was absolutely correct. Acting as conductor was the FBI, who, in its own words, initiated a program "centered around espousing to the public, both white and black, on a nationwide basis the abhorrent aspects of the organization and its racist, hate type teachings."[22] This program was complemented by efforts to dispel the leadership by planting seeds of mistrust. In 1962, the FBI discovered tension between Malcolm X (Little), then national representative of the NOI, and the Messenger. Resolutely, the bureau decided to intervene with a program that "could possibly widen the rift between Muhammad and Little and possibly result in Little's expulsion from the NOI."[23] This program, later boosted by SAC (special agent in charge), Chicago, as "the most notable" of all "factional disputes" they had "developed,"[24] constituted in part the background to the assassination of Malcolm X. In August 1967, the disruptive efforts of the FBI directed against the NOI were incorporated in a broader and more systematically conducted counterintelligence program against "black nationalist hate groups." The explicit purpose was "to expose, disrupt, misdirect, discredit, or otherwise neutralize the activities of black nationalist, hate type organizations and groupings, their leadership, spokesmen, membership and supporters . . . "[25] In March 1968, the program was extended to include long-range goals, such as to "prevent the coalition of militant black nationalist groups" that "might be the first step toward a real 'Mau Mau' in America, the beginning of a true black revolution" and to "prevent the rise of a 'messiah' who could unify and electrify the militant black nationalist movement."[26] Translated into practice, this meant that the FBI collected intelligence through a tightly woven net of informants and technical and microphone surveillance, and then used that information to destroy the NOI. Agents engaged in writing a series of anonymous letters, furnishing derogatory information about the NOI to loyal journalists, creating factional disputes within the NOI as well as between the NOI and the Black Panther party, and a number of similar covert actions.

The FBI plan did not work out. "For years," SAC, Chicago, complained, the bureau "has operated a counterintelligence program against the NOI and MUHAMMAD . . . despite these efforts, he continues unchallenged in the leadership of the NOI and the organization itself, in terms of membership and finances, has been unaffected."[27] The FBI never did realize that their actions were perfectly suited to the eschatology of the NOI. When Elijah Muhammad and other Muslims were imprisoned,[28] when local police forces assaulted Muslim temples,[29] when the bureau launched media campaigns, or when other actions of the FBI became known to the NOI through double agents,[30] the Muslims reacted with no surprise. The bureau was but one part of the forces of evil who in the Latter Days are supposed to behave in this manner. All instances of repression only proved Muhammad to be correct: the white man *is* the devil. Assisted in this manner by the

FBI, the Nation of Islam became established as the largest black nationalist organization in the United States and retained the structure roughly delineated here until 1975.

DEATH AND RESURRECTION

According to official medical documents, the Messenger of God died of congestive heart failure on February 25, 1975.[31] He was succeeded by his son, Wallace D. Muhammad (b. October 30, 1933), later renamed Imam Warith Deen Muhammad. He received unanimous acclamation by 20,000 believers gathered in Chicago for the annual Savior's Day festivities, commemorating the birth of W. D. Fard. With astonishing speed, Wallace Muhammad initiated a process of Islamization, moving the NOI toward orthodox Sunnism. This process has been described elsewhere,[32] making a summary description of the essential features sufficient. Imam Muhammad transformed W. D. Fard from God to "witchdoctor,"[33] sent by Iblis, Satan, to misdirect the African Americans.[34] The position of Messenger of God was given over from Elijah Muhammad to Muhammad Ibn Abdullah, the last Messenger in orthodox Islam. The economic empire was dismantled and the army dissolved. Some nationalistic features were temporarily preserved in a milder and more authentic Islamic fashion. The African Americans were still Islamic by nature, not as an organic body of God but as *Bilalians,* underlining historical affinity instead of revealed divinity. Bilal Ibn Rabah was a black Abyssinian slave in the service of Umayyah Ibn Khalaf of Mecca. He was one of Muhammad Ibn Abdullah's first followers, and after being bought and released by Abu Bakr, he became a close companion of the Prophet. Bilal had a melodious voice and was made the first *mu'adhdhin,* reciter of the call for prayer. The fact that a black former slave was an early compatriot of the Prophet is given tremendous importance: It is the black man who is calling the world to God.[35] Racism in American society and religion was still condemned, but resistance less outspoken. Portrayals of God are un-Islamic. A commitee was even formed to urge churches to remove all images of whites portrayed as divine.[36] The quest for a separate territory was transformed into a wish to form a "New Medinah," somewhat analogous to the Amish community, integrated in society with a degree of autonomy.[37]

Other aspects of the former nationalism were totally disbanded. The de-deification of the African American was accompanied by a de-demonization of the Caucasian. Black and white became brothers under a colorblind God and Caucasians were allowed to become members.[38] Renamed The World Community of Al-Islam in the West (WCI) and later The American Muslim Mission (AMM), it replaced former criticism of the United States with patriotism. Imam Muhammad claims that the Muslims are loyal Americans, and has even made a serious attempt to connect Islam with the Founding Fathers. Said Wallace Muhammad: "The Constitution of the United States is basically a Qur'anic document. Its principles were presented to the world over 1400 years ago by the Prophet Muhammad."[39] As "the final step" of transformation, Imam Muhammad urged his followers to dissolve the organization and drop the name American Muslim Mission. "The hangover from yesterday of 'Black Nationalist' influence is something we have to get rid of," Imam Muhammad said, "because it was in conflict with the open society and democratic order of an Islamic community."[40]

The process of transformation was forced ahead at the expense of the movement's unity. Many Muslims felt their world-view shaking. Many left the NOI with a feeling of abandonment and turned back to the street. A large number responded enthusiastically when Minister Farrakhan declared his decision to rebuild the Nation of Islam.

Minister Louis Farrakhan Muhammad was born under the slave name Wilcott in the Bronx, New York, on May 11, 1933. His mother was from Saint Kitts in the eastern Caribbean and was at the periphery of the movement of Marcus Garvey. Louis Wilcott was given a violin at the age of 5 and soon proved to be a gifted musician. He toured with the Boston College Orchestra before encountering calypso and discovering his talent for performing and singing. Louis was working as a night club artist at the Blue Angel in Chicago in 1955 when he was invited to hear Elijah Muhammad. Later the same year, he joined the mosque in Harlem, which was led by Malcolm X, who told him to either give up music or Islam within thirty days. Farrakhan says he made up his mind immediately, but used the time for consideration to give a last series of shows. The very last night, Louis X showed his audience the full range of his talent in a splendid crescendo, not knowing a top manager to be present.

The manager went to Louis X in his dressing room, offering

him a lucrative contract to be signed the day after. Tempted, Louis went to bed and was given a vision: "And in that vision I saw two doors. Over one door was written 'success.' I could look into that door and I saw an amount of gold and diamonds which represented, of course, riches that would accrue. But there was another door, and over that door was the word 'Islam.' And it had a black veil over that door. And in the vision I choose the door of Islam."[41] Walking through the door behind the black veil, Farrakhan encountered an avenue of success, strewn with obstacles and trials. He made a fast career in the NOI. He served as lieutenant in the FOI and as assistant minister in Harlem before becoming captain of the FOI and later minister of the Boston mosque. Minister Farrakhan was assigned the delicate task of rebuilding the Harlem mosque after the assassination of Malcolm X, whose death was blamed on the Muslims, and became national representative of the NOI. As with Malcolm X, Louis Farrakhan is a verbal virtuoso and possesses, in the sociological sense of the word, great charisma.[42] His sermons are high-quality performances in which he uses the skills of his former occupation. He is a preacher-artist, an entertainer, and a stand-up comedian with a serious message. His speeches have a structure analogous to classical compositions. Farrakhan starts by displaying a theme, which is repeated in various versions, high and low, building toward a dramatic finale, making use of all instruments, leaving his audience at the same time enthusiastic and exhausted.

When the death of Elijah Muhammad was announced, many observers had speculated on the possibility of Farrakhan becoming the Messenger's successor. The anticipated struggle for power in the NOI was called off when Farrakhan pledged loyalty to Wallace D. Muhammad, declaring him to be "the will of God," trained to assume leadership.[43] Minister Farrakhan soon found himself disfavored under the new head. He was moved from Harlem to "a dirty little place" on the West Side of Chicago with a former assistant as his new boss.[44] While Wallace D. Muhammad carried out his Islamization plans, Farrakhan was sent on speaking tours to the Caribbean and Africa. Observing the existence of ghettos and racism even in Muslim countries, Farrakhan realized "the necessity for a specific message to black people."[45] Elijah Muhammad "never intended for us to follow completely what is called orthodox Islam", Farrakhan said,[46] which is why he began criticizing the direction taken by Wallace Muhammad. In a speech on November 8, 1977, Minister Farrakhan officially declared his intention to reestablish the Nation of Islam, "on the platform of the Honorable Elijah Muhammad."[47]

Though Farrakhan in the name of black and Islamic unity stopped short of condemning Wallace Muhammad as a tricknologic tool for white America, other brothers were less diplomattic. "Wallace is a modern day Absalom," Brother Frederick X explained, "turning against his father, destroying the Kingdom David established. And you know what happened to Absalom . . . "[48] The course of events is explained not only scripturally, but more important by references to the prophecies of Elijah Muhammad. After a sermon before 40,000 African Americans at Randall's Island in September 1974, Minister Farrakhan said in exaltation to the Messenger "that it looked like soon we were gonna capture New York City for Islam." Elijah Muhammad, tells Farrakhan, "put his head down, and he looked so sad, and he said 'Brother, the time is soon coming when you may go to the mosque, and you will not find a believer there other than yourself.' "[49] It was hard to understand at that moment, but in less than a year and a half Farrakhan was persona non grata in the mosque he had headed and the rostrum was occupied by unbelievers. Farrakhan now understood why the Messenger had assigned him the difficult task of rebuilding the mosques in Boston and Harlem and what was presently expected of him:

> the building of the mosque in New York, the rebuilding of the mosque in Boston, was preparation. Now Elijah is gone. His son is in power. The Nation takes a totally different turn. People are disillusioned, angry, bitter, because everything that they suffered and sacrificed for is gone. And it is into that backdrop that I again came to rebuild his work. Not a mosque but his work. And here we are, all praise is due to Allah.[50]

THE MESSIANIC AGE HAS BEGUN

Farrakhan's claim to be the rightful heir of Elijah Muhammad as his spiritual son is supported by a new doctrine of belief that has dramatically accentuated the eschatology. A moment of skepticism was present already at the first announcement of the Messenger's death. "We who believe . . . won't accept anything until we see his body" said a relative when confronted with the news.[51] Sister Tynetta Muhammad, presently a leading theologian in the NOI, describes a vision she was given the evening of February 25, 1975: "I dreamed that the Honorable Elijah Muhammad sat upright on the funeral bench where he had been lain with the sheet wrapped across his body in the style of the Ihram garments worn by the Pilgrims during Hajj. When I saw him sitting in this position, I exclaimed several times, he is not dead!"[52] The Messenger of God is alive. Now, other prophecies of his can be correctly interpreted.

Clara Muhammad, wife of the Messenger, died in 1972. Shortly afterward, Elijah Muhammad gave a lecture and said: "There was a great prophet whose wife died. And three years after his wife died, the End came."[53] The congregation, not knowing exactly what prophet Elijah Muhammad had referred to, believed the Judgment to be coming in three years. Now, the NOI knows that the prophet that Elijah had referred to was the prophet Muhammad. Three years after the death of his wife, Khadidja, came the end of the Meccan period. The prophet Muhammad learned of a death plot, and he took flight. From that point began the Medinan period, where an independent Islamic nation came into existence. Farrakhan believes Elijah Muhammad "was made to appear as though dead," but escaped a death plot conducted by his enemies, a flight introducing a modern Medinan period, an era of independence for the Nation of Islam.[54] This is the point of departure for the development of a new theological creed of the NOI that has an interesting historical parallel.

As related previously, W. D. Fard presented himself as a prophet and Elijah Muhammad became his dedicated disciple. Upon Fard's disappearance, the relationship transformed when Fard was identified as God and Muhammad as his Messenger. Now, Elijah Muhammad has disappeared and has been identified as *the Messiah*. The relationship between Muhammad and Farrakhan was transformed from Messenger and his disciple into Messiah and his Prophet, his principal witness. "This," Farrakhan said, "is the crux of the theology that I represent: the Messiah is alive. He is in the world. The power of God is present in America with me." Continues Minister Farrakhan, "my work is to make his great commission known. To say to the Jews who are looking for the Messiah, to say to the Muslims who await the Mahdi, that Elijah Muhammad is not Messenger of God. That he is the Messiah that the whole world is looking for. And that I and my work in America is the witness that the Messianic age has in fact begun."[55]

Followers of Imam Wallace Muhammad accused Farrakhan of preaching what he knew was a lie when speaking of Elijah Muhammad as alive. They asked him for proof. Had he met him? Had he spoken to him? For seven years, Farrakhan relied on scriptural argumentation before he was given a vision confirming the truth of his position. On September 17, 1985, Minister Farrakhan was in the quiet Mexican hamlet of Tepotzlan, close to an Aztec temple on top of a mountain. In the vision, he walked up to this temple together with some companions. When he got to the top of the mountain a UFO appeared. Farrakhan directly realized the importance of the moment. According to the cosmology of the NOI, God supervises humanity from a large, constructed planet called the *Mother Plane*. In the Bible it is known as *Ezekiel's Wheel*. It contains an entirely new civilization and a number of smaller wheel-shaped spacecrafts carrying bombs, which will be used to destroy the old civilization in the Final Battle. Farrakhan was called from the circular plane and told to come closer. When he did, a beam of light brought him up into the plane, which took off. The pilot of God docked on the Mother Plane, which is "like a city in the sky." Farrakhan was allowed into a room, empty except for a speaker in the roof. Elijah Muhammad's well-known voice spoke to Farrakhan through the speaker. He authorized him as the *criteria* (Arabic: *farrakhan*) of God, obliged to guide the people of His choice through the Latter Days.

"As he begins to talk to me," Farrakhan narrated, "it was as though a scroll was rolled down inside my head." On the scroll were words of God in cursive writing. Farrakhan continues:

> [the scroll] was being put in me. That is there, and I know it is inside, and under the right circumstances things will come out of me that I have never thought of before. But if you give me questions I give you answers. If you come back with light, what you think is light, God will bless me to shed light on anything that you already know. Because some thing has been put in me, not just for my immediate community, but for . . . the entire world.[56]

This makes Farrakhan a prophet and his words the words of God. Farrakhan is surrounded by a staff, writing down or recording his sayings, which become subject to an intensive scriptural interpretation. With al-Mahdi (Master Farad Muhammad) and the

Messiah (Elijah Muhammad) present in the world, the Messianic age has truly begun. This is the time when prophecy is being fulfilled. Farrakhan is standing at the tomb of Lazarus—the African American—and calling him back to life. He is the lamb in the midst of four beasts that cannot hurt him. He is in the midst of America proclaiming the Messiah to be a black man, who

> will return in power now, just as the scriptures say, and you will see him come in the clouds of heaven having big power. Not coming in clouds—clouds means planes. With power to deal with his enemies, which are America and the Western world in general. The wrath of God is coming, and my [Farrakhan's] job as a student is just to warn America: if they continue in their path, they will be destroyed.[57]

The world is now experiencing the countdown to Armageddon. Earthquakes, floods, drought, epidemics, wars, and starvation are all signs of the Messianic labor pains accompanying the birth of a new era. According to the understanding of the NOI, the imminent destruction of the present world order is directed from the *Mother Plane*. A nucleus of leading devils knows the wrath of God coming from out of space. This is why reports of UFOs are classified. This is why billion of dollars are invested in militarizing space and the science of astrology. The Strategic Defense Initiative continues to receive an enormous budget despite nuclear disarmament. This is because Star Wars was never intended as protection from the secular missiles of the Soviet Union, but as a devil's shield against the holy missiles of divine retribution.

When the space shuttle Challenger in 1986 was to be sent out in space its true mission was to gather intelligence in a naive quest to prevent the destruction of Babylon. But the devil plans, and Allah plans. Challenger exploded 72 seconds after takeoff. This is not circumstantial but refers to Surah 72 of the Holy Qu'an in which the event is described. Surah 72 is titled "the Jinn," that is, the devil, and verses 8–9 read: "And we pried into the Secrets of Heaven; But we found it filled with stern guards and flaming fires. We used, indeed, to sit there in [hidden] stations, to [steal] a hearing; but any who listens now will find a flaming fire watching him in ambush."

All efforts of the devil to preserve his race by challenging God technologically or militarily are doomed to fail. But there is another way for the white race to survive. There is a small, but real, possibility for the white race to be saved, which is connected to a doctrine recently developed. As in all religions there is a discrepancy between theory and practice, leading to a problem of theodicy that has to be satisfactorily solved. If God is black and has a covenant with His black people, why did He have them experience the enormous burden of white supremacy? Why did they have to go through the cataclysm of slavery? What could possibly be the meaning of 6000 years of oppression? Pondering these questions, the new NOI arrived at the following understanding.[58]

In the cosmogonic act, God created the positive and the negative. This duality is integrated in all things created, from the finest particle of matter to the largest planet. The dialectic of good and evil was present within the Original People. They were created out of God's substance, but metaphorically like the planet they emerged on, they were not made perfect. There is a wobble in the planet's motion. God compensated for this wobble by making the planet obedient to a law that lessens the effects of the friction produced by the motion. Should the planet disobey she would cause her own destruction. The wobble in the black man's nature is the possibility for doing evil, compensated for by making the Original People obedient to Islam. The harmony in the first civilization was not perfect. There was a tendency to underestimate the power of evil that reduced the understanding for the necessity of Islam. There arose a tension, a friction in the motion of humanity.

God, whose plan is the perfection of humankind, decided in His omniscience to conduct an experiment, to teach the Original People their innate potential for good and evil. By self-knowledge blacks can ennoble their divine capacity and become like gods, but first they must learn to know how to defeat evil. Mr. Yakub, who believed himself to rebel against God when he grafted the devil, performed the will of God. What he actually did was to extract the negative from within the black man and graft a humanlike creature out of the pure concentrate of evil. Although in the anthropology of the old NOI there was an unsurmountable chasm between the nonwhite and the white, there is today an element in common. The white originated in the black, who originated in God, which indirectly makes the Caucasians created and leaves them a road of salvation.

"You cannot reform a devil," Farrakhan told his audience. "All the prophets tried and failed. You have to kill the devil."[59] The

Nation of Islam's philosophical understanding of reality postulates the primacy of ideas. In their own way they have reached the same conclusion as Michel Foucault when he inverted the classical saying "the body is the prison of the soul" to a significantly different statement: *"the soul is the prison of the body."*[60] The blacks are mentally imprisoned by erroneous ontological misconceptions of self, keeping them down as so-called inferior Negroes at the bottom of the ladder in the hierarchy of races. When they change their conceptions and understand their true divinity, the surrounding reality will automatically change in accordance.

In the same manner, the white man is not physically but mentally the devil. Black and white have been transferred from the biological to the psychological level, in which the colors now represent different attitudes and patterns of behavior. It is no longer necessary to kill the white man in a physical sense for the devil to be exterminated. "It is not the *color* of the white man that is the problem," Farrakhan continued in his lecture, "it is the *mind* of the white man that is the problem. The mind of white supremacy has to be destroyed."[61] The past 6000 years of white world hegemony has been a pedagogic experience effectively teaching the Original people about themselves. They have been ruled by their own potentials for evil, which has caused a friction in their motion, destructive enough for returning to Islam and crying for God's intervention. When saved, the blacks will never again let the devil within loose, which is why the hereafter will be truly a paradise. The pale-skinned tools of education have thereby served their purpose and can be removed. In His mercifulness, God gave the devil a possibility to avoid the physical battle of Armageddon by the presence of the Messiah. All it takes is for the Caucasians to condemn their evil origin and the evil they have caused throughout history and pay tribute to Elijah Muhammad as their Savior and Messiah.

Farrakhan has, however, a pessimistic view of the present leaders' propensity to give up white supremacy. "Unfortunately," he said, "the world rulers are so upset over their loss of power that they really don't give a dog about a new world reality. If they're gonna lose power they'll take the whole world down with them."[62] According to the eschatology of the NOI, the battle of Armageddon already has begun and will ultimately transpire into the physical phase, should the devil not commit suicide and let the white vehicle bow down to the will of God.

The apocalyptic perspective pervades the attitude of the NOI and explains the seemingly paradoxical or controversial position taken in a number of areas. Discussed under separate headings will be the relation between the Nation of Islam and the orthodox Muslim community, the alleged anti-Semitism of the NOI and its cooperation with extreme white nationalists, and last the perceived role of the NOI in the modern black American community.

"SOON WE SHALL SEE WHO IS MISGUIDED": THE NATION AND ORTHODOX ISLAM

Islam is a tolerant religion, harboring within its broad limits rich spectra of different tendencies and understandings of the religious creed. Despite this, the Nation of Islam has to be defined as heretical from an orthodox perspective. C. Eric Lincoln, writing about the old NOI, concluded that "it was not orthodox Islam, but it was by all reasonable judgments proto-Islam,"[63] thus indicating the logic of the course taken by Wallace Muhammad. The NOI is an important part of a black rediscovery of Islam. Islam has a long but somewhat invisible African American history. Apart from a small number of free adventurers, the vast majority of African Muslims were brought to the new continent as slaves. Austin estimates that 10–15 percent of the human cargo arriving in North America were Muslims.[64]

Apart from isolated instances,[65] Islam as an organized religion did not survive in the land of the unbelievers. The rise of Islam in the 1930s cannot be related to a fading "memory of Islam" as Lincoln suggests.[66] It can rather be seen as a logical consequence of the rediscovery of Africa. When blacks started to study their pre-American history they encountered Islam. If open-minded, the student could very likely arrive at a positive evaluation of the religion, as did the Christian black nationalists W. E. Blyden and Bishop Turner.[67] In Islam they could find a powerful faith traditionally opposed to European expansionism and supremacy. Islam could thus serve as a vehicle of black unity and resistance, as it did for the Nation of Islam.

In the first phase, the element of resistance was the single most important object. The creed was more a negation of Christian dogma than it was Islamic. Through studies of the Qur'an and a gradually increasing dialogue with Muslim theologians, the knowledge of orthodox Islam grew. When the Messenger left the visible world, his son Wallace rapidly continued the process of Islamization, purging all heterodox remnants. Farrakhan, maintaining the legitimacy of the distinctive features in the creed of Elijah Muhammad, split and reestablished the old NOI, as described earlier. Minister Farrakhan is, however, neither unaware nor unaffected by the orthodox criticism of the movement. The Nation of Islam has an extensive network of contacts with radical Islamic nations and organizations. This cooperation has led to a transformative process of the NOI along two lines of evolution:

1. *Externally,* the outward show of the NOI has moved closer to orthodox Islam. Members now master Islamic rituals, such as prayer and fasting, and appear not to be at odds with the local population when traveling in Muslim countries. In the United States, there is today a double set of religious services. Open meetings for the black community have kept the old churchlike structure. The audience sits on benches, listens to sermons, and gives an offering. In this way the NOI avoids distancing itself from the surrounding black culture, in line with their wish to be in the midst, not at the side, of the black community. First-timers should feel at home and not alienated by exotic furnishing and ceremonials. Members are invited to conduct their daily prayers and listen to the Friday prayer in the mosque. In Mosque Maryam, the national headquarters in South Side Chicago, a traditionally decorated mosque is situated on the first floor, below the hall for open meetings. Friday prayers are often led by a guest Imam from Africa and have a complete orthodox structure. Farrakhan declared this outward Islamization to be in line with the will of Elijah Muhammad, who, wise of timing, never himself introduced it, but left it to be conducted by his chosen successor.[68]

2. *Internally,* the differences in dogma are defended by polished religious argumentation. The different interpretations of the religious creed of the NOI and orthodox Islam are so far apart that they are irreconcilable. One of them has to be reformed. Acknowledging this, the apocalyptic perspective gives Farrakhan the confidence to assert the correctness of the NOI. It is the so-called orthodox Muslims that have deviated from the path of God. They have to repent and follow the superior

guidance of the Honorable Elijah Muhammad if they wish to survive Armageddon.

According to Minister Farrakhan, God chooses prophets from among the people in different periods of time. The prophet delivers a message from God for the people to obey, accommodating their pattern of behavior and thinking to His will. The message is related to the specific conditions characterizing the time people are living in. The world is in a constant process of transformation. When times change, religion has to change. If religion does not evolve in accord with the general evolution, it ceases being guiding and progressive, and it becomes impeding and oppressive instead. This, according to Farrakhan, is exactly what has taken place in orthodox Islamic countries. The Arabs deny God's intellect when asserting a timeless interpretation of the revelation given to Muhammad Ibn Abdullah. Should not God understand that the world He has created changes? The rigid and incomplete Arab understanding of the Qur'an caused the once leading Muslim countries to stagnate. All this is written in the divine Book of History, in the Scriptures and in the Hadith (collection of Traditions). In two Hadith, the Prophet Muhammad mentions the time we are now living in. One refers to the latter days, when the sun of Islam will rise in the West. The other relates to the specific people honored to realize its fulfillment. Muhammad said, "I heard the footsteps of Bilal going into Paradise ahead of my own." The interpretation of this hadith is evident. "He didn't mean his own personal footsteps," Farrakhan explained, "he was white. He was an Arab. And he was saying that it is the Blacks who are going to lead the Arab world back to the faith that they had forsaken, and lead them into the Paradise their God promised to them by the prophet Muhammad (PBUH) and the Qur'an."[69]

The racism that in the era of the Devil has penetrated every religion, including orthodox Islam, mentally blocks the road to salvation opened by God. As has the Christian longing for the return of Christ, the Muslim eagerness to hail the Mahdi has been clothed in racial terms. They all expect him to appear as white. Farrakhan, believing this to be psychologically deep-rooted, asks the waiting peoples of the world: "Would your latent or dominant racism stop you from accepting your salvation? That is the greatest trial of all for the whole world. Can you accept Mahdi and Messiah as Black people? If you can't, then you go out with this world as it goes out."[70]

Apart from the heavy argument that the Mahdi and the Messiah were raised from among African Americans and founded the NOI, making their interpretation of Islam correct, the truth is further confirmed by scriptural exegesis. As do many other Islamic factions, notably Shi'is and Sufis, the Nation of Islam acknowledges the existence of two Qur'ans. One manifest, exoteric; one hidden, esoteric. The latter is the most significant and can be ready only by means of a numerological analysis, using the hidden "Mathematical Code of the Holy Qur'an's Revelation."[71] The key to the code was placed by God in a pyramid before He put the Original People to sleep. It was to remain undiscovered until the latter days when prophecy was to be fulfilled. The final phase was introduced with the departure of the Honorable Elijah Muhammad. In the same year the Qur'anic code was discovered.[72] Without giving an account for the research leading to the discovery, the conclusion can be revealed: The code is based on the number 19. "Islam is Mathematics and Mathematics is Islam."[73] Based on the code and the work of Rashad Khalifah and Mexican mystic Rodolfo Benavides, Sister Tynetta Muhammad has elaborated a method for exegesis adopted by the NOI, attesting the validity of their beliefs, in the following manner.

The "death" of the Honorable Elijah Muhammad was traumatic news, rocking the foundation of the Nation of Islam. The drama is described in the Qur'an, the esoteric significance of which can be correctly understood by using the code. Separating the prefix *19* from the year 1975 points to Sura 75, "The Resurrection." Verses 7–12 (= 19) read: "when the Sight is dazed, and the moon is buried in darkness. And the sun and the moon are joined together—that Day will Man say: 'Where is the refuge?' By no means! No place of safety! Before thy Lord alone, that Day will be the place of rest." The meaning is clear. The perception of the believers was dazed, that is, confused. They were made to think of the Messenger as dead. But it was no more than an eclipse. He was resurrected and joined with God, his refuge from the enemies seeking his death and the resort for the true believers, who can rest in confidence of their Lord. But there is more to understand from the event. Divide the figure of the year in this way 1/97/5, and read Sura 97, verses 1–5. It is the "Night of the Majesty" that "is better than a thousand months" when "angels descend" and that leads to "the rising of the morning." The event in which Elijah was rescued by descending angels thus signals the end of the sixth millennium of Devil's Rule and the dawn of a new world order. In 1975, al-Azhar University was exactly 1000 years old. *Thousand* corresponds to the teachings of Elijah Muhammad, in which the earth is said to burn in 390 years and cool off in 610. These numbers resolved individually, $3 + 9 + 0 + 6 + 1 + 0$, equal 19. The year when the Prophet Muhammad received his first revelation is 610. Remove the zeros, reverse 39, and add it to 61; and 154 appears. 154 is the number of lessons delivered by Master Farad Muhammad. The number 154 connects to the code by adding $15 + 4$. Separate the prefix 19 from the year of Elijah Muhammad's departure and reverse the number given; this makes 57, that is, 19 multiplied by 3. Furthermore, $57 + 57 = 114$, which represents the number of Suras in the Qur'an ($= 19 \times 6$). Add a 0 and we get 570, the date of Prophet Muhammad's birth. The number 570 is a multiple of 19×30, which gives us another date, 1930, corresponding to the year when Master Farad chose to make his first appearance.

The preceding represents only a cursory glimpse of the exegesis conducted through the mathematical method based on the number 19. Through the code, religious pillars of the NOI, such as the true identity of Master Farad and Elijah Muhammad or the work of the Wheel, are affirmed. As is evident from this, the NOI does not hesitate to use the Holy Qur'an translated into the English language. Although the scholars of the NOI do read Arabic, knowledge of the language of Muhammad Ibn Abdullah is not a prerequisite for deciphering God's hidden messages. The keys to a proper understanding of scripture are carried over into every tongue by the code, which is expressed in the universal language of mathematics, because the message of God concerns us all:

> In God's Supreme Wisdom, He uses many means and methods in disclosing His Identity to the people who have been ruled by falsehood. He comes speaking out of the many languages and tongues of the world's religious communities, and undergirded with an underlying linguistic code common to all, so that none will offer the excuse that he was unable to understand the Message or the Message-bearer.[74]

The code becomes an additional argument against mainstream Muslim efforts to monopolize their interpretation of Islam and the Qur'an as the only legitimate one. The orthodox Muslims have had the Qur'an but not the key for its understanding. According to Minister Farrakhan, they resemble the donkey carrying a cargo of gold on its back: The ass does not understand the value of the load, which turns into a burden.[75] They deny the significance of the code placed in the scripture revealed to Muhammad for the world to know, which is why they correctly can be repudiated by the words of God in the Holy Qur'an: "Ye People of the Book! Why reject ye the Signs of God, of which ye are (yourselves) witnesses?"[76]

JEWS, NAZIS, AND THE NATION OF ISLAM

Farrakhan is recurrently in the midst of unfavorable media attention caused by some of his statements. Rare is the effort to comprehend what he really is saying, for which the religious context must be taken into consideration. Perhaps most has been written on the subject of Farrakhan's alleged anti-Semitism. When Farrakhan decided to support Jesse Jackson in his presidential campaign of 1984, the course of events initially went smoothly. Many Muslims registered to vote for the first time,[77] Farrakhan's Syrian connections helped Jackson free the captured American pilot Lt. Goldman,[78] and the Fruit of Islam vowed to protect Jackson after a series of death threats.[79] When Jackson referred to Jews as *Hymies* and New York as *Hymietown* in an off-the-record conversation with black *Washington Post* journalist Milton Coleman,[80] the success turned to its opposite.

Jackson's excuses were snowed under Farrakhan's untactical statements. In a radio broadcast he called Coleman a traitor and, although saying that "no physical harm" would come to him "at this point," warned him that "one day soon we will punish you with death. You're saying when is that? In sufficient time, we will come to power right inside this country—one day soon."[81] This, of course, is a rhetorical statement referring to the eschatological teachings of the NOI, and should not be literally and secularly interpreted—even though the secular nimbus of power implicated seems to be a desired sideeffect. To understand statements like these in a profane context, black English sociolinguistics has to be taken into consideration. As Gumperz has shown, *to kill* in the context of black political rhetoric is a metaphor.[82] Translated to standard English the previous statement of Farrakhan means something like "to put him out of influence and respect." This interpretation is supported by Farrakhan's own explanation, when he later asked for a meeting with Coleman. He denied ever threatening the reporter and said all he intended was to "put social pressure" that ostracizes him "in the black community."[83]

A second controversy later arose from statements of Farrakhan in the same radio sermon. Some Jewish critics had called him *Hitler*. Farrakhan said "Hitler was a great man. He wasn't great for me as a black person, but he was a great German, and he got Germany up from the ashes of her defeat (in) The First World War." He further stated that he was not "proud of Hitler's evils against the Jewish people" and ended by saying "don't compare me with your wicked killers."[84] The media concentrated on the word *great* and neglected the obvious effort of Farrakhan to distance himself from the Hitler comparison. They blasted the story in big headlines like "Jackson Pal Hails Hitler—Hitler Was Great, Says Jackson Pal."[85] Farrakhan says he understands why the Jews are concerned about what people say about Hitler "because the way [people] look at Hitler may mean the way that they look at the victims of Hitler." What Farrakhan tried to do is to force the black holocaust on the agenda, too: "Jews are sensitive because of their suffering, but we are all sensitive and we have all so suffered. . . . We as black people, look at our loss. Conservative estimators suggest 100 million in the middle passage. Who will weep for us?"[86] Again, the apocalyptical perspective remains dominant. If the white world, in which the Jews are included, does not recognize the evils done against the Original People, the physical battle of Armageddon cannot be avoided:

> If I was Jewish I would say "never again." I wouldn't like to see a Hitler coming up again. What I say to Jewish people is you can never say to God never again. Because we don't control his power. We may be able to stop another Hitler. But if God decrees an oven for us all, no one can stop it. And if you read the Torah as I read it, or read the Gospel as I read it, or read the Qur'an as I read it, God promised water in the destruction in the days of Noah, but he promised a baptism of fire in the destruction of the present world 'cause this world is totally out of order. You cannot say to God "never again," He's gonna put us all in an oven if we're not getting' this damn thing straightened out, and quick.[87]

Another controversy centered on Farrakhan allegedly calling Judaism a *gutter religion* and *dirty religion*.[88] He was not, however, referring to the religion as such. Farrakhan spoke about the misuse of religion: the human habit of gaining worldly power and riches by oppression and exploitation in the name of religion. This is not limited to Judaism, but concerns all other world religions: Christianity, Buddhism, Hinduism, and Islam. Only Jews seemed to be sensitive and alert enough to pay attention to the fierce voice from the black community. "The unclean is our action hiding behind God's name, Jesus' name, Muhammad's name," Farrakhan stated, "we're killing and destroying each other in the name of God. . . . Cheating, stealing, deceiving in the name of God—that's dirty religion."[89]

What basically lies behind this controversy is religion and identity. All statements made by Farrakhan relating to Jews and Judaism have to be seen in the context of his religious teachings. The Nation of Islam in a way represents black Zionism, expressing a religious hope for a promised land. The belief that the blacks are the chosen people and the true keepers of the covenant implies competition between two parties with exclusive claims to being the principal actors of the Bible. "The Jews don't like me 'cause I'm saying they're not the chosen people of God," Farrakhan said.[90] He emphasized he was not an anti-Semite, but a theologian: "All I said to the Jews was 'You are an impostor.' You are not the real people of God. I said these Black people who have suffered 400 years fulfilling the scriptures, these are the people that God is to visit and rise from a mental death."[91] The point is further reinforced by the recent cooperation between the Nation of Islam and the black Original Hebrew Israelite Nation, whose members contribute with articles in the *Final Call,* the organ of the NOI.[92] The opposition Farrakhan experiences from the (white) Jewish community and American mainstream media becomes a confirmation of his speaking the truth. The media are the modern day scribes and the Jews the modern pharisees eagerly trying to crucify the modern Savior.[93]

The alleged anti-Semitism has been related by various media to the idea that the Nation of Islam represents a sort of black Nazism or fascism. Supporting this argument, the connection between the NOI and various white-extremist right wingers has been emphasized. British National Front (NF) hailed Minister Farrakhan in a photo essay penned by NOI spokesperson Wali Abdul Muhammad in NF magazine *Nationalism Today.*[94] In a campaign National Front printed posters with Farrakhan's picture and the words

"Louis Farrakhan. He speaks for his people. We speak for ours."[95] Farrakhan accepted a donation from Ku Klux Klan leader Tom Metzger.[96] Nation of Islam representative Abdul Alim Muhammad spoke at a LaRouche conference in December 1990.[97] The Nation of Islam was—together with German neo-Nazi groups—in Baghdad in January 1991 to pledge support for Saddam Hussein in the Gulf conflict.[98] On the basis of these kind of reports, journalists have established as truth Nation of Islam participation in a "new alliance" between Islamic fundamentalists and neo-Nazis[99] and even a "new Axis" connecting Libya, neo-Nazis, and the NOI.[100] Although these contacts undeniably exist, the nature of the relationship has not been analyzed. The "alliance theory" is based on an incomplete understanding of the religious motives underlying the Nation of Islam's position. The relationship between the NOI and white extreme nationalism has to be seen in the context of the former's apocalyptic perspective.

Answering a direct question on the relationship between the NOI and the aforementioned white extreme nationalists, Farrakhan denied any direct contacts, although attesting to a level of mutual understanding:

> I have never met with any of them and their leaders. I have never written to them, nor have I received any correspondence from them. [But] they see integration as the destruction of their race and their people. And since I represent the Honorable Elijah Muhammad and his plan not of integration but of separation, they feel that they have common cause with me, though there is no linkage of myself with the KKK or any of these groups that you name. But I must tell you that I have got respect for any white man who wants to keep his race white, 'cause I certainly wanna keep mine Black.[101]

This line of reasoning has historical counterparts in the ideas of Malcolm X and Marcus Garvey. Malcolm repeatedly confessed his preference for the open white racist, the wolf, compared to the concealed white racist, the fox.[102] Marcus Garvey regarded the Ku Klux Klan as "better friends" of his race than "all other groups of hypocritical whites put together." Garvey liked "honesty and fair play" and believed that "potentially, every whiteman is a Klansman . . . and there is no use lying about it."[103] Underlying this argument is a conviction concerning the inner character of the white man, uniting Malcolm, Garvey, and Farrakhan. Minister

Farrakhan vows to "always defend the black community" but believes whites attacking blacks to be an expression of normal behavior, a predisposition "in the nature of white men."[104]

The increasing racial antagonism is only a sign of the time we are living in. In the transitory period leading to the final battle, the nations are supposed to separate. As the Bible puts it: "In that day every man will go to his own and find refuge under his own olive and fig tree." According to Minister Farrakhan,[105] the National Front–directed racial violence "is all part of the drama, the worldwide drama the prophets foretold." The Original People have to wake up from their mental slumber, realize the evil nature of the Caucasian and move out of Babylon for the final phase of divine retribution to begin. The Ku Klux Klan and the National Front are to be erased in due time, but they stand forth as temporarily useful. They are pedagogically perfect in their role as obvious devils. And although Farrakhan says he "don't approve of their violence against our people," he believes their violence to be prophetic: "It is fulfilling prophecy to make it uncomfortable for black people to stay here."[106] The apocalyptical perspective also explains Farrakhan's support for Saddam Hussein. In the eschatology of the NOI, the Final Battle begins in West Asia as a conflict between Muslims and non-Muslims, whites and nonwhites. Expecting the End to come any day now, Farrakhan made what appears to be a hasty conclusion. "This," he said, "is Armageddon."[107]

WARNING TO AMERICA

There is yet another element in common between the secular Ba'ath party of Iraq and the Nation of Islam. They both have an organic conception of race. The members of a race will normally think, behave, and act in coherency. This view on race can be traced to nineteenth century theories that focused on "race"—in this context used not in the modern biological sense but in the meaning of German *Volk*, as distinct "personalities" that each in its own way contributed to the perfection of humankind. The influence of von Herder, Schleiermacher, von Treitsche, and Guizot on classical black nationalists like Alexander Crummel, W. E. Blyden, and W. E. B. DuBois has been noted by Moses.[108] The organism theory dominated in black nationalism from the Emancipation up to Marcus Garvey and was adopted by the Nation of Islam. As in the classical variety, the organic race is structured as an authoritarian collectivism, with a supreme head governing the body. History is believed to move in circles, with different races taking turns as world leaders. Implied is a de facto acceptance of the ascribed inferior position from which a practical route out of misery is prescribed. Despite the revolutionary separatist rhetoric of Minister Farrakhan, an analysis of his recommendation for what has to be done shows the NOI to be advocates of a predominantly acculturative ideology. It can be understood as a project of *autocivilizing* that, if successful, would perfectly accommodate the black community to conservative middle-class standards.

According to Farrakhan, he is living in a "declining civilization" with all the signs of the "breakup of society" with "the social fabric beginning to pull apart."[109] America is falling and is going to be destroyed by God if the government does not radically change its policies and the people do not totally reform. Farrakhan regards the present standard of the black community to be far from the original divine civilization. The African Americans "are living a criminal life," Farrakhan said, "a very wicked and savage life here in America. Though we have the potential to be wonderful Muslims our condition is such that no civilized society wants us to be a member."[110] He condemned the morals of black youths, saying: "Your heads are full of reefers, your veins so full of heroin and your noses so full of cocaine or you're so busy at the party chasing one another sexually that you become a modern Rome." There is no meaning for blacks hoping for a change through traditional means of politics. "No politician can save anybody," Farrakhan said, "politicians are in no saviour business. Politicians are hoodlums. No whore can save you."[111]

The only route available to the black community is "racial uplift" under the guidance of the Nation of Islam. As for the old NOI, the social interim program established constitutes a recognition by society of the organization's abilities. The FOI became renown as *Dopebusters* when clearing a rundown section of black Washington from drug dealers.[112] Minister Don Muhammad, responsible for NOI coordination in the East Coast, is one of several Muslims rewarded for successful rehabilitation programs for drug addicts and criminals.[113] Committed to "build a Black economy" and make blacks "self-sufficient," the POWER (People Organized and Working for Economic Rebirth) program was established with the "purpose of restoring Black people in America to their original industrial and commercial greatness."[114] The re-creation of the economic empire has begun with enterprises in various areas, such as shampoo and body-care products, fish imports, restaurants, banks, and so forth,[115] but the NOI is still far from its former economic strength.

Praising conservative values, such as God, nation, and the nuclear family, the NOI members regard themselves as moral knights defeating the dragon of decadence. "God raised a group from among us [the decaying black community] and gave us life," Farrakhan said, "and we are the witnesses of Elijah Muhammad. Clean-cut, sharp, disciplined, non-smoking, non-drinking, non-dope using, strengthening the family."[116] This, in the eyes of Minister Farrakhan, proves that only blacks can take care of blacks, because only blacks really care about blacks. They are divine by nature and if let alone they will act in accordance. If unaffected by white society they will be able to re-create the original unity of the divine black body. That is why separation is the only solution to the social problems in the United States.

Farrakhan told the Congress and the President to give up their worries for the African American: "Let our Black brothers out of prison, give us your poor . . . give them to me—Let my people go."[117] Farrakhan continued: "We can reform the convict, you can't. We reform the drug addict, you don't. We reform the alcoholic and the prostitute. You don't. We take the poor and give them hope by making them do something for themselves. You don't. We are your solution."[118]

The alternative is the imminent destruction of America as we know it. "God Himself is angry with America"[119] and has sent the Messiah to judge the world and lead the community of believers to the promised hereafter:

> And I saw a new heaven and a new earth; for the first heaven and the first earth were passed away. . . . And I saw the holy city, New Jerusalem, coming down from God out of heaven, prepared as a bride adorned for her husband. And I heard a great voice out of heaven saying: . . . God himself shall be with them, and be their God. And God shall wipe away all tears from their eyes; and there shall be no more death, neither sorrow, nor crying, neither shall there be any more pain: for the former things are passed away. And he that sat upon the throne said, Behold, I make all things new.[120]

NOTES

1. They have been renown as "the Black Muslims," thanks to the work of the foremost authority of the NOI during the leadership of Elijah Muhammad, C. Eric Lincoln. As the members themselves consider the proper name to be "the Nation of Islam," they will here be spoken of under the name of their choice.

2. C. Eric Lincoln wrote his dissertation, *The Black Muslims in America* (Boston: Beacon Press, 1961; updated 1973). The Nigerian E. E. Essien-Udom wrote *Black Nationalism* (Chicago: University of Chicago Press, 1962). For the New NOI under the leadership of Minister Farrakhan, no monograph is yet available, but a number of valuable articles have been written by Lawrence H. Mamiya, notably "From Black Muslim to Bilalian. The Evolution of a Movement," *Journal for the Scientific Study of Religion* 2, no. 6 (June 1982) and "Minister Louis Farrakhan and the Final Call: Schism in the Muslim Movement," *The Muslim Community in North America*, ed. Earle H. Waugh, Baha Abu-Laban, and Ragula B. Quereshi (Edmonton: University of Alberta Press, 1983).

3. Elijah Poole was born in Sandersville, Georgia, October 7, 1897, and married Clara (b. Evans, November 2, 1899, Georgia) in Cordele, Georgia, 1919.

4. For the Nation of Islam during this initial time, see Erdmann D. Beynon "The Voodoo Cult Among Negro Migrants in Detroit," *American Journal of Sociology* 43, no. 6 (May 1938); and Lessons #1, #2, of W. D. Fard. The Prophet of God had a number of additional aliases, but these are the ones most used by the NOI.

5. The first practice was for the reconvert to sign a request for his original name, which was attested and given by God. Later, God became less generous in granting the members knowledge of their original Islamic names, and the famous X was adopted as a symbol for the original surname, lost during slavery. X also symbolized the mystery of God, the divine power latent in the black person's nature and manifest through the NOI. As the society of believers grew, it became necessary to add a figure for distinguishing among several with the same name, for example, James X, in the same local mosque. They became known as James X, James 2X, James 3X, and so on, in chronological order of their applications for membership.

6. Muhammad University of Islam, *Year Book No. 2*, 1973. pp. 24 ff.

7. This is based on Elijah Muhammad's *Message to the Blackman* (Philadelphia: Hakim's Publications, 1965); *The Fall of America* (Chicago: Muhammad's Temple of Islam No. 2, 1973); and *Our Saviour Has Arrived* (Chicago: Muhammad's Temple of Islam No. 2, 1974), and articles by the Messenger in "Mr. Muhammad Speaks," 1966–1975.

8.   Among these we find all Rastafarian tendencies, the African Orthodox Church, and various "Ethiopian" and "Abyssinan" Churches.

9.   There are a number of "Black Hebrew" sects proclaiming the blacks to be the real Jews and the principal actors of the Scriptures. Apart from their stronghold in the industrial northern United States, there are congregations in the Caribbean and Israel. The Black Hebrews (not to be confused with the Falashas from Ethiopia) in the Promised Land are mainly migrants from the United States, notably from New York, and have encountered hardship and racism in the motherland. Many (white) Jews do not accept the black immigrants' Hebrew identity, which is why they can be said to have moved from a perceived second-class citizenship in the United States to a second-class citizenship in Israel.

10.   NOI was not the first black nationalist religion to claim Islam as the natural faith for the African American. An important predecessor was the Moorish Science Temple of America founded by Noble Drew Ali (aka Timothy Drew) in 1913. They claim the blacks to be Moorish, heirs to the ancient Asiatic Moabite nation who ruled Mecca and inhabited Asia, Africa, and America before the European conquest. Noble Drew Ali, inspired by Sufism and gnosticism, authored a Holy Qur'an as scriptural base for the creed. The Moorish religion had its height in the 1920s, ending with the death of the Prophet in 1929. Thereafter the movement split into several competing factions, ruled either by a prophet believed to be Noble Drew Ali reincarnated, or by a sheikh, spiritually guided by Ali.

11.   This concept was created by Imam Wallace Deen Muhammad as a part of the transition of a large section of the NOI toward Islamic orthodoxy.

12.   Louis Farrakhan, "The Origin of the White Race: The Making of the Devil," speech delivered at Mosque Maryam, Chicago April 23, 1989.

13.   Muhammad, *Message to the the Blackman,* p. 161.

14.   Ibid., p. 174.

15.   Lincoln, *The Black Muslims in America,* 1973 ed., p. 97.

16.   Muhammad, *The Fall of America,* p. 97. Due to a 1934 conflict with educational authorities, these schools are authorized as private schools.

17.   See Muhammad, *Message to Blackman,* pp. 237–240.

18.   Elijah Muhammad, *The Flag of Islam* (Chicago: Muhammad's Temple of Islam No. 2, 1974).

19.   They are not armed but master the marshal arts. The female counterpart, the Muslim Girls Training–General Civilization Class (MGT-GCC), confines its activities to female education and discipline and is not supposed to participate in the external defense of the NOI.

20.   FBI Files 100-6582-45, 9/1/43, and 100-6582-151, 11/9/43.

21. Bernard Cushmeer, *This Is the One: Messenger Muhammad. We Need Not Look for Another* (Phoenix: Truth Publications, 1971), pp. 39–40.

22. FBI File 100-448006-(?); Chicago File 100-36535 sub B, 4/22/68.

23. FBI File 105-24822-133. Memorandum from J. F. Bland to W. C. Sullivan, 2/7/64.

24. FBI File 100-448006-626, SAC, Chicago to Director, FBI, 1/22/69.

25. FBI File 100-448006-(?) From Director, FBI to SAC, Albany, 8/25/67.

26. FBI File 100-48006-17, 3/4/68.

27. FBI File 100-448006, Chicago file 157-2209, 4/22/68.

28. Elijah Muhammad was arrested a number of times, but imprisoned only once for failure to register for the draft during World War II. He was arrested in 1942, sentenced to five years but was released on parole in 1946. (FBI file 105-248-22-25, 8/9/57.)

29. This happened a number of times, notably in Los Angeles, 1962, and New York, 1972, when the outcome was bloody. (See Muhammad, *Message to the Blackman*, pp. 216–217; *New York Times* [April 15, 1972]; "Mr. Muhammad Speaks" [April 28, 1972])

30. Some of the FBI informers reconverted while infiltrating the Nation of Islam and turned against their employers (Farrakhan, interview, May 18, 1989).

31. State of Illinois Medical Certificate of Death #605408 dated February 25, 1975: "The cause of death was congestive heart failure and arteriosclerotic disease."

32. C. Eric Lincoln, "The American Muslim Mission in the Context of American Social History," in *The Muslim Community in North America*, ed. Waugh, Abu-Laban, and Quereshi; and "The Muslim Mission in the Context of American Social History," in *African American Religious Studies*, ed. G. Wilmore (Durham, N.C.: Duke University Press, 1989); Mattias Gardell, "Religiös nationalism och nationalistisk religion: om den senaste utvecklingen inom politisk islam i det svarta USA," *Svensk Religionshistorisk Årsskrift*, no. 3 (1988).

33. Sidney R. Sharif, *The African American (Bilalian) Image in Crisis* (Jersey City, N.J.: New Mind Productions, 1985), p. 95.

34. Ibid., p. 71.

35. For the history of Bilal Ibn Rabah as described in orthodox Islam, see Muhammad Abdul-Rauf, *Bilal Ibn Rabah* (Takoma Park, Md.: American Trust Publications, 1977).

36. Sharif, *The African American Image*, p. 115; *Muslim Journal* (August 20, 1987; September 4, 1987).

37.   Brother Loqman, conversation, August 28, 1987; and Brother Abdullah, conversation, August 30, 1987.

38.   Warith D. Muhammad (Warithduddin Wallace), *Challenges That Face Man Today* (Chicago: W. D. Muhammad Publications, 1985), p. 150, "Mr. Muhammad Speaks" (July 25, 1975).

39.   Sharif, *The African American Image*, p. 118.

40.   Warith D. Muhammad, *Focus on Al-Islam* (Chicago: Zakat Publications, 1988), p. 82.

41.   Farrakhan, interview, May 11, 1989.

42.   *Charisma* here is not used in the original Weberian meaning, as a mystic inherent quality, but should be understood as a social process, a dialectical relationship between an individual and a group, resulting in the gradual construction of leadership flavored with extrahuman qualities being ascribed to the leader.

43.   *Chicago Daily Defender* (February 27, 1975).

44.   Farrakhan, interview, May 18, 1989.

45.   Farrakhan, interviewed by Carlos Russell, *Chicago Daily Defender*, Big Weekend Edition, (February 11, 1978).

46.   Farrakhan, interview, May 18, 1989.

47.   *Chicago Daily Defender*, Big Weekend Edition (December 3, 1977).

48.   Brother Frederix X, conversation, May 12, 1989.

49.   Farrakhan, interview, May 11, 1989.

50.   Ibid.

51.   *Chicago Daily Defender* (February 26, 1975).

52.   Tynetta Muhammad, *The Comer by Night* (Chicago: Honorable Elijah Muhammad Educational Foundation, 1986), p. 84.

53.   Farrakhan, interview, May 11, 1989.

54.   Ibid.

55.   Ibid.

56.   Farrakhan, interview, May 18, 1989.

57.   Ibid.

58.   The coming description is taken from ibid. and his speeches "The Origin of the White Race: The Making of the Devil," April 23, 1989, and "The Dawn—A New Beginning," February 1989, both delivered at Mosque Maryam, Chicago.

59.   Farrakhan, "The Origin of the White Race."

60.   Michel Foucault, *Discipline and Punish: The Birth of the Prison* (Harmondsworth: Penguin Books, 1979; first published 1977), p. 30.

61.   Farrakhan, "The Origin of the White Race."

62.   Farrakhan, interview, May 11, 1989.

63.   Lincoln, "The American Muslim Mission in the Context of American Social History," p. 224.

64. Allan D. Austin, *African Muslims in Antebellum America* (New York: Garland Publishing, 1974), pp. 29–36.

65. As on Selapo Island and St. Simon Island, where a team of researchers in 1940 found descendants from small congregations of Muslims. See *Drums and Shadows*, Georgia's Writers' Project (New York: Doubleday-Anchor Books, 1972; first published 1940), and Albert J. Raboteau, *Slave Religion* (Oxford: Oxford University Press, 1978).

66. Lincoln, "The American Muslim Mission in the Context of American Social History," pp. 219–221, and "The Muslim Mission in the Context of American Social History," pp. 344–345.

67. Bishop Turner praised the Muslim teachers in West Africa (Edwin S. Redkey, *Black Exodus*, [New Haven, Conn., and London: Yale University Press, 1969], p. 44), and Blyden repeatedly informed his audience of the difference in attitude toward the Africans in the two religions: "The Negro came into contact with Christianity as a slave and as a follower at a distance. He came into contact with Mohammedanism as a man, and often as a leader" (Edward W. Blyden, *Christianity, Islam and the Negro Race* [Edinburgh: Edinburgh University Press, 1967; first published 1887), p. 231). Sharply critical of the version of Christianity spread by the colonial powers in Africa, which in the eyes of Blyden cemented inequality between intruders and aborigines, he provocatively stated that "Islam extinguishes all distinctions founded upon race, color or nationality" (Blyden, quoted in Hollis Lynch, *Edward Wilmot Blyden. Pan-Negro Patriot* [London: Oxford University Press, 1967], p. 74).

68. Farrakhan, interview, May 18, 1989.

69. Farrakhan, interview, May 11, 1989. *PBUH* means Peace Be upon Him.

70. Ibid.

71. Tynetta Muhammad, *The Comer By Night*, p. 81.

72. Ibid., pp. 16–17, 81.

73. Ibid., p. 78.

74. Ibid., pp. 72–73.

75. Farrakhan, conversation, May 19, 1989.

76. The Holy Qur'an 3:70 (translation and commentary by A. Yusuf Ali [Islamic Propagation Centre International, 1946]).

77. *Chicago Defender* (February 11, 1984). This was a new policy. The old NOI condemned all participation in the electoral system of the devil. For the attitude of the old NOI, see E. Muhammad, *Message to the Blackman*, p. 218.

78. *Chicago Defender* (January 3, 1984; *Newsweek*, (January 16, 1984).

79. *Chicago Defender* (February 27, 1984).

80. *Washington Post* (February 11, 1984; February 22, 1984).

81. *Washington Post* (April 3, 1984; April 4, 1984).

82. John Gumperz, *Discourse Strategies* (Cambridge: Cambridge University Press, 1982), pp. 187–202.

83. *Washington Post* (April 6, 1984).

84. *Washington Post* (April 12, 1984).

85. For the media reactions, see Jeff Roby, "The Rainbow in 1984: The Jackson-Farrakhan Alliance," *The Honorable Louis Farrakhan: A Minister for Progress* (New York: New Alliance Productions, 1987; first published 1985), p. 33. In a CNN interview of 1990 by Larry King, Farrakhan said "great being an adjective does not have a moral quality attached to it. The Mexican earthquake of 1985 was *great* and the devil too is *great.*

86. Louis Farrakhan, "A Time of Danger: The Signs of the Fall of America," speech delivered at the University of Maryland, March 29, 1989.

87. Ibid.

88. *Chicago Defender* (June 28, 1984); Farrakhan, ibid.

89. Farrakhan, ibid.

90. Louis Farrakhan, "Power at Last . . . Forever," speech delivered in Washington, D.C., July 22, 1985.

91. Louis Farrakhan, "The Crucifixion of Jesus: The Destruction of Black Leadership, speech at Mosque Maryam, Chicago, March 26, 1989.

92. *Final Call* (May 11, 1989).

93. Farrakhan, "The Crucifixion of Jesus: The Destruction of Black Leadership."

94. *Searchlight* (December 1989).

95. *Searchlight* (September 1987).

96. *Searchlight* (December 1986).

97. *In These Times* (January 30, 1991).

98. *Dagens Nyheter* (February 2, 1991).

99. Ibid.

100. *Searchlight* (September 1987).

101. Farrakhan, interview, May 18, 1989.

102. Malcolm X, "God's Judgement of White America," in *The End of White World Supremacy,* B. Karim ed. (New York: Seaver Books, 1971, reprinted speech from 1963), p. 137.

103. Marcus Garvey, *Philosophy and Opinions II, The Philosophy and Opinions by Marcus Garvey. Or, Africa for the Africans,* ed. Amy Garvey (Dover, Mass.: The Majority Press, 1925; reprinted 1986), p. 71.

104. Farrakhan, interview, May 18, 1989.

105. Ibid.

106. Ibid.

107. *In These Times* (February 6, 1991).
108. Wilson J. Moses, *The Golden Age of Black Nationalism* (New York and Oxford: Oxford University Press, 1978), pp. 21–22, 48–50, 133–135.
109. Farrakhan, "A Time of Danger: The Signs of the Fall of America."
110. Farrakhan, interview, May 11, 1989.
111. Farrakhan, "The Crucifixion of Jesus: The Destruction of Black Leadership."
112. See *Final Call* (July 31, 1989). The minister of the Washington Mosque, Dr. Alim Muhammad, also represented an innovation in NOI attitude toward politics when he decided to run for Congress (*Final Call* [May 31, 1990]).
113. Minister Don Muhammad, interview, June 8, 1989.
114. NOI POWER Proclamation.
115. See *Final Call,* Special Edition, 5, no. 13.
116. Farrakhan, interview, May 18, 1989.
117. Farrakhan, "The Origin of the White Race: The Making of the Devil."
118. Farrakhan, interview, May 18, 1989.
119. Louis Farrakhan, *Warning to the Government of America* (Chicago: Honorable Elijah Muhammad Educational Foundation, 1983), p. 26.
120. Revelations 21:1–5.

CHAPTER 3

Urban Muslims: The Formation of the Dar ul-Islam Movement

R. M. Mukhtar Curtis

THE EARLY ATTRACTION TO ORTHODOX ISLAM

About forty years ago Rajab Mahmud, Ishaq Abdush-Shaheed, Yahya Abdul-Kareem, Hasan Abdul-Hameed, Sulayman Abdul-Hadi, Luqman Abdul-Aleem, and others made up an amorphous group of New York African American converts to Islam.[1] Like many other African American converts in the New York area, they came into Islam by way of an immigrant connection or a "jazz route": many Muslims living in Harlem during the late 1940s and early 1950s were musicians.[2] The converts frequently socialized at restaurants run by Muslims from the Caribbean and at clubs that featured Muslim entertainers or those attracted to Islam at one time or another such as Dakota Staton, Charlie Parker, and John Coltrane.

When the converts socialized they often discussed the necessity for a Dar al-Islam, an area where Muslims could practice and live an Islamic life as the norm without fear or apprehension.[3] This was their answer to the racism, segregation, and caste system of America that came to the forefront of the national consciousness with such events as the lynching of 14-year-old Emmett Till and the rise to prominence of Martin Luther King and Malcolm X.[4] Underlying the bombings of Negro churches and homes, the lynchings of African Americans, and other forms of resistance by white America to integration was the attitude that black Americans were "beings of an inferior order, and altogether unfit to associate with the

white race, either in social or political relations; and so far inferi-
or, . . . they had no rights which the white man was bound to
respect."5

Many urban African American youths reacted by assuming an
identity or ideology that had un-American or anti-traditional-
American aspects; one of these was a turning away from Christian-
ity.6 They perceived that "whites believed that Christianity was
their exclusive faith, . . . [that] there was segregation throughout
Christendom, . . . [and that] Negro religion [was] merely a Jim
Crow wing of Christianity."7 In a speech at the National Press
Club in Washington, Martin Luther King, Jr. noted with shame
that "the church is the most segregated major institute [sic] in
America."8 As a consequence many African Americans turned to
one form or another of black nationalism whose primary propo-
nents at the time were Malcolm X and the Honorable Elijah
Muhammad, leader of the Nation of Islam (NOI).

Although Dr. King had been quite successful in spearheading
the civil rights movement as a vigorous one of political activism,
his theme of nonviolence was rejected by black nationalists and
many others after his assassination. Nonviolence as a response to
brutality and aggression in the real world of most blacks is an
admission of subordination and weakness as it is in the real world
of many whites and as is manifested in American foreign and
domestic policy.9 Within the African American community the
sentiments of Malcolm X about nonviolence were the popular
alternative to King's stance:

> Never turn the other cheek until you see the white man turn
> his cheek. The day that the white man turns the cheek, then you
> turn the cheek. If Martin Luther King was teaching white people
> to turn the other cheek, then I would say he was justified in
> teaching Black people to turn the other cheek. That's all I'm
> against. Make it a two-way street. Make it even steven. If I'm
> going to be nonviolent, then let them be nonviolent. But as long
> as they're not nonviolent, don't you let anybody tell you any-
> thing about nonviolence. No. Be intelligent.10 . . . Tactics based
> solely on morality can only succeed when you are dealing with
> people who are moral or a system that is moral.11

The New York converts to Sunni Islam and those who joined
them had black nationalist philosophies similar to those of Malcolm X. Many of them were former gang members. Some had

spent time in prison, a few matriculated in college, and all distrusted both the government and Christianity, as did Malcolm and many others within the African American community. The converts believed, as did Malcolm, that Islam unambiguously affirmed qualities and behaviors that they considered essential for a strong and viable African American community. One of these was responsible manhood. Within Islam manhood emerged distinct from femininity and included a theological right of self-defense, self-respect, and family leadership. Passages from the Qur'an and hadith concerning self-defense and self-respect were well known and explicit: "And those [believers] who, when an oppressive wrong is inflicted on them, (are not cowed but) help and defend themselves . . ."[12] "God has made your blood, properties, and honor inviolable . . ."[13]

In addition, the Nation of Islam, with direction from Malcolm, developed the prototypical black defense corps, the Fruit of Islam (FOI), for protection against police brutality and aggression from both racists and elements within the black community. Wherever the FOI had a chapter, it was usually respected if not feared by the African Americans in the vicinity. Members of the community knew not to insult or make passes at women who were affiliated with the "Black Muslims," for they had a policy of physical retribution. This was their reaction to the immoral treatment and low status that black women in general had suffered in America. One of their texts states, "Until we learn to love and protect our women, we will never be a fit and recognized people on the earth. The white people here among you will never recognize you until you protect your women."[14] Subsequently, converts to orthodox Islam recognized both the necessity for an organ similar to the FOI to protect their families and the fact that Islam sanctioned such a body as long as it was governed by orthodox Sharia precepts.

Although Sunni Muslim converts rejected the theology formulated by Elijah Muhammad, they—like all other African Americans—appreciated his and Malcolm's idea that African Americans had to control their own community affairs.[15] Similarly, the concept that African physical features are beautiful and that blacks should take pride in Africa as the motherland received almost universal acceptance throughout the black community. Such ideas had been totally absent from Christian rhetoric until the rise of black nationalism.

In the 1950s black nationalists decried the Christian portrayal of Jesus as a white man with European features. This exclusivist conception, supposedly divinely affirmed, with which white people could identify and feel superior to nonwhites, was another reason for black American disaffection with Christianity.[16] The concept of a white man as the son of God who is a manifestation of Him contrasts with Islamic monotheism and its precept of anti-anthropomorphism.[17] This difference between the two religions was not lost upon African American converts. Indeed, a key attraction for African Americans was Islam's disavowal of racism: "We created you from a single (pair) of a male and a female, and made you into nations and tribes that ye may know each other (not that ye may despise each other). Verily the most honored of you in the sight of Allah is the most righteous of you."[18]

THE FIRST "DAR UL-ISLAM"

The main, if not the only, regularly functioning Sunni Muslim mosque in New York in the late 1940s and early 1950s was the Islamic Mission of America, Inc., located at 143 State Street in Brooklyn.[19] It was started by Daoud Faisal, a West Indian, along with a few Yemeni seamen. Shaykh Daoud was the director, and Maqbul Ilahi, a Pakistani, was the religious scholar. The Islamic Mission featured classes on Islam and Jum'ah, the weekly Friday congregational prayer.

The immediate stimulus to form Dar ul-Islam was dissatisfaction with Shaykh Daoud. Some of the converts believed he was overly concerned with "being accepted by America" and perceived him as an agent of status quo politics. They thought that he despised them and considered them minimally Muslim. These African Americans accused him and the mosque leadership of being "either unaware of or unresponsive to the needs of the indigenous people in whose midst they had settled."[20] He was preoccupied, they believed, with visiting Muslims in prison, conducting marriage ceremonies, and performing duties not devoted to aiding African Americans. They wanted energies focused on Islam as the "uplifting force for the poor and downtrodden within the New York slums and ghettoes."[21] Shaykh Daoud apparently had no intention of mounting an Islamic dynamic that would challenge or attempt to become independent of Western society. These, however, were goals of the African American Muslims.

Articles entitled "Dar-ul-Islam Movement" published in the 1970s in *Al-Jihadul Akbar*, the journal of the movement, state that Rajab Mahmud, Ishaq Abdush Shaheed, and Yahya Abdul-Kareem founded the Dar-ul-Islam concept in 1962.[22] The converts still attended the State Street Mosque, but for prayers other than Jum'ah, and as a place to congregate on Fridays after Jum'ah, they designated other locations as their Dar ul-Islam mosque. The first of these was established at 1964 Atlantic Avenue in Brooklyn in 1962. The first Imam of the brotherhood was Rajab Mahmud; Yahya Abdul-Kareem was in charge of missionary activities or "amir of tabligh (propagation)".[23] A pledge or *bay'ah* was constructed and taken by most of the brothers.[24] The "Dar-ul Islam Pledge" read:

> In the name of Allah, the Gracious, the Merciful; Allah is the Greatest; Bearing witness that there is no God but Allah and that Muhammad (peace be on him) is His Messenger, and being a follower of the last Prophet and Messenger of Allah, I hereby pledge myself to the Shariah and to those who are joined by this pledge. I pledge myself, by pledging my love, energy, wealth, life and abilities. I also pledge myself to the Majlis (Imamate), whose duty is to establish, develop, defend and govern according to the precepts of the Shariah. (Amin).[25]

At a dinner held in the summer of 1963, practically all of the forty to fifty brothers present took or retook the pledge, and as a symbolic show of solidarity all placed their signatures on the table spread.

Due both to a fast growing congregation—"150 brothers" in a matter of months—and the loss of the lease to the Atlantic Avenue site, a new place of prayer was located on Downing Street. Here, said *Al-Jihadul Akbar*, the brotherhood faltered due to "internal disorders" arising from "personality conflicts, misunderstandings of the religion, worldly desires, and the misuse of knowledge."[26] This meant that there were sharp disagreements, that some continued to have sexual relations outside of marriage, and that some believed that certain behaviors deemed illegal according to Islamic law were considered permissible. For example, until 1968 more than a few members of the group did not believe that they had to give up smoking marijuana because English translations of the Quran do not specifically mention this drug, and the earlier revealed verses concerning intoxicants do not ban them outright: "They ask you about intoxicants and gambling. Say there is great sin, but some benefit in both of them; the sin, however, is greater than the benefit" and "do not approach prayer while intoxicated, [wait] until you know what you are saying."[27] Some of the Dar Muslims interpreted this to mean that marijuana was allowed or that Muslims had the right to withdraw gradually from drinking alcoholic beverages as the early Muslims did. The lack of discipline of these converts concerning sobriety—a trait opposite to that of the true believer—and unstable financial resources hindered progress toward a cohesive organization. Hence, a number of brothers did not stick to either the brotherhood or basic Islamic principles.

After the loss of the lease to the Downing Street location in 1965, the group used 777 Saratoga Avenue near Livonia in Brownsville, East New York, as their gathering place. At this location, however, the group broke apart and the "first Dar" ended. The brothers went their separate ways and stopped meeting. Yahya referred to the group's demise as an "upheaval."[28] Apparently a continuation of the problems encountered at the Downing Street mosque, the lack of specific goals and an effective organization to meet them, and failure to comply with basic Islamic precepts doomed the group to break apart. Yahya emerged from this situation as a leader with a group of loyal companions. Muslims of the area continued to use the apartment at Saratoga Avenue to socialize until August 1972.

TRANSITION TO THE SECOND DAR UL-ISLAM: THE CONTEXT

In the United States, laymen unfamiliar with the history and theology of Islam have usually identified all African American Muslims as "Black Muslims," a term popularized by C. Eric Lincoln for the members of the Nation of Islam formed by Elijah Muhammad and now headed by Louis Farrakhan.[29] Sunni Muslims abhorred the group and hated to be mistaken for its followers. To prevent this misidentification, Shaykh Da'ud in 1967 announced that all of the African American Muslims who attended the Islamic Mission had to carry Sunni Muslim identification cards. Those who chose not to comply "did not have to come back" to the State Street mosque ever again. His good intentions notwithstanding, many of the men whom he addressed regarded this decision as patronizing and arrogant. They felt that he was paternalistic enough to order African

Americans to carry identification to distinguish themselves from other blacks, but he obviously felt no authority over Arabs and Pakistanis to ask—much less command—them to be distinguished from their non-Muslim compatriots or from white Americans.

His dictum stimulated the latent sense of frustration that had prevailed among the African American Muslims since the first Dar ul-Islam brotherhood had disbanded. They felt they had put themselves in a subordinate position by having to attend the Islamic Mission without having any authority within it. Indeed, one of their failed goals was to tend to the needs of African Americans independent of outside control and to produce an alternative to the Nation of Islam. They had not produced a counterculture to American society including its morality—or lack thereof—and de facto caste or segregation systems. They wanted to establish an Islamic community for themselves whose activities would revolve around a mosque that would be open for prayer twenty-four hours a day.

The context of the frustrations of the African American Muslims and their resulting goals must be taken into account. For example, by 1967 the "black power" slogan was popular within the African American community. It meant different things to different people, but in general it connoted a more militant, if not aggressive and belligerent, stance for its supporters.[30] It meant that black people should control their own affairs and destiny and should protect themselves and fight their enemies. While he was the head of the Student Nonviolent Coordinating Committee, Stokely Carmicheal helped to spread the black power concept. He remarked to a group of his supporters that:

> When you talk of "black power," you talk of bringing this country to its knees. When you talk of "black power," you talk of building a movement that will smash everything Western civilization has created. When you talk of "black power," you talk of picking up where Malcolm X left off. When you talk of "black power," you talk of the black man doing whatever is necessary to get what he needs . . . we are fighting for our lives.[31]

Also, in the summer of 1967 the United States suffered the worst racially motivated civil disturbances in its history. There were more than 40 riots and more than 100 smaller incidents. The National Advisory Commission on Civil Disorders headed by Otto Kerner studied them and produced its report for President Lyndon Johnson in March 1968. Among its conclusions were that the

United States was moving toward two societies, one white, one black, separate and unequal; that white racism was the most fundamental cause of the riots; and that around half of the disturbances were precipitated by police violence against blacks.[32]

By 1967 a number of black self-defense groups had formed both to monitor and fight the police if necessary and to protect their communities overall. The three most prominent ones were the Black Panthers, the Deacons of Lowndes County in Alabama, and Simba Wachuka (Swahili for "young lions") popularly known as the army of the US organization headed by Ron Karenga.[33] These groups were modeled after the Fruit of Islam, the paramilitary of the Nation of Islam. The African Americans' decision to attempt again to build an independent Dar ul-Islam community thus drew its impetus not only from their commitment to Islam, but also from an African American nationalistic consciousness that was popular during the time. Shaykh Da'ud's paternalistic dictum to them to carry Sunni Muslim identification cards was the proverbial straw that broke the camel's back.

THE DAR UL-ISLAM MOSQUE

In its failed attempt to build a new Islamic community, the brotherhood had continued attending the Islamic Mission for Jum'ah. Following Shaykh Da'ud's announcement in 1967, and for the first time ever, the converts held a separate Friday prayer. This was a significant statement of independence. The converts chose not to defer to the larger mosque. "Their action implied that they no longer recognized the legitimacy of the Islamic Mission to hold the Jum'ah prayer for the benefit of all of the local community; they believed that the mosque failed to meet everyone's religious needs. Hence, five to seven brothers, Yahya Abdul-Kareem included, prayed within a one-bedroom flat on Lewis Avenue in Brooklyn. It was a modest place; the tenants shared a bathroom and kitchen. This time the men were more determined to build an Islamic community: the vibe [i.e., ethos] was to adhere to Qur'an and sunnah; no compromise. Remember! All of us had come from gangs and jail [and we knew the meaning of no compromise]."[34]

When the people became too numerous to meet for the Friday prayer within the Lewis Avenue location, Bilal Abd al-Rahman offered his four-room apartment in the 100 block of Saratoga Street in the Ocean Hill district of Brooklyn. Two months later the

Muslims outgrew his place, forcing them to move the Friday prayer to another Brooklyn location, 240 Sumpter Street. Two rooms of Jamil Abdur-Rahman's five-room apartment were used for the mosque. In 1968 Yahya was elected Imam. By all accounts this was where the Dar really "took off." The apartment was open for prayers twenty-four hours a day. Classes in Islam and elementary Arabic were taught. The brothers considered it their Islamic duty to pray the predawn and one of the after sunset prayers, *maghreb* or *'isha'*, within the mosque. Those who wanted to live at the mosque to affirm their commitment to the Islamic way of life, or who necessarily had to live there, were allowed—even encouraged —to do so.

BIRTH OF DAR UL-ISLAM, THE MOVEMENT

A clash with the United States government later that year compelled the New York brotherhood to seek unity with other African American Muslim communities and to organize their own police force. The conflict began when four white FBI agents arrived in the predominantly black Brownsville section of Brooklyn in an unmarked vehicle. Three of them entered an apartment house. They caught the attention of five or six Sunni Muslims. When they saw the men coming out of the building accompanying a fellow Muslim in handcuffs and shackled at the feet, the Muslims confronted the arresting officers. The captive managed to escape.

Shortly thereafter, the neighborhood was flooded with federal agents, police, and plainclothes detectives. Some agents came to the mosque. The guard asked them to follow the Muslim custom of removing their shoes. The agent closest to the guard bent down as if to comply, but brandished a .38 caliber pistol instead and arrested the doorman. The Feds then proceeded to trash the mosque claiming that they were looking for the fugitive. The Muslim community was outraged. Imam Yahya commented on the incident in *Al-Jihadul Akbar* and explained why he thought the FBI did not give the mosque the same respect as he thought they would have given a church frequented by white people:

> There was an incident in 1968 with the F.B.I. when the mosque had been violated by the American police—by the Federal authorities, and the outcry from that was due to the provocation— to their provocation. . . .
> . . . the reason we were attacked was basically out of igno-

rance of the federal government about Muslims, about sanctity of the Mosque, and ignorance in their relationship of how to deal with Muslims. That's part of it. They attacked the mosque on the precept that they were supposed to be looking for a draft dodger who was related [i.e., alleged] to have been Muslim. They alleged that we hid him in the mosque [and they wanted] to see if they could find this "alleged Muslim"—Allah protect us.

To be honest, I think it has a racial basis because most of these people [i.e., whites in positions of authority] have a tendency to . . . regard Blacks in particular as being . . . [no]thing other than [whites' racist perceptions of] Blacks. When they look upon American Blacks they don't look at his [sic] religion or his character. All they can see is that he is Black and they look back to the past history and they see him always as being the [servile] subject of the society instead of looking upon him as a man or the person that he might be. That's why (I feel personally) they disregarded the sanctity of the Mosque.[35]

Imam Yahya's perception of the attitude of whites and the government agents is reminiscent of Justice Taney's words mentioned earlier; namely, that since black Americans are regarded as beings of an "inferior order, . . . they had no rights which the white man was bound to respect."

Although a delegation of Muslims met with the regional head of the FBI to resolve the incident, it roused the brotherhood to redouble efforts to realize a national Dar ul-Islam federation. Delegations went to various cities to encourage Muslim communities to join the movement. Ratification of affiliation was by word and sometimes by a handshake.[37] Cleveland was the first to join under the leadership of Imam Mutawwaf Abdush-Shaheed. Philadelphia was the second under Imam Ali Ahmad. With New York these communities were the largest of the movement.

In August 1972 the New York brotherhood made 52 Herkimer Place in Brooklyn its mosque. The location was acquired from a childhood friend of Imam Yahya named Ben Banu. The name chosen for the mosque was Ya-Sin, a term consisting of the names of two Arabic letters corresponding to the English Y and S. It is also both the first verse and the name of the thirty-sixth chapter of the Qur'an. Because this chapter is considered to be the heart of the Qur'an, one of its verses seemed especially apt to the converts, for they considered the text directly related to them, their families, and their African American brethren. It reads: "[This Qur'an was revealed] in order that thou [Muhammad] may warn a people whose fathers were not warned, and who, therefore, remain heedless."[37] Thus, the mosque was named Ya-Sin because it was to be the heart of the Dar ul-Islam Movement as the chapter Ya-Sin was to the Qur'an and because the movement was to spread the Islamic message among blacks in particular, for they were those whose fathers had not been warned.

When it moved to Herkimer Place the brotherhood became more organized. Responsibilities were delegated to newly created ministry positions: Propagation (Da'wa), Defense, Information, Culture, Education, Health and Welfare, and Protocol.

The ministry of defense and its paramilitary Ra'd (Arabic for thunder) were very important. Ra'd was similar to the defense corps of other militant organizations that were involved in violent confrontations such as the Fruit of Islam, the Black Panthers, and the army of the US organization. All young males were required to take self-defense training and the best of them were chosen for Ra'd. Members drew various assignments ranging from providing personal bodyguards and building security, to protecting the females or dealing with those who insulted them, to administering punishments to those who broke the laws of the community. Ra'd members were supposed to be the exemplars of the community. More than anyone else, they were truly to fear none but Allah and His displeasure; they were to "hear and obey" without question.[38] The Ya-Sin mosque administration believed that Ra'd was a force superior to other similar groups not only because of the members' skills, but also because of their superior discipline and higher standard of morality. The founders had achieved one of their goals.

By the mid-1970s at least thirty-one mosque-based Sunni Muslim family communities were affiliated with the Dar ul-Islam Movement. They were located principally in cities along the eastern seaboard and in all of its larger metropolitan areas.[39] Dar ul-Islam was the largest indigenous Sunni Muslim group in the United States until 1975, when Warith Deen Muhammad proclaimed Sunni Islam as the religion of the Nation of Islam bringing 100,000 members into the fold.[40] Each community had its own Imam and Yahya Abdul-Kareem was the Imam of the Dar ul-Islam Movement. After the affiliation of a new Dar community, it organized itself into ministries like those at Ya-Sin mosque. To formalize the federation, a contract of allegiance modeled after the Medinah treaty of the Prophet of Islam was used.[41] This treaty and the pledge mentioned earlier were regarded as lifelong commitments similar to the pledges Muslims gave to the Prophet and the early caliphs. Enforcement of these declarations was through moral suasion, but they were regarded very seriously; breaking one's word is an indication of hypocrisy.[42] (The treaty is reproduced in this chapter's appendix.)

ISLAMIC EDUCATION

Imam Yahya studied under Hafiz Maqbul Ilahi of the Islamic Mission and from 1963 to 1969 with Dr. Fazlur Rahman Ansari, said to be a Sufi Shaykh from Pakistan of the Qadiriyah *tariqah*.[43] Once the Dar-ul-Islam movement was underway in the late 1960s, the Imam offered a class appropriately labeled *the Shaykh's class* in which he taught material learned from Ansari and from texts on Sufism such a *Kashf al-Mahjub* [Illumination of the Veiled], ʿAwarif al-Maʾarif [Masters of Mystical Insights], *Futuh al-Ghaib* [Revelations of the Unseen] and *Memoirs of the Saints*.[44]

The Shaykh's class was the highest a student could attain; only those who were recommended by their Imam or someone already in attendance and whom Yahya approved could attend. The class was taught on Thursdays and Sundays. Each student wore a blue thobe or jallabiyah, a loose, shirtlike garment extending to the lower part of the leg. After five years of acceptable matriculation, a student's name was supposed to be recommended to the Sufi order. If accepted the student had to serve two years somewhere else under observation in a kind of practicum. It is unknown if anyone did this.

Requisites for this class were the first two courses of the Minhaj (educational) "program" series: Maʾrifat Allah (knowledge of Allah) and Islam. The others in their required order were entitled Angels, Books, Prophets, Punishments of the Grave, and Taqdir and Qadar (preordainment). Except for the fourth, these titles correspond to the terms denoting the basic beliefs in Islam.[45] Students could attend these classes and the Shaykh's class concurrently.

The Philadelphia community became influential in the area of education. The text that they used for an introductory course, *Mubadi al-Islam: Fundamentals of Islam*, was adopted by many other mosques throughout the movement.[46] The two classes following this, Fundamentals I and II, were adopted by other communities also. Teachers used passages from *The Religion of Islam* and *The Tenets of Islam* for the first and *Origins and Development of Islamic Institutions* and *Islamic Law and Constitution* for the second class.[47] Teaching methodologies were unconventional. Except for the introductory course popularly known as Mubadi', teachers usually did not tell the students the names of the texts being used. Classes resembled traditional Islamic learning circles wherein students and teacher sat in a circle on the floor of the mosque. The core of the session was the teacher dictating from his notes the partial text from one of the readings. Students were required to write and eventually memorize this. Teachers were those who had taken the class previously.

ETHOS: PURITY, INDEPENDENCE, AND ELITISM

Because the era of Malcolm X and the rhetoric that characterized him and the black nationalist movement spawned Dar ul-Islam, published articles by the group often carried a theme of liberation from racism; for example,

> The Dar-ul Islam movement and community have found that Blacks, Indians and Spanish speaking people are the best adherents to [the] laws of God Almighty in America. . . .[48]

> Mahmud, Abdush Shaheed and Abdul-Kareem were motivated by a sincere love for Islam and by a sincere love for the people from which they . . . had sprung. They knew that there was a natural affinity between Islam and the poor . . . and realized the ability of Islam to be an uplifting force for people, such as the poor and downtrodden of New York's slums and ghettoes.[49]

Actually, there was no particular plan to address "the needs of the indigenous people" except for an opportunity to practice Islam within the Dar ul-Islam Movement and to gain the deific benevolence that believers thought might accrue as stated in the article "Dar-ul-Islam Movement": "[the founders] endeavored to mobilize the people, to change what was in their hearts so that Almighty God Allah might change the condition of the people."[50]

Westerners would characterize the Dar ul-Islam movement as fundamentalist, because the faithful put a premium upon praying at the mosque, covering women according to Qur'anic precepts, and the avoidance of the major sins, the *kaba'ir*. These include violations of Islamic monotheism, the most serious of which are praying or making supplication to any entity except to God-Allah,[51] illegal sexual relations, and lying.[52] A trait the Dar shared with traditional Muslim groups was the eschewal of political participation.[53] This characteristic was part of a broader goal, however, which was to avoid friendship with and dependence upon non-Muslims and to maintain a distance from Muslims who appear to have such relationships. This theme of disassociation was explained in a homily by Imam Yahya, "Take Not the Unbelievers for Friends" (Qur'an, 5:90).[54]

Furthermore, Muslims should feel disaffection toward coreligionists—male and female—who associate with or dress like non-Muslims. Thus, physical appearance to Dar members was an important barometer of a Muslim's adherence to the precepts of the religion and concomitantly to one's devotion to the Sunnah or normative practice of the Prophet of Islam.[55] Members frequently cited the hadith, "Whoever imitates a people is among them."[56] Less frequently they referred to the narration that labels shaving as anathema.[57] Therefore, Muslim men—foreign and indigenous—who succumbed to occupational and cultural demands to be beardless and women who did not wear a covering headpiece were considered to be brazenly disobedient to God and in love more with the norms and mores of non-Muslims than with Him and His commandments.[58]

A few influential members of the Dar harbored antipathy toward the brothers who attended college. They were regarded as being too close to the enemy and not to be trusted because of their perceived white mannerisms, diction, nonprison or stable family background, and ease of persona with whites who were educated or "successful." In private, older influential members referred to their college educated brethren as *young boys*.[59] "In retrospect," said one former Dar member, "there was jealousy toward them." Dar members did not perceive their attitude as blameworthy, for they believed that Allah would establish a new Islamic state with Muslims like them—if not with them and trusted Dar ul-Islam members only—at its core and helm.[60]

Members of the movement often viewed Muslims with Western

degrees and professional Muslims, particularly those who were immigrants, as Muslim "Uncle Toms" who were imitating and ingratiating themselves to the West. They were seen as running toward disbelief or Jahiliyah, pre-Islamic ignorance, for they often violated certain Islamic precepts. Their offenses were said to include the men being beardless, women dressing not according to Islamic principles, and parents forcing their daughters to dress without the *khimar* (Islamic headcovering). Other violations were the obtaining of interest bearing loans, selling or drinking alcohol, and socializing with non-Muslim men and women. Dar members also believed that most nonindigenous Muslims were too fearful and respectful of U.S. government authority.

On the other hand, many Muslim immigrants and their American-born offspring viewed blacks as stupid if not uneducable, deserving of being despised, and only minimally Muslim. Thus, there was friction between these two groups and interaction between them was kept to a minimum.

THE SUFI ENDING

In 1980 Ya-Sin moved from Herkimer Place to Van Siclan. Two years later the group suffered a tumultuous change in direction; Imam Yahya declared that the Dar had ceased and was part of an "international Jama'at al-Fuqrah" under the leadership of a Shaykh Mubarik Ali Jilani Hashmi.[61] Yahya abdicated his authority and leadership. His former followers now consider themselves Sufis with an ethos and precepts unparalleled in the former Dar. Many members of the movement did not accept Jilani, including the community in Atlanta led by Imam Jamil Abdullah al-Amin, formerly H. Rap Brown, chairman of the Student Nonviolent Coordinating Committee after Stokely Carmichael. Others from around the nation who chose not to follow had to start their communities anew. They formed another federation that may be more than half the size of the former Dar. There is no title or official name for the new group. They refer to themselves simply as the *jama'ah* or the "national *jama'ah*." Jamil is its leading Amir or Imam and members of this group share little common ground with their former coreligionists. The Ya-Sin mosque on Van Siclan ceased operations, and its building was sold in the mid-1980s.

CONCLUSION

Islam offered to Dar members a lucid, divinely ordained value system with a promise of rewards and punishments in this life and the hereafter. It included a set of daily behaviors that distinguished a practicing Muslim from others. The believer required no skills in deconstructionism to understand Islamic monotheism nor was one's worry that the divine text, the Qur'an, was subject to alteration, an ipso facto litmus test for revelation. The second Islamic criterion, the Prophet's behavior, also not subject to revision, was made available in hadith translations.

The simplicity of the basic tenets of Islam and its consonance with certain aspirations of blacks, particularly those who desired a culture and polity separate from and not dominated by white America, made Islam and the Dar attractive. The converts personified many of the individual attributes associated with Malcolm X, such as a readiness for self-defense, a disciplined traditional morality, and an exemplary strong African American manhood. These were manifest in the brothers' attempt to have their own mosque separate from the Islamic Mission, the decision not to return there, the statements by Yahya concerning the FBI's disrespect for the mosque, and the building of the movement consequent to the FBI incident. Traditional moral values and Islamic attire within the context of an unsympathetic environment suggests the strength of the female Muslims.

On a societal scale the hope was that the Muslim communities would become independent and self-contained with their own political, judicial, economic, and defense systems. The ultimate earthly hope was that the Dar faithful would form a sovereign state. Their professed methodology was to live by Qur'an and Sunnah, and to disengage from American institutional life as much as possible while gradually providing the community with replacement institutions and services. Their hedge against such high hopes was to understand that sovereign statehood was not a necessity as much as an Islamic perspective, a principle taught by Fazlur Rahman Ansari, the Sufi who taught Imam Yahya, and by the latter in his classes on Thursday and Sunday.

The venture into aspects of Sufism was related to changing "what was in their hearts" to gain certain benefits; but the preoccupation of this process is introspective. It becomes antithetical to social change because the Sufi in an antagonistic society can find fulfillment with a change in perspective or with the discovery of inner or transcendent truths while issues of governmental and financial import become less important; the perspective of many Sufis is to learn to live despite oppressions instead of gaining control over them.

Identifying the impediments that both hampered Dar-ul-Islam and led to its dissolution requires more research, but provincialism probably was a factor. Distrust of both those who were not Muslim and Muslims who were too close to the "enemy" in appearance or manner limited the resources available to the group. This was not unintentional; part of their philosophy was to be self-reliant. Factors accounting for distrustfulness were as much a function of a street-black cultural index as they were of Islamic values. Islam became a counterculture as a complement to the African American culture as understood and represented by the leadership and opinion makers within the Dar.

Although there was a necessity for a *bay'ah* to ensure dependability, further research will also have to establish whether it became a negative factor, as that possibility is discussed by Bilal Philips:

> establishing the *bay'ah* prematurely will likely reinforce any narrow-mindedness and extremism present among the leadership or membership and eventually create a closed elitist group. Such a group, once created, becomes unable to benefit from knowledgeable non-members because non-members are branded as outsiders and thus untrustworthy. Eventually . . . [malevolent forces] may introduce a deviant idea, which will spread quickly and unopposed through the ranks due to their close[d]-mindedness and eventually they may end up committing atrocities against Muslims in the name of Islam.[62]

The personal Dar-ul-Islam pledge was comprehensive and, if taken literally, a lifelong contract of indenture. It is conceivable that complexities arose both in members' personal lives and for the group as a whole in applying the phrase "according to the precepts of the Shariah," for no intelligentsia has developed that has both the credentials of traditional Islamic scholarship and the ability to apply it aptly within African American or Western cultures.

Nonetheless, the existence of the Dar and the families who helped begin it might represent a first in United States history. The

movement was a true Sunni Muslim group predominantly composed of African Americans who successfully imposed upon themselves a number of Islamic precepts, including moral principles like
chastity and family integrity, within a society that does not encourage these values.

NOTES

Heartfelt thanks to the Hanover College Faculty Development Committee for the Minor Research Grant that enabled the initial research for
this paper, to Shaykh Sayed Abdul-Hadi of Philadelphia for his time and
access to his library, to Denise Johnson for reading this work, and to S. A.
Jackson of Indiana University for reviewing this paper and offering many
beneficial suggestions. Of course, all errors and shortcomings are mine.

1.   Arabic terms and names like Yahyah will be spelled according
to either the way the person named or the publication of his or her group
spells it, e.g., Yahya; otherwise, transliterations will be similar to the style
used by Arabic linguists but without distinctions between emphatic con-
sonants and their nonpharyngealized equivalents.

2.   Roi Ottley, *New World A-Coming* (1943; reprint ed., New
York: Arno Press and The New York Times, 1968), p. 56.

3.   *Dar al-Islam* refers to the "land or realm wherein Muslims live
by the law of Islam" as opposed to Dar al-Harb or "land of war," wherein non-Muslim government and moral values dominate. The publications
of the group usually spell the name as *Dar-ul Islam* and sometimes *Dar-ul-Islam*.

4.   See George A. Davis and O. Fred Donaldson, *Blacks in the
United States: A Geographic Perspective* (Boston: Houghton Mifflin,
1975), p. 112: "Patterns of residential and educational land use are the
most common examples of the spatial *caste system* [against blacks] in the
country" (my italics.); Bertram Karon, *The Negro Personality* (New
York: Springer, 1958), pp. 1–7 and Chap. 2, "The American Caste System"; Bertram Doyle, *The Etiquette of Race Relations in the South: A
Study in Social Control* (Chicago: University Press, 1937).

5.   Words of Chief Justice Roger Brooke Taney of the Supreme
Court of the United States quoted by Frank B. Latham, *The Dred Scott
Decision, March 6, 1857: Slavery and the Supreme Court's "Self-Inflicted
Wound"* (New York: Franklin Watts, 1968), p. 30.

6.   Cf. Na'im Akbar, *Visions for Black Men* (Nashville: Winston-
Derek, 1991), pp. 69–73; George Breitman, *The Last Year of Malcolm X:
The Evolution of a Revolutionary* (New York: Schocken Books, 1967),
pp. 56 and 147.

7. Simeon Booker, *Black Man's America* (Englewood Cliffs, N.J.: Prentice-Hall, 1964), pp. 108–109.

8. Ibid., pp. 116–117.

9. This is not to mention that within the African American community nonviolence as a response is often interpreted and despised as a homosexual trait. See Charles E. Silberman, *Criminal Violence, Criminal Justice* (New York: Vintage Books, 1978), pp. 523–530.

10. Bruce Perry, ed., *Malcolm X: The Last Speeches* (New York: Pathfinder, 1989), p. 149.

11. George Breitman, ed., *By Any Means Necessary: Speeches, Interviews, and a Letter by Malcolm X* (New York: Pathfinder, 1970), p. 43.

12. Qur'an, 42:39. English renditions of Quranic passages are from *The Meaning of the Glorious Koran* by Mohammed Marmaduke Pickthall (New York: Penguin Group, n.d); *The Quran*, trans. T. B. Irving (Brattleboro, Vt.: Amana Books, 1991); *The Holy Qur'an*, ed. The Presidency of Islamic Researches, Ifta, Call and Guidance (Medinah, Saudi Arabia: Ministry of Hajj and Endowments, 1410 A.H.); and *The Holy Qur'an*, trans. A. Yusuf Ali ([n.p.]: The Muslim Student Association, 1975).

13. *Sahih* [Muhammad ibn Isma'il] *al-Bukhari*, (Beirut: Dar Ihya' al-Turath al-ʿArabi, 1958), 8:18.

14. Elijah Muhammad, *Message to the Blackman* (Chicago: Muhammad's Temple No. 2, 1965), pp. 58–61.

15. On the theology of the Nation of Islam see Zafar Ishaq Ansari, "Aspects of Black Muslim Theology," *Studia Islamica* 53 (Spring 1981): 137–176.

16. A common view in the 1960s and early 1970s; see Harding, "Black Power and the American Christ."

17. See Qur'an, 2:255; 42:11; 112.

18. Qur'an, 49:13.

19. See Akbar Muhammad, "Muslims in the United States" in *The Islamic Impact*, ed. Yvonne Yazbeck Haddad et al. (Syracuse, N.Y.: Syracuse University Press, 1984), pp. 208–210.

20. "Dar-ul-Islam Movement," Articles 1 and 2. There are three editions of this article; all are entitled "Dar ul-Islam Movement." Articles 1 and 2 are identical, have the subheading "The Real Muslims Stand Up!", are a brief indulgent early history of the group, and are followed by a page captioned "Medina Treaty," the Dar agreement federating a mosque.

Article 1 is from the July 1974 edition of *Al-Jihadul Akbar*. Article 2 is part of an unnumbered and undated eight-page insert apparently from a special printing. The third article is an edited version of articles 1 and 2 leading into an interview with Yahya Abdul-Kareem. Citations to these will refer to Article 1, 2 or 3. The last publication of *Al-Jihadul Akbar* was in spring 1980.

21. Ibid.

22. Ibid.

23. Article 3, p. 9.

24. The models for this are the two pledges of Aqabah and that of al-Ridwan during the lifetime of the Prophet and the pledges given to the four caliphs after him. See Abd al-Malik Ibn Hisham, *The Life of Muhammad: A Translation of Ibn Ishaq's Sirat Rasul Allah*, trans. Alfred Guillaume (New York: Oxford University Press, 1955), pp. 198–205 for the first two pledges (see Qur'an 60:12) and pp. 503–504 and 686–687, respectively, concerning al-Ridwan and Abu Bakr.

25. "Dar-ul-Islam Movement," all articles.

26. "Dar-ul-Islam Movement," Articles 1 and 2.

27. Qur'an, 2:219 and 4:43. The verses of prohibition are 5:90–91.

28. Article 3, p. 9.

29. Eric C. Lincoln, *The Black Muslims in America* (Boston: Beacon Press, 1961). Americans commonly believe a Muslim to be a foreigner and an Arab in particular. Hence, the improper uses of *Moslem* for them and *Muslim* for followers of Elijah Muhammad and Sunni African Americans.

30. Alton Hornsby, Jr., *Chronology of African-American History: Significant Events and People from 1619 to the Present* (Detroit: Gale Research, 1991), p. 127.

31. G. Roberts, "From 'Freedom High' to 'Black Power,'" *The New York Times Magazine* (Sept. 25, 1966), p. 6, quoted in James Haskins, *Profiles in Black Power* (New York: Doubleday, 1972), p. 193.

32. Bradford Chambers, ed., *Chronicles of Negro Protest* (New York: Parents' Magazine Press, 1968), pp. 300–301.

33. The Black Panthers were a militant African American organization organized by Huey P. Newton and Elridge Cleaver in 1966. Members believed in defending themselves and the black community by open conflict with the police if necessary. On their demise, see Chap. 9, "The Only Good Panther," *Racial Matters: The F.B.I.'s Secret Files on Black America. 1960–1972* (New York: The Free Press, 1989) by Kenneth O'Reilly.

Ron Ndabezitha Everett-Karenga founded the U.S. organization in the mid-1960s emphasizing African American culture and black nationalism. He was also the originator of the African American holiday, Kwanzaa.

34. Interview with Bilal Abdur-Rahman.

35. Article 3, page 9.

36. Ibid.

37. Qur'an, 36:6; the hadith mentioning Ya-Sin as the heart of the Quran do not meet the standards of sahih "sound (free from deficiency)" hadith. See Isma'il Ibn Kathir, *Tafsir al-Quran al-'Azim* (Beirut: Dar al-Andalus, 1983), 5:598.

38. See Qur'an, 2:150, 2:285, 5:27 ff, 5:44, 76:7–10.

39. Dar ul-Islam mosques were located in New York, Massachusetts, New Jersey, Ohio, Pennsylvania, Maryland, Virginia, Washington, D.C., North Carolina, South Carolina, Alabama, Georgia, Michigan, Illinois, Colorado, Ontario, Trinidad, the West Indies, and Alaska.

40. Hornsby, *Chronology of African-American History*, p. 111. Imam Warith Deen of the American Muslim Mission was named at birth after Wallace Delaney Fard who propagated the foundations of Islam to the then Elijah Poole. After Fard's disappearance in 1934, the Nation of Islam said he was God in person and Allah, even though his physical features were not black or Negroid. Whites were said to be "devils."

Wallace, like Malcolm X, was a seventh child. This was significant to each of their families. Since his childhood Wallace was expected to inherit his father's position. Upon assumption of leadership, "his ultimate goal," says C. Eric Lincoln, has been "complete orthodoxy" and "to eradicate completely the Black Nationalist image." Concerning Warith Deen, Z. Ansari said that "[his] influence and followers have been reduced by Louis Farrakhan's extraordinary demagogic skill" ("W. D. Muhammad: The Making of a 'Black Muslim' Leader," *American Journal of Islamic Social Sciences* 2 [December 1985]: 245–262).

41. W. Montgomery Watt, *Muhammad at Medina* (New York: Oxford Univiversity Press, 1956), pp. 221–225; Ibn Hisham, *The Life of Muhammad*, pp. 231–234.

42. Hypocrisy (*nifaq*) in Islam is different from the popular concept of the term in English, where it means to say one thing and do another. The hypocrite is one who consciously and falsely claims belief in Islamic monotheism or the Prophet of Islam.

43. *Tariqah* (lit. "way" or "manner"): a religious order whose members stress following God in a mystical or inner sense.

44. Interviews with Imam al-Amin Abdul-Latif and Shaykh Sayed Abdul-Hadi (1991). Ali ibn Uthman al-Juliabi al-Hujwiri, *Kashf al-Mahjub*, trans. Reynold Nicholson (Leiden: E. J. Brill, 1911; reprint ed., London Luzac, 1936, 1959, 1967; Lahore: Islamic Book Foundation, 1976). Umar ibn Muhammad al Suhrawardi, 'Awarif al-Ma'arif, trans. H. Wilberforce (Lahore: Sh. Muhammad Ashraf, 1973). Abd Al-Qadir al Jilani, *Futuh al-Ghaib*, trans. Aftab al-Deen Ahmad (Lahore: Sh. Mu-

hammad Ashraf, [1972, 1967]). Muhammad ibn Ibrahim Farid al-Deen, *Tadhkirat al-Awliya 'Memoirs of the Saints' of Muhammad ibn Ibrahim Farid al-Deen*, trans. Reynold Nicholson (London: Luzac, 1905–1907).

45. Muslim ibn al-Hajjaj ibn Muslim al-Qushayri al-Nisaburi, *Sahih Muslim*, trans. Abdul Hamid Siddiqi ([n.p.]: Academy of Islamic Research and Publications, n.d.), 1:1–2; *Sahih Muslim*, ed. Muhammad Fu'ad Abd al-Baqi (Dar al-Ihya' al-Kutub al-'Arabiyah, Isa al-Babi al-Halabi, 1955), 1:28–29.

46. Muhammad ibn [Abd al-Wahhab] Sulayman al-Tamimi, trans. Ahmad Jalal and Muhammad Ghaly (Riyadh, Saudi Arabia: Ri'asat Idarat al-Buhuth al-'Ilmiyah wa-al-Ifta' wa-al-Da'wa wa-al-Irshad, n.d.).

47. Ahmad Ghalwash, *The Religion of Islam*, (Supreme Council for Islamic Affairs, 1966). Ali Musa Raza Muhajir, *The Tenets of Islam* (Lahore: Sh. Muhammad Ashraf, [1969]). Amir Hasan Siddiqi, *Origins and Development of Islamic Institutions* (Karachi: Jamiyat al-Fallah, [1962]). Abul Ala Maudoodi, *The Islamic Law and Constitution* (Karachi: Jamaat-e-Islami Publications, [1955].

48. "Dar-ul Islam is a Community," *Islamic News: Special Anniversary Edition*, n.d. This publication was published by the Philadelphia mosque, it reprinted this article and others from *Al-Jihadul Akbar*.

49. "Dar-ul-Islam Movement," all articles.

50. Ibid. The article cites the translation of the verse as "Allah will never change the grace which He hath bestowed on a people until they change what is in their very soul." The exegesis of this, however, refers first to conditions that proceed from good to bad.

51. *Sahih al-Bukhari*, 9:4. Prayer and supplication to icons, amulets, saints, their pictures, and even to the Prophet of Islam himself is considered polytheistic. Other major sins are disobedience to parents and murder. Outside of self-defense against non-Muslims and declared warfare, the taking of human life is permitted as atonement for murder, apostasy, male homosexuality, and extramarital sexual relations.

52. *Sahih al-Bukhari*, 3:224–225; Qur'an: 25:68.

53. Rafiq Zakaria upbraids this self-imposed position, "Where Muslims are in a minority . . . the attitude of the fundamentalists is quite clear; they should learn to live as second class citizens and avoid participation in politics or administration." *The Struggle Within Islam* (New York: Penguin Books, 1988), p. 27.

54. Yahya A. Kareem, "Take Not the Unbelievers for Friends," *Al-Jihadul Akbar* (Spring 1400 A.H., 1980): 13–14 and 23–26.

55. In *Kitab Iqtida' al-Sirat al-Mustaqim Mukhalafat Ashab al-Jahim*, Ibn Taymiya argued vigorously that Muslim imitation of others is proscribed. Ibn Taymiyah provided one exception; see Ahmad Zaki Hammad, *Islamic Law* (Indianapolis: American Trust Publications, 1992),

p. 24. Muslim faith is disaffirmed upon disbelief in the compulsory nature of the behavior and commands of the Prophet of Islam for Muslims; see, for example, Qur'an, 4:80, 48:17.

56.   *Man tashabbaha bi-qawmin fa-huwa min-hum*: cited from the hadith collections of Ahmad ibn Hanbal, *al-Musnad*, and Abu Da'ud Sulayman al-Sijistani, *al-Sunan*, by Fazlul Karim in *al-Hadis [A Translation and Revision of al-Mishkat al-Masabih by Muhammad ibn Abd Allah al-Khatib al-Tibrizi]* (Lahore: Muhammad Ashraf, n.d.).

57.   *Sahih al-Bukhari*, 9:198.

58.   On injunctions mandating having a beard, *Sahih al-Bukhari*, 7:206; Qur'anic injunctions on women's attire: 24:31, 33:59.

59.   *Young boy* is a slang term whose core meaning pertains to "inexperience" whether it is in a particular area or to the age of someone relative to the age of someone older. Here the term refers to life or street experience less than to actual age.

60.   Qur'an, 24:55 presents the promise of political sovereignty to the believers.

61.   *Fuqra* is a corruption of the Arabic plural *al-fuqara*; the singular is *faqir*. The literal meaning is one who is poor, impoverished. A popular usage of it refers to the Sufi who is poor in comparison to his Lord, a meaning derived from Quranic passages like: "O mankind! It is 'you that have need' [*al-fuqara*] of Allah; but Allah is the One who is free of all wants, worthy of all praise (al-Fatir, 35:15)."

62.   *Tafseer of Soorah al-Hujaraat* (Riyadh: International Islamic Publishing House, 1988), p. 88.

CHAPTER 4

Tradition and Innovation in Contemporary American Islamic Spirituality: The Bawa Muhaiyaddeen Fellowship

Gisela Webb

INTRODUCTION

The purpose of this study is to shed light on the historical development of Islamic movements in this country by addressing an area
that has thus far received little attention: the "mystical dimension"
of Islam (*tasawwuf*, Sufism) as it has manifested itself in the contemporary American context. It is surprising that there has been
virtually no scholarship on Sufism in America, but this can be seen
in light of three factors.

First, the field of study of Islam in America is quite new, and in
general there is a lack of awareness of the growth of Islamic religion
in this country. Most Americans think of Islam as consisting of
foreign-born Muslims and their families, and they do not see converts to Islam as somehow fully integrated into the Islamic community.

The second factor is the coinciding of the emergence of Sufi
groups in America with the 1960s interest and population of "religions of the East," and the suspicion (among academics, "anticult"
groups, and traditional Muslims alike) that American Sufi groups
were perhaps merely "counterculture" or (now) "new age" religious phenoma.

The third factor, which is thoroughly addressed in James Morris's "Situating Islamic Mysticism: Between Written Traditions and Popular Spirituality,"[1] is the lack of attention given to the role of the "holy personage," the *wali Allah* (the "Friend of God"), in contemporary studies of Islam in general. Morris observes that until very recently this was "the central focus of popular religious and devotional life in virtually every region of the Islamic world." He reflects on the lack of discussion of the historical development of "classical" mystical literature, which, as he points out, emerged subsequent to—and in light of—oral traditions, and not the other way around. Similarly, little work has been done on the relationship of these traditions (oral and written) to their actual use in the lives of both "ordinary" and "learned" Muslim individuals and communities.[2] This situation, as is the case with the "new religious groups," clearly points to the lack of consensus within the scholarly community and traditional religious institutions themselves about the status of "popular" religion. It is very difficult to address the issue of "popular religion" without entering into arguments over what constitutes "authentic" religion or "traditional" religion or "spirituality" (as opposed to "mysticism") or "orthodoxy," who is defining the terms, and so forth. One of the objectives of this study of a living and successful Islamic community in America is to provide food for further reflection on these very issues.

This study is an introduction to the life and teachings of the twentieth century Sri Lankan Sufi teacher Bawa Muhaiyaddeen and the community—the "fellowship"—he founded in 1971 in the Overbrook section of Philadelphia.[3] The Bawa Muhaiyaddeen Fellowship consists of about 1,000 members, a handful of whom live on the premises of the mosque, which was erected by the members themselves in 1984, two years before Bawa Muhaiyaddeen died. It is an extremely heterogeneous community, with members from a wide variety of racial and cultural backgrounds, ages, and professions. Some are "born Muslims" from abroad and others are Americans from Jewish, Christian, or nonreligious backgrounds.[4] The fellowship has gone through a variety of states, from its early days, when it was hardly identified (by members or others) as an "Islamic" community, to its present existence as a visibly thriving community. It now has scheduled daily prayers, classes on the Qur'an, Arabic language, and Qur'anic recitation, resources for all stages of community life (rituals for celebrating the birth of a baby, marriage, death), and perhaps most important for this community, books and scheduled talks (now on videotape) by their late founder, Bawa Muhaiyaddeen. The emergence and continued existence of this group raises a great many social and religious questions.

The questions on which this research has been focused relate to the connection between traditional Islamic approaches to spirituality and that of Bawa Muhaiyaddeen. What is the relationship of Bawa's theological and philosophical perspective to traditional schools of Sufi thought, particularly the Qadiriyya line, which Bawa claims as his "spiritual lineage"? In what ways does he perpetuate fundamental Islamic doctrines and practice? How does Bawa utilize the Quran, hadith, and other traditional sources of Muslim piety? What is the religious language, imagery, and style through which Bawa communicates his vision? To what extent is the language and imagery on which he draws a reflection of his own cultural-historical background, and to what extent is he responding to the American milieu? To what extent does Bawa function in the traditional role of the Sufi shaykh (teacher)? What are the means by which Bawa's teachings are inculcated in the community? Can any conclusions be drawn with regard to the question of whether Bawa Muhaiyaddeen and the fellowship function in a "conserving" manner vis-à-vis "the tradition" or whether they depart from traditional Islamic values and practice?

Answers to such questions must be sought in the interrelationship between the theoretical aspects of Bawa's works (e.g., his teachings on the nature of God, creation, the human being, revelation, the shaykh-disciple relation, etc.) and the "institutions" or cultural forms utilized by Bawa and his community.[5] The goal of this chapter, therefore, is twofold: to highlight a few major elements of Bawa's "mystical theology," namely his conceptions of *tawhid* (the unity and transcendence of God), *qutb* (the "pole" or axis), and shaykh (teacher, master); and to introduce the matrix of cultural forms through which spiritual teaching actually takes place within this particular community—including the chronological development of Bawa's teachings and spiritual practices within the community. Questions related to the issue of community practices have been prompted by the concerns of both history of religions and anthropology. First, in what ways do the rituals of the Bawa Muhaiyaddeen community reflect traditional Islamic ele-

ments of faith (daily prayers, fasting, almsgiving, pilgrimage, commemoration of the Prophet Muhammad's birthday)? In what ways
do the community's rituals reflect traditional elements of "mystical" Islam (the *dhikr*, the esoteric invocation of the name of God;
commemoration of the "patron saint" of Bawa's order, ʿAbd al-
Qadir al-Jilani of eighth century Baghdad; commemorative vigils
in honor of Bawa's death; litanies of the Divine Names)? Second,
what are the genres of discourse utilized by Bawa (e.g., myths,
aphorisms, symbolic narratives, poetry, songs, didactic prose)?
What is their relation to traditional or South Asian Muslim spirituality? Third, how is the idea of the sacred reflected in the "aesthet-
ic" dimension of community life (use of music, sacred space, the
decorative arts used in architectural spaces, books, dress)? How do
these cultural forms reflect the "American" culture in which the
community is situated? Fourth, with regard to the ongoing education of the community, how are Bawa's teachings and Islamic values communicated to the children and to new members? How do
the ongoing functions of support, advice, and spiritual guidance
take place since Bawa's death?

The work on this project has been carried out both through
"field research," interviewing members at the community's
mosque and educational complex in Philadelphia, and through an
examination of Bawa's discourses, so as to relate the methods of
spiritual teaching he employed to traditional modes—both classical and popular—of Sufi teaching and to see if there have been any
shifts of emphasis in the thought or practices in the community
over time. This research has been greatly aided by the fact that
Bawa maintained an unusually open form of "esoteric" Islam and
that the archivists at the fellowship have been extremely helpful in
making available to the public written collections of his teachings
—as well as audio- and videotapes of his discourses. Although
Bawa's oral discourses were in Tamil interspersed with English and
Arabic, the talks were immediately translated by a team of American and Sri Lankan translators, literally at his side (as the videos
reveal), and they continue to be edited for possible errors in translations.

It becomes evident that, although Bawa's teachings contain
"traditionally" controversial elements associated with a *wahdat al-
wujud* ("unity of being")[6] interpretation of *tawhid,* the methods of
transmission of these teachings clearly fall within the bounds of

Islamic orthopraxis. The emergence and continued existence of the Bawa Muhaiyaddeen Fellowship, therefore, provide a "living" example of the dynamic process of transmission-transformation-integration of Islam in America. The fellowship furthermore models a contemporary example of the traditional role Sufism has played in the transmission of Islam itself. Finally, an understanding of the development and functioning of this group sheds light on the issue of the relationship between "popular" and "classical" forms of Islamic mystical teaching.

THE HISTORICAL DEVELOPMENT

There is a collective affirmation among those who were close to Bawa that the content of his teachings is no less than a continuation of the "oral transmission" that began with a first resonance of the divine self-disclosure (*tajalli*). The content of that transmission was the "*La ilaha illa Allah*," which is translated in the "classic" Sufi manner as "There is no reality but The Reality"[7] that is, "Only you, Oh God, are the Real, the Truth (*al-Haqq*)." Another interpretive theme permeates Bawa's teachings and his followers' self-expressions, as evidenced in fellowship discussion "meetings" and literature: the "movement" from interior, hidden, unmanifest (*batin*) modes of being to externalized, manifest (*zahir*) modes of being, the latter of which themselves become vehicles of reintegration-realization. This "movement" is seen in the historical development of the community as well as on ontological, cosmological, and individual "levels" of "being."

The history of Bawa's emergence as a teacher and the development of his community in America can be seen as the movement from less articulated, implicit identification with Islam to a more articulated, explicit identification. Although this chapter will focus on the Bawa Fellowship in America, it is important to note that Bawa was well known as a spiritual teacher in Sri Lanka well before his arrival in America. What is known of Bawa as a teacher begins in the 1940s when a small group of Tamil Hindus in northern Sri Lanka on their way to a Hindu pilgrimage site encountered this wandering ascetic emerging from a jungle. They viewed Bawa as a holy man and asked him to be their teacher. He agreed and, after another three-year period as a wandering ascetic, began a very informal, nonpublic, teaching that focused on the development of the "exceptional qualities" of justice, charity, and wisdom. He used stories to illustrate his teachings, incorporating the tales of the Hindu Puranas for his original group of listeners. This characteristic of using the religious image world of his audience as his teaching tool continued throughout his life and travels. He was referred to as *swami*, or *guru*, or *Bawa* (Father). His disciples came to include a small pocket of Muslims in Jaffna, and members recall Bawa's early activities as including a good deal of "removing spells, casting out demons, and generally chasing out things that got in the way of people's lives."[8] As his following grew, Bawa began to utilize more Qur'an and hadith and *hadith qudsi*[9] material. His work remained centered in northern Sri Lanka until the 1960s. He revealed little of his own "history" and maintained that he had no formal education or religious instruction. Certain Muslims in the South, trained in "orthodox" (albeit with a Sufi orientation) Islam in Columbo, began traveling regularly to Jaffna. They saw Bawa as a divinely inspired shaykh (teacher, master), possibly even one of the "*awliya*" (the "saints," the "friends" of God).[10] In this period Bawa began to be identified with the "*qutbs*," the highest spiritual teachers of the Sufi tradition (the function of which will be discussed later). Meanwhile, in Jaffna in 1955 Bawa laid the foundation for a mosque near Mankumban. With this event came the beginning of a clear connection of Bawa's teachings with Islam, although he insisted that there was to be no distinction of people because of "race, color, or religion" at his discourses and that people of all religions could pray in the mosque as long as non-Muslims respected the *salat* times as designated for Muslim prayer.[11] Furthermore, in 1967, a group of Muslims in Columbo began to formally organize meetings that included listening to and "studying" Bawa's discourses, the Serendib Sufi Study Circle, which still meets today.

THE PHILADELPHIA FELLOWSHIP

In discussions with original members of the Philadelphia "fellowship" and in listening to Bawa's discourses between 1964 and his death in 1986, one sees both a constant connection made with the spiritual lineage of 'Abd al-Qadir al-Jilani (d. 1166), the "sober" Hanbali preacher-saint from Baghdad, and a movement made from the institution of the silent *dhikr*[12] to the institution of the loud *dhikr* and then to more formalized instruction on Islamic liturgical forms. It also appears that not a few members see this process as analogous to the process of God's self-disclosure—resonance, that is, "the hidden" need or desire (as in "I was a hidden treasure, and I loved to be known"[13]), an "externalization" in the world of forms and differentiation.

When Bawa came to America in 1971, it was at the request of a young woman in Philadelphia, who as a result of an "inner" experience began a search for a spiritual teacher. She heard about the Sri Lankan teacher through an Asian graduate student studying in Philadelphia and wrote to Bawa over a two year period 1969–1971. He agreed to an invitation to come to the United States and arrived on October 11, 1971. The original members describe how, in those early days, Bawa, situated in a small row house in west Philadelphia, was a counselor-teacher with no formal spiritual practices. Many of the original members speak of themselves as belonging to that generation of 1960s "spiritual seekers" in America. This formative period is remembered for Bawa's "giving"—of his time ("In the fifteen years of his Philadelphia stay, he never had a private moment except when he went to the bathroom"), his love ("It was like someone actually manifesting 'He who abides in love abides in God and God in him'"), his counsel, and even his financial assistance. One hears many testimonies of Bawa's "cleaning us up and getting us off drugs." Bawa's main teaching at that time was simply "to remember God at all times," and he would sometimes recommend saying "*La ilaha illa Allahu*" as a tool—"not as a mantra or yoga"—to help remember God. Most of the early American members say that they had no idea that this language of "remembrance" had anything to do with Islam. Many American members have told me that in looking back now, they see that all along there was the language and imagery of the Qur'an, hadith, and *tasawwuf*—but they did not recognize it as such, save a few members who were familiar with Sufi literature. As one member said, it was five years before Bawa said, "This is Islam." Without exception, the original members of the community maintain that it was Bawa's "love in action," his capacity to teach "what we needed, when we needed to hear it, and how we would be able to hear it," that won their affection and commitment.

The beginning of a more clearly articulated connection with Islamic practice in the American fellowship took place in 1976. On

August 11, at 4:30 A.M., Bawa called together the collection of members (now at the group's Overbrook location in Philadelphia) and taught a more formal practice of the *dhikr*. The tapes of these discourses are still played periodically to introduce-reintroduce-participate in the original time-space of the teaching. In fact, the series of tapes is annually played during August, on the dates of the original transmission, at 6:00 A.M. The practice that was taught consisted of

1. Washing oneself as an outward preparation and symbol of inward purification.

2. Fixing one's intention within oneself, saying, "I intend to worship."

3. Offering certain formalized prayers and Qur'anic verses: the traditional "I take refuge with God from the accursed Satan," the *basmala* ("In the name of God, the Merciful, the Compassionate"), the recitation of the *fatiha*, the opening sura of the Qur'an, the recitation of three short Quranic suras—*nas, ikhlas,* and *falaq.*

4. Focusing on the "*dhikr* Allah" itself. This involved (and it is still one form of *dhikr* practiced) a rhythmic purification-pushing out of negative breath-energy with the left "side" of the body (left nostril, etc.) while saying the "negation" part of the *kalimah* (*La ilaha,* "Nothing else is"), followed by breathing in through the right "side" of the body (right nostril, etc.), the positive breath symbolically associated with the "positive" assertion of the *kalimah* (*illa Allahu,* translated as "Only you Are, God").[14] In the videotapes of Bawa's teaching of the *dhikr,* the sound of the *La ilaha* can be seen and heard to drift away until there is pure stillness. As one member said, "On a good day, we (too) would be in stillness."

5. Giving "*salams*" ("Peace be with you") after the *dhikr,* looking directly at the other person "in the eye" and really carrying the intention of "unity" and "peace", were all considered by Bawa to be a crucial part of this practice. Men were to greet men, women to greet women, and women were asked to cover their hair for prayer. Thus some of the traditions of Islamic practice became established, and this early morning silent *dhikr* continued from 1976–1978 in the American fellowship.[15]

The "*dhikr Allah*," the silent *dhikr* (*zikr* is the spelling used in fellowship literature) is described by Bawa in the language of a precision of consciousness—as sharp as a knife, an act of unswerving attention to the dispelling of the mind, desires, all "sections" of the world and self (through the process of the aforementioned rhythmic breathing, the drawing in and expelling of breath) such that "When he is at that point. . . . The man does not exist. He is nothing." This of course is a reference to the well-known principle in *tasawwuf:* that the self, the ego, the *nafs*, must "die before you die." One must "focus with faith and certitude on that one point, . . . all the senses will be anesthetized . . . the *qalb* (heart) will focus on God. . . . This *dhikr* is not done by earth, fire, water, air, ether . . . it cannot be done through religion, race" (in other similar statements, caste). And in an allusion to a well-known *hadith qudsi*,[16] Bawa describes how in this *dhikr*, in this state of the "god-man, man-god," in this "death before death," one "sees Him through His own sight, speaks to Him through His tongue, communicates to Him with His qalb."[17] Bawa's language of "merging" and "unity" with God—and its understanding-legitimation through such *hadith qudsi*—places Bawa in the line of such figures as Bistami, al-Hallaj, and Ibn ʿArabi, whose ecstatic expressions and teachings form a historical constant in the Islamic tradition, albeit a controversial one.[18]

Bawa continued to travel back and forth to Sri Lanka, and there he began to teach formal Islamic (Arabic) liturgical prayers. Many American disciples accompanied Bawa to Sri Lanka to continue their "learning of wisdom." Taped discourses indicate that as early as 1974 he was discussing the nature and reason for a number of types of *dhikr*. His teachings therefore can be seen as moving in a direction that includes a societal, communal understanding of the meaning of *tawhid* (the affirmation of God's unity and transcendence) and *ittihad* (unity). He began to lead the still more "externalized" early morning "loud *dhikr*," which he called the *dhikr jaliy*.[19] In a series of discourses in Sri Lanka, he discussed the significance of the major forms of *dhikr*, the *dhikr jaliy* was described as a necessary concession and blessing to the very human needs connected to the "section" of the world: "it intermingles with the world and base desires and cravings," and "it is on the level of the intentions of the world."[20] It is clear in this discourse that there are "degrees" of prayer attuned to persons' capacities, their "stations."[21] Bawa's discussion on *dhikr* is Muslim theology framed in the language of prayer and devotion:

> Understanding this and praying this in the right manner is good. / For those who do this *dhikr* there is no treasure other than God. . . . / There is no *rahmat* or wealth other than God . . . / There is no other than Allah's love . . . / There is no sustenance other than Allah's sustenance . . . / There is no intention other than the intention of Allah . . . / There is no worship other than the worship of Allah . . . / There is no glory other than the glory of Allah . . . / There is no yearning other than yearning for Allah . . . / There is no bliss other than the bliss of Allah . . . / There is no other love or praise other than the praise of Allah / Everything is His glory, His story."[22]

As with many of his discourses, Bawa ends this one with a spontaneous song that expresses the teaching in a poetic manner, proclaiming the beauty of waking up at three o'clock in the morning, when "you can hear the resonance and the sounds of the birds," when "angels and saints and *qutbs,* and prophets, and atoms . . . and everything . . . , birds, snakes, . . . frogs . . . fishes . . . all worship. Come and worship that One."

With the "loud *dhikr*," Bawa began to utilize the traditional invocation of the Names of God and other blessings in repetitions of 33, 99, and 100 times.[23] The loud *dhikr* has been streamlined over the years because of members' work patterns, from three-hour sessions to one-hour sessions now, either preceding or following the *fajr* (early morning) prayer.

In 1981 in the United States Bawa proceeded to institute the five-times-a-day *salat* prayers, including the requirement of an Imam (a leader of congregational prayers) trained in the Islamic tradition such that the Qur'an could be recited, prayers led, and the *adhan* (the call to prayer) done properly. There are a variety of discourses on the significance of the "five-times" *salat,* with the "inner" significance of these "five *waqts*" (the five times) being related (ontologically and epistemologically) to the natural progression of "stages" in the spiritual life.[24]

In 1982 Bawa began discussions on the building of a mosque in Philadelphia. As with the mosque in Jaffna, it would be referred to as God's house (*bayt Allah*), where, on the one hand, people of all colors, races, and religions could pray except during Islamic liturgical times, and on the other hand, it was stipulated that the forms of liturgical prayers should be observed strictly according to the "*shariah* (Islamic law) . . . and *sunna* (custom) of the Prophet so that a Muslim from any part of the Islamic world would feel comfortable worshiping in the mosque." The prayers would follow the Hanafi *madhhab* (school of law). A mosque was built within six months, with virtually all work done by the members of the fellowship.[25] Bawa designed it, based on the Sri Lankan mosque model.[26]

The stages of Bawa's teachings suggest a movement from a focus on an (individual) interior experience of consciousness—the radical ontological implication of the "first *kalimah*" that only Allah can be called *the Real*—to more manifested, externalized, formal, and traditionally Islamic expressions of community rituals. This community emphasis is interpreted as an "integrative" manifestation of *tawhid,* the divine unity that paradoxically "comprehends" all, yet in whom there is no distinction, race, class, or religion. The community is also seen as the arena in which the *nafs* (the lower self) can be trained and purified and in which the virtues, the names and qualities of God, can be cultivated and manifested in this world. Bawa describes the character of this coming together in the mosque as a state of peace, unity, compassion, which is the "state of Islam,"[27] and that this "Iman-Islam" is a reflection the divine unity itself.

TAWHID

Bawa's type of spirituality spans the (probably artificial) categories of speculative and devotional-ascetic. He has a very complex, subtle *wahdat al-wujud*[28] metaphysics that is expressed in the traditional (medieval-neoplatonic) ontological and cosmological framework of an effusion of being from the One to the many—with a gradation of levels of being from the original effulgence of God to the elemental levels. Yet the teachings are always connected to devotional practices and an ascetic style, which Bawa instituted as means of integrating and reflecting these teachings in everyday life—both at the community and individual levels.

Bawa's teaching on God's unity and transcendence (*tawhid*) must be understood in light of his discussions on the origin and nature of the created order. The origination of being is framed in an Ibn Sina[29]–Ibn 'Arabi cosmological model of generation of being in which the created orders come into existence with an original act of intellection of God's "wanting to be known" (in reference of course to the well-known *hadith qudsi*) through which there emerges a first "resonance," described as "the explanation that comes out of God when God began to know God's self." This "understanding of God" is the origination and purpose (ontologically, phylogenically, and epistemologically) of the *insan*, the human being. Whereas all other creatures "naturally" worship God, only *insan* can understand Him (and thus the dialogue of *insan* praising God and God praising *insan*).[30] The first emergence of God's being—"His history"—is identified with the *nur al-Muhammad*, the "Light of Muhammad," the Eternal Muhammad, the Inner Muhammad, which is the logos-word-"first resonance" through which and in which all things exist.[31] This is the "ontological level" of unity that is associated with Bawa's teachings with the countenance of God, God's beauty, the ninety-nine names (with many precedents in "classical" teachers of *tasawwuf*, such as Ibn ʿArabi's "*wahidiyyah*" level).[32]

Bawa utilizes the mystical theories about the *mims* (*m*s) of Muhammad's name and the word play–symbolism of "*ahad-ahmad*,"[33] which is based on a *hadith qudsi* much used by the Sufis: "*ana Ahmad bila mim*" "I am Ahmad without the m"; i.e., *ahad*, One).[34] Bawa also utilizes word play in the Tamil language: *muham* in Tamil means "face" or "countenance" and *aham* means "heart." Thus Bawa will say, " Muhammad is the beauty of the heart reflected in the face."[35] Through such word play Bawa speaks of the "inner reality" of Muhammad as being both "caused by," yet in an ontological proximity to the Divine,[36] in that the Light of Muhammad, the Inner Muhammad, is the first reflection, or "countenance," of God's very being. This understanding of Muhammad includes the dimension of causality, as Bawa saw reflected in the *hadith qudsi*, "Nothing would have been created without you, Muhammad." As we shall see, the "inner reality of Muhammad" is also the state of the person who has "realized wisdom," the one who has realized that original, primordial unity with God and thus externalizes, reflects it through his or her "countenance," the reflection of the names and qualities of God. Furthermore, it is the embodying of the "names and qualities of God" in the small details of daily life that constitutes the essence of the Shariah for Bawa,[37] the way one should be in the world.

One should say that this language was not always met with passive acceptance—especially among Muslim visitors who were either unfamiliar with or who rejected such explanations of God or Muhammad. In one of the many taped question and answer meetings with members and visitors, this formulation of the nature of Allah and Muhammad was greeted with a gasp by a visiting Muslim who was clearly concerned about Bawa's explanations of the "inner" dimension of the Islamic belief and practice—that people might not do the "outer" requirements of the *'ibadat* (worship and service to God)—and who interspersed his question with long quotations from the Qur'an in Arabic. Bawa's sharp retort was a discourse on the unlimitibility of the ("inner") Qur'an:

> the Quran is not just commanded: it *is* the Rahman of Allah. . . . No one can bear and lift up the Quran. . . . No one can even say one *alif* in the whole world. . . . The Haqiqat Muhammad is Allah's Face. . . . No one can ever finish reciting the Quran . . . [and referring to well-known hadiths]. If all the oceans were made into ink and all the trees made into pens, . . . the Quran could never be finished. . . . Nothing would be created without you, Muhammad . . . Allah is one alone. All belongs to Him. What do you have that belongs to you? . . . When this is understood, you have *iman*.[38]

One sees in Bawa's teachings that the ontological levels of origination of being have corresponding "states" in the *insan* (the human being). The "level" of Allah-Muhammad, the Nur al-Muhammad, is that which is mirrored in the *insan al-kamil,* the realized person: "That unity found within all creation is Islam. For both the beginning and the end, Islam came in the form of unity. It came through Prophet Muhammad, through Nur Muhammad, through Ahmad . . . when Allah said 'Oh Muhammad, without you I would not have created anything, then or now.' . . . The state of a true man, the true form of Adam comes into being once wisdom resplends. The heart becomes radiant and shines in the face as the beauty of that face, that is the state of Muhammad."[39] This "Allah-Muhammad," the "form of Adam," is that of God in the person which speaks through the person who is in prayer-*dhikr.* It is that in the individual which returns to unite with its source.[40]

It should be noted that these "theoretical" teachings are found in the midst of devotional literature, such as the fellowship's collection of meditations on the *Asma' ul Husna, The Ninety-Nine Beau-*

tiful Names of Allah.[41] That is, the externalization of the virtues (the qualities of God) in the life of the individual and the community is not only a manifestation of the "Allah-Muhammad" state, but also the vehicle of the "return" to that origin. "We must do the work of Allah's compassionate qualities." "Taking the form of God's qualities and doing Allah's duty *is* the (inner) Quran."[42] The "reality" of Allah's *rahmat*, the "inner" Qur'an, the Muhammadan reality-beauty are thus theologically identified as the source, method, and return to that primal source of unity.

The teaching of this "wisdom" (*hikmah*) takes place in the community life in a variety of ways. We have mentioned Bawa's own discourses, which were often responses to particular questions of members or visitors raised in the context of fellowship "meetings." These meetings are still regularly scheduled events in which members gather to reflect on/try to understand/share/articulate these teachings to each other and to new members. At the meetings it is evident that the ongoing articulation of these teachings is considered to be an ongoing articulation-resonance of the "original" resonance—an aspect of "Allah's duty," "Allah's compassion," the *Nur al-Muhammad,* and hence, literally, a part of Allah's "oral transmission." Bawa often communicated these teachings symbolically through stories, songs, and allegories—many of which are "populated" by the beloved figures of 'Abd al-Qadir al-Jilani, Uways al-Qarani,[43] Fatimah, Ali, Moses, and Gabriel—the last of whom always seems to be the target of Allah's and Muhammad's reminding of Muhammad's place in the cosmic hierarchy vis-à-vis Gabriel's. One example is the charming story of Gabriel arriving to deliver a Sura (Qur'anic revelation) to the Prophet. Muhammad is not home, but his daughter Fatimah is, and she greets Gabriel with "*as-salamu alaikum,* younger brother of my father." Gabriel becomes upset, seeing himself as "the elder," and he does not return the *salams.* When Muhammad returns home, Fatimah asks who is the "older one," to which Muhammad responds (to Gabriel) with a teaching on the *nur al-Muhammad,* the primordial first resonance of Allah that existed-exists even prior to the "Angel of Revelation."

The "teaching of wisdom" also takes place as part of the cycle of *mawlids* (celebrations) in honor of the Prophet's birthday which are held every year from the first through the twelfth of the Islamic month of *Rabi 'ul-Awwal.* Interspersed in the prayers, songs, and *salawat* (blessings) in honor of Muhammad are readings from the *sirah* (the life of the Prophet as recorded in the traditional biographies), all recited in Arabic. A revealing manifestation of the plurality of perspectives in the community regarding such issues as the appropriateness of the *mawlids,* as well as the justification given by Bawa for instituting them, is a small pamphlet made available for the 1991 *mawlids.* In it Bawa spoke of the worthiness of celebrations in praise of God's mercy as shown through the lives of the prophets and saints.[44]

QUTB

The concept of the *qutb* appears in Bawa's more theoretical, didactic discourses as well as in his symbolic stories whose characters include the *anbiya'*-prophets and the *awliya'*-saints as well as the myriad of creatures from the jungles, deserts, and forests that "speak" of the "psychological-analytical" aspect of the process of attaining "wisdom" and the realized state of the *insan al-kamil.* Again, to situate this aspect of Bawa's work within the tradition, one only need refer to the most accessible texts on *tasawwuf* (e.g., al-Muhasibi, Hujwiri, Ghazzali, Ibn ʿArabi) to see early tendencies toward keen self-observation—always under the guidance of the shaykh—that includes various states and stations, whose goal is the prefigurative Quranic eschatological *al-akhira–yaum al-qiyama–fana* experience,[45] when "We have rent your veil, so your sight today is keen" (Sura 50:22).

The *qutb* (literally, "pole" or "axis") is the term used by many Sufis to indicate a spiritual leader, the highest member(s) in the "hierarchy of saints," a system of ranking going back at least to Tirmidhi (d. c. 932 A.D.).[46] The *qutb* is sometimes referred to as *ghauth* (help) and is considered to be a "center" of spiritual energy. The term has a variety of uses in Bawa's teachings, all of which correspond ontologically to the same "essential" reality. Using the model of interiority, externalization, integration, one sees three meanings—levels of *qutb.* The first is that aspect of Allah's resonance, which, having "originated" from the "hidden" divine treasure in a "movement-level" of self-disclosure (*tajalli*) that is the *nur al-Muhammad,* now exists as that "power" of Allah's very being that is the "explainer." It is often referred to as divine wisdom or divine analytic wisdom, the wisdom that explains.[47] It also refers to a "developmental" stage in Bawa's spiritual psychology: it is the sixth "stage" (called here the *qutbiyyat*) in the ascending levels of consciousness that exist potentially within the *insan*. It is "the wisdom which explains the truth of God. It is the power which awakens all the truths which have been buried."[48] The *qutbiyyat*, then, is primarily that which "differentiates," which analyzes, which discerns the truth, the "subtle" knowledge of things. The *qutbiyyat* is the "interface" of God's knowing and human knowing, and it functions analogously to Suhrawardi's Tenth Angel Intellect,[49] which is an individuated, particularized knowledge of God (namely, *insan*'s knowledge of God, self, and world, but more important, God's knowledge of God, self, and world known "through" the person, thus rendering *yaqin* and *haqq*—certitude, truth). Therefore, the *qutb*, or *qutbiyyat*, plays the integrative role of the inner teacher through which one comes to understand that there is no God but The God, no reality but The Reality. It is that faculty which makes possible a realizing of the eschatological clarity of vision and hence, self-judgment.

However, the "spiritual reality" of the *qutb* has been "externalized"—manifested—in the form of the saints and *qutbs*, including 'Abd al-Qadir al-Jilani, the twelfth century Baghdadi preacher who was called *muhyi al-din* (reviver of the faith)[50] and is perhaps the most popular and venerated of Islam's "saints" the world over, especially in the Indian subcontinent.[51] Bawa claimed to be in Jilani's spiritual lineage, although there seems to be no formal *silsilah* connection to the Qadiriyya order. However, for Bawa and his community, 'Abd al-Qadir al-Jilani is the exemplar (in the most Eliadean sense of participation in the state-reality of the paradigm) of a particular type of spirituality, characterized by certain emphases in his life and teachings. For example, part of the received tradition of Jilani with which Bawa identifies is the very ascetic stance he takes toward the "glitter" of the world (it is noteworthy that in the descriptions of the illusory character of the world and human self-deception, Bawa will utilize terms such as *maya*, instead of, say, *ghurur*[52]). Bawa also mirrors Jilani's discussions on the prayer of the heart (*qalb*), the internal prayer that purifies the heart, referring to a hadith in which Muhammad describes a piece of flesh in man's body, which when purified, whole body is purified; when it is impure, the whole body remains impure. "That piece is the heart."[53] Bawa echoes Jilani's (and other Sufis') language of the *qalb* as the source of true prayer–true *dhikr*, especially Jilani's comparison of the heart to the place of worship: "Its mosque is the *qalb*. Its congregation is the conglomeration of all internal forces in man. It recites with spiritual tongue the Names of God's Unity (*tawhid*). Its *imam* is a deep spiritual urge in the heart (*al-shawq fi'l-fu'ad*). Its *qiblah* is the unity of Godhead (*ahadiyyah*). The *qalb* and *ruh* are constantly in this prayer."[54]

The thrust of Bawa's discourses on the human activity of "analyzing"—of discerning—is that the "spiritual organ" through which the *qutb*–divine luminous wisdom speaks is the heart (in contradistinction to the mind), and the heart, to use another favorite metaphor (of Bawa and other Qadiris of the Indian subcontinent) is the taproot from which flows the "pure" water whose source is "deep" and ever-renewing.

Special devotion to Muhyi al-Din 'Abd al-Qadir al-Jilani can be seen in the daily life of the community through the daily morning "loud" *dhikr*, for example, in the invocation of *qutbs:* "O Primal ruler Muhaiyaddeen, throne of God, O Seat of God's authority, showering God's grace. O Saint Muhaiyaddeen, shelter of peace and tranquility from Allah, O Awliya' Muhaiyaddeen."[55] (If one senses an identification of Bawa Muhaiyaddeen with the "reality" of "Muhaiyaddeen" as manifested in 'Abd al-Qadir and the heart-as-seat of-knowledge, one is correct.) There are also *mawlids al-qutb*, celebrations in honor of 'Abd al-Qadir al-Jilani at the anniversary of his death, which last from the first through the eleventh of the month of *Rabi 'uth-Thani*. The *mawlids* commemorating Bawa Muhaiyaddeen's death overlap with the last days of the *mawlids al-qutb*, and the overlap is seen as symbolic of the identity of functions of the two "Muhaiyaddeens." Similar to the *mawlids* for the Prophet, each evening consists of a series of prayers, songs, readings of stories and legends of 'Abd al-Qadir (some in English, most in Arabic), and many *salawat* (blessings) to the Prophet and Jilani. Well-known stories such as the story of "'Abd al-Qadir and the Robbers" (whose virtuous qualities led to their "conversion") are included. One of the songs used was taught by Bawa himself (Tape 5 Songs, "The One Who Rules Baghdad"). It is evident that in this yearly ritual of devotion, the direction of the prayer is to the "primal" *qutb*, who is "eternally" the revivifier of the faith, which is manifest in the *anbiya'*, *qutbs*, and *awliya'*, who is most presently manifest in Bawa Muhaiyaddeen. There is a place for heartfelt veneration and supplication of the historical saint of Baghdad, but one perceives in the overall feel of the song that Bawa uses the veneration and supplication of the Baghdadi saint as a means of effecting a "melting of the heart," a metaphor traditionally used by Sufis to suggest the process of the death of the ego and, with it, all that separates *insan* from *insan* and *insan* from God. One also notices a purposeful ambiguity in the supplication of the twelfth century saint; is Bawa referring to the historical *Muhaiyaddeen-qutb* or the eternal *qutb*-ruler of the inner city of Baghdad? Clearly it is both:

> Oh that light that was born in this world. . . . Oh that one who came before the twelfth century [Jilani lived from 1088–1166] . . . who came to unite all people. . . . Oh that golden one . . . Oh the one who rules in Baghdad . . . When I cry with melting heart. Oh that one who understands that state, give us grace . . . you are that *qutb* for the entire universe. . . . Oh that honey, that fruit that is understood in our hearts. . . . You said you went to the Maldives. . . Oh protect us and give us your grace . . . so that our hearts will resonate with your grace. . . . Oh the heart . . . at the moment it is suffering. Oh that exalted one . . . come and dispel the sorrows of the poor. Oh that honey who can dispel our darkness. . . . Oh give us that state of *iman.* . . . so that the effulgence of Allah will be known. . . . We need your grace. . . . the One who rules Baghdad.[56]

It is clear that *Baghdad* is the human citadel in which the throne, the heart, the seat of knowledge of all the universes (the elemental aspects of the world and individuals and the "spiritual" universes) is located. Similarly, in a number of discourses, Bawa uses the legend of "The Qutb on the Maldive Islands" as an allegory about the "divine analytic wisdom" within the person that travels through all the recesses, the infinite oceans of being—the exterior and inner worlds—to analyze and render illumination of one's state, one's imperfections, how to progress, and so forth. The *qutb* is also that which fights and kills the "ghosts," "demons," and "idols" within the self.[57] It should be noted that these wisdom stories, the morality tales, the allegorical tales of the *qutb,* form an important ongoing teaching tool for the community, including the children. At children's meetings (weekly discussions with the children in the fellowship, led by regularly alternating members, men and women, who were close to Bawa), these stories are utilized for instruction; and they often form the material for theatrical productions performed by adults and children for the community at annual events, such as "Anniversary Day," the yearly celebration of Bawa's arrival in the United States.

SHAYKH

A constant theme in the history of Sufi literature is the necessity of following a shaykh (teacher). The authentic shaykh of Muslim piety is considered to be the successor of the Prophet, embodying the grace, knowledge, and authority to guide disciples on the spiritual path. Becoming a member of a Sufi order has traditionally meant entering a bond between master and disciple that is permanent, surviving even death.[58] The literature is also replete with warnings about persons who claim to be shaykhs but are not.[59] The "real" shaykh is described as the "physician of the heart," the teacher who helps the disciple to return to that primordial state of unity with God (the "day of the covenant," *yawm al-mithaq*)[60] that can happen only through the training of the will and the cultivation of the qualities of God. Yet the particular style and vision of the *shaykh* and the manner in which the disciples embody his teachings render the distinctive characters of the various Sufi orders.

The "inner dimension" of a "true shaykh," as Bawa understood it, includes the necessity of the teacher to have realized the station of the *insan al-kamil.*[61] Bawa's own teachings and the community's descriptions of Bawa's station and function speak of his having attained this "death of the ego" as well as his identification with the essential reality of the "*qutb-muhaiyaddeen*" such that Bawa himself could be an "explainer" and a "pointer" to God.

Regarding the manner in which Bawa understood his relationship to the members in the fellowship, a number of published discourses are devoted to the subject of the importance of finding a "true" shaykh, and they are clearly a response to both the spiritual "claimants" in Bawa's own Sri Lanka and the proliferation of guru figures in the United States that his late 1960s–early 1970s American audience was encountering. Bawa differentiates between the teachers of the "four hundred trillion, ten thousand forces, miracles, spirituals, prayers, mantras, and magics," the teachers and

ascetics who take marijuana and opium and alcohol, who teach
about spirits, about the mind, about the five elements, about
"causes and effects," and the way of a "gnana" or "kamil sheikh,"
whose role is compared to that of "the father":[62]

> There is a way that a father raises his child. . . . That loving
> unity [which exists between father and children] is a very, very,
> very precious study. It . . . has nothing to do with spiritual
> things. . . . The father teaches the children to imbibe the qualities
> of the father, the father teaches the actions of the father, the
> father teaches the children that original work. . . . The father
> teaches patience, tolerance, . . . the explanations of his own ex-
> perience. . . . The father transmits that beauty to his children
> and teaches them. The father's teaching never ends. For until he
> finally reaches his Father, he embraces his children and takes
> them along to his Father. The father's study takes you to the
> unity of God, while the guru's study teaches you to unite with the
> earth and to unite with maya. . . . The two are completely oppo-
> site. . . . You must try to learn your father's qualities, his actions,
> his words, his customs, and his habits that he teaches to his
> children.[63]

In other discourses he speaks about the shaykh's role in giving
wisdom as "shading and comforting the travelers crossing the desert of the world"[64] and the function of cutting away certain tendencies, actions, and thoughts in the disciples.[65] The shaykh is to
teach the qualities of patience, tolerance, peacefulness, compassion, and tranquility[66] and give to the disciple the "sword of wisdom" to "battle each section in a different way."[67] (Indeed, the
often repeated combination of virtues of "*sabur, shukur, tawakkul,*
and *al-hamdu li-llah*" now form part of one of the musical compositions regularly sung at the children's educational meetings.)

One of the most striking ways in which Bawa teaches about the
"father's love" is through imagery of the mother's nurturance, specifically the image of the baby suckling from the mother's breast.[68]
This metaphor is also used in discourses regarding the disciple's
manner and attitude in doing the silent *dhikr.*

> The father has two breasts. With one he gives the milk of wisdom
> and with the other he gives you love. . . . Whoever is hungry
> must search for and come to the place where his hunger can be
> satisfied. The nipple is the same for everyone; it is not small for
> one and large for another. The amount you receive depends upon

the manner in which you draw from it. If you do not receive enough, perhaps the fault is in your concentration or effort. If you are distracted, looking here and there while trying to nurse, you will not be able to finish. . . . You should not be jealous and think, 'That person is drinking . . . she is doing well, but I am unable to get the milk I need." Just as an infant drinks the milk gently without hurting either the mother or himself, you must have the same gentleness and love when you draw milk from your father. If you draw gently, the milk will flow.[69]

Another such image of the "skaykh as mother" is seen in Bawa's descriptions of the protective role of the shaykh.

A monkey carries its baby close to its body wherever it goes . . . when danger is imminent . . . the mother will jump from tree to tree, carrying the baby to safety. The little one is protected as long as it does not let go of the mother. . . . Similarly, if you hold on tightly to the qalb of the sheikh, then when any danger comes he will jump away from it. . . . Everything depends on how you cling to the sheikh. . . . Like that, if . . . you hold onto the sheikh with the grip of faith, certitude, and determination, you will not slip. . . . To develop that conduct, those actions, and those qualities of love, compassion, patience, tolerance, peacefulness, and equality—to gain that grip and establish that state of peacefulness is indeed difficult. It is easy for a child to put dirt on its head and roll playfully in the mud or sand, but it is difficult for the mother to bathe and cleanse the child. . . . The difficulties of a shaykh are a hundred times more difficult than those of a mother. You are always rolling in impurities, sin, fire, and hell. It is a very difficult task for the sheikh to take you and bathe you every time you dirty yourself. You do not experience the difficulties that the sheikh undergoes; it is not difficult for you, so at least try to hold onto him like the baby monkey.[70]

Bawa's role as transmitter of wisdom, protector, caretaker, cultivator of "good qualities" extended into areas that became emulated, institutionalized, and continued after his death. These institutions are understood to be the duties (*'ibadat*) and the practices of the shaykh and are seen as metaphors for "inner work" that has an externalized social dimension, whose "doing" leads to the "unity of Islam." For example, Bawa cooked for the fellowship. Members fondly recall how through this humble activity, Bawa fostered the qualities of servanthood to God and fellow human beings. Moreover, he taught the members how to cook. His recipes have been collected in a book (*The Tasty Economical Cookbook*) and are designed for feeding between 50 and 200 people. The book is introduced with a metaphysics of eating that describes not merely what is *halal* and *haram*, but the "qualities" that certain foods and spices have that become part of one's character, behavior, and health. Cooking is seen as a "traditional" science, a part of the process of analyzing and "knowing" the self. Food and cooking become teaching metaphors on those elements of the world to which individuals are attracted and that they consume—for better and for worse. In the tradition of only the most ascetic of Islamic spirituals, Bawa taught that it was better not to eat meat. He spoke of the Islamic rituals associated with slaughter as being given to Muhammad in order to *curb* the amount of slaughter to animals by making it difficult, and he suggested that it was much more difficult to slaughter the "beasts" inside.[71] Furthermore, members speak of how Bawa insisted that people learn to cook as part of taking care of each other and those less fortunate, as well as a way to learn to cooperate and work together as a community. The kitchen is still part of the almost-sacred space of the first floor of the "fellowship," with cooking "duties" shared and rotated, often accompanied by tapes of Bawa's discourses. Bawa's original dishes are available for all who attend events at the mosque and fellowship activities.

One of the metaphors Bawa frequently used when speaking about the disciple's process of cultivating the good (divine) qualities was that of farming—the process of clearing the field, digging a well to get and retain water, cultivating the garden (of the heart, *qalb*). He asked the community to buy land for the purpose of building a burial ground for members as well as for farming so that individuals would learn about cooperation, unity, taking care of those who were needy, and burying members according to Islamic custom. Land was purchased in Coatesville, Pennsylvania, and there is now a thriving farm where there are regular community "work days" and "*zikr* days," where children have a summer camp, and importantly, where Bawa is interred. The community has built a *mazar* (shrine) reflecting traditional Islamic architectural style. It is a simple white stucco room with copula and a green marble floor. The specific area under which Bawa is buried is covered with a dark green cloth embroidered with golden calligraphy of Qur'anic verses. An *'urs* ceremony is held at the *mazar* in the month of *Rabi'uth-Thani* each year to commemorate Bawa's death. The *mazar* is used for private prayer and reflection and serves as the focal point—the "well spring"—around which the individual and communal "farming" is maintained.

Further work needs to be done specifically on what constitutes sacred space at the fellowship. Certainly the mosque serves that function for the community at large (including those visitors from the Philadelphia area and abroad who are not "Sufi oriented"). However, it is quite clear that Bawa's room is sacred space. His bed, the locus of many of his discourses and much of his counsel— day and night, as members say, even through the worst of his ongoing respiratory problems—is still the place where members gather for "meetings," discuss "wisdom teachings," share experiences (and dreams), offer each other "support," and "remember." Individuals also use this room for private reflection. Members often kiss Bawa's pillow as they enter the room. Women and children especially populate this room during the *mawlids*, for women may not share the social space of the male readers during this time. It is quite clear from the way the use of space has evolved—and from what many women have shared—that there is special significance to the fact that the closest "presence" to the shaykh had no gender barriers beyond traditional practices of modest dress—covering the hair for women and clean, loose clothing that covers the arms and legs. In Bawa's room, which is white with green trim, are his green chair, his bed, and his artwork (which consists of iconographical representations of his stories and letter symbolism referring to the *Allah, Nur, Muhammad* "realities," all of which deserve attention as modes of transmission of teachings). The room also has a large television and video equipment with which Bawa's teachings were taped and are still being viewed. The ease with which Bawa and his original members used the video and audio media is clearly a sign of the historical and social context of Bawa's American disciples. Such use of "the media" was disconcerting to me during my first visits to the mosque complex (track lighting and other media equipment in the meeting room and bedroom) and seemed to be a clear "innovation"[72] of contemporary American influence. However, in watching and listening to the discourses and in witnessing the daily life cycle of the community, one sees in fact a correspondence between Bawa's mode of teaching and the pattern of the popular Sufi teachers before him, who used the vernacular and indigenous cultural forms they encountered, transforming them into media of transmission of Islamic spiritual teachings and values. Clearly the fellowship, in utilizing Bawa's original tapes—whether they be of Bawa teaching silent *dhikr* or Bawa talking to the children—sees them as the ongoing "oral transmission" of the original primordial resonance that all the *anbiya'*, *qutbs,* and the *awliya'* have communicated. Therefore, the Islamic (and *tasawwuf*) beliefs, practices, and institutions that continue to be enculcated in community life are, for the members of the Bawa Muhaiyaddeen Fellowship, no less than the living presence of the shaykh.

DEMOGRAPHIC TRENDS, FUTURE DIRECTIONS

As was stated, the Bawa Muhaiyaddeen Fellowship consists of approximately 1,000 persons. There has been no formal "census," and many people attend fellowship and mosque activities without becoming "registered" members. It appears, however, that although there was a slight decrease in the American membership after Bawa died,[73] the total membership remains about the same or has perhaps increased, due to additional numbers of foreign-born Muslims and American Muslims (including African American Muslims)[74] who attend the mosque's Friday prayer services but who do not necessarily become involved with meetings and activities directly related to Bawa and his teachings. In fact, on a variety of levels there is more interaction of the fellowship with the "Islamic establishment" of Philadelphia and abroad. First, some of the newer members of the "mosque congregation" who have had traditional Islamic training have become resources for those in the community who wish to know more about the traditional Islamic sciences. Thus, during a given month there might be a special series of classes on *fiqh* (Islamic jurisprudence), taught by local Muslim professors and offered parallel to the regularly scheduled meetings devoted to Bawa's teachings. Second, over the past year there has been more interaction between the fellowship and other Muslim communities in the area as the fellowship mosque leadership now participates in citywide meetings of the Imams of the Philadelphia mosques. Third, there have been visits from representatives from Islamic countries and educational institutions who seem to be taking an interest in understanding the goals and work of the Bawa Muhaiyaddeen Fellowship.

This increased interaction with the larger Islamic community has, not surprisingly, caused a good deal of individual and community soul-searching about the future of the community. There is clearly a friendly diversity and discussion of views on how best to assure the continuation of Bawa's particular vision of "Iman Islam." Members continue to turn to Bawa's discourses as the primary source of guidance and describe how Bawa's teaching and conduct will be the "norm" by which any proposed changes in the fellowship will be measured. Indeed, Bawa left a great many discourses and directives pertaining specifically to the ongoing conduct of the community and mosque. For example, very early in the community's history, Bawa established the structures for governance of the organization. In 1972, he set up a Board of Directors and an Executive Committee as the ongoing administrative bodies, and bylaws were written. The Executive Committee members would vote on policies for the fellowship (including the building of the mosque). The Philadelphia fellowship would remain the geographic center of the organization, with the Serendib Sufi Study Circle as its "sister organization." As the number of branches grew,[75] each one would have a president, secretary, and treasurer who would be voting participants at Executive Committee meetings. These policies are still in effect today.

Bawa also gave a number of directives that have become especially important as the demographics of the community have changed (e.g., the aging population, the growth of the mosque attendance). For example, he gave specific directives for burials and the establishment of men's and women's burial committees to carry through traditional Islamic burial customs.

Although Bawa did not pass on his function as shaykh two Imams were appointed to lead Friday prayers and assist in other religious observances and communal needs. Bawa left a number of directives on the rules and etiquette of the mosque and on the roles and responsibilities of the Imams—including the nature of *jum'a* (Friday) talks. For example, he maintained that the correct pronunciation of Arabic prayers by the Imam was of grave importance and that the *jum'a* talks should not be used to beat people down but rather to "melt the heart."

The emergence and continued existence of the Bawa Muhaiyaddeen Fellowship provide a living example of the process of transmission of Islamic belief and practice in the contemporary American context. Bawa shares in the lineage of the inspired Sufi shaykhs of Islam who took Islam to regions far removed from the geographic and cultural context of the Arabian peninsula. His work included elements traditionally associated with the Sufi teacher; namely, (1) teachings on the "inner" or esoteric meaning of the *kalimah,* the *"La ilaha illa Allah"*; (2) a method that involves renunciation of attachment to whatever separates the human being from Allah; (3) a "subtle" analysis of the self through a mode of knowledge associated with God's knowledge or wisdom, such that one can understand (and correct) the various motivations that inform one's actions; and (4) teachings on what constitutes correct conduct in the world (the "shariah"), that is, manifesting the virtues associated with the qualities of God as a means of both "externalizing" the inward reality of God's "unity" and becoming "reintegrated" in the primordial unity. However, although his teachings contain the philosophical underpinnings of "classical" "learned" Sufism, Bawa's mode as a shaykh was that of the mystical leaders in popular Sufism who spoke to "the masses" through the story, the inspired song, practical wisdom, individual spiritual counsel, and exemplary conduct (*adab*), and who in turn received devotion from their followers that continued after their death.[76]

The Bawa Muhaiyaddeen Fellowship will face the kinds of challenges that all religious communities experience when their charismatic founder dies: new members who did not experience the "encounter" with the inspired teacher, varying interpretations of the original teachings, and struggles for power. The tendency of human beings and societies toward "disunity"—toward "disintegration"—is addressed in a variety of Bawa's discourses, and to these discourses on the "state of unity which is Islam" members will undoubtedly turn as the challenges associated with time and growth arise.

To be in Islam is to act with virtue, modesty, compassion, peacefulness, forbearance, Allah's three thousand gracious qualities. His unity, His tranquility, and His equality, Islam embraces all equally in both joy and sorrow. If one is hungry, all are hungry. If one is sad, all are sad. If one is happy, all are happy. In this state of Islam, if we have a quarrel with somebody after the afternoon prayer, we must make peace, and embrace each other by the time of the early evening prayer . . . if we have this intention with every breath, if we can acquire His qualities and His actions, then that is the state of Islam lived by true believers.[77]

All who have faith in God are striving for the same thing. There-fore, we must have no divisions of race, religion, or caste, for wherever there are separations we can never see God. Only in the place where no divisions exist can one see God. . . . Be within the state of God's peacefulness and try to give peace to the world. Be in the state of God's unity and then try to establish unity in the world.[78]

NOTES

I wish to thank the many members of the Bawa Muhaiyaddeen Fellowship who shared their time, knowledge, and memories of Bawa. My appreciation also goes to the Seton Hall University Research and Faculty Development Council for their support in this project.

1. James Morris, "Situating Islamic Mysticism: Between Written Traditions and Popular Spirituality," in Robert Herrera, ed., *Mystics of the Book: Themes and Typologies* (New York: Peter Lang Publishing, 1992).

2. Ibid. Morris provides a discussion of the historical and ideological significance of various paradigms that have permeated the field of studies of Islamic mysticism. See also Steven Katz, "The 'Conservative' Character of Mysticism," in Steven Katz, ed., *Mysticism and Religious Traditions* (New York: Oxford University Press, 1983), pp. 3–61.

3. Philadelphia became the central location for his American followers. Bawa had already developed a large group of disciples in Sri Lanka, the central location being the Sufi Serendib Group in Columbo. His travels between the two locations continued after the foundation of the American group.

4. Bawa's original "disciples" in America were Americans. When Bawa came from Sri Lanka, a small number of Sri Lankans came to the United States with him. The ethnic diversity of the community continues to grow, especially at mosque salat services.

5. That is, at least as important as the theological and philosophical questions posed by Bawa's work is the issue of Bawa's teachings in light of what has been called the *Islamic humanities*, "the socially imbedded and historically changing matrix of forms—institutions, rituals, myths and stories, poetry, music, implicit values, and expectations—through which . . . transmission of spiritual teaching actually takes place within" particular Muslim families or local social groups (James Morris, "Situating Islamic Mysticism"). This approach presumes (in agreement with Morris's position) that to present merely the ideas and theories of "mysticism" without an understanding of the very "human" ways in which these teachings are transmitted and received would, in fact, distort

the teachings themselves and prevent an accurate assessment of those teachings.

6. *Wahdat al-wujud* refers to a line of thought associated with the well-known expositor of Sufi doctrine, the late twelfth-early thirteenth century Andalusian Ibn ʿArabi. Ibn ʿArabi maintained that all things of the created order are "*tajalliyat,*" manifestations or "theophanies" of the Divine. Ibn ʿArabi's own writings are voluminous and complex and have been subject to a variety of interpretations by both Muslim and non-Muslim scholars. There is perennial discussion on whether Ibn ʿArabi's "unitive" view of reality might compromise the idea of a "radically transcendent" God, which is part of the traditional creedal understanding of the Divine. For a good summary introduction of Ibn ʿArabi, see Annemarie Schimmel, *Mystical Dimensions of Islam* (Chapel Hill: University of North Carolina Press, 1975), pp. 263–274.

7. See William Chittick, "Ibn ʿArabi and His School," in S. H. Nasr, *Islamic Spirituality, Manifestations* (New York: Crossroads Press, 1991), pp. 49 ff.

8. The member who related this portion of the history made the point that "today" we might call these things (the demons, ghosts) *psychoses* with the "psychoanalytic" goal of getting rid of the "ghosts" (those fears, attachments—those things that bind us to the past and to all that is not "Real.") Many members see in Bawa's coming to the West a meaningful union of "traditional" and more modern psychoanalytic understandings of "the demons" that haunt us.

9. Hadiths are narratives that relate the sayings and actions of the Prophet Muhammad. These narratives are for Muslims a primary source (along with the Qur'an) of authoritative guidance for all areas of life, individual and communal. The *hadith qudsi,* the "divine sayings" are a category of hadith especially important in Muslim piety. The *hadith qudsi* is considered to be a saying of the Prophet in which God speaks in the first person and has an exalted position between the Qur'an and the hadith. See S. H. Nasr, *Islamic Spirituality: Foundations* (New York: Crossroads Press, 1989), pp. 97 ff.

10. The different titles, the "ranks" of sainthood, have a long history in Islamic mysticism, beginning with Tustari (d. 896) and Tirmidhi (d. c. 932). See A. Schimmel, *Mystical Dimensions,* pp. 56–57.

11. Fellowship Audio Recordings, ARS 6802-01, 1968, "Tawhid," "Death Before Death:" ARS 6400-01 A, 1964. "Muhaiyaddeen Abdul Qadir Jilani," "Zikr," "The Five Faruls (furud)."

12. *Dhikr,* the Arabic term for "remembrance," signifies the Sufi practice of invoking the name of God, the focus of the variety of practices that have developed as part of the quest toward "realization" of the meaning of the Islamic "creedal" statement: "There is no God but God."

13. One of the most beloved of the *hadith qudsi* (the "divine sayings"), utilized in Sufi explanations of "how the many originated from the One."

14. Again, one should note that this traditional association of "the left" with the "negative" pole and the first part of the *kalimah,* and "the right" with the "positive" pole of the *kalimah* can be seen in much of the vernacular Sufi poetry of the Qadiriyya, as pointed out by A. Schimmel in *As Through A Veil, Mystical Poetry in Islam* (New York: Columbia University Press, 1982), p. 143. Schimmel also mentions another metaphor used in vernacular poetry of the Indian subcontinent, that of the *dhikr* as taproot, the source of water that makes the divine plant grow "in the heart"—a theme much used by Bawa. See Bawa Muhaiyaddeen, *Come to the Secret Garden* (Philadelphia: Fellowship Press, 1985). Note the drawn-out long *u* in Allah*u,* which Bawa described as the "sound of resonance," in a discourse played on the last day of the 1991 *Mawlid al-Qutb.*

15. It is noteworthy that during the years 1978–1980, the political events in the Middle East prompted Bawa to take an active letter-writing role, corresponding with Khomeini, Begin, Sadat, and Carter in an effort to effect a peaceful resolution to the variety of troubles in the region. He encouraged members of the fellowship to join together in their concerns and political actions toward peace and "goodwill."

16. See William Graham, *Divine Word and Prophetic Word in Early Islam* (The Hague: Mouton and Co., 1977).

17. ARS 7404-05, "How to Do Zikr," 4/21/74, Sri Lanka. Again, this is a reference to still another favorite *hadith qudsi,* in which "God said: . . . (when my servant draws near to me) . . . I become his ear with which he hears, his eye with which he sees, his hand with which he grasps, and his foot with which he walks" (Quoted from W. Graham, *Divine Word and Prophetic Word in Early Islam,* p. 173).

18. As with the concept of *tawhid,* where some among the Muslim "orthodoxy" have seen certain expressions of a "unity of being" ontology as suggesting a compromise of God's radical distinction (i.e., transcendence) from "the natural order," the concept of a "unitive" spiritual experience, in which claims are made that suggest a "unity" or union with God, has also been a point of contention in Islamic theology. Bistami, al-Hallaj, and Ibn 'Arabi were among those figures in Islamic history whose spiritual "locutions" included this unitive-experiential dimension. See Carl Ernst, *Words of Ecstasy in Sufism* (Albany: State University of New York Press, 1985), pp. 1–6, who notes that the inspired and ambiguous utterances of the mystics of Islam must be understood in terms of the context in which their mystical vocabulary developed.

19. ARS 7404-05D. The tape is labeled *Zikr Jalali.*

20. ARS 7404-05D.

21. This teaching is reminiscent of the attitude expressed in Ibn Arabi's *Tarjuman al-Ashwaq,* in which the body and the passions are viewed as vehicles to the knowledge of God: "The soul loves the body because all her knowledge of the Truth is gained through her imprisonment in the body and through her making use of it in order to serve God." *Tarjuman al-Ashwaq.* trans. and ed. R. Nicholson (London: Theosophical Publishing House, 1911), p. 126.

22. ARS 7404-05D.

23. APT 9004-01, "Morning Zikr After the Night of Power in the Mosque of Sheikh M. R. Bawa Muhaiyaddeen."

24. The 1974 date of this discourse in Sri Lanka clearly indicates the earlier assimilation of and familiarity with Islamic practice in the Sri Lankan group. Indeed, there was the mosque in Jaffna. ARS 7404-05, 1974, Part II, "The Significance of Zikr."

25. Michael D. Schaffer, "Mosque Was a Labor of the Heart," *Philadelphia Inquirer* (September 6, 1984). See also Amy Linn, "The New American Muslims," *Philadelphia Inquirer* (July 10, 1988).ep

26. More work needs to be done on Bawa's "aesthetics-as-teachings." One should add that the movement from interiority to externalization has meant a certain movement from unity to distinction in terms of the use of space (a whole topic unto itself). The "sacred space" in the early days consisted solely of Bawa's room, literally around his bed or "downstairs," a larger meeting room. During Bawa's discourses, this space was occupied by men, women, children, together in the "presence of the *shaykh,*" and this practice continues in the "meetings," where members discuss-share-learn Bawa's teachings. During the *salat,* the men and women are in traditional fashion separated in the mosque by a veil. A "gray" area in the use of social space seems to be such events as the *mawlids,* during which the readings are done, not in the mosque, not in Bawa's room, but in one of the teaching classrooms. Women (except for children) are excluded from this space and must sit in the hallway or go into Bawa's room where closed-circuit television provides viewing and participation. On the other hand, the larger meeting room also televises the readings, but men and women sit together here. Another emerging development in the use of space and rituals one can see is that at the events revolving around Bawa and his teachings, such as the "meetings," the *mawlids,* and the *dhikr,* one sees less attendance of non-American Muslims.

27. APT 8404-06 4/84. "Love and Unity in Islam," and "Islam and Congregational Prayer."

28. See notes 6 and 18.

29. Ibn Sina, known in the Latin West as Avicenna, is the eleventh

century neoplatonic Muslim philosopher whose emanationist ontology forms the backdrop—and sometimes point of departure—for all future Islamic philosophy and mysticism. His ontology, his "philosophy of Being," stresses God's transcendence, and his cosmology affirms the relationship of all beings to Absolute Being, the effusion of all beings from their source. See S. H. Nasr, *Three Muslim Sages* (Delmar, N.Y.: Caravan Books, 1976).

30. ARS 8606-06, 6/86, "Search for the True Beauty of Insan, with Many Hadith, inc. Gabriel and Fatimah, Ali, and Khidr Nabi."

31. A variety of hadiths understood to be related to this subject. "The first thing God created was Light," "The first thing God created was my Light"; "I was a prophet when Adam was still between clay and water," "If it were not for you, Muhammad, I would not have created the heavens."

32. In Ibn ʿArabi's writings the "level of being" associated with God in His "inclusive Oneness" (*al-wahidiyyah*) is sometimes referred to as the level of the divine names (*asma al-ilahiyyah*). This is contrasted with the undifferentiated oneness or unicity (*al-ahadiyyah*) of God. See T. Izutsu, *A Comparative Study of the Key Philosophical Concepts in Sufism and Taoism* (Tokyo: Keio Institute of Cultural and Linguistic Studies, 1966). See also Annemarie Schimmel, *As Through a Veil*, p. 195.

33. *Muhammad* and *Ahmad* are both forms of the Arabic *hamida*, to praise. *Ahmad* is sometimes referred to as the esoteric name of the Prophet.

34. Schimmel, *As Through a Veil*, p. 194. See Rumi's use of this word play.

35. Bawa Muhaiyaddeen, *Islam and World Peace* (Philadelphia: Fellowship Press, 1987), p. 151. That is, the word play is used to speak of the "inner meaning" of Muhammad. The Light of Muhammad is the first externalization of the Divine Absolute, hence, the symbol of God's "countenance." In Sufi literature, the heart (*qalb*) is the "inner Throne" of Allah, the "place" of intimate knowledge-experience of God in the individual. This tradition of the heart-as-locus of intimate colloquy with God is an important theme in Sufi literature since the time of Tustari, and it is present in the teachings of ʿAbd al-Qadir al-Jilani.

36. This *Ahmad bila mim* tradition has been used in both "high" and "popular" mystical literature since the thirteenth century and the interpretations always refer to a unitive-causal relation between Allah and Muhammad. That is, the letter *mim* is the only "barrier" between Allah, the One, and Ahmad, Muhammad. The *mim*, because of its sperm shape, is sometimes seen as a symbol of the source and agency of creation. See Schimmel, *Mystical Dimensions of Islam*, pp. 419–420.

37. Islamic "law." For a description of the conduct that Bawa de-

scribed as embodying the shariah, refer to Tape ARS 8605-22, "Interview with Two Professors from Connecticut." A list of 100 modes of conduct is recited by Bawa when he was asked about his conception of the Shariah.

38.   ARS 7508-03, 8/75, "Imam-Islam."

39.   Bawa Muhaiyaddeen, *Islam and World Peace*, p. 102. The "true form" should be understood in the multivalent sense of essence, archetype, reality, the realized human being who has returned to that primordial state of perfect unity and knowledge of God. (In Sufi literature this is sometimes seen as a recapitulation of the Quranic *yawm al-mithaq* of Sura 7 171, the "Day of Covenant," the day of *alastu*, the "primordial time" in which the human heart truly "witnessed" to its Lord.)

40.   Bawa Muhaiyaddeen, *Asma' ul-Husna, The Ninety-Nine Beautiful Names of Allah* (Philadelphia: Fellowship Press, 1979), p. 196. For a more complete description of the various "names of Muhammad," see page 136.

41.   Ibid. The meditations on the Ninety-Nine Names are followed by teachings of Bawa, hadiths, and legends about such familiar figures as Fatimah, Gabriel, Ali. In other texts, these metaphysical teachings are framed through stories with other Islamic and Sufi exemplars, such as 'Umar, Abu Bakr, and al-Ghazzali.

42.   Ibid., p. 145.

43.   In Sufi lore there are a number of stories about Uways, who is supposed to have lived in Yemen, who never met Muhammad, but whose piety and devotion were known to the Prophet. For later Sufis he became the prototype of the inspired Sufi who has been guided solely by divine grace, knowing the Prophet without outward connection. Thus the *uwaysi* is the mystic who has attained illumination outside the regular path and without mediation and guidance of a living shaykh. Bawa tells many delightful and poignant stories about Uways and clearly identifies with this form of attainment of knowledge of the "inner" truth of things. Tape ARS 7508-03, 8/23/75, "Iman-Islam Bawa Takes Two People on Hajj, Man Who Saw Muhammad."

44.   Bawa's method of gradually introducing more clearly articulated Islamic practices, coupled with an insistence on tolerance among the members toward each other's differences in understanding, cultural background, etc., has resulted in a "plurality" of degrees of participation in events centered around Bawa and events centered around the mosque.

45.   *Al-akhira, yaum al-qiyama,* and *fana* are all terms found in Qur'anic eschatological material. They refer, respectively, to the ends of things (the hereafter), the day of resurrection, and annihilation (or passing away of all things but God). In Sufi literature these terms often also speak of the individual experience of annihilation of the ego, the lower self.

46.   Schimmel, *Mystical Dimensions of Islam*, 57.

47. Bawa Muhaiyaddeen, *Asma'ul Husna*, p. 201.

48. Ibid.

49. Shihab al-Din Yahya Suhrawardi, *al-Shaykh al-Ishraq*, "master of the philosophy of illumination" (d. 1191), whose theories included the formulation of an explanation for the "descent of being" from "Absolute Being" through the various orders of "angelic" light (the "powers" of God) to the elemental level of existence, posits the "Tenth Angel-Intellect" as the archetype of humanity, whose epistemological function is identified with the figures of Gabriel and Khidr; namely, that to denote that individuated power of God within the individual which explains the subtle understanding of events, texts, situations, persons, oneself, etc. See Gisela Webb, "The Human/Angelic Relation in the Philosophies of Suhrawardi and Ibn 'Arabi" (Ph.D. diss., Temple University, 1989), pp. 47–84.

50. It is from the translation of the Arabic, *muhyi al-din*, that the name Muhaiyaddeen comes.

51. Schimmel, *Mystical Dimensions of Islam*, p. 247.

52. Qur'anic term referring to the "multilayered self-deception" that is part of the human condition. "Man's conscience itself becomes so perverted that, through long habituation with particularized interests and persistent worship of false gods, the holy seems unholy, and vice versa" (Fazlur Rahman, *Major Themes of the Quran* [Chicago: Bibliotheca Islamica, 1980], p. 107.)

53. See Bawa Muhaiyaddeen, *Islam and World Peace*, pp. 59, 68. Bawa: "Within this innermost heart is a peace of flesh where the eighteen thousand universes, the heavens, and His kingdom are found. . . . there the angels, the heavenly beings, prophets, and lights of Allah prostrate before Him. . . . This piece of flesh within the heart contains the wisdom which can discover that palace of Allah." ". . . there is a tiny piece of flesh in the heart which worships Allah, looks at Him, hears Him, and prays to Him. . . . This is the throne of the true believer."

54. Quoted in S. H. Nasr, *Islamic Spirituality, Foundations*, p. 114.

55. Quoted from the fellowship's handout of the translation of the "Morning Zikr."

56. Tape 5 Songs, "The One Who Rules Baghdad."

57. ARS 7202-09, 2/72, "Qutb on Maldive Islands." The ghost, demons, and idols are interpreted by many in the fellowship in language that unites "spiritual" and "psychoanalytic areas"; i.e., the past attachments, the fears, the mind's tricks and desires, the pseudo-gods that block the integration of the self and thus the original unity and peace of "Islam."

58. S. H. Nasr, *Sufi Essays* (New York: Schocken Books, 1977), p. 59.

59. W. C. Chittick, *The Sufi Path of Love* (New York: State University of New York Press, 1983), pp. 120–121.

60. This a reference to and Sufi interpretation of Sura 7:171.

61. The "realized" or "perfected" human being. See Bawa Muhaiyaddeen, *Sheikh and Disciple* (Philadelphia: Fellowship Press, 1983).

62. Bawa Muhaiyaddeen, *God, His Prophets and His Children* (Philadelphia: Fellowship Press, 1978), pp. 16–17. The quoted transliteration is the one used in the text.

63. Ibid., pp. 17–18.

64. Bawa Muhaiyaddeen, *Sheikh and Disciple*, p. 11.

65. Ibid., p. 18.

66. Ibid., p. 23.

67. Ibid., p. 25.

68. Ibid., pp. 51 ff.

69. Ibid., p. 52.

70. Ibid., pp. 85–88.

71. Bawa Muhaiyaddeen, *Asma' ul Husna*, pp. 182–183 (on the *qurban*).

72. I use the word *innovation* precisely because of its ambiguous character when discussing developments of Islamic groups in America. The nonspecialist should be aware that the Arabic term *bid'a*, innovation, has a negative connotation when pertaining to changes in religious custom. In American English, the term has developed an almost implicitly positive connotation.

73. Bawa was quoted by a member as saying that "that those who come to the fellowship for me, for food, for the social part will leave, but those who come for God will remain."

74. A number of the earliest disciples of Bawa's were African American. Bawa's insistence on "unity" of "race, religion, class, caste" translated into a visible number of interethnic or interracial marriages.

75. During the 1970s Bawa was invited to several public speaking engagements. The pattern was that people who took Bawa as their shaykh, their teacher, usually moved to Philadelphia. Those who could not move near the shaykh established branches. Some of the branches emerged as Philadelphia members moved to other areas of the country, particularly after Bawa's death. There are branches in Boston, Connecticut, New York, Pennsylvania, Kansas, Iowa, Michigan, Wisconsin, California, Canada, England, Nigeria, and Sri Lanka. Branches have membership of approximately 7–18 in the various individual locations.

76. This reverence, of course, is manifested in the *mazar*, the shrine, which, too, forms an important part of the "Islamic landscape."

77. Bawa Muhaiyaddeen, *Islam and World Peace*, p. 93.

78. Ibid., pp. 37–39.

CHAPTER 5

The Five Percenters: A Teenage Nation of Gods and Earths

Yusuf Nuruddin

ORGANIZATIONAL STRUCTURE AND DEVELOPMENT

The Five Percenters are a splinter group that broke away from the Nation of Islam (NOI) in 1964, under the leadership of Clarence "Pudding" 13X. The name is derived from their belief that they are the chosen five percent of humanity who live a righteous "Islamic" life and thereby have manifested the "true divine nature of the black man who is God or Allah." This group rather than the NOI was primarily responsible for disseminating, popularizing and re-interpreting the "Lessons" or teachings of Elijah Muhammad among the adolescent generation of the sixties in the New York metropolitan area. In the twenty-five years since, the influence of The Five Percent Nation or The Nation of Gods and Earths (as they are now known) has grown enormously—many of the lyrics in contemporary rap music make direct reference or strong allusion to Five Percenter ideology.

The actual size of the Five Percent Nation is difficult to gauge. New York City is the center of the movement; it began in Harlem and rapidly spread to all of the outlying boroughs. Yet the organization is loosely knit and it is difficult to distinguish a member from an interested sympathizer. Numerical estimations are further complicated by the fact that offshoot or cognate groups exist that espouse a similar ideology; one such group is the Zulu Nation in the South Bronx. Certainly in the metropolitan area the Five Percenters number in the thousands and perhaps in the tens of thousands. The extent of the influence in New York City may be judged, qualitatively if not quantitatively, by an oft-repeated comment that was coined in the seventies: "Just about all of Brownsville is righteous!" The statement was accurate in its assessment and, perhaps, ominous in its implications. In the sprawling Brownsville ghetto in Central Brooklyn, the "righteous" ideology of the Five Percent Nation has become a dominant, pervasive and potentially permanent feature of the black adolescent subculture. Brownsville—even more than Harlem—is characterized by impoverishment and decay. It is a fertile environment for the flourishing of a black supremacist ideology which speaks directly to disenchanted youth. If the spiral of urban poverty and decay continues unabated, all of the inner-city neighborhoods might succumb to the Five Percent Nation in domino-like fashion.

The size and geographical distribution of the Five Percent Nation throughout the rest of the United States is a matter of conjecture. From its original Harlem headquarters it has spread far, first travelling throughout the penal institutions of New York State, then to cities along the East Coast and gradually even to the West Coast. (In the mid-seventies an acquaintance from a relatively small New England city—Springfield, Massachusetts—mentioned (with disdain) its influence in her home town.) One indication of the movement's cultural influence on black America can be seen in a popular black movie of the mid- seventies entitled "The Watts Stax Festival." In a short segment of this movie comedian Richard Pryor is portrayed as a Five Percenter-styled character from Los Angeles, who eloquently, in street corner dialect, rails against the "tricknology" of the white man, the ill effects of consuming pork, and other such evils. Organizationally, the Five Percenter Nation has only begun to spring up in West Coast cities such as Los Angeles and San Diego during the past two years (1987–88), yet by the mid-seventies the ideology, colorful terminology and the spellbinding oratorical style of the Five Percenters, in one form or another, had become a familiar and integral part of the African American inner city experience across the nation.

For twenty-one years (1967–1988) the headquarters of the Five Percent Nation was located at the "Allah School in Mecca" on the corner of Adam Clayton Powell Boulevard and 126th Street in Harlem. (In Five Percenter parlance, Manhattan—especially Harlem—is known as Mecca, Brooklyn is known as Medina and

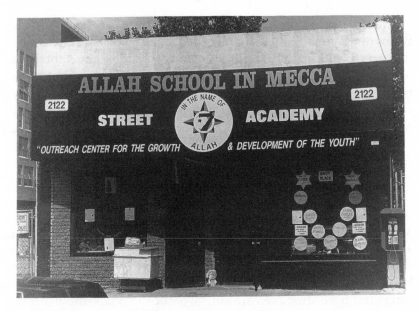

the other boroughs have equally descriptive names.) The headquarters in "Mecca" was a two-story brick building painted black with the name *Allah* emblazoned in huge gold letters above the entrance. Next to the word *Allah* was the smaller gold-painted caption: "The Black Man Is God." At these "Mecca" headquarters lessons were prepared and disseminated and leaders studied incessantly until they became sharp-tongued, quick-witted, and well-polished articulators of the ideology. The Five Percenters were politically powerful enough to request and obtain, as a bona fide youth organization, the use of city-owned facilities for their meetings and activities. They won this recognition from municipal government officials because they were too large and potentially too disruptive to be ignored. As is true of street-fighting gangs or "social clubs" that the Five Percenters somewhat resemble, social workers and other city officials preferred to cooperate with them in an effort to channel their energies toward achieving constructive ends rather than to ignore them or try to fight with them. This was the policy at least until 1988, when the City of New York terminated the tenancy of Allah School in Mecca.[1]

Organizationally the Five Percenters developed a simple but highly efficient and effective system of communication. The Allah School in Mecca was the central office from which the lessons were distributed. Schools in Medina (Brooklyn), The Desert (Queens), and Pelan (the Bronx) also have disseminated Lessons.[2] The schools function as meeting places for all members, and non-members are barred access. Once a month members from each of the boroughs hold boroughwide convocations called *Parliaments* in local public school buildings or public parks. These Parliament sessions are open to the general public and they provide a democratic forum for any member of the Nation to speak to the entire assembly. At a typical Parliament hundreds of youths may be present.

In recent years, the Five Percenters have turned to the print and the electronic media as means of mass communication. Five Percenters tend to dominate the rap music industry. Rap artists such as Rakim, Big Daddy Kane, and Lakim Shabazz now record hit albums with titles such as "Pure Righteousness," with album covers displaying the Five Percent Nation flag and lyrics which "drop Science" (teach Five Percenter lessons) on their audience.[3] The Five Percenters have also taken advantage of the radio talk-show format to disseminate their ideas. WWRL is a black-oriented AM station in New York devoted almost entirely to religious broadcasting, mostly in the form of gospel music and live or taped sermons from various congregations. But at two o'clock in the morning twice a week the Five Percenters rap away to whomever is awake and listening. As masters of the spoken word, the avenues of rap music and talk shows are a natural course of evolution for the movement.

Surprisingly, perhaps, members of the Five Percent Nation have also turned to journalism. In recent years they have launched at least two publications. The first entitled *Behold The SUN OF MAN* was essentially a newsletter which appeared around 1985 but was rather short-lived. In June of 1987, *The WORD*, a sixteen-page bimonthly tabloid, made its debut. (The title plays on a contemporary slang expression, "Word!", which in conversation is an emphatic response from a listener that affirms or underscores the *truth*, incisiveness, or cogency of the speaker's statement.) The paper, which sells for a dollar per copy, is very difficult to find because of production and circulation problems. It is further hampered by the poor quality of its typeface and ink. Only the most dedicated reader will strain his or her eyes to read an issue thoroughly. This is unfortunate as the paper is in fact lively, informative and well-researched and has a broad scope of news coverage and feature articles.

The back page of the newspaper is often devoted to a statement of beliefs and program reminiscent of the back page of *Muhammad Speaks*. Under the banner "What We Teach" are listed the following nine points:

1. We teach that Black People are the Original People of the Planet Earth.
2. We teach that Black People are the Mothers and Fathers of Civilization.
3. We teach that the Science of Supreme Mathematics is the key to understanding man's relationship to the universe.
4. We teach Islam as a natural way of life: not a religion.
5. We teach that education should be fashioned to enable us to be self-sufficient as a people.
6. We teach that each one should teach one according to their knowledge.
7. We teach that the Blackman is God and his proper name is Allah (Arm Leg Leg Arm Head).
8. We teach that our children are our link to the future and they must be nurtured: respected, loved, protected and educated.
9. We teach that the unified Black Family is the vital building block of the Nation.[4]

Under the heading "What We Will Achieve" are listed three points which are extensively defined and elaborated: (1) National Consciousness (i.e., Black Nationalist Consciousness); (2) Community Control and (3) Peace.

The early issues of *The WORD* featured a lengthy three-part history of the movement which concentrated on the biography of the founder Clarence "Pudding" 13X, whom the Five Percenters refer to as *Allah*.[5] According to the biography, Clarence 13X (1929–1964) was born Clarence Smith in Danville, Virginia. He derived his nickname "Pudding" from his mother who called him "Put" as a child. (Other sources claim that he derived the name because he was a gifted conversationalist—his "rap" was so smooth and sweet that people would swallow his words like pudding.) During childhood he experienced the typical incidents of racial prejudice and discrimination that occurred in the segregated

south. One such incident, in which his father had a violent altercation with a white man, affected him deeply.

In 1946 he moved to Harlem with his family and eventually
married. In 1950 he joined the army and served in the Korean War.
While he was in Korea, his wife Dora joined the Nation of Islam.
When he returned he also accepted the teachings of the Nation and
became a member of Temple No. 7 in Harlem which was then
under the leadership of Minister Malcolm X. Having learned kara-
te while in the service, he first distinguished himself in the NOI as
a martial arts instructor, and rapidly rose to the rank of lieutenant
in the military training unit known as the Fruit of Islam (FOI).
Soon afterwards he also gained recognition for his proficiency in
memorizing the lessons. His hypnotic speaking style earned him
promotion to the position of student minister, for which he was
congratulated in person by Elijah Muhammad who travelled to
New York to meet him.

In the early sixties he began to encounter troubles in the NOI
when he started to doubt, and eventually rejected, the doctrine that
W. D. Fard was Allah. He reasoned that Fard could not be God
because the NOI lessons stated the Original Man or Black Man
was God and by appearances Fard was not black. He re-interpreted
the lessons of the NOI and began to teach that it was not Fard, but
the black man collectively, who was God. In 1963 he was reprimanded and ordered to stop teaching by Captain Joseph of the
FOI. This was also the year that Minister Malcolm X was suspended for his comments on the Kennedy assassination. It was a
time of turmoil in Temple No. 7, and in the NOI in general. With
this leadership problem in the background, and his own differences
with the NOI authorities growing increasingly irreconcilable,
Clarence 13X left the NOI.

Some of the brothers in the Temple left with him, most notable
among them one who later became known as Justice. With Justice
as his right-hand man, Clarence 13X devised a plan to go out into
the streets and teach and organize the masses of black youth who
had never been reached by the NOI. Together Clarence and Justice
invented the system called the Supreme Alphabet and the Supreme
Mathematics, and introduced this system along with the re-
interpreted NOI lessons to a group of nine youth who became
known as the First Nine Born.[6] When these First Nine Born became well-versed they were instructed by Allah (Clarence 13X) to

each teach ten youth younger than themselves. Through this method, hundreds of youth were brought into the movement that was first known as Allah's Nation of the Five Percent.

In 1967, a year marked by racial violence in New York City, the Lindsay administration created a Task Force to reach the real black leaders in the community in order to prevent further violence. Clarence was one of the community leaders with whom the Mayor's Task Force developed ties. The New York Urban League assisted in the negotiations with the Mayor's Task Force. A building was secured for the Five Percenters, first known as the New York Urban League Street Academy and eventually called the Allah School in Mecca.[7]

On the night of June 12, 1969, Clarence was gunned down by seven bullets in East Harlem, the assailants unknown. A police spokesman quoted in the daily newspapers alleged that the NOI was behind the assassination because they wanted to do away with rival splinter groups. Minister Louis Farrakhan, then leader of Muhammad's Temple No. 7 in Harlem, emphatically denied the police account, stating that the "white power structure" was attempting to instigate hostilities between the two groups so that they would destroy each other. The murder was never solved and speculation still persists as to the identity of his assassins. The Five Percent Nation initially experienced a period of disorganization after their leader's death, and no individual stepped in to fill Clarence's shoes. In 1971 the organization regrouped under collective leadership and began to initiate several activities to "show and prove" that "Allah" (Clarence) could not die as long as his teachings were still alive.

IDEOLOGY

The ideology of the Five Percent Nation is based upon the reinterpreted lessons of the Nation of Islam. The teachings of the NOI were presented to its members in catechism (question and answer) format; the grouped sets of questions and answers were designated as a lesson. In total several lesson sets representing about a hundred catechism questions and answers constituted the core doctrine of the NOI. The first ten questions and answers were known as the Student Enrollment Lesson allowing students to "earn their X." This X symbolically replaced their "ex-slave name" and made them full-fledged members of the NOI. As a member proceeded up the ranks of the NOI, he was required to master more difficult Lesson sets. The NOI Student Enrollment Lesson began thus:

1. Who is the Original Man? The Original Man is the Asiatic Black Man, the Maker, the Owner, the Cream of the Planet Earth, the Father of Civilization, and God of the Universe.

2. Who is the Colored Man? The Colored Man is the Caucasian (white-man), or Yakub's grafted devil, the Skunk of the Planet Earth.

3. What is the population of the Original Nation in the Wilderness of North America, and all over the Planet Earth? The population in the Wilderness of North America is 17 million, with 2 million Indians making it 19 million; all over the Planet Earth is 4,400 million.[8]

After "processing" or "earning their X" the NOI members proceeded to memorize several other Lesson sets including Lost-Found Lesson No. 1 which consists of fourteen questions and Lost-Found Lesson No. 2 which consists of forty questions. This second set of Lost-Found Lessons teaches a naturalist theory of the universe which denies the idea of life after death as well as the existence of a "mystery god."[9] The only resurrection possible is a revival from "mental death" (ignorance and superstition). Those who believe in a mystery god are mentally dead. The only "god" is man himself; it is the "devil" (white man) who has tricked 85 percent of humanity into believing in a god whom they cannot see, so that he can "make slaves [of them] . . . rob them and live in luxury." This exposition leads into a series of three important questions from which the Five Percenters draw their self-conception:

14. Who are the 85 percent? The uncivilized people; poison animal eaters; slaves from mental death and power; people who do not know who the Living God is, or their origin in this world and who worship that direction but are hard to lead in the right direction.

15. Who are the 10 percent? The rich slave-makers of the poor, who teach the poor lies to believe: that the Almighty, True and

Living God is a spook and cannot be seen by the physical eye; otherwise known as bloodsuckers of the poor.

16. Who are the 5 percent? They are the poor righteous teachers who do not believe in the teachings of the 10 percent and are all-wise and know who the living God is and teach that the Living God is the Son of Man, the Supreme Being, or the Black Man of Asia, and teach Freedom, Justice and Equality to all the human family of the planet Earth; otherwise known as civilized people, also as Muslims and Muslim Sons.[10]

These beliefs are the core of the Five Percenters' identity and ideology. They believe that 85 percent of humanity is bent on self-destruction because of their involvement in vice and immorality and their lack of true self-knowledge. Thus they also refer to the self-destructive 85 percent as "Destroy-Powers," i.e., those who foolishly destroy their own divine powers or creative abilities, talents and potential. They destroy not only their own individual power but the collective power of the race as well. (One of the popular rap records of 1989 is a cautionary message addressed to black youth entitled "Self-Destruction.") The Five Percenters also believe that 10 percent of humanity have knowledge and power but use it wickedly to deceive and exploit the 85 percent. In this category, they place the "white devil" as well as orthodox Muslims "who teach that Allah is a spook," Christian ministers and any others who "tell lies to the poor." Finally they view themselves as the Five Percent who have self-knowledge (knowledge of their "divinity" or unlimited potential for great achievement as a race) and who use their knowledge creatively to unleash the untapped resources of, or under-utilized powers of the black man. Hence they refer to themselves also as *Build-Powers*. Furthermore, they believe that once a man has mined his own hidden talents or achieved mastery of his own inner powers, he is a God in the sense of being a Creator of his own destiny. (This concept is related to ideas expressed by humanistic psychologists, such as Abraham Maslow, in terms like *self-actualization* and *transpersonal self-realization*.)[11] Hence, most members refer to themselves as Gods rather than Five Percenters. A Five Percenter is actually a "new-born" or someone who has just begun to study the knowledge but has not yet applied it. A God is one who has applied this self-transformative knowledge, or in their own parlance, one who can "show and prove" that he is God. In accordance with their professed divinity they adopt divine or "righteous" names such as "Universal God Allah," "Born Islam," "Allah Supreme," "Divine God," "Understanding Allah," "God Allah Mind," "Forever Allah," etc., emblazoning these names on sweatshirts and even going through court proceedings to gain legal recognition of them.

One area in which all Five Percenters or Gods have exhibited remarkable mastery or self-actualization is the ability to communicate effectively. As conversationalists they are unequalled. The fascinating, even mesmerizing, appeal of the movement to the youth comes from the Five Percenter's eloquent and spell-binding usage of African American inner-city slang. Using the potency and the vitality of the black dialect they open up new avenues of logic and thinking, or original ways of perceiving the world. For example, a Five Percenter will "break down" (analyze) the word *knowledge*: "It means 'know the ledge.' A man who has knowledge of self knows his strengths as well as his limitations, he knows how far to go. A person without self-knowledge doesn't know his own boundaries or limitations, therefore he'll take things to excess, like alcohol, or drugs, and he'll go off the ledge, he'll go off the deep end."[12] Similarly he can give you new insights into the meaning of the word *wisdom*: "Wisdom is a wise word spoken by a wise person. If you break down "wisdom" you get 'wise the dome' or 'wides the dome' See the dome is the brain. Wisdom wisens the dome and it widens the dome."[13]

Words are also "broken down" into acronyms to reveal hidden truths. Five Percenters illustrate that the black man is divine by unfolding the secret meaning of the word "man": *My Almighty Name*. This human/divine relationship is further corroborated by unveiling the name of Allah which means *Arm Leg Leg Arm Head*.

When dozens of these novel concepts come at you in the rapid-fire, mile-a-minute talking pace of a Five Percenter it is a mind-expanding experience . . . a visit to another world where normal rules of logic are suspended and an entirely new set of rules apply. The terrain of this world is landscaped by the mythology provided in the lessons of the NOI, and the "divine sciences" created by Clarence 13X, the Supreme Alphabet and the Supreme Mathematics. The Supreme Alphabet is a system in which every letter is given a mystical meaning: *A* stands for Allah, *B* is Be or Born, *C* is See, and so forth on down to *X* which is Unknown, *Y* which is "Why?"

("the question most asked by the Eighty-Five Percent") and *Z* which is Zig Zag Zig. Each mystical meaning of a letter has a moral or parable connected to it. The Supreme Mathematics is a corresponding numerological system. The Supreme Alphabet and the Supreme Mathematics are the building blocks of the Five Percenters' semantic word play. For example, the letter *F* in the Supreme Alphabet stands for "Father." According to the logic of the Five Percenters:

> If you "break-down" [i.e., analyze] "Father," you get Father. Now a man can fat[ten] he or her—I could fat a man and I could fat a woman. When I say I could fat a man, that means I can give him proper knowledge of self; that means I'm fattening him, you know, to show and prove that he's the Almighty True and Living God. When I fat the woman, I can give her a baby. See I can make a baby in one day, but a woman has to return it back to me in nine months. Soon as you plant your seed into the woman, in all reality, the baby's already born. But she's got to return it back to me in nine months. See, that shows and proves right there that the black man is the most dominant force in the universe.[14]

Sexism aside, there is a strange and twisting logic in this kind of interpretation which is at once both nonsense and much sense. Koestler, in his treatise on creativity, calls such thinking *bisociation*; De Bono, a cognitive psychologist, calls it *lateral thinking*.[15] Both emphatically state that such thinking breaks up the imprisoning old habits of routine logic or vertical thinking, allows the generation of original ideas, and is the key to the processes or insight, discovery and creativity. An example of such insight is found in the word-play surrounding the letter *U* in the Supreme Alphabet which stands for "You," "Universe" and "Understanding." If you "break down" the word "universe" you get *U* '*N*' *I* verses [i.e., 'you and I converse'] to bring about Supreme Understanding." The insight here is that the universe is defined through social discourse and shared understandings that each culture has the right to construct its own worldview or definition of reality. This insight parallels prevailing concepts in the sociology of knowledge.[16]

A rich example of the interplay between the lessons of the NOI and the Supreme Alphabet is found in the interpretation of the letter *K* which stands for "Knowledge," "King," and "Kingdom": "For surely I'll be the King of my Kingdom. The Planet earth, in all reality, is my Kingdom but I gave it to the devil for six thousand years. The way you break down "King" is 'King I Now God' which means that 'I am the King who now ac-knowledges myself as being God.'"[17]

The Supreme Mathematics is also used by the Five-Percenters in "breaking down" the Supreme Alphabet. In the Supreme Mathematics: "One means Knowledge; two means Wisdom; three means Understanding; four means Culture; five means Power; six means Equality; seven means God; eight means Build-Destroy; nine means Born; ten means Knowledge-Cipher."[18] Hence K, which is the eleventh letter of the alphabet, is also broken down as "one-one" or the "knowledge-knowledge degree for a King is one whose 'Knowledge' is ac-knowledged." According to this same logic, Wisdom plus Knowledge or two plus one yields three which is Understanding which also corresponds to U, the twenty-first (21st) letter of the Supreme Alphabet. One of the cornerstones of the Alphabet is, of course, I or "Islam" which is the ninth degree or the "Born-degree"—when one is born into Islam, one recognizes that "I Self-Lord Am Master" or that "I Surely Love Allah and Mathematics."

The Five Percenters' worldview constitutes an example of pro-tonationalism—an undeveloped nationalistic ideology which functions as a precursor to a developed nationalistic ideology. (One must note, however, that the political analysis in the newspaper The WORD demonstrates a rapid movement towards a developed nationalistic ideology.) The impulse toward nationalism is clearly seen in the fourteenth degree of the Supreme Alphabet, "Now" or Nation":

> Now is the time for the Black man to wake up and come into the realization of Islam, which is his true and righteous Self, which is his true Nature and his true Nation. Fourteen is the "Knowledge-Culture degree," when a man ac-knowledges his culture he is going to see the Power. And the Power is the Truth and the Truth is the Light. Before a man can see the Light he must find the switch and before we put on Our Light we must find our switch—we must ac-knowledge Our Culture.[19]

The idea of this cultural nationalism, which is to be found in or expressed through religion, is again reinforced in the fourth degree or "Culture degree" of the Alphabet. D or "Divine" is "the Sacredness of One Culture and that Divine Culture is Islam."

Geneva Smitherman in *Talkin and Testifyin: The Language of Black America* (1986), observes that

> . . . black talk is never simple cocktail chit-chat but a functional dynamic that is simultaneously a mechanism for learning about life and the world and a vehicle for achieving group approval and recognition. Even in what appears to be only casual conversation, whoever speaks is highly conscious of the fact that his personality is on exhibit and his status is at stake . . . for the speaker must be presented in a dazzling, entertaining manner. Black speakers are flamboyant, dramatic and spectacular; speakers and raps become symbols of "how to get ovah."[20]

The "streetology" of the Five Percenters, i.e., their style of street corner philosophical dialogue, is a quintessential expression of the "black talk" which Geneva Smitherman describes. Great outdoor disputations and debates take place as Five Percenters vie with the unconverted, as well as with one another, over major issues or subtle distinctions. These street corner debates draw crowds of young men as onlookers, in a time-honored tradition that goes back to Plato. As Smitherman points out, the speakers are artistic and eloquent in their manner of oral presentation. It is difficult to convey this artistry in a written exposition because the oral rhythm, cadence and improvisational techniques are missing. Intonation and spontaneity play an important role in determining the rhetorical quality and vitality of a streetologist's rap.

Smitherman has pointed out that the modes of discourse of black English have their roots in the oral tradition of West African culture. This heritage is expressed nationally both in the syntactical structure and idiomatic rules of black English and in the fusion or unity of the sacred and secular, which are perceived as existing on a continuum in the traditional African worldview. Smitherman has also observed that there are several particular verbal strategies, rhetorical devices, and expressive rituals. The Five-Percenter's "streetology" represents the mode which Smitherman has termed *signification*:

> Signification . . . refers to the verbal art of insult in which a speaker humorously puts down, talks about, needles . . . the listener. . . . It is characterized by exploitation of the unexpected and quick verbal surprises. . . . It is subtle and . . . has the following characteristics: indirection; circumlocution; metaphorical-imagistic, humorous, ironic, rhythmic fluency and sound;

teachy but not preachy; directed at person or persons usually present in the situational context; punning, play on words; introduction of the semantically or logically unexpected.

Signifying can be a witty one-liner, a series of loosely related statements or a cohesive discourse on one point. It can exhibit all or a combination of the characteristics just cited.[21] Smitherman also states that ". . . Another unique characteristic of signification is that it can be . . . heavy, that is, a way of teaching or driving home a cognitive message . . . without preaching."[22]

In the streetology of the Five-Percenters all of the above characteristics are present, although the insults or put-downs are generally directed at "the Caucasian white man" rather than the black members of the audience. This distinction, however, is a matter of shift of emphasis, for the black audience as members of the "uncivilized" Eighty-Five Percent do not totally escape a typical Five-Percenter tirade. The point of the Five Percenters' rap, however, is to drive home the cognitive message that black people are colonized and oppressed by the Ten Percenters, "the rich slave-makers of the poor," and to sway the Eighty-Five Percent over to the ideological viewpoint of the Five Percenters rather than to alienate them. The fusion of secular and sacred in the metaphors that the Five Percenters employ is representative not only of the traditional African worldview but of the millenarian or "nativistic" tradition as well.[23] The sacred metaphors of this cultural protonationalism, or religious protonationalism, actually couch a rudimentary class and racial analysis of the existing social structure. The term *Ten Percenter* is applied by the Five Percenters in reference to either whites or blacks. Hence "rich slave-makers of the poor" or "bloodsuckers of the poor" are those who would be called "white imperialists and neo-colonialist black bourgeoisie" in a more developed nationalist ideology.

Another peculiar feature of the Five Percenters' ideology is the creative adaptation from Tasawwuf or Sufism of the spiritual science, called *Hurufa-i-jay-Hurufa-Ab-jay*. This science of interpreting mystical meanings from each letter of the Arabic alphabet has been adapted by the Five Percenters in their Supreme Alphabet to apply to the Roman alphabet used in the English language. In Hurufa-i-jay-Hurufa-Ab-jay, for example, the first letter of the Arabic alphabet is mystically interpreted as Adam or First Man and a spiritual lesson is applied to this interpretation. In the same way the Five Percenters have applied a spiritual (and political) lesson and interpretation to the letters in their Supreme Alphabet. This spiritual science of Hurufa-i-jay-Hurufa-Ab-jay finds its counterpart in Hasidic Judaism in the Kabbalistic science of the Path of Letters. The Supreme Mathematics which is an esoteric numerological system also has counterparts in Sufism and Kabbala as well as in the philosophical-mathematical system developed by Pythagoras.

In each of these esoteric systems—the Kabbala's Path of Letters, the Hurufa-i-jay-Hurufa-Ab-jay, the Supreme Alphabet, the Supreme Mathematics, and the Pythagorean numerology—the basic premises are that the Divine Letters or Numerals constitute the fundamental elements or underlying principles of Reality. Therefore they are the keys to divine knowledge, wisdom and understanding. By using these keys man may unlock the secrets of the physical universe through the study of the atom and its constituent elements. Hence, the students of various esoteric systems often refer to them as spiritual or divine sciences.

In the Nation of Islam, where pragmatism was a reigning philosophy, any member who probed deeply and intensely into the lessons or any other esoteric system in search of hidden secrets was called a "Scientist," a term which simultaneously connoted awe and respect for the person's knowledge and a dismissal of such behavior as eccentric or oddball. When members of the NOI are asked about the Five Percenters, the standard reply is "Oh, they're Scientists!" The Five Percenters themselves acknowledge this characteristic when queried about the major distinction between themselves and the NOI. Their standard reply is "We science-out the Lessons and they don't." One manner in which they "science-out" the Lessons is by "Showing and Proving":

> Anyone can say "I'm the Asiatic Black man, the Maker, The Owner, The Cream of Civilization and God of the Universe"— even a white man could say that—but that doesn't make him the Original Man . . . you have to be able to "show and prove it," because Knowledge and wisdom is the truth but understanding is the proof and without the proof there is no truth.[24]

In "showing and proving" a concept or a lesson, the Five Percenters "break it down" in the same fashion that they "break down" the Supreme Alphabet.

The easiest way to get a feeling for what this kind of "showing and proving" is all about is to hear it from the mouth of a "God" himself. The following excerpts are from an interview which I conducted in 1977 with a tall, dark-complexioned, seventeen-year-old youth named Sincere Allah who spoke smoothly and with authority. The text loses much of its original flavor in transcription from tape to paper because the rhythm of the Five Percenter's rap is more engaging to the ear than it is to the eye. The almost hypnotic cadence of the spoken rap comes across as rather choppy when read. The reader is asked to better understand the appeal of the movement itself.

Sincere Allah was asked why the group calls itself the Five Percenters:

> *Sincere Allah*: Well, see, a Five Percenter is one who strives for perfection. A man, you know, has got to go from the Alphabets to the "1 to 10" [i.e., questions "1 to 10" of the Student Enrollment Lesson]. Once a man goes from the Alphabets to the "1 to 10," once he goes past that, then he can say he's God. Because then he can Show and Prove it. But, if a man says he's a Five Percenter, he's saying he's striving for perfection. That's why I say I'm not a Five Percenter. I'm God. Because a Five Percenter is a person who strives for perfection. I've already got perfection. Once a man deals with reality, he's dealing with perfection, right there. The Five Percenters . . . they're striving like a New Born. [*New Born* and *Baby* mean those who are only starting to learn the Five Percenter doctrine.] And you might tell them, you know, "Prove that you're God." He couldn't prove it, because he's striving for his. That's the difference between the Five Percenters and God.
>
> *Interviewer*: What about the Eighty-Five Percenters? And the Ten Percenters?
>
> *Sincere Allah*: Oh, yeah. Eighty-five Percenters . . . them the ones we used to call them *Build Powers* but now we call them *Destroy Powers* because, you know, once a man starts getting further in his lesson, then he'll fully understand. See before we used to call them Build Powers. See, I'm a Build Power because, you know, I want to build my powers. Eighty-five Percenters or Destroy Powers is a man who destroys his powers, each and every day by dealing cocaine, dealing with dope, you know, he'll be out there playing basketball, out there gambling, but he don't want to get into his books and learn about himself. That's what we call Destroy Powers. See, he's got the chance to be this, you know, to

be God, but he don't want to do this, you know? He wants to live that fast life, and make the money. He says, "Well if I'm a Five Percenter, or I'm God, but that ain't putting nothing in my pocket, so why should I take up this?" So, you know, he'll be living that fast life.

Now a Ten Percenter, they know what the True and Living God is. But they teach that the True and Living God is a spook, you know? I've got a lot of them on my block, and when they see the Five Percenters, you know, or the Gods manifesting the truth to little babies, they'll start sticking pins in the Baby's head, they'll tell the little Baby, "He's a thief. He took something from me. He ain't no God. He's been to jail." Like, I've been to jail, so the people try to down me. They go around the block telling people I'm not God because I stole from this, I stole from that. I know at one time, I was stealing, you know, because I didn't know myself. But now that I know myself, I stopped all that. You know, because a man, he learn from his mistakes. You know, like all these Ten Percenters, like Pope Paul is a 33-1/3 degree [33rd degree Mason]. That's like [in the NOI Lost-Found lesson No.1] when Musa (Moses) went to the caves of Europe to civilize the devil . . . them's the Jews, he only gave them 33-1/3 of the knowledge [according to the NOI Lesson, Moses came and taught the savage white devils, who had been cast out of the Holy Land into the caves of Europe, how to live a civilized life as well as some of their forgotten evil tricknology]. . . . A Mason's supposed to get 33 degrees, right? Well there are 360 degrees—that's knowledge, wisdom and understanding. 120 degrees worth of knowledge, 120 degrees worth of wisdom, and 120 degrees worth of understanding. And that's 360, right? That's 100 percent exactly. But a Mason only has one-third of that 33 percent. Actually you only have one man in the world today who has 33-1/3 percent, and that's Pope Paul, that's why all the presidents go to him. . . . He's the ruler of the world now . . . the presidents get the orders from him, in all reality, but they don't let you know this.

One of the themes most offensive to Sunni Muslims is the claim of the Five Percenters that the Black Man is God. Sincere Allah addressed this matter by "sciencing out" the NOI Student Enrollment Lesson, referred to by Five Percenters as [Questions] "One to Ten" or "Degrees One to Ten":

> *Sincere Allah*: One to Ten? The first degree, right, says "Who is the Original Man? The Original Man is the Asiatic Black Man.

The Maker, the Owner, the Cream of the Planet, Father of Civilization and God of the Universe. The reason we ask who is the Original Man is because the original means first. Black means dominant, right? They say Asiatic; Asiatic means mind and body. The maker: what you make, you own . . . we're makers of the earth, so therefore, we own the earth. We gave the Devil 6000 years to rule it. When Yakub, when he made the Devil he looked up at his people and he said, "Yeah, I'm going to make a nation that shall rule your nation for 6000 years." Well in all reality, he been here for more than 6000 years." In all reality he's only ruling those who don't know theirselves. This is why we say we gave the Devil 6000 years to rule. Well, in all reality, his time is up. It's like he tries to go to the moon, see the life on the moon, and tries to go to these different planets, because he knows his time is up. Then, the second degree says, "Who is the colored man?" . . . The colored man is the Caucasian white man: Yaukub's grafted devils of the planet earth. The reason why I say "colored" is because the white man takes on many shades of disguise or false colors.

He might have blond hair and blue eyes; gold mustache, silver . . . you know . . . you see, that's a colored man. Back in the days they used to call us colored. Well, the people realized who they were. . . . You know Black People used to be ashamed of being black. As soon as I call you black, you're ready to kill me. But now the people have woke up. Now they know that black is the most dominant force in the universe. Then, in the third degree, it says "What is the total population of the Original People, here in the wilderness of this North America?" . . . Here in the wilderness of this North America, a total of 17 million plus 2 million Indians makes it a total of 19 million. That's when they say Christopher Columbus, right, he discovered the poor part of the planet earth, which was North America. And when he came here he found the Indians here, so therefore, he discovered, nothing. Cause when you discover something that mean that nobody ever been there before, you know? But this the white man teaches in the school.

Then the fourth degree says, "What is the total population of the colored people in the wilderness of North America?" . . . Here in the wilderness there was a total of 103 million.

All over the planet earth, the original people got 4 billion, 400 million; (4,400,000,000) the Chinese and Japanese, all these are original people. They got three shades of the black man: black, brown, and yellow. After that it's grafted. That's why we're the most powerful people in the universe, and, on the planet earth. Then the fifth degree says, "What is the area in square miles of the planet earth?" The area in square miles of the planet earth is 196,940,000 square miles. Now, the way I see that right, only showing and proving right, like, you give me a piece of paper I could show you, like, years in it. In the 196,940,000 square miles, you've got the year 1960 in there; you've got the year 1964 and 1969. Now, the way I see it is when Allah— Knowledge was born by equality, born back to the culture, to the cipher [this is the numerological analysis according to the Supreme Mathematics; knowledge = 1, equality = 6, born = 9, culture = 4, cipher = 0, i.e., 1960 = knowledge − born − equality − cipher] only showing and proving that year 1964 when Almighty God Allah (Clarence 13X) when he left the temple, you know, in 1964 he showed and proved that the black man was God. Then, in 1969, that's when Mayor Lindsay offered him a lot of money and a certain amount of cars, you know, to stop teaching the babies; stop teaching it. So, he said "No. God can't be bought or sold." So they took him out of here. They figured they would kill him and his whole teachings would be stopped. See, they only killed his body. See, his body didn't manifest itself to the kids. It was his intelligence.

The rap never becomes stale or obsolete because it grows organically—each new generation rids itself of dead slang phrases and incorporates new ones. In 1966, the greeting was "Peace B'Allah" [pronounced "ba-lah"]—a contraction that I never really figured out, although some possibilities are "Peace, By Allah," "Peace Be Allah," of "Peace Brother of Allah." Today the greeting is "Peace, God." When one of the early Five Percenters uttered a profound truth, his cohorts let out choruses of "There it is!", "There it was!", "There it goes!" as if to signify that the spoken truth was rapidly ascending into the cosmos. Today one would hear choruses of "Word!" Other expressions of the eighties include "Ain't no puzzle!" [i.e., That's not hard to understand"] and "What's today's mathematics?" [i.e., "What's today's date?—to which the answer must be given in terms of Supreme Mathematics]. Even the Supreme Alphabet is not above change. In 1966, for example, Z stood for "Zelda Zee—a woman who is weak and wicked for she has not the knowledge, wisdom or understanding of self." By the late seventies, Z stood for "Zig Zag Zig—a snake who wanders to and fro, ever deviating from the right path back to the wrong path." The movement has become so widespread that according to some sources there are now Puerto Rican Five Percenters who have created a version of the Lessons in Spanish.

The letter *H* in the Supreme Alphabet stands for "He or Her." The parable or moral is that "He or Her has the power to build or destroy depending on whether they have knowledge of self or don't have knowledge of self." "He," however, seems to have more power than "her." In The Nation of Gods and Earths, men are the Gods and women are the Earths. As the Earth revolves around the Sun, so does a woman revolve around her man. The insignia or "Universal Flag" of the Five Percenters is a stellated circle circumscribing the numeral 7 which is superimposed over a star and crescent. In the Supreme Mathematics seven is the number of perfection and signifies Allah. Only men can attain the level of perfection signified by the seven. A woman's number is six, which is the highest level that she can attain. Six in the Supreme Mathematics is (ironically) Equality. However, Equality is "broken down" into E-Quality which refers to Earth Qualities or bad E-Qualities depending on how they use their "magnetic," i.e., their magnetism or power of sexual attraction. They can use their "magnetic" to lure one man after another simply to satisfy their own lusts (like weak and wicked Zelda Zee), or they can use their "magnetic" to reproduce, or to bear "God's" baby. Through reproduction they fulfill their womanhood and become like the Planet Earth because the Earth is productive and brings forth life. Three-fourths of the woman's body must be covered by clothing, just as three quarters of the earth is covered by water. Hence many of the Five Percenter women look just like Muslim women—they wear khimars or head coverings and long loose fitting garments. In fact, a female Five Percenter, unlike a male Five Percenter, is a "Muslim" because she bears witness that her man is "Allah." Five Percenter Earths are also known as Queens (Q standing for Queen or Quality) and bear righteous names such as "Queen Star Asia Peace Refinement" and "Princess Learn Her Earth." There seem to be a number of Earths or Queens in the Five Percent Nation, as a tide of unwed teenage mothers in Brownsville are bearing children whose names are listed on birth records as "Born Allah," "True God," "True Mathematics," "Always Be Allah," "Queen Culture Nation," and so on.

As the Five Percenter's political ideology becomes more developed, they increasingly identify with the aims and aspirations of the Nation of Islam. Although members of the old Nation would dismiss them as "Scientists," Minister Louis Farrakhan in his October 1985 Madison Square Garden address to a overflow crowd of 25,000 New Yorkers at one point specifically addressed his "beautiful brothers and sisters of the Five Percent Nation" in a message of unity. Several hundred Five Percenters in the crowd cheered in response. Some Five Percenters now say that the only difference between themselves and Farrakhan's NOI is the latter's strict dress code (e.g., suits and bow ties).

As the Earths cover their hair and wear ankle length dresses and as the "Gods" often wear kufis (traditional Muslim skullcaps), Five Percenters are sometimes mistaken for Sunni Muslims. Frequently the Muslim greeting "Salaam Aleikum" is returned by the Five Percenter greeting "Peace, God". There is a great deal of tension between Five Percenters and Sunni Muslims. The former in the eyes of the latter are committing "shirk" or the unforgivable sin of associating partners with Allah, and the latter in the eyes if the former are Ten Percenters because they "teach that the True and Living God is a Spook." Because Five Percenters view Islam as just a natural "way of life" rather than a religion, they "break down" the term *Sunni Muslim* to mean "Soon to be Muslim," (i.e., not yet Muslim and still hung up in the useless performance of a lot of rituals). Young Muslims who attend public high schools often encounter Five Percenters and engage them in petty debates and name calling. The young Muslims refer to the Five Percenters as "nickleheads" (Five Cents) and the Five Percenters in turn call them "Dimes." They "play the dozens" (an inner city game of repartee) with one another, e.g., "Ten Percenter, you still diving on the floor?" (i.e., "Are you still prostrating yourself in prayer?").

Adult Sunni Muslims have never forgotten the brutal murder in 1977 of a Sunni Muslim in his Brooklyn home in front of his wife and children. A group of Five Percenters, after knocking on his door on the pretext of making peace over an earlier altercation, shot him in the back of the head. There is a bitterness that still lingers and though the older Sunni Muslims would like to redirect these misguided youth, they tend to ignore them instead in order to avoid a major war between the youth and the elders of the black community, in which there clearly would be no winners.

Yet there appears to be another relationship between Five Percenters and Sunni Muslims if one looks at the community and its development. The Five Percent movement is basically a youth movement, an adolescent phenomenon. Its structure is designed especially to appeal to youth. While there are some adults in their thirties who call themselves Five Percenters it is rare; as people age the fun seems to wear thin and a desire for mature expressions of spirituality and political commitment develops. A substantial number of Sunni Muslims in their thirties today were the Five Percenters of the mid-sixties and early seventies. Whether or not this pattern will continue is difficult to assess. The fact is that in the past decade Sunni Muslims have lost community because of their internecine conflicts, stagnation and ambiguous stance on nationalism, although they are beginning to gain some of it back with their anti-drug campaigns. Five Percenters, on the other hand, have made some giant steps with the publishing of a national newspaper. the movement has become more cohesive and more ideologically sophisticated, and great emphasis is being placed on the importance of higher education and long-range planning. I am left pondering Sincere Allah's closing comment: "The Cream (of the Planet Earth) will always rise to the top."[25]

NOTES

1. "Harlem Landmark Threatened," *The WORD* 1, no. 8 (November 1988), p. 1 [unsigned article]. In an editorial accompanying this article entitled "Allah's Schools Close," God Kalim states that over the years there have been closings of six schools in New York City: four schools in Brooklyn, and one each in The Bronx and Queens. Two schools in Springfield, MA and one each in Newburgh, N.Y., and Beacon, N.Y., have also been closed.

2. Staten Island, the fifth borough of New York City, is known as The Oasis but I have no information on whether a school ever existed there.

3. Charlie Ahearn "Lakim Gets Busy Dropping Science," *The City Sun* 6, no. 17 (April 26, 1989), p. 13. See this article for a more detailed exposition of Five Percenter lyrics in contemporary rap music.

4. "What We Teach," *The WORD* 1, no. 2, (July 1987), p. 12.. Early issues of the tabloid were twelve pages; later issues were expanded to sixteen.

5. Beloved Allah, "The Greatest Story Never Told," Parts 1–3, *The WORD* 1, no. 2 (July 1987), p. 3; 1, no. 3 (Aug./Sept. 1987) pp. 6–7; and 1, no. 4 (Dec./Jan. 1988), pp. 6–7.

6.   The first student, whose "righteous" name was originally Kar-
riem but later changed to Black Messiah, was chosen because of his
ability to attract other youth and his very dark complexion which indicated that he was a pure Original Black Man. Black Messiah brought the
rest of the First Nine Born students to Clarence. Their righteous names
were Bisme Allah, Uhuru (Swahili for "Freedom"), Al-Java, Dihoo, Ar-
Rahiem, Sha-Sha, Ubeka and Salaam. Many of the first generation of Five
Percenters adopted concocted "Arabic-sounding" names, such as Sha-
Sha, Al-Java, etc.; later generations began to all call themselves Allah.

7.   It is reputed that an out-of-print book entitled *The Mayor's
Man* (author unknown) gives an early history of the Five Percenters, and
details the role played by Barry Gotherer, Mayor Lindsay's aide (the
mayor's man), who was the Task Force member assigned to work with the
Five Percenters. Gotherer coordinated the negotiations for securing the
street academy building.

8.   Student Enrollment Lessons of the Nation of Islam.

9.   Question #8 asks "What makes rain, hail, snow and earthquakes?" The answer is a lengthy detailed technical exposition on evap-
oration, distillation air currents, atmospherical conditions, etc. In questions #9–13, students are taught that there is no Mystery God who
makes it rain, hail, snow, etc., and that man has searched for such a God
for "trillions of years" but was unable to find him because none exists.

10.   Lost-Found Lesson No. 2 of the Nation of Islam.

11.   Robert Assagioli, *The Act of Will*, Penguin, 1974, pp. 119–122.

12.   Interview with Two Five Percenters; Sincere Allah and King
Allah, 1977.

13.   Ibid.

14.   Ibid.

15.   Arthur Koestler, *The Act of Creation*, Macmillan, 1964,
pp. 657–660. Edward De Bono, *Lateral Thinking* Harper and Row,
1970, pp. 9–14.

16.   See Peter Berger and Thomas Luckman, *The Social Construction of Reality*, Doubleday, 1966.

17.   Interview with Two Five Percenters: Sincere Allah and King
Allah, 1977.

18.   Ibid.

19.   Ibid.

20.   Geneva Smitherman, *Talkin and Testifyin: The Language of
Black America*, Wayne State University Press, 1986, p. 80.

21.   Ibid, pp. 118, 121.

22.   Ibid, p. 120.

23.   See Yonina Talmon, "Millenarianism"; and Anthony Wallace,
"Nativism and Revivalism"; both in the *International Encyclopedia of
the Social Sciences*, Crowell, Collier, Macmillan, 1968.

24. Interview with Two Five Percenters: Sincere Allah and King Allah, 1977.

25. Ibid.

PART 2

The Mosaic of Islamic Communities in Major Metropolitan Centers of the United States

CHAPTER 6

Muslims in Los Angeles

Ron Kelley

INTRODUCTION

Any overview article purporting to discuss as broad a subject as Muslims in Los Angeles is a project of precarious proportions. For virtually any generalization made in a community so extraordinarily diverse, some exceptions can be found. Within the community here, featuring a wide variety of distinct cultural backgrounds from the farthest corners of the earth, Islam and its unifying influence notwithstanding, Muslims are very different from each other.

This simple observation is a delicate point for those brotherly Muslims who emphatically insist otherwise, citing the five pillars of Islam as proof of homogeneity and courteously taking visitors aside in their respective mosques to underscore the core tenets that are common to all, including the idealized Muslim creed: "There is no difference between any Muslim. We are all the same." Although such words are theologically correct and appreciated, with all due respect this chapter is mostly about differences.

At no other time and in no other place have Muslims from so many different ethnic and cultural backgrounds come together to live their faith within such a myriad of cultural, psychological, and environmental obstacles, other Muslims sometimes not the least of them. Whatever else it is, this grand confluence of Muslims in Los Angeles is an experimental challenge in the honing of Muslim identity, the search for the purest meaning of Islam devoid of extraneous cultural baggage, and the continuous testing of both the faith itself and the dream of communal unity.

135

POPULATION SIZE

Since the United States census does not request religious information in its surveys, there is no way to ascertain accurately the size of
the current Muslim population in Los Angeles. The seminal, and
best known, mosque in the area—the Islamic Center of Southern
California—has attempted to estimate local Muslim numbers by
survey, tabulation of Muslim-sounding names in phone books, and
other methods, all to no avail. In one humorous case, in telephon-
ing a state government agency for population data on local Muslims, an Islamic Center official was taken down a long and circuitous path through a maze of departments and subdepartments,
each bureaucrat referring the inquirer to yet another office. At
length, not knowing to whom he was speaking, the last bureaucrat
in the chain advised the caller to contact the Islamic Center of
California, the very place from which the question was originating.

Maher Hathout, spokesman for the Islamic Center, estimates
that some 500,000 Muslims live in the area. The Los Angeles
County Commission on Human Relations estimates 200,000 local
Muslims in a 1991 report.[1] Whatever the total number, the term
Muslim, as it appears in such estimates, is a relative term, usually
referring more to an individual's socioreligious heritage than to his
or her actual religious practice. Most researchers agree that only a
small percentage of the Muslims in Los Angeles are actually practicing the faith and active in the local mosque network. The largest
Muslim groups in the immigrant community here are Arabs, Indo-
Pakistanis, and African Americans. Although there is a very large
local community of Iranians, they are predominantly secular.[2]

MOSQUES

The largest Islamic centers in the Los Angeles area are the Islamic
Center of Southern California (I.C.S.C.) and the Islamic Society of
Orange County. Both have approximately 1,000 active members,
but their respective influences in the broader Muslim community
here go far beyond those numbers. The I.C.S.C. estimates that they
"reach," in some form, 10,000 Muslim families.

The most active, influential, and best known mosque is the
I.C.S.C. Founded in 1961, it has changed sites over the years from
the Hollywood Hills to Boyle Heights to its current location, for

the past fourteen years, in a remodeled insurance warehouse on Vermont Avenue. The center provides marriage, burial, and counseling services, as well as weekly prayer programs, social activities, Ramadan and other services, and Zakat collection and distribution to the poor. Two full-time schools are sponsored—a preschool at the mosque site and an elementary program in Pasadena. Part-time education programs include Arabic instruction and religion classes at five different sites in the city.

The most distinctive aspect of this mosque, however, is its broadly based commitment to "outreach" activities, geared both to Muslims spiritually floundering in America and to correcting negative stereotypes about Islam within the non-Muslim public. The center sponsors a half-hour television program on Saturday mornings, hosts non-Muslim religious leaders at the mosque in multireligious panels about public and international affairs, and provides speakers to discuss Islam at the request of churches, schools, and community associations. A sister organization, the Muslim Public Affairs Council (now independent, but born of I.C.S.C.), pursues political activities throughout the broader American community, addressing local and international concerns, lobbying the mass media and, rarely, politicians, and advising Muslims about their electoral rights in this country.

In maintaining such a high public profile, the I.C.S.C. is unlike most other mosques—particularly the small ones—that, in the face of a mostly negative public perception of Islam, typically seek to draw as little attention to their community as possible. In times of international tension, the Los Angeles center is usually the local scapegoat for American hostility toward Islam, attracting crank phone calls, hate mail, and occasional bomb threats. Whenever local journalists seek an Islamic reaction to international events, they turn to an Islamic Center spokesperson for an interview. In this regard, the center is generally perceived by many non-Muslims as representing the entire local Islamic community.

Not all local Muslims embrace the Islamic Center and its programs, however, particularly not those who envision a good mosque to more carefully follow the religious contours of Islamic centers in their respective homelands. The Los Angeles center has a reputation for a religious agenda that *adapts*—but does not, its leaders insist, *compromise*—the Islamic faith to the peculiar conditions here in America. In this regard, it is one of the rare mosques to display the American flag. Friday prayer is led not by an officially accredited "Imam" but by Maher Hathout, the religious director, who is a doctor by profession. Members are concerned that the term Imam has a negative association in America with revolutionary Iran and that most such religious leaders, often from Egypt or Saudi Arabia, usually speak very limited English and cannot adequately comprehend the complex problems facing Muslims in America. Furthermore, men and women at I.C.S.C. are not positioned behind curtains or segregated in different rooms for prayer, and although women must keep to the rear and most wear some form of head covering in the mosque, veiling is not enforced by center officials as mandatory.

Forty miles away in Garden Grove, the other large mosque complex—the Islamic Society of Orange County—sometimes attracts up to 1,500 people for Friday prayers. Founded twenty-five years ago, its programs include one of the largest Islamic schools in the state with over 300 full-time students from preschool to eighth grade. The society also publishes a monthly magazine and sponsors a radio program each weekend.

These two major Islamic organizations in Los Angeles and Garden Grove—as well as smaller centers—do not always agree on some of the more practical Islamic matters. For a recent Eid al-Fitr prayer marking the end of the Ramadan fast, for instance, the two mosques did not concur on the exact date to conclude that Islamic month. The L.A. center chose one day, and the Garden Grove mosque chose the next, causing its members to fast for an extra twenty-four hours. With Ramadan's conclusion traditionally based on the rising of the new moon, confusion and controversy can be created for Muslims in America over whether the new moon should be literally sighted here, in the homeland, or Saudi Arabia, or, even differently, by scientifically projected times decided upon months earlier by astronomical calculations. For the Garden Grove society's part, the leadership chose to wait until the moon could be sighted above them.

The Islamic Center of Southern California lists thirty-one local Islamic centers, mosques, and organizations on a recent mailing list. The Orange County Society cites forty-two. Some mosques are not listed on either tally. Very small or pioneering Islamic centers are often in a state of flux, losing leases or members of their congregations (particularly students who return to their homelands).

Local Imams and religious leaders tend to estimate the current number of mosques in the greater Los Angeles area to be somewhere between thirty and forty, although two individuals cited numbers over fifty.[3] No doubt the highest numbers reflect a liberal interpretation of the word *mosque,* which usually connotes a site for communal Islamic prayer distinct from a home environment. Over a dozen of these mosques have been involved in sending leaders to regular dinners to discuss community issues and problems.

Because of Islamic injunctions against receiving or paying interest, most mosques are financially creative in avoiding such payments. One Islamic center, for instance, solved the problem by having a wealthy member buy the building outright and await repayment —with no interest—from the congregation. Others conclude that compromises must be made in the American milieu, and that these are Islamically sanctioned.

Most mosques in Los Angeles are rooted in Sunni Islam, but seven are "Twelver" Shi'a (not including an Ismaili "Sevener" center in Irvine). These are located in the cities or areas of Bell, Cudahy, Pico-Rivera, Pomona, Southgate, Watts, and Los Angeles. Mosques that claim to transcend Sunni-Shi'a categories tend to be Sunni-oriented, if for no other reason than the important commemorations that distinctly define the Shi'a faith are ignored. Some groups that define themselves as Muslim are not considered Islamic by others and, hence, usually are not counted as part of the general mosque network, such as the Nation of Islam in Los Angeles and the Ahmadiyya organization in Chino. There are also Sufi organizations, including three such centers in the Iranian immigrant community. Muslim student groups, of course, meet for religious programs at a variety of local colleges and universities.

CONFLICTS IN THE COMMUNITY

Although many local Muslim leaders highlight the idealized Islamic creed of a unified, egalitarian circle of homogeneous believers irrefutably based on the "five pillars" of Islam, the extraordinary ethnic, cultural, and racial diversity of Muslims in Los Angeles poses critical challenges to the desired model of dedicated communal unity. Among the factors mitigating against the dream of a locally empowered Muslim solidarity are stresses upon the Muslim family, cultural fragmentation, political fragmentation, religious fragmentation, and gaps between immigrant Muslims and African American believers.

Stresses upon the Muslim Family

Children are particularly subject to intensive peer-group pressures in non-Muslim environments. Women are besieged with American pressures to become increasingly independent and autonomous. Men face continuous threats to their traditionally patriarchal authority.

For many women from other countries (particularly from the Third World, Muslim and non-Muslim), great strength must be marshaled to defy the secular standards that define a very different kind of woman here in America, underscoring personal independence, autonomy, and provocative sexual allure. In cases of divorce here, traditional Muslim women sometimes find themselves in the unfamiliar role as breadwinners. If the woman wears a head covering, finding employment in the non-Muslim environment can be difficult. In other situations, when women are called upon by necessity to aid economically in supporting the family, extraordinary tensions can be introduced into the traditional family unit. Such a scenario often implicitly impugns the male authority of the head of the household who may, for whatever reason, have had difficulty in finding employment.

In their homelands most immigrant Muslims were part of closeknit extended families, and individual roles and expectations were clearly defined along traditional patriarchal lines. For those Muslims who spent their early years in Pakistan, Iran, Palestine, Malaysia, and other countries, these traditional roles have been intricately woven into their expectations for their children. For those raised here, however, subjected to the continuous barrage of non-Muslim values, trying to balance the pressures between old and new cultures can be extremely stressful.

"The kids (of immigrant Indo-Pakistanis) come into the house wearing Levi 501's," says one American convert to Islam. "They take off their makeup and jackets. They put on their Indian clothes—they're kind of like pajamas. And then they eat Pakistani curry and their parents think everything's OK. They don't know that when their kids walk out of the house, they're totally American." Relations between children and parents can become seriously aggravated, especially for those children who, growing older and more independent, rebel against Old World ways. In a much publicized case in a small town three hours north of Los Angeles a Yemeni immigrant shot and killed his 13-year-old sister when she began ignoring her father's demands that she stay away from typically American youth activities, particularly dating. Although an extreme example, many Yemenis familiar with the case were reluctant to condemn the slaying.

A common point of friction, too, is that most immigrant Muslim parents insist that their children marry not only within the same faith, but also someone from the same country. Largely estranged from their parents' homelands, and with the enforced segregation of young men and women by many local mosques, some young people find themselves in extraordinarily difficult positions. Dawud Abdullah, an American convert to Islam and president of the Islamic Center of South Bay in Lomita, has been called to mediate disputes of this kind for a number of immigrant Muslims. He notes that most immigrant children spend all their public school time and other day-to-day activities integrated with non-Muslim Americans from various backgrounds and histories. If young Muslim women and men are regularly segregated from prospective spouses in the local mosque system, he argues, is it any wonder that so many Muslim children become attached to non-Muslims and desire to marry out of the faith?

Within the past year, three cases of child-parent conflict over marriage partners have been brought to his door. In one case, a local psychologist called the mosque in support of a Muslim patient to ask if it was true, as the young woman's father insisted, that a Muslim woman could never under any circumstances marry a non-Muslim. Abdullah agreed that it was not acceptable, but noted that the simple solution—if the young woman's prospective American groom would consent—would be for the young man to become a Muslim. Informed of this option, the father would have none of it. Not only did he decree that his daughter must marry a Muslim, but he also demanded that she also marry an Afghani like themselves or be disconnected from the family forever.

Recognizing such problems, some mosques have set up programs where young Muslim men and women can meet each other under chaperoned conditions. At the Islamic Center of the San Gabriel Valley, for instance, initial steps include filling out a form itemizing the desired qualities of a prospective spouse.

Cultural Fragmentation

Muslims from all over the world find themselves reexamining the practice of their faith here. Some try to separate genuine Islamic tenets from variant expressions of cultural tradition imported from their respective homelands. Others hold dearly to such cultural variables as genuine Islamic expressions in their lives.

"Children pick up things from their parents early," said one local American convert to Islam, married to a Pakistani immigrant. "My sister-in-law's 4-year old daughter came up to me one day and said, 'Auntie, if you learn one word of Urdu (the Pakistani language) every day, pretty soon you'll be a Muslim. She had already equated an aspect of culture with being Muslim. I think alot of adults are the same way." With her own child, her husband's insistence that their baby's hair should be shaved three or four times like other Pakistanis before letting it grow was a source of conflict. Where, she asked him, does the Qur'an say to do that?

A common complaint by local (particularly American) Muslim activists is the tendency of Muslims in Los Angeles to cluster together along cultural, ethnic, and linguistic lines, seeming to emphasize these distinguishing characteristics over the unifying tenets of the faith. American converts are often attracted to Islam as a vital, active, idealistic, and humanitarian faith. A majority of immigrant Muslims often are more inclined to be passively insular, or even lax, about their religious beliefs.

Although Islamic centers, by definition, have open-door policies for all believers, there is a tendency for small groups to break away from larger, more diversified mosques to form new ones within their own specific ethnic communities, inevitably preserving very specific culturally interpretive nuances of Islam: modes of dress, sermons in the native tongue, homeland foods at social functions, and other esoteric expressions. In this sense, many mosques, while officially decrying such insulation and perhaps even having a board member or two from different backgrounds, are founded and centered on ethnic identity. In one case, for instance, an Egyptian decided to leave a mosque that he felt was too politically controlled by Saudis and, hence, religious conservative. He was much disillusioned subsequently to find the socio-religious discourse in the next mosque he began attending to be dominated by the suprareligious discourse of Palestinian politics. In one of the larger mosques, factional struggles for directive power surfaced when cultural distinctions were interwoven with different political agendas between Arabs and Indo-Pakistanis.

Muslim children can be caught in overlapping cultural webs, pulled from different directions. Even at the Islamic Society of Orange County's full-time Orange Crescent school, small children can be faced with conflicting role models. When formally credentialed non-Muslim teachers instruct science, math, and English classes, Muslims in traditional roles follow up with Arabic and religious instruction.

Role models even within the local Muslim community may be confusing for youngsters. "Many times my daughter asks me why some other Muslims don't wear the hejab," says a local Iranian woman, supportive of her country's Islamic republic.

> That's the question in her mind and it's important. She understands the difference between Christianity and Judaism and Islam; the others don't have the hejab. But we do. But she doesn't understand why some other Muslim women don't do it. That's in her mind, constantly, pounding. And so I'm going to take her home to Iran and she'll find out more about Islam. . . . But yes. I've had difficulties with her. She said, "Mommy, I can't wear a hejab when I'm 9 (when her mother wants her to wear it). How can I go to school? The children will make fun of me."

Political Fragmentation

Deep political divisions separate many local Muslims, from the centuries old Sunni-Shi'a schism to allegiance and identification along Iranian-style, Saudi-influenced, intra-Arab, nationalist, or other lines. Strong Yemeni animosity for Saudis, for example, is rooted in allegedly poor treatment of Yemeni sojourners in Saudi Arabia and a festering border dispute between those neighboring countries. Over the years, in the highly factionalized local Iranian community, incidents between pro-Khomeini Muslims and various Iranian secularists have been common. After the killing of over 400 Muslim pilgrims during riots in Mecca by Saudi authorities in 1987, Iranian-led Shi'a demonstrations were a yearly rite at the Westwood Saudi Embassy. In the wake of the Iranian revolution, many Persian members of the Moslem Student Association quarreled with others and pulled out to form their own organization: Moslem Student Association—Persian Speaking Group. In the local Iraqi community, immense distrust of other Iraqis stems from suspicion that agents of Saddam Hussein's regime are planted in their ranks here. Mosques, too, can come under various political suspicions. A widespread rumor, for instance, claims that, years ago, some of the leadership of the Islamic Center of Southern California were also members of a Masonic order.

Despite predictions that Muslims will soon be the second largest religious community in the United States, they have been unable to unite as an effective lobbying force, relative to their large numbers. Often compared to American Jewish organizations, Muslims, as a political force, are comparatively invisible.

One of the most sensitive political undercurrents in the international Muslim world is the issue of Saudi Arabian influence. More particularly, this concern addresses the fabulous wealth and attendant self-interest of the Saudi monarchy, its repressive government, and its disproportionate economic power in interpreting the tenets of Islam according to its own conservative sect, Wahhabism. (One local African American Imam who spent six years studying Islam in Saudi Arabia personally witnessed forty public beheadings in a plaza by the local mosque, as well as an execution by stoning, a number of women executed by firing squad, and a host of hands dismembered.)

Locally, these and other international tensions translate directly into the mosque system. Although the Saudi government has embarked in recent years upon a policy to keep most of its own students at universities in the homeland, a number of Los Angeles (and national) mosques and Islamic organizations have, in varying degrees, received economic support from Saudi foundations, corporations, and individuals. Whatever Saudi intentions, many Muslims view such philanthropy as innately political. Although no mosque leaders openly admit to Saudi influence in their organizations, a widespread perception among the rank and file is that inevitably "strings are attached" to Saudi donations. In this regard, it is widely believed that when Saudis contribute money to Islamic organizations in the United States, they exert control or directly install loyal individuals to be officially involved in the group's leadership. In one case, a recognized elected religious leader was allegedly ousted from his position by the sway of Saudi influence. A number of local mosques bear the taint of such accusations, including a prominent Imam who is commonly believed to be under direct employ of Saudi benefactors. True or not, for many in the local Muslim community his reputation most assuredly precedes him.

In another case, a group of disgruntled individuals broke away from a mosque they considered to be far too closely tied to the local Saudi embassy (highlighted by what was felt by some to be Saudi propagandizing in the mosque in preparation for the Persian Gulf War) and started their own Islamic center only a mile away. At yet another Islamic site, the elected president of the organization was incensed upon receiving a letter from the Saudi embassy that blithely requested the home phone numbers and addresses of all the mosque's board members.

During the Persian Gulf War most local Muslims were against the invasion of Kuwait by Saddam Hussein, but also against the prospect of a United States–led attack on Iraq. Many were appalled at U.S. troops in Saudi Arabia. A few Muslims here began meeting with non-Muslim peace activists and joined in protest demonstrations and peace vigils. Within the local Islamic community, Muslim peace activists were unsuccessful in attempting to attract local mosques into a united stand against the impending war. A central problem, as many activists saw it, was the reluctance of Muslim leaders who were economically beholden to the Saudis to take such a public stand.

In recent years Saudi organizations have also been involved in sponsoring national conferences and gatherings of Imams, including a meeting in Los Angeles that resulted in physical scuffles between staff organizers and protesting Shi'is who felt their version of the faith was being severely slighted. At a mosque on the westside, an Egyptian activist was confronted by mosque officials and his papers were torn up when he dared to hand out flyers after Friday prayer accusing the Saudi government of torturing its own people.

A number of years ago, in the academic world, a prestigious local university was faced with a scandalous threat when, in donating a large sum of money to institute a Near Eastern Studies Center program, the Saudi benefactors sought to exert undue influence in specific faculty appointments. At another juncture, members of the local Iranian exile community in opposition to Iran's Islamic Republic likewise were willing to advance economic aid to the university for similar reasons.

Playing financial politics behind the scenes of local Muslim institutions can be extraordinarily divisive. The president of a large Islamic school in Los Angeles claims that in bids for control over the past twenty years, government officials from Saudi Arabia, Kuwait, and Iraq have offered to completely or partially subsidize his independent organization. The Libyan embassy, for its part, refused to release a $100,000 check for the school from a Libyan Islamic organization when school leaders, on principle, would not sign a paper guaranteeing that the school would never criticize the Libyan government. A group of Iranian businessmen even offered $1 million to the school president if he would admit to them, privately, that he was really a Shi'i Muslim. (He was not.)

Highly vulnerable economically, in recent years the African American Muslim community has been of particular interest to Saudi philanthropists. Scholarships are provided worldwide for Muslims to study in the Saudi homeland. Also 300 fares were established for (mostly) African American Muslims to perform the hajj in Mecca. This program was eventually scrapped, however, at the request of African Americans who felt that the once-in-a-lifetime trip should not be free but rather should involve personal struggle. At the site of Masjid Bilal, the seminal (now orthodox) African American mosque in Los Angeles, King Fahd himself has committed $7–8 million to build a new mosque. Plans have already been developed and donated by an architect in Ridayh. Masjid Bilal leaders were alerted to the rumored threat of a Shi'i demonstration against a symbolic groundbreaking ceremony at the proposed mosque site featuring a speech by an official from the Saudi embassy, but no such demonstration materialized.

For their part, African American leaders usually bristle at suggestions of covert foreign influence in their religious and Educational organizations and accept Saudi gifts at their religious face value, seeing no problem with getting a small share of the vast Muslim oil wealth for their own impoverished communities and the noble service of Islam. Judging by the modest storefront mosques in the Los Angeles African American community, however, it is clear that such reputed economic aid has not, thus far, been substantial. Certainly it does not filter far into the broader African American Muslim community.

Religious Fragmentation

There remains a wide range of interpretive practice of Qur'anic teachings in America, from, for example, women interpreting religious texts to dictate the wearing of facial veils to those who go to mosques with no head covering whatsoever. Sunni-Shi'a dissonance is an obvious division, religiously and politically.

The mix of culture in confounding religious uniformity can be considerable. One local African American religious leader was appalled to find himself in a debate with a Pakistani friend over whether there was enough time to pray quickly at a community college. Whereas the African American understood the requirements of the prayer to last a few minutes, his immigrant friend perceived the necessity of a considerably longer series of prayers, as is the practice in his homeland.

In another case, the principal of an Islamic school deemed it necessary to leave a Syrian wedding reception when an American bellydancer made her gala entrance to entertain the predominantly Muslim crowd. Although the bride and groom were fairly religious, the popularity of such entertainment at weddings in their homeland outweighed any objections they might have religiously held. The principal, however, was not from Syria and could not reconcile such a display, culturally or otherwise.

The question of the hejab, modesty, and women's role in an American context can be a subject of considerable controversy and epitomizes the many conflicts between traditional views and adaptive practices. At a mosque in San Gabriel, for instance, Rene Hai was elected (on a write-in ballot, mostly by women) to be one of the few female members of a mosque's Board of Directors in the city. Her election met with stiff opposition from a number of immigrant men. Somewhat paradoxically, at the Shi'a Jafaria Hall, American convert Lorraine Mirza and her daughter became the first Jafaria members to don the hejab for all public appearances, ultimately inspiring the predominantly Pakistani congregation enough that about a third of the female congregation now follow her example.

Although many local Muslims view the very idea of a fashion

show to be morally repulsive and in direct contradiction to Islamic principles that publicly shield attention from women, some young Muslim women are finding ways to compromise in putting on such presentations. At the Islamic Society of Orange County, for example, a group of women hold an annual Islamic fashion show, this year entitled Women Under Cover. Although men were barred from the show, a videotape was made for the viewing by other women in the Muslim community.

In another case, a Pakistani student association at a local university sponsored a fashion show at a weekend celebration of Pakistani Independence Day. In front of a mixed audience of about 300 Pakistanis, 10 Indo-Pakistani women paraded about on a stage as fashion models while a loud wave of rock music guided their synchronous motions. There were many Muslim women in the audience, but none were participating models. Rather than courting trouble in the Muslim community, organizers selected models of Sikh, Christian, and Hindu descent. In the African American Muslim community, social gatherings have sometimes included relatively modest male and female dancing, an emphatic taboo for some in the broader Muslim community. In the secular Iranian community, a Persian beauty contest—minus bathing suit displays—was even ironically held at a local westside nightclub during the important Shi'i mourning period of Moharram. The next year another Persian beauty contest was held at the St. Bonaventure Hotel, sponsored by a Hindu businessman married to an Iranian.

In the importation of Muslim traditions from the homeland to Los Angeles, a curious circumstantial transition takes place with women who choose to wear a classical headcovering. In the homeland, because it is a common sight, such dress serves the purpose of discretely blending women in with the crowd. In the United States, however, the sight of a woman walking down the street wearing various veils is a magnet for attention. Unlike Muslim men who can blend into American culture more anonymously, such women are easily recognizable and can be potential scapegoats for international tensions and negative stereotypes about Islam. Clearly it sometimes takes courage for a woman to so publicly advocate her faith.

Animosity in these cases does not come just from Americans. One Iranian woman related the experience of being harassed by individuals from her own country here, supporters of the deposed Shah, who equated her dress with empathy for the politics of Iran's Islamic Republic. Older women in the local Iranian community are given more latitude in wearing traditional Islamic dress here. It is presumed to be entirely a religious expression. For younger women, however, veiling is considered by many in the largely secular, Iranian community here to be not only a religious statement, but also a political (usually anti-imperialist) statement.

At the more religiously conservative end, the international evangelical group Tableeghi Jamaat continuously makes its way through the local Islamic system from a base at the Inglewood mosque near the Los Angeles airport. Regular programs are held at the center on Friday nights. Founded in Pakistan, it consists of Muslims from all over the world who commit days, weeks, or months to the task of drawing wavering Muslims back into the faith and, where practical, proselytizing.[4] One of their most common tactics is to suddenly show up in small groups at the homes of Muslim individuals who have not been seen at a mosque lately. Typically dressed in long white robes, turbans or caps, and bushy black beards in emulation of the prophet Mohammed, Tablighi volunteers travel in groups. Upon arriving in Los Angeles they soon spread out into mosques throughout the city, state, and country, usually sleeping in bedrolls on the floor of host Islamic centers and cooling with whatever facilities are available. Apolitical, the Tablighi Jamaat religious agenda reflects a zealous, Old World conservatism, typically interpreting the Qur'an and religious texts in the most literal way. For some, images of animate objects are not allowed and a beard is understood to be obligatory for righteous Muslim men. Women's place in Islam is a sensitive topic and females are not allowed at the mosque whatsoever during male Tablighi visits there.

Not all Los Angeles mosques are receptive to Tablighi agendas. There have been occasions when the group is courteously made unwelcome, usually with mosques citing logistical and insurance problems against the prospect of the visitors intruding upon their Islamic center.

For some staunchly conservative Muslims, the very presence of immigrant Muslims in America is, by definition, a contradiction in terms and an indictment of their religious commitment. According to this view, all Muslim immigrants came to America not with

Islam but rather material and economic advancement foremost on their minds. Finding the material comforts here to be far more desirable than in the homelands, the Muslim doctors and engineers then decided to stay rather than return to help people in the place they came from. How Islamic, critics complain, is that?

In this view too, in the face of availability of alcohol, casual sex, and other temptations of a decadent American society, the pious Muslim is tested at every corner, and Islam cannot help but be compromised in this country. Some Muslims never reconcile the uncomfortable adjustments that must be made here, from having mortgages for homes (Islam forbids interest) to the relative difficulties of securing halal meat. Given, too, the Qur'anic injunction against alcohol, the preponderance of Muslim-owned mini-marts that sell inebriates also causes friction, both within the religious community and in the conscience of the offending individual. In one case, an older Arab who finally made it for the first time to Mecca for the hajj was emotionally and spiritually crushed when his American employer telephoned him, only 30 miles from Mecca, and insisted that he return to California to face an impending emergency in the company. Dumbstruck, robbed of his first hajj, the devout Muslim returned to America religiously unfulfilled. For over a year he was tortured with the notion that God had interrupted his hajj because of sinful behavior in America in his younger years.

For others, however, Islam is understood to be an adaptive, flexible faith. These individuals view themselves as religious pioneers in this country. Long-term immigrants here and American converts are often at the vanguard of this movement. At the organizational level, the Islamic Center of Southern California best manifests this perspective.

"There are some people who would like to tamper with the religion and break the rules that we consider unbreakable," says Maher Hathout of the Los Angeles center. "There are also those who want to make a replica of Saudi Arabia, Pakistan, or Egypt here. But people are not subject to the same temptations and challenges here as the homeland. When they see we are changing some practices to fit the society here, they call us liberals. We claim we are abiding by divine direction, not traditions. Manmade traditions are not sacred."

Class and Cultural Gaps Between Immigrant Muslims and African American Believers

Until the mid-1970s, immigrant Muslims and African American practitioners had very little to do with each other. Few African Americans were orthodox Muslims, and as policy, the Nation of Islam excluded non-blacks from their organization. For their part, the immigrants perceived the NOI, based on the "messenger of God" status of their founder Elijah Mohammed and other tenets, to be un-Islamic.

In the 1970s many African Americans moved into orthodox Islam to join a largely immigrant religious community with a very different cultural history. Hence, beyond the quiet unity of communal prayer in the mosques and the pleasantries of solidarity meetings by local religious leaders, relations between rank and file immigrant and African American Muslims can sometimes be strained.

In contrast to the African American community, which is predominantly rooted in poverty and the working class, a significant proportion of immigrants here are highly educated professionals and business people. Some are even from wealthy families in their homelands. (Born in Ghana, Imam Tajuddin Bin Shu'aib of Masjidus Salaam notes that, upon arriving to America, he was struck by the distinctive American sight of some Muslims—predominantly immigrants—wearing three-piece suits in the major mosques for prayer.) Immigrant grocery and other shop owners—Muslim and non-Muslim—in impoverished African American neighborhoods are often perceived by the indigenous population as economically exploitive, taking from the local community but investing nothing back. Although many Muslim leaders emphatically pride themselves upon the perceived lack of racism in their community, it is common for economically prosperous immigrants to associate African Americans with an undesirable socioeconomic class. For their part, some local African American Muslims emphatically insist that the blight of racism knows no religious barriers and that many immigrant Muslims here, too, have long been raised with the myth of white supremacy, struggling to identify with colonial powers in their homelands and bringing their prejudices here.

Religiously, many immigrant Muslims perceive African Americans as being largely ignorant novices to the faith, to be sincerely appreciated but in need of guidance. The seminal Nation of Islam movement is often cited as a misdirected case in point. For their part, some African Americans perceive immigrants to be aloof, class conscious, distant, and overly directorial. As avid Qur'an-reading converts, African Americans often claim keener insight into the faith than many of their immigrant brethren. Too many newcomers to America, they argue, confuse their respective cultures with the tenets of Islam. Immigrants are largely perceived to have become Muslims by passive osmosis in their homelands. "African American Muslims are their conscience here," says one local Imam. Although there are those African Americans who have adopted especially Arabic clothing as their own, many bristle when Arab Muslims exhibit excessively chauvinistic tendencies based upon the fact that the Qur'an is written in Arabic. (According to a prominent Central Valley Yemeni, for instance, the original mosque in Bakersfield—120 miles north of Los Angeles—was broken apart by disagreements between African Americans and Arabs over the degree to which English should be used in prayers. In the dispute, an immigrant group pulled out and formed its own mosque.) A common problem, too, is the many contradictory statements made by well-meaning Muslims from different countries trying to direct African Americans toward proper religious etiquette. One African American religious leader even noted the immigrant tendency to take photographs with believers in his community to prove immigrant evangelical efforts and to aid in raising funds from wealthy Muslim countries for further Islamic expansion projects here. He later laughed in citing the occasions of immigrant Muslims nervously calling his mosque for physical help when being harassed by militant groups such as the Jewish Defense League.

Unlike most immigrant Muslims, many African Americans continue to support the notion of a militant disciplinism. This expression is rooted, and best exemplified, in the Nation of Islam and, particularly, in its Fruit of Islam youth organization which includes a range of iconography borrowed from the military, including marches, drills, martial arts training, captains, lieutenants, organizational hierarchies, and saluting superiors with a hand upraised and a click of the heels. Although this attitude has been considerably diffused by the transition of many African Americans into the less overtly politicized arena of orthodox Sunni Islam, the idea that Islam reflects both an efficiently ordered system and a source of physical as well as spiritual empowerment remains popular.

Using the prophet Mohammed as the model for a noble warrior ethic and paradigm, Islam is commonly conceptualized in the African American community as a particularly "manly" enterprise, nonaggressive, but quick to defend honor, dignity, and moral righteousness. Much of this attitude stems from the self-perception that the broader African American community—subject to centuries of oppression, racism, and discrimination—is in catastrophic social, material, moral, and spiritual disarray. Hence, the road to recovery of a lost identity cannot help but involve a very tight order via the dedicated Muslim aim of raising the broken community back onto its own feet again.

Another reason for this pseudo-militaristic scenario is that simply to survive in some of the most violently undisciplined areas of urban America, Muslims must be fully streetwise, prepared and able to defend themselves against the baser elements of a heartless America, physically as well as spiritually. In this regard, for example, Imam Abdul-Aziz at Masjid Assef has even designed a particular uniform for young men under his tutelage, complete with shoulder patches, and has held, for defensive purposes only, classes in the use of firearms. The reputation of African American Muslims in this regard stretches far beyond religious networks. To paraphrase a local religious leader at the Terminal Island Corrections Institution in San Pedro: "For better or for worse, Christians can be easily perceived as wimps in this kind of environment. Turn your cheek, and all that. But no one messes with Muslims, especially in the prison system."[5]

All of this leads to yet another important difference between largely reticent immigrant Muslims and African American believers who are willing to "make waves" and "rock the boat" wherever necessary in the sociopolitical scene. The African American community at large is highly sensitized to social injustice as an outspoken minority group, quick to voice complaint about any wrongdoing. Most immigrant Muslims, however, come from undemocratic, and often despotic, homelands where voicing mere opinion can endanger not only the speaker, but his or her entire extended family. Hence, although it is emphatically sanctioned within their community for African Americans to decry injustice, immigrant Muslims (particularly more recent ones) are much more likely to keep low profiles in matters other than those that involve Islam itself.[6] Immigrant Muslims often function here as products of political socialization in their homelands, real or imagined concern for deportation and government harassment, and the omnipresent presumed threat of losing their secure American socioeconomic status here.

In the days before there were Muslim chaplains in the prison system, stereotypes of Middle Easterners offered one Christian Arab an opportunity for self-protection while serving a prison term in the L.A. area. A group of African American Muslims identified him as an Arab and, presuming all Arabs to be Muslim, solicited his teaching of Arabic, Islamic advice, and leading of Islamic prayer. Happy to find such a protective brotherhood in such a dangerous environment, the Christian played out the ruse through his entire prison term.

THE AFRICAN AMERICAN MUSLIM COMMUNITY

Any attempt to address the development of Islam in the black community must inevitably center on the Nation of Islam, the first officially organized (albeit controversial) Muslim group in Los Angeles. In 1956, predating formal immigrant Muslim organizations by five years, the Nation of Islam founded Temple #27. In that year there were only ten such (then called) temples in the entire United States. At the NOI's peak in the mid 1970s, there were over 200.

Abdul Kareem Hasan, today the Imam of Sunni-oriented Masjid Bilal[7] in south central Los Angeles, has deeper roots in the Nation of Islam movement than any other locally active Muslim leader. Joining the NOI on the East Coast in the mid 1950s, he rose through the ranks and was ultimately sent to Los Angeles as the western regional director in 1971. When he arrived there was only a single storefront center. Within a year membership had doubled to 1,000. Three more temples were soon opened in the area and at its peak in the mid-1970s Nation of Islam programs in Los Angeles regularly attracted 2,000 people. In 1973 the organization purchased the old Elks auditorium on Central Avenue, the largest building owned by African Americans in Los Angeles. It had three floors, a balcony, and six storefronts.

With the death of Elijah Muhammad in 1975 and the move-ment of his son and successor Warith Deen Mohammed to ortho-dox Sunni Islam, Kareem Hasan, like all other NOI members, was faced with a profound reevaluation of his entire religious belief system. Over the next few years many NOI members followed W. D. Mohammed into orthodox Islam, some left the Muslim com-munity completely, and others eventually reconstructed the Nation of Islam organization along past tenets. In 1983 the old Elks build-ing was determined by local authorities to be structurally unsound to resist earthquakes. Confronted with a $250,000 fee by structur-al engineers just to evaluate the building, the financially strapped community was forced to tear it down at a cost of $17,000. The site today is largely a parking lot with a small structure serving as a temporary mosque until Saudi funds are confirmed for a perma-nent structure. In Los Angeles the best known splinter group from the original Nation of Islam (under the leadership of Louis Far-rakhan) exists in a single storefront center on Western Avenue under the administration (from Alaska to Omaha) of the western regional director, Wazir Mohammed.

Although Sunni African Americans depict the Nation of Islam as sparsely supported, the NOI still maintains a high public profile, particularly in relation to its leader, Louis Farrakhan, and his so-ciopolitical appeal to the black community. Recent confrontations with police in Los Angeles, however, have drawn public attention on their own accord. Early in 1990, stemming from a traffic ticket, thirteen members were involved in a violent fracas with twenty-five police officers. Within the month a second incident left Oliver Beasly dead, shot by police. For their part, NOI members claim continuous harassment by police in the black community, even citing incidents of officers enforcing trivial city codes against mem-bers stepping illegally into the street, selling bean pies. Resultant progress in conferences with police officials, Nation of Islam repre-sentatives, and other activists in the African American community were by all accounts unprecedented.

SHI'I MUSLIMS IN LOS ANGELES

The seven "Twelver" Shi'a mosques in the Los Angeles area have been founded, respectively, by Pakistanis, Lebanese, East Africans (of Indo-Pakistani descent), Iraqis and pro-Islamic Republic Ira-nians, and two by African Americans. The reasons for the variety of Shi'a mosques include geographical factors and variant cultural and ethnic traditions, as well as different religious interpretations or political views, in particular allegiance to the religious model and political goals of Iran's Islamic Republic. (The Lebanese and Pakistani Shi'a centers, for instance, are a mile apart and the Iranian and Iraqi-based mosque is less than five miles from either of them. All are in Hispanic neighborhoods.) Although most Shi'a mosques have, from time to time, congregational overlap as an expression of Shi'a unity, degrees of interaction and cooperation among mosques vary depending on the concern at hand. Although all such mosques have cooperated in planning demonstrations against Saddam Hussein, for example, their actual practice of Shi'a Islam (particularly during Moharram) may technically vary. The Iraqi-based mosque in Pomona, Ahl Beit, for instance, has a much more progressive agenda than other Shi'a centers. Women at Ahl Beit are not separated into a different room for prayer, some have been known to formally address the mixed congregation, and the elicitation of communal mourning during Moharram is considerably less inspired than most other places.

The oldest Shi'a mosque in Los Angeles (and one of the oldest in the United States), Jafaria Hall, is located in a Hispanic neighborhood in Cudahy. In the late 1970s members of the local Shi'a community began to meet in homes for the practice and preservation of particularly Shi'a programs. Of common concern was the fact that children of Shi'is here had no recourse but to send their confused children to Sunni Islamic centers for religious training. As the meetings grew larger, halls were rented throughout the city for important occasions and the community continued to grow. During the Iranian revolution local interest in Shi'a Islam particularly accelerated. Likewise, the community began finding widespread American hostility and suspicion directed toward them and the group had increasing difficulty in securing formerly rented halls for Shi'a programs. Requests to use the established Islamic centers of the fundamentally Sunni mosque network for expressly Shi'a practices were routinely denied, usually with the argument that such activity was divisive for the broader Muslim community here.

At Jafaria Hall, the predominantly Pakistani gathering has fashioned a detailed, small-scale replica of Hussein's shrine in Karbala and a symbolic deathbed that is carried about the mosque in procession during Moharram. Among local Shi'is, too, many Pakistanis are among the most zealous strikers of their bare chests in the ten-day empathy with Imam Hussein's martyrdom.

Originally inspired by the Iranian Islamic revolution and, particularly, by its championing of social justice for the oppressed of the world, small numbers of African Americans have become attracted to the Shi'a Muslim faction. Two mosques, Masjid Al-Rasool and Masjid Assef, reflect such interest. Masjid Assef, founded by Imam Abdul Aziz, is actually a room on the second floor of a small office building. The small mosque is particularly distinctive with its photographs of Elijah Mohammed, Malcolm X, and the Ayatollah Khomeini on the walls. Abdul Aziz is new to Shi'a Islam, coming under its influence several years ago after a personal involvement first with the Nation of Islam and then with Sunni practice. With the aid of a local Shi'i Imam from Iraq, Abdul Aziz visited Iran alone, was impressed by what he found there, and returned to forge a new Shi'a organization in an African American neighborhood. Thus far it is a fledgling community of about fifty members, focusing particularly on the aimless and disenfranchised youth of the area.

Beginning a new mosque in an impoverished urban neighborhood can raise a number of different challenges. Soon after the mosque's founding, members were called upon to defend themselves and physically confront an armed gang of teenagers lined up across the street who resented a new organized presence in their criminal territory. Over time, Imam Abdul Aziz counted more than one former gang member in his Shi'i membership.

IRANIANS IN LOS ANGELES

Any discussion of Islam in the large Los Angeles Iranian community must immediately consider the faith's widely perceived political, as well as religious, basis. Most Iranians (75,000–500,000 depending upon whom you talk to)—Muslims, Jews, Bahais, Armenians, and others—came to Los Angeles in the wake of the Islamic revolution in their homeland. Given the fact that as few as 10 percent of the secular-oriented Iranian Muslims in L.A. may actually practice their religious heritage on a day-to-day basis, Islam is often merely considered to be a negative force that cost local immigrants and refugees their possessions, occupations, life-styles, and sometimes loved ones in the homeland. Islam in the local Iranian context is, hence, always framed in political discourse.

The extraordinary politicization of Islam among Iranians here has mitigated against a community-based mosque being founded. Although an Iranian mosque and cultural center has been proposed, widespread public animosity among Americans toward Iranians has hindered its development past discussion stages. Perhaps even more important, within the local Persian community, many fear such a religious site would be an inevitable magnet for continuous political controversy.

Islam does, however, express itself in the local Persian community in a variety of forms. There are, for instance, a few hundred Iranian immigrant supporters of Iran's Islamic Republic in the southern California area. Years ago there was a more firmly established community, but due to personality clashes, internal politics, and differences in religious opinion, core members have split apart into two major congregations.

The first group—the Moslem Student Association–Persian Speaking Group—is predominantly an organization of Iranian students and former students who regularly meet in homes and local universities for religious, social, and political activities. Their largest event is the yearly anniversary of the Islamic Republic, where lecturers from the United States and abroad extol the virtues of the Iranian revolution and the future of the Islamic movement. They have also been active in staging various public protest marches, including those against the Saudi Arabian embassy in Westwood and in support of the Iranian revolution.

A second Islamic congregation is under the leadership of Sayed Morteza Ghasvini, an Islamic cleric who fled his Iraqi birthplace, survived an assassination attempt by agents of Saddam Hussein in Kuwait, and immigrated to Iran in the early years of the revolution to partake in its religious revival. Speaking fluent Arabic, Persian, and English, Sayed Ghasvini became a judge in the Iranian Islamic legal system and was a leader at a Tehran mosque. With the invitation of a group of religious Iranian students in Los Angeles and with the encouragement of peers in Tehran, Sayed Ghasvini made his way to America to start an Islamic teaching center. Recently his group purchased a small church in a Hispanic neighborhood in the city of Southgate and renovated it to fulfill its new function as a Shi'a mosque. Before this building was acquired, prayers, lectures, and discussions were held at his home until unsympathetic neighbors called the police to demand enforcement of local zoning codes. Important religious occasions requiring additional space were observed in local public school halls and cafeterias.[8]

Earlier in the year, during the fasting month of Ramazan, the group gathered in a small grade school hall to pray and have a potluck dinner. During the night Morteza Ghasvini related the tragic Shi'i tale of the suffering of the martyred Imam Hussein and his woeful associates. When the story began in Los Angeles, the lights were turned out to enhance the somber mood, and the audience could freely weep and moan in relative privacy. Heads were bowed, and men and women were encouraged to release their accumulated sense of loss and melancholy. After a period of sobbing and wailing, the men all rose and stood in a group at the front of the hall to begin rhythmically thumping their chests ("sineah zadan") in unison, chanting in Persian, and shouting exaltations to the beloved, martyred Imam.

Sayed Ghasvini's core Los Angeles congregation is approximately half native-born Iranian and the other half mostly Iraqi. Religious services are conducted, alternatively each night, in Persian and Arabic. Ghasvini speaks for a while in one language, then the other. Members of the audience respond, in turn, with the corresponding language, depending on their respective ethnicity.

Missionary projects for Sayed Ghasvini in the American community have been realized only slowly. Thus far, he has aided an American convert in securing permission to study Islam in the holy Iranian city of Qom and has influenced an African American Muslim leader to establish a small Shi'a mosque in the local African American community. His dream is to begin a local Islamic university.

Not all religious Muslim Iranians adhere to the current sociopolitical and religious agenda of the Islamic Republic. One of the best known examples of a less restrictive, more adaptive Islam in California is Mohammed Nemazikhah, a professor of dentistry at a local Los Angeles university. A few years ago he and a group of friends, desiring to maintain their Islamic faith, began holding religious recitals every Thursday night in his home in the San Fernando Valley. News of this regular religious meeting spread rapidly by word of mouth. Today, during important Ramazan and Moharram nights, over 300 people follow him in prayer, severely straining the capacities of his large home.

These weekly gatherings are entirely open. Friends tell friends, and all are invited to Nemazikhah's home for a free dinner, catered by a local Iranian restaurant, and recitals of Islamic prayer. He is careful to point out that his home is not a mosque and that he makes no pretense of being a religious leader. He merely invites people to gather in prayer, to help them regain something spiritually lost in their transition to America. The range of visitors who appear Thursday nights is considerable. Though non-Iranians are rare, it is far from a traditionally Islamic crowd. Older women in classical head-to-toe chadors sometimes attend, but so do business people and fashionably dressed women who look like they just interrupted a shopping trip. A few women unpack a chador for brief moments of prostration in an unobtrusive side room in the classically prescribed manner of Islamic prayer and then pack away the modest gown again. Many gatherers, however, ignore such traditional prayers and simply await Nemazikhah's recitals. For many visitors, the Thursday night services provide an opportunity to revitalize their waning Islamic faith here in America without having to identify with the overt politics of the Islamic Republic. Across town, in Beverly Hills, Dr. F. Hormozi has opened his home every Friday night for Qur'anic readings and religious discussion for the past thirty-five years. Once a board member of the Islamic Center of Southern California in its early years, Dr. Hormozi became disgruntled with distracting factionalization and formed his own society—the Moslem Brothers of America—in the mid-1960s. Over the years he claims to have aided up to 1,000 American converts to Islam and to have been the organizer for a hajj group that included the first visit to Mecca of African American Muslim leader Warith Deen Mohammad.

Still another variant form of Islamic restoration and renewal in the Los Angeles Iranian Muslim community is the interest, particularly among the intelligentsia, in the Sufi tradition of ascetic mysticism. There are at least three formal Sufi meeting places in Los Angeles.

For a recent Eid al-Adha holiday, when traditional Muslims slaughter sheep in commemoration of Abraham's willingness to follow God's order to slay his son, one of the local Sufi orders held an observation at their center in Burbank. This group of about 100 were adherents to the teachings of the Oveyssi Shahmaghsoudi line, a largely genealogical lineage of forty-two Sufi masters going back to the prophet Mohammed. In 1990, between 3,000–5,000 people from all over the world reportedly gathered for their revered leader's birthday observance in the desert city of Lancaster, a hundred miles north of Los Angeles.

Dressed in white, men on the left side of the room and women on the right, the group gathered beneath a chandelier to face a poster-sized, blue neon-framed color transparency of a revered Sufi leader and listen to their spiritual director lecture on transcendent themes. Later, when the room was gradually darkened, the local leader ("pir") led his audience in a cycle of memorized songs, chants, poems, and prayers. As the recitals continued, the group responded with deeper and deeper intensity. People began swaying back and forth, weeping and shouting, releasing an avalanche of unguarded emotions. This rhythmic, contagious chanting culminated with the group joining hands, raising them above their heads, and repeatedly exhorting—in a kind of wild cheer—the name of God, Allah. The the group quietly sat down, the dim lights returned, and tea and pastries were served by five male attendants. For fifteen minutes, as tea was served and the glasses were recovered, there was absolute silence. Then, after parting remarks by the speaker, the audience backed away from the altar, accepted a wrapped gift of grapes and cucumbers, and went home.

Less than 10 miles away, another Iranian group, the Nimatullahi order, practices Sufism in a very different, more meditative manner. As one of a dozen Nimatuallahi centers in the United States, the "khaneghah" in Mission Hills usually attracts 30–40 members on Thursday and Saturday nights, including a few Americans. Ecstatic expression is not accentuated.

Under the leadership of the organization's only shaykh in America, Dalavar Karaien, members first sit in meditative postures against the walls of the center, listening to traditional Iranian music in dim light. Next, about half the members turn to traditional Islamic prostration prayers toward Mecca; others choose to leave the room. Another tape is played, this time a lecture by the Nimatullahi master Javad Nurbakhsh and English translation tape follows. Finally, on occasion, a dinner is placed on the floor before the congregation. The food is served and eaten in total silence except for the shaykh's brief directives to begin and conclude the meal. As the leader leaves, the congregation rises in homage and he meets with members for private consultation behind a curtain in another area.

With the obvious exceptions illustrated previously, most Iranians in Los Angeles who routinely refer to themselves as Muslims are not particularly religious. They still consider themselves linked in some manner to the Islamic creed, following Muslim traditions at least to some extent in marriage and funeral ceremonies. There are, however, no major communal events or organizations around which they unite. In other words, they are not, of themselves, a distinctive *community*, as are Iranian minority groups here (Jews, Bahais, Armenians, and others). Most cultural events and holidays at which they might gather, such as No Ruz and Sizdah Bidar, are shared in tradition with other Iranian ethnic and religious groups, partly because these celebrations predate Islamic development in Iran. In this sense, secular Muslims in L.A. are more socially disenfranchised than other Iranian ethnic and religious groups that left the homeland for America.

MUSLIMS AND NON-MUSLIMS

Among the most curious kinds of limbo immigrant Muslims must face is the fact that Arabs, Iranians, Indo-Pakistanis, and some other racial groups are not legally considered minorities in America, although they are often treated like them. In the eyes of the government, they are part of the dominant culture, entitled to no minority benefits. However, they still reap the negative consequences of being considered cultural "outsiders."

The most common problem faced by Muslims in America is their mass media image for violence, terrorism, medievalism, and other sensationally negative stereotypes. For the American public, largely ignorant of the tenets and background of Islam, there follows a typically prejudicial, and sometimes hostile, perception of Muslims here.

These attitudes are manifest in many forms, sometimes reaching the broadest public arena. In 1990, for instance, the Islamic Center of Northridge ran into much publicized trouble with would-be neighbors and the very city of Los Angeles. The story began in the late 1970s when a group of about ten Indo-Pakistani families in the San Fernando Valley found the 50 mile roundtrip commute to the Islamic Center of Southern California to be excessive. Following the development pattern of many other mosques, the group began meeting at homes for Islamic programs and, later, at a member's nursery school in Sepulveda. Within two years they pooled their resources and bought a home at what they imagined would be a good site, eliciting no trouble from neighbors, on a busy street corner across from a gas station in Northridge. But when they applied for zoning changes to convert the structure into a small mosque, their request to the City Council was denied. Seeking advice from the city for a suitable site, they next located a three-bedroom home for sale next to a church. In applying for rezoning permission again, the small Islamic community was surprised to find opposition from even the church next door, whose representative called the proposed mosque "a conflict of interest" for the neighborhood.

Ultimately, after considerable effort and energy, their request for rezoning was approved. Within ten years, however, the community had grown too large and they began looking for a new site upon which to build, from the ground up, a Muslim religious structure. An empty parcel of land was tentatively decided upon in Granada Hills. Anticipating from past experience the usual neighborhood resistance to the dreaded idea of a mosque in their midst, the Muslims hired an American-born consultant and lobbyist to troubleshoot possible obstacles. Sure enough, once again concerned neighbors surfaced to complain and worry, ostensibly citing inevitable noise and pollution problems from a new public structure in the area. The Islamic Center felt it had no choice but to hire an engineering company, recommended by the city, to do a traffic and noise study at a cost of $5,000. Zero environmental impact by a proposed mosque upon the local neighborhood was found. Eventually the mosque proposal for construction was passed by the Los Angeles City Council, but with forty-four imposed conditions, the highest number of restrictions ever placed on a house of worship of any kind in the entire city. Included was the condition that the mosque blend in with the local Spanish architecture.

According to Mohammed Mohuiddin, president of the Islamic Center of Northridge, the mosque seemed destined to look like "a Spanish warehouse." At this point, however, a *Los Angeles Times* reporter took up the story of covert, city-sponsored discrimination and the inability of a minority religious faith to build a religious center the way it chose, including a traditional minaret. The mayor of Los Angeles, Tom Bradley, soon became publicly involved in the defense of religious freedom in the city and the *Los Angeles Times* followed the initial story with a number of sequential articles and an editorial in support of the proposed Islamic center.

The Muslims who were involved never jumped on the political wave that rushed to defend them. The issue of the minaret, says President Mohuiddin, was never really very important and was championed more by the newspaper reporter than by the Muslim community itself. In a public relations minefield, most Muslims simply sought to build their mosque, Spanish-style or otherwise, as expeditiously as possible, circumnavigating the implicit distrust and suspicion so typically directed at them, eager to prove themselves good, and undemanding, neighbors.

Prejudice, suspicion, and discrimination have been focused even more ominously upon Muslims by a number of government agencies in Los Angeles. During the Persian Gulf War, local Muslims and other minority groups were infuriated, and effectively alerted the local media when the FBI began selectively interviewing Arab Americans here, searching for covert ties and allegiances to Iraq and Saddam Hussein as well as evidence of planned terrorism. In earlier years, Lorraine Mirza, an outspoken Shi'i activist and director of the Pakistani-American Friendship League, was shocked to discover through local news reports that the Los Angeles Police Department had held her and her organization (as well as a number of others) under illegal surveillance.

In a recent protest demonstration against Saddam Hussein on the holy day of Ashura, Imam Mojai of Masjid Al-Rasool, a Shi'a mosque in the African American community, angrily told fellow Muslims that he was being harassed by the FBI, who had called to warn that they had discovered "serious threats' against him. Nisar Hai, local director of the United Muslims of America, an antidiscrimination group, has a large file of harassment and discrimination cases against Los Angeles Muslims, ranging from derogatory jokes anonymously circulated over far-reaching computer systems to specific complaints by Muslims who have been mistreated in stores for their traditional attire. In the last five months of 1990, after the Iraqi invasion of Kuwait, nineteen hate crimes (actual violation of law) against Muslims were recorded by the city of Los Angeles.

Simple harassment surfaces in many forms. In one case police squad cars circled a traditionally dressed Muslim woman and her daughters in Long Beach after a caller reported that three Muslim women with shotguns were walking around the neighborhood. They were, in fact, carrying carpet cleaning equipment. During the Persian Gulf War, Muslims in the phone book with the last name of Hussein were subjected to threatening phone calls at all hours of the night. In other cases, Muslims have faced covert harassment by anonymous neighbors demanding the enforcement of obscure city laws and bureaucratic regulations. One day a local Muslim received word from the California Department of Motor Vehicles denying his innocent request for a personalized license plate that said "4 Jihad," the name of his son. Even the site of the state Republican convention was found to be canvassed—seat by seat— with anti-Islamic literature.

CONCLUSION

Despite efforts by some in the local Muslim community to unify its members into a broadly based religious federation and an effective political lobby to protect its rights and interests, Muslims in Los Angeles have remained highly fragmented along religious, cultural, and political lines. The exact shape and form the local Muslim community takes over future years is a particularly poignant issue for many older immigrant generations who struggle to imbue in their children the nuances of Islam from their homelands.

Ultimately, the socioreligious course of Islam in this country will be decided by today's Muslim children, who are continuously called to weigh their divergent histories against their common problems here. In this sometimes painful process of conflict resolution, throughout the playgrounds, schools, and colleges of Los Angeles, as well as in front of the omnipresent TV set, a commonly adapted American Muslim identity is steadily being formed.

NOTES

This chapter is based on over fifty tape-recorded interview sessions with over seventy Muslims living in Los Angeles, including twenty-one Imams or presidents of Islamic centers and six officials of other Islamically linked organizations, as well as a number of other informal discussions with members of the community. The author has visited over thirty mosques in the local area. The discussion largely focuses on Muslims in relation to the local mosque system. Those entirely beyond the mosque network tend to blend into the surrounding American society and are difficult to identify as, distinctly, Muslims. This problem is intrinsic to even local religious activists who would like to know authentically the size of their community here.

1.   During a recent Eid prayer to end the Ramadan fasting (one of the most important communal gatherings of the year), the two main mosques in metropolitan Los Angeles each attracted 8–10,000 people, predominantly adults. Other major Eid gatherings were sponsored by a center in the San Fernando Valley, which attracted 3,000 people, and a Rowland Heights mosque, which gathered 2,000 Muslims to the Los Angeles County Fairground. The seminal African American mosque, Masjid Bilal, and Islamic Center of Riverside each drew another thousand.

2.   Imam Safir Sadik of Masjid Ibaadalluh estimates that of the 300,000 Muslims he believes to be in the area, 10 percent are actively religious. Nayereh Tohidi's surveying the local Iranian community found only 10–13 percent responded affirmatively to questions regarding daily personal practice of Islam in Los Angeles.

3.   When ten Imams or other religious leaders were asked how many mosques there are in Los Angeles, no two respondents cited the same figure. The author has thus far visited over thirty mosques (from converted warehouse space and small storefronts to large permanent structures) and believes there are less than forty in the greater Los Angeles area.

4.   As noted by many Muslims, Tablighi enthusiasm and salesmanship can be extreme. Within minutes of meeting one Tablighi gentleman at the Inglewood Mosque, the author was given a Muslim name and, henceforth, over protest, introduced to others by this given name.

5.   Islam has a noteworthy presence, particularly through African Americans, in the U.S. prison system. Malcolm X discovered the Nation of Islam behind bars, as did many others who found, in their understanding of the faith, keys to sociopolitical action.

In the late 1980s the state and federal prison systems began experimenting with the hiring of Muslim chaplains to augment other religious leaders in tending to the religious needs of the incarcerated. No less important was the prison authority's interest in religious leaders' functions as counselors and calming troubleshooters. Imam Adbdul Hafiz, a Sunni scholar, became the first of six current Muslim chaplains working in western U.S. prisons.

Because prison officials' only contact with Islam had been through convicted criminals, the Muslim chaplain program was closely watched. Among such administrators, Islam was commonly perceived to be a "prison religion," operating like a gang, a mutual protection society. With stereotypical repercussions from the Iranian hostage crisis of 1979–

1980 and an earlier beheading of an Oklahoma prison guard by prisoners who claimed to be Muslims, Imam Abdul Hafiz struggled to destroy a range of ridiculous preconceptions by prison guards and wardens and became an important ambassador for Islam. Walking the delicate line between prison staff and inmates, the Imam has over the years successfully proven his credibility to both of them.

Initially working in a federal penitentiary in Lompoc where inmates faced the rest of their lives behind bars, his congregation included 150 men. Ten were dedicated members of the Nation of Islam, 30–40 were members of the Moorish Science Temple of America (originally from the East Coast, particularly Washington, D.C.), and the rest were Sunnis.

Eventually transferred to the minimum security facility at Terminal Island in San Pedro, he leads prayer and counsels about thirty dedicated Muslims who regularly come to Friday prayer and another fifteen or so with some interest in Islam. Most are African American, but there are also three Iranians, a Turk, two Afghanis, two Cubans, and a Mexican American. Different Muslim sects at the Terminal Island facility freely interrelate, sometimes joining together for Friday prayer. Demarcations among different Muslim groups in the federal penitentiary system, however, are much more rigid.

6.   There are exceptions, of course, to immigrant political passivity. Such expressions rarely leave the Muslim community to reach non-Muslim Americans, however. The Islamic Association for Palestine, for example, recently held its second national celebration of the Palestinian Intifada. In Los Angeles, over 700 people gathered from all over the state to hear a series of Arabic presentations, including visiting Sheikh Khalil Al-Kuka's call for armed struggle against Israel and support for the Palestinian Muslim political organization, Hamas. Suspected of being a potential spy of some kind, the author was not allowed to photograph or tape record any of the proceedings. No one present at the meeting, including members of the organization's hierarchy, were willing to be interviewed, even informally.

7.   All mosques in the African American Islamic community in Los Angeles trace their historical lineage or leadership to Masjid Bilal except Masjid Al-Mumim, a Sunni Islamic center that was, in very small numbers, an early contemporary of the Nation of Islam in L.A.

8.   On one occasion during a Moharram observance, a group of 200 people had to move from the Bellflower High School gymnasium to its cafeteria because the gym had been reserved by a local American group's bingo game.

CHAPTER 7

The Muslims of San Diego

M. K. Hermansen

San Diego has many of the features that one expects of large south-ern California cities. Until recently there has been no strong central sense of downtown core but rather a loose association of a number of smaller cities that grew together over time. A feeling of discon-nected sprawl and vast distances that must be navigated by car predominates. Unlike the major urban centers of the northeast, the Muslims of San Diego would find it difficult to spatially recon-stitute the communities of the home countries due to the southern California urban pattern of horizontal rather than vertical expan-sion.

The demographic makeup of the Muslim community of San Diego has changed dramatically over the past two decades. Some estimates of the Muslim population exceed 50,000.[1] Although this is possible considering that San Diego with a population of 1.7 million is the seventh largest city in the United States, others feel that 20,000 would be a more realistic figure.[2] What appears to be the relatively limited number of participants in formal Islamic reli-gious activities at mosques or Islamic centers (some 2,000 gener-ally attending the special community prayers on the Eid holiday and 500–600 going to regular Friday noon prayers) may be ex-plained in several ways. The number of Muslims as a whole in San Diego appears to be inflated due to the many Christian Iraqis and non-Muslim Iranians who have migrated here but naturally are not connected with mosque activities. Second, even the Muslim Ira-nians who have migrated in large numbers to southern California generally tend to be from the more Westernized classes, who fled

169

the revolution and do not participate in formal Islamic religious activities in America. A third factor is a kind of voluntarism that pervades Muslim as other religious groups in America. Muslims often feel they can choose or not choose to actively participate in Islamic religious activities at the institution of their choice. For the majority participation is not considered a religious requirement.

The "local" dimensions of the Muslim presence in San Diego are influenced both by the origins of those who come here and the character of the city itself. Despite the overall population and Muslim presence in San Diego, community organization seems to be at least a decade behind that of other comparable urban areas. This delay may have interesting consequences for the future development patterns of the community. As one member noted, "We have had a chance to learn from the mistakes of Los Angeles and Orange County." Because there is a relatively high degree of cooperation and interaction among the fairly recently established local mosques, for example, it may be possible to avoid such problems as politicization and divisions along ethnic lines.

The Muslim community of San Diego is affected by being a satellite of Los Angeles, some 100 miles away. Many of the ethnic groups have not reached the critical population mass that would allow for extensive social networks and sufficient marriage partners being available locally for the next generation. This is especially evident among groups who traditionally do not intermarry, such as Pakistanis and Afghans. Even the Iranians, who in numerical terms are by far the largest Muslim ethic group,[3] function as the furthest southern outpost of a Persian community centered in Los Angeles and stretching south through Orange County into San Diego County. Many Muslim families from San Diego drive to Los Angeles to celebrate festivals with a larger community in order to keep ties with a more extensive network of friends and relatives. This has served to discourage the formation of an active community in San Diego.

IMMIGRATION PATTERNS
AND COMMUNITY DEVELOPMENT

Several factors make San Diego attractive to Muslims. Its Mediterranean climate and its landscape are reminiscent of many areas of the Middle East. Several of the universities in the area, including the University of California at San Diego (UCSD), San Diego State, and many other private institutions[4] now offer graduate degrees in medicine or engineering, concentrations of high priority to foreign students. The matter of graduate studies is particularly significant because foreign professionals are more likely to settle in a community than return to their homeland or migrate in search of employment.

Because much of the industry in San Diego has been military or defense oriented, for which the hiring of U.S. citizens is mandatory, it has often been difficult for immigrant engineers or technical experts who do not have citizenship to find employment. A small number of Muslim immigrants originally came to the area because of an offer by the U.S. Navy of U.S. citizenship to foreign nationals who served for a certain period. For the most part, however, unlike many other cities in the northeast, or even Los Angeles or San Francisco, San Diego had and continues to have a core of Muslim professionals to establish institutions for Muslim immigrants equal to that of other large U.S. cities.

The first Muslims to settle in this area were probably the agriculturalists who migrated in the early part of the century. In 1912, for example, a Punjabi from Jullundur, India, named Shahabuddin came with his cousin to the San Francisco area, where he studied agriculture at the University of California in Berkeley.[5] He later moved to the El Centro area in the Imperial Valley agricultural region, about 110 miles east of San Diego, where he became a successful farmer with a substantial acreage. Shahabbudin was part of a group of Punjabis, a majority Sikhs but some Muslims, who came at the end of the first decade of this century in search of adventure and fortune.[6] The early Punjabi immigrants generally were known as *Hindus* regardless of their religious orientation.[7]

In the early 1920s the Muslims on the West Coast still had no mosque of their own and used to travel from all parts of the state to gather and celebrate the festival days. Presumably the Imperial Valley Muslims would go to the Stockton area, where there was a larger community. Eventually a Mohammedan Club was established in El Centro, where members would meet in a space above a local bar for social and religious gatherings. In 1952, after the partition of India and the creation of Pakistan, Muslims in the Imperial Valley pooled resources to buy a building in El Centro which was used for various Islamic functions. A small section for burials was also purchased in the Evergreen Cemetery there, where tombstones with Arabic writing can still be seen today. Such sites, which exist in a number of California cemeteries, were known as *Hindu plots*, an interesting anomaly because Hindus traditionally are cremated and in fact only Muslims are buried in these plots.[8] Only a few Muslims still live in Imperial County; most of them are recent immigrants and not descendants of the first settlers.[9] A Sikh community still exists there and maintains a local temple.[10]

Most of these early Punjabi settlers were young men who married locally, usually Mexican women.[11] Several factors accounted for this choice. East Indians were forbidden to own land because of the California antialien acts of 1913 and 1920. Technically, having a Mexican American wife hold the land in her name was not a solution, because a married woman's legal status was considered to be the same as her husband's, but this was often overlooked in Imperial County.[12] (East Indians were declared Caucasian but not "white" by the Supreme Court, and thus after 1923 were ineligible for citizenship.) And between 1923 and 1946 they were not allowed legally to immigrate to the United States, so those who were in this country could not bring brides from abroad.[13]

Miscegenation laws remained on the books in California until 1948, allowing county clerks to deny applications for what they considered mixed marriages. Alliances between Hispanic women and Punjabis were not so problematic, however, because both were considered to be "brown" by the surrounding Anglo culture.[14] Very few of the Punjabi Muslims observed the prescribed prayers or the fast of Ramadan, and few had Qur'ans or prayer rugs. For a brief time there apparently was an Arabic class for children brought up in El Centro.[15] Ultimately the children of these mixed marriages assimilated to American culture, generally adopting the Roman Catholicism of their mothers and losing any sense of Islamic identity.[16]

After the partition of India in the late 1940s some of the relatives of these early settlers came to this part of California because of family connections. The remoteness and limited facilities of the El Centro area, however, soon caused them to disperse to the larger cities in California in search of education and professional employment. One member of the San Diego Muslim community recalls leading the funeral prayers during the 1960s for some of the El Centro oldtimers.[17]

Since the 1960s there have been waves of immigration to San Diego by Muslims seeking employment and to escape turmoil at home. An Arab American community has been in existence in San Diego since the 1950s, but immigration substantially increased after 1967. Because the early Muslim immigrants did not necessarily plan to settle in this country they focused on ethnic rather than religious ties and did not establish formal Islamic institutions. Although the percentage of Muslim Arab Americans is increasing, the majority are still Christian.[18] There is also a community of about a thousand Sunni Muslim Iraqi Kurds in the city, segmented along political lines. A recent (1993) plan proposes establishing a Kurdistan Islamic Center backed by funds from the Saudi embassy, a move with clear political overtones for the community.

A substantial demographic shift in the Muslim community in San Diego occurred with the influx of Muslim students from abroad in the late 1970s. These students were often Islamic activists from the Arabian Gulf or Syria. A member of the community estimated that there may have been up to 500 Kuwaiti and 300 Saudi students, most of them attending United States International University. (One story has it that the Kuwaiti government eventually came to feel that the students attending that university were becoming too politicized and withdrew its financial support.) A mosque for this student community functioned for a time in the Mira Mesa area in north San Diego, and social clubs served the large Saudi and Kuwaiti populations.

The Iranian students in the San Diego area received a good deal of public attention during the hostage crisis of 1979–1980. Some 200 attended a march sponsored by the Iranian "Moslem Student Association" to protest the admission of the Shah to Mexico for medical treatment; there was a three-hour disturbance involving rival groups of Iranian students at San Diego State University; a wave of threats by Americans against local universities urged suspension of their Iranian students. Ensuing social and economic pressures and systematic visa crackdowns greatly reduced the numbers of these students over the next several years.[19] In any case, the religiously oriented Muslim community of San Diego experienced little impact from the large influx of Iranians into southern California in the postrevolution period because few of them participated in religious activities.

In general the influx of Muslim students in the 1970s radically changed the character of Muslim social activities in the San Diego area, culminating in the early 1980s when stricter codes of behavior were imposed at Islamic activities and the participation of women became more limited.[20] The shift in population and the difference in focus between the settler Muslims and the students led to tensions in 1984 and events that one member termed a *break up*. At issue were concerns of ethnic identity, differing political agendas, and whether one was transient or settled. Most of these matters were resolved over time as the activists and students either moved on or became permanent residents, many of whom are now U.S. citizens.

While the main Islamic center of San Diego attracts about an 80 percent Arab clientele, most of the local South Asian Muslims also participate in its activities. Two of the five positions on the center's board, for example, are currently held by South Asians. The leadership of the center has adopted a conscious policy of trying to involve those who voice opposition to its activities and policies. The center has kept a watchful eye on the 1992 experience of the Orange Country Islamic Center when a relatively hard-line faction attempted to remove the director for primarily ideological reasons. Although that case seems to have been resolved through legal recourse,[21] San Diego members are trying to avoid such a split in their own center. The strategy of appealing to American legal structure was also employed in San Diego during a critical period when the new Islamic center was opened. A number of individuals objected to one or another aspect of the constitutional structure of the society, but the constitution that had been set up and ratified under American law served as a check on these potentially destabilizing activities.

After the Iranians the largest group of Muslim immigrants to come to San Diego were the Afghan refugees, some of whom were encouraged by the INS to settle away from the more established Afghan communities in the San Francisco and Washington, D.C., areas. Only a few Afghans were in San Diego in the 1980s, but they have grown rapidly over the past decade to some 600 families or 3,000 individuals. Many who held degrees and government positions in Afghanistan now must run businesses or work in social service industries. About a third of the Afghans are Shi'a; they hold their own informal ceremonies in rented halls or large homes during Muharram but have no formal mosque or permanent Imam and pray with the Sunnis. In 1990 an Afghan Refugee Cultural Council was founded to preserve the Afghan language and culture. Presently classes are held for about sixty children on Saturdays in a rented facility. The group states that it sponsors primarily cultural rather than religious functions and seeks to prevent more conservative religious and political factions from dictating what types of activities are appropriate. Although not technically a mosque,[22] the center does provide a context for a number of religious activities such as mawlids (ceremonies to honor the Prophet), fatihas (formal gatherings after funerals), and lifecycle ceremonies. About 100 families participate in and contribute to the support of the center; currently there are plans to expand its social and educational activities.

Recently a number of African Muslim refugees have settled in San Diego. Many of them are from Somalia, including the present president of the Islamic Society, Hassan Abukar. During 1992 the number of Somalis in San Diego increased from "fewer than 200 to more than 1,000, most of them arriving under U.S. refugee policies for family reunification."[23] The San Diego Somali community has now become the largest concentration in the United States. Most of them come from Ogaden, a territory disputed between Somalia and Ethiopia. Socially and religiously they have interacted primarily with the immigrant community. This may change as an anticipated 1,000 more Somalis arrive in 1993. Most of the refugees have settled in east San Diego where they have occupied entire apartment complexes. The children generally attend weekend Qur'an classes at a center in the neighborhood founded by a Somali scholar of Islam; the Musalla mosque on Winona Avenue serves as a community center.

The history of this center is interesting from the perspective of community formation. It was initially organized by an African American with Sufi inclinations and functioned as a mosque and served for Sufi assemblies on Thursday nights with a wide range of participants: African Americans, Somalis, Arab American Naqshbandis. In 1989 an unfortunate incident occurred when one of the participants in the Sufi session was shot and wounded near the mosque in mysterious circumstances. This has led to a diminution of Sufi activities and a shift in the mosque's function so that it has become primarily a community religious center for the area's Somali population.

According to one community leader, local Somalis represent three main orientations: traditional, Islamist, and Westernized elite. The Islamists are called *wadaad* by their compatriots. This term in the context of traditional Somali society signifies a Sufi-affiliated religious leader who often functions as a neutral and respected peacemaker during clan disputes.[24] In San Diego the so-called *wadaads* tend to be Somalis educated in Middle Eastern universities where they have absorbed current Islamist ideas and aspirations for an Islamic state. Most (perhaps 70 percent) of the refugees in San Diego are characterized as "traditional" and therefore, although identified with Islam, they do not share an activist or political agenda. This division of interests has led to the formation of two local Somali associations, the original Somali Community of San Diego and a more Westernized Somali Society of San Diego, which broke away in 1992 because it felt that the original group had too much Islamist (*wadaad*) influence on its executive committee. In the near future it is likely that the Somalis will establish a larger religious center to serve their community.

Perhaps because San Diego has not been an area that offers the cultural resources to attract artistic or spiritually inclined persons there are fewer Anglo American Muslim converts in comparison to, for example, the Bay area. A number of American women are married to immigrant Muslim men; a support group for them functions sporadically.[25] Although the African American Muslim community was established quite early, it does not seem to be expanding through conversion at a significant rate.

In summarizing the impact of immigration patterns on the constitution of the particular San Diego community, one notes the effect both of the origins of the immigrants and the shifts of attitudes of the host environment since the arrival of the Punjabi pioneers some eighty years ago. The pressures to assimilate to a dominant Anglo version of the American way have given over to greater tolerance of racial and ethnic diversity, increased pluralism, and legal and political recognition of the rights of minorities. With this decline in pressure to identify with the dominant culture and an increasing pool of potential spouses with similar cultural backgrounds, endogamy among the Muslim immigrants and their children is likely to increase even among those who are not particularly religious. This does not, of course, preclude the further Americanization of each subsequent generation.

COMMUNITY CENTERS AND MOSQUES

The first locally based organization for immigrant Muslims in the city was the Islamic Society of San Diego. It was founded through the efforts of a small core of Muslim professionals, primarily of South Asian origin. According to one account, a few members of this group divided the local phone book into four sections in 1971 in order to call about 200 households with Muslim-sounding names to try to initiate some community activities. This early group first met for a picnic lunch in a local park, and then decided to constitute a society.[26] A bulletin of this early society, called *The Islamic Reporter* and first published in early 1973, memorializes the first forty persons to constitute the society. Nearly all appear to have been of South Asian origin.[27] Previous to this time Eid prayers and meetings had been held at private homes.

The first full-time center-mosque was a home on Curry Drive near the San Diego State University campus that had previously been owned by Dr. Abidullah Ghazi, a Muslim of Indian origin who taught Islamic studies at the university and founded a branch of the Muslim Student Association there.[28] This house was purchased in 1973 by the community to serve as a center with donations collected through pledges, rummage sales, and other fundraising efforts.[29] The Muslim community continued to meet in this house until the late 1980s. The number attending Friday prayers grew so large that they were usually held at the local recreation center, and Eid prayers were held in Balboa Park or on the lawn of the recreation center. Church halls or gymnasiums were rented for social functions and lectures. Women's meetings were held at the home of Zarina Bari, a Pakistani American, from 1973 to 1984. Today both the Islamic Society and the various mosques sponsor women's activities.

Until recently the Muslim community as a whole has had a very low profile in the city. Relatively few established professionals participated in its functions, and the style of the institutions up to the inauguration of the local Islamic center in 1990 was very "foreign" in terms of language, customs, and outreach. The Islamic center has adapted to its new space with an accommodation of its style in terms of welcoming visitors, issuing a glossy computerized newsletter, and participating in interfaith events.[30] The new Islamic center has a very "modern" feel and features a sparkling new angular building, computers, a book store, spacious offices, and other facilities.

With the visibility of the new center and heightened awareness of the Muslim community on the local scene due to the Gulf War of 1991 and community shock at a recent bomb incident at the center, at least some segments of the local community are becoming interested in the Muslim presence. Evidence for this includes an increase in the amount of newspaper coverage of community activities and the fact that increasingly representatives from the mosque have become a part of local interfaith networks.

On August 28, 1990, the impressive mosque in the new Islamic Center of San Diego was officially inaugurated. Located at Balboa Drive and Highway 805 in a prestigious area of the city called Clairemont it is conveniently situated near a major freeway exit and can be seen from the highway as a large, imposing, modern structure, with its dome, crescent and minaret distinguishing it as a mosque. The two-story building is 27,000 square feet, with a mosque on the upper level and facilities for women, offices, a cafeteria, a book store, and a library. It claims to be "the largest center on the West Coast."[31]

The land for this center had been bought from the nearby Atonement Lutheran Church in 1983 for $535,000. It appears that eventually this church will close and offer to sell its remaining property to the Muslims. The core contribution for the Islamic center was a generous donation from an anonymous Saudi patron, who made the request that the mosque be called Masjid Abi Bakr al-Siddiq. In the course of acquiring permission to build from the city a series of hearings were held. At this time a number of objections to locating this center were raised, one on the part of a health club over a mile away, which contended that the Islamic center would be excessively noisy. Others feared that the call to prayer would disturb the neighborhood. The presiding judge actually requested that the *adhan* be played in court to assess its impact, despite the fact that it would not be made outside the building or otherwise broadcast or amplified in a public way. A number of Christian and Jewish religious leaders initially were opposed to the building of the mosque. All of these objections proved to be insubstantial and construction finally began in 1987; the center was formally inaugurated in 1990.

Since 1984 the center has had both a full-time director of

religious affairs, Sharif al-Battikhi, and a full-time Imam, Abdussatter al-Zoobi. In early 1992 Mr. Zoobi returned to Lebanon, leaving Imam Battikhi as the full-time director and Imam until he resigned from the position later in the same year. Shaykh Sharif al-Battikhi was originally from Jordan and has a degree in Islamic law from the Islamic University of Medina.[32] Currently the funds for all salaries are raised locally, although in previous times the Rabita, a Saudi-sponsored religious body, paid part of one Imam's salary. The 1989 constitution of the society provides for a five-member Board of Trustees and a five-member Board of Directors. As this is somewhat of a transitional stage in the development of the center, some members of the board have been activists from L.A. rather than local residents. Eventually it is likely that all directors and trustees will be elected by members of the Islamic Society. The trustees and the directors meet weekly on Fridays, and community meetings for all members-at-large are held perhaps twice a year. Membership in the society is available to those who subscribe at the rate of $60/year per person or $120 per family. Some Muslims have complained about this system of membership dues, saying that it is not practiced abroad and that "during the time of the Prophet, membership was not a custom". There are currently 280 members in the society. The Islamic center's land and building are legally owned by the North American Islamic Trust as a waqf, common practice for North American Centers affiliated with this organization.

The activities at the Islamic center include lectures, Iftar (breaking the fast in Ramadan) dinners and talks, Eid prayers, a food bank, and the performance of marriages, funerals, and conversion ceremonies. A youth group with some thirty-five participants meets regularly at the center. Previous attempts to start such groups by concerned families featured events either at the universities or in private homes. A mosque "Sunday school" was attended by seventy-four pupils in 1991. In 1992 an initial step was taken toward developing a full-time kindergarten through sixth grade education with the enrollment of twenty-seven pupils in an "Islamic elementary" kindergarten to second grade program.[33] By 1993 the school was ready to extend its range to grades five and six. A curriculum issue facing the school is the teaching of the Arabic language. Some feel that it is hopeless to attempt to instruct children in Arabic in the limited time available. Although some prefer "prep" classes that would enable children to recite the necessary Arabic prayers, more traditional members aspire to actual language instruction. A possible future expansion of the program would feature after school Islamic day care activities.

A number of the San Diego mosques sponsor women's groups. The group at the Islamic Society currently meets on Friday nights and has two sections, one for English and one for Arabic speakers, each with about fifteen participants. The 1993 ballot for electing women to the Islamic Center woman's committee stated that nominees must wear hejab (full Islamic dress) and practice the five pillars, among other requirements.

At a typical Friday congregational prayer during Ramadan 1991 the attendance in the women's section was predominantly Arab (perhaps 120), with a handful of Pakistanis, a few Afghanis, and a very few African American and Anglo American Muslims. Practically all of the women wore traditional or ethnic dress. The male congregation (700) differed in ethnic composition with a high proportion of South Asians and Afghans. The difference in male and female attendance probably is due to local custom in certain home countries, according to which women do not attend the mosque for Friday prayers.

The Iftar dinners during Ramadan are held in a large cafeteria. Individual members of the congregation or groups, for example the Pakistan Association, sponsor each dinner, often in commemoration of an event such as the birth or death of a family member, or simply for the religious merit of feeding persons who are breaking their fasts. During the first year such dinners were held, males and females were served at separate lines and sat in separate halves of the hall, but no partition was used. More recently a folding partition has been added and segregation is more strictly observed. Maximum attendance for dinners in 1991 was about 350 persons; that number has now (1993) surpassed 500.

In addition to Masjid Abi Bakr there are a number of other places of prayer in the community: Masjid al-Taqwa, serving a primarily African American congregation, is the oldest mosque in urban San Diego. It is located at 2575 Imperial Avenue in San Diego. Its history goes back to the 1940s when it was established in a house on Clay Avenue in San Diego as Masjid #8 in the Nation of Islam. It is claimed to be the first NOI mosque west of the Mississippi and thus the first on the West Coast. One of the early founders of this congregation was Yusuf Abdullah, who after becoming a follower of Elijah Muhammad in 1949 went to Chicago in 1950 to attend Saviors Day.[34] He was recognized by Elijah Muhammad and given the name Yusuf. For a time he ran a popular Muslim restaurant in the city. The early group was harassed by the police. In 1951 a group of followers scuffled with the San Diego police in the courthouse and were jailed, during which time the women of the community kept the mosque running.[35]

The present building was bought in the 1950s and expanded in the 1970s. When Warith Deen Muhammad assumed the name The World Community of al-Islam in the West for his movement in 1977, some 400 local families joined in a celebration of this merger under the auspices of Imam Daniel Adnan.[36] In 1979 the name became the American Muslim Mission. Throughout these shifts the building continued to function as a center. In 1987, for example, a weekend conference was held on eating and slaughtering halal meat at which Warith Deen Muhammad was present. Presently it also houses the Clara Muhammad School which has grades K–6.

In addition to the Friday congregational (*juma*) prayer, which is generally attended by about forty persons, there is a Tuesday lecture called *talim*, a women's group called the Muslim American Women International (M.A.W.I.) that meets at private homes every other week, and a Qur'an study group on Fridays. The permanent Imam of the congregation is Aqeel el-Amin. This group prays the Eid prayers with the larger congregation at Masjid Abu Bakr. The mosque includes a large hall that can be expanded through folding doors. It is finished in masonite and painted in two shades of green. The atmosphere is enhanced by burning incense, small carpets and scrolls of Qur'anic calligraphy decorating the walls, and a rack with Qur'ans and Islamic literature. The hall is carpeted, and taped lines mark the rows for prayer. The street outside contrasts with the clean and peaceful interior of the mosque because it is in a rough and derelict section of town.

One of the more interesting activities of this center is outreach to the local military bases. Imam Aqeel was recently interviewed for a TV series on Muslims in the military and his activities have been written up in *The Muslim Journal*. For the past five years a *dawa* (missionary) team has been going to the Naval Training Center's religious complex at Camp Pendleton, just up the coast from San Diego in Oceanside, California. They also visit the Miramar base and hold bimonthly sessions at the Camp Pendleton brig. Conversions in the military are said to be occurring at a steady rate.[37] According to Imam Aqeel, most of these new Muslims are only temporarily posted to San Diego and then are sent elsewhere or return to their original homes. Many had originally heard of Islam through followers of Minister Farrakhan. The local San Diego *dawa* group perceives that part of its function is to correct misinformation about the religion. It is responsible for the sale or distribution of an estimated 100 Qur'ans (the Yusuf Ali translation) a month to the public, military, or those in prison. Little concrete outreach has been made to the Hispanic community due to a lack of Spanish-speaking Muslims and appropriate materials in Spanish.

There is a sense of solidarity and dedication in this community although it is relatively small, remaining steady in membership and possibly even shrinking. According to the Imam it is preferable to have "a few sincere Muslims rather than a whole *masjid* full of insincere ones." Still he acknowledges a need for a more intensive *dawa* effort, noting that "the Farrakhan people are doing more using black nationalism and black pride as a message; we could do more."

Al-Ribat al-Islami is an institution begun by thirteen persons with the aim of founding a charitable organization to help needy Muslims, particularly American Muslim women who are divorced or single mothers, in the San Diego area. Later they expanded their work to include religious activities. The institution was incorporated as a nonprofit organization in 1984.

The first center was a two-bedroom apartment off 70th Street, established near San Diego State University at a time when a number of members were students there. The living room was used as a mosque and open for the five daily prayers. One bedroom was an office and the other a lecture room. A two-bedroom house on Saranac Street near the old apartment was purchased in 1985. Among activities offered at this mosque-center are lessons in Islam for men and women (separately), marriages, divorces, and funerals, outreach activities such as distributing free Qur'ans and Islamic literature and giving lectures at local schools, sponsoring guest lectures, accepting the declarations of faith of new Muslims, collecting donations of money and clothing for needy persons and disaster relief abroad, and charitable assistance to needy Muslim women in the local community. Social gatherings include Thursday night meals provided for those who regularly fast on this day, as well as Friday and Saturday evening meals and programs.

In late February 1991 the old house was demolished and construction began on a new center, which was opened in late 1992. Funds for this were solicited from the local community, including the congregation of Masjid Abi Bakr, which encouraged the creation of this new center, and from donors abroad. Some question the necessity for a center only twenty minutes from the larger mosque. It may be that this smaller center promotes a more intense feeling of community and also appeals to a younger, largely student, clientele. Its location near San Diego State University and the mosque on Curry Drive means that it draws a number of people who live and work in this area. One finds both Islamic activist and Sufi trends among its multiethnic congregation. The rather loose organization of the Rabat (there is no constitution regarding the election of a board and no Imam or elected director) led to some opposition from those who want a say in its direction.[38] At one time Saudi students were able to raise funds to help maintain this center but it appears that interest abroad in supporting this type of project is waning.

Masjid Nur is located on 50th Street in east San Diego. It was started by three brothers of Indian Muslim origin, who are active in the Tablighi Jamaat, with the support of other South Asian well-wishers. In 1985 they purchased a house on 50th Street in a rather tough neighborhood known as east San Diego. It is a high-crime, drug, and gang-infested area. Although this section of San Diego is largely black, it also serves as the first residence of refugees from Southeast Asia, the Middle East, and Africa.

Masjid Nur has a full-time Hafiz (Qur'an reciter and teacher) from India, Arabic and Urdu classes, and an intense Ramadan program including recitation of the entire Qur'an over the thirty nights of the month of fasting. There are no facilities for women, as Tablighis traditionally require their women to keep strict customs of Purdah (segregation of the sexes). In the Tablighi spirit, Masjid Nur promotes conversion and outreach to lapsed Muslims. One program operates primarily for African Americans. For a time a dormitory adjunct to the mosque permitted new "brothers" to live in a communal atmosphere and experience an intense immersion in a traditional Muslim way of life. Currently new Hispanic and African American Muslims are placed more informally to live with bachelor Muslims whom the mosque's directors feel will represent role models of an exemplary Muslim life-style. There is also an outreach program to Tijuana, which one major activist from Masjid Nur characterized as fertile ground for the expansion of Islam due to the failing grip of Catholicism, the generally depressed conditions, and pervasive anomie. A small mosque was founded in Tijuana as part of this activity; it has functioned sporadically but has had trouble keeping going due to problems with established local leadership and supervision and finding landlords willing to rent space for Muslim activities.

Masjid Nur attracts Muslims of various ethnic groups from the east San Diego area who wish to pray close to their homes. It is creative in reaching out to nonimmigrant communities. Its Tablighi style and the fact that it is the project of specific individuals make it less appealing to some of the immigrant and African American Muslims. Some of the latter have objected to the cultural style of Masjid Nur, for example its segregation-exclusion of women. Friday services attract well over a hundred persons and had to be moved to a larger space at a recreation center on nearby 44th Street. Recently attendance at this Friday congregation was boosted when a large group of Afghanis shifted participation from the Islamic Society to this group after they were refused permission to hold a celebration (mawlid) honoring the birth of the Prophet in the Islamic Society's facility. The leadership style of Masjid Nur is devotional and relies more on the personal charisma of the leaders than that of the Islamic Center or the Ribat. Tablighi shaykhs occasionally visit from South Asia and there are connections to a South African madrasa. Members of this congregation have a pattern of holding their Eid prayers separately from the rest of the community.

The Musalla is located in the entertainment suite of an apartment complex on Winona Avenue. It was first established by "Brother Dawud," an African American Muslim, who was the manager of this ninety-one unit complex in east San Diego, the area of town with the highest crime rate and a location where many new immigrant groups initially settle. About 90 percent of the occupants are recent immigrants from Somalia. The building was previously notorious as "the worst property in San Diego" in terms of drugs and crime. As the number of Muslim tenants in the complex increased, Dawud arranged for the entertainment room to be converted into a place of prayer and an additional studio unit became the location of a Qur'anic school on the weekends. The mood of the mosque is devotional and the five prayers are offered, although most of the congregation prays at the Friday prayer at the main Islamic center mosque. A local Sufi Naqshbandi group used to hold sessions here on Thursday nights, which were attended by as many as fifty men. At that time a curtain was drawn so that those Muslims who were not participating in the ceremony could use the mosque as well. Sufi activities have now been discontinued and Dawud has moved on, but the space continues to be used as a religious community center.

Many of the Somalis are especially active in Islamic affairs. One of the most striking is a Qur'anic school established in late 1990. Held on Saturday and Sunday mornings, it is now attended by well over 100 pupils ranging in age from preschool to teenage. Classes are taught in traditional learning circles, where students gather at the feet of their teachers. The room is crowded, and the classes are divided according to five levels of proficiency and by gender with the girls' classes at one end of the large room. About 40 percent of the pupils are girls. Many of the children in the advanced class have learned half of the Qur'an by heart.

The five or six teachers are not paid and no tuition is charged. In addition to memorization of the Qur'an the children are taught hadith, Arabic language, Islamic norms of behavior, and Somali language and cultural traditions. During the week other activities such as lectures, adult study groups and English classes are held in the same space, attended by ten to forty people. A vacant unit is used for women's religious classes on Saturday and Sunday mornings, regularly attended by over thirty women. The male teacher is screened off by a curtain, and the women wear exclusively "Islamic" rather than traditional Somali dress. In November 1992, the Winona complex was taken back by the bank and sold to a new owner, who is working with various government and resettlement agencies to make his buildings function as social centers as well as residential housing. A Head Start program is slated to open in the Winona complex, and the owner is developing another complex on Bates Street called Casa Hermosa.

Muslims of San Diego (MOSD) is a group of relatively liberal Muslim professionals with a largely Indian and Pakistani leadership. This group used to sponsor lectures and dinners, which were attended by both men and women. With the founding of the Abi Bakr center this group has largely been assimilated, facilitated by the more accommodating position on women's participation at the larger center.

Muslim Student Association groups exist at United States International University, the University of California at San Diego, and San Diego State University. As the number of first-generation American Muslim students increases, these groups are becoming more active. The local student associations have begun to coordinate their activities across the various local campuses, and meetings of the leaders are held at the main Islamic center. One issue recently raised among the student leaders was how assimilationist the groups should be and whether their purpose was to inform or to convert American students.

Islamic activities at the Richard J. Donovan Correctional Facility in Otay Mesa are expanding. By 1992, 149 of the 4,600 inmates identified themselves as Muslim.[39] Statewide, some 7 percent of prisoners are Muslim. The former director of the Islamic Society, Sharif M. Battikhi, visits the prison once a month, and Alan Khan serves twenty hours a week as a volunteer chaplain. Muslim prisoners worship and study Arabic together. They have permission to eat after sunset during Ramadan but no other special concessions to Muslim dietary rules are made.

Al-Basit Academy is run by Islah Abdul Hafeez, an African American Muslima. It currently is attended by thirty students, primarily African American and both Muslim and Christian, and is located on Winnet Street in Encanto, a district in San Diego. According to Islah Abdul Hafeez it started as an alternative to gangs and drugs and now holds classes from kindergarten to high school. Islam is taught as part of the curriculum. In January 1991 the school was involved in a zoning dispute that attracted significant local media coverage, particularly because this period coincided with the war in Iraq and a bomb had been found in the Islamic Center of San Diego the previous week. The school is visible in its neighborhood because Hafeez wears full Islamic dress and the students black and purple uniforms. The City Council voted to allow the school to continue operating despite zoning violations due to the good work being carried on and heightened community sensitivities to anti-Muslim incidents.

The Nation of Islam continues to function in San Diego, where it operates a center under the original NOI name, Mosque #8. It is located on Imperial Avenue, five blocks from the original center, which is now Masjid Taqwa.

Although the Iranian community in San Diego is very large with an estimated 45,000–60,000 members,[40] many of the Muslim Iranians who immigrated here after the revolution wanted to escape religious pressures at home. In comparison to Los Angeles, a larger percentage of San Diego Iranians are Muslim, with a smaller minority of Jews, Bahais, or Armenians (Christian). One reason that religious institutions serving the Shi'a Muslim community are relatively few in number is that many of these immigrants came from the more Westernized stratum of Iranian society, a class that in the Pahlavi era was not religiously observant. La Jolla, one of the elite cities in San Diego county, is well known as home to Iranian emigres; producers of the local Middle Eastern television program estimate that 10 percent of the businesses in La Jolla are Iranian owned or managed. Iranians in San Diego tend to travel to Los Angeles for cultural or religious events and that limits the development of a distinctive community in this area. Although a small number of the local Iranians came from the prerevolutionary elite, one member of the community characterized the majority as being from the business or nouveau riche background. Again this would tend to slow the development of cultural and religious organizations in San Diego.

Some Iranian Muslims who want a religious function such as a marriage performed would feel comfortable going through one of the local mosques. In other cases, particularly at death ceremonies, a Shi'i religious functionary may be invited from the L.A. area, or one of the more knowledgeable persons from the San Diego Iranian Shi'a community might assist. In 1990 a group was established to promote religious knowledge among Iranian Shi'i immigrants. Normally about twenty persons participate in mixed gatherings; a session lasts some three hours and includes reading the Qur'an in Arabic, an explanation and discussion in Persian, a question and answer session and a recitation of the Du'a-yi Kumayl, and a prayer of Imam Ali. Up to 100 persons may participate in major religious holidays such as Ashura. Community members also travel to Los Angeles to participate in sessions there. Many families hold religious-cultural functions in their homes for personal friends; usually these are women's rituals such as sofreh and rauzeh ceremonies.[41]

Since the establishment of the Islamic regime Iranian Muslims have shared facilities with the African American community at Masjid Taqwa. About forty participants attend weekly meetings, which have a rather activist, pro-government political stance. From the mid-1970s to 1986 a small group of Hizbullahi students lived communally near San Diego State University. They maintained a hot-line with Iran, conveying messages about the Ayatollah Khomeini's decrees. In the postrevolutionary period the mood of the emigre community has been to associate support for religious activities with a pro-Islamic regime stance. Groups of like-minded acquaintances have now begun to meet in each other's homes for religious and cultural activities. This home-study model may develop as a trend for Shi'i Iranian Muslims for whom large religious gatherings carry the threat of being politicized.

A number of Sufi movements function mainly among immigrant Muslims. The major group is a branch of the Naqshabandi tariqa with Syrian connections. Sessions are held in private homes and at the Musalla. Female relatives of the participants may be initiates but they do not participate in the ceremony. Information about this group spreads through personal contacts.

Currently no Sufi groups appeal primarily to Anglo Americans, although a small group of followers of the Persian Nimatullahi order headed by Dr. Jawad Nurbaksh is trying to establish a center in a northern suburb. They disseminate information by placing their magazine, *Sufi*, in "new age" bookstores and by putting up small signs for special events at the universities. Up to the present most of the participants are Iranian immigrants. There are apparently some other small traditional Sufi groups functioning locally among the immigrants from Iran.

The Islamic Information Center of the Americas is run by Muhammad Zaki, a member of the San Diego Muslim community who produces video programming about Islam in English, Spanish, and Arabic, shown on the public access channels in San Diego and some channels in the Bay area. The unique aspect of his work is the specific targeting of the Latin population.[42] He is particularly well prepared for this task because, as the son of Egyptian diplomats, he spent a long period in the Spanish-speaking world and he is married to a woman from Columbia.

Zaki's Spanish programs are sent to Islamic centers in Latin America, where they are used in outreach courses in film, communications, and computer-generated animation. Many are question and answer sessions about Islam and the teachings of the Qur'an. In others he takes scripts based on talks by popular Islamic speakers such as Jamal Badawi, translates them into Spanish, and inserts appropriate graphics and segments from other films to illustrate them for the television audience. He also prepares pamphlets in the Spanish language for public information purposes.

In terms of outreach to the local community, Zaki focuses both on San Diego and Tijuana, Mexico, where he estimates that there is a population of 400 Muslims.[43] Although his programs generate a certain volume of inquiries about Islam, he notes that the most successful form of involving Hispanics in the religion is through personal contact and that this takes a full time commitment. Many of the Hispanic Muslims, in fact most of them in this region, are women who have married male Muslim immigrants. Zaki cites a number of instances where the marriage of a Hispanic woman to a Muslim ultimately has led to a string of other conversions among her relatives. He agrees that overall the number of such women in the San Diego area over the past ten or fifteen years is about 100. He also characterizes these couples as somewhat transient in the area because the men are often students or move here in search of a supportive Muslim community to help them get established, but ultimately they migrate elsewhere.

Some efforts have been made to target Tijuana for Muslim outreach, but there have been problems with fund raising on this side of the border, finding able and committed Spanish-speaking leaders, and obtaining a suitable space that the owners are willing to rent to a Muslim organization. Muhammad Zaki recently returned from Spain, where he recorded about twenty interviews with new Spanish Muslims to use in his programs for the Spanish-speaking audience. He also is collecting images of Muslim and Muslim-influenced monuments in Spain and Latin America to illustrate his videos for the Latin audience with the rich contributions of Muslims to Spanish history and culture.

A number of other organizations and informal groups, although not directly religious, affect the Muslim presence in San Diego. Various ethnic subgroupings among the Muslims have formal or informal organizations, for example a Saudi club where social functions and weddings are held and where Saudi women can socialize with each other. A number of other Arab nationalities, either separately or collectively, hold functions that may or may not have some religious content. A group of Kuwaiti women, for example, used to meet for social and religious observances. A new Pakistan association was recently formed that, although cultural in nature, also sponsors some religious activities such as Iftar (fast-breaking) dinners at the Islamic center. In addition, a small support group has been formed for American women (Muslim and non-Muslim) who are married to immigrant Muslims.

SUMMARY

There is a fair amount of communication and shared participation among the Muslim institutions in San Diego. A core of devout persons are connected to all of the mosques, pray at each at least occasionally, and personally know all segments of community leadership. In contrast to certain other Muslim communities in the United States there is no strong sense of ethnic rivalry or ideological conflict among the various centers.

If we were to generalize from trends within this very specific and local context to possible tendencies among Muslims in America, several observations could be made. Very few of the Muslim youth, especially the American-born teenagers of Muslim parents, participate in the life of the community, and the majority are assimilating very rapidly. The few who do attend functions with their parents tend to be young South Asian women. This suggests that in the coming years when a larger group who are children today begin to reach adolescence, some sort of youth activities will need to be established for this age group, as has occurred in the L.A. area. These activities have to be appropriate, in style and intellectual engagement, to teenagers who live and attend schools in modern American society.

A second observation relates to women's participation. Imam Aqeel el-Amin of Masjid Taqwa commented on the importance of the participation of women in his congregation and made a more general observation that in American culture it is usually women who pass on the religion. Although this has not usually been the case in the Islamic tradition it would appear to be true among Muslims in the United States based on patterns in the emergent community. The more strict Muslim literalists who do not bring their wives to the mosque are also not going to bring their children, and ultimately they will assimilate. The Muslims who practice Islam intertwined with cultural performances, such as in the Barelvi or Shi'a traditions, where the women conduct their own religiocultural rituals in the home, probably have more chance of successfully passing on the religion to the next generation. As a consequence all groups may come to recognize a greater need for the participation of women in Muslim religious life and institutions in America. The connection to the North American context through marriage to American women emerges as an interesting pattern, at least in San Diego. The Islamic Center, Ribat, and Masjid Nur all have persons in prominent leadership roles as founders or presidents who are married to American Muslim women. In contrast, the Imams who have come to San Diego thus far have all come from overseas and do not have that sense of permanent membership in the community or the direct connection to the North American context through marriage.

Finally, based on developments since 1992, it seems likely that increased segmentation of the San Diego Muslim community will occur, particularly along ethnic lines. Currently Kurds and Somalis are moving toward establishing their own Islamic centers and Afghans will likely follow. It will be interesting to continue to trace how these new centers respond to the challenges which political and class differences pose to bringing together individuals within an ethnic grouping. It seems that the more consciously Islamist members of the community will prefer to affiliate along ideological internationalist lines whereas the more traditional Muslims will choose to constitute predominantly ethnic Islamic centers. As for the "silent majority," who are nonparticipant Muslims, some seek to preserve dimensions of ethnicity such as language and traditions through cultural centers rather than religious institutions whereas others seek to assimilate to American culture as rapidly as possible.

NOTES

1. Editorial, *The San Diego Tribune* (February 8, 1991), p. B-10.
2. Interview December 11, 1991, with Hasan Abukar, director of the Islamic Society. The *San Diego Union* cited a similar estimate of 20,000 (November 14, 1992), p. B-8.

3. Estimates of the Muslim Iranian population vary from 15,000 to 60,000.

4. Including United States International University, which traditionally has had a large clientele of students from the Middle East and Iran.

5. Karen I. Leonard, *Making Ethnic Choices: California's Punjabi Mexican Americans* (Philadelphia: Temple University Press, 1992), pp. 24 ff.

6. Rajani Kanta Das, *Hindustani Workers on the Pacific Coast* (Berlin: De Gruyter, 1923), p. 20. Leonard located a manuscript census for Imperial County, 1910, which noted eighteen men of Indian origin, eight of whom were Muslim; he says that the Moslem Association of America founded in Sacramento in 1919 had a branch in the Imperial Valley among whose stated aims were "social improvement, Americanization, reform and education," p. 89. See also *Making Ethnic Choices*, p. 47. Statistics indicate that 30,000 acres were leased by Indian (Sikh and Muslim) agriculturalists in the Imperial Valley in 1921. See "The Sikhs of El Centro: A Study in Social Integration" by Robindra C. Chakravorti (Ph.D. dissertation, University of Minnesota, 1968), p. 11.

7. Karen I. Leonard, "California's Punjabi-Mexican Americans" in *The World and I* (May 1989): 615; and "Pioneer Voices from California: Reflections on Religion, Race and Ethnicity" in *The Sikh Diaspora*, ed. N. Gerald Barrier and Verne Dusenbery (Delhi: Manohar, 1989), 122 ff. Leonard notes that almost none of them were actually Hindus, about 10 percent were Muslims and the rest were Sikhs. *Making Ethnic Choices*, p. 30.

8. Karen I. Leonard, "Mourning in a New Land. Changing Asian Practices in Southern California," *Journal of Orange County Studies* 3–4 (Fall 1989–Spring 1990): 62.

9. A survey of this population in 1959 located eighty Punjabi men living in the Imperial Valley, fifteen of whom were Muslim and the rest Sikh. C. Scott Littleton, "Some Aspects of Social Stratification Among the Immigrant Panjabi Communities of California," in Ralph L. Beals, ed., *Culture, Change and Stability* (Los Angeles: University of California Press, 1964), pp. 109–110.

10. Chakravorti found sixty-five Sikhs living there in the late 1960s (p. 57).

11. Leonard has traced 304 such marriages; she calculates that in southern California 93 percent of the wives of Punjabis were Hispanic. "Pioneer Voices," pp. 122–123.

12. Leonard, *Making Ethnic Choices*, p. 56.

13. Lawrence A. Wenzel, "The Identification and Analysis of Certain Value Orientations of Two Generations of East Indians in California" (Ed.D. dissertation, University of the Pacific, 1966), pp. 26–38.

14. Leonard, "Pioneer Voices from California," pp. 121, 134.

15. Leonard, *Making Ethnic Choices*, p. 130. This arose out of the efforts of one of the Hispanic wives, Julia Deen, apparently the only wife formally to accept Islam (no. 30, p. 267).

16. See Chakravorti, "The Sikhs of El Centro"; Yusuf Dadabhay, "Circuitous Assimilation Among Rural Hindustanis in California," *Social Forces* 33 (December 1954): 138–141.

17. Interviews with Zarina Bari, May 25–26, 1991.

18. San Diego has the second largest (after Detroit) Iraqi population in the United States (est. 15,000), many of whom are Chaldean Christians. *San Diego Tribune* (February 8, 1991), p. B-10.

19. There were also large numbers of Iranian and Palestinian students in San Diego at that time who, although Muslim, were not active participants in the religious community.

20. This in distinction to earlier days when, according to the memory of early participants in the community, a group of dancers from the local Middle Eastern night club danced at a rummage sale to help raise funds for the mosque.

21. The current director, Muzammil Siddiqi, won the right to remain in his position.

22. At the institution of the council there was some debate as to whether the major facility should be a mosque. The majority involved in the initial meeting concluded that this was impractical because it could not be kept open for the daily prayers and there was no qualified Imam.

23. David Smollar, "Add Somalis to Polyglot Scene," *Los Angeles Times*, San Diego County Edition (October 26, 1992), p. B-1.

24. I. M. Lewis, "Sufism in Somaililand: A Study in Tribal Islam," in *Islam in Tribal Societies*, ed. Akbar S. Ahmad and David M. Hart (London: Routledge and Kegan Paul, 1984), pp. 140 ff.

25. See M. Hermansen, "Two-Way Acculturation: Muslim Women in America Between Individual Choice (Liminality) and Community Affiliation (Communitas)," in *Muslims in America*, ed. Y. Y. Haddad (New York: Oxford University Press, 1991), pp. 188–201.

26. Anwar Dil, "A Note on the Early History of the Islamic Society of San Diego, California," unpublished paper, p. 1.

27. *The Islamic Reporter* (January 1973), pp. 4–5.

28. Ghazi later moved to the East Coast and now runs Iqra, a Muslim educational foundation in Chicago.

29. Dil, "A Note," p. 2.

30. A notable precedent was an interfaith meeting convened by the National Conference of Christians and Jews at the Islamic Center on February 7, 1991, and attended by representatives of the Baha'i, Buddhist, Christian, Hindu, Jewish and Muslim communities. *San Diego Union* (February 8, 1991). The Islamic Society now participates actively in inter-

faith organizations. It plans to hold a special open house for its neighbors in the Clairemont area to make them more comfortable with its presence and discuss issues of common concern.

31.   Interview with Hassan Akubar, *Salaam: A Magazine of the Islamic Center of San Diego* 1 (Ramadan/March 1991).

32.   The center is currently advertising nationally for a replacement Imam. There are in addition three full-time and two part-time employees.

33.   The new program was written up in the local newspaper in "Mosque School Teaches Kids a Fourth 'R'—Religion," *San Diego Union* (November 14, 1992), p. B-8.

34.   Aqeel Al-Amin, "Yusuf Abdullah—Pioneer of Islam," *Muslim Journal* (September 30, 1988).

35.   Yusuf Abdullah's grandson Sagan Penn was later to become well known in a case in which he was prosecuted for shooting a San Diego police officer who had stopped and hurled racial epithets at him. Penn was ultimately acquitted, but his case served as a reminder of harassment to the community.

36.   *San Diego Union* (August 14, 1977), p. 16.

37.   A news item that received national coverage was the accusation of an African American Muslim, Mr. Shaheed, of mutiny during the Gulf War. Charges subsequently were dropped but the Imam was consulted as a mediator.

38.   After one Friday prayer in 1993, for example, a leaflet was distributed by some disaffected persons (falsely) accusing the institution of being sponsored by the Saudi Arabian secret police.

39.   "In Allah They Trust: Otay Mesa Prisoners Turn to Islam for Peace, New Path," *San Diego Union* (November 13, 1992), p. C-1.

40.   "By the estimate of one publisher of a local Iranian newspaper, San Diego County is home to 60,000 of his countrymen." Lawrence Osborne, "Slabs of Persia," *San Diego Reader* 22, no. 12 (April 1, 1993): 22.

41.   These are sessions in which recitations are made invoking and lamenting the tragic deaths of the Imams, food is cooked and distributed, and vows that have been fulfilled are commemorated.

42.   "Minarets over Zona Norte," *The San Diego Reader* (July 26, 1990), p. B-1.

43.   Interview Muhammad Zaki, June 1, 1991.

CHAPTER 8

Muslims of Seattle

Miriam Adeney and Kathryn DeMaster

Seattle is a young city; the first boatload of settlers docked here in 1851. Although the population of the greater Seattle area is less than 2 million people, it is the biggest urban center between Montana and San Francisco. Sizable cities like Tacoma, immediately to the south, and Bellevue, just a few miles east, and the larger city of Vancouver, Canada, three hours north, make this a major urban corridor. In general, these cities stretch north and south along waterways: Vancouver along the Pacific Ocean and several rivers, Seattle and Tacoma along Puget Sound, Bellevue along Lake Washington. This elongation has implications for the community life of Muslims in the city.

Seattle faces outward. It is the major hub in the contiguous forty-eight states for Alaskan business. Seattle also sees itself as a Pacific Rim city. Much of Washington state's production is raw materials: grain, timber, apples, and other fruits and vegetables. A large proportion of this is marketed to Asia and the Middle East. The biggest industry in Seattle, the Boeing Aircraft Company, sells globally. The second biggest employer in Seattle, the University of Washington, abounds in international connections. Quite a number of East Asian garment factories have headquarters in Seattle.

East and Southeast Asians make up a significant portion of the city's population. Because Seattle is a sister city to Tashkent in Uzbekistan and hosts an intensive Uzbek language and culture program at the University of Washington, Soviet Muslims visit periodically and have developed friendships with Seattle residents. Several hundred Afghan refugees have settle in Seattle, resulting in visits to and from Mujahideen.

MAJOR MUSLIM CENTERS

Muslims of Seattle have four major places for Friday prayers: Sheikh Abdul Kadr Idriss Mosque, also known as the Islamic Center of Seattle; the Islamic International House at the University of Washington; the Islamic School; and the South Seattle Islamic Center. The Idriss Mosque is in the north end of the city, and the Islamic International House and the Islamic School are in the middle.

Communities of Muslims, mainly students, are found in the western areas of Tacoma and Lacey. Students also constitute most of the Muslim population of eastern Washington, primarily in Spokane and Pullman. In the tri-cities area of central Washington there are settled families of Muslims, drawn by employment in a nuclear installation. Estimates of the number of Muslims in Seattle vary from 4,000 to 10,000. Of these, a mosque spokesperson estimates that there are 1,500 "committed" Muslims.[1]

South Seattle Islamic Center

The oldest center currently in use is the South Seattle Islamic Center. During the early 1960s, two Muslim men working for the Boeing Aircraft Company noticed each other skipping lunch during the Fast of Ramadan. One was a Pakistani, the other an Iraqi. They introduced themselves to each other and began to exchange social visits in their homes. Gradually other Muslim families were included.

In time this group decided that they needed a mosque. A number of families began to save money, wanting to put a down payment on a building without having to pay interest on a loan. For about a year they each saved $100 monthly, and finally bought a two-story house on a half-acre of land in south Seattle. This became a place of prayer, worship, and community life for Muslims of various ethnic backgrounds.

When the major mosque was built in north Seattle in 1981, most Muslims in the area began to worship there. The South Seattle Center now serves primarily as a worship and educational center for the Chams, a distinctive population of Muslims from Indochina. Nevertheless, some Arabs and others who work at the Boeing aircraft plant in the nearby suburb of Renton also use this mosque for Friday *salat*.

Islamic School

In 1980 the Islamic School was opened in the South Seattle Islamic Center. Five Anglo American and African American women who had converted to Islam saw the need for Islamic education and organized the school. "American Muslim women have accepted a responsibility interfacing Islam with the non-Muslim community," says Amina Saleh, a local Muslim mother, acknowledging that American women have been major movers in many of the local Muslim community projects. A Muslim lawyer put the women in touch with the information they needed to become an accredited school with nonprofit status. One family knew a Pakistani woman in Florida who was a certified teacher. She became the first instructor. Mohamed El-Moslimany, the Egyptian husband of one of the five women, happened to be in Kuwait during this period, where he solicited donations for the school. With this "seed money" the committee bought a van and initial curriculum materials.

The response of the immigrant community was very positive. According to Rafia Khokar, one of the five founders, "Just about every family who had a child in that age group sent their children to that first school." The men were more guarded in their enthusiasm than the women, but they gave financial support. The north-south elongation of Seattle, however, meant that Muslims living in the north end needed something more convenient than the South Seattle Center. During the first year of operation founder Ann El-Moslimany traveled to Kuwait for fund raising. Her success meant that in 1981 the community was able to purchase a former Hebrew school building in the more central area of Capitol Hill, where the Islamic School subsequently moved.

Today the Islamic School is a private, full-time elementary school accredited by the school district. It can accommodate 300 students, but there are at present only 25, ranging from preschool through fourth grade. Financing remains an issue. The annual tuition of $1,575 covers only 60 percent of expenses, with the remaining 40 percent donated by sponsors. The students, children of resident families, have come from Pakistan, Afghanistan, Egypt, Palestine, Kuwait, Ghana, Ivory Coast, Mali, Australia, and various parts of the United States. Non-Muslim students also are accepted.

The teachers have come from a variety of ethnic backgrounds, from Singaporean Chinese Muslim to Ethiopian. On occasion, non-Muslims have been hired to teach in the school or in the day care center, but normally in the school itself all the teachers are Muslim. The curriculum covers standard subjects, as well as Arabic language and Islamic studies. Accommodation is made for daily and Friday prayers. "Islam as a twenty-four-hour way of life" is a goal of the co-administrators Mohammad and Ann El-Moslimany, emphasizing the importance of upholding high ethical standards. Religious instruction permeates the whole curriculum, rather than being taught as a separate subject, with Qur'anic verses brought up whenever they apply. Muslim greetings, blessings, and proverbs are incorporated into daily speech. When the Middle East is in the news, and particularly when media coverage is biased, teachers make it a point to present what they consider to be a more balanced and well-rounded view.

Reflecting on why the five founders felt the need for a separate Islamic School, Rafia Khokar says, "*We* wanted to be the influencing factors in our children's lives, and we wanted to share that with others." Protecting their children from negative influences in American culture was not a primary goal. Rather, she says, "We wanted to be in a powerful position because we felt they needed to be trained for leadership roles."

What is wrong with public schools? The separation of church and state is confusing to teachers, Rafia suggests. Teachers are restricted from teaching in areas that deal with questions of morality. "What I see is that when you've got a good teacher she's strangled," Rafia comments. "I don't think public schools are about building character, they're about passing along information."

By contrast, the goals of the Islamic School are

1. To provide an environment that centers on God, and teaches our place in his creation.
2. To help children excel in leadership.
3. To nurture the brotherhood of Muslims.
4. To teach knowledge of the Arabic language.
5. To provide an academically rigorous curriculum.

"You just want your children to be God-fearing and sensitive," Rafia concludes.

Beyond its educational function, the school also serves as a general religious center. Several communities make the Islamic School their location for prayer and worship, including a group of Somali immigrants, a Shi'a group of twenty-five–fifty people, and an African American group of about twenty people.

Islamic International House

A number of Muslim student associations are present on the campus of the University of Washington. The Muslim Student Association has 30 dues-paying members and performs services for about 100 students. The Muslim Arab Youth Association (MAYA) sponsors occasional *halaqas* for discussion and brainstorming on Saturdays after *maghrib* (evening prayer). MAYA also organizes the students to help them attend the annual large national student convention in December.

The International Muslim Student Association (IMSA) started as a Persian-speaking and Shi'a group. Now it includes Sunnis and non-Persian speakers. Because its focus is political rather than religious, it has moved into a complementary role in relation to the other groups. There are also ethnically based Muslim student groups, such as the Cham Muslim Students Union.

During the early 1970s, Muslim students at the University of Washington met regularly at a Methodist church in the university district. With financial help from Kuwait, donated through the North American Islamic Trust, around 1980 a committee was able to buy a large fraternity-style house near the university. This is not a regular dormitory, but provides temporary housing for arriving students and visitors. The house is a center for Friday prayers, teaching, social gatherings, and spiritual advice. It introduces non-Muslims to Islam. House affiliates give out informational literature, respond to media coverage, write occasional articles for the university newspaper, and maintain a daily office hour. Arabs are the most involved ethnic group, followed by Indo-Pakistanis.

Because of some administrative difficulties, the West Coast representative of the North American Islamic Trust visited in October 1991 to mediate a dispute between U.W. Muslim students and community members. An interim governing board was appointed to serve for one year, with the aim of developing "a system that transfers the authority to the local community based on policies and procedures instead of individual whims."[2]

Periodically Muslim students at the university organize a *dawa* program to provide information about Islam. Such an activity took place for four days in October 1991. Booths were set up in a large room in the central student union building, where books and pamphlets about Islam were made available. At one end of the room, rows of chairs were arranged in front of a podium where prominent local Muslims gave talks throughout the day and engaged their listeners in discussions. A number of university students perused the exhibits, many were non-Muslims with internationally focused majors. On the grounds in front of the student union building members of the politically oriented IMSA engaged in loud soapbox-type oratory, targeting especially U.S. support for Israel.

The Islamic Center

The major mosque was built in 1981, endowed by a Saudi whose daughter lived in Seattle. Today it is sometimes crowded during Friday prayers, with estimates of as many as 400 attendees. The overflow congregation is forced to pray in the basement. Striking against the sky are the octagonal dome and narrow minaret. Both are sheathed in copper and topped with crescents. As one commentator describes the building:

> Clear-cut volumetric composition is one of the building's chief attributes: through careful massing the small building appears much larger and assumes a public importance unusual for its size. . . . The building's classical air is no accident: the architect derived the proportions using the Golden Section . . .
> The red brick walls are banded with buff brick and pierced by tall glass-block windows, which are topped with concrete lintels in the shape of Moorish arches. An abundance of brass, copper, and celadon green ceramic tile highlight and define the main entry.[3]

Inside there is a large room for *salat*, with a latticed balcony for the women. In the basement is a room for ablutions, a large space for social activities, and a room for the women's *halaqa* with a separate entrance from outside. The mosque commands attention as it sits on a corner lot and forms a transition between a busy retail shopping street and a residential neighborhood.

The mosque is governed by a democratically elected committee. It has a constitution that specifies the offices of the Executive Committee and the procedures for the annual elections; any Muslim who pays membership dues of $10 per month may vote. In addition to the Executive Committee, there are committees for Shura Council, Islamic Education, Zakat, Cultural-Social Functions, and Sisters. The Imam is not a professional scholar but a graduate student who volunteers his service. At present, the muezzin and the custodian are the only employees of the mosque.

The largest ethnic group at the mosque is Indo-Pakistani, with the Arabs second in size. Many other backgrounds are also represented. This is, however, a Sunni mosque. Shi'is are welcome to come and pray, but not to introduce distinctive doctrine. Also, there is an unwritten rule that no political activity is to be allowed in deference to the U.S. policy of separation between church and state.

Activities at the mosque include Friday night *halaqa* after *salat*, children's classes on Sunday mornings, and occasional youth or student meetings. A Muslim Women's Association called Sisters United Through Islam has recently been formed and holds occasional potluck dinners on Saturdays. In calling the downstairs part of the building the *community center* or *community area*, members recognize that the mosque is important as a cultural center even for Muslims who are not religious.

During the *halaqa* after *salat*, men and women meet in separate rooms. They start with a short prayer, then take turns around the circle reading the Qur'an. The goal usually is to attempt to memorize sections of the Qur'an. The meaning of a passage also may be discussed. Religiously knowledgeable people may break into the reading to correct pronunciation or expound on a point. In addition to *halaqa* meetings, the women have other gatherings to discuss such subjects as parenting and CPR. Eid celebrations, especially the *Eidul-Fitr*, the Feast of Breaking the Fast, are coordinated through the mosque but held in larger facilities. As many as 1,500 people have participated in this celebration.

The mosque also publishes an eight-page English-language news magazine several times a year, featuring articles on such subjects as financial investment, the Qur'an and the Sunna, and topics of current political interest.

CHAM MUSLIMS

A unique presence that distinguishes the Muslim community in Seattle is that of several hundred Chams, Muslims from Viet Nam and Cambodia. They first arrived in Seattle in 1978, fleeing the Khmer Rouge and the Vietnamese Communist regimes. Out of 1,000 Chams accepted by the United States in the first influx, about 400 came to Seattle, with more arriving from 1979 to 1982. Today it is estimated that there are at least 100 families of Chams in Seattle.[4] Many of the men are employed in the fishing industry, in auto mechanics, or in interior remodeling. Women often work in sewing factories or in seafood-processing plants.

Chinese records and Sanskrit inscriptions make mention of the kingdom of Champa in southern Viet Nam as early as the second century A.C.E.[5] Chams speak a Malayopolynesian language, the only sizeable group to do so in mainland Asia north of Malaya.[6] Their earliest known kingdoms were Indianized civilizations with Hindu rulers. From the ninth century on the Chams found themselves "sandwiched between two powerful and frequently aggressive neighbors—the Khmers of Cambodia and the Vietnamese of Tonkin—and had to fight hard for survival."[7] When the Vietnamese won, Sinicization went forward. From 1400 on Islam moved into this milieu, spreading out from Malacca in Malaysia through traders, teachers, and intermarriage.

Over 50 percent of the Seattle Chams came from three villages in Indochina. The decision to emigrate was a communal one. The elders met together and encouraged an exodus, mainly of the youth, in light of the suffering that they were enduring under the Khmer Rouge in Cambodia and the Communists in Viet Nam. Chams were singled out for torture and barbaric mass killings because they were a minority ethnic group, because their claim to be from the historic "kingdom" of Champa smacked of aristocratic pretensions, and because they insisted on being religious. One way the Khmer Rouge detected them was by observation at community meals. Anyone who washed in a ritual way or who did not eat pork would be suspected of retaining Muslim allegiance and would be killed. In Viet Nam the Cham wanted to escape from compulsory military service in the army of an atheistic regime. It is estimated that in a three-year period, from 1974 to 1977, the total population of Chams dropped from 1 million (60,000 in Viet Nam, 700,000 in Cambodia and the rest elsewhere) to 200,000.[8]

When they first arrived in the United States, then, the Chams came with a sense of heritage, destiny, and community support and communal obligation. In the early days they had no idea how to find other Muslims. In Pike Place Market, Seattle's renowned central farmer's market, some of them discovered a shop sign in Arabic. Going into the store they met Muslims from Pakistan. "We were so happy," reported one of the Chams. "They were like family to us, [even though] we couldn't communicate."[9] After this initial contact local Muslims came to visit them, among them Iraqi-born Jamil Abdul-Razzaq and the American convert Ann El-Moslimany.

At that time, in the late 1970s, Muslims were meeting in the older two-story home that became known as the South Seattle Islamic Center. Since then the more substantial mosque in north Seattle has been built, and most Muslims now pray there. Because the Chams live in Ranier Valley in south Seattle, however, they continue to meet in South Seattle Islamic Center. Here the elongation of the city along north-south waterways correlates with ethnic differences to encourage separate worship centers.

In contrast to Muslim students and immigrants from some other countries, Chams have maintained a strong sense of community cohesion. In Seattle they live close together, many occupying adjacent units in the same government-subsidized apartment complexes. As a result of having to struggle for their identity throughout their history they maintain a strong allegiance to Islam and are deeply devout.

Because even the South Mosque is too far to visit very often, the community recently has purchased another two-story house just blocks away from their major apartment complex. They intend to transform this into a mosque, school, and general center. Right now classes are held on Sundays for the children at the South Seattle Mosque. It is reported that some 10-year-old Cham girls have learned to recite the entire Qur'an in Arabic and have gone to Malaysia to compete in Quranic recitation competitions where they have won over native Arabic speakers. A few Cham parents hope to send their children to universities in the Middle East.

Because they were able to keep their extensive community support system intact when they immigrated, because preserving their distinct identity is something they have had to struggle for so hard and long, and because they prize orthodoxy and piety, the Cham hope to create a true Islamic neighborhood in Seattle.

OTHER MUSLIM COMMUNITIES

A Druze community of about 200 is located in Seattle. In 1908, seventy-six Druze men met in that city to start the first Druze organization in the United States. Some were new immigrants to the United States; others had come from other states. No Druze women lived in Seattle in those early years. The organization founded in 1908, El-Bakurat El-Dirziat, was a social and cultural association. Its officers were Hassan Farris, Milhem Bshir, Hussein Kassem Yahia, and Salim Najm Jaber. For worship, these men met each Thursday night, "the eve of Friday," in a designated home. Here they prayed and read the book of wisdom, *Al-Hikma*.[10] During the 1960s a wave of Druze families arrived, with still more arriving in the 1970s and 1980s, especially after the beginning of the war in Lebanon. Because they are a small community, there is no official worship center. Each family prays at home although they do celebrate Eid al-Adha, their only religious holiday, as a group. A close-knit community, they also socialize together a great deal throughout the rest of the year.

Several thousand Iranians live in the greater Seattle area. About fifty Shi'i families are known to practice their faith in Seattle itself. They meet for worship at the Islamic School, where they rent space. During Ramadan they sponsor activities two or three nights a week. They also meet to celebrate the birthdays of Imams and prophets. During Moharram up to 100 people may gather for the evening events. Because they lack an Imam, these Shi'is govern themselves by an executive committee composed of five elected officers. They operate within the guidelines of a local constitution. Elections are annual, and a majority vote decides an issue.

Alongside the regular worship meetings, the group runs a Sunday school for their children. Looking to the future, they make it a point to worship in a combination of Arabic and English. "All languages are God's languages," says Masood Irani, an engineer and a member of this worshipping community. "So we try to use English/Arabic, and try to stay away from Persian, Urdu, Afghan, Pushtu. . . . We're English-speaking. That is our goal. We defeat ourselves otherwise. We must create a religious culture based on the English language. We are *American* Muslims: we need to see it that way for our kids."

African Americans in Seattle number only about 50,000, and many are dispersed throughout the general population. Muslim African Americans worship with other Muslims or in small groups of their own. Syid Askia is one who meets with about twenty other African Americans for regular Friday prayers at the Islamic School. Askia has watched the Nation of Islam for many years. "When

Warith D. Mohammed took over the leadership," Askia says, "there was now no excuse not to be a Muslim." He formally accepted the faith in 1976. At that time a group of African American Muslims were worshipping in a local school building on Martin Luther King Way in Seattle. Askia joined them. With the national change of leadership and reorientation, he remembers tremendous confusion, fragmentation, decentralization, and falling away. However, in his view, this was also a positive time for releasing energy and realizing potential, for relearning religion. Now his group is "trying to internalize the message."

Askia believes indigenous American expressions of Islam are vitally important. Islam in Seattle is dominated too much by immigrants, students, and visitors from outside the country, he believes. Many of these people are "mesmerized by the West" and do not adequately empathize with how African Americans have had to struggle to overcome their environment. Many immigrants came from colonized countries and therefore view religion in a different way. Some immigrants come from countries where everything is provided and thus tend to depend on donations. "Even Northgate Mosque was a gift from outside." Such people are not used to having to create their own "conscious community situation," says Askia, who also feels that too much use of Arabic can create a "priest class."

Askia reflects on what being a Muslim means to him in the American context. "Al Islam by contrast took away the inferiority complex (nurtured by racism), the biggest blockage to performance." Now the challenge is to create a model Islamic community through education, business, propagation, and empowering individuals. "Our motto is: If you see a dirty glass, set a clean one next to it; don't blame the dirty glass," he suggests. Askia points to models in Atlanta and Oakland, but observes that African American Muslims in Seattle have not been as successful in moving toward this model community because "there is not a lot of collective *anything* here." Also, African American Islam often has grown stronger by absorbing the poor, he says, but this does not work so well here because "Seattle is a very generous city."

MUSLIMS IN THE AMERICAN COMMUNITY

In the past few decades, there have been some incidents of prejudicial behavior from non-Muslims. An anonymous telephone call announced a bomb threat at the north mosque. A couple of shots have been taken at the building, and some beer cans thrown at it. At Seattle Pacific University, a Free Methodist school, there was an exchange of heated comments in 1985 when some students objected to Muslim students praying on the Christian campus. Occasionally an individual has been asked, "Why don't you go back where you came from?" Muslims in Seattle as elsewhere express their sense of frustration when only Jewish "experts on the Middle East" are featured in national and local media and resource information centers.

Overall, however, anti-Muslim incidents stand out as exceptions. Seattle Muslims often try to be involved in local events, addressing schools and organizations and influencing local libraries, media, and cultural institutions. Speaking as president of the American-Arab Anti-Discrimination Committee in 1987, Riad Kayyali said, "In Seattle, we are very lucky that there is really a decent atmosphere for everyone to express their opinion."[11] According to news reporter Carol Ostrom, "Seattle, say those monitoring violence against and harassment of Arab-Americans, is an oasis of reason and understanding compared with many other cities, partly due to efforts by groups such as the Church Council of Greater Seattle and individual influential churches." In 1986 a formal coalition was formed by the Church Council of Greater Seattle, the Islamic Center of Seattle, and the Western Washington Board of Rabbis. This occurred in the aftermath of a visit from the late Meir Kahane, then a controversial member of the Israeli Parliament. As key members have moved away, however, the coalition no longer is active.

The Seattle Public Library has made efforts to improve its Islamic collection and reach out to the Muslim community. It has purchased Islamic books and audiovisual materials, published lists of books on Islam for both adults and children, sponsored an Islamic art display and a talk on Islam's contributions to the sciences, and hosted a workshop for children on the Eid holiday. During the Gulf War, the Seattle Public Library was "one of the few libraries in the United States prepared to help people cope with the trauma of the Gulf War," according to Amina Saleh, one of the founders of the Islamic School.

The Seattle Children's Museum included a series of workshops on the Eid during its Africa exhibit in the summer of 1991. The

University Bookstore, one of the largest west of the Mississippi, has introduced a section on Islamic books and continues to expand its selection of titles on Islam.

Focus on Islam is a TV talk show which airs at 9:00 P.M. Sundays on TCI Public Access Channel 29. The host is a second-generation Seattle Pakistani. It is an issues-focused educational program with a discussion format. Local Muslims appreciate the fact that it is on the air, but give it mixed reviews in terms of quality. The public station does not want to use tapes developed elsewhere, but requests local production. The station previously did run a series of tapes by Jamal Badawi, an internationally known apologist for Islam. These tapes are now available through the Seattle Public Library, thanks to a local American-born Muslim who made the connection.

A particularly difficult issue for Muslims in the United States relates to burial of the dead. Islam calls for burial on the day of death, but government regulations make this difficult. Over time the Muslim community in Seattle has worked out arrangements with certain funeral homes that are able to provide this service to the Muslim community. Currently some effort is underway to buy a cemetery for Muslims. In Mt. Pleasant Cemetery, which is now used, a section is set aside for Muslims.

To illustrate community relations in this part of the country, we note in conclusion two incidents related by local Muslims. Whether apocryphal in details or not, these contemporary legends are cited by local Muslims to illustrate the way they feel about their place in community life in Seattle. The first concerns a Palestinian from the West Bank who has been attending Washington State University in Pullman. Recently Israel called the student home. When he arrived, he was tortured and detained in custody. His American wife sought help from the community. To get the Palestinian back, the local sheriff issued a warrant for his arrest. The sheriff sent out an All Points Bulletin to pick up the young man. Soon the U.S. government was asking for the return of this "offender." Israel sent him back and he was reunited with his wife and supportive community. In another case, a gas station in Seattle hired a Muslim. Eventually, the Muslim wanted to move on. When he did, the owner asked for another Muslim to fill the position. "I'm willing to pay $1.00 more per hour if necessary," he is reported to have said. "I want a Muslim because I want somebody *honest*."

NOTES

1. Interviews with many Muslims in Seattle were conducted during October and November 1991 by Miriam Adeney, Kathryn DeMaster, and Robin Poling.

2. "Community News," *Al Huda: Newsletter of the Islamic Center of Seattle* 14, no. 7 (November 1991), p. 8.

3. David Schraer, "Northgate's Mosque: A Monument on the Strip," *Arcade* 2, no. 2 (June–July 1982), p. 2. The "golden section" to which Schraer refers is the most famous axiom for achieving pleasing proportion in the history of architectural design. According to this axiom developed by the ancient Greeks, "a line should be divided into two unequal parts of which the first is to the second as the second is to the whole" (*Encyclopedia Britannica* Vol. 17, p. 5).

4. Timothy McCarthy, Islamic Lecturer, South Seattle Islamic Center, interview, October 1991.

5. Brian Harrison, *South-East Asia: A Short History* (New York: Macmillan and Co., 1967), p. 12.

6. Robbins Burling, *Hill Farms and Padi Fields: Life in Mainland Southeast Asia* (Englewood Cliffs, N.J.: Prentice-Hall, 1965), p. 121.

7. Harrison, *South-East Asia*, p. 35.

8. Ibid.

9. Carol Ostrom, "The Moslem Way," *Seattle Times* (March 16, 1989), p. E-4.

10. Sami Abulhosn, notes from personal research in Seattle Druze records, November 1991.

11. Carol Ostrom, "Arab-Americans Find Seattle Accepting, with Exceptions," *Seattle Times* (October 24, 1987).

CHAPTER 9

To "Achieve the Pleasure of Allah": Immigrant Muslims in New York City, 1893–1991

Marc Ferris

The World Trade Center bombing catapulted a tiny cell of New York City's Muslim community into the national spotlight. This attention distorts the fact that representatives of almost every Muslim country in the world have created a distinctive Islamic tradition in New York City since the early twentieth century. The city's Islamic activities have largely taken place in Queens and Brooklyn, far from Manhattan's glitter, which camouflaged the religion's presence from most New Yorkers. Since the mid-1960s, the Muslim population in New York City has increased dramatically due to immigration, conversions, and high birthrates while Islam has spilled across the city's borders to the rest of metropolitan New York, New Jersey, and Connecticut.

Although the region's Muslims provide the vital services that keep the city's economy humming, Islamic organizations are difficult to track. After suffering decades of negative media stereotyping and hostility, dedicated networks within New York's immigrant Muslim community began making a discernible effort to revel in their heritage and spread Islam to a wider audience in the mid-1970s. Since 1980, when the city contained eight or nine mosques, immigrant Islamic associations have multiplied across the five boroughs of greater New York so quickly that by 1991 there were at least twelve immigrant mosques in Queens, fifteen in Brooklyn, two in the Bronx, six in Manhattan, and two on Staten

Island. Deriving an accurate census of Muslims living in New York City's five boroughs is more difficult than counting mosques; realistic estimates range from 300,000 to 600,000.[1]

Africans brought to the Americas during the colonial era probably introduced observance of Islamic law to the city, and Muslim seamen and other temporary migrants may have left their mark as they passed through the New York port in the late 1800s. However, white journalist Alexander Russell Webb organized the city's first documented Islamic institution. Born in Hudson, New York, in 1847 and named United States counsel to the Philippines forty years later, Webb converted from Christianity in Manila after corresponding with Bombay Municipal Council Member Budruddin Abdullah Kur in 1891.[2]

The next year Saudi Arabian businessman Hajee Abdullah Arab visited Manila and pledged to support Webb's missionary activities for Islam in the United States. Webb took the indirect route home to make fundraising trips in India, where he received money from "some of the wealthiest and most influential merchants in Bombay," and in Turkey, where he also made connections in high places. After Webb returned to New York City in 1893, he established the American Moslem Brotherhood at 30 East 23rd Street and soon attracted attention as the "Torch Bearer of Islam."[3]

Assisted by John H. Lant, Erwin Nabakoff, and Leon Landsburg, along with business manager Harry Jerome Lewis and librarian R. Othman White, the "Yankee Mahometan" also founded the Moslem World Publishing Company, which issued at least twenty-six volumes of the *Voice of Islam* and the *Moslem World: Dedicated to the American Islamic Propaganda* between 1893 and 1895. Nefeesa M. T. Keep edited the periodicals and served as the company's secretary.[4]

Dissension within the organization ultimately undermined Webb's efforts. On July 12, 1894, Nefeesa Keep locked herself in the *Moslem World*'s editorial offices and accused Webb of financial chicanery. Keep alleged that Webb failed to pay her and other staff members, that he used misleading tactics when soliciting funds from abroad, and that he bought a lavish farm and land in upstate Ulster County with money earmarked for spreading Islam throughout the country. His credibility damaged by Keep's accusations, Webb again found it necessary to confront charges of irresponsible money handling when the Nawab of Basoda, the "ruling Prince of India" who claimed to represent Webb's financial backers, arrived in New York City to check on his investment's spiritual returns. The Nawab accused Webb of squandering $140,000 to $150,000, although the two never met.[5]

Traveling to Webb's farm in Ulster Park after the Indian prince sailed off, a New York Times reporter found the "Torch Bearer of Islam" inhabiting a "miserable house." Webb admitted to the journalist that his impact upon American religious culture had been slight, pleaded hardship, and claimed that he had only received $20,000 from abroad. Recounting his first few months in New York City, Webb characterized most of his early associates as "sharks," solely interested in bleeding the American Moslem Brotherhood's treasury. Webb further asserted that his former assistant, John H. Lant, attempted to seize control of the American Moslem Brotherhood's finances by circulating a newsletter throughout India that highlighted Webb's supposed financial ineptitude. The *Times* reporter claimed that Lant shadowed the Nawab of Basoda around New York City, begging the prince to pay past wages supposedly owed to him by Webb.[6]

The *New York Times* pounced on this sordid story with a full-page, illustrated feature and ridiculed the whole cast of characters, heralding the "Fall of Islam in America" and gleefully relating the "Story of a Mussulman Propaganda That Came to Grief." Webb passed the rest of his days in relative obscurity, excepting his 1901 appointment by the Sultan of Turkey as Honorary Consul General of the Turkish government in New York. Even without the Moslem Brotherhood's internal strife, few Americans were receptive to Webb's message.[7]

Although most turn of the century New Yorkers ignored Islam, historic circumstances soon brought permanent Muslim settlers to the city. In 1907 Polish, Russian, and Lithuanian immigrants to Williamsburg, Brooklyn, founded the American Mohammedan Society, New York City's first institution organized around a mosque. Members probably worshipped in rented space until 1931, when they bought three buildings, 104, 106, and 108 Powers Street, making the Mohammedan Society the first corporate body to purchase property in New York City with the express purpose of practicing Islam.[8]

An Islamic outpost in New York for one generation, the society claimed an average of 400 members through the 1950s. Over the years, descendants from this insular Eastern European Islamic community dispersed across the tri-state region, and their Williamsburg neighborhood changed, attracting Hasidic Jews after World War II and Puerto Ricans and African Americans during the late 1950s. Now, in the 1990s, the association's elderly leaders face a challenge keeping the group together. Subsequent generations born to parents active in the Mohammedan Society, which changed its name to the Moslem Mosque during the 1960s, have mostly intermarried or found other interests.[9]

Americanization has even affected the mosque's elders, whose European heritage gave them the opportunity to assimilate quickly. Few other immigrant or African American Muslims know about or visit Powers Street, and the mosque is isolated from other Islamic activities throughout the city. In 1991, the group counted about 200 "book members," but the core of active constituents is shrinking. On a given Friday or Sunday, as many as forty elderly members may show up for prayers during pleasant weather, but a turnout of twenty is considered normal. Some leaders believe that their only hope is to keep the mosque going long enough to be able to hand the organization over to their children, should they eventually accept religion.[10]

In 1938 the Works Progress Administration's *New York Panorama* declared that the Powers Street Muslims administered the city's "only real mosque." Ten years before, however, Moroccan-born Sheik Daoud Ahmed Faisal came to the United States via Grenada and began organizing the city's second bona fide mosque, the Islamic Mission of America for the Propagation of Islam and Defense of the Faith and the Faithful. Faisal's plans languished until the Islamic Mission of America in 1939 rented a brownstone at 143 State Street, Brooklyn Heights, incorporated with New York state five years later, and bought the building in 1947. Located one block from Atlantic Avenue, the heart of Arab New York since the mid-1940s, the Islamic Mission has remained one of the city's preeminent Islamic institutions for almost half a decade.[11]

Somewhat ambitiously, Faisal deliberately referred to his mosque as a *mission*. Turning the tables on Christian foreign missionaries, who have tried to alter behavior patterns in Muslim lands, Faisal attempted to change the way Americans viewed God. Imam Faisal criticized aspects of American society that countered Islamic values, exhorting his followers not to "allow the glitters of this material world to lead you away from Islam." Conversion, the improvement of his religion's image, and the dissemination of the message of a just, compassionate God remained central to Faisal's goals for the Islamic Mission.[12]

Critical to Faisal's program was the Institute of Islam. Although a fading, painted wooden sign stands outside the mosque advertising the institute's presence, the school's main period of activity was between 1950 and 1965, when it offered daily, two-hour-long, year-round Islamic and Arabic classes for children and adults. Somewhat boldly for the politically volatile 1960s and early 1970s, the Imam explicitly designed his organization "for the enlightenment and liberation of the African and Asiatic people residing and born in the United States and in the Americas." Setting out to "educate, enlighten, and inform" Americans about Islam, Shiek Faisal presided over an unusually active mosque and school.[13]

From the late 1950s through the mid-1960s, when the Islamic Mission was one of the city's only immigrant mosques, Faisal ministered to a 300-member congregation, which included a significant share of diplomats, businessmen, and university students. During the 1970s, however, the mosque began to attract blue-collar Muslims. Statesmen and students ceased making the trip to Brooklyn and devout worshippers at the Islamic Mission sometimes derided members of the well-educated professional community as "Muslims of Holiday" or "Muslims of Friday."[14]

Faisal's labors on behalf of Islam were even more remarkable because, after he left State Street at 5 P.M., the Imam worked full-time for the federal government as an Amtrak official. Faisal's wife, Sayedah Khadijah, assisted at the mosque by chairing the Muslim Ladies' Cultural Society and providing other support. Since 1950 Mohamed Kabbaj, who came to New York City from Morocco in 1949 and worked for the Voice of America, assisted Faisal with the Islamic Mission's day-to-day administration. Kabbaj oversaw the Institute of Islam, served as president of the mosque's "Muslim Fraternity," and became the Mission's Imam after Faisal's death in 1980.[15]

One of the Islamic Mission's legacies was to bring African American and immigrant Muslims together. Faisal's mosque served as a forum where African Americans received exposure to the

Sunni tradition and were offered an alternative to Elijah Muhammad's Chicago-based Nation of Islam. Stressing that "all Muslims are brothers," Faisal attempted to promote harmony and interaction within the city's Islamic community. But space limitations at the Mission's austere three-story building virtually dictated that Faisal's institution would spawn several splinter groups and offshoot mosques. Most of these were Brooklyn based, including the Dar-ul-Islam movement during the mid-1960s, an African American Sunni organization that challenged the Nation of Islam's primacy in New York City, and Masjid Al-Farouq, bought by the mostly Yemeni Islamic Brotherhood, at 552–54 Atlantic Avenue in 1977.[16]

The relocation of the United Nations to Manhattan in 1952 magnified Islam's presence in the city. Publicity lavished upon ambassadors and dignitaries from Islamic countries by the local and national media during the 1950s enhanced the religion's image and some New Yorkers realized for the first time that they had Muslim neighbors. Although the New York Times rarely portrayed Islam in a flattering light, captioned pictures and short blurbs about Ramadan rituals and burgeoning local Islamic organizations in the newspapers demystified Islam and made Muslims more human to average New Yorkers.[17]

This move was important because the average New Yorker's perception of Islam has been more influenced by diplomats and doctors than by taxi drivers in Queens, no matter how many immigrant Muslims distribute Islamic tracts or convert brownstones, stores, and basements into mosques. Under the auspices of the Pakistani League of America, Pakistani diplomats sponsored well-attended Ramadan ceremonies at their local headquarters and at several Manhattan hotels throughout the 1950s. Aided by their home governments and private donations, professional Muslims from such diverse nations as Egypt, Pakistan, and Indonesia established the association that eventually built the city's most visible mosque—albeit after almost forty years of fund raising and planning.

In 1952 Manhattan's Muslim community organized the New York Mosque Foundation to raise money. Optimism surrounding this mosque project ran so high that the foundation established the Islamic Center of New York in 1955, which was temporarily quartered at Pakistan House, 12 East 65th Street, home of the Pakistani delegation to the United Nations. The foundation charged its Islamic Center with developing the religious, social, and educational programs that the group planned to transplant into the proposed building.[18]

Headed by University of Cairo professor Mahmoud Yousef Shawarbi, a Fulbright scholar at Fordham University, the Islamic Center's Executive Council first attempted to fill the demand for an Imam's services themselves. In November 1955 Dr. Shawarbi's successor, N. Saifpor Fatemi, who chaired Princeton University's Department of Oriental Languages and Literature, announced that the city's first mosque would be located somewhere on the west side of United Nations plaza and that work would commence within one year, "Allah willing." Although it took the Mosque Foundation until 1991 to complete their building at 96th Street and Third Avenue, the fact that representatives from a cross section of the world's Islamic nations united for a common purpose in New York City during the 1950s was significant.[19]

As progress toward completing the new mosque dragged and the need for a full-time organization became more acute, the foundation purchased a four-story building at 1 Riverside Drive in 1957, where the group has operated—almost without incident—for over thirty years. Soon after, the Executive Council imported Dr. Muhammad Shuraiba to New York, the first of an unbroken line of Imams from Cairo's prestigious Al-Azhar University recruited by the Islamic Center.[20]

In addition to these developments, other changes strengthened the practice of Islam throughout New York in the 1950s. African American Islamic influence in the city probably can be dated to the interaction between members of Marcus Garvey's camp and Noble Drew Ali's Moorish Science Temple in the 1920s. But interest in Islam among African Americans grew substantially after the Nation of Islam opened their Mosque #7 in 1946 at the Harlem YMCA. Certainly, the Nation of Islam repelled most immigrant Muslims, who questioned Elijah Muhammad's allegiance to the Qu'ran and Islamic orthodoxy. But the conversion to Islam by significant numbers of mostly Christian, native-born African Americans coincided with the immigrant Muslim movement to strengthen the city's Islamic network, exemplified in part by the Mosque Foundation, the Islamic Center, and the establishment of the city's first Muslim Student Association at Columbia University in 1956. [21]

Pakistani immigrant Abdul Basit Naeem, who lived in the Park

Slope section of Brooklyn, chronicled Islam's growth in New York City during the 1950s and the interaction between African American and immigrant Muslims in his journal *The Moslem World and the U.S.A.* Although solely responsible for producing the *Moslem World*, Naeem was more than a publisher; along with selling tapestries, prayer rugs, Islamic texts, religious articles, and handbags, he also performed marriages and taught Arabic and religious classes.[22]

Sowing the seeds for future interactions between African Americans and immigrants, as well as revealing the interest shown by the African American community in Islam, Naeem moved the site of his lessons from Brooklyn to Harlem in 1957. Not surprisingly, Naeem prayed at the Islamic Mission of America, where African Americans and immigrants regularly mixed. He published writings by Nation of Islam leader Elijah Mohammed and publicized the mosque's various activities in *The Moslem World*. Although Naeem's journal focused primarily on the immigrant community, he clearly included African Americans within the city's Islamic fabric, indicating the degree to which the religion has united people of widely differing backgrounds in New York City since at least the 1950s.[23]

Malcolm X, who arrived in New York City to serve as Imam at the Nation of Islam's Mosque #7 in 1954, brought Islam more attention during the early 1960s than the religion had ever received. But the most significant event to affect the city's immigrant Islamic community during the twentieth century occurred in Washington, D.C., where President Lyndon Johnson ratified the 1965 Immigration Act increasing quotas from non-European countries that were virtually excluded by law since 1924. Once the law took effect New York City attracted floods of Muslim immigrants from Guyana, Africa, the Middle East, and the Indian subcontinent. Later supplements to this human tide included Muslims from almost every country with a significant Islamic presence. Dedicated Muslims who came to the city in the wake of the Immigration Act rented buildings formerly used as stores, apartments, schools, and factories for Islamic gatherings, or simply prayed in each other's homes. After adjusting to American life and carving their niche in the city's economy, they began to build lasting Islamic institutions between 1969 and 1975.[24]

By the late 1970s and early 1980s, mosques and other organizations rapidly multiplied across the city. Between 1983 and 1991 the city's immigrant Muslims constructed two new mosques, broke ground for another, and organized approximately thirty more. Established largely by Pakistanis in 1976, the Islamic Center of Corona (Masjid Al-Falah) built New York City's first structure planned and conceived as a mosque at 42-12 National Street, Queens. The group first met at 101-03 43rd Avenue until they finished the new facility in 1983. Attached to a Jehovah's Witness Hall and down the street from a spiritualist Christian center, Masjid Al-Falah's modest dome and minaret hover above a largely Puerto Rican and Colombian neighborhood. The Islamic architectural features are grafted onto a square two-story building, which houses two levels of prayer rooms and a funeral parlor in the back lot.[25]

Masjid Al-Falah's carpeted main prayer space can accommodate 200 tightly packed bodies, if necessary, although a typical Friday service attracts 40 to 50 men, who generally represent a wide range of ethnic identities. A women's prayer room, completely hidden behind smoked-glass, sits invisibly behind the austere main prayer hall. A majority of Pakistanis make up the Board of Directors and its Managing Committee, which oversees day-to-day operations. The Masjid's Imam is also Pakistani, although Bangladeshis exert a secondary influence within its leadership.[26]

It is not surprising that working-class Pakistanis played a leading role in erecting the city's first mosque. Often more devout and usually possessing a better command of English than most other Muslim immigrants, Pakistanis have promoted Islamic observance in New York City since the 1950s. In addition to building the city's first mosque, Pakistani newsstand owners and restaurant workers helped institute at least six other houses of Islamic worship throughout the city during the 1970s and 1980s, mostly in Queens, and organized such proselytizing groups as the Islamic Circle of North America, formally established in 1971 to propagate Islamic teaching.

A Pakistani-dominated organization was also involved in the construction of Queens' new mosque at 137–64 Geranium Avenue in 1991. Founded in 1975, the Muslim Center of New York first rented an apartment at 41st Avenue in Flushing, then purchased a $75,000 house in 1979, and finally bought an adjacent single-family home in 1987 for $350,000 "in cash." After demolishing the houses, the group started building their Mosque and Community Center on May 21, 1989.[27]

Muslim Center officials designed the new 18,600 square foot concrete complex to provide adequate prayer space for over 500 worshippers, a community hall for Islamic functions, and educational facilities to host daily and weekly classes. They also planned the building with separate stairways and prayer spaces for men and women, a caretaker's apartment, a "full fledged administrative office," and two rental units. For the center's ground-breaking ceremony, mosque leaders solicited responses from the Queens borough president and the neighborhood's congressional representative, who wrote letters of congratulations, and the mayor, who showed up at the event in the midst of a heated reelection campaign. The local mass media ignored the event, probably because the mosque's Queens location is not glamorous.[28]

In contrast, Manhattan's first mosque, the Islamic Cultural Center of New York, at Third Avenue and 96th Street, with its impressive minaret and dome, received great fanfare after it hosted Eid-al-Fitr services for the first time in its new building on April 15, 1991. The direct descendent of the New York Mosque Foundation's efforts during the early 1950s, the "Mosque of New York" symbolizes Islam's ascendancy in New York City. Although likened to a Mariott hotel and flanked by a housing project to the north and a generic apartment tower across Third Avenue, the Islamic Cultural Center's mosque stands near the crest of a gently tapered hill and commands a distinguished presence on its nondescript block. The mosque's dedication served as a source of pride and interest for most of the city's Muslims and was particularly associated with the Persian Gulf oil states, especially Kuwait. Even though representatives from forty-six Muslim nations served on the organization's Board of Trustees, Mohammad A. Abulhasan, named permanent representative of the state of Kuwait to the United Nations in 1981, chaired this body and raised a large portion of the money that finally completed the building.[29]

Completing the city's most visible mosque took almost forty years. Even after the New York Mosque Foundation purchased the 96th Street plot in 1966, the group advertised the mosque's imminent completion four times between 1967 and 1989. Several disputes mired construction in delay, including charges that the mosque's leaders fired an Iranian contractor for hiring a Jewish firm as technical consultants. Modernists and traditionalists on the board also clashed over the edifice's architecture, which resulted in a compromise plan drafted by Skidmore, Owings and Merrill.[30]

Even with the embarrassing construction snags, the Islamic Center's new mosque signalled the rising Muslim population in New York City. The organization's transition to the new building from 1 Riverside Drive presented some logistical problems, although the center was still keeping the Upper West Side mosque open for Jum'a prayers in January of 1992, and will probably continue to maintain the building. Hoping to make a measurable impact upon the city's religious culture, the Islamic Center has planned to sponsor educational cultural outreach programs designed to introduce New Yorkers to Islam. Future goals include building a school and Imam's quarters next to the mosque.[31]

Sandwiched between the affluent Upper East Side and Harlem's southeast border, the Islamic Center occupies a unique position to further bind the African American and immigrant Muslim communities. This is not an easy task because each group is so culturally distinct. However, relations between the two communities remain cordial, with several examples of intergroup cooperation. The Nation of Islam rarely appealed to New York City's immigrant Muslims and even today most mosques in primarily African American neighborhoods seldom attract outsiders. Moreover, as John Jay College African American Studies professor Yusuf Nuruddin has noted, some foreign-born Muslims display "a racist attitude that is no different from the attitude of Europeans toward African Americans." But since Elijah Mohammad's son and successor, Warith Deen Mohammad, dissolved his organization and encouraged followers to adopt the Sunni tradition in 1985, relations between the two communities have improved.[32]

On the whole, Islam has done more to unite than divide its practitioners in New York City. The most significant bond that all of the city's Muslims share is their minority status. Being more recently established in New York than most other mainline religions has goaded many Muslims to work hard building institutions and spreading their faith. For the city's religiously active African Americans and immigrants alike, mosques assume the central role in Islamic life and serve symbolic functions. Even though mosques have sprouted seemingly overnight across Queens and

Brooklyn—where most of the city's non-professional immigrant Muslims live—it is impossible to determine the extent to which members of the city's Muslim population avail themselves of their services and activities or attend to religious duties such as Islam's five demanding "pillars."

The city's immigrant-founded mosques are as impossible to generalize about as the people who pray in them. Each institution displays varying degrees of organizational cohesion, ranging from hierarchical, tax-exempt corporations that can navigate the city's labyrinthine bureaucratic maze so as to successfully build a mosque to groupings that gather irregularly in someone's basement. Most of the city's mosques attract an amalgam of regular congregants, shopkeepers from the local neighborhood, or perhaps a few cab drivers in the vicinity during Jum'a.

One of the city's only mosques to attract a trickle of outsiders was the American Association of Crimean Turks, which has been located at 45-09 Utrecht Avenue, Borough Park, Brooklyn, since 1970. Founded as a private social club in 1961, it provided a means for the Crimean Turks to maintain their heritage. After they bought their building in 1970, the foundation of that heritage has increasingly focused on Islam. Like the Crimean Association, some of the city's other mosques serve as fraternal, immigrant-aid, and social organizations as well as places to observe Islamic laws in a group setting. For instance, the Islamic Brotherhood, which governs Brooklyn's Masjid Al-Farouq, serves multiple roles within a community constantly welcoming new members unfamiliar with New York City life.[33]

But no matter how blurred the national makeup of worshippers at the vast majority of New York City's immigrant mosques may be, most of the city's Muslims vigorously profess kinship by dint of religion regardless of historic enmities or present-day class and political alignments. In 1987 a New York Times reporter cited Muslim World League associate director Dawud Assad as saying that "Muslims from disparate countries . . . are finding that in America they can establish ties around their religion rather than their nationality." Certainly, New York City's unique polyglot has provided Muslims from around the globe the opportunity to pray together at local mosques. Nowhere on earth are Muslims from so many different backgrounds living in such close proximity, a situation that accentuates commonalities rather than differences.[34]

Good relations between Sunnis and Shi'is exemplify intra-Muslim unity within the city. Shi'i organizations date from at least the late 1970s, when researcher Lois Gottesman documented the existence of a Shi'a Mosque and the Shi'ite Association of North America, both in Queens. Also during the late 1970s, Maxine Fisher located the Bohra Jamaat of the Eastern United States, a group of about seventy Indian Shi'i families that met monthly at a rented hall, as well as an East African group of Ismaili Shi'is. In the 1980s, Earle Waugh identified a Shi'a Muslim Association of North America at 108 53-63 62 Drive, Forest Hills, Queens.[35]

Today, Shi'is represent a tiny minority within the city's Muslim community, numbering perhaps 8,000 in the metropolitan area and 2,500 in the five boroughs. Shi'is worship regularly at Sunni Mosques, including Masjid Al-Falah, and the reverse is also true. In addition to the Iraqi-based Al-Khoei Foundation in Jamaica, Queens, which refashioned a pre-existing building with a minaret and other Islamic features, another group of Shi'is, known as the Islamic Guidance, prays in a building in front of Brooklyn's Masjid Al-Farouq. This organization includes Iraqis, Pakistanis, Indians, and East Africans.[36]

Most of the city's immigrant mosques now attract eclectic congregations. For example, the Elmhurst Muslim Society, organized in 1969 by Pakistanis in the basement of an abandoned school building at 85–37 Britton Avenue, regularly welcomes Muslims from Syria, Afghanistan, Egypt, and Bangladesh to Friday prayers. At the same time it is also true that the city's Islamic institutions are usually organized by people who share more in common than religion, because nation of origin and primary language also define the identities of most Muslim New Yorkers.

One of the city's oldest immigrant mosques, the Albanian-American Islamic Center of New York–New Jersey, also presented an example of tolerance to the Muslim community. About 50,000 Muslims in the New York metropolitan region left Albania to escape persecution from Inver Hoxha's Communist government, which declared Albania an atheist state in 1967. Led by Imam Isa Hoxha, New York City's Albanian Muslims converted a former mansion at 1325 Albemarle Road, Flatbush, Brooklyn, into a mosque in 1972. Although Albanians owned and administered the building and oversaw the center's programming, they overlooked ancient animosities and welcomed Turks to religious observances.

Pakistani and Arab neighbors regularly attend Jum'a prayers as well.[37]

Also typical of the newly established immigrant mosques now flourishing in New York City is Masjid Fatima, founded primarily by Pakistani taxi-drivers and mechanics in 1987 at 58th Street and 37th Avenue, Woodside, Queens. Occupying the basement of a car services garage and located in a desolate factory district, Masjid Fatima attracted about 250 worshippers each Friday during 1991. Arabs make up almost half of Masjid Fatima's congregation while the rest came from India, Pakistan, and Bangladesh; several African Americans and some Anglo Americans pray there as well. Collections pay the rent, support the congregation's Imam, and give the mosque's leaders hope that they will one day buy or construct their own building.[38]

Most newly established, and rapidly overflowing, immigrant mosques in New York City share this yearning. On November 2, 1991, for example, the mostly Pakistani Islamic Center of Brighton Beach (Masjid Omar), at 230 Neptune Avenue, Brooklyn, held a fund-raising dinner at a local high school to finance their $120,000 building expansion plans. Even mosques organized by professionals shop for mosque sites. The Islamic Society of mid-Manhattan's Uthman bin Affan Mosque, an Egyptian group that meets at area hotels for Friday prayers, has solicited donations from the Muslim World League, foreign governments, and private individuals to buy their own structure.[39]

Islamic organizations unaffiliated with a particular mosque, such as the Islamic Circle of North America (ICNA), the Muslim Foundation of America, Inc., and the Islamic Foundation, Inc., Center of the Islamic Movement of Queens, a *dawa* group organized by Muslims from all over the world in 1990, have also increased their activities within the community. Of the three, the Islamic Circle has sponsored the most ambitious program, which includes the establishment of ten branches in the United States, two in Canada, and one each in the Caribbean and London.

Updating Sheik Faisal's goals for his Islamic Mission of America, the Islamic Circle aims to "achieve the pleasure of Allah through establishing the Islamic system in this land." To fulfill this goal, and to assist their coreligionists, ICNA provides Muslim banking and matrimonial services, publishes and distributes tracts about Islam, operates a mail-order video and book trade, and has published its periodical, *The Message*, quarterly since the mid-

1970s and monthly since 1989, among other local, national, and international projects. Illustrating ICNA's zeal, the group estimates that only one-tenth of the Muslims who live near a mosque regularly attend prayers, so the group plans to computerize a Muslim Data Base "to reach to these 90% Muslims who are not involved in any Islamic activity [sic]." [40]

Another group, the Muslim Foundation of America, focuses its efforts locally, sponsoring an annual banquet at the Roosevelt Hotel and the United Muslims' Day Parade, which has marched through midtown Manhattan one Sunday each September since 1984. Also contributing to the city's Islamic flavoring, in 1976 the Mecca-based Rabitat opened its New York City branch of the Muslim World League and Council of Masajid, which makes financial and other support available to eligible mosques, among other programs.

Islam's vigor in New York City is also demonstrated in other ways. *The Minaret,* a biweekly newspaper established by Indian immigrant Mohammad Abdul Munim in 1974, continues to attract local advertisers. Beginning in the 1980s Muslims took to the city's parks en masse to celebrate Eid-al-Fitr. Muslim Student Associations at local universities and colleges, which date to Columbia University in 1956, exhibit varying levels of enthusiasm and influence. While Columbia's organization remains the city's most influential MSA, Muslim student groups also exist at City College, Queens College, New York University, St. John's University, the College of Staten Island, York College, and Brooklyn Polytechnic Institute.[41]

One of the most significant recent examples of Islam's flowering in New York City during the early 1990s has been the effort to spread *dawa* among Latinos by PIEDAD (Propagacion Islamica para la Educacion y Devocion de Ala'el Divino). Founded in 1987 by Khadijah Abdelmoty, a Puerto Rican immigrant to New York City and convert to Islam in 1983, PIEDAD has reacted to the increased interest in Islam among Latino women married to Muslims and young Latino men in prison. Ms. Abdelmoty relies upon networks of localized support groups, acts as a mediator between Latino Muslims and the rest of the city's Islamic community and also serves as an information outlet. PIEDAD has worked with the Islamic Circle of North America on Spanish translations of the Qu'ran and other Islamic literature.[42]

Although the group has begun reaching out to the whole

Spanish-speaking Muslim community, which is centered in New York City, Ms. Abdelmoty designed the organization as a women's group. Women who convert to Islam and marry immigrant Muslims face unique adjustment problems, and PIEDAD has addressed such issues as employment outside the home, day care, child rearing, and marriage disputes. The group's activities stimulate dialogue about the role of women in society, a thorny and potentially volatile subject among many immigrant Muslims.[43]

The conversion to Islam by African Americans, Latino Americans, and even Anglo Americans presents a unique situation to foreign-born Muslims. With the infusion of new blood, Muslims may be welcoming people into the religion who may eventually weaken Islam's cohesion and orthodoxy. As American Muslims accept those from different backgrounds into the fold, these converts will either change Islam or be changed by it.

The American impact upon Islamic practice will remain an important issue for several generations, but the most pressing potential problem faced by New York City's foreign-born Muslim population is whether or not they will allow American society to dilute their Islamic culture and values. New York City's Muslims are still a minority that exerts a relatively small impact upon mainstream American culture. Like other immigrants to the United States, those Muslims who plan to stay in America for several years must grapple with assimilation and Americanization. Most Muslim New Yorkers strike a precarious balance between religious, national origin, and American identities; many proudly assert their status as Islamic Americans and face the prospect that time may erode their sense of self. Certainly, New York City exposes its residents to the most concentrated dose of American culture and vice available. At the same time the city's settlement pattern—and sheer size—has allowed immigrants to carve out neighborhoods that foster, rather than inhibit, recognizably distinct immigrant cultures. It will be interesting to see how—or if—Islam adapts to American society in New York City.

Homogenization threatens Islamic purity in the United States and the city's first-generation immigrants must sometimes battle hard to instill Islamic values in their children and grandchildren. Even though the city's Islamic groups have begun to complete their longed-for mosques, some parents still fear that American society will "devour" their children. And with good reason: New York

City's secular lures have always attracted second-generation immigrants from around the world to shed tradition and identify with the generic aspects of American culture. At the city's 1991 Muslims' Day Parade I noticed one child marcher dressed in a Teenage Mutant Ninja Turtles tee-shirt clutching his colorfully robed mother's hand.[44]

Beginning in 1977, several concerned Muslims with the means to effect change expressed their determination to establish full-time schools, where they planned to provide their children with a sense of Muslim history and identity. Schools have existed as adjuncts to mosques for years, but now separate institutions, analogous to Catholic schools, have also rooted themselves in Jersey City, in Queens, and in Westbury on Long Island. Struggling with limited resources, most of the city's Islamic schools still remain in fledgling status.[45]

The Al-Iman Elementary School at 137-11 89th Avenue in Jamaica, Queens, a branch of the Shi'i Imam Al-Khoei Foundation at 89-89 Van Wyck Expressway, Jamaica, Queens, enrolled its first eighty-five pupils in September 1991. Under the leadership of Iraqi principal Fadhel Al-Sahlani, the school's African American, Latino American, and immigrant prekindergarten, kindergarten, and first to sixth grade students attended a full-time program reflecting "a traditional SAT preparatory course of study." Al-Iman supplemented these classes with Islamic studies, including "Qu'ran, Hadith, History, Ethics, and Beliefs." The seminary currently charges a modest $950 tuition per year and plans for future expansion.[46]

Schools founded by African American Muslims, including the city's two Sister Clara Muhammad schools, which operate at Masjid Malcolm Shabazz (102 West 116th Street) and Masjid Nuruddin (105-01 Northern Boulevard, Jackson Heights, Queens), also promote intra-Muslim interaction and are much better established than schools created by immigrants. Al-Madresa Al-Islamia, another African American administered full-time school located since 1977 in Crown Heights, Brooklyn, presently enrolls some 135 students, including African American, Latino American, and American-born sons and daughters of immigrant parents.[47]

New Yorkers have generally afforded foreign-born Muslims freedom of worship and education, but certain events have triggered hostility toward immigrant Islamic institutions. In the wake of the 1979 Iranian hostage crisis, assailants torched the Islamic Center of Corona's old building at 101–03 43rd Avenue in Queens, causing light damage, and the police reported several other bias crimes involving Muslims. Even in the new structure, Masjid Al-Falah suffered another vandal's attack on Halloween night 1985. Someone lit a fire in the mosque, attempting to burn down what was then the organization's one-story building, although the fire never caught.[48]

Hints that tensions between Muslims and non-Muslims did not occur solely in response to world events included a July 1988 assault outside the mostly Pakistani and Indian Islamic Center at 50-11 Queens Boulevard. Accused by mosque worshippers of being "rude and nasty," the police could not determine exactly what triggered the violence between one group of Muslims and another of Latino men. Police captain Maurice Collins claimed that the fight stemmed from a "clash of cultures" and a "general state of mistrust and animosity" and surmised that the brawl evolved from an earlier traffic accident. The center's Imam, Anwer Ali, believed that as the neighborhood's Jewish and Italian character gave way to a mixed immigrant flavor, many recent, mostly Puerto Rican, newcomers targeted the Indians and Pakistanis for taking away jobs, housing, and commerce. But Imam Ali also admitted that misperceptions about Muslims by average Americans probably contributed to the viciousness of the assault, and claimed that the attackers shouted vile slurs against Islam and Muslims. As disturbing as this incident was, the Police Department's bias unit, created in 1981, investigates relatively few bias crimes directed against Muslims or mosques.[49]

Partially mitigating hostility toward Islam in New York City was the arrival of 8,000–10,000 Afghan refugees after the 1978 Soviet invasion of Afghanistan. Led by Habibullah Mayar, the city's Afghans swelled the ranks of worshippers at Queens and Brooklyn mosques and organized the Afghan Community in America to rally public opinion and government support behind the Mujahadeen rebels who fought the Soviet Army. The presence in New York City of Muslims given immediate sympathy by the city's news media and lauded as allies in the fight against Communism by President Reagan elevated Islam's image in the minds of some New Yorkers.[50]

Internally driven by the desire to obey and observe Islamic law and externally motivated by what many of them perceive to be a hostile environment, New York City's Muslims have labored to ensure that Islam will evolve into a significant social force within the five boroughs. Beginning in the 1980s, after the Iranian revolution, the fear of terrorism, the Salman Rushdie affair, and the World Trade Center incident have created a feeling of urgency among the immigrant Muslim New Yorkers. They had responded by attempting to fight negative stereotyping and to play a more pronounced role in local affairs. Negative experiences aside, New York City has provided fertile ground for the world's most cosmopolitan Muslim population to forge a flourishing, unique, and inclusive Islamic community.

NOTES

1. A City University of New York study counted 300,000 Muslims in the state, and the Islamic Mission of America's Imam Mohamed Kabbaj figured that 2,500,000 lived in the New York metropolitan region.
2. Shalom Staub, *Yemenis in New York City* (Philadelphia: Balch Institute Press, 1989); *New York Times* (October 3, 1916; December 1, 1895).
3. *New York Times* (July 14, 1894; December 1, 1895); *New York Tribune*, (February 24, 1893).
4. *New York Times* (October 8, 1893, July 14, 1894, December 1, 1895); *New York Tribune* (February 24, 28, 1893). *The Union List of Serials in Libraries of the United States and Canada*, 3rd edition, Edna B. Titus, ed. (New York: H. W. Wilson and Co., 1965) ed. Edna Brown Titus, 3d ed. (New York, 1965), lists that Webb published more than twenty-six volumes of *The Moslem World* and gives dates as 1893+. Webb wanted to publish weekly, but could barely issue a monthly, by himself, in December 1895.
5. *New York Times* (July 14, 1894; December 1, 1895).
6. *New York Times* (December 1, 1895).
7. *New York Times* (December 1, 1895; October 1, 1901).
8. *Book of Conveyances*, Brooklyn City Register, Block 2781, Lot 12; conversations with Mosque officials.
9. Conversations with Mosque officials.
10. Conversations with Mosque officials.
11. *New York Panorama: A Companion to the WPA Guide to New York City* (New York: Pantheon Books, 1984; reprint of 1938 edition), p. 117. Shiek Daoud Ahmed Faisal, *Islam the True Faith: The Religion of Humanity* (New York: by the author, February 1965), pp. 97, 110. Faisal,

who was born on October 8, 1892, of a Moroccan father and a Jamaican mother, twice stated that the mission's founding date is 1928, which is probably the date he came to the United States. Conversations with Islamic Mission of America Imam Mohamed Kabbaj. *Book of Conveyances*, Brooklyn City Register, Block 270, Lot 19.

12. Faisal, *Islam The True Faith*; p. 17; conversations with Imam Kabbaj.

13. Faisal, *Islam The True Faith*, pp. 96 B, 110; conversations with Imam Kabbaj.

14. Faisal, *Islam The True Faith*, p. 78; *New York Times* (January 9, 1956); conversations with Imam Kabbaj.

15. Fasial, *Islam The True Faith*; *New York Times* (September 1, 1952); conversations with Imam Kabbaj. The federal government created Amtrak in 1973.

16. Faisal, *Islam The True Faith*, p. 15; *Book of Conveyances*, Brooklyn City Register, Block 186, Lot 25.

17. *New York Times*, (June 25, September 1, 1952; May 24, November 14, 1955; January 9, 1956; October 26, 1957).

18. New York Telephone Company, *Manhattan Telephone Directory, 1952–53*; *New York Times* (September 1, 1952), vaguely referred to a "drive to be started for funds to build [a mosque in New York]"; *New York Times* (May 24, 1955).

19. *New York Times* (November 14, 1955).

20. New York County, Hall of Records, Room 205, Block and Lot Book; the only incident at the center was an alleged takeover by five African American Muslims, *New York Times* (December 7, 8, 1966).

21. Robert A. Hill, ed., *The Marcus Garvey and Universal Negro Improvement Association Papers* (Berkeley: University of California Press, 1983), vol. 5, p. 681, n. 4; information supplied by officials at Masjid Malcolm Shabazz, name given to Mosque #7 in 1976; *New York Times* (October 26, 1957).

22. *The Moslem World and the U.S.A.* 2, no. 5–6 (May–June 1957).

23. Ibid.; in 1957, for example, Naeem advertised the Mission's annual bus trip to its upstate retreat and model Islamic village at East Fishkill, which Imam Faisal bought for $100,000 in 1955 with help from the Saudi Arabian government; Faisal, *Islam The True Faith*.

24. These include the Elmhurst Muslim Society (1969), the Islamic Circle of North America (formally chartered in 1971, but active since 1968), the Albanian American Islamic Center of New York–New Jersey (1972), and the Muslim Center of New York (1975).

25. Discussions with Imam Paracha.

26. Conversations with Imam Paracha; among those present for afternoon prayers on Friday, November 29, were about forty men, includ-

ing several Pakistanis and African Americans, some Arabs, a Malaysian, an Indonesian, four Anglo Americans, two young African American boys, a 3-year-old girl who wandered about while her father worshipped, and several elderly men, who supplicated for about eight minutes before abruptly splitting up. A circle of ten men sat for another five minutes engaging in religious discourse.

27. "Muslim Center of New York, Souvenir, Ground Breaking Ceremony and Fund Raising Dinner, May 21, 1989," privately published.

28. Ibid.

29. *New York Times* (April 16, 1991); Jonathan Traub, "The Road to Mecca," *New York Magazine* (June 24, 1991), p. 40; *Resalah: The Bulletin of the Islamic Cultural Center of New York* 1, nos. 1–3.

30. *New York Times* (February 17, 1967; January 2, 1968; October 28, 1984; May 29, 1987; September 15, 1988; September 26, 1988; October 21, 1988); Traub, "The Road to Mecca," pp. 38–39.

31. Conversations with Mosque officials; *Resalah* 1, no. 1–3.

32. Traub, "The Road to Mecca," p. 41; Zaheer Uddin, "Did '80s Teach Us Anything? An Overview of Islam in North America," *The Message International* 13, no. 8 (January 1990).

33. Conversation with an Association official; the city's other Turkish Masjid, the Fatih Mosque at 59-11 8th Avenue, Brooklyn, attracts Muslims from around the globe to Jum'a prayer like most of the city's other Mosques.

34. *New York Times* (April 28, 1987); in fall 1991, I observed this phenomenon during Friday prayers at 1 Riverside Drive, at the Islamic Mission of America, at the Islamic Cultural Center's Mosque of New York, and at Masjid Al-Falah, as well as at the Muslim World Day parade.

35. Lois Gottesman, *Islam in America: A Background Report* (New York: American Jewish Committee, Institute of Human Relations, 1979); Earle Waugh et al., *The Muslim Community in North America* (Edmonton, Canada: University of Alberta Press, 1983), p. 288; Maxine Fisher, *The Indians of New York City: A Study of Immigrants From India* (New York: Heritage Publishers, 1980), pp. 148–149.

36. Estimates supplied by Al-Khoei Foundation.

37. *New York Times* (November 13, 1972); conversations with Imam Hoxha.

38. Conversation with a mosque official.

39. Flyers circulated by the Islamic Center of Brighton Beach, Inc., and the Islamic Society of Mid-Manhattan.

40. ICNA pamphlet, "An Introduction to I.C.N.A." November, 1991; Zaheer Uddin, "Did '80s Teach Us Anything?"

41. *New York Times* (May 19, 1985; July 14, 1989; October 26, 1957).

42. Conversations with Khadijah Abdelmoty; PIEDAD literature.

43. Ibid.

44. Uddin, "Did '80s Teach Us Anything?"

45. *New York Times* (November 25, 1977).

46. Al-Khoei Foundation brochure for the Al-Iman Elementary School; the group first opened a New York City branch in 1978.

47. Conversation with a Sister Clara Mohammad School official, who claimed three immigrant Muslim students attended the Harlem school, and the Queens school enrolled a significantly larger proportion; conversation with Principal Abdul Basir.

48. *New York Times* (November 22, 23, 1979); conversations with Imam Paracha; Police Department of New York City, Bias Incident Investigation Unit.

49. *New York Times* (July 7, 1991); conversations with Police Department's Bias Incident Investigation Unit officials.

50. Eleanor Lerman, "Home Free," *New York Daily News Magazine* (July 24, 1988); "Afghan Refugees Are Supported," *West Orange Chronicle* (New Jersey) (January 14, 1988); "Holy Name Treats Refugee," *Teaneck Suburbanite* (November 8, 1989); "Bronxville Hospital Treats Afghan Freedom Fighter," *Gannett Westchester Newspapers* (December 12, 1986); "Afghans in the City, Deeply Bitter over Summit, Try to Help Homeland," *New York City Tribune* (January 1, 1988); "U.S. Afghans Suspicious of Soviet Pullout," *New York Newsday* (May 16, 1988); Thomas Kean, governor of New Jersey, proclaimed March 22, 1988 as "Day of the Afghan Refugee."

CHAPTER 10

Activities of the Immigrant Muslim Communities in Chicago

Asad Husain and Harold Vogelaar

Chicago, one of the most important service, information, and high-tech centers of North America and the largest city in the Midwest with a population of over 6 million, contains an estimated 300,000 Muslims. However, a thorough case study of Muslims in Chicago has never been done, nor does this paper purport to be one; this study depends on (1) oral tradition; (2) early Muslim newspapers; (3) unpublished dissertations written for the Anthropology and Sociology Departments of the University of Chicago; (4) an unpublished monograph of Asad and Asifa Husain; and (5) newsletters and published materials of different Muslim organizations in Chicago.

WAVES OF IMMIGRANTS

First Wave, 1885–1893[1]

The first group of Muslims came to Chicago during the late nineteenth century, neither in large numbers[2] nor with the idea of staying permanently. According to Dr. Abdul Jalil al-Tahir, they came because "The homeland was in the grip of the feudal system until the civil war between the Christian Syrians and the Muslim Palestinians which took place in 1860. The peasants were rapidly losing proprietorship in the soil and becoming serfs. Christian Syrians and Muslim Palestinians sought security elsewhere."[3]

It was never the intention of these new Muslims to live permanently in Chicago. Their goal was to amass as much wealth as possible in the shortest time and then return to the homeland to enjoy it in peace and quiet. They wanted to remain as foreigners and had no desire to be assimilated into American culture and society. They segregated themselves and chose to live in an isolated area on the border of the African American district in the southern part of the city.[4] Here they settled down and only gradually developed relations with their neighbors. Though aware of Islam and Islamic practices, they did little more than keep the faith and offer prayers separately, not in congregation (jama'ah).

Most Muslims who came to Chicago in the late nineteenth century were farmers, laborers, and peddlers. Many of them sold goods on the street or operated small shops. They had little formal education and their knowledge of Islam was extremely limited. Because they planned to return, many did not bring their families. Those who stayed here tended to marry within their own group; a few also married into the Spanish, Mexican, and Jewish communities.[5] Because they did not want their children to become Christian, some actually sent them home for religious education. Most of the children growing up here did in fact assimilate into the society, although with only a few exceptions they did not become Christian.

These early Muslim immigrants in Chicago left no significant sign of their existence in the history of this city. Their practice of Islam was minimal, and they did little to propagate Islamic ideology in this area. Their efforts to mix with the local population were tenuous. A few of the early families are still surviving and have identified themselves with one or other of the Islamic groups in Chicago, but most have blended into the American melting pot.[6]

Muslims of this early period organized a few social clubs, such as the Bytinyia Society that in 1924 was given the name Arab Club. The purpose of these clubs was to teach children the Arabic language and Islamic values to make the younger generation aware of their cultural heritage. Some wished to concentrate on Palestine, so another club was established, called the American Arab Aid Society, whose purpose was to provide financial help to Palestinian refugees. According to Imam Kamil Advich of the Yugoslav (Bosnian) Muslim Community, people from his country established the first religious society in Chicago in 1906 under the name *Khairat ul-Umma*.[7]

It appears that the intention of all these clubs and societies was to provide a respectable place for religious teaching for Muslims with the hope of eventually building a mosque for prayers. However, formal religious education for children remained minimal, and no mosque was established. As a result children grew up knowing little of their faith. As the current brochure of the Islamic Foundation School puts it: "Of those Muslims who came here in the first quarter of this century, their children are almost 100 percent lost."[8] Still, for some, religion did serve as a locus of identity as they assimilated in the American culture and society.[9]

Second Wave, 1917–1945

By the turn of this century, the political climate of Europe was getting more and more cloudy. The disarray of the Ottoman Empire encouraged the Arabs to nurture the idea of nationalism, a force that eventually broke apart the brotherhood of Islam. At the beginning of the twentieth century the Ottoman Empire was neither an Islamic state in the true sense of the term nor Arab or Turkish as a nation. The relations of the ruling Turkish elite with minorities were becoming harsh; they treated their non-Turkish fellow Muslims no better. The breakup of the Ottoman Empire after World War I resulted in the emergence of several nation states and the migration of some Arabic-speaking people to the United States on Turkish passports.[10] Many of these settled in the Great Plains area, including Chicago. With the emergence of the Communist State in Russia, some Muslims from Central Asia also came to America.

Third Wave, 1945–1965

The end of World War II brought two major changes in the world: the redrawing of many national boundaries and a communications revolution. The strain caused by the loss of earlier forms of identity plus the facility to travel seems to have triggered a new wave of migration. The first arrivals were those who had suffered repression in East European countries and the Soviet Union, followed by people from the Indian subcontinent after the partition of India in 1947 and the "police action" by India in Hyderabad state in 1948. The establishment of the state of Israel in Palestine in 1947, with the resulting political instability, ideological confusion, and internal conflict in the Middle East, was a major factor in the emigration of thousands of Muslims to America from the Arab world. Later, the separation of Bangladesh from Pakistan and the Civil War in Lebanon caused many more Muslims to seek refuge in the United States. Recently, the breakup of the Soviet Union has brought many Muslims to America and the current fighting in the Balkans may bring more from Bosnia and Herzegovina to the Chicago area to be with their families who have settled here during the first half of this century.

Arrival of Students

After World War II a large number of students came to study in the United States, many of whom eventually settled in this country. Students from many parts of the Muslim world came to Illinois and Chicago. On January 1, 1963, a group of them met at the University of Illinois at Urbana to formally establish the first Muslim Student Association of the U.S.A. and Canada (MSA) as a central organization for all Muslim students in North America. This eventually gave birth to the Islamic Society of North America (ISNA) and other Muslim professional organizations that have branches in Chicago. Presently there are Muslim student organizations in almost every college and university of Chicago.

Fourth Wave, 1965–Continuing

The Immigration Act of 1965 signed by President Lyndon Johnson allowed families of immigrants to come to the United States. Many Muslims took this opportunity to sponsor their relatives to emigrate. As a result, the greater Chicago Muslim community presently includes people from at least the following countries: India, Pakistan, Yugoslavia, Syria, Jordan, Lebanon, Palestine, Egypt, all countries on the Arabian Peninsula, Tunisia, Libya, Algeria, Morocco, Iran, Malaysia, Indonesia, China, Turkey, the former Soviet Union, the Balkans, Albania, and Cambodia.

The five major schools of Islamic law are well represented among Sunni and Shi'a Muslims in Chicago, though differences among these schools are not given much importance. There is a trend in the younger generation to emphasize direct Islamic teachings from the Qur'an and hadith rather than to follow the different schools of thought. Those who are born in America feel strongly that Muslims should be called American Muslims and should not be linked to their parents' country. This trend is growing and eventually will lead to only one Muslim group known as American Muslims with English as their main language and Arabic as a second language to study the Qur'an and offer prayers.

DEVELOPMENT OF COMMUNITY ORGANIZATIONS

The Muslim community derives its strength and support at the grass-roots level through its membership, which is composed of Muslims from many countries who speak many languages. Their main objectives are to invite both Muslims and non-Muslims to Islam, to develop Islamic character and values among Muslims of all ages, to provide services to the Muslim community in the fulfillment of its religious, cultural, social, educational, and welfare needs, and to promote and strengthen cooperation among different Muslim groups and organizations pursuing similar objectives. The Muslim population of Greater Chicago can be divided into the following categories:[11]

1. Family: married 46 percent, single 18 percent, children 34 percent, undisclosed 2 percent, mean family size, three.
2. Occupation: medical doctors 8 percent, engineers 17 percent, other professionals 20 percent, skilled and unskilled laborers 6 percent, students 35 percent, undisclosed 14 percent.
3. Geographical representation: Asia and Africa 82 percent, United States 3 percent, Europe and others, 3 percent, undisclosed 12 percent.
4. Distribution in metropolitan Chicago: northern Chicago 59 percent, southern Chicago 13 percent, western suburbs 18 percent, northern suburbs 6 percent, southern suburbs 4 percent.

In the greater Chicago area, more than forty Islamic centers in various locations serve the population of Muslims in the surrounding area. These centers are used by Muslims of different countries according to the ethnic makeup of the neighborhood. Some centers serve Muslims predominantly from the Indo-Pakistan subcontinent, others have their membership primarily from Arab countries, yet another represents the Eastern European Bosnian community, and so on. Each center also has other nationalities represented. The Arabs who came in the late nineteenth century generally lived in the southern part of Chicago, whereas those Arabs who came after World War II established themselves in the northern part of Chicago and the suburbs. Similarly, the Bosnian community from Yugoslavia settled in the mid-northern areas of the city and many moved to northern suburbs such as Northbrook. The Indo-Pakistani community that came to the United States after World War II generally settled in the northern part of Chicago and subsequently moved to the northern and western suburban areas.

All the Islamic centers in Chicago described here are incorporated as not-for-profit organizations and are governed by their own trustees or boards of directors elected by the membership on a regular basis. They are supported by donations from the community through fund-raising dinners, bazaars, bake sales, and personal donations. In addition most have received support from international Islamic organizations located outside the United States as well as from Muslim countries such as Saudi Arabia and the Gulf States.

Organizational Structure

The five largest community or Islamic centers in the Chicago area are situated in different parts of the greater city area. In between these, other smaller centers have been established as significant numbers of Muslims moved into those areas.

Most of the smaller centers in one way or another have followed the same principles of structure and activities as the larger and older ones. Their major activities and services are run by committees, including planning, budget, constitution, human resources, investments, book service, community service, cooperative funds, community development, rehabilitation and welfare, literature development, speakers bureau, outreach, adult education, library, women's and youth groups, Friday prayers, religious affairs, special events, fund raising, membership, publication, public relations, media relations, Sunday schools, full-time schools, and others.

All organizations are structured into a general body, Trustees or Board of Directors, and an Executive Committee. All except one are membership based, and the members who pay dues have rights and obligations toward the organization. The organizations follow a written constitution passed by their general body. With the exception of two centers, none has an Imam who is in the employ of the center and responsible for the religious activities. The philosophy of each center is to serve the cause of Islam in this country and help the new generation to understand their Islamic heritage and cultural and linguistic background within the framework of the American political, social, and cultural environment. Almost all the organization's general bodies elect the Board of Directors, Board of Trustees, or Executive Committee. Committee chairpersons are appointed by the president of the Executive Committee; they, in turn, select the committee members. Differences that emerge from inevitable internal politics generally do not affect the overall working or running of the organization. At times, when conflict is personalized, frustration and anger are precipitated, but seldom does it appear to destroy the purpose of the organization or its working condition.

MUSLIM COMMUNITY ORGANIZATIONS

The Muslim Community Center (MCC), Chicago

The Muslim Community Center, considered to be the largest and one of the oldest among all the centers, was established in 1969 in Chicago. In the early stage its activities were conducted wherever they were able to find space. Some of the colleges and universities, such as the University of Chicago and Illinois Institute of Technology, allowed the Muslims to use school facilities for their activities, which helped in getting recognition within the student community.

MCC was organized by former MSA members and newly arrived immigrants, mostly from the Indo-Pakistan sub-continent, and a significant number of other ethnic groups. The first MCC building at 1651 North Kedzie was purchased in September 1972,[12] after which the activities of MCC expanded rapidly. A Sunday School was set up for the children, and regular Friday (Jummah) prayer and Tarawih prayer during the month of Ramadan were established. Membership grew, aided by the beginning of a community newsletter, called *The Message*.

After several years of operation, some members who were coming from the suburbs wanted to establish a center closer to where they lived. This led to an important debate with those who thought there was no need for a different organizational structure or center. Eventually the suburban residents established the new center in a peaceful manner using the organizational structure they preferred. However, MCC kept its own democratic process of operation and continued to grow. In less than six years the community outgrew the building. In 1982 a much larger building at 4380 North Elston Avenue was purchased, which currently serves the Muslim community through a wide variety of activities. According to Syed Najiullah, the current president, MCC now has 1000 members; the entire operation is funded by donations, membership dues and special fund-raising dinners.

In 1989 MCC purchased a school building in the suburb of Morton Grove to use as an education and youth center. Although objections to the purchase were raised by a local community organization, the people of Morton Grove in a local referendum overwhelmingly approved the purchase. A full-time school was started in the fall of 1991, according to Professor Abdul Majid, a member of the Board of Education, beginning with kindergarten, first and second grades. The school has grown to 125 students up through the fifth grade and 40 children in a preschool. The school has its own Board of Directors and consultant to develop curriculum. The expenses for the school are met by tuition, donations and a $100,000 annual subsidy from MCC. The school functions under the regulations of the Illinois Board of Education; all of the teachers are certified by the state.

MCC provides activities for the youth, including two places on the Board of Directors, a youth room, sports activities and an annual week-long youth camp. MCC women are active participants in the Board of Directors, teachers in the weekend schools, and all activities of the center. The weekend schools, broken into four shifts, educate over 800 children. An evening school, called Dar ul-Uloom meeting four evenings a week, teaches about sixty children to read and memorize the Qur'an and basic Islamic teachings.

With the growth both in activities and in the number of Muslims in the neighborhood there is already a need for a larger building.

The Islamic Foundation

In the late 1960s Muslims started moving to the western suburbs of Chicago to have better schools and less crime; by the mid-1970s their numbers reached into the thousands. In 1974 a group formed an organization under the name Islamic Foundation. The founding trustees had philosophical differences with the organizational structure of MCC, and according to Abdul Hameed Dogar, one of the founders of MCC, the Islamic Foundation developed a totally different organizational concept with no membership or dues and no concept of election. The structure is based on twenty-one founding trustees who were considered life trustees, although some have since retired and others have been nominated to fill the vacancies.

In 1976 the Islamic Foundation purchased eight acres of land on which they intended to construct their center. Before anything was built, however, a public school in Villa Park came up for sale and was purchased by the foundation in 1983. This building is now the headquarters of the Islamic Foundation and the first full-time Islamic school, established in 1987.

The full-time school began with kindergarten and first grade. Inamul Haq, the principal of the school, said they plan to add one grade every year to the existing school. Presently the school has 160 students with twelve full- and part-time certified teachers, both Muslim and non-Muslim. The children who attend come from a radius of 15 miles and receive education in both Islamic and secular subjects. Occasionally minor issues have arisen in the coeducational school with regard to preference for Arabic terminology or South Asian language and on the question of the proper head covering for girls. According to Principal Haq, the Arabs like to see the girls use *hejab* whereas the Indo-Pakistanis like *duppata*.[13]

Another important activity that recently developed at this center and is generating a lot of interest among young people is a dialogue between parents and their American-born children on the issue of the educational philosophy of the center and the cultural and social problems of this country.

Mosque Foundation, Bridgeview

Mosque Foundation was established in the early 1970s mainly by Arab immigrants, both second and third generation and those who came after World War II. For over a decade Mosque Foundation functioned in different locations by meeting in rented areas in universities and colleges and sometimes in the basements of its members. The majority of this Arab population lived in the southwest portion of Chicago, including the suburbs. Many established their businesses and stores as well as their residences in this area. During this period of its development the foundation went through ups and downs; in 1983 it finally purchased a piece of land and became the second center in Chicago to construct a mosque from the ground up.

Located at 7306 W. 93rd Street in Bridgeview, its membership is currently over 500. This includes some non-Arab Muslims, although basically the center caters to the Arab Muslim population, according to Bassam Osman, a member of the Board of Directors. The twenty-four member board consists of seven elected every year for a three-year term, an elected president, the past president, and the Imam.

According to Osman, the expenses of the various activities are raised through donations, membership dues, dinners, and so on. Mosque Foundation has weekend schools where 300 children are educated both in Arabic and English. No women have been elected to the Board of Directors although women have the right to vote in the elections and the constitution has no restriction on their membership on the board. Women have established their own committees, and a youth organization has been formed to cater to the needs of the younger generation.

Islamic Cultural Center of Greater Chicago (ICC), Northbrook

One of the earliest community centers for Muslims, in this case primarily from Yugoslavia (Bosnia), was founded in 1954 at 1800 N. Halsted Street. On March 21, 1976, they moved to 1810 N. Pfingsten Road, Northbrook, where the first phase of the Islamic Cultural Center, consisting of a school, library, administration offices, nursery and social hall, was completed. This building was the first constructed in the Chicago area as a traditional mosque with a dome and minaret. The membership is mostly from Bosnia, although many other ethnic groups participate in their activities as evidenced in the recent election of an Arab president. ICC has an Imam who takes care of the religious affairs of the community.

American Islamic Association (AIA), Mokena

The association, established in 1979, used a rented school for its initial activities in the south suburban areas of Chicago. According to the chairman of its Advisory Committee, Mansoor Mozaffar, the main purpose of AIA was to provide an Islamic education for the Muslim children of that area and carry out religious activities for the people living in a 175 square mile area of the southern suburbs. Mansoor feels that the 14 acres of land purchased by the association at St. Francis Road and 88th Avenue in Mokena eventually could be developed into a beautiful summer camp for the entire Muslim community of Chicago. AIA operates on the same structure as the other centers with similar activities.

Islamic Society of Northwest Suburbs (ISNS), Rolling Meadows

ISNS, located at 3890 Industrial Drive, was organized in 1982 when a number of Muslims moved into the area. According to Quadir Husain Khan, ISNS President, these Muslims generally work in various firms and industries in that area. Most of the activities are geared toward establishing weekend schools for children; they follow the same pattern of activities as the other centers.

Shi'a Community

The community of Shi'a Muslims is small but growing, and includes a few Isma'ilis and Dawoodi Bohras. The two Shi'a organizations in Chicago are the Husaini Association of Greater Chicago and the Midwest Association of Shia Organized Muslims (Masoom). Syed Asad Ali Rizvi, chairman of the Husaini Association, estimates that there are several thousand Shi'is living in Chicago and its suburbs. The Husaini Association, the largest Shi'a center in Chicago, was established in February 1972 and soon after purchased a building at 3109 N. Washtenaw.

The organization, which consists primarily of Indo-Pakistanis, is guided by Maulana Azki Husain who is resident *alim* (scholar, teacher) in Houston, Texas. It is governed by an elected Board of Directors with a chairman and an Executive Committee with a president and executive members. The board has recently adopted a Jaafri Fiqh–based constitution establishing a six member Board of Trustees, five of whom are nominated by Maulana Azki Husain for life and one elected from the Board of Directors to serve for two years.

Their activities include the observation of ten days of Muharram commemorating the martyrdom of Hazrat Imam Hussein, the grandson of Prophet Muhammad; according to Shi'a Muslim custom they also observe a forty-day mourning period for the Imam every year. These forty days are spent in commemorating the life of

Imam Hussein and the entire family of the Prophet Muhammad. Other activities include seminars on different topics concerning Islam and the development of Shi'a philosophy, a sex-segregated Sunday school for seventy children, an annual Hajj trip, potluck dinners, observance of the fast of the month of Ramadan, and the two Eid celebrations.

Although the Shi'a population is small in relation to other Muslims in Chicago, differences among members of the Husaini Association led some to begin a new separate organization. The Masoom Association was established April 26, 1975, at 6111 W. Addison Street, Chicago. Revenues come from rental of apartments that the organization owns as well as the mosque fund. The association arranges the annual Hajj trip and provides the Shi'a community information regarding pilgrimage to the grave of Imam Hussein at Karbala, Iraq. Their activities include the Muharram events as well as organizing a short procession in the streets on 10 Muharram in which all Shi'a groups participate. Both of these Shi'a groups are active and have monthly newsletters. The community has a publication center run by an Iraqi scholar of Shi'a philosophy, Maulana Muhammad Husain Jalali.

There is also a very small but closely knit Shi'a group known as the Dawoodi Bohra Community. According to Hakim Taiyebi, who is a member of the Board of Directors of the community, only 600 Bohras live in the Chicago area. In 1977 they purchased a center known as Al-Markaz-us-Saifee, located in suburban Chicago at 7009 W. Madison in Forest Park. They bought five acres of land in Hinsdale to build a masjid, the cornerstone of which was laid in October 1990 by His Holiness Dr. Syedna Mohammed Burhanuddin Saheb, the head of the worldwide Bohra community with headquarters in Bombay, India. According to Taiyebi, the head of the organization in Chicago is 'Amil' Behlul Bhai Saheb, who was appointed by Burhanuddin. The organization has a seven member board nominated by Bhai Saheb and approved by Burhanuddin.

The major function of Bhai Saheb in Chicago at present is to run a Deni (religious) school for seventy–eighty children. Most members observe the month of Ramadan with prayer and fast breaking, sharing a meal provided free to the entire community. Unlike other Shi'a groups who observe the ten days of Muharram as days of mourning, the Bohra celebrate the first of Muharram as New Year's Day in which they distribute food and exchange gifts.

The Bohra community is membership based, and it is expected that every person must be a member of the organization. The membership fee is prorated depending on the condition and financial situation of the individual. They do not have fund-raising dinners as do other organizations, but instead organize several dinners a month contributed by members of the organization for which donations are voluntary. There are two subsidiary organizations, the Anjumane Burhan Women's Association, whose purpose is to help the parent organization in any way necessary, and the youth organization known as Shabab. According to Taiyebi, the members of the community are very close to each other and are always ready to help in time of need.

Sufi Orders

Of several Sufi orders in Chicago, the largest is the Naqshabandi. These Sufi *tariqa* groups meet for *dhikr* (remembrance of God) in various mosques and private homes. Many non-Muslims have converted to Islam through these religious orders.

EDUCATIONAL ACTIVITIES

Providing an Islamic education to youth and adults is the aim of every Islamic center and is taken very seriously. The weekend Islamic schools are run and taught by the educated members of the community, which has given incentive to the parents to bring their children to the center to reinforce the teaching of Islam at home. Classes are organized for children aged 5 through 14. The younger children are placed in coeducational classes but the older children are separated by sex. There are separate educational activities for the older youth. Adult programs are offered in English as well as in other languages. The major subjects taught in the Sunday schools are Qur'an, Islamic principles, life of the Prophet Muhammad, Arabic, and Islamic etiquette. Advanced classes are offered for the older children in Islamic law, Islamic history, relations between Muslims and non-Muslims, ethics of marriage and family, biographies of Islamic personalities of the Muslim world, comparative study of the Islamic and American democratic and secular values and institutions.

Evening schools were established for children whose parents wanted them to learn to read and memorize the Qur'an; this training has encouraged some children to become Hafiz (one who has memorized the entire Qur'an). Some of these schools also teach explanation or exegesis of the Qur'an, Qur'anic laws, and the Arabic language. The goal and purpose of such institutions is to prepare American Muslims to have their own American-educated Hafiz and Islamic scholars instead of inviting such men from other countries of the world. A few of these young boys and girls have become Hafiz and it is hoped that when they advance in their schooling, they will help others to become scholars. Many centers offer four- to six-week summer schools with four to six hours of classes per day for both boys and girls. Children age 12 or older are separated by gender in the classroom.

The question of whether or not to establish full-time schools was debated at length among the members of the community. Some felt strongly that there was no need for such Muslim schools. They argued that it would be very expensive to purchase land and buildings and to equip the schools properly, and it would be difficult and expensive to train qualified teachers. Some of them felt that such schools would create a Muslim elite because only the rich could attend and, worse still, might promote isolationist tendencies that would prevent a healthy integration of Muslims among themselves and into the American society. Others argued strongly that a beginning must be made sometime, somewhere, and that if even 1 percent of the Muslim children attended such schools, they would provide future leadership for the community. They deplored the environment of this country as contrary to Islamic values and specially harmful for children. They also believed that boys and girls should be educated separately.

In the end the establishment of such full-time Islamic schools was inevitable. Many parents felt strongly that they should provide an education for their children in which all subjects were taught as in the public schools along with Islamic subjects within an Islamic environment. Islamic schools in the Chicago area now include the Islamic Foundation School (elementary); MCC full-time school (elementary); Universal School (grades K–12); Al-Aqsa Girls' School (grades 6–12); and the College Preparatory School of Illinois (grades 7–12). Older boys and girls are always separated by sex. The intention is to expand the elementary schools gradually, extending them to all the grades of a high school. All these schools are approved by the governing authorities of the state of Illinois, have certified teachers both Muslim and non-Muslim, and are run under strict Islamic discipline. Each school has its own governing body. Parental input is considered extremely valuable; all have active Parent-Teacher Associations.

The Madrasah Ta'lim-ul-Islam (Institute of Islamic Education), established as a residential school in 1991, is unique in its philosophy with the sole purpose of developing a comprehensive Islamic studies program to produce American-educated scholars, Hafiz (memorizers) of Qur'an, specialists in Islamic law, and leaders for the communities who are educated in comprehensive Islamic studies. The institute was established by Maulana Abdullah Saleem, a highly educated scholar in Islam from the famous Islamic School of Deoband in India. The sources of funding are the same as the centers except tuition is charged each student. The faculty of the school is educated in India as well as in the United States. A large number of Muslims are anxious to see their children, at an early age, acquire a solid Islamic education. For that purpose the curriculum is prepared by the Maulana himself. An important feature of this school is that it is residential, which helps the children to learn Islamic manners at an early age.

The same reasons and goals operating in the development of Islamic elementary and secondary educational programs also led to the establishment of the American Islamic College (AIC) in 1983. AIC is unique in its mission and purpose. It is a four-year institution approved by the Illinois Board of Higher Education to grant Bachelor of Arts degrees in Islamic Studies and Arabic Studies and to grant the two-year Associate of Arts degree with concentration in various disciplines such as computers, business, Arabic and Islamic Studies. It is located on Lake Michigan at 640 W. Irving Park in Chicago.

AIC's general studies program includes the disciplines of computer science, sociology, economics, geography, history, political science, and the natural and social sciences. In addition to the general studies program, a wide range of courses is offered in Arabic and Islamic studies. Among the former are language and grammar, classical and modern literature, and directed reading in an area of specialization. In the area of Islamic studies, courses in history, Qur'an and hadith, Islamic thought, economics, jurisprudence, and ethics are offered.

AIC is a culturally diverse institution with students from North

America, Muslim and non-Muslim, as well as from countries such as Bangladesh, Ghana, Gambia, Jordan, Kuwait, Pakistan, and Togo. The strength of the college lies in its Islamic environment and its well-trained and experienced teaching staff. Small classes with a student/teacher ratio of about 7/1 give students ample opportunity for discussion and individual attention. Every semester ten to twenty community members are attracted to an extension course offered in a local center. Despite a number of problems over the ten year history of the school, the college is making progress in attracting students to its programs of study. The first graduation ceremony was held in 1987 with seven graduates.

The AIC library has a large collection of Islamic and Arabic books. Students are offered a total Islamic environment through a dormitory and a mosque on campus. AIC facilities, including an auditorium seating over 1,000, are open for all organizations and are used especially for youth meetings. AIC is the only institution of its kind in North America that is run solely by Muslims. A Board of Trustees and a Board of Directors govern its policies.

PRAYERS

At some sixty locations in Chicago congregational Friday prayers are offered, many of which also have the regular congregational prayers five times a day. Depending on the locale, the *khutba* (sermon) may be delivered in Arabic, English, Urdu, or some other language. Younger Muslims are generally more comfortable with the *khutba* in English and have insisted on it. Most universities and colleges in Chicago provide rooms for Muslim students to offer Friday prayers. Many businesses and hospitals also provide space to conduct Friday prayers or allow time off to their Muslim employees to attend these prayer services.

During the lunar month of Ramadan, Muslims fast during the day and perform the special congregational evening *tarawih* prayers offered in nearly every Islamic center and mosque. The Hafiz recites the entire Qur'an from memory during the prayers in the course of the month. The two major Islamic celebrations, those of Eid al-Fitr and Eid al-Adha, are well attended by Muslims from all walks of life and ethnic backgrounds. Some 10,000 gather annually in McCormick Place to offer their special Eid prayers. In recent years some outlying centers have held their own Eid prayers.

BOOK STORES AND PUBLISHERS

The largest Islamic book store, publisher, and distributer of Islamic books in the city is Kazi Publications, located at 3023 W. Belmont. It carries books representing all the philosophical viewpoints present in the Muslim communities and is the oldest Islamic book store in Chicago. IQRA International Education Foundation, 831 S. Laflin, Chicago, publishes a large number of books especially in the educational fields. IQRA also operates a bookstore and reading room at 6410 N. Campbell in an area where a large number of South Asians live and shop. Two special programs of IQRA are the IQRA Book Club and the Ansar of IQRA.

Sound Vision, a division of Islamic Circle of North America, established in August 1988, produces educational Islamic video and computer programs for children as well as adults. These are marketed through seminars, conferences and advertisements in magazines. It is located at 843 W. Van Buren, Chicago.

Every major Islamic center in Chicago sells books and other Islamic cultural items.

INFORMATION SERVICES

Islamic information is provided by the Institute of Islamic Information and Education, 4390 N. Elston Avenue, Chicago;[14] Islamic Information Center, Des Plaines; Islamic Circle of North America, Bellwood; Islamic Culture Center, Oak Lawn. These organizations provide information and literature to Muslims and non-Muslims, help new Muslims learn about Islam, develop political and media consciousness among Muslims, correct misinformation and stereotyping of Muslims in textbooks, the media, and society, and provide speakers on Islamic topics to non-Muslim groups. These organizations work together to coordinate activities and share resources.

ISLAMIC MEDIA

The first Arabic newspaper, *The American Star*, was established in 1868 in New York. *The Muslim Journal*, a national English weekly newspaper, published in Chicago by the African American Muslim community, was established in 1979. In the early stages the goal was to inform African Americans about Islam and world affairs. *Unity Times*, a bimonthly newspaper in English established by Hamedullah Khan, primarily gives news about Pakistan but also gives information concerning Muslims living in America. *The Pakistani*, published monthly in Urdu and English, is directed to the Urdu speakers in Chicago. Although it caters to the interests of Pakistani Muslims, it does print activities of Muslim organizations in Chicago. In 1989 a newsletter initially called the *Islamic Support Group News* was started by a group of American converts to the faith. Beginning as a single page, it has grown to more than twenty pages and, under the new name *The American Muslim*, now has nationwide circulation. There are also a few Arabic newspapers published in Chicago.

Increasingly the media in the Chicago area offer specialized programming of interest to the Muslim community. Station 1330 AM provides an hour of radio program in Arabic at 2 P.M. Monday through Friday. An Urdu program, "Paksarzameen," airs on Friday 8–9 P.M. on radio 1590 AM. A weekly Arabic TV program for one half hour can be seen on Channel 26, at 3:30 P.M. on Saturday. On Saturday morning on Channel 26 from 9:40 to 10:00 A.M. an Islamic program is produced by the Foundation for Religious and Cultural Reflections. A number of Islam-oriented programs are available on cable TV.

COMMUNITY AFFAIRS

A large number of social programs have been initiated by various groups. They are mostly funded by the generous Zakat (charity) collected by the community and the various centers. Most Muslims pay their zakat to their centers to be used according to Islamic law. Many centers arrange clothing collection drives for distribution to those in need. During the month of Ramadan, at the time of Iftar when the Muslims break their dawn to dusk fast, free meals are served daily to the community and the needy at a number of the centers free of charge. On Thanksgiving Day some centers cooperate with other non-Muslim organizations in providing food for the homeless.

A large number of intercultural and interfaith marriages are taking place involving Muslims. In the latter cases the non-Muslim partner usually accepts Islam. Most of the larger Islamic centers are authorized to perform marriages; they also provide counseling in marital disputes. Most marriages are performed on the model of the home country of the parents and are extremely traditional. Some of the younger generation, however, object to the traditional weddings and want to design their own.

Many centers in Chicago provide adult education programs and seminars, and organize Islamic conferences. Two such major conferences held in the recent past were the Conference on Muslim Community Development in 1978, and the Conference in 1977 honoring the twelve-hundredth anniversary of Shaykh Bukhari, considered the most authentic compiler of hadith (the sayings or traditions of Prophet Muhammad). Both conferences attracted Muslims from all over America.

According to Islamic law Muslims should consume only the meat of cattle and poultry that are slaughtered according to Islamic law. There are a large number of such halal meat shops in the city, which also specialize in local and imported ethnic foods. The Islamic Food and Nutrition Council of America, Bedford Park, established in 1983, promotes the halal food system, provides advisory services to local and national food catering agencies such as hotels and airlines, and publishes a news and views periodical.

CEMETERIES

In some local cemeteries areas are set aside for the burial of Muslims. Since no cremation or embalming is allowed in Islam, burial usually takes place the same day on which the death occurs. Many funeral homes cooperate in allowing the Muslim family to prepare the body for burial according to Islamic requirements. In addition, they also provide facilities to perform funeral prayers on their premises. City Hall has approved that the funeral prayer can be performed in the centers as well.

DIALOGUE GROUPS

Many Muslims are active participants in programs for interfaith dialogue and conversation. Some have been involved in the Council for Parliament of World Religions, preparing for a centenary international conference in Chicago in 1993. Muslims join Christians and Jews in interfaith dialogues to create a better atmosphere for living together in the city of Chicago. The Conference for Improved Muslim-Christian Relations was founded in 1985; Catholics, Protestants and Muslims have participated in planning programs that serve the educational and social needs of all their community members. The Christian-Muslim Dialogue Committee holds regular discussion meetings in churches, mosques, and at the American Islamic College. Every year an annual fellowship dialogue and banquet is held in Chicago. The Muslim community joined in the Interfaith Day of Fasting and Prayer held in Chicago on March 31, 1992, to protest the cancellation of Illinois Transitional Assistance Program.

ETHNIC MUSLIM ORGANIZATIONS

The Consultative Committee of Indian Muslims of the United States and Canada (CCIM) is an organization that tries to help solve problems of Indian Muslims, such as those that arise when anti-Muslim riots occur in India, as well as the problems of education and economic underdevelopment of Indian Muslims. CCIM has tried to keep the Indian Muslims in America informed of these events and to demonstrate and protest against discrimination of Indian Muslims in India. They also make presentations to the government of India and the Indian embassy in the United States. Other such organizations with similar goals are the Gujrati Muslim Association and a large number of organizations based on national and linguistic affiliations such as Pakistan Federation of America, Indus Society of North America, Arab Association, Hyderabad Association, Palestine Association, Egypt Association, and Organization of Muslims for Palestine. Though the Urdu language is not spoken by Muslims alone, there are associations that support the language through literary conferences and Mushaerah (poetic symposia). All these organizations are extremely busy in their cultural, social and political activities. The membership of most of these organizations consists of Muslims and non-Muslims.

WOMEN

Muslim women are quite active in community life and in the Islamic centers. The Muslim Community Center has elected women as members of the Board of Directors. Although other centers constitutionally allow women's participation none have been elected so far. Women are, however, present in the schools, PTA, and a variety of committees at the various centers; they also organize their own women's educational programs. They teach in the Sunday schools and those who are certified teachers also teach in the full-time Islamic schools. Many Muslim women who specialize in highly skilled professions participate in various affairs outside the Muslim community; a large number of Muslim women are medical doctors, some of whom have private medical clinics. Some are lawyers. Most of the Muslim women professionals are active in their respective associations. A great number of Muslim women teachers are in the Chicago Public Schools as certified teachers and bilingual teachers. None of the centers has a strict dress requirement, although there is a separate women's section for prayer in every center.

YOUTH

All Islamic centers, schools, and colleges have established active youth groups with a range of activities such as voluntary services for the Muslim community, summer youth camps, regular seminars and debates, educational programs, recreational activities, and athletic programs. Some of these groups publish their own newsletters, expressing their views on Islamic topics, national and international issues, and local and national activities. The Muslim Youth Council of Chicago has been organized by the youth themselves to coordinate the efforts of all the youth organizations in the area, generally involving boys and girls in the planning. The Muslim Youth Camp is a recreational and educational program where boys and girls travel to a private campground and live in an Islamic environment for one week. During this camp the educational programs are coeducational but the recreational programs are segregated allowing full involvement of both sexes. Adult counselors are present in the camp and well-known teachers are invited to give lectures.

The national organization Muslim Youth of North America has a very active Chicago chapter. They recently organized a successful week long program which was held at American Islamic College.

POLITICAL PARTICIPATION

The Muslim community of Chicago is just beginning to enter into the political systems of the Chicago area. The candidacy of Harold Washington for mayor in 1983 provoked every minority group in the city of Chicago to participate actively in the political processes in Chicago. At that time the Muslims of Chicago established an organization known as the League of Muslim Voters. The league and many other individual community members worked for Washington's election. This was the beginning of Muslim involvement in politics in Chicago. Mayor Washington appointed several Muslims in different areas in an advisory capacity. After Washington's tenure Muslims supported Richard M. Daley for mayor. Mayor Daley has appointed several Muslim industrialists and educators to various committees in an advisory capacity. Governor Edgar and the state treasurer have also selected several Muslims for their advisory councils.

Muslims have participated in the Democratic and Republican conventions of 1988 and 1992 as delegates and have taken serious interest in the activities of both political parties. In the recent local school council elections in Chicago, several Muslims were elected. The political participation of Muslims in the Chicago area, however, is not yet reflective of the size of the Islamic community.

COORDINATING ORGANIZATION

The idea of establishing an Islamic organization at the intracommunity level was first conceived at a representative gathering of Muslims in Cedar Rapids, Iowa, in 1952. As a result, the Federation of Islamic Associations (FIA) was formally established in 1954 in Chicago.[15] The FIA survived for a while but did not receive the endorsement of the new organizations formed by recent Muslim immigrants, due to the perception of many that those within the federation did not act Islamically.

The Muslim Student Association (MSA) did bring most of the Muslim students into its fold, and most of the Islamic or Muslim centers later established were the creation of former MSA members. The MSA gave rise to the Islamic Society of North America (ISNA) with headquarters in Plainfield, Indiana. Although ISNA established its branches in different states it has not succeeded in becoming the umbrella organization of all "centers" in the United States. Another national group with branches in various states is the Islamic Circle of North America (ICNA). Recently, the National Coordinating Committee has been established for more or less the same purpose.

None of the several attempts made to coordinate the activities of all the Islamic organizations in Chicago has yet been fruitful, although it appears that continuing efforts will be made. Thus far neither the FIA, MSA, ISNA, nor ICNA has been able to provide the leadership necessary for bringing together these organizations in any kind of umbrella organization.

While the annual convention of ISNA does attract Muslims from most Islamic centers of America, providing the spectrum of a national coordinating body, ISNA fails to harness this gathering in establishing direct communication with the Islamic centers of America. Perhaps it would be advisable for ISNA to initiate the idea of a confederation of all Muslim organizations in America. This would provide the local organizations relative independence to function as they wish but still maintain a link with ISNA. At the same time it would be helpful if the two national organizations, ISNA and ICNA, could first coordinate efforts among themselves to reach out to other organizations. In general, the several attempts that have been made to coordinate the activities of all the Islamic organizations through a single body have not met with much success, for a variety of reasons.

1. *Leadership*: In any community organization, whether ethnic, religious, social, or political, the issue of leadership emerges in the context of a consideration of the philosophy of the organization of the coordinating body. Philosophically and fundamentally, Muslims are united on the issue of Allah, the Qur'an, and the finality of prophethood, but are not always in agreement over questions of interpretation and approach. Hence, it has not yet been clarified which organization and under whose leadership coordination will start.

2. *Representation*: Chicago has more than forty Islamic centers and organizations, some of them much older and larger in membership and thus financially better off than the majority. It is natural, therefore that the larger groups tend to have more say and even dominate the smaller groups, particularly as they

have more available resources and thus the potential for great impact. Some larger organizations support the position that representation in a coordinating council should be proportional to the number of members. The smaller organizations naturally feel that any contribution they could make in this sort of representative structure would be negligible.

3. *Funding*: Funding has always been an irritation among the larger and smaller groups. Proportionally, the larger or more financially sound groups will contribute more and hence demand a greater influence within the organization. A scheme for collecting funds for a coordinating council has not yet been developed. Unless this happens, funding for a coordinating council will be difficult if not impossible.

4. *Projects*: The most significant problem is the selection of which specific kinds of projects the coordinating group would undertake and how those could best be determined to promote the good of the entire Muslim community in Chicago.

5. *Headquarters*: This is a relatively minor issue, yet insofar as location carries certain prestige, it has the potential for creating further friction among all the participating organizations.

The time is ripe for the establishment of such a coordinating body in Chicago, and those who feel strongly about it will continue to make further attempts. But the fact is that until these fundamental issues are properly and Islamically settled it will be difficult to establish a successful coordinating effort. Recent modest efforts to form a Council of Islamic Organizations faced opposition due to differences on just such issues as have been mentioned already.

CONCLUSION

It is fair to say that the Muslim community of Chicago is religiously vibrant, financially sound, educated, and active. It plays a significant role in the development and prosperity of the city of Chicago. The Muslim community has a large number of highly skilled professional men and women in various specializations. They are medical doctors, engineers, nuclear scientists, educators at both the school and university level, scientists, and social scientists; and they are contributing to the well-being of the city of

Chicago both financially and intellectually. The Muslim community also has a significant number of business people who own or operate grocery stores, restaurants, travel agencies, industries, and other kinds of business enterprises, as well as those with service-oriented, semi-skilled labor, and other jobs. The Pakistani community managed to accomplish the renaming of a street in Chicago after the founder of Pakistan, Mohammed Ali Jinnah.

The community is financing and operating various kinds of voluntary, charitable, and community organizations such as Islamic centers, mosques, educational institutions, and youth activities. The variety and quality of these voluntary associations and activities is a good indication of the social and ethical ethos of the community.

Every community, however, must experience certain ups and downs. The Muslim community is no exception. They have their own problems, which they sort out among themselves intellectually through a democratic process of concensus involving seminars, debates, arguments, and writing. But they do it in a democratic fashion as the need arises. Some are funding their centers and coordinating their activities. They still have no powerful media or voice for the community as a whole, which ultimately is necessary if it is to express its concerns about its own people as well as about the general population of the city at large.

Muslims are becoming more socially and politically conscious of their duties and rights as U.S. citizens; they participate in demonstrations against things they do not like and for things they do like that occur on the local, national, and international scene. Increasingly they confront issues that concern them as Muslims and Americans, discussing the pros and cons of such matters individually and collectively, sometimes in heated debates on the question of methodology. Although the Muslim community has one religion, it has many languages and different points of view, as well as ethnic entities based on their geographic, linguistic, and other sociocultural origins that divide them sharply. In spite of this, the work of their Islamic centers does not suffer. These debates are seen as healthy for the development of the community, the understanding, enrichment, and refinement of their Islamic values and religion, and for their socialization in the larger American society. The debates are generally about the approaches of dealing with different issues.

The Muslims are a new ethnic and religious community in comparison with other older groups. They are anxious to build a future for their children, to maintain their religion as well as their American identity, and to establish a unified community in close relationship with other religious and ethnic communities in the Chicago area. These goals can be accomplished only if the Muslims and their organizations realize their past mistakes of ignoring the 80 percent of the Muslim population who are not involved in their activities. If the Muslims of Chicago are to be a positive force in the larger context of the city of Chicago, it is imperative that they critically analyze their own actions before venturing into the larger arena. The onus is on the Muslims of America in general and the Muslims of Chicago in particular to make a serious and conscientious effort to bridge the gap between the 80 perent and the 20 percent of their own population without undue concern for the political, social, cultural, and other differences that may tend to divide them.

NOTES

The authors acknowledge the input and assistance in finalizing this paper of Mary C. Ali, registrar, American Islamic College, and the editorial comments of S. Waqar Ahmed Husaini, vice president for development, American Islamic College, and visiting scholar, Hoover Institution on War, Revolution and Peace, Stanford University, California.

1. Lawrence Oschinsky, "Islam in Chicago: Being a Study of the Acculturation of a Muslim Palestinian Community in That City" (Ph.D. diss., University of Chicago, 1952).

2. Abdul Jalil al-Tahir, "The Arab Community in Chicago Area, A Comparative Study of the Christian-Syrians and the Muslim-Palestinians" (Ph.D. diss., University of Chicago, 1947). By the end of the nineteenth century there were nearly 100 Muslim families in Chicago, which, with an average of five persons in each family, would total about 500 Arab Muslims.

3. Ibid., p. 2.

4. At the turn of the century, several Palestinian Arabs from the village of Ramallah came to Chicago and settled down here in the furnished rooms in the neighborhood of 18th Street and Michigan Avenue (Oschinsky, "Islam in Chicago," p. 23).

5. Ibid., p. 27.

6. Asad Husain and Asifa Husain, "Islam and Non-Muslim Soci-

ety, A Case Study of Islam in the United States of America," unpublished paper read in the Muslim Community Development Conference, Chicago, March 1978.

7. Personal interview of Asad Husain with Kamil Advich in 1978.

8. Islamic Foundation brochure, n.d., p. 5.

9. Husain and Husain, "Islam and Non-Muslim Society," p. 16.

10. M. A. Rauf, "Islam and Islamic Institutions in North America," *Impact* 6–77 (April 9–22, 1976).

11. "Muslim and Community Development Project" (Chicago: 1977), Muslim Community Center Masjid Planning Committee, p. 10. These figures are based on a 1977 survey but we are assuming the figures are approximately the same in 1992 with minor variations.

12. Ibid., p. 11.

13. *Hejab* and *duppata* both are forms of headcovering.

14. According to its founder and manager Dr. M. Amir Ali, the institute has the following goals: (1) to elevate the image of Islam and Muslims in America by removing misinformation and defamation from textbooks, reference books and the media, and to combat misinformation; (2) to invite the indigenous American population to open their hearts for Islam using the positive methods of Qur'an and Sunnah; and (3) to educate and train new indigenous Muslims in Chicago and make efforts into the Muslim community at large. The institute opened the first street-level reading room in Chicago in 1988.

15. Husain and Husain, "Islam and Non-Muslim Society," p. 14.

CHAPTER 11

The Muslims of Indianapolis

Steve A. Johnson

INTRODUCTION

In 1933, Pierre Crabites, representative of President Taft in Egypt, wrote the following:

> In envisaging this possibility of Mohammedanism becoming a black spot upon the American horizon it should not be forgotten that Islam today is making more converts in the world at large than any other religion. The Moslem faith may be particularly strong among backward peoples, but it is not a dying religion. Right here in Egypt, where there are 14,000,000 Mohammedans and 1,000,000 Christians, Jews, and Agnostics, Mohammedanism is, I am told, making practically a hundred conversions to one effected by the combined Christian Churches.
>
> I got these figures from a source which is most sympathetic to Christian Missions. They frighten me. They do not mean that Jesuit Fathers, Christian Brothers, Presbyterian clergymen and Anglican Missionaries are not doing good work. They are. But their converts are not gained in reassuring numbers from among Mohammedans.
>
> If these converts return to the United States, the ardent spirit of the neophyte and the sermons which they will preach make me shudder at the consequences which I see in store for America.[1]

Crabites's fear may have been prophetic. Some researchers have concluded that by the early part of the next century Islam will be the second largest religion in America, the number of Muslims then exceeding the number of Jews.[2] Historically, the midwestern states have been an important area for Islamic institutional devel-

259

opment. Yet, although considerable material has been written on the Muslims in midwestern cities such as Detroit (Dearborn), Toledo, and Cedar Rapids, to date the Muslims in Indianapolis have been mentioned only in passing and then primarily simply to note that the headquarters of the Islamic Society of North America is in a suburb of Indianapolis.[3]

In this study, I will focus on three areas with respect to this relatively neglected group of Muslims: (1) a history of the establishment and growth of Islamic institutions in Indianapolis, (2) a description of the Islamic institutions and their activities, and (3) an account of the interrelations among the Muslim groups in the city.

ESTIMATE OF THE MUSLIM POPULATION IN INDIANA AND INDIANAPOLIS

Indiana has a significantly greater percentage of African American Muslims than the national distribution and a significantly lower percentage of Eastern European Muslims (and to a lesser extent a lower percentage of Asian and Subsaharan Muslims). The percentage of Middle Eastern–North African Muslims in Indiana is roughly equivalent to the national average. Oral reports among Muslims set the 1990 number of Muslims in Indianapolis at approximately 2,000.[4] That figure is identical to a 1978 oral report estimate given by Ali Abu Talib of the Indianapolis Muslim Association.[5]

BRIEF HISTORY OF ISLAMIC INSTITUTIONAL ESTABLISHMENT IN INDIANA

Islamic institutions were established in Indianapolis roughly between the 1940s and the 1980s. In general, the African American Muslim institutions were begun in the 1940s and 1950s, and the immigrant Muslim institutions were established from the 1960s through the 1980s. Perhaps the first among the proto-Islamic institutions established in the city was a temple affiliated with the Moorish American Science Temple movement, apparently instituted in the early 1940s.[6] Within the next decade, the Nation of Islam, under the leadership of Elijah Muhammad, became a significant presence in Indianapolis. The first among the immigrant

Muslims to arrive in Indianapolis were the Ahmadiyya (Qadiani) Muslims from India, who apparently had only a marginal presence in terms of numbers and longevity. The group was established in the early 1960s and had disappeared by the 1970s. In the 1970s two major developments took place within the Indianapolis Muslim community. In 1973 al-Fajr mosque was bought to house Sunni African American Muslims who were not associated with Elijah Muhammad's movement. Then in 1975 the Muslim Students' Association (MSA) moved its headquarters from Gary, Indiana, to Indianapolis. In the summer of 1982 MSA was incorporated into a larger umbrella Islamic organization called the Islamic Society of North America (ISNA), located on a 124-acre field in rural Plainfield, Indiana, in the western suburbs of Indianapolis.

HISTORY OF THE PROTO-ISLAM–AFRICAN AMERICAN INSTITUTIONS

Moorish American Science Temple Movement

Little is known about the origins of this group in Indianapolis. A March 1959 newspaper article described the group as flourishing in Indianapolis with a temple headquarters at 796 Indiana Avenue.[7] Another temple was located in Indiana Harbor, Indiana.[8] The leader of the group, Grand Governor J. Blakely-Bey, lived nearby on Beauty Avenue. The group emphasized love toward their Christian "brothers" and taught that they were members of the Moabite Tribe in North Africa before they were brought to the United States as slaves. They held that the Moabites were part of the Moorish race and were all Muslims. The group held a worship service on Friday evening and a Qur'an study class on Sunday afternoons. On January 8 a gift exchange was held in the temple in commemoration of their American prophet, Noble Drew Ali. By the early 1960s the area was cleared to build the Indianapolis campus of Indiana University, in particular the School of Medicine. What happened to the group and its members is unknown.

The Nation of Islam

African American Muslims claim that the establishment of a temple of the Nation of Islam was hindered by the Indianapolis city police. Thus the first group was organized informally in the city in

1959 in homes and stores along Indiana Avenue. Eventually a headquarters was set up at 2905 Clifton on the northwest side of the city. On the front of the building was a sign that read, Muhammad's Mosque, and a red flag with a white star and crescent was painted at the top of the doorway. In the windows were signs announcing the lectures to be given by Elijah Muhammad in Chicago. Muslims say Elijah was never permitted to come to Indianapolis. On the one occasion when an attempt was made to have him speak in the city, the police allegedly coerced building owners not to rent space to the Muslims. One author describes the group as follows:

> The black-supremacy Muslims are here where the white-supremacy Ku Klux Klan once ruled. Few in number, the Muslims hold meetings in Negro homes and stores along garish, neon-lighted Indiana Ave., once the black belt of Indianapolis, which starts with a pawn shop (Sack's) and ends with a hospital (General). About the Muslims, Richard Caine of the police department's Internal Security Division says, "They don't want to integrate. They want to exterminate."[9]

In 1964 it was reported that there were only 25 members of the "Black Muslim movement" out of a total black population of about 102,000.[10] The group held its weekly service on Sundays at 2 P.M., at which time an Imam from Chicago would address the members, and also met on Wednesday evenings.[11]

Throughout the 1950s and 1960s the NOI in Indianapolis remained relatively insignificant numerically. In fact, much of the black community itself was not pleased to have the group in the city. King Muhammad (King Preston), a member of the group said, "It was nothing for so-called Negroes to sick dogs on us while we were selling papers."[12] Before Wallace Muhammad assumed leadership of the movement when Elijah Muhammad died in 1975, each member of the movement was required to sell 300 of the movement's newspapers, called "Muhammad Speaks." It was not uncommon for the police to arrest members selling the papers, accusing them of disorderly conduct, loitering, and occasionally of resisting arrest.[13]

In 1971 the movement was struck with violence. Within the local organization a rift had developed between the younger and the older factions of the group over financial matters and leadership style. The result was that Daniel Green (Brother Minister X), leader of the mosque then located at 25th and Central Avenue, and Leonard Thomas Clark, Jr., were both killed. The murders remain unsolved due to lack of evidence, witnesses, and suspects.[14]

Membership in the group did not increase significantly until after the death of Elijah Muhammad and the ascendancy of his son, Warith (Wallace) Deen Muhammad as leader. In March 1981 Warith Deen Muhammad brought Muhammad Siddiq to Indianapolis to establish a Muslim community in the city in line with the new directions in which he was taking the movement. Muhammad Siddiq had already served as director of education for the University of Islam in Harlem and as an Imam in Tallahassee, Florida. The first mosque was established at 2931 Central Avenue. The year after his arrival, membership had increased to between 150 and 200. In less than five years there were 60 to 75 regular attendees for Jumah prayer, 70–100 for Eid prayers, and an estimated 1,000 or more individuals who had taken Shahada. The local masjid had public religious services on Fridays and Sundays at 1 P.M., and held community awareness meetings at 7 P.M. on Tuesdays. It also had one public radio program on WGRT FM, Saturdays at 9 P.M.

In July 1983 Siddiq's group opened an AMMCOP chapter, a cooperative-buying venture operated by the American Muslim Mission under W. D. Muhammad. In September 1984, W. D. Muhammad visited Indianapolis and spoke at a Roman Catholic center in support of the AMMCOP chapter, but the enterprise was short lived.[16] To help raise funds a small restaurant was run at the front end of the masjid. However, throughout its history it has struggled financially.

Although the group had signed a ten year lease for their storefront mosque, in 1987 they were ousted from the building. Thereafter they met in several locations, such as the Martin Center (a small struggling black university of approximately 500 students whose president, Fr. Boniface Hardin, is a black Benedictine monk with a reputation for years of civil rights work in Indianapolis), Siddiq's home, Catholic churches, a YMCA, and Crispus Attucks school. They recently acquired the property at 2040 E. 46th Street for their new Islamic center, which they are calling the *Daniel Muhammad Islamic Center* (after the Daniel Muhammad who was murdered in 1971).

Muhammad Siddiq reports that his group has received tremendous acceptance from the Christian community. In fact, Siddiq has a leadership position in a "Concerned Clergy" group of minority clergy. He is active in *dawa* and social justice issues particularly as they relate to racial issues in Indianapolis (he has been very outspoken on alleged unjust police action toward blacks), and frequently speaks at local universities and recites al-Fatiha on a local radio program.

Siddiq reports that his group's relationship with ISNA and the immigrant Muslim community has always been distant, some times more so than others. On special occasions, such as the Eid prayers, the indigenous and immigrant communities gather together, but recently even these relations have become strained. The more conservative immigrant community insists upon the strict separation of the sexes at the Eid prayer, whereas the indigenous community wants to attend as families with husband, wife, and children sitting together. The indigenous community has developed a rather negative attitude toward ISNA and what they perceive to be ISNA's "dominate them or ignore them" attitude toward their community. Siddiq reports that relationships with ISNA were at their best when Iqbal Unus was ISNA's secretary general, but since Dr. Unus has become too ill to serve in that capacity, things have deteriorated. Relationships were at an all time low under the ISNA leadership of Ahmad Zaki, allegedly a member of the Egyptian Ikhwan al-Muslimun (Muslim Brotherhood). Among the grievances Siddiq's community lists against ISNA are the following.

1. The cultural isolationism and Arab hegemony in ISNA reveals "subtle racist tendencies among many immigrant Muslims."
2. No books by W. D. Muhammad are displayed in ISNA's library and no such books are distributed through NAIT's Islamic Book Service.
3. Black Muslims are treated by the ISNA immigrant community as though they had second-class status.
4. The "scholarly" and "social" works of W. D. Muhammad are not credited at any level by ISNA.
5. ISNA has attempted to dominate and take credit for the work that the followers of W. D. Muhammad have done among prison inmates in Indiana (Siddiq mentions that Ihsan Bagby

and Umar Hattab have been instrumental in turning power over the prison *dawa* work to a Muslim brother in Gary rather than acknowledging Siddiq's group and the work they were already doing).

6. ISNA does not appropriate any of its funds to help with the social problems of the inner city.

7. ISNA has no interest in the problems of the inner city, which is witnessed to by the fact that its headquarters is located in the suburbs (Siddiq refers to the headquarters as a "white elephant" in the suburbs that benefits only a minimal number of Muslims and an even smaller number of indigenous Muslims).[17]

Muhammad Siddiq's group has recently become overshadowed by a very active Muslim group with ties to Louis Farrakhan. The group, under the leadership of James 2X, enlists young men to stand at busy intersections along 38th Street in the city selling *The Final Call* newspaper and soliciting funds in the name of helping to fight drugs in the inner city. Before becoming a minister under Louis Farrakhan, James 2X, formerly James Madlock, was a football player, first for Purdue University and then for the New York Giants. After being introduced to Farrakhan's version of Islam while a sophomore in college, he went to Atlanta and joined Mosque #11. From Atlanta he came to Indianapolis and aggressively worked to establish study groups. James 2X became more visible as an outspoken critic of the trial of Mike Tyson, who was convicted of rape in Indianapolis. His group operated a book store called, Black Is Back, but the store closed in 1992. Now the organization runs a restaurant and a small button production business.[18]

Al-Fajr Community

Another African American Muslim group in Indianapolis is the al-Fajr mosque established in 1973. Historically it has been closely aligned with ISNA, although at times it also has been disgruntled by ISNA's lack of monetary support. Al-Fajr was originally located at 3700 Sherman Avenue, but in 1986 it moved to an old house at 527 Leon Street on the near east side of the city. Until the past few years the al-Fajr group has had poor relations with Siddiq's group. However, as W. D. Muhammad moved toward orthodoxy, and more important as followers of W. D. Muhammad joined the al-Fajr group, the two have moved closer. The al-Fajr mosque, particularly with the help of Ismail Abdul Alim, an active African American Muslim, and John Sullivan, an Anglo American convert who was employed by ISNA until 1986 to direct the prison *dawa* program, has produced a talk show about Islam through a local cable television station. Their members, most notably Omar Hattab, have at times helped ISNA on fund-raising expeditions to Saudi Arabia, Kuwait, and the United Arab Emirates. Apparently, stories told by indigenous Muslims about the success of *dawa* within the American population make fund-raising efforts more effective. This fund-raising strategy, however, has had negative impact on the indigenous community's perception of ISNA. A prevalent undercurrent within the indigenous community is that, although ISNA uses them to raise money for *dawa* and to maintain their organization, the indigenous Muslims do not benefit concretely from the fund raising. As a result indigenous Muslims are willing to use ISNA's facilities when it is to their benefit, but they feel the relationships is, and will remain, superficial.[19]

The Leon Street group is building a mosque near a Baptist church at 2900 Cold Springs Road. The new mosque will sit on 2 acres at the northeast side of a 17-acre upscale housing development, whose houses are being designed by M. Mazen Ayoubi, Syrian owner of Architecture International Consulting, which has built mosques in Chicago; Dayton, Ohio; Ann Arbor, Michigan; Tallahassee, Florida; Charleston, West Virginia; Columbus, Missouri; and the Hampton Roads area of Virginia.[20] The Board of Trustees of the mosque project is composed of Haroon Qazi, a famous mosque, as well as long time members of the Al-Fajr mosque and Essam Ismail, the director of ECIB, a business housed in the ISNA headquarters, and reportedly a member of the Egyptian Ikhwan al-Muslimun. The cost for the mosque is $500,000. To date the North American Islamic Trust (NAIT, the financial wing of ISNA) has loaned $100,000 toward the project, and another $60,00 was donated by the World Assembly of Muslim Youth (WAMY), with headquarters in Saudi Arabia and reportedly run by members of the Saudi Arabian Ikhwan al-Muslimun.[21] This contrasts sharply with reports from Ihsan Bagby, former director of ISNA's Islamic Teaching Center (ITC) who affirmed that the project is being funded solely by Muslim individuals.[22] Unfortunate for the housing development, only one of the plots of land in the development has been sold, and now the model home has had to be put up for sale because even Muslims are not buying the land.

Bilalian Student Alliance

There is one additional African American Muslim group in Indianapolis: the Bilalian Student Alliance, formed at Indiana University-Purdue University at Indianapolis (IUPUI) as an official student group to "educate and sensitize the university to the truths about Al-Islam and the concerns of Muslims."[23] Under the leadership of Kenneth D. Majied, a computer consultant at IUPUI, the group has been relatively quiet, particularly when compared to the activities of the Muslim Student Association (MSA). When in April 1992 the MSA presented a series of lectures on Islam, including the topic of African Americans and Islam, the Bilalian Student Alliance was neither visible in the program nor apparently participated in the presentations on the topic.

HISTORY OF THE IMMIGRANT MUSLIM INSTITUTIONS

The Ahmadiyya (Qadiani) Muslims

An Ahmadiyya temple was established on the near northeast side of the city in an economically depressed area at 2248 Yandes Street by 1960. The first leader or *muballigh* of the group was Aminullah Khan, a Pakistani and a graduate of the Missionaries Training University in Pakistan. Khan impressed Hoosiers with his soft amiable demeanor. However, apparently the group was short-lived, although no particulars are known about its demise.[24]

Muslim Student Association—Islamic Society of North America

In the mid-1960s, some five Arab and Indo-Pakistani Muslim families formed a chapter of the Muslim Student Association at the newly formed Indianapolis branch of Indiana University. A Pakistani professor of physics, Khurshid Alam, is credited with forming the MSA chapter by enlisting Ray Dault, the director of the Student Union on the Medical School campus of the university, to serve as the faculty sponsor of the organization. In actuality, the wives in cooperation with Nuri Alam, an Anglo American convert to Islam and wife of Khurshid Alam, organized and conducted the bulk of activities. For example, the MSA formed a Sunday school for the children using space in the Krannert Building of the university. They also organized the Friday prayer at the Union Building at the Medical School, invited prominent Muslim student activists (many of whom later went on to achieve national prominence as MSA and ISNA officials) such as Ahmad Sakr and Jamal Badawi to serve as khatibs, and produced a newsletter of the *qutbs*.

Several factors have been noted as contributing to the first death, and of what came to be several deaths, of MSA in Indianapolis. One interviewee reported that when Khurshid Alam was denied tenure at the university and subsequently moved to Saudi Arabia, the activity declined. Another reason given is that there was infighting within the group along ethnic lines—Arabs versus Indo-Pakistanis.[25]

The MSA remained relatively inactive throughout the remainder of the 1960s and 1970s until the Iranian students organized in the late 1970s and early 1980s in support of the Iranian Revolution under Khomeini. University officials were apparently skittish about the group's activity; when a group of Muslim women approached the university about establishing a Muslim Women's Association in 1984 there was mild, but short-lived opposition. Eventually three female Anglo American converts established the organization and began to hold meetings and to organize. The women included Nuri Alam (who had returned from Saudi Arabia and was completing a degree in computer technology), Carol L. Stone (a graduate student in biochemistry), and Habiba Ali (a secretary to Essam Ismail at ISNA). Chief among their activities were periodic "ladies' nights out" in which both African American and Anglo American women converts went to movies, had dances in each other's homes, or met at a Pizza Hut for dinner. Some of their more serious activities included annual retreats that appear to have been threefold in their emphasis: social, religious-spiritual education, and political action education. The "sisters" conducted research and not only presented lectures to each other, but also invited outside speakers to address such topics as abortion, writing effective press releases, nuclear freeze issues, and reaching out to non-Muslim women. The group began to invite sisters from neighboring states, and soon a small number of women from cities such as Chicago, Dayton, and Cincinnati began to attend the retreats.

As the Muslim Women's Association began to grow beyond the

handful of Indianapolis Muslim women they met opposition from two fronts, although closer examination reveals the fronts shared a common base; namely, ISNA. One front was the Arab Muslim women (largely the wives of ISNA officials), who viewed the association as exclusionist and as contributing to *fitnah* (chaos or disorder within the Muslim community). The other front was ISNA leadership within the headquarters at Plainfield, Indiana. For example, the association's first scheduled retreat was held at the ISNA headquarter's grounds (500,000 square meters of farmland just off I-70 between Indianapolis and Terre Haute). On the day of the retreat, however, the headquarters said the space reserved for the meeting had been given to another meeting of "brothers." At subsequent ISNA Majlis as-Shura meetings it was stated that the association duplicated the ISNA Women's Committee and would do nothing but create *fitnah* and divide efforts. The sisters of the association took the position that the Women's Committee was inactive and a mere tool for the male ISNA officials to propagandize the sisters to be submissive to men.[26] By 1986 the association was effectively dead and the MSA was in the hands of young undergraduate Arab men students, particularly a small group of Syrian students who were either employed by ISNA/NAIT or served as volunteers at the headquarters.[27]

Chronologically overlapping the Muslim Women's Association was the formation of the Association of American Muslims (AAM), an organization of Muslim converts. The AAM's membership consisted of Anglo American women who were employed as secretaries at ISNA/NAIT and university students at Purdue and Indiana University, many of whom were very active in the university MSA chapter. The group was informal, providing an opportunity for Muslim converts to gather and simply have fun. Knowing that the ISNA headquarters would be upset with the AAM, the members deliberately decided that rather than actual leadership it would have a fictional president, whose history and personality were the topic of one of the early meetings. The group's prediction about a strong response from ISNA was correct. Tariq Quraishi, then director of the Islamic Trust Publications division of the North American Islamic Trust, allegedly wrote a vitriolic letter condemning the group as divisive and racist. The AAM did eventually develop a newsletter that was favorably received by the Salafi community in the United States, Canada, Kuwait, and Saudi Arabia. By the mid-1980s, however, with Ahmad Zaki's ascendancy to the presidency of ISNA and the subsequent termination of the employment of a number of the Anglo American Muslim women from the headquarters, the group had dwindled to two or three individuals producing a newsletter.

In the mid-1980s the MSA at Indiana University–Purdue University at Indianapolis received new life when a small group of young female second-generation, primarily Indo-Pakistani, Muslim students assumed leadership. The daughter of Dawood Zwink, Anglo American convert and a vice president of ISNA, became the president of the organization. She was assisted by the daughter of a Pakistani medical doctor, the daughter of the ISNA secretary general, and the daughters of ISNA employees. The group keeps a low profile at the university, but they have been somewhat successful in reaching out to professors and moderating the views toward Muslims; their wearing of *hejab* adapted to Western tastes makes them a prominent presence at the university. One newspaper account of some of the members highlighted their ability to combine their ethnic-Islamic heritage with their American identity.

> Favorite foods? Pizza, brownies, and grape leaves. . . .
> "We're sort of like teens from the 1950s. Sort of like *Leave It To Beaver*," he says with a smile. "Or *The Brady Bunch*," someone else chimes in.
> And while they enjoy rock music, they switch the radio dial if the sound is heavy metal, Satanistic or rap.[28]

The national Muslim Student Association, begun in Peoria, Illinois, in 1963, moved its headquarters from Gary, Indiana, to Indianapolis in 1975. The MSA was formed by individuals, primarily students, who had participated in their home countries in such organizations as the Ikhwan al-Muslimun (individuals from the Sudan, Iraq, Syria, and Egypt comprising the bulk of the membership) and the Jamaat Islami of Pakistan. Many of the early MSA activists claim that the organization was run on a purely voluntary basis and that it did not accept money from overseas governments, but evidence indicates otherwise.[29] From the beginning of the MSA in Indianapolis at least the salaries of some of the Muslim workers were funded through foreign Muslim government agencies. This issue has always been a difficult one for the MSA. The organization was started to serve, at least in part, as a training ground for foreign Islamic activity among Muslim students studying in the

United States and Canada, yet it did not want to appear to be aligned with any foreign Muslim activity and thereby raise suspicions. Former MSA/ISNA headquarters employees also state that the leaders of MSA were instrumental in forming FOSIS, the European equivalent of MSA with its headquarters in England.

From the beginning of MSA until the Iranian Revolution the organization had both Sunni and Shi'a members. Ilyas Ba-Yunus, former president of ISNA, reportedly claims that three of the MSA presidents were Shi'a. However, with the Iran-Iraq War the Muslims became polarized, and those who were donating money to MSA began to pressure the organization to condemn the Shi'a. Anti-Shi'a literature was published and propagated. If elections in mosques held in trust through the North American Islamic Trust of the MSA appeared to be going Shi'a, then NAIT reminded the mosque that the property was in the hands of MSA. As a result, another organization, called MSA/PSG or Muslim Student Association–Persian Speaking Group, was formed in opposition to MSA.

In 1982 the MSA was incorporated into the Islamic Society of North America along with numerous other Muslim organizations: Islamic Teaching Center, American Muslim Scientists and Engineers (AMSE), American Muslim Social Scientists (AMSS), Islamic Medical Association (IMA), Muslim Community Association (MCA), Foundation of International Development, Muslim Youth of North America (MYNA), Malaysian Islamic Study Group (MISG), and Muslim Arab Youth Association (MAYA).[30] The formation of ISNA occurred one year after the formation of the International Institute of Islamic Thought (IIIT) in Reston, Virginia. IIIT became the think-tank of Muslim activists; many of the employees and founders were former activists within MSA. Some persons opposed to activist Islam have charged that IIIT promoted the formation of ISNA as an umbrella organization so that IIIT could have more effective control over Islamic work in the United States and Canada. Some former ISNA employees allege that ISNA's perpetual financial problems may be designed by IIIT so that it can dismiss unwanted workers under cover of financial problems. In this way, IIIT could maintain control over the grassroots Islamic activity but not be encumbered with the daily problems of administering those activities. The Majlis ash-Shura, the ruling committee of ISNA, typically contains a number of IIIT employees.

The ISNA headquarters actually employs very few individuals. In addition to the secretary general, there is the director of education, the director of the Islamic Teaching Center, the director of fund raising, a secretary for AMSS/AMSE, a groundskeeper, and a handful of secretaries. Less than 5 miles east of the ISNA headquarters is its financial wing, the North American Islamic Trust. NAIT has more employees than ISNA working in such departments as the Islamic Book Service, American Trust Publications, and the Audiovisual Center. In addition, NAIT used to run a credit union and still is involved in the Amana Mutual Fund organized through the Unified Company in Indianapolis.

Through the Islamic Teaching Center, ISNA has begun on a limited basis to reach out to the greater Indianapolis community. For example, in 1991 a coalition of ten Muslim groups in Indiana, including ISNA, joined the Indiana Interreligious Commission on Human Equality. This marked the first time that any Islamic organization was represented in any statewide ecumenical or interfaith organization.[31]

An organization whose members frequently engage in *dawah* or outreach work for ISNA is the Islamic Society of Greater Indianapolis (ISGI). ISGI was formed in the early 1980s to meet the educational and social needs of the immigrant Muslim community in Indianapolis in ways that the ISNA headquarters could not. It meets at the ISNA headquarters, typically on Sundays, for one half-day. ISGI children also frequently participate in the Muslim Youth of North America. Thus the children receive their Islamic education progressively through ISGI, then MYNA, then MSA as they enter the university. In the past, ISGI sponsored a free health clinic for Muslims through the ISNA headquarters. A number of its members are actively engaged in Christian-Muslim dialogues within the city, and a few have begun to venture into Muslim-Jewish dialogue. On occasion an Indianapolis rabbi has been invited to speak at the ISNA headquarters.

Despite the efforts of ISNA and ISGI to reach out to the non-Muslim community, relations remain strained at best. Plainfield is only a few miles from a sizable Ku Klux Klan population. Elements of a milder version of that world-view can be seen among a number of the surrounding population. Consequently, rumors about the ISNA headquarters are always in the community and frequently surface when Middle East tensions are present, sometimes leading to acts of vandalism committed against the ISNA property. Among the rumors about the ISNA headquarters are that under the mosque is a large firing range where Muslims practice in preparation to overthrow the U.S. government or that it is involved in gun running or drug smuggling to support foreign armed struggle. ISNA's response has been to install a state of the art security system to protect itself against violence.

During the Iran-Iraq War, ISNA attempted to moderate ill feelings by portraying itself as a Sunni organization and distancing itself from the Shi'a and Khomeini's regime. A similar attempt was made in the 1991 war in Kuwait when the ISNA president offered to help intervene as a fellow Muslim with Saddam Hussein on behalf of the United States and for the peace of the global community. Editorial responses to this gesture in the *Indianapolis Star* in January 1991 were generally favorable. That was a difficult time for the local immigrant Muslims, many of whom had family members in the Middle East, including Iraq and Kuwait. They naturally opposed any aggression toward their family members, but on the other hand did not want anyone to question their American identity and commitment to the United States. As an Iraqi professional said, "Anything I say betrays someone."

MUSLIM RELATIONS

As Muslims attempt to forge a cohesive community out of their varied backgrounds, divisions do remain between and within Muslim groups. The clearest division is between the immigrant and the indigenous communities. These two groups tend not to socialize with each other. They worship together usually only on Eids, and even then they differ about the format. By and large, the immigrant community is financially better situated than the indigenous, largely African American community. The groups live on opposite sides of town, worship in different mosques, and have different interests.

Within the immigrant community there is also a clear split between conservatives and liberals. Muslims, primarily Arabs, who arrived earliest to the city as well as some of the Pakistani and Indian physicians tend to be more liberal. Many of their children date and marry outside the faith. Some within this group have even hidden their Islamic identity to get jobs in the religiously conservative Midwest, whereas others struggle to understand what their identity is. For example, in 1991 a young second-generation Egyptian man raised in Indiana began his seminary studies toward ordination in the Methodist church. During his first semester, he discovered that although he had been raised a Christian, his father was indeed a Muslim and was offended by his son's desire for ordination. The young man withdrew from seminary and is still experiencing a crisis of identity.

Those immigrant Muslims who do practice Islam (in terms of participating in Jumah prayer, fasting, and keeping Islamic names) are likely to be associated with ISNA in some fashion. This group tends to be religiously conservative and is composed primarily of Arabs and Indo-Pakistanis, some of whom have a Muslim movement background.

Thus the major divisions among Muslims are generally along conservative-liberal, socioeconomic, and immigrant-indigenous lines. Among the indigenous Muslims, the division seems to be related to the choice made between Warith Deen Muhammad or Louis Farrakhan as leader. The new group of second-generation Muslims tends to be in a category by itself. Combining ethnic Islamic and American identities, they tend to be more liberal than the larger conservative immigrant community without having assimilated to the degree that the more liberal immigrant community has. They have developed their own unique brand of living Islam with confidence, and they can communicate with Americans on their own terms. One of the most striking features of this group is the central position given to women in leadership roles. In fact, the women lead the MSA chapter at the university in Indianapolis, and young women are actively leading the ISNA youth group, MYNA.

CONCLUSION

Islam at an institutional level in Indianapolis is in flux. The last five years have seen the rise of the Farrakhan-led version of the African American Muslim movement and what may be the concomitant waning of influence within the African American community of the Wallace Muhammad version. The next few years will afford the opportunity to witness the results of the former's more isolationist stance versus the latter's more assimilationist approach.

Within the immigrant Muslim community alternatives to the

ISNA-led movement have been developed, especially among more liberal immigrant Muslims. It yet remains to be seen exactly what form Islam will take among the second generation Muslims. To date they appear to be developing an effective balance, if not integration, of their dual cultures.

The Muslim women, particularly the Caucasian converts, are more difficult to characterize. At the institutional level, for example in their interaction with ISNA, there appears to be a marked decrease in activity. However, at a personal level many of the women are finding new ways to balance their various priorities, including their professions, families, and personal relationships with other Muslims.

NOTES

1. Pierre Crabites, "American Negro Mohammedans," *the Moslem World* 23 (July 1933): 284.

2. Yvonne Y. Haddad, *A Century of Islam in America*, The Muslim World Today, Occasional Paper No. 4 (Washington, D.C.: Islamic Affairs Programs, 1986), p. 1.

3. Abdo A. Elkholy, *The Arab Moslems in the United States: Religion and Assimilation* (New Haven, Conn.: College and University Press, 1966); Yvonne Y. Haddad and Adair T. Lummis, *Islamic Values in the United States* (New York: Oxford University Press, 1987); Ahmad Naserdine, *History of American Moslem Society* (Toledo, Ohio: The Islamic Center of Toledo, 1970).

4. Rebecca Bibbs, "Muslim Leaders Point to Public Misconceptions," *Indianapolis News* (August 25, 1990), p. B-5.

5. Eunice McLayea, "Black Muslims Change Image, Encourage Membership of Whites," *Indianapolis Star* (September 3, 1978), sec. 3, p. 11. Recent estimates of the number of Muslims in America range from 2 million to 8 million, with the most reliable 1986 estimate being approximately 4 million (Carol L. Stone, "Estimate of Muslims Living in America," in Yvonne Y. Haddad, ed., *The Muslims of America* [New York: Oxford University Press, 1991], pp. 25–36). However, such estimates of the Muslim population are rough and imprecise at best. This caveat noted, Stone's method for estimating the Muslim population, when used, yields a 1980 Muslim population of approximately 30,000 in the state of Indiana, which is approximately 0.56 percent of the total state population. The same method when applied to provisional 1990 census data indicates a Muslim population still of 30,000 in Indiana and 4,000 for the capital city of Indianapolis (*Census '90: Quick Release Reports, Pub-*

lic Law Data: PL Report #1 Indiana/Counties/Places [Bloomington: Indiana Business Research Center of the Indiana University School of Business, 1991], pp. 1, 4). The 1980 census indicated that the distribution of Muslims, indicated as percent of total Indiana Muslim population, by area of origin is as follows: African American (54.8 percent), Middle Eastern/North African (27.1 percent), Eastern European (7.7 percent), Asian (5.2 percent, and Subsaharan (4.6 percent). This distribution differs significantly (X^2 = 11901.91, ***p < .001) from the U.S. Muslim distribution as estimated by Stone (Eunice McLayea, "Black Muslims Change Image, Encourage Membership of Whites," *Indianapolis Star* [September 3, 1978], sec. 3, p. 11).

6.   J. Gordon Melton, *The Encyclopedia of American Religions*, 3d ed. (Detroit: Gale Research Inc., 1989), p. 840.

7.   Lee Flor, "Hoosier Moslems Worship Allah, But Are at Peace with Christians," *Indianapolis Times* (March 7, 1959), p. 6.

8.   Melton, *The Encyclopedia of American Religions*, p. 840.

9.   Irving Leibowitz, *My Indiana* (Englewood Cliffs, N.J.: Prentice-Hall, 1964), pp. 63–64.

10.   Al Bolin, "Here's What Black Muslims Are Doing in Indianapolis," *Indianapolis Times* (March 8, 1964), p. 3.

11.   Mohammed A. Rauf, Jr., "What the Black Muslims Are Doing in Indianapolis," *Indianapolis Times* (February 22, 1965), p. 3.

12.   McLayea, "Black Muslims Change Image," p. 11.

13.   Bolin, "Here's What Black Muslims Are Doing in Indianapolis," p. 3.

14.   McLayea, "Black Muslims Change Image," p. 11.

15.   David McCarty, "Mission: Dispel Poor Image," *Indianapolis News* (June 26, 1982), p. 8.

16.   Edward McKinley, "Muslim Criticizes Welfare," *Indianapolis Star* (September 23, 1984), p. B-10.

17.   Imam Muhammad Siddiq, interview with author, Indianapolis, January 29, 1992.

18.   James Muhammad, *The Final Call* (May 4, 1992), p. 30.

19.   Muhammad Siddiq, interview with author, Indianapolis, January 29, 1992.

20.   Carol Elrod, "Muslims to Build Mosque, School on Northwestside," *Indianapolis Star* (February 3, 1990), p. A-11.

21.   Abdulaziz Arif, telephone interview with author, Indianapolis, April 1992.

22.   Elrod, "Muslim to Build Mosque," p. 11.

23.   "Chapter Sensitizes IUPUI to Muslim Truth, Concerns," *Sagamore* (February 3, 1992), p. 2.

24. Marjoe Creamer, "Moslems Open Mission To Convert Hoosiers," *Indianapolis Times* (November 13, 1960), p. 4.

25. Nuri Alam, interview with author, Indianapolis, October 1991.

26. Zeba Siddiqui, *A Guide for Muslim Parents Living in North America* (Indianapolis: American Trust Publications, 1976).

27. Nuri Alam and Carol L. Stone, a series of interviews with author, Indianapolis, October 1991–January 1992.

28. Ruth Holladay, "Muslim Teens: East Meets West for Central Indiana Teens Who Follow the Islamic Faith," *The Indianapolis Star* (July 22, 1990), p. H-8.

29. Letters dated between May 2, 1978 and July 13, 1979, addressed to "The Muslim Student Association of the U.S.A. and Canada" at P.O. Box 38, Plainfield, Indiana, 46168, and signed by Faraj Senoussi Abedsaid, the Financial Counselor for the Embassy of the Socialist People's Libyan Arab Jamahiriya in Washington, D.C., state clearly that the money was to cover "the monthly salaries of the persons" mentioned in attached lists. It included the names of MSA activists and leaders, some of whom later became leaders of the Islamic movement in the Sudan and one who became a president of the Islamic Society of North America.

30. Gutbi Mahdi Ahmed, "Muslim Organizations in the United States," in Yvonne Y. Haddad, ed., *The Muslims of America*, pp. 11–24.

31. "Muslims Join Human Equality Organization," *Indianapolis Star* (January 17, 1991), p. B-2.

CHAPTER 12

Diversity in Rochester's Islamic Community

Tamara Sonn

Rochester's Islamic community, like its Christian and Jewish counterparts, reflects the diversity of the ethnic backgrounds of its members. However, due to a greater proportion both of recent immigrants from various Muslim countries and recent African American converts to Islam, that diversity seems more apparent than in the Jewish and Christian communities. The processes of assimilation and identity formation have not had as long to take effect as they have among Jewish and Christian citizens of Rochester. Moreover, some of the diversity of the city's Jewish and Christian communities can be accounted for by sectarian differences. The Protestant sects are distinguished by varying beliefs, rituals, and organizational frameworks, as are the Ukrainian and Greek churches from the Roman Catholic churches, for example, and the Orthodox and Reform temples from each other and the Conservative Jewish community. By contrast, Rochester's three major mosques are all Sunni, making the ethnic diversity among them even more apparent.

The purpose of this chapter is to present some observations about Rochester's diverse Islamic community, both from the standpoint of members of its various segments, and from persons who are not Muslim. Research is based primarily on interviews with individuals representing different Islamic groups in the Rochester area.

279

SOURCES OF DIVERSITY IN ROCHESTER'S SUNNI ISLAMIC COMMUNITY

The predominant differences among Rochester's Sunni Muslims are ethnic. In some cases, their organizations vary with the groups countries of origin. The major communities are African American, Arab, Pakistani, and Turkish. These differences become evident in two ways. First, there are linguistic and overall cultural differences. The *khutba* (sermon) at the Turkish mosque is delivered in Turkish, whereas that at the African American mosque is in English. The Islamic Center's *khutbas* are also in English, as are administrative and social meetings, owing to the diversity of native languages represented in the center's membership. Urdu, Arabic, Pashtu, and Persian are frequently heard in group conversations.

Ethnic differences are also evidenced in the differing degrees to which Muslims have been assimilated into the overall Rochester community. The degree of assimilation often varies with the length of time the community has had a visible presence in Rochester. The Turkish community, for example, was established when some 200–300 families immigrated in the late 1960s, attracted primarily by Rochester's men's clothing industry. It is now a familiar feature in Rochester's multicultural landscape. The African American Islamic community was established in 1960, and although it experienced a great deal of harassment in its early years, it has been well established since the mid-1960s. The Islamic Center is relatively new, and is not necessarily considered the "center" by the older communities.

The level of assimilation also seems to vary according to the degree of ethnic identity assumed by the communities' mosques. Members of mosques with obvious national, cultural, or ethnic identity tend not to be as deeply integrated into American culture. The Turkish mosque, for example, was established in 1980. Previously, Turkish Muslims had worshipped with other Muslims in a room made available at the University of Rochester's Interfaith Chapel. The Turkish mosque is run by the Turkish Society of Rochester and obviously stresses its ties to the home country. Its Imam is Turkish, administrative and social meetings are generally carried on in Turkish, and zakat is collected regularly and sent to support projects in Turkey. Many of the older members of the Turkish community do not speak English.

The Islamic Center, established at its current location in 1985, also sends zakat remissions abroad, although not exclusively; determination of the recipients of zakat funds is generally based on need. According to an officer of the center, significant portions of the funds have been sent to Bangladesh, Pakistan, and Kashmir. The Iraqi Kurds also received Islamic Center support, as has Rochester's main African American mosque, Masjid Taqwa. The Islamic Center, therefore, is not specifically identified with a single ethnic group; most Turks belong to the Turkish mosque and most African Americans belong to Masjid Taqwa.

The ethnic identity of certain mosques tends to be reinforced by the fact that they serve as community centers for new immigrants and converts. Indeed, recent immigrants often find themselves gravitating toward the mosque, even if they were infrequent attenders in their countries of origin. This is a common phenomenon among minority communities. When they are in "diaspora"— that is, no longer able to rely on national identity as such or on direct attachment to a homeland—religious identity often takes on heightened importance. Those without ethnically identified mosque affiliation on the other hand, tend to be more integrated into the Rochester community as a whole, or into other groups reflecting their culture of origin. This is evident especially in the case of pluralistic cultures, such as that of Arabs. Rochester's Palestinians have a nonsectarian community center, for example, a chapter of the National Association of Palestinian Americans.

In this context the African American Sunni mosque, Masjid Taqwa, represents an interesting dimension of cultural diversity. It is considered an integral part of American culture by members of recent immigrant communities (such as Pakistani or Arab), but of a unique aspect of American culture, African American. For that reason, both the Islamic Center and the Turkish mosque tend to leave community outreach programs (*dawa*) to the Masjid Taqwa. "You are much better at *dawa* than we are," Imam Abdel-Malik Hasan of Masjid Taqwa quoted Islamic Center representatives' frequent statements to him. The Imam explained that what they mean is that African Americans know American culture and are thus better equipped to transmit Islam to the community. However, that outreach is by nature rather limited. Masjid Taqwa indeed carries on active outreach. It has operated its own Sister Clara Muhammad School since 1979. Teaching classes through grade six, it is accredited through grade eight, and expects to expand to the eighth grade level by the end of 1992. With a standard academic curriculum, plus Islamic studies and Arabic language, the school currently has sixty-five students. Its graduates consistently have performed above average upon entrance into public high schools and frequently go on to college. The school is entirely support by zakat offerings from members of Masjid Taqwa, as well as individual donations from members of the Islamic Center, as well as tuition. It therefore provides an invaluable service for the Islamic community, but those who choose to benefit from this service are virtually entirely from the African American community. Non-African American Muslims generally send their children to public schools or secular private schools.

The same is true of the second major area of Masjid Taqwa's active outreach efforts: prison programs. Imam Hasan himself worked for five years full time as chaplain in New York's federal prison system. He now personally visits the federal prison twice monthly, and the mosque has trained Imams for three major county and state correctional facilities. The conversion rate from these outreach programs is extremely high, reports the Imam. Yet again, the success rate is highest among African Americans. Islam seems to provide for them spiritual solace, self-respect, dignity and religious inspiration, as well as a sense of cultural identity. And again, the unique identity of African American culture in Masjid Taqwa is intensified.

This pattern is also evident in the third major area of outreach activity for Masjid Taqwa: high schools. Upstate New York high schools have been the focus of increased activity among several other groups identifying themselves as Muslim, which have particular appeal to African Americans. Dominant among them, according to Imam Hasan, are the Five Percenters and the Ansaru Allah. The Five Percenters, or the Five Percent Nation, are a group founded by Clarence 13X "Puddin'" Smith who split with the Nation of Islam in the turbulent 1960s. The name is based on identity with the 5 percent of the human race identified by Elijah Muhammad as neither the exploiters (10 percent of the human race) nor the exploited (85 percent of the human race), but the poor and righteous teachers of the truth that "the Black man is God, and the women are the field in which to produce their nation."[1] The Ansaru Allah, led by Imam Isa al-Haadi al-Mahdi in Brooklyn, seems to teach a combination of Islamic doctrine and black nationalism, emphasizing the acquisition of wealth. According to Imam Hasan, who does not identify these groups as truly Muslim, both are increasingly active in upstate New York. The Five Percenters are particularly visible in Albany and Newburg, New York, and have begun recruiting converts in Rochester's high schools. Masjid Taqwa is making a concerted effort to reach high school students, therefore, to clarify understandable confusion about the teaching of Islam and to present what it believes to be the truly Islamic path to dignity and piety. Imam Hasan reports that many of their high school converts come from among those previously drawn to the Five Percent nation or Ansaru Allah community.

The pattern of conversion to Islam in Rochester, therefore, seems to strengthen the ethnic identity of Masjid Taqwa as African American. Indeed, among the over 200 families belonging to Masjid Taqwa, only three individual members are white. By contrast, the Islamic Center focuses its outreach on interfaith dialogue. Although the Islamic Center is very active in this regard and its efforts are highly effective in opening communication among Rochester's various faith communities, these activities generally do not result in conversion to Islam. Most of the increase in the Islamic Center's membership is due to immigration and reproduction, whereas Masjid Taqwa's growth is through the high conversion rate among African Americans.

ARE ETHNIC DIFFERENCES A PROBLEM?

Ethnic differences in general do not seem to be problematic in themselves. For example, Masjid Taqwa sees itself as a part of specifically African American culture, which it recognizes as a unique culture within the cultural mix of the United States. "We have our own culture," the Imam stated, "and it is perfectly understandable if non-African Americans prefer to associate with participants in their own cultural communities." But when cultural differences coincide with distinctions in socioeconomic levels, ethnic differences can be confused with class distinctions and sometimes with prejudice identified with ethnic or socioeconomic differences.

For example, members of Rochester's African American mosques tend to characterize themselves as more zealous regarding Islamic injunctions, such as those against the consumption of pork and alcoholic beverages, than members of other mosques. Some regard participation by certain members of the Islamic Center and the Turkish community in commercial enterprises that include the sale of pork and alcoholic beverages as laxity in the practice of Islam. Members of the Islamic Center, on the other hand, tend to be perceived as more prosperous and more successful, working within Rochester's professional and commercial community. Some of its members even regard the underrepresentation there of members of the African American Islamic community as self-induced, the result of laziness or ineptitude. In an interfaith discussion of Islam and national identity, some Christian students suggested that perhaps the African American Muslims' apparent preference for their own mosques stems from the long heritage of racist prejudice they have suffered in the United States. A member of the Islamic Center replied, "Racism in the United States is a thing of the past." When asked about the success of David Duke's recent campaign in Louisiana, he replied, "I agree with David Duke. Welfare is killing this country. These people live off the dole and don't live for anything but handouts." Although the exponent of this position described it as a political stand rather than racism, this kind of attitude is often characterized by those who oppose it as a kind of racism since by far the largest community represented among welfare recipients is African American. It should also be noted that economic frustration in the United States has fostered a growing intolerance of welfare and its recipients among a broad spectrum of the population; it cannot be identified with any particular religious group.

Some members of the Islamic Center indicate they are aware of the different perceptions that are held of the various Rochester mosques, but feel that charges of ethnic prejudice are unwarranted. The Islamic Center is open to all Muslims. Membership includes people from all over the world. Among the Arabs, Palestinian families make up the majority (some 35–40 families out of total of nearly 500 families). There are also African American and Turkish families who are members of the Islamic Center, rather than the Turkish or African American mosques. Forty percent of the Center's membership is Pakistani.

However, according to an officer of the Center, 75–80 percent of the administrative and financial support of the center is provided by Pakistanis. (The center's current Imam is also Pakistani.) When asked why this is so, the official replied that it is because the

Pakistanis as a group tend to be more highly educated and professional than other ethnic groups represented in the center. Many of the Pakistani families are two-career families, with both the husband and the wife educated and professional. This high-profile participation has apparently led to the perception by some that the Islamic Center is dominated by Pakistanis. The center officer noted that Egyptian members also are mainly educated and professional and likewise play a leading role in the center's administration, but that there are fewer of them.

Another aspect of tension among the communities was revealed in an incident several years ago when some African American families wanted to leave the primarily African American Masjid Taqwa and join the Islamic Center. A representative of the Islamic Center said concern was expressed by some members of both mosques that because these families were well placed in Rochester's professional community, it might look as if the Islamic Center had recruited Masjid Taqwa's members, or were competing for members of th Masjid Taqwa, or that the families had "defected" to the Islamic Center. The informant indicated that the Islamic Center felt it had thus been put in an unfair position because it could not and did not want to turn anyone away, but it also did not want to inflame ethnic or racial tensions.

As noted previously, since then African American families have become members of the Islamic Center, and feelings of distrust have, for the most part, faded. Still, perception of the degree of ethnic clinquishness within Rochester's Islamic community seems to vary from generation to generation. Older members of all three of Rochester's Sunni mosques, when questioned, expressed awareness that there had been tensions among ethnic groups, but believed that these were a thing of the past. Relations among the various groups were cordial and even warm now, the elders believed.

Among groups of students from all three mosques, on the other hand, there was open concern about several aspects of ethnic diversity. Students from both the Islamic Center and the Turkish mosque, for example, expressed skepticism about African Americans' Islamic authenticity. "They probably weren't Muslim in Africa and even if they were, they lost touch with it in America. Then they suddenly discover Islam and adopt it as a way of gaining some kind of ethnic or cultural identity," as one student put it. Other

members of the group generally concurred. "Even when they come
to the Islamic Center," another added, "they stick together and
they act different." When questioned about the nature of this "acting different," the student said, "They sit together in the back and
talk during the *khutba*." It was pointed out that the Pakistanis tend
to sit together, as do the Egyptians, and so forth, and that some
younger members of the Masjid Taqwa think Islam is just a matter
of cultural identity for immigrant Muslims, too, because "they
don't even bother with *dawa* and sell *haram* [forbidden] food in
their stores," as one African American Muslim put it. Students
from the Islamic Center and the Turkish Center had to smile in
recognition of those allegations. Some acknowledged that that is
what they accuse their parents of all the time. "They come to
America and 'make it' [economically] and they show everyone how
successful they are by making the *hajj* [pilgrimage to Mecca]. But
they don't even know what *ijtihad* is and have never heard of the
need for *tajdid* or *islah!*"[2]

Two Turkish students in the group agreed that the adults go to
mosque just to show off their fancy cars and clothes to their countrymen, but at the same time, "they try to teach us that we're the
best Muslims because we're Turkish." They pointed out that they
knew that Pakistanis taught their children that Pakistanis were the
best Muslims, Egyptians taught that Egyptians were the best Muslims, and so on. The students generally agreed that this tendency
on the part of the older generation is both a result of social isolation in a primarily non-Muslim country and a cause of intensifica-
tion of that isolation.

It should be stressed that the perception of snobbishness or
single-ethnic dominance, even among students, is not universal
with regard to Rochester's Islamic Center. Other members interviewed, Persian, Palestinian, and Egyptian, expressed no feelings of
discomfort over ethnic diversity in the Islamic Center. It was described as warm, welcoming, and supportive; and its diversity perfectly representative of both Islamic universalism and principles of
tolerance. "Ethnic differences are irrelevant among believers,"
commented an Iranian student.

Interestingly, the positions of the Arab and Turkish communities seem to be quite different from each other. The Turkish
Center tends to be considered anamolous. It is well established and
keeps a low profile and is considered more cultural and ethnic than

racist or even sectarian in identity. Indeed, a public appeal for aid for victims of the recent earthquakes in Turkey elicited a sympathetic response from the Rochester community as a whole. Moreover, the use of the Turkish language in services is generally considered the Turks' right, even though it tends to automatically exclude non-Turks. Turkish Center members tend not to be identified with specific political or social issues. The Arab community, by contrast, has a higher profile stemming mainly from interest in the Arab world's ongoing political struggles. On most issues, the Islamic community reflects the range of opinion one would expect in any diverse sector of American society. For example, the Islamic community tended to be divided on the issue of the Gulf War. On the issue of Palestinian statelessness, and more specifically, Israeli occupation of Jerusalem, there is far greater unanimity. In any event, the Arabs are an integral part of the Islamic Center, although it does not serve as an Arab cultural center. The Arab cultural community tends to be nonsectarian; Muslim Arabs frequently socialize with other Arabs, whether Muslim or not. This phenomenon is particularly evident among Arab students in Rochester, whose several colleges and universities host dozens of Arab students annually.

Indeed, there is a growing feeling of cooperation and community among the various mosques. All the communities have had problems to deal with. The primarily immigrant communities of the Turkish mosque and the Islamic Center generally identify their major problems as similar to those of other immigrant communities in the United States—dealing with legal immigration issues, establishing economic and cultural ties—rather than specific issues of local prejudice. The African American community, on the other hand, has had to deal concurrently with the extreme racial prejudice that plagues many urban centers, as well as organizational and economic problems. The African American Islamic community began in Rochester in 1960 as followers of Elijah Muhammad. For the first few years of their existence, they were routinely harassed by police. For one thing, they had trouble finding a landlord to rent to them. Having tried dozens of locations and even offering to pay extra rent, they were informed by one potential landlady that she had been instructed by the FBI not to rent to their group under any circumstances. (Eventually, a landlord defied the unlawful order.) When they planned meetings, police cars would gather at the designated place, clear the sidewalks, and frequently prevent people from entering the meeting. Matters came to a head on February 1, 1963, when police demanded entry into a meeting, claiming to have a report that someone inside had a gun. Imam Hasan reports that his people had searched all attendees (fewer than seventy), and that the report was false. Nevertheless, arrests were made and nineteen men were charged with five felonies each, including unlawful assembly, inciting to riot, and resisting arrest. Still, the community grew and developed. After 1975 they moved away from the teachings of Elijah Muhammad in favor of the mainstream Islam taught in the American Muslim Mission of Elijah Muhammad's son Imam W. Deen Muhammad.

Some open rifts have developed among the Sunni Muslim communities. Ill feelings were aroused, for example, when members of the African American mosque protested the sale of pork and alcoholic beverages, as mentioned earlier by the students, in stores owned by members of the Islamic Center in the depressed inner-city neighborhood that Masjid Taqwa calls home. According to the elders of both communities, however, that issue is no longer a real problem. Members of both communities also have come to accept the Turkish community's desire to maintain cultural cohesion by establishing its own mosque.

Among current problems is the evidence of perceived "racism" on the part of some members of the Islamic Center toward one another. As one Pakistani student put it, "Pakistanis are the worst racists . . . even though they would never admit it." His statement was made in the context of a discussion of anti-Arab sentiment and was meant to refer to a sense of cultural superiority. This view was reflected in comments by other non-Arab Muslim students and is reminiscent of instances of non-Muslim America's anti-Arab sentiment. Several Turkish and Pakistani students complained about being mistaken for Arabs. They expressed exasperation at the American habit of identifying Muslims with Arabs and, further, identifying Arabs with terrorists. Although these students generally recognized that the fault lies with the misinformation of the American populace, some nonetheless wanted to clarify that they are not Arabs. Similarly, many non-African American Muslim students expressed a desire to distance themselves from the African American Muslim community, not because of their own prejudice, they said, but because of Americans' inability to distinguish among the various groups of African Americans calling themselves Muslims (i.e., among such groups as Louis Farrakhan's Nation of Islam, as well as some of the other splinter groups mentioned previously).

Still, the overall emphasis today is on cooperation among the communities. Communal celebrations of feasts such as Eid al-Fitr (feast ending the Ramadan fast) are jointly planned, and held at the Islamic Center. Only the Turkish community chose to celebrate the end of this year's Ramadan fast separately, and that much to the chagrin of some of its younger members. The issue of communal solidarity among Rochester's Sunni Muslims, in fact, constituted the thrust of this year's sermon at the celebration. The Islamic Center's Imam Shafiq called on Rochester's Muslims to overcome their cliquishness and come together as a unified and mutually supportive community:

> Islam speaks of unity of Muslims. Disunity in Islam is close to *kufr* (disbelief). We all believe in Allah (SWT), the Holy Qur'an, Muhammad (SAWS) as the last messenger and prophet of Allah. We all face the Ka'ba for prayer five times a day. We all believe that no race, culture, ethnicity or geographical location will come to our rescue on the day of judgment. It is *iman* (faith) and *amal* (deeds) that are counted. Everyone of us knows the hadith: "There is no superiority of an Arab over a non-Arab, a white man over a black man except in *taqwa* (fear of Allah SWT)." But our actions are contrary to all our belief systems and faith. This problem of ethnicity must be arrested. . . . [In North America] mosques and Islamic centers are built in the name of Muslim countries. Mosques and Islamic centers are built in the name of ethnicity and controlled by the same ethnic group. There are some Muslim countries who support such ethnic approaches. The situation is such that one ethnic group is not ready to pray with the other even on Eid day. Thanks to Allah (SWT), Muslims of North America have become conscious of this problem of ethnicity. Yet I see no organized effort to solve this problem. We must act fast before our ethnic differences become so severe that they cannot be resolved.[3]

Interestingly, there is a growing sense among African American Muslims that they are coming into their own. Imam Hasan readily acknowledged mistakes that had been made in the early days of American Muslims' efforts to find the true faith. He expressed appreciation for the generous help of shaykhs and scholars from

Mecca, Egypt, Pakistan, and even Libya who for years made themselves available to give spiritual guidance to the emerging American Muslim Mission. Now there is a palpable self-confidence at the mosque, a recognition that they are now in a position to reciprocate. Imam Hasan expressed confidence that African American Muslims can now offer guidance and example to those Muslim communities, both in North America and abroad, who seem to have lost touch with the vital spirit of Islam. Members of the Turkish Mosque seem to be grappling with issues of assimilation, particularly differences between the older and younger generations. Representatives of the Islamic Center seem to be focusing on educating the Rochester community about Islam and overcoming negative stereotypes of Muslims in America. The African American Sunni community, on the other hand, seems to look to the future with the assurance of one that has weathered its worst storms. To those who have become complacent in their Islam, who relegate their Islam to cultural identity or ritual practice, indeed, perhaps African American Islam can provide living example of the communal transformation, the call to justice and universal human dignity, that characterized the generation of the Salaf.

CONCLUSIONS

Ethnic differences evident among members of Rochester's Sunni Islamic community appear to parallel those of other ethnic and national groupings in America's cities. Even among Roman Catholic churches in Rochester, some are still predominantly Italian, some are Polish, and so on. As assimilation proceeds, these differences tend to become less apparent. Nevertheless there is, despite fading ethnic identities among various Roman Catholic parishes, an overall sense of belonging to a broader, indeed universal, community. There is virtual unanimity on doctrine, projects are undertaken on a diocesewide scale, and families easily move from parish to parish when they relocate to different neighborhoods. This kind of solidarity is largely a function of a well-defined tradition of hierarchy in Roman Catholicism, one level of which is represented by the Rochester diocesan bishop. The Sunni Muslim community thus far has no such well-defined tradition of hierarchy to rely on for communal identity. Indeed, there is no clergy, as such, in Sunni Islam. It is therefore not surprising that as developing communities in a predominantly non-Islamic environment, Muslims seek solidarity among their conationals or coreligionists. It appears that, when there is an identifiable ethnicity, such as that of the Turks, solidarity becomes more attractive and thus more dominant. However, where there is no such ethnically identified center, religious identity as a feature of cultural identity appears to supersede that of nationality and becomes more central.

The very existence of two levels of loyalty that compete for allegiance is considered threatening to some Muslim integrists and is blamed for much of the disunity in which the Islamic world finds itself today. On the North American scene, where the Muslim community is being reconstituted in a primarily non-Muslim land, the salient feature appears to be the absence of a single Islamic authority, of a recognized tradition of hierarchy, to provide a communal identity broader than that of one's ethnic group. There is no local or regional body of religious scholars or jurisprudence for Rochester's Muslims, dealing with social issues faced daily by the various ethnic communities. Although there are national organizations of Muslims, especially among academic groups, none has acquired exclusive legitimacy or taken a dominant or centralizing role. Nor is there even an established vehicle for recognizing or legitimizing such an organization if one were to emerge. The existence of various international bodies of Muslims, such as the Organization of Islamic Conference, does indicate that there is a high degree of international solidarity among Muslims or an intensive effort to deepen that solidarity. Indeed, the past century of Islamic intellectual history can be described as a discussion of whether or not, or how, Muslims should deal with the end of a unified Islamic religiopolitical entity: how to maintain Islamic universalism in a world of geopolitically limited nation-states. The divisions within Rochester's Sunni Islamic community are no doubt a reflection of this broader pattern, heightened by their status as religious and cultural minorities.

NOTES

1. Imam Muhammad Armiya Nu'Man, *What Every American Should Know About Islam and the Muslims* (Jersey City, N.J.: New Mind Publications, 1985), p. 32.

2. *Ijtihad* is fresh interpretation of revealed Islamic principles for

implementation in changed-changing circumstances. It, along with *tajdid*, renewal, and *islah*, reform, is a major theme among modern Islamic thinkers.

3. From "Summary of the Eid Khutba," April 1992, by Dr. M. Shafiq of the Islamic Center of Rochester.

CHAPTER 13

The Islamic Center of New England

Mary Lahaj

THE IMMIGRANT GENERATION

The Islamic Center of New England was the long-range dream of seven Lebanese Muslim families who immigrated in the 1900s from different regions of Lebanon to Quincy Point in Quincy, Massachusetts. They were among the first wave of Muslim immigrants who entered America from the Middle East in the years 1875 to 1912.[1] Two of these seven families were from the Shi'a tradition; the majority were Sunnis.

During the period between 1880 and 1925 almost 90 percent of the Arab immigrants to come to America were Christians from Mount Lebanon.[2] The majority of Lebanese who settled in the Quincy Point neighborhood were Melkite Christians. Most of the Lebanese immigrants, Christian and Muslim, met for the first time in Quincy. Although their initial concern was earning a living, as a minority group they soon established strong social ties along ethnic and linguistic lines and started to form a community.

Lacking in training and skills and impeded by a language barrier, both groups of Lebanese immigrants made slow progress adjusting to American life. The religious orientation of the Lebanese Christians, however, made their integration into American society easier than that of the Muslims. The Christians had two churches in Boston, Our Lady of the Cedars (Maronite) and Our Lady of the Annunciation (Melkite). Those living in Quincy Point accepted the local Roman Catholic church, St. Joseph's, as their parish. The Muslims, on the other hand, had no institutions to help them assimilate or support them in the process of social integration.[3]

They were therefore unable to fulfill such Islamic communal obligations as praying over the dead, reading the Qur'an, weekly congregational prayers, and obligatory charity. One of the immigrants,
Mohamed Omar (Awad), pushed for the group to get organized,
and because he could read and write, he became a leader in the
nascent community. Omar knew religious history and the Qur'an,
and his peers depended on him for such things as citing the moon
at the beginning and end of Ramadan, counseling, marrying, and
burying, as well as reading and writing all of their correspondence
in Arabic. Omar became the first official leader (Imam) by consensus, serving until 1982.

In Quincy, where the pool of marriageable Muslims was small,
marrying outside the faith was tolerated. Of the immigrant generation, two of the seven men married American Christians, one went
back to Lebanon to find a bride, and one was married before he
left and later sent for his wife. Others married Muslim women they
met in America. As their children grew to marriageable age, unions
were arranged from among the seven families, including two
Sunni-Shi'i mixed marriages. Because of their common ethnicity,
the children of the immigrants never realized that there was any
difference between them until they became adults and learned
about sectarian variations.

In the second generation, interfaith marriages occurred more
frequently. Every family experienced conversions of American
women who married Muslim men; American men also converted,
but with less frequency. By the third generation, most members of
the seven founding families married outside their religious and
ethnic groups. It should be noted, however, that the divorce rate is
very high among members who married outside their faith and
that all those interviewed in this study cited the social importance
of having a mosque where young people can meet and marry their
own kind.

In 1931 the Quincy neighbors decided to organize a social club
called the *Sons of Lebanon*. The purpose of the club was to teach
children the Arabic language, help immigrants learn English, collect funds for charity, and discuss common concerns. But when the
Christians appeared to identify with the Lebanese state carved out
of Syria by France, and wanted to use the Lebanese flag that pic-
tured the cedars of Lebanon as the emblem of the Quincy group,
the Muslim minority within the group objected. They wanted to

use a flag that represented a united Arab world. The question of which flag to use stirred up old-country political, nationalistic, and religious loyalties. This tension pointed to the fact that there really were two separate religious identities or traditions, which necessarily involved different political-geographic loyalties peculiar to the complex history of Lebanon-Syria. One man, whose father was a founding member of the Sons of Lebanon, put it this way: "One Arab would say, 'We don't want to walk under the Lebanese flag!' And the other would say, 'Well, we don't want to walk under the sword of Islam.'"[4]

The national and political differences between the Christian Lebanese and the Muslim Arabs motivated the Quincy Muslims to redefine their community and to form a social club and charitable organization of their own. In 1934, aligning themselves with other Arabic-speaking Muslims in Boston, Sunni and Shi'i, they founded the Arab American Banner Society which was chartered on November 9, 1937, under the provisions of the business corporation law of the commonwealth. Because according to state law one must be a citizen to sign a state charter, some founding members who were not citizens were unable to sign on. The first president of the club was Eassa Ali. The constitution of the society, written in 1937, states in Article I, Section 2, that "The purpose of the Society shall be the preservation of the racial identity among the Arabs in the United States and its development in accordance with the highest principles and traditions of American life and education; and to aid the Arabic countries in the fields of politics, education, and economics."

Like other Muslims residing in America at the time, the Arab immigrants in the words of C. Eric Lincoln "seemed content, or at least constrained, to keep Islam within the parameters of their ethnic associations."[5] In the constitution no reference is made to religion, although there is clear evidence of concern for Arab nationalism. At the time the constitution was written, the Arab world had been colonized by Western powers, undermining any hope for unity among Arab countries. The immigrants' disapproval of this situation was reflected in Article II of their constitution, which states that the privilege of membership in the society is extended to all those who "desire independence for the Arab countries . . ." In Article V, the constitution also makes it clear that the Muslims saw the possibility of integrating Arab-Islamic and American values. It states: "The Society shall endeavor to conduct a school to teach the Arabic language and to educate our youths in the fundamentals of American Democracy . . . in accordance with the highest principles and traditions of American life and education."

Thus the earliest efforts of the immigrant generation, both Christian and Muslim, to preserve their ethnic identity reflect a certain insecurity felt by many immigrants coming to America. Both Christians and Muslims attempted to reaffirm their ethnic identity by forming strong community ties and social clubs. Through the organization of the Arab American Banner Society the Quincy Muslims were able to act on their need for religious community. And by pooling their limited resources as a community they were able to fulfill at least one of the pillars of Islam, the obligatory giving of alms (zakat).

Recognizing the need for a meeting place the society purchased a house at 470 South Street in 1937. The immigrants gathered there in the evenings to socialize and to hear Mr. Omar recite the Qur'an or poetry about the life of the prophet Muhammad. These social gatherings, as well as the annual picnic to raise money for charity (muharrajan), were the main activities of the society from 1937 to 1952. The struggle for survival in America, however, consumed most of their time and energy, and during World War II, frustrated by waning interest, they allowed their social club to die out.

After the war their children reactivated the Arab American Banner Society. As educated professionals and business people they enjoyed increased economic and social status typical of the experience of second-generation Americans. Unlike their parents, many of the American-born Muslims were removed from the roots of their ethnic and religious heritage. They generally were not able to speak Arabic or read the Qur'an very well, if at all. They had no knowledge of religious law or history, and only one had ever been inside a mosque. Many of the Arab American Muslims from the original seven founding families showed no interest in any Islamic instruction.

Furthermore, the family life of the second generation was altered permanently once they had moved away from the Quincy neighborhood and from the homes of their parents, where religion traditionally had been passed along. The constraints of mixed marriages added to their inability to provide a solid religious base for their families. They understood that their children were growing up in a religious vacuum, with no sense of religious community, no religious education, and no social setting conducive to finding a marriageable Muslim. The second-generation Muslims thus faced the challenge of how to assert their religious identity in a pluralistic society where they were an ethnic and religious minority. With whatever knowledge and resources they had, they resolved to unite the community in a stronger sense of in-group identity.

THE AMERICAN-BORN GENERATION

In 1952, even though they did not always agree, the two generations of immigrant and American-born merged to reorganize the Arab American Banner Society with newly elected officers. From 1952 until 1963 business meetings were held in a neighborhood restaurant, Ma's Lunch, owned by one of the founding families, followed by informal religious lessons. Prayers—congregational, holiday, and burial—were held in private homes. By sharing these occasions, members of the community were helped to understand their religious obligations to each other and to their children, as well as the need for greater group cohesiveness.

Meanwhile throughout these formative years the founders of the society were recognizing that local community involvement was necessary for the survival of any institution in America. The second generation produced leaders who were socially integrated into American society. Aziz Abraham, president of the Banner Society for eleven years, was a businessman with bureaucratic and diplomatic skills who was able to diffuse arguments inside the community. As president he attended local political activities at the State House as well as the inauguration of the mayor and city counsel.[6] Women were also an integral part of community leadership. Fatima Allie was both treasurer and secretary of the society for ten years. A teacher and school principal, she was meticulous about the treasury, the writing of the constitution, and the minutes of the board meetings. Sam Hassan, who alternated with Abraham as president, was a well-respected and unifying force in the community. According to his peers his strong leadership abilities kept the organization on the straight path.

Early in this phase of its life the community began to conceive the importance of building a mosque. Motivations were both internal and external. "I think this generation wanted to relate to a church," said one long-time member. "When people asked us what church do you go to, it would be embarrassing to say, 'We don't have a church.' The kids would come home and say to their parents, 'How come we don't have a church?'"[7]

Relating to a church was what might be called an outwardly directed motivation. Because there was no other model, the Muslims fashioned themselves in many ways after the religious communities of the Christians and Jews. To build a mosque would, in some respect, "nationalize" their religious community in the same way a church symbolized the Christian community in America. After the mosque was in fact built, many of the programs were clearly influenced by, and therefore geared toward, American traditions and holidays. On May 2, 1965, children were given May baskets to celebrate the Islamic New Year. On Memorial Day of that same year, the center held prayers for all its deceased members. Halloween parties and sock-hops were organized with the hope of recapturing the interest of the Muslim youth.[8] There were also several inwardly directed community motivations for building a mosque. Muslims wanted to be able to pray together, to educate their children in Islamic religion and customs, and to provide a place where their children could socialize with each other.

The society faced two questions in regard to establishing a mosque. The first concern was whether they should build a new structure or buy an existing building. And if they did decide to build, they questioned whether to do so with whatever money was available or to wait until they had saved enough to finance the whole project. In 1961 the ambitious decision was made to level the house at 470 South Street and build anew. At the time they had $5,000.[9] With this decision made, the society's fund-raising efforts gained momentum.

In the phase preceding the actual building of the mosque, from 1957 to 1963, the core of community leaders did much to raise money and draw attention to their group. The Arabic secretary Haj Muhammad Omar (first generation) promoted the society in two Arabic-English newspapers circulated in America, *As-Sameer* in Brooklyn, New York, and *Nahdat Al-Arab* in Detroit, Michigan.[10] Publicity specifically drew the attention of other Muslims in America, attracted scholars and dignitaries to the area, and generated donations to the future mosque. In 1961, King Saud came to

Boston for an eye operation. The society was invited by the state legislature to send representatives to his reception. During the king's recuperation, members paid him a visit at the hospital. Mohamed Omar wrote a poem for the occasion, which the king asked him to read aloud. Eid cards were exchanged in the upcoming holidays. In February 1962, King Saud donated $5,000 to the society for their mosque.[11]

Outside of this major donation, the primary sources of funding for the mosque were donations and pledges made by the seven founding families. During this period before the construction the founders of the small Muslim community in Quincy were plagued by lack of funds. The American-born Muslims also relied on donations from their business associates, lawyers, doctors, priests, rabbis, and neighbors. Fund-raising activities were open to non-Muslims and modeled after similar "church" events.[12] The largest fund raiser was the annual picnic or *muharrajan*. It gave Muslims from distant locations a chance to congregate and pledge money toward the mosque. As a result of these various efforts to solicit pledges and donations the bank balance was nearly $20,000 by the end of March 1963.

In 1962 the society hired a local architect to design a mosque, and work was started on the building in spring 1963.[13] Pressured to make payments to the contractor for the work in progress, members reluctantly succumbed to the idea of taking out a small mortgage, an idea that they had resisted because interest is forbidden in Islam. The mosque was completed in February 1964. The list of guests invited to the building dedication in October 1964 included representatives from the Quincy Council of Churches, all state and local officials, four Imams from Detroit and one from New York, and the director of the Islamic Associations of the United States and Canada. The main speaker was Shaykh Mohamad Jawad Chirri, director of the Islamic Center of Detroit.[14]

In 1962 society president Aziz Abraham had determined with the help of legal counsel that a new corporation needed to be formed with new by-laws and constitution. Thus the Banner Society became the Islamic Center of New England, organized with a board of eight directors and four officers. Sam Hassan and Aziz Abraham were the leaders of the center.

Throughout the 1960s the center was inundated by requests from across the country for financial and informational help from other Islamic groups interested in building mosques and establishing community centers. Hassan and Abraham traveled to New Jersey and Connecticut to give speeches about how to build a mosque. In addition Abraham sought support and acknowledgement for the center from other Islamic organizations in America. In the early 1960s, the center joined the Federation of Islamic Associations in the United States and Canada (FIA). The FIA, founded in 1952 by Lebanese Americans from Cedar Rapids, Iowa, kept Muslims abreast of the growth of Islam in America, sponsored youth camps, established full-time accredited schools and monitored the media.[15] From 1963 to 1981, the center sent delegates to the annual FIA convention.[16] Dawud Assad, president of the FIA from 1975–1977, relied heavily on the support of groups like the Islamic Center of New England. He became friends with Sam Hassan when they served together as first and second vice presidents of the FIA in 1967. When Assad was president in 1977, Abraham became treasurer. In later years, Assad became the director of the Muslim World League and helped the Quincy group to find a trained Imam.

During the 1960s, many Muslim students entered the United States for university study. In their quest to maintain relations with other Muslim groups they established the Muslim Student Association in 1963, which the Quincy group joined that year. These students made available Islamic materials from early sources that had not been translated into English prior to the 1960s.[17] The MSA has continued to publish educational books and pamphlets written by Muslim scholars for English-speaking people. The Muslim students in Quincy helped organize community events at the Islamic Center such as lectures in English and Arabic on such subjects as the importance of prayer and the celebration of *mawlid an-nabi* (the birthday of the Prophet) in the Arabic tradition, and Arabic classes for the children. The Muslim students encouraged the small group of founders to learn more about Islam.

About this time the leadership of the center began to advertise its activities in local papers, at airports and hotels; perhaps as a result of this as well as other efforts Muslims flocked to the center. The mosque membership tripled between 1964 and 1974. The community became a heterogeneous mix of transient and permanent immigrants from many different countries. (Currently twenty-seven countries are represented in what is the fifth wave of Muslim immigrants to the United States, 1967 to the present.)[18]

One of the dimensions of the heterogeneous nature of the Islamic Center has come through its relationship with Harvard University, begun in 1940 by Abu Nuri, an African American convert to Islam who in 1965 became a member of the center and later vice president of the board.[19] One founding member and board officer of the center stressed that one of the most valuable contributions the students have made to the community has been their ability to teach the Arabic prayers to adults and children by using phonetics. The current religious director of the center, when asked his opinion of the relationship between the Muslim students and the indigenous Muslim community, expressed his feeling that their religious background was a great asset to the community.

By 1967 new immigrants were taking up positions on mosque committees; the founding members and their families by then were outnumbered by the recent immigrants. As one founding member put it, the mosque was now seen as one for "all Muslims," not just for their own children. The building was expanded in 1968 to double the size of the prayer room and social hall. The original members began to be made acutely aware of the fact that some of their fund-raising activities, including raffles, card games, Chinese auctions, and the sale of liquor at the annual picnic were frowned on by newer members as un-Islamic. Sam Hassan, then president, stated that there was tremendous pressure from the Muslim students and recent immigrants to stop these activities. In 1967 he "decreed" that all of the activities considered by the community consensus (*ijma*) to be Islamically improper would be discontinued forever.[20]

However, conformity to Islamic standards was a gradual process. With what little Islamic education they possessed, the immigrant generation had taught their children the importance of paying the obligatory charity and giving it to the less fortunate Muslims overseas. But American Muslims had learned other methods of raising money from the example of churches and synagogues. Whether or not to give to charities overseas became the subject of heated debates between generations, especially at the time when money was being raised to build the mosque. The second generation argued that if the community were ever going to have such an edifice it was important to remember that "charity begins at home." Imam Omar argued that money used to build a mosque should come in Islamic ways. When the debate ended in 1967, everyone feared that fund raising would be impossible. But the women, who had always participated in the efforts to raise money, responded again by finding new ways to do so. The women of the American-born generation reorganized the Ladies' Auxiliary and established new fund-raising activities that were Islamically appropriate, such as luncheons, dinner parties, banquets, bake sales, and an international food fair and bazaar. Through this process the mosque at once became more Islamic. Yet because women in Muslim society do not traditionally become involved in mosque activities, even this showed clear overtones of accommodation to the host culture.

The 1960s, then, were a period of transition during which the identity of the community changed radically. It was a time when the expense of building and maintaining the mosque had overextended the small community of Arab Americans. Because of the influx of Muslim immigrants, the small, ethnic community became large and heterogeneous. Simultaneously, an interdependence developed between the indigenous and immigrant Muslims. Although the founders were outnumbered, they still maintained control in leadership positions. In the following decade, they became receptive to the more knowledgeable members of the community. Relying on this new source of knowledge and themselves as the traditional community authority, the founders set out to build a strong Islamic community.

THE ISLAMIC COMMUNITY 1970

In the early 1970s the mosque leadership came under the influence of Muzammil Siddiqi, a student from India studying at the Harvard Divinity School in the 1960s and a member of the Harvard Islamic Society. (Siddiqi currently is the director of the Islamic Center of Orange County, California.) He served on the Board of Directors from 1973 to 1976 and was also assistant to Imam Mohamed Omar from 1974 to 1977. Under his guidance, the center became increasingly Islamized and more attractive to Muslims. Islamic cultural practices were adopted, such as prayer schedules, proper Islamic dress in the prayer room, men and women's funeral committees and *wudu* (washing) rooms, and weekly *khutbas* (sermons) on Fridays given by Islamic scholars and students in both English and Arabic. The leaders also indigenized certain American cultural usages. A scholarship fund was established, a Boy Scout troop was formed, an office secretary was hired, and

Muzammil Siddiqi and Imam Omar were licensed as Justices of the Peace.[21]

At this time, fund-raising efforts focused on rich Muslim countries. Immigrant members traveling for business or pleasure would bring with them expansion plans for the mosque. Major donations were received and recorded. Between 1975 and 1979 donations were received from Iraq, Libya, Kuwait, and Saudi Arabia (the last agreeing to give the mosque $100,000, which was actually received in 1981).[22] These donations allowed for some significant additions to the mosque. In 1974 it expanded to add a library and office space. A multicolored dome was added to the top of the building. A *minbar* (movable staircase or speaker's podium for the Imam to use during the Friday *khutba*) was built. Efforts were made to add a traditional niche in the wall that faces Mecca, but the niche with its protruding wall would have exceeded the limit of the Building Code of Quincy. Money was donated to build a minaret, but it was never constructed.

In September 1977, the center bought land for a Muslim cemetery in Candia, New Hampsire. Due to zoning complications, the project never reached fruition and the land was sold.[23] In 1988 twelve cemetery plots were purchased in the Knollwood Cemetery in Canton. That number has now increased greatly. According to the Quincy *Patriot Ledger* the center currently "has an agreement with Knollwood for use of 2,000 grave sites during the next thirty years, with the option to buy more."[24]

After numerous attempts to find a format, a suitable curriculum, and capable teachers, the Islamic Sunday school was finally organized under the leadership of Abdul Karim Khudairi. Dr. Khudairi was elected to the Board of Directors in 1970 and served as president of the Board from 1980 to 1989. By 1974, seventy-five young people and twenty-five adults were enrolled in the school program. That number increased to 140 in 1990 and reportedly over 300 in 1991. In 1975, because more space was needed to accommodate the growing student body, the city of Quincy consented to allow the mosque Sunday school to have seven classrooms at the local elementary school. The basic format of the school includes four grades for children in four subjects: Qur'anic Arabic, Qur'an recitation, history of the prophet Muhammad, and religion. There are extra classes for adults in the interpretation of the Qur'an.

Up to the 1970s, to become a member of the center a Muslim

would pay annual dues making him eligible to vote in the election for new board members. In April 1977 a membership committee was formed with the goals of increasing membership and monitoring community growth. It has been the responsibility of the committee to ascertain which members are registered and have paid, registered but have not paid, or not registered at all. The biggest problem has been communicating to newly arrived Muslims that one has to pay to become a member of the center. Paying membership dues is an American custom, but in the Quincy community it has raised problems because according to Islamic tradition every Muslim is automatically a member of the community. The matter cannot be solved by asking Muslims who are not members to "join", because they consider themselves to be members already.

Here we have another example of the indigenization issues the community faces. The subcultural response has been to refuse to pay membership dues because they see it as part of the influence of a non-Muslim society and inappropriate to Islamic culture. Another such example of indigenization comes in the changes made to the traditional practice of voluntary giving (sadaqa). Many of the Muslims object to regularized or public giving, especially in such ways as having an offering plate passed in the prayer room. They prefer that giving be voluntary, and are offended at being asked to give, because that changes what was formerly voluntary into something mandatory. The issue then is not how much to pay but whether to pay at all. When voluntary donations do come in, the board has to decide if such donations could or should be put toward donors' membership dues, making them eligible to vote. This raises such questions as how the donation would be enumerated or broken down, and how this alteration would be communicated to sensitive donors. In 1990 it was estimated that the membership dues represented only 6 percent of the entire mosque income.[25] The current list of paid and unpaid registered members is numbered at 589 families. As an index of community growth, estimated figures of how many Muslims attend Eid prayers indicate that more and more Muslims are using the mosque on holidays such as Eid-ul-Fitr (feast after the month of Ramadan) and Eid-ul-Adha (feast of the sacrifice, after the pilgrimage to Mecca), rather than being a part of the membership. In April 1990, the attendance at Eid-ul-Fitr was estimated to be over 3,000.[26]

During the now fairly lengthy course of its history the mosque has experienced a good deal of turbulence, and its leaders often have been challenged. In 1977, as the membership increased, the community experienced what they perceived to be the attempt at a kind of coup by Muslims outside the group of founding families. A close study of the amendments and by-laws reveals how the leaders responded to the changing community constituency and the threat of takeover.

In the original constitution of the Islamic Center, Article V states that a person can become a board member after a three-month membership. In 1966, in response to the growing hetero-geneity of the community, Article V was amended to read that a consecutive four-year membership was required for eligibility to become a board member. Some, however, came to feel that these eligibility requirements were too stringent. In 1975 one of the board members, Iranian Shi'i physician Fereidoun Azizi, tried un-successfully to change the by-laws. Then in January 1977 he be-came president of the mosque. At his urging, the founders agreed to review the constitution, and by amendment they reduced the term of membership required for eligibility from four to two con-secutive years.

Dr. Azizi was well respected in the community, having been highly educated in Shi'i schools of law and having served on the Religious Committee. However, when he became president and tried to fill board vacancies with other Shi'is who were new to the community, the founders, both Sunni and Shi'i, became alarmed that he was trying to move the ideological base of the mosque from the practice of the Sunni tradition to that of the Shi'a tradition. Azizi also wanted the required term of membership to be less than the two years upon which the founders had decided. In Quincy community authority traditionally had been in the hands of the founding members. In addition, historically, the social cohesion of the community was based on the fact that its founding members were all "Arab Muslims," with no interest in Shi'a domination. With the controversy that ensued after his attempts to change the system, in 1977 Azizi resigned and left the center.

A second attempt at takeover came rapidly on the heels of the first. It concerned the religious director from 1976–1978, Muzam-mil Siddiqi's younger brother Mudassir Siddiqi. After Muzammil Siddiqi left the mosque in 1976 to work for the Muslim World League, Mudassir, a student at Harvard Law School, became

Imam Omar's assistant, and later the first official religious director of the mosque. With the help of Muzammil Siddiqi, the center received a subsidy from the Muslim World League to pay Mudassir's salary. Mudassir Siddiqi, an energetic director, accomplished much in the community, handling work that the elderly Imam was unable to do. However, it is the general consensus of those interviewed for this study that an incompatibility arose between the expectations of the religious director and the founders. At the heart of this incompatibility was the reluctance of the founders to surrender their authority to the most knowledgeable member. When the founders were unwilling to give the expected tacit authority, a power struggle ensued. All the respondents in this study refer to this period as the first time their community was ever divided.

The divisive issues were the degree of authority the religious director should have and the scope of his duties and responsibilities. Recognizing that Mr. Omar was still the official Imam, limits as to what Siddiqi was going to be expected to do were imposed by the American leadership. Questions were raised as to whether Siddiqi should be working throughout the New England area or confining his responsibilities to the center. There seemed to be little agreement on the geographical scope of his duties or the conditions under which the Muslim World League had agreed to pay him.

Early in 1978, after much dissention and little conclusive agreement, the leadership decided to remove Mudassir Siddiqi from this position. The community consensus was honored as the matter was brought before the general membership for a vote. In an effort to resolve matters, Siddiqi arranged for many of his supporters to attend the meeting, pay their dues, and vote. But in spite of these last-ditch efforts, the majority voted to dismiss him. The leaders immediately amended the by-laws of 1962, requiring that dues be paid well in advance of the November election.[27]

As a result of this threat to community cohesion, when knowledge was used as authority, the indigenous leadership resolved to maintain their authority in the community. However, because of the rapidly growing and increasingly diverse community, the need for further knowledge was great. No one knew better than the indigenous leadership that their limited knowledge was inadequate to cope with questions pertaining to life in a non-Muslim society and the legalities of Islamic law. For example, the board wrestled over the problem of what to do about interest accrued from the mosque savings account. It is forbidden in Islam to charge or receive interest. Many questions were raised over this one issue: Should they keep a savings account? What should be done with the interest money? Is it legal to give it away as charity to families overseas? Can it be given to the mosque as a donation?

The founders determined to find a trained Sunni Imam to give them the knowledge to deal with such questions. Because they realized that a knowledgeable scholar was likely to come from a Muslim country, various issues were raised. How would a foreign Imam respond to a secular society? Would he impose a cultural interpretation of Islam on the community? How would he go about the intricate process of establishing and maintaining community cohesion? In 1982, the Muslim World League sponsored ten "orthodox" Imams from Lebanon, a majority of whom were trained at Al-Azhar University in Cairo, to provide religious leadership in America. Dawud Assad, director of the Muslim World League in New York, recommended Talal Eid to his long-time supporters and friends at the Quincy Center.

THE COMING OF THE IMAM-RELIGIOUS DIRECTOR

Talal Eid came from Tripoli, Lebanon. In 1974 he received his degree from the School of Legislation and Law at Al-Azhar University, and in the late 1970s was appointed to the mosque in Tripoli as a full-time Imam. Unwilling to support the civil war in Lebanon, Imam Eid applied for a position in America. The chief Islamic scholar (Mufti) of Lebanon nominated him to the Muslim World League (of Mecca) for appointment to a mosque in America. Imam Eid arrived with his family in March 1982 at the age of 30. He remains today the religious director of the center. He is the only graduate of Al-Azhar University in the New England area and chairs the Majlis As-Shura Religious Committee of the Islamic Council of New England. In June 1991, he received his Master of Theological Studies degree from the Harvard Divinity School.[28]

After their experience with different leadership styles in the 1970s, the founders took steps to protect the mosque from anyone who would assume tacit authority. The first guidelines for the duties and responsibilities of the religious director were worked out by the board. Under Article V of the constitution the terms of office of the religious director, including the length of his tenure, are determined by the board with the approval of the general membership. In accordance with the corporate format, the board views the Imam as a salaried functionary of the mosque. The title religious director most likely corresponds to this perception of his role in the corporation. The sphere of his influence within the community is restricted to the realm of religious matters and does not include administration. Among his duties Imam Eid lists leading the prayer, teaching school, giving lectures and the Friday sermon, participating in interfaith activities, performing burials, witnessing marriages and conversions, and doing family counseling.

The Imam was not insensitive to the precautions taken by the founders to restrict his role. He understood that anyone bringing Islamic knowledge to an isolated community has to be very careful. When he first arrived, Eid suggested to the board to hang a curtain in the prayer room to separate the men from the women. At first the board agreed; but later, after much protest by both American-born Muslim women and immigrant women, the board decided to table the issue rather than jeopardize unity. The Imam saw that his role is to cooperate with the board. He learned that "if Imams try to change people, confront them too often, or press them too hard, they will alienate themselves from the community and become ineffectual."

Eid's advice to new Imams is to find out what the people expect from them rather than to focus on what they expect from the people. The Quincy Muslims were not eager to make changes in the ways they did things. For example, weddings of American-born Muslims (usually to non-Muslims) were modeled after American church weddings. They were held in the prayer room where friends and families (non-Muslims included) gathered to observe the vows.[29] After the Imam's arrival the American-born founding families continued to requires this type of wedding. The Imam honors these requests, even though he prefers that anyone who enters the prayer room be purified in the Islamic tradition by performing the ablution (*wudu*). He is willing to allow the imitation of American weddings because he believes it will die out on its own as he teaches the children of the American-born Muslims (fourth-generation founding families) about Islamic etiquette and the proper use of the prayer room.

The influence of Christianity on the practices of the Quincy Muslims is evident in other ways. Because most people do not work on Sunday, they are free to attend the congregational prayer at the mosque on that day rather than on the traditional Friday. In the summer, however, the opposite is true. Sunday prayers are not well attended whereas large numbers come on Fridays. Because the Islamic school does not meet in the summer, this reversal would seem to indicate that Muslims are making a special effort to bring their children to Islamic Sunday school. It is also the case that the role of the Imam is coming to be more like that of the Christian clergy. The Imam, for example, now spends about one-third of his time counseling married couples.

Overall, Imam Eid's greatest impact has been in increasing the knowledge of Islam among the members of the community. He believes that the growth and unity of the community corresponds to the degree of knowledge of its members. The youth, whose interest is always a concern, have also returned to the mosque in recent years. Increasingly they are coming to adopt many of the traditional Islamic values.

With the arrival of the Imam attendance at the mosque on both Sundays and Fridays increased fivefold. In 1986, a fourth expansion of the center was completed, adding a duplex next door to the mosque. One side functions to house the Imam and his family; the other side is rented to Muslims with the income used to supplement the Imam's salary. Presently the primary function of the mosque is as a place to pray. Social and economic needs are met minimally. The center needs to expand to make it more attractive to the youth. Currently the space for social-recreational activities to bring young people together is inadequate. There is not enough money in the zakat fund to meet the demands of indigent community members or students seeking money for higher education. And there is not yet a full-time Islamic school to meet the social and educational needs of Muslim families. When more Islamic institutions are built, Imam Eid foresees an increased role for the mosque and thereby for Islam in the lives of the Muslims in America.

Because Imam Eid receives part of his salary from the Muslim World League, which is funded mainly by Saudi Arabia, the question might be raised as to the league's possible influence on him and his work in the mosque. Thus far there does not seem to be any conflict of interest. In the American context of the separation of church and state, the Imam enjoys political immunity. He regards his relationship to the Saudis as between an employee and employer. Because of the great diversity in the Quincy Muslim community the prayer room is likely to be filled with Saudis, Iranians, Iraqis, Kuwaitis, and many others. It is imperative that the Imam not take sides in international political conflicts. Although the role of an Imam in a Muslim country is politicized, immigrant Muslims have come to appreciate the more neutral role of the Imam in America, knowing that if he were to take sides it would cause serious divisions among the members of the community.

Imam Eid feels that the mosque, like other religious institutions in America, should promote a more "humanistic" approach to world conflicts. Common goals that religious leaders share with their congregations and each other should be valuing human life and having sympathy for its unnecessary loss, abhorring of the killing or holding of innocent people, advocating peace and justice, and fostering compassion and understanding for all people. He acknowledges, however, that the politics of prayer and peace practiced by the clergy (including the Imam) in America are not always without controversy.

THE ISLAMIC COMMUNITY, 1980s AND 1990s

As soon as the mosque was built, non-Muslim students came from churches, elementary and high schools, and colleges to tour the building or to request that someone from the mosque come to talk to them about Islam.[30] Although the response to the genuine interest of the non-Muslim community has been positive, interfaith activities rarely have been initiated by the Muslims. A notable exception to this was the work of Dr. Abdul Karim Khudairi, president of the center from 1983–1989. Giving interfaith relations high priority, Khudairi initiated meetings with organizations such as the National Conference of Christians and Jews, and in more recent years he formed the Islamic Interfaith Committee which meets on a regular basis with the Massachusetts Council of Churches.

In 1985, when international tensions were high, interfaith activities increased at the Quincy mosque. After "Muslims" were reported to have taken hostages aboard a TWA plane and demonstrators burned the Ayatollah Khomeini in effigy outside the mosque, a public relations committee was formed at the center.

The committee observed that the demand for information about Islam corresponded directly to international incidents involving Muslims. Since the revolution in Iran, which generally heightened awareness of Islam among Westerners, bad publicity has been a driving force for positive interaction between non-Muslims and Muslims in America. Sensational news such as the threat to kill the author of *The Satanic Verses*, as well as the Gulf War of 1991, have continued to spark interfaith activities.

Another goal of Abdul Karim Khudairi's administration in the 1980s was to organize the Islamic Council of New England, headquartered at the Islamic Center. In 1985 Khudairi organized the first Islamic Conference of New England, an annual event sponsored by the council and attended by an average of 400–500 Muslims from all over New England. There were twelve charter members who joined the council in 1983, and two more who joined in 1985.[31] Today, the council is an umbrella organization of eighteen mosques and Islamic societies in New England. In the August 1991 issue of the *Islamic Forum*, Dr. Khudairi stated the goals and objectives of the council: "To establish a forum in which each of the independent Islamic centers or societies from the New England area could come together and exchange views of common concerns, develop strategies and programs for achieving common goals, to strengthen the unity and harmony amongst the Muslims, to represent the Muslim community at the regional level with one united voice and force and much more."[32]

The Quincy Center has served as a training ground for many of the Islamic leaders who are now members of the Islamic Council. One interesting example is Shakir Mahmoud, an African American who converted to Islam in 1964 and is now the Imam of the Masjid al-Qur'an in Dorchester, Massachusetts (formerly Temple #11 in Boston, once assigned to Malcolm X). Influenced by the experiences of Malcolm X and motivated to learn for himself about "orthodox Islam," Shakir went to the Islamic Center for instruction. In 1973 he became a member of the mosque and served on the Board of Directors from 1977 to 1978. In 1982 an Egyptian engineer and member of the Islamic Center of New England organized the Islamic Society of Boston, a grouping of all the Muslim student associations in the area for mutual assistance.

On March 30, 1990, during the month of Ramadan, a fire destroyed the Islamic Center of New England, although the concrete exterior remained intact. Damage was estimated at more than

$500,000. Investigators have never determined if it was the work of an arsonist. Insurance money covered the cost of repairing the center[33] and an outpouring of sympathy and financial assistance came from the surrounding communities, both Muslim and non-Muslim. A year after the fire the leadership of the center became interested in purchasing a 7.5 acre lot and large mansion in Milton, Massachusetts. Their intention was to build a prayer room and social hall that could each accommodate 1,000 people and to use the land to build a school and a camp for the youth. Negotiations, however, fell through in July 1991.

Reception to the possibility of the fast-growing Muslim community moving to the city of Milton had not been completely favorable. A few residents of the prestigious Milton neighborhood who came out against the center made themselves an easy target for allegations that prejudice and discrimination drove their resistance. In their own defense, they claimed concerns over an increase in traffic.[34] The center filed a suit against those involved, based on religious and country-of-origin discrimination, but recently the leadership decided not to pursue the suit.[35] As of November 1991 the land was bought by the Milton neighbors. As of December 24, 1991, the membership of the center approved the board's purchase of 55 acres of farmland in Sharon, Massachusetts, at a cost of $1.15 million.[36]

It is tempting for observers to want to categorize a religious community as having a specific location somewhere on the scale of liberal to conservative. To try to do this with the Islamic Center of Quincy, as perhaps is somewhat true for any American Muslim community, leads to a rather superficial description of Muslim life in America. As one prominent Muslim leader stated: "I resist the temptation to categorize a community. We are shaping Islam in America, working together, and learning from each other in an effort to find and fashion our own medium way. What makes it impossible to categorize a certain community as 'liberal' or 'conservative' is that Islam itself is socially liberal, as exemplified by its concern for the welfare of all defenseless societal members, while it is simultaneously morally conservative."[37]

NOTES

1. Yvonne Y. Haddad and Adair T. Lummis, *Islamic Values in the United States* (New York: Oxford University Press, 1987), pp. 13–14.

2.   Brent Ashabranner, *An Ancient Heritage—The Arab-American Minority* (New York: Harper Collins Publishers, 1991), p. 24.

3.   ". . . [The Muslim] immigrant to North America . . . [and] his identity, so long as his neighbor had any opinion at all, was shrouded in mystery. At times he was 'Syrian', at times, 'Turk'" (Earle H. Waugh, "Muslim Leadership and the Shaping of the Ummah: Classical Traditon and Religious Tension in the North American Setting," in *The Muslim Community in North America*, ed. Earle Waugh, Baha Abu-Laban, and Regula Qureish [Edmonton: University of Alberta Press, 1983], p. 13).

4.   Noel Haddad, interviewed August 7, 1991, Weymouth, Massachusetts. The current Imam of the Quincy mosque notes that the phrase *al-raya* [banner] *al-Arabiyya* is a name that the immigrant generation had translated into English. It was the name of a party in the Arab countries that had raised the Islamic banner after the downfall of the Ottomans (Imam Talal Eid, interviewed July 11, 1991, Quincy).

5.   C. Eric Lincoln, "The American Muslim Mission in the Context of American Social History", in *The Muslim Community in America*, p. 219.

6.   Islamic Center Archives, secretary's minutes, February 18, and January 12, 1964.

7.   Fatima Allie, interviewed July 16, 1991, Weymouth, Massachusetts.

8.   Islamic Center Archives, secretary's minutes, Decade Files, 1963–1969.

9.   John Omar, interviewed August 3, 1991, Kingston, Massachusetts.

10.   Islamic Center Archives, "Quincy Mosque Rises," *American-Arab Message*. Editor's note: "The preceding article was reprinted from the *Patriot Ledger*; Saturday, April 27th, 1963." English and Arabic used.

11.   Islamic Center Archives, "King Saud Cancels Swampscott Rest; No Reason Given," *Patriot Ledger* (January 27, 1962).

12.   Islamic Center Archives, "Quincy Point, Whist Party," *Patriot Ledger* (October 12, 1961).

13.   Islamic Center Archives, James J. Collins, "N.E. Islamic Center Builds Quincy Mosque," *Boston Sunday Globe* (June 9, 1963).

14.   Islamic Center Archives, "Members Praised at Dedication of New Islamic Center in Quincy," *Patriot Ledger* (October 18, 1964).

15.   Islamic Center Archives, "Quincy Islamic Center Observes Mosque Dedication Anniversary," *Patriot Ledger* (November 6, 1967).

16.   Islamic Center Archives, secretary minutes, Decade Files, 1963–1969 and 1970–1979.

17.   Imam Talal Eid, interviewed July 11, 1991, Quincy.

18.   Haddad and Lummis, *Islamic Values in the United States*, p. 14.

19. The Harvard Islamic Society was organized in 1958 by Abu Nuri, Syed Nadwi (from Pakistan), and Ahmed Osman (from Sudan), all of whom bcame members of the center in the 1960s. Ahmed Osman buried Malcolm X in New York after his assassination in 1965.

20. (Haj) Sam Hassan, interviewed August 6, 1991, Sandwich, Mass.

21. Islamic Center Archives, Justice of the Peace certification, personal files of Mohamed Omar, May 23, 1963.

22. Islamic Center Archives, treasurer's report, 1981. Also, secretary's minutes, Decade Files, 1970–1979.

23. Islamic Center Archives, secretary's minutes, Decade Files, 1970–1979.

24. Also some 500 gravesites are available to the center at the Forest Hills Cemetery in Jamaica Plain" (Peter Halesworth, "Islamic Center Looks at New Sites," *Patriot Ledger* [August 22, 1981], p. 8).

25. Islamic Center Archives, secretary's minutes, general membership meeting, November 1990.

26. Ann Doyle, "Mosque Determined to Be Rebuilt from Ashes," *Patriot Ledger* (May 12, 1990), p. 53.

27. Islamic Center Archives, secretary's minutes, Decade Files, 1970–1979.

28. Imam Talal Eid, interviewed July 11, 1991, Quincy.

29. The first wedding to take place in the mosque was right after it was built in February 1963, by the Derbes family, American-born generation.

30. Islamic Center Archives, Barbara Shea, "Needham Students Tour Religious Center," *Patriot Ledger* (December 5, 1966).

31. Islamic Center Archives, Articles of Incorporation and By-Laws of the Islamic Council of New England, 1986.

32. Current council members include Islamic Centers of Quincy, Boston, and Wayland, Mass.; Connecticut and Hartford, Conn.; Merrimac Valley and Salem, N.H.; Rhode Island and Providence, R.I.; Boston (universities), Cambridge, Western Massachusetts, Holyoke, Mass.; Greater Worcester and Worcester, Mass.; the New England Muslim Sisters Association, Worcester, Mass.; Masjid Al-Qur'an, Dorchester, Mass.; Masjid Ar-Razzaq, Providence, R.I.; Islamic Community of Fairfield County, Norwalk, Conn.; Mosque of New England, Seekonk, Mass.; Society of Islamic Brotherhood, Boston, Mass.; Islamic Center of University of Connecticut, Storrs, Conn.; Islamic Association of Greater Hartford, Hartford, Conn.; Masjid Muhammad, New Haven, Conn.; and the Islamic Society of Amherst Area, Mass.

33. Islamic Center Archives, Brian Carr, "Arsonist Hits Area Mosque," *Patriot Ledger* (March 30, 1990), p. 11.

34. Islamic Center Archives, Ellen Nakashima, "Neighbors Buy Site Sought by Mosque," *Patriot Ledger* (July 27, 1991), p. 1.

35. Islamic Center Archives, Ellen Nakashima, "Muslims Sue, Property on Hold," *Patriot Ledger* (October 4, 1991), p. 1–2.

36. Stacey Wong, "Islamic Center Approves Buying Farm in Sharon," *Quincy Partriot Ledger* (December 24, 1991).

37. Dr. Cader Asmal, interviewed by telephone, September 11, 1991, Weymouth, Mass.

CHAPTER 14

Muslims of Montreal

Sheila McDonough

The Muslim community in Montreal, Quebec, Canada, is young and active and has experienced many new developments during the decade of the 1980s. There seems every reason to suppose that the vitality the Muslim people of this city exhibit and express will give birth to new forms of Muslim existence in this distinctive setting. Many of them are notably future-oriented as they busy themselves organizing, fund raising, promoting new institutions, and encouraging new patterns of involvement and interaction with the wider society in which they find themselves.[1]

Quebec is currently in the midst of debate as to the form of its future relations with the rest of Canada. These discussions will actively affect the situation of Muslims and other immigrants, because the Quebec government is giving increasing preference to immigrants who are native Francophones. One can expect that in the future the Muslim community here will be predominantly French speaking and that their cultural links will become stronger with France and North Africa. The laws of the province are such that even those immigrants who have an English-speaking background have to send their children to French schools. A new Muslim school established by members of the community must offer instruction in French, although the children also get some classes in Arabic and in English.

Presently about 50,000 Muslims are in Montreal, more or less evenly divided between those of South Asian origin and those from the Arab world. There are also smaller groups representing other geographical areas. Although a few Muslims from Syria and Leba-

non came to Montreal before World War II, the community began
to develop more rapidly in the early 1950s when a number of
immigrants from South Asia and the Arab world, mainly professionals, began to arrive. The oldest mosque in the city, the Islamic
Centre of Quebec (ICQ), dates back to 1958. The community used
a series of rented buildings until it was finally able to establish the
current center in 1965. It has been rebuilt twice since then, and
there are plans for further expansion. In the 1950s and 1960s the
Pakistanis and other South Asians were the more numerous group
and were active on the board of the ICQ and in other community
affairs. More recently, because South Asians are normally English
speaking, they have tended to go elsewhere in Canada, as Quebec
has become more predominantly Francophone. During the 1970s
and 1980s immigration from Lebanon and North Africa has increased significantly. These French-speaking Muslims usually find
it easier to adapt to Quebec society than do those who speak only
English.

The ICQ, an attractive suburban building, is the oldest Sunni
mosque in the area. It is licensed for marriages and funerals and
for the registration of births. Most Montreal Sunni Muslims take
advantage of the facilities of the mosque, particularly with respect
to funerals.[2] It has a large prayer hall, with a separate screened
section for women. Those currently administering the ICQ have
determined that it should be used for prayer only, not for other
community purposes. This is an issue of great concern to the Muslims of the city. Before 1976 women were involved in governing
ICQ, but since that time the more conservative element, particularly the Tablighi Jamaat, has tended to dominate the affairs of the
mosque and women have not played an active role.

In addition to ICQ there are eight other Sunni mosques in the
Montreal area, as well as a number of groups who meet for prayers
in apartment. The second mosque built in the city is that owned by
the Muslim Community of Quebec (MCQ), which dates from
1979. As with the ICQ, South Asian Muslims have been prominent
in the leadership, although persons of other ethnic backgrounds
also have been part of the life of the MCQ from the beginning. The
premises of MCQ have been expanded a number of times and are
still undergoing change and development because the Muslim
school shares the same space. The MCQ leadership has understood the role of the mosque in society differently from that of the

ICQ. The MCQ facility is intended to serve as a community center as well as a prayer hall. Several rooms are used for public lectures, discussion groups, children's celebrations, and monthly potluck suppers. The prayer hall is shared by men and women, with the women praying behind the men. A few women have been members of the Council of Trustees of the MCQ.

Muslims from many different ethnic and linguistic backgrounds participate in the functions of the MCQ. It is not uncommon for participants to break up into smaller groups to talk in Arabic, French, or English, according to their interests. Muslims attending such functions commonly address one another as brother or sister, as is characteristic of North American Muslim life. Public lectures are usually attended by both men and women, with women sitting at the back, although for other functions men and women generally meet separately.

Many diverse activities take place on the premises of MCQ. The prayer hall is regularly used; small groups meet early Sunday mornings for devotions. Marriages are performed there. Food is served on various special occasions. Sometimes local politicians are invited to take part in public meetings in the center. Teachers and students from Protestant schools occasionally visit MCQ or other mosques as part of their study of world religions, as do students from the colleges and universities of the city. During the recent Gulf War members of MCQ were involved in a number of ways in speaking to the greater Montreal community about Islam and Muslim values and concerns.[3]

There are now seven other smaller Sunni mosques in Montreal in addition to ICQ and MCQ. The two downtown mosques, the Fatima Masjid (1976) and the Umma Masjid (1983), were founded by Arabic-speaking Muslims. The Imam of the Umma Masjid is a French-speaking Muslim from Lebanon.[4] At present both mosques are overcrowded at prayer times because of the number of Muslim workers in the downtown area. Although the Fatima Masjid is a Sunni mosque, it is also used by the Iranian Shi'a. Another mosque is in an apartment; this is a small group, which calls itself *Ansar Allah*, whose outreach activity includes distributing material in metro stations. Four other mosques are in the more remote suburban areas of the South Shore, North Shore, and West Island sections of urban Montreal. Although the conceptual differences about the role of a mosque help differentiate between ICQ and

MCQ, the raison d'être for most of the other mosques is mainly geographical.

In 1980 a small group of Muslim men calling itself the Muslim Welfare Organization (Falah i Muslimin) agreed to give $1,000 each to have funds available to help Muslims in need; they have continued as a service group helping different mosque communities and aiding Muslim students.[5] The group has now bought land for a new and much larger downtown mosque that would also have a lecture hall and reading rooms and would hold 5,000 people in the prayer halls. They have raised considerable funds and hope to begin work on the new mosque within the next year. They envision that this mosque will serve as a center for worship as well as for the intellectual and cultural life of the Muslims of the city. It is also intended that the mosque be financially self-supporting; to this end a number of stores will be built along the sides of the mosque building.

The four other mosques, located in the suburbs, are smaller in size, usually consisting of a small house made over into a prayer hall with a few rooms for offices and discussion groups. Each of the suburban centers serves as a prayer hall and a meeting place for the local Muslim population.[6] The one in Montreal North was established mainly by Algerians and other North Africans who live in the area. They consciously set up their governing board so that all the major participating ethnic groups would be represented.[7] In that part of the city the Muslim community is predominantly Francophone.

When the small new Masdjid Makkah al-Mukarramah opened in 1988 in the West Island suburb its by-laws determined that it would not belong to any particular individuals but to God and the Muslim community. Mosque management is to be by a committee (majlis al-shura) whose members are chosen for a limited term. Every year there are to be general elections through which at least five of the fifteen members of the Majlis would be replaced. This arrangement is typical of the Montreal mosques and indicates a concern to avoid domination by individuals or groups in the management of the mosque. In this small masjid there is a resident Imam from South Asia who studied in Saudi Arabia and is fluent in both Urdu and Arabic and thus is able to communicate with the various immigrant Muslims who come to see him.

There is also a Shi'a mosque in an area of the city fairly close to downtown. The participants in the life of this mosque are mainly Ithna Ashari Shi'a from South Asia. Many of them came to Canada from Africa after the South Asian communities had to leave various African countries. This building is financially self-supporting, with apartments above the meeting rooms. (Women gather in a separate room, with TV coverage of the ceremonies in the men's prayer hall.) The mosque has a constitution outlining its governing structures.[8] A director and joint director of religious affairs are appointed annually. The former gives advice to the association in matters of the Shariat of the Ithna Asheri Ja'fari faith, binding on all members unless a ruling, *fatwa*, to the contrary is obtained from the leader of the center of the faith (A'lam, Mujtahid-e-Azam) or his recognized successor.

Another Shi'i group, the Ismaili's, have a Jamaat Khana in a suburb near the city center and a small one on the West Island. Most of them came to Montreal from South Asian communities that had to leave Africa.[9] Some are from French-speaking African countries, many having an excellent French education. Despite the close similarities in Ismaili thought and practice between the French- and English-speaking members of the community, there is recognizeable difference in cultural attitudes between those who are products of the French educational system with its closer ties to European culture and those with English educational experience.

The Ahmadiyya Movement in Islam, a nineteenth century sectarian movement of Indian origin, also has a small center in a suburb of Montreal. They regularly sponsor interfaith discussions on contemporary issues. The usual procedure is to have representatives of all the major traditions speak to an issue, with a member of the Ahmadiyya community speaking last. These regular interfaith conversations make the Ahmadiyya community known to the other religious groups in a more systematic way than is typical of most Islamic communities.

The main Sufi group active in Montreal now is the Burhanniya movement of Egypt and the Sudan, although a few other groups hold meetings.[10] A cofounder of the group became interested in Sufism while a student in Cairo when he heard Sufi preaching in a mosque. The Sufi brotherhood for him was a path of devotion and service that he understood to come from the authority of the saintly leaders of his order. The other founder of the Montreal group is a French-Canadian who converted to Islam when he was a student at the University of Montreal.[11] The center that they set up in 1987 consists of the lower part of an apartment; the Egyptian leader, his French-Canadian wife, and their children live upstairs. Ritual devotions, *hadra*, are performed every Saturday night, and discussions take place on weekends. Regular participants are mainly Egyptians, Sudanese, and Somalis, along with some French Canadians. Immigrants are often newly arrived from Africa, and the intensity of their chanting is reminiscent of their African religious experience. Many of the participants are students or fairly young working men who have found in this group a community in which African and French Canadian members clearly share fellowship and mutual acceptance.

In addition to the mosques and Sufi groups there are other forms of voluntary association among Muslims in the Montreal area. All four of the universities of the city, two English and two French, have Muslim student groups. There are also two local Francophone voluntary associations, the Comité Maghrébin de Recherche et d'Information (CMRI),[12] and the Centre des Études Arabes pour le Developpement (CEAD).[13] The CMRI president is Moroccan; the CEAD leadership tends to be Lebanese and Egyptian, both Muslim and Christian. Both groups sponsor research and public conferences and lectures; the events are mainly in French, although CMRI has held several large bilingual conferences dealing with issues of the stereotyping of Muslims in the local press.

THE CANADIAN EXPERIENCE

The requirements of Canadian law necessitate a financially responsible administrative board for mosques as well as a constitution. A membership list is necessary, because the members are responsible for election of the board. Many Muslims use the mosques for prayer and other activities without becoming members and appreciate the opportunity to visit different mosques and to pray in different places. In the Quebec context, however, the legal requirement of membership lists in itself encourages participation in one particular mosque community.

In both Sunni and Shi'a mosques the Imams or directors of religious affairs are responsible to the board. The expectation for Sunnis is that the Imam will have had some madrassa training, but there is no job description that emphasizes an authoritative chain of command in terms of decisions or advice. In the Sunni case, advice on matters of religious law usually is given in terms of traditional understanding of the classical schools of Muslim religious jurisprudence. In the MCQ, the constitution states that in matters of conflict with respect to *fiqh*, the Council of Trustees is the final arbiter.[14] In the Shi'a case the line of authority is explicit. Shi'a refer not only to the traditional jurisprudence, but also to a particular living individual who is considered the ultimate authority on matters of religious law, whereas Sunnis give final authority to the judgment of a local group of respected persons. Traditional Sunni and Shi'a differences with respect to authority are thus adapted to the new situations of voluntary associations in a secular nation. The diversity of ethnic backgrounds that characterizes the Muslim community in Montreal is further complicated by language differences. Although English is spoken in the business and professional worlds in certain parts of the city, Quebec is explicitly a French-speaking province of Canada. In commerce of any kind, French is essential. English speakers increasingly have to be able to function in French, but the converse is not the case. Therefore French-speaking North African or Lebanese Muslims may never learn English unless they have a particular reason to widen their cultural contacts. In the community life of the mosques these various differences are worked out in an ad hoc manner. Arabic is often the medium of conversation if neither French nor English is mutually understood. Muslims are well aware of their differing ethnic backgrounds and are concerned to transcend these differences to achieve a more satisfactory experience of common life and practice.

Differences in the performance of ritual are not particularly significant among Muslims of varying ethnic backgrounds with respect to the basic practices of prayer and fasting. They can and do pray together at the appropriate times in a mosque without worrying about what part of the Islamic world their neighbors may come from. It is rather in matters such as marriage rituals and extra forms of prayer (as distinct from the five daily prayers) that diversity in practice is more apparent. For example, many members of the Bangladeshi community participate in a ritual entitled *Milad-i-Nabi*. This ritual of remembrance of the Prophet Muhammad in its Bangladeshi form is unknown to some of the Arabs, and in Montreal generally involves only South Asian Muslims.

Differences among Muslims can spring from a number of

causes: linguistic background is one issue, but the historical background of the particular group can also influence its relations with others. In the early 1970s, at the time of the conflict between Pakistan and Bangladesh, immigrants from the latter area were understandably averse to too much socialization with Pakistanis. Many of the recent Bangladeshi immigrants have been refugees without much money or status. Now, however, there are several Bangladeshi Muslims who are well-known figures in the wider Muslim community in the city. In the South Shore mosques, where there is a significant South Asian population, Bangladeshis tend to be quite well integrated within the larger group.

South Asian and other cultural and linguistic groups are also divided in their attitudes to the Tablighi Jamaat. This movement, strong at ICQ since the late 1970s, has the largest number of participants among Muslims in the area. The Tablighi movement originated at a Sufi shrine in Delhi.[15] The original aim was to encourage devout Muslims to volunteer to visit semi-Islamized villages outside of Delhi and encourage the rural people to purify their ritual and moral practices from non-Muslim elements. The movement is now widespread in South Asian countries, as well as in North America, Europe and the rest of the Muslim world.

Those who value the Tablighi movement see it as an effective revival and a way to return lax Muslims to practice of their religious duties. Those who are less sympathetic tend to see the movement as anti-intellectual and unreasonably conservative with respect to practice. Tablighi members are encouraged to serve the needs of their fellow Muslims through such means as visiting in prisons and calling on Muslim homes to invite renewal of faith and commitment to ritual life, the latter practice appreciated greatly by some Muslims and disliked by others.

As the differences of opinion about the Tablighi movement indicate, varieties in ritual and other forms of Muslim life exist not only among Muslims from different countries, but also among those from the same country. I experienced this kind of difference not long ago when I took students from a class to observe a Burhanniya Sufi service or *hadra*. One of the students in my class, an Egyptian (as is the cofounder of the Sufi movement in Montreal) but from the reformed (*salafiyya*) tradition,[16] was upset by the ritual he observed and found the Sufi practices very distasteful.[17] The differences in these perspectives go back to Ibn Taymiya's critique of Islamic practices in the fourteenth century, and have continued to divide Muslims ever since.[18]

This issue is particularly contentious among young Muslims in Montreal at present. The "reformed tradition" condemns reverence for saints (*walis*), pilgrimages to tombs of saints, and prayers of intercession, and calls for a return to beliefs and practices of the first generation of Muslim believers. Activist Muslims in Montreal tend to disparage the Sufis as representing a corrupted form of Islam and accuse them of losing the original Islamic vision and adhering to a perspective that wrongly leads to passivity in the face of imperialist foreign domination. The Sufis, on the other hand, know that they have spiritual lineages through their masters that go back to the time of the Prophet. They tend to see themselves as practitioners of spiritual exercises whose validity is timeless, and whose end is liberating personal transformation.[19] They seek an ecstatic loss of self, and they trust the wisdom of their spiritual guides. Members of the Montreal group see themselves as part of a long heritage of Muslim devotional life; they have cassettes of the chanting of other groups in the Arab world and Europe and are very aware of the bonds of fellowship with Sufis elsewhere. Sufis have no problem in taking part in regular prayer services with other Muslims at the various mosques of the city. The problem comes, as is the case with the Shi'a, in other forms of religious expression, such as the *hadra*, that have developed over the centuries.

The Comité Maghrébin de Recherche et d'Information has sponsored a trilateral committee of Muslims, Jews, and Christians. At the time of the publication of Salman Rushdie's *Satanic Verses* this group produced a paid advertisement for the Montreal press, signed by local people from all three communities, recommending a balanced attitude following United Nations recommendations on respect for culture.[20] Another press release contained the endorsement of twenty-five Montreal Muslim organizations, incuding the Sunni mosques, the Shi'a organization, the Aga Khan Council of Quebec, five ethnic associations, three student organizations, and several smaller welfare associations. This release regretted the Canadian government's decision to permit import of Rushdie's book and urged the government to appoint a board of Muslim scholars and others conversant with the Islamic faith to review the volume and restore the embargo on its circulation.[21] "As Canadian citizens," the press release read, "we resent having to explain our right to register our outrage over this insidious and scurrilous attack on our religious beliefs . . . under a well contrived effort to denigrate Islam."

The perception conveyed by this statement, that of being misunderstood and denigrated by the wider community, seems to be one of the strongest forces uniting Muslims in the Montreal context. Canadian Muslims are angered at much of the media coverage of Islam, and many of them have had unfortunate experiences of personal discrimination. They may disagree on many issues, but in the matter of unfair or inaccurate stereotyping of them and their culture there is virtual unanimity. During the Rushdie affair some of them tried to hold a public meeting to explain their views, which was disrupted by shouting and calling for death to Rushdie on the part of a few. Order was restored by Qur'an recitation and the meeting continued, but the media focused almost entirely on the shouting minority. Thus the intention to convey to other Canadians a moderate Muslim perspective was frustrated, and once again the public heard only the voice of the extremists. The Centre des Études Arabes pour le Developpement tends to focus its activities particularly on public lectures and conferences in French concerning Lebanon, the Palestinians, and problems in the Arab world. Several Quebec students have formed a group calling itself Salam, which has visited Lebanon and the Palestinians. During the recent Gulf War CEAD and Salam provided resource persons for those wanting information about the Arab world.

Some changes in public perception of Islam in Montreal seem to be taking place. Canadian radio, TV, and newspapers all make use of Muslims to give a local Muslim perspective. Although the stereotyping problem is very real, there is also considerable local effort among journalists, teachers, social workers, and others to consult Muslim opinion and to promote better knowledge of Islam. For the first time in 1991 I heard the local radio announcing the beginning of Ramadan and explaining the ritual. In the local children's hospital notices on every floor explain the meaning of Ramadan. A Montreal-based ethnic television channel regularly shows programs produced by local ethnic groups, and Muslims often participate in broadcasts of religious groups on Vision TV. Radio broadcasts by ethnic and religious groups, including Muslims, are produced one night a week.

Just as the ethnic diversity of the Montreal community reflects the ethnic diversity of the Muslim world as a whole, so also the diversity in respect to perceptions of women's roles reflects the variety of attitudes and practices of the wider Islamic civilization. At one end of the spectrum is the Tablighi Jamaat, which maintains that faithful practice of Islamic duties requires separation between the sexes. There are Muslim women in the city who rarely leave their homes and have almost no contact with any persons other than family members. At the other end are the women who work outside the home or for voluntary associations. Some women would never go out without covering their heads, whereas others on principle refuse to wear headcoverings. Because of the ambiguity and diversity of attitudes and expectations with respect to gender roles found in the Muslim community, it is sometimes necessary to make special or ad hoc arrangements to accommodate differing perspectives.[22]

CMRI and CEAD both have held conferences on issues relating to Muslim women in Canada and in the wider world community. Guest speakers and discussion groups on Muslim family life and the role of Muslim women are sponsored regularly in the various mosque and student communities. The national Canadian Muslim Women's Association, which has a local branch in Montreal, also sponsors lectures and discussion groups. At one such public lecture on Muslim family life an invitation was made to any young men in the audience considering marriage to consult with members of the association who might facilitate the meeting of potential marriage partners. Summer youth camps and student associations have also helped to bring eligible young people together.

Women interested in changing perspectives of women's roles are more likely to be active in the voluntary or ethnic associations than in the mosque communities. Among the South Asians are many who admire the leadership capacities of such women as Benazir Bhutto and Khaleda Zia, the current leader of Bangladesh.[23] South Asian and Arab women immigrants, many of whom are university graduates, differ among themselves as to the degree of their involvement with mosque or other voluntary associations. Some are involved in the South Asian Women's Centre, whose members are Hindu, Christian, Muslim, and Buddhist.[24]

A readiness to be critical of traditional attitudes is characteristic of many of the Muslim women who are concerned with changing the status of women.[25] Others perceive the wider society as immoral and threatening and encourage their sisters to separate themselves from the corruptions of that outside world.[26] The characterization of the wider society as dissolute and threatening to the moral purity of Muslims seems to be a significant facet of Muslim adaptation to North American life. One finds Muslims talking about the dangers of secular humanism, a phrase characteristic of fundamentalist Christian critique of contemporary social values. The tendency to characterize the wider society as impure in contrast to what is understood to be the purity of one's own religious tradition is common to Islam, Christianity, and Judaism. It finds particular focus in the concern for moral breakdown associated with changes in family patterns.

Some of the conferences sponsored in Montreal by CMRI and CEAD have tried to present a global vision of the varying circumstances of Muslim women. In 1985, for example, CMRI sponsored a four-day meeting entitled, Muslim Women of the Third World and Canada, with both provincial government and federal support. The Women's Division of the National Filmboard of Canada provided documentaries for the occasion, which featured guest speakers from Bangladesh, Egypt, Pakistan, and Algeria discussing women's issues in their respective countries. Government and local representatives talked about Canadian issues such as social services for immigrant women. The papers were later published by CMRI.[27] In November 1987, CEAD sponsored a seminar on the theme, Arab Women and Women Here, Accomplishments and Challenges of the 80s. The papers were published in French by CEAD.[28] Workshops dealt with women's activities in Tunisia, Egypt, Palestine, and Lebanon. The conference explicitly related its work to the United Nations sponsored meetings in Mexico City and Nairobi. CEAD has also published a dossier on "Women in the Arab World," which includes articles from the local press as well as writings by Muslim women.

The problem of transmitting traditional values to the youth is an issue that receives a great deal of attention in the respective mosque communities. On this basis Muslims have argued for and eventually received some measure of provincial support and recognition. Catholic schools provide either catechism or classes in moral education, and the Protestant schools have a curriculum on moral and religious education that is intended to be pluralistic and deal with all religious traditions. There are also a number of private Jewish schools that receive some state support, as well as other private schools accommodating specific ethnic groups.

In 1985 a Muslim school was established on the premises of MCQ. The school began with kindergarten classes and now offers all the primary grades. There is a plan to begin high school classes very soon. The curriculum is the provincial French curriculum with the addition of classes in Islam and Islamic history. English and Arabic are also taught. The school's principal is a Nigerian educated in an Islamic school that consciously aimed to make education the equivalent of that received in British schools in Nigeria.[29] The school presents an appearance of disciplined and well-organized purposefulness. Children seem emotionally secure and relaxed in their environment. At one graduation children representing some twenty different nations came in the dress of their countries of origin and presented short recitations and songs. It is too early to begin to evaluate the impact of this educational structure on the students, but it seems probable that the young people will graduate from it with a sense of their own identity as Muslim citizens from Quebec and Canada. The school experience is designed to stress religious rather than ethnic or racial identity.

Among the Muslims of Montreal, as elsewhere in North America, there is little consensus as to the exact meaning of Islamic education. There is clear agreement, however, that the Qur'an and Sunna should be well understood and that students should have some knowledge of Islamic history. Islamic ritual practice is taught, and there is emphasis on the unity of Muslims across their ethnic diversity. Most parents hope that their children will have a secure sense of their identity as Muslims. There is a book store and small reading room in the MCQ, where a variety of books on Muslim subjects can be found by authors such as Mawdudi and Sayyid Qutb, Iqbal, and Amir Ali.

Views about an appropriate Islamic education are influenced by contacts with the larger Islamic community. A number of local Muslims attend lectures on Islamic subjects sponsored by different groups with different perspectives. Muslims who are active in mosque affairs in Montreal sometimes attend meetings of the Islamic Society of North America (ISNA).[30] Visiting speakers also pass through the city and give talks on various aspects of current Muslim thought. The thinking of the Muslims of Montreal can be assumed to be moving in roughly the same directions as typify many well-educated Muslim professional people.

The Canadian Muslim community experiences diversity not only through its complex mixture of immigrants, but through conversion to Islam of both French- and English-speaking Canadians. To the extent that there is interfaith marriage it is usually of French-speaking Muslim men and French Canadian women. A journal, *Le Monde Islamique*, edited by a French Canadian convert, is intended as a vehicle to make Islamic values known to the wider community and to help facilitate a new sense of brotherhood. Some of the French-speaking Muslims have been actively involved in sponsoring public discussion of Islam; they have several times invited Roger Garaudy to Montreal to give public lectures. Garaudy, a French Roman Catholic theologian known particularly for his efforts to reconcile socialist economic analysis with Christian faith, has recently become a Muslim and has been actively writing and speaking about his new vision for the world.[31]

The group that publishes *Le Monde Islamique* also recently has opened an Islamic Information Centre near the French Université du Québec at Montreal. The center is concerned with familiarizing the public with Islamic culture and the Islamic world. Its brochure states that it aims to participate in dialogue, which it sees as necessary, if not mandatory, to the fostering of an accurate understanding of Islam. It has a reading room with books and cassettes available for interested persons. Students who have gone there for information usually have found themselves well received.

In a great variety of ways, then, the Muslims of Montreal are adapting to life in the Canadian environment. Recently they helped celebrate Eid by having a sugaring-off party (eating sugar from the fresh sap of maple trees) and picnic in the woods near the city, the traditional Montreal mode of greeting the end of winter.

The leaders of most of the mosque communities and of the voluntary associations are mainly first-generation immigrants. Many of them have been active for more than twenty years in their efforts to establish viable new Muslim institutions in the Quebec context. Their primary intention has been to transcend ethnic and other differences and to work for a unified sense of Muslim identity. In spite of occasional differences of opinion, they have seen their efforts bear fruit in the effective functioning of these institutions.

NOTES

1. Harold Barclay, "The Muslim Experience in Canada," in *Religion and Ethnicity in Canada*, ed. Harold Coward and Leslie Kamamura (Waterloo, Ont.: Wilfred Laurier University Press, 1978), pp. 101–113. See also Daood Hasan Hamdani, "Muslims and Christian Life in Canada," *Journal Institute of Muslim Minority Affairs* 1, no. 1 (1979): 51–59.

2. The Muslims of Montreal still have not acquired satisfactory land for their own graveyards, probably because of local prejudice. They have been refused land several times, but reasons for the refusal have not been given.

3. The local press, both English and French, ran articles about the Montreal Muslim community in an attempt to develop greater awareness in the general public of the Muslims in their midst.

4. Two articles about this mosque in the local French press are Jules Béliveau, "Un infidèle chez les musulmens de Montréal," *La Presse* (April 4, 1987), p. 1; and Martin Pélchat, "Pèlerinage à la mosquée, angle St. Laurent-Maisonneuve," *Le Matin M* (March 10, 1987), p. 8. See also "L'Islam au Québec: Lecoctail Mahomet," *L'Actualité* (June 1988), pp. 50–58.

5. The current president is a retired teacher from the Montreal area who originally came from south India.

6. An insightful discussion of the changes in religious roles can be found in Earle Waugh, "The Iman in the New World: Models and Modifications," in *Transitions and Transformations in the History of Religion*, ed. F. E. Reynolds and S. N. Ludwig (Leiden: E. J. Brill, 1980), pp. 125–149.

7. The young Algerian who drove the car on my visit to that mosque told me that he rarely came into any part of the city other than the "quartier" where he lived, worked and interacted with the other Muslims in the area.

8. This document, entitled *Shiane Haidery International Inc. Constitution and By-Laws*, was distributed to members in March 1990.

9. Azim Nanji, "The Nizari Ismaeli Muslim Community in North America: Background and Development," *The American Ismaeli, Special Edition* (New York: Imami Ismailia Council for the U.S.A., 1986). See also Raymond Williams, *Religions of Immigrants from India and Pakistan* (Cambridge: Cambridge University Press, 1988).

10. The card of the local group reads "Le Tariqa el Borhanniya el Dousouqia el Shahouliya Disciples du Sheikh Mouhammad Othman Abdouh el Borhani, Montreal." Their founder, Muhammad al Burhan, was born in the Sudan in 1902. The oder is a reformed order of the Shadhiliya

tradition. For an exposition of the meaning of Egyptian Sufi ritual, see Earle Waugh, *The Munshidin of Egypt: Their World and Their Song* (Columbia: University of South Carolina Press, 1988).

11. He told me that through the influence of the French scholar Rene Guenon (see *The Crisis of the Modern World* [Lahore: Suhil Academy, 1981]) and his critique of the spiritual emptiness of modern Western society he came to study Eastern religious life and finally joined the Muslim student group in his university and accepted Islam. Later he traveled to Europe and discovered some Sufis at the mosque in Paris, with whom he learned to chant in Arabic.

12. In a press release handed out at one of its conferences, CMRI defined itself as "a non-profit organization for intercultural education that attempts to go beyond instant information and to offer, Canadians and Quebecers alike, opportunities for thought, exchange, and for respect towards our differences." CMRI is located at C.P. 451, Succursale Cote St. Luc, Montreal, H4V 2Z1.

13. CEAD is located at 1265 Berri, Montreal, H2L 4X4. It advertises itself as offering workshops on subjects such as Arab women, Islam and minorities, development, Egyptian literature, Lebanon and Palestine. Booklets and cassettes on these topics are available.

14. This constitution was approved by the Council of Trustees, October 18, 1984.

15. For a discussion of the origins of the movement, see Anwar al Haq, *The Faith Movement of Maulana Ilyas* (London: Allen and Unwin, 1972). In its origins in India, the movement was apolitical and still tends to be so. In this respect it has differed from the more politically activist neotraditionalist groups such as the Jamaat Islami founded by Mawlana Mawdudi.

16. For an explanation of *salafiyya*, see John Esposito, *Islam, The Straight Path* (New York: Oxford University Press, 1988), pp. 132–136. *Salafiyya* refers to the companions of the Prophet and is a term used by reformers in Egypt. It indicates both a desire to recreate the moral purity of the original Islamic community and an imperative to recover Islamic vitality as first urged on Muslims by the nineteenth century activist Jamal al-Din Afghani.

17. See Nekki R. Keddie, *An Islamic Response to Imperialism* (Berkeley and Los Angeles: University of California Press, 1983).

18. I was told that there was a heated argument at the Fatima Masjid in Montreal one evening among Muslims of the Salafiyya and others as to whether or not Sufism is acceptable as a valid Muslim perspective on life.

19. For background information on Sufism, see Annemarie Schim-

mel, *Mystical Dimensions of Islam* (Chapel Hill: University of North Carolina Press, 1975).

20. See, also, Fatima Houda-Pepin, director of CMRI, "Les Versets Sataniques et l'Islam" in the Montreal newspaper *Le Devoir* (February 18, 1989), p. 7.

21. The government had briefly put an embargo on the book because of Muslim protest, but then reversed that decision.

22. One Bangladeshi woman, who has been active on the governing board of a South Shore mosque and has organized many activities for the community, recently organized a public meeting to celebrate the *mi'*raj or ascension of the Prophet. The guest speaker, an Arab, was not willing to be introduced or thanked by her, although she conducted the rest of the meeting. A man had to come to the stage to introduce and thank the guest.

23. See "The Destiny of Benazir Bhutto" in the local journal *Newsviews* 2, 3, 11, 4, & 5 (1986). A group of young South Asians discussed the new female leadership of Bangladesh in their journal *Montreal Serei* 5, no.2 (1991).

24. Their statement of goals reads as follows: "The South Asian Community Centre is an organization to help women achieve their full potential in Quebec and Canadian Society, and it offers them help to become independent." It provides a number of services, including a support network for battered women, job searching and vocational counseling, counseling on family, legal, immigration and health related issues, and settlement programs for refugees and new immigrants.

25. An article in the ladies' section of *Payambar*, newsletter of the Pakistani Association of Quebec, written by a Muslim woman, argued that women were achieving better status and recognition in India as compared to Pakistan (*Payambar* 3, no. 5 [1987]). Another periodical dealing with women's issues is *Bulletin d'Organisation Nationale des Femmes Immigrantes et des Femmes Appartenent a une minorite visible du Canada*. See Ghazala Shaheen and Cecilia Gonzales, "Clothing Practices of Pakistani Women Residing in Canada," *Canadian Ethnic Studies* 13, no. 3 (1981).

26. In March 1986, I had the occasion to hear an American Muslim woman lecturing at MCQ on the problems of society such as teen-age pregnancies, drugs, violence, abortion, and sexual corruption, advising Muslim women to reject the lures of the impure outside world.

27. *Muslim Women in the Era of Islamism: Proceedings of the International Symposium on Muslim Women of the Third World* (Montreal: CMRI, 1987).

28. *Les Femmes dans le Monde Arabe* (Montreal: CEAD February

1985). See also *Femmes Arabes et Femmes d'ici Acquis de Defis des Anées '80* (Montreal: CEAD, 1988).

29.   He reports having grown up in a situation in which Muslims had to struggle to prove that Islamic education need not be intellectually inferior to the standards of the British educational system. After leaving Nigeria he studied in Saudi Arabia and subsequently at McGill University in Montreal where he obtained an M.A. in Islamic studies. He is currently working for a doctorate.

30.   ISNA holds annual meetings in St. Catherine's, Ontario. At the 1985 meeting, the topic was Islamic Education and Family Life. The Council of the Muslim Community also has met annually since 1973; in the 1985 meeting in Guelph, Ontario, the members agreed on a number of projects relating to Muslim education.

31.   Garaudy maintains that he has not changed religion but that he has changed culture. The ultimate truths about God and humanity are the same for Christians and Muslims, he says, but European Christianity has become linked with the economic imperialism of the European Common Market over against Third World countries. See Roger Garaudy, "Pourquoi je suis Musulman," *Le Monde Islamique Special Roger Garaudy*. This lecture was originally given at a conference in Seville in July 1985. A charter of Seville was put forward giving a vision of future development among Muslims. See "Pour un Islam du XXe Siecle (Charte de Seville)," *Le Monde Islamique*, 1, no. 5 (July–August 1987).

PART 3

Ethnic Communities in Metropolitan Settings

CHAPTER 15

The Shi'a Mosques and Their Congregations in Dearborn

Linda S. Walbridge

When Abdo Elkholy carried out his well-known study of Muslims in the Dearborn-Detroit area[2] the highly visible split between the Sunni and Shi'a communities was just occurring. The Islamic Center of America, the first of the Shi'a mosques, had just been built several miles from the Southend of Dearborn, where most of the Muslims lived. This mosque seems to have beckoned the Lebanese Shi'a northward, as over the years they have migrated closer to the Islamic Center.

East Dearborn, the northeast quarter of this city which now numbers close to 100,000 people, is a far more prosperous area than the Southend and not nearly so isolated. The houses, usually of sturdy brick construction, are middle class in appearance. Lebanese own and operate most of the establishments on Warren Avenue, the main shopping area, and they increasingly attract non-Arabs to their shops and restaurants. Indeed they can be said to have rescued that part of Warren avenue from decay. Although the Arabs of the Southend often wear the colorful clothing of Palestinian and Yemeni villages, one sees little of the "peasant" look in east Dearborn. The people in this neighborhood wear "modern" clothes; that is, Western or contemporary Islamic dress.

Since Elkholy's study two more Shi'a mosques have opened their doors; the Sunnis, displaced by the Yemeni Zaydi's in the Southend, occupy a small building in East Dearborn. The Shi'a themselves have undergone significant changes largely because of the Lebanese Civil War and the Iranian Revolution. The Lebanese

337

Shi'a are a far more complex group than they were fifteen or twenty years ago, reflected in the changes that have taken place in their mosques. How the mosques originated and the role they play in uniting and dividing the community are the subject of this chapter.

HISTORICAL BACKGROUND

The Shi'a have always been a minority in the Islamic world and never constituted a majority in any country until the Safavids came to power in Persia in the sixteenth century. Although like most Sunnis they adhere to the Qur'an and the central tenets of Islam, their rituals and much of their religious law have evolved separately.[3] In the eleventh century Twelver Shi'a began to appear in areas where they apparently had never been before, including Jabal 'Amil in the south of Lebanon. Moojan Momen[3] speculates that these people may have been converts from the Isma'ili branch of Shi'a, a sect that had become particularly hated in the Muslim world. When the Safavids of Persia brought clerics from South Lebanon to teach Shi'a to their newly conquered people during the reign of Shah Abbas, the sphere of influence of Shi'i clerical learning moved eastward. Lebanese men aspiring to become religious leaders went to Najaf and Qum. The Lebanese people themselves, however, became increasingly isolated from these great centers.

There are few references to the Lebanese Shi'a before the advent of the Lebanese Civil War. Mikhayil Mishaqa, a fiscal manager to the Shihabi emirs of the nineteenth century, wrote a history of Lebanon in the eighteenth and nineteenth centuries and occasionally mentions the Shi'a. But he says that in those days "it was the custom among clansmen to distinguish followers not with regard to sect, but rather with regard to allegiance and loyalty."[4] This would indicate that until the beginning of this century the Shi'a aligned themselves with their Christian or Sunni Muslim compatriots according to the exigencies of the situation. It was not until the so-called Great Powers intervened in Ottoman affairs that we begin to see strict divisions among the various religions and sects.

That the Shi'a have been the poorest and most backward of the confessional groups in Lebanon seems undisputed. The economic success that Lebanon experienced in the nineteenth and twentieth centuries certainly was not evenly shared among all groups and regions of the country.[5] A. R. Norton says that "even as recently as the 1950s, the Shi'a seemed most notable for their invisibility and irrelevance in Lebanese politics." He cites studies indicating that the Shi'a had the lowest per capita income and were the most poorly educated and least represented in professions and businesses.[6] According to Joseph Olmert, in 1961 Bint Jubeil, a capital in a district in the south with a population of 10,000, had only two doctors, no pharmacy, no electricity, and only eleven telephones.[7] The increasing poverty of the rural areas forced large numbers of Shi'a to the Beirut slums where they lived in miserable conditions.[8]

It was to this scene that Seyyid Musa Sadr, an Iranian-born cleric from an illustrious clerical family, arrived. Learned in the religious sciences but also a man of action and pragmatism, he pitted himself against the quiescent clergy and the powerful feudal leadership and became the spokesman of the "oppressed" in Lebanon. Although he actively sought to bridge gaps between sectarian groups, he ultimately saw that the Shi'a would need to fight on their own. Eventually he established Harakat Amal (the Movement of Hope), which began as a social movement but in 1974 became an armed militia, one of many in Lebanon. This movement grew after Seyyid Musa disappeared during a visit to Libya in 1978.[9]

Conflicts with the Palestinians, retaliatory raids on the South by the Israelis, the Iranian Revolution, and finally the Israeli invasion of Lebanon in 1982 all served to arouse a new sense of religious fervor in some elements of the Shi'i population in Lebanon. New radical groups have emerged, but they are generally considered to be under the umbrella of the Hizbullah movement, which is Iranian based and has aspired to transform Lebanon into an Islamic Republic modeled after the revolutionary government in Iran. Amal and Hizbullah have fought bitter battles for regions with large Shi'i populations.

Lebanese Shi'a can now be found in areas throughout the world, with especially sizeable communities in Australia, Montreal, and Sierra Leone. The processes by which they are establishing their religious roots are recorded by writers such as Michael Humphrey,[10] Baha Abu-Laban,[11] Van Der Laan[12] and others. But the largest concentration is in Dearborn. The majority of them are members of what Sharon Abu-Laban refers to as the *differentiated cohort*; that is, those who came since 1968 and who have been affected by the prestige of Arab oil wealth and the recent surge in Islamic identity.[13]

IMAM CHIRRI AND THE DEVELOPMENT
OF THE ISLAMIC CENTER OF AMERICA

In 1988, on the twenty-fifth anniversary of the opening of the Islamic Center of America, a booklet was produced and distributed to the Shi'i Muslims of the Detroit-Dearborn area recounting the way in which the Islamic Center, the Jamia, came into being. It is a tale of frustration, fortitude, and sacrifice. The story states that because of the guidance of "the ever present, beloved Imam, Mohammed Jawad Chirri, the community united for the most part." It further states that "the people contributed to the new Center with a humble zeal reminiscent of the first Muslims." The community underwent a metamorphosis.

By the 1940s the Shi'a community in Dearborn was in need of strong leadership if it was to survive as an independent faith and not be subsumed by Sunnism, something that it has resisted in the rest of the world for centuries. Before the arrival of Shaykh Chirri, there was no true Shaykh or Imam[14] to serve the community, which at that time, according to an informant, consisted of about 200 Muslim families. These were mostly Lebanese, Syrians, and Palestinians, both Shi'i and Sunni. The ceremonial and spiritual needs of the Shi'a were met by a Shi'i from the Lebanese village of Bint Jubeil, Sheikh Khalil Bezzi. Yet my informants tell me that Shaykh Bezzi did not limit his ministrations to the Shi'a but took care of the religious needs of all Muslims, "not only in Dearborn but all over the country and regardless of whether they were Shi'ites, not Shi'ites or whatever." Illiterate when he came to the United States, he went briefly to Najaf to study Arabic and the Qur'an, then returned to America to serve here in the role of religious leader although not in a full-time capacity. My informants describe Bezzi in saintly and heroic terms, although he is a far different kind of hero than Chirri. Rather than being revered for his learning and ambitions for the community, he was distinguished for his humility and almost anti-clerical behavior.

Shi'i clergy in Lebanon are a class apart from the rest of society. They do not labor but simply perform clerical duties such as preaching, giving eulugies, contracting weddings and divorces, and the like. But Bezzi did something unusual for a Lebanese shaykh, which no self-respecting shaykh in Dearborn would do today: he made a living driving a truck from store to store selling vegetables. He refused payment for his religious services. In the 1950s, one of my informants and a small group of other believers pooled their money to buy him a car. They left the vehicle in front of his home and the keys with his wife. When shaykh Bezzi arrived home and found the car, he telephoned one of the men responsible and told him that he had half an hour to come to get it. If he did not come by then, said Bezzi, he would divorce his wife for having accepted the gift. The car was picked up and returned to the dealer. Many of today's shaykhs in Dearborn would not shun such tokens of prestige and privilege.

Michael Gilsenen writing about the Ulama in South Lebanon in the 1950s presents a picture of the clerics as being "the local socially prominent group."[15] Landowners with a monopoly on knowledge and literacy, they formed an elite that did not question the status quo and did not fight for the rights of the Shi'a. In great part because of the revolutionary efforts of Musa Sadr in the 1960s, who was very much in disagreement with this type of cleric, the role of the Ulama in Lebanon changed significantly. Sheikh Bezzi was no revolutionary, but neither was he a quiescent religious leader content to make a living by performing ritual services. From all accounts he seems to have been an idealistic missionary whose interest was not in converting new souls to Islam, but in serving those already in the fold.

The early Shi'a in this area with whom I have spoken like to stress the fact that there was very little Shi'i-Sunni division in the community; there is actually strong resistence even to discussing this topic. But obviously a distinction was made between the two sects even in the earliest days. It is interesting, for example, that Shaykh Bezzi is seen as the religious leader of this community, even though other preachers, Sunnis, were active in the area. In fact, the earliest accounts of Islamic activity in the Detroit area are of that dominated by Sunnis.[16]

The growth of Islam in this area actually coincides with the growth of the Ford Motor Company in southeastern Dearborn, where a mosque was built in the 1930s. Though this mosque was supposedly open to all Muslims, it was dominated by Sunnis; a year or so after its establishment the Shi'a rented a hall a few blocks away. They named it the Hashemite Hall. It was to the Hashemite Club that Shaykh Chirri came to teach. He says that when he arrived in Dearborn in 1949 he too was involved with the predominantly Sunni mosque, which at that time had a large Lebanese congregation. Shaykh Chirri also resists discussing Sunni-Shi'a differences, at least with outsiders.

Elkholy accuses Chirri of having "encouraged the physical as well as the spiritual separation between the two sects in the Detroit community. Now the community has two separate religious institutions, the mosque for the Sunnis and the Arabian Hashemite Club for the Shi'ahs."[17] Elkholy's information is not entirely correct. The Hashemite Club existed before Chirri's arrival. The earliest history of Islam in the Detroit area indicates that there was always a consciousness that the Shi'a had to remain somewhat distinct, though obviously the line between the two major sects had grown rather fuzzy. At the Hashemite Club such Shi'a holidays as the birthdays of the Imams (the line of successors after the Prophet) and of the Prophet's daughter were not celebrated. There were instead parties and dances and classes for children. But the very fact that there was an institution that took the name of the Prophet's family, Hashem, suggests that this community grasped the significance of keeping their separateness alive.

What is most striking about Elkholy's account is that he tells the story of the community from a Sunni perspective. His is a history of the community, but it is only one history. The Shi'a of Dearborn, with their three mosques, their plans for a school and their obvious prosperity, have their own interpretation of what occurred. History is often mythical and the myths are what motivate people and shape a community. For the victorious Shi'a, Shaykh Chirri was not a man of selfish designs but a self-sacrificing hero who braved all odds to establish Islam in America. It is this image that prevails and probably will continue to do so.

When Sheikh Chirri arrived in America he found an immigrant community of primarily Ford factory workers who clung to their Islamic identity, perhaps praying, avoiding pork when possible, and asking for the services of a Sheikh on ceremonial occasions. This is a community whose gatherings were more social than religious. He also found a group that was not academically oriented and that had given in to the temptation to follow many of the easier paths offered by American life. Certainly the intricacies of the Imami Shi'a eluded them. Chirri, with his scholarly credentials, taught his people reverence for the saints and symbols of the Shi'a. "Without Shaykh Chirri there would be no Islam in America" is a commonly heard expression of gratitude about this man who is now quite elderly.[18] As for the Shi'a-Sunni split, Chirri is not considered at all to blame. One informant told me that visiting shaykhs from Lebanon encouraged the division, not he.

I was told that from the beginning it was Chirri's aim to build a mosque. However, he ran into resistance in the community and left for Michigan City, Indiana. Fortunately for the Dearborn Shi'a a small band of loyalists stood by Chirri and gave him sufficient encouragement for his mission. Chirri returned to Lebanon, befriended someone who had access to President Abdul Nasser of Egypt, and solicited from Nasser enough money to motivate the fledgling band of Shi'is to begin the task of actually constructing a mosque. It is interesting to note that Chirri did not turn to the Shi'a religious leadership in Najaf, but went to the outstanding Arab political leader of the time, who was a Sunni.[19]

The history of the building of the Islamic Center of America is replete with stories of sacrificial giving. Fund-raising dinner reaped increasingly greater rewards and, I am told, some individuals even remortgaged their homes so as to be able to contribute. Finally in 1963 the center on Joy Road in Detroit was completed and its doors opened. Its domed exterior and minaret give it a mosquelike appearance, but its interior is plain in the extreme, with arid rectangles of rooms as often as not filled with folding chairs and formica topped tables. In the receiving area is a receptionist's desk in front of the shaykh's office. And on either side of the room are book shelves, containing among their volumes works written over the years by its director Imam Mohammad Jawad Chirri with titles such as Shi'ites Under Attack, The Brother of the Prophet, and a book about Imam 'Ali. There is no mistaking this for a Sunni mosque.

THE ISLAMIC CENTER OVER THE YEARS

If the mosque has changed over the years, it is primarily in terms of the appearance and behavior of those who frequent it. A photograph of a children's class in 1965 shows a group of school age children dressed in their "Sunday best." The girls, sitting among the boys, wear crisp, frilly dresses and all but one has on a fancy bonnet.

The older members of this community now laugh at themselves when they look back at this earlier era. "The women used to wear curlers in their hair to the mosque!" more than one person told me. Such a thing would be inconceivable today. Those in this earlier community did not think about wearing Islamic dress. Even simple traditional scarves were a rarity. Furthermore, a photograph of Shaykh Chirri dating from the 1960s shows him in a suit and necktie, with an aba around his shoulders, which is not the typical garb of today. He did wear a turban, but would even forego this when out in public.

Styles of clothing are not all that has changed. One informant who was still a young girl when the mosque opened remembers going there for parties and dances. It was common to hold traditional Lebanese weddings at the Islamic Center, with music and singing and dancing. Traditional kinds of weddings take place today in rented halls, certainly not in the local Shi'a mosques. A woman who came here from Jabal Amil in the 1950s said that a few people had even started sneaking alcohol "under the table" at the weddings. That she should have told me such a thing horrified her 30-year-old son. I assured him I knew that things had changed dramatically since then.

Indeed they have. Shaykh Chirri is responsible for some of these changes. He reportedly weaned people slowly to the ways of Islam. "He never pushed us too hard," are the words of one of his admiring early followers, who went on to say that Chirri did not want to scare away the youth by being too strict. He feared that if they seemed to look and behave too differently from the larger society, it would make them uncomfortable and might drive them away from Islam.

It appears that once the Islamic Center of America was established the Shi'a community developed in a fairly predictable fashion. The membership became largely assimilated into American society. Small in number, they wanted to learn English as soon as possible. Their children may have grown up speaking Arabic, but few received instruction in reading and writing the language.

Certainly the leadership, hand picked by Shaykh Chirri himself, became quite prosperous. The community appeared to be concerned with remaining distinctively Muslim, but in a way that also fit with American society. Shaykh Chirri became known among his constituents as someone who understood America and Christianity. Members of this community who remember the Sunday school programs at the Hashemite Club and later at the Islamic Center have told me that they learned a great deal about Christianity from Chirri. On Christian holidays they would be given lessons explaining these occasions. Throughout the years Chirri was interested in teaching Islam to Americans and was supported in this by his congregation. Yet he seemed to confuse "Christian theology" with American viewpoints on religion, and thus was not greatly successful.

Shaykh Chirri has long been the spokesman for the Shi'a of Dearborn and Detroit. Interviewed on the radio and by newspapers, he has had his opinion sought on current events involving the Arab world and Islam. The issues that Chirri addressed to his followers and in public reflect how strongly he has been affected by world events. One man who was a child in the Southend in the 1950s when Chirri was preaching there recalls that the Sheikh did not advocate a political struggle for Palestine. He told his listeners that they must resign themselves to the reality of Israel. No doubt this message was meant to encourage the immigrants to get on with their life in America. But it also suggests that he was very sensitive to Islam's image in this country and did not want Islam to be seen as anti-American.

The death of Nasser in 1970 evoked words of praise from Chirri for the Arab leader that show the extent to which he was affected by the pan-Arab movement that Nasser advocated. The *Garden City Guide-Journal* on October 1, 1970 quotes Chirri as saying that Nasser was "a barrier between communism and the Arab people." The anticommunist sentiments again reflect his pro-American stance.

By the 1980s Chirri was having to defend the Shi'a against the rising tide of feelings engendered by events in the Middle East. His remarks quoted in the newspapers show that he was walking a thin line. After the hijacking of the TWA plane in Beirut, *The Detroit Free Press* stated that Chirri "does not condone the hijacking but that it did not surprise him." He was quoted as saying ". . . it is like the cat that is sleeping. If you tread on it, should it amaze you that it bites you? If two or three people hijack because Israel is holding their brothers, should you be amazed?" By the 1980s the political situation in the Middle East had escalated to the point where Israel was definitely seen by the members of the Muslim community as an enemy. By then the number of Muslims in Dearborn was so great that consideration for their feelings was paramount in the minds of any cleric.

But what to say about the Iranians? This was and is a delicate issue. Iran and the Lebanese kidnappings and bombings obviously have been a thorn in the side of Chirri and those closest to him. An article in the *Dearborn Times-Herald*, July 25, 1985, about the kidnapping of Americans in Lebanon reports Chirri as saying, "The Shi'ites are good people who should not be judged for the actions of a few." He left the interviewer with the sense that the Shi'a of Dearborn "should not be confused with Iranian Moslems who advocate fiery revolution in the name of Islam." The press wanted Chirri's views again when the Satanic Verses issue erupted. Interviewed on television, Chirri condemned Salman Rushdie "as a dog that should be killed," and one informant said that he was encouraging people to take their protest against Rushdie into the streets. The fact that they did not shows the rather conservative tendencies of the center's congregation.

The Islamic Center is a house of worship for both the old and new immigrants, and tensions exist between the two. Those who are assimilated, although acknowledging themselves to be Muslims, tend not to identify strongly with their Lebanese heritage. Some express great American patriotism and even animosity toward Iran and the rule of Khomeini and his successor clerics. Even those who are inclined to be sympathetic to the goals and ideals of the Islamic republic are averse to participating in the political divisions that plague Lebanon. A majority of the newcomers also wish to leave behind the problems of Lebanon, but it is far more difficult for them to do so.

THE ISLAMIC INSTITUTE

That by the mid-1980s Sheikh Chirri could no longer claim to speak for all Shi'a is underscored by the fact that in 1985 the Islamic Institute was opened. Situated on Warren Avenue in east Dearborn, in the very heart of the Shi'i Lebanese community, its director is Shaykh Abdu'l Latif Berri, a young eloquent Najafitrained shaykh from Tibnin in south Lebanon. The Islamic Institute (Majmah) was not built as a mosque, but was converted from a business building and revamped to meet various social, educational, and spiritual needs of the community. Like the Islamic Center, the institute also lack visual reminders of Middle Eastern mosques. The main meeting room is usually lined with collapsable tables and folding chairs. During social occasions where food is to be served the tables have paper table cloths, styrofoam cups, and plastic utensils. For various occasions the walls may be adorned with plaques of locally produced calligraphy and occasionally one finds a large photograph of Khomeini dominating the room. But during Ramadan and holy day observances the aura of the building changes. At those times the large congregational room is strewn with prayer rugs. While some of the believers (the brothers and sisters as the "core" group call themselves at this mosque) engage in prayer, other clusters of men and of heavily veiled women, usually with toddlers and infants in tow, visit among themselves in various corners of the room. This room is not where *salat* (obligatory prayer) is performed; Shaykh Berri leads the prayer upstairs in a room that faces Warren Avenue. When it is lit up at night one can see from the street the men, and on very rare occasions a few women in the back row, going through their prostrations.

Shaykh Berri states that the institute was never intended to be a mosque as such, but was meant for more educational purposes. He does not want outsiders to think that it had begun as an open breach with the Islamic Center. Yet it is common knowledge that its opening was in reaction to the center. As one well-informed woman stated, "Shaykh Berri was divorced from Shaykh Chirri." Berri actually started out as a preacher in the center, but he left after a short time because of disagreements with Chirri and the center's Board of Directors. Relations between the two shaykhs are still extremely strained, although it is apparent that there is communication between the mosques and that there is at least no open animosity.

Those who supported Shaykh Berri's establishment of the institute had been deeply affected by the revolutionary form of Islam advocated by the Islamic Republic of Iran. For this group, who represent all regions of Lebanon, the Islamic Center had become too tolerant of Western ways. Several people have told me that the center has become "like a church." They object to the lack of rigor there in such matters as women's dress and sexual segregation. Innovations such as Sunday services also draw criticism. The core membership of the Majmah opts for a strict interpretation of Islamic law: women's hair, arms, and legs must be covered; men and women should not shake hands (there are even some who would prefer not to shake hands with Kuffar (unbelievers or non-Muslims); men and women should not sit together at the services; women are not to join men during the prayer; men (and also women) should refrain from wearing gold jewelry; women should save their makeup for their husbands' eyes only; and *mut'a*, a temporary type of marriage sanctioned only by Shi'a, should at least have the believer's approval.

It is not that one cannot find these strict attitudes shared by some at the center. More people attending the institute, however, believe in this kind of conservative interpretation. Unlike the center, the institute has not experienced in its brief history a period of assimilation into mainstream society. Therefore there is not the American-Lebanese divide that there is at the center. No assimilated Muslims hoping for a dialogue with Christian Americans are to be found at the institute. Keeping the Lebanese Muslims on the straight path is the main goal for both the institute and the center. Yet among some of the members of the center there is still a longing to continue what had been started before the refugees descended on them: the building of a community that is at once truly Islamic and truly American.

It is commonly said that the center is more sympathetic to the Harakaat Amal of Lebanon; the institute generally is seen as being closely aligned with the Hizbullah movement. However, in the past five years or so that it has been open, the institute obviously has undergone some changes. When one attends the institute for social reasons or for such events as Ramadan, 'Id al-Fitr, and Ashura, it appears that the community represents a fairly broad spectrum of political interests. Only when there are special adult education programs or when events in Iran such as the death of Khomeini or the Iranian earthquake occur does one become very conscious of the Hizbullah approach to Islam.

Most peole in this community, however, are not actively involved in either Amal or Hizbullah, and many try to avoid Lebanese politics. More than a few have told me that they do not attend any regular services at the mosques because both are too political, yet I also found people who try to avoid the Amal-Hizbullah dispute by attending both the center and the institue to show that they are not "prejudiced."

THE ISLAMIC COUNCIL OF AMERICA

The Islamic Council of America is another story. It was opened in winter 1989, but some months went by before it was even noticed by many members of the community. The structure, which is situated in part of a row of two-story brick commercial buildings, served as a store before its recent transformation to a house of worship and study. Immediately off the street on the north side of this rather narrow structure is a room used for *salat* and preaching. The south side, again with a door entering from the street, is a gathering room where one might go for Iftar (suppers during Ramadan) or for general types of meetings. During Ramadan this room is reserved for the women and children, while the men congregate in the prayer room to hear Shaykh Mohammad Ali Burro, the director of the Islamic Council, speak. The council does not differ from the center or the institute in its simplicity.

Some features, however, do differentiate it from the other two institutions, the most striking of which is that no one attends it who is not in strict conformity with the rules of Islam, at least as regards outward appearance. This is a mosque not only for the type of *Hejab* that has become common among the new breed of Arab fundamentalist Muslims but also for the Iranian *chador*. The *chador* may also be seen at the institute, but often it will be worn with a lacy scarf to counteract the effect, at least on general holidays and social occasions. This is not the case at the council. One does not find a trace of women's hair (or arm or leg) showing here. The men are often bearded, dress in open collared shirts, and maintain a serious demeanor. Again, one can find men who look like that in the halls and prayer rooms of the institute, but they may be sitting next to a person whose approach to Islam differs significantly from their own.

It is hard to say exactly what would happen if a woman appeared at the council in fashionable Western clothes and a hat. At this point it is unimaginable that any woman would attempt such a thing. I have never seen a woman at the council, except for myself, who does not wear a *chador* or *hejab* as a matter of course. An informant told me of an occasion when Shaykh Burro, who at the time was preaching at the center, publicly and emphatically reprimanded a woman for not wearing a headcovering at a memorial service. She was a Lebanese Christian friend of the deceased.

Another striking feature of the institute is the office of the director, Shaykh Burro. The new carpeting and long, sumptuous sofa are not as remarkable as the fact that one must remove one's shoes before entering this room. This is an Iranian custom, not Lebanese, and another indicator of the extent to which Shaykh Burro's approach to Islam has been marked by the Ulama of Qum where he lived for approximately seventeen years.

Like Shaykh Berri, Shaykh Burro began his work in the Dearborn community at the center, but found it lacking. He disapproved of women who tied scarves on their heads, much as Catholic women did before the 1960s, and sat at tables with men. Men were even seen greeting women with a handshake. Informants tell me that Shaykh Burro expressed his astonishment that even men who had made the hajj would do such a thing. His final break with the center came, though, over a more substantial issue involving the authority of what the Shi'a call a Marji'-taqlid. In Shi'a Islam there is a hierarchy of clerical leadership based on superiority of learning. By the eighteenth century there was a religious elite referred to as *mujtahids* who could practice ijtihad, that is, make religious decisions based on reason. Eventually a hierarchy of *mujtahids* was instituted and the concept of Marji'ayat-i-taqlid-tamm became institutionalized.[20] Superiority in learning is generally held to be the primary prerequisite for the selection of a *marji'*, though there is no clear cut set of criteria that governs the choice. In fact, charismatic leadership is an extremely important factor for determining who holds this role of leadership in the community. Ultimately, it decides which *marji'* to follow. In Dearborn the majority of Shi'a were *muqallad* to Ayatollah Abu'l Qasim Khu'i of Najaf until his recent death, although a substantial minority also followed Khomeini during his lifetime.

In summer 1989 Ayatollah Khu'i made an offer of several million dollars to the Islamic Center to build a Islamic school in the greater Detroit area. The offer, delivered by Shaykh Burro, was made on the condition that the school in question was to be under the jurisdiction of the Khu'i Foundation. The Islamic Center turned down the offer on the grounds that, when it built a school, that shool would be controlled locally by the Board of Trustees of the Islamic Center. The offer was then taken to Shaykh Berri and the Islamic Institute, who accepted it. Plans are now under way to build the school.[21]

Shaykh Burro is the only religious leader in the community whom I have heard berate other religious groups. During a single speech he condemned the Sufis, the Ahbaris,[22] and the Babi-Baha'is. At the other mosques occasional criticisms may be leveled at Sunnis, but generally these are intended to counteract accusations made by the Sunnis against the Shi'a and are not wholesale condemnations of Sunni Islam.

THE DIVISIONS OF THE COMMUNITY

The differences among the three mosques as outlined are related to how "Shariah minded"[23] the mosque leadership and the congregations tend to be, how much emphasis they place on following carefully the religious law. None of the Shi'i shaykhs in Dearborn would say that the Shariah is not important. Yet there are differences in the ways in which they follow the law based on whether they feel it is appropriate to consider the cultural context in which people currently live. This context refers both to America and to Lebanon.

The Deanborn Lebanese Shi'a, far from Najaf and other centers of Shi'i learning, have developed a religious identity uniquely their own. Although maintaining the central elements of Shi'a Islam, they have adapted the religion to their special surroundings. Now they are at an interesting crossroad. Those who are more Shariah minded would like to see a "pure Islam" established in America. They wish to deculturize Islam and to deny that the society in which they live has any bearing on the religion they practice. This group tends to be affiliated with either the institute or the council. For others cultural context is very important. Many of the immigrants with a traditional approrach to religion, both early and more recent, would like to see their Lebanese customs maintained, although most of them recognize that some accommodations have to be made to American society. The Islamic Center tends to attract people for whom some acknowledgment of cultural identity is important.

There is not a sharp dichotomy in Dearborn between the Shari-ah minded and the traditionalists. There are degrees within each group. Yet in interviewing and speaking more casually with people, I got the clear sense that the people themselves tend to see the community more or less in terms of this kind of division. Further-more, each group sees itself as "following the true Islam."

The Shariah minded are almost invariably critical of Muslims who do not properly cover themselves and follow strict dietary laws, who hold festive weddings in halls, and the like. They object to a "life-cycle" approach to Islam, in which older people assume the marks of religion and thereby gain prestige in the eyes of the people. For example, the idea of waiting until one's later years to go on pilgrimage is considered reprehensible. Everyone knows that after pilgrimage one must be more conscientious about performing one's religious duties. To wait until the later years when it is less inconvenient to pray and wear a scarf and pay religious taxes signals a lack of true commitment to Islam, say the Shariah minded. They feel that the traditionalists carry out religious duty only through habit and do not "seek out the truth" for themselves.

The traditionalists generally are of the opinion that the Shariah minded, who are frequently referred to as *Hizbullah* whether or not they are aligned with this movement, are ruining religion. Reli-gion should be between the believer and God, who will judge the heart of each individual. Traditionalists see themselves as attempt-ing to live up to the laws of their religion to the best of their ability and recognize that they will become more religious as they grow older. They believe that the Shariah minded often succumb to so-cial pressure and do not obey God's laws because of what is in their hearts. The latter are also accused of blindly following Iran in religious matters. This accusation is commonly heard in relation to *mut*'a (temporary marriage). Although *mut*'a is not completely alien to the Lebanese, neither has it been a well-established and highly regarded practice. It is not that *mut*'a has suddenly gained complete respectability among the Shariah minded of Dearborn, but that there is a strong effort being made in this direction.

It should be noted, though, that whereas the traditionalists find fault with their more legalistically minded coreligionists, they also express some ambivalence about their own approach to reli-gion. Bare-headed women are often not certain that their decision to forego the scarf is religiously correct. One woman expressed envy of women who feel comfortable wearing the scarf. She knew that covering her head is a religious duty, but simply could not bring herself to carry it out. Others struggle with their "prayer problem," the fact that they pray during Ramadan but do not follow through with this obligation for the rest of the year. Some people express a concern that the religious practices and observances of the Shariah minded are supported by religious texts although they themselves are either unwilling or unable to make the kinds of commitments that the texts sanction. Those who do follow most of the laws are sometimes sensitive to not appearing too extreme in the eyes of Americans. They feel that the Hizbullahis distort religion and thus give it a bad name. Yet it is apparent that the assertive brand of Islam found in this community does tend to set the standard for behavior and that most people are now at least more conscious of religious law than they might otherwise have been. This influence is particularly apparent in matters of female modesty. Women who used to swim or wear shorts in public in Beirut will not do so in Dearborn for fear of criticism.

THE RESPONSE OF THE MOSQUES TO THE PEOPLE

The mosques may reinforce the different approaches to religion in the community, but it cannot be said that they created them. The attitudes of the congregations of the three mosque communities have been strongly influenced by events in Lebanon and other parts of the Middle East and have taken quite different forms.

The Islamic Center continues to be the most flexible over what might be called legalistic laxity. The new director, who recently arrived from Lebanon, before conducting an engagement ceremony urged several bare-headed women to cover their hair. The women laughed good naturedly as they pulled scarves out of their purses. The philosophy of the center is not to push too hard, but hard enough so that the center cannot be accused of being un-Islamic.

The most recent of the mosques, the Islamic Council, was created as a refuge for those who were not willing to make any compromise with society whatsoever. Shaykh Burro has allowed none. As he said to me during an interview, "There are two types of Muslims: the ones who are very strict, and those who call themselves Muslims but do not observe the rules." He feels that there is no reason for Muslims not to follow all the teachings of Islam. This message is unmistakable for anyone who crosses the threshold of the Islamic Council.

The Islamic Institute also officially supports a rigorous form of Islam. Classes held at the institute teach that one must follow precisely what a *marji taqlid* or exemplar prescribes in his writings. Those who regularly attend the institute seem keenly concerned with knowing and following the laws of religion. Some of these same people may be found in meetings at the Islamic Council as well. The director of the institute, Shaykh Berri, most certainly advocates a strict approach to religion. Yet he also shows some flexibility, recognizing that not all the Muslims in his congregation are going to be so rigorous in their application of the law. A case in point is a woman who grew up in Beirut and developed a taste for Italian styles. Never one to go out of the house unadorned with makeup and jewelry, she told me that she asked Shaykh Berri if makeup were permissable for women. Knowing full well that it was hopeless to ask this woman to throw away her mascara and eyeliner completely, he instead opted to encourage her to pray and to follow the rules that forbid wearing makeup while at prayer. In this way he did not alienate her, yet gave her sound religious advice. The leadership at the institute seems to have recognized that by being too rigid in its insistence on strict Islamic behavior it runs the risk of alienating many of the Lebanese Muslims in the area.

SUMMARY

The Shi'a of the Dearborn-Detroit area built their own mosque, the Islamic Center of America, in the early 1960s several miles north of Dearborn's predominantly Arab Southend, where a Sunni mosque already existed. Since that time the Shi'a Lebanese have tended to settle in the more prosperous northeast quarter of Dearborn, where two more Shi'a mosques have been established.

The two most recent mosques have strongly reflected the assertive Islam that has become dominant in the Middle East since the 1970s. The Muslims who frequent these mosques tend to strongly emphasize the legalistic aspects of Islam. In fact, the services held at one of the two mosques, the Islamic Council, draw only this sort of person.

A kind of dichotomy exists in the Dearborn community, then,

between the highly "Shariah minded" and those with a more traditional approach to religion. Although the distinction is not clear-cut, the community tends to see itself in this light. Accusations are made by traditionalists that the Shariah minded are "Hizbullahis," who blindly follow Iran, whereas the traditionalists are accused of being just that: followers of tradition who have not thought through their religious beliefs. Regardless of any resentments, though, the Shariah minded do set a standard for the community, especially in terms of female modesty.

The mosque leadership is faced with the dilemma of deciding how strictly they should insist on people following the laws. The Islamic Center, even though it has become more conservative over the years, still remains the least demanding of the three mosques. The latest mosque, the Islamic Council, has given a clear message that the person who does not completely follow all Shi'a law is not truly a Muslim. The Islamic Institute, although emphasizing the law, has managed to attract a number of more traditional types to its general gatherings, as the leadership there refrains from being openly critical of those who do not maintain the strictest standards of Islamic behavior.

NOTES

This chapter is based on research conducted for my doctoral dissertation. The research involved participating in mosque events and other community activities, interviewing religious leaders, and carrying out fifty intensive interviews with Shi'i adult men and women. I lived in Dearborn for three years (and in an east Dearborn neighborhood for two years) to carry out this research and came to know many people on an informal basis.

1. Abdo Elkholy, *The Arab Muslims in the United States* (New Haven, Conn.: College and University Press, 1966).

2. Said Amir Arjomand in *The Shadow of God and the Hidden Imam* (Chicago: University of Chicago Press, 1984), p. 1, argues that Twelver Shi'a "can be fruitfully considered 'a world religion' as conceptualized by Weber . . . that is as an autonomous intellectual pattern or belief system, which is embodied in meaningful social action and enfolded in sentiments."

3. Moojan Momen, *An Introduction to Shi'i Islam* (Oxford: George Ronald, 1985), pp. 90–91.

4. Mikhayil Mishaqa, *Murder, Mayhem, Pillage and Plunder: The*

History of the Lebanon in the Eighteenth and Nineteenth Centuries, Wheeler M. Thackston, Jr., trans. of *Muntakhabat min al-Jawab* 'ala iqtirah al ahbab. Lebanese Ministere de l'Education Nationale et des Beaux-Arts (Beirut: Catholic Press, 1955; New York: State University of New York Press, 1988).

5.   Charles Issawi, "The Historical Background of Lebanese Emigration 1800–1914," paper presented at the Centre for Lebanese Studies Conference on Lebanese Emigration, St. Hugh's, Oxford, 1989.

6.   Augustus Richard Norton, *Amal and the Shi'a: Struggle for the Soul of Lebanon* (Austin: University of Texas Press, 1987), p. 14.

7.   Joseph Olmert, "The Shi'a and the Lebanese State," in Martin Kramer, ed., *Shi'ism, Resistence and Revolution* (Boulder, Colo.: Westview Press, 1987), pp. 189–201.

8.   Samir Khalaf and Guinain Denoeux, "Urban Networks and Political Conflict in Lebanon," in Nadim Shehadi and Dana Haffar Mill, eds., *Lebanon: A History of Conflict and Concensus* (London: Centre for Lebanese Studies, 1988), pp. 181–200.

9.   See Fouad Ajami, *The Vanished Imam: Musa Al Sadr and the Shi'a of Lebanon* (Ithaca, N.Y.: Cornell University Press, 1986).

10.   Michael Humphrey, "Community, Mosque and Ethnic Politics," *Australian and New Zealand Journal of Sociology* 23, no. 2 (July 1987): 233–245.

11.   Baha Abu-Laban, "The Lebanese in Montreal," paper presented at the Centre for Lebanese Studies Conference on Lebanese Emigration, St. Hughs, Oxford, 1989.

12.   Laurens Van Der Laan, "Mobility and Migration of the Lebanese in West Africa," paper presented at the Conference on Lebanese Emigration, St. Hugh's College, Oxford, 1989.

13.   Sharon McIrvin Abu-Laban, "The Coexistence of Cohorts: Identity and Adaptation Among Arab American Muslims," *Arab Studies Quarterly* 11, nos. 2–3 (Spring–Summer 1989): 45–82.

14.   A true Shaykh in Shi'i terms is one who has been trained at one or more of the holy cities such as Najaf in Iraq or Qum in Iran. The term Imam is also used to designate a religious leader, but because this term refers also to the Twelve Imams of Shi'a and some people in the Dearborn community do not like their religious leaders to assume this title, I have elected to use Shaykh.

15.   Michael Gilsenan, *Recognizing Islam* (New York: Pantheon Books, 1982), p. 72.

16.   See Barbara Aswad, "The Lebanese Muslim Community in Dearborn, Michigan," paper presented at the Centre for Lebanese Studies Conference on Lebanese Emigration, St. Hugh's, Oxford, 1989; Alixa Naff, *Becoming American: The Early Arab Immigrant Experience* (Carbondale: Southern Illinois University Press, 1985), p. 299.

17. Elkholy, *The Arab Muslims*, p. 77.

18. Shaykh Chirri is now retired. The new director is a recently arrived cleric from the Beka'.

19. For further discussion of this matter, see Linda Walbridge, "Shi'ism in an American Community" (Ph.D. diss., Wayne State University, 1991).

20. Muhammad Jawad Chirri, *The Shi'ites Under Attack*, (Detroit: Harlow Press, 1986); Muhammad Jawad Chirri, *The Brother of the Prophet* (Detroit: Islamic Center of Detroit, 1979). See Abbas Amanat, "In Between the Madrasa and the Marketplace: The Designation of Clerical Leadership in Modern Shi'ism," in *Authority and Political Culture in Shi'ism*, ed. Said Amir Arjomand (Albany: State University of New York Press, 1988), pp. 98–132. The concept of *marja'ayat-i-taqlid-timm* means complete authority of one's religious leader (a *majtahid*) over the entire community. The concept began to evolve in the eighteenth century and became institutionalized in the nineteenth.

21. For more on the issue of the Khui's School and the role of the *marji'* taqlid in Dearborn, see Walbridge, "Shi'ism in the American Community," pp. 107–150.

22. The Akhbaris are a school of thought in Shi'a Islam that once dominated the Shi'a. In the eighteenth century they were challenged by the Usulis, who argued for far greater authority of the clergy. The Akhbaris were violently persecuted in the Shi'a religious centers by the Usuli religious establishment who came to dominate Iran. Akhbaris can still be found in India, Bahrain, and in southern Iraq.

23. See Marshall Hodgson, *The Venture of Islam*, vol. 1 (Chicago: University of Chicago, 1974), p. 238.

CHAPTER 16

Bektashi Tekke and the Sunni Mosque of Albanian Muslims in America

Frances Trix

Albanian Muslims are often forgotten in surveys of Muslims. In the United States they are eclipsed by the more numerous Muslims of Arab and other Asian background, while in Europe, they are obscured by the atheist policy of the current Albanian regime. Therefore, it is not common knowledge that Albania is the only European country ever to have a Muslim majority (70 percent Muslim, 20 percent Orthodox Christian, 10 percent Roman Catholic).[1] Nor is it common knowledge that, during this century, thousands of Albanian Muslims immigrated and continue to immigrate to the United States and Canada from their Balkan homeland.

Albanian immigrants to America, both Christian and Muslim, have settled principally in New England, the New York area, and the industrial cities of the Midwest. And whereas Boston became the center for Orthodox Christian Albanians, and New York eventually the political center for all Albanians, Detroit became the organizational center for Muslim Albanians. It was in Detroit that the first Albanian mosque in America was organized in 1949, and in the Detroit area that an Albanian Bektashi Tekke, a Sufi center of the Bektashi Order, was founded in 1953. Both the mosque and *tekke* continue to the present, and their relationship and religious practices, particularly those of the *tekke*, constitute an unusual and intriguing aspect of Islam in America.

This chapter will focus on these two Albanian Muslim institutions, the first Albanian mosque and the Albanian Bektashi Tekke of the Detroit area, as a means of highlighting the Albanian Muslim experience in America. Previous studies of Albanian communities in America have looked at the Albanian immigrant experience in general, with cursory notes on Muslim institutions[2] or specifically at the Orthodox Christian experience.[3] None has looked exclusively at Albanian Muslims in America. Therefore primary sources have been important. These include interviews with Albanian Muslim immigrants and their children and grandchildren in the Detroit area, Balkan publications of Albanian nationalist societies of the late nineteenth and early twentieth centuries, and booklets of various anniversaries and congresses of the pan-Albanian Federation of Vatra and of the Albanian American Moslem Society. In all areas, my research has been facilitated by my twenty-year association with the Bektashi Tekke and study with Baba Rexheb, leader of the *tekke*.

The most unusual aspect of the Albanian Muslim community in relation to other Muslim groups in this country is the existence of the Sufi *tekke* with community functions and the interaction of mosque and *tekke*. To focus on this, the chapter begins with a brief description of the mosque and *tekke*. This is followed by an overview of Albanian Muslim immigration to America, and an account of organizational growth within the Albanian Muslim community in Michigan. Against this demographic and institutional background, the Albanian mosque and *tekke* are presented in more detail, including information on their differing functions, their membership, leadership, and the question of their continuity in the American context.

SPOTLIGHT ON THE MOSQUE AND TEKKE

The first Albanian mosque in America is a handsome domed building with minaret, located in a small suburb on the eastern edge of Detroit. The Imam of the mosque, Vehbi Ismail, is from northern Albania, but lived and studied in Cairo before coming to the United States. His children are grown, and he now lives with his wife in a house adjacent to the mosque complex. He conducts the weekly prayers and the two major holiday celebrations at the mosque: Bajram i Madh ("the Big Holiday"), known in Arabic as *Eid al-Fitr*, the holiday that comes at the end of the fast of Ramadan; and Bajram i Vogël ("the Little Holiday"), known in Arabic as *Eid al-Adha*, the holiday that commemorates Abraham's willingness to sacrifice his son. On the actual day of these holidays, there is *salat* in the mosque, with the prayers in Arabic and the sermon in Albanian and English. Participants include mostly Albanians, but also other Muslims from Pakistan, Egypt, and Turkey who live on the east side of Detroit. On the Sunday following these holidays there is a public gathering at the mosque with prayers, speeches, and a large communal meal for 300 to 400 people, almost all of whom are Albanians.

In contrast, the Albanian Bektashi Tekke is found to the south and west of Detroit in a much more rural area. Its central building was once a farmhouse, and its grounds include 18 acres planted in soybeans, fruit, and other vegetables. Its leader, Baba Rexheb, is of the celibate branch of the Bektashi Order that in Albania was always more revered than the other branch that allows its leaders to marry. Baba comes from southern Albania where he received a classical Ottoman education in the Qur'an, Arabic grammar, and Persian and Turkish literature. He also lived in Italy and in Egypt before coming to the United States. He resides at the *tekke;* and his *turbe*, where he will be buried, has already been built on *tekke* grounds. The *tekke* is a striking building in traditional octagonal form with gardens. Baba conducts the twice daily prayers, the initiation ceremonies for those seeking closer association with the order, sessions of *muhabbet* ("love") or *zikr* (remembrance"), wherein God is praised through changing poetry, and the two major *tekke* holidays: Ashure, which commemorates Hussein's death at Kerbela, and Nevruz, a New Year's celebration. The ten-day mourning period that precedes Ashure includes a selective fast, daily readings from an Albanian adaptation of a sixteenth century Turkish work, and special ceremonies on the tenth day attended by the initiated members. On the Sunday following Ashure there is a public gathering of 300–500 people in the large basement room of the *tekke* with prayers, speeches, special Ashure food, and a large communal meal.

From this brief overview of the mosque and *tekke* leaders and holidays, it would appear that the mosque is Sunni, the *tekke* Shi'i. Indeed it is appropriate to categorize the Albanian Mosque as Sunni. Its Imam comes from Shkodra, a city in northern Albania that prior to the Communist takeover was known to be strongly Sunni Muslim and Roman Catholic. It is much more problematic, however, to say that the *tekke* is specifically Shi'i. In fact, its leader specifically refuses that appellation and notes that traditionally Bektashis have found error in both Sunni and Shi'a perspectives. Instead Bektashis look to a mystical interpretation of the Qur'an with veneration of *ehli beyt*, the family of the Prophet. And in contrast to the Imam, Baba comes from the southern Albanian city of Gjirokastër that has long been the home of several Bektashi *tekkes*, as well as other Sufi orders and Orthodox Christians. (Historically, the Bektashi Order is a Turkic Sufi order founded in the thirteenth century in Anatolia. It has been known throughout its history for its tolerance of different religions and the humor with which it characterizes its more legalistic fellow Muslims.)

Along with the question of Sunni-Shi'a categorizations, there is the more practical question of the relation of the mosque with the *tekke* among Albanian Muslims. Attendance patterns reveal that some Albanian Muslims attend only the mosque, and others attend only the *tekke*, but many attend both. And the tradition of the Imam's attendance at *tekke* celebrations and the Baba's attendance at mosque celebrations further contributes to a sense of cooperation.

But before looking closer at the relationship of the mosque and *tekke*, it is useful to have some background on the people who make up their congregations. Where do the founding members, the clerics, and the continuing members come from in the context of Albanian immigration to America?

WAVES OF ALBANIAN MUSLIM IMMIGRATION TO AMERICA

The founding members of both the mosque and the *tekke* come from the earliest wave of Albanian Muslim immigration to America. These immigrants were men from small towns in the regions of Korçe and Gjirokastër in the southern part of Albania. In immigrating to America these Muslim Albanians were following in the footsteps of their Orthodox Christian compatriots, also from southern Albania, who had started coming to America in the last part of the nineteenth century. Thus the first Albanian to come to America was an Orthodox Christian who arrived in 1884,[4] and the first Muslim Albanian to come to America, according to the Detroit community, was Orhan Ali of Voskop, a village in the vilayet of Korçe, who came here in 1905.[5]

But it was only after 1914 that Albanian Muslims started coming to America in any number.[6] The event that precipitated their arrival was the invasion of southern Albania by Greece in 1913. Albania had been under the rule of the Ottoman Empire for 500 years, and many Muslim Albanians had held low-level administrative positions under their fellow Muslim Turks. With Albania's declaration of independence from the Ottomans in 1912 and the ensuing invasion by the Greeks, however, many Muslim Albanians in the south lost their means of livelihood.

Like their Christian compatriots, the Muslim Albanian immigrants came principally to the mill towns and shoe factories of New England. With the advent of World War I, they also moved westward to factory towns of the Midwest. They lived together in rooming houses known to them as *konaks*, sharing close living space and saving for their return to their homeland. The pattern then was for single men to come to America, either as bachelors or as married men whose wives remained in Albania, and work for a period. They then returned to Albania, sometimes to stay but often to return to America for more work. As a result there are many instances in the Albanian Muslim community in Detroit where two generations of the same family were both born in the Balkans. Fathers came to America to work, went back, fathered children, and then returned to America, with their sons following them later.

The first wave of Albanian Muslim immigration lasted from 1915–1925. Then there was a hiatus in new immigration until after World War II. This can be accounted for by the imposition of the quota system in immigration regulations, but also by what appeared to be somewhat improving conditions in Albania and later by the Italian invasion of Albania and the advent of World War II.

The second wave of Albanian Muslim immigrants to America came from 1945 to 1960. They differed from the earlier group in that they came principally for political rather than economic reasons. Many had been allied with anticommunist resistance groups in Albania such as Balli Kombëtar. When the Communists gained power in 1944, they were forced to flee for their lives. They also differed from the earlier immigrants in that they came not just from the towns of southern Albania, but from all regions of the country and all classes of society. The clergy of both the mosque and the *tekke* are from this second group of Albanian Muslim immigrants.

The third wave of Muslim Albanian immigrants was from 1962 to 1989. This group has taken advantage of nonquota immigration regulations and is principally from Albanian populations outside the country in the republics of Yugoslavia, especially the Prespa area of Macedonia, and the Kosovo region of Serbia. These minority populations are found outside Albania because when the Great Powers drew Albania's borders after World War I they left half of all Albanians in the surrounding countries of Greece and Yugoslavia. The Prespare, that is the people from the Lake Prespa region of Macedonia, have been particularly active members of both the mosque and the *tekke*.

But what numbers can be associated with these three waves of Albanian Muslim immigration to the United States? Unfortunately official statistics are practically useless. For the first period of immigration, from 1915–1925, there was no separate country listing for Albanians—rather they were recorded as Greeks or Turks or as nationals of the country they sailed from. And never was religious affiliation indicated. Still, by the late 1930s, the Albanian population in the United States was estimated to be in the range of 35,000 to 60,000 people,[7] most of whom were Christian. Given then that Christian Albanians greatly outnumbered Muslims in the early period of immigration, and that Muslim Albanians tended not to intermarry nor to bring families but to return to Albania, a conservative estimate of the Muslim Albanians in the United States in the late 1930s is somewhere around 5,000.

As for numbers for the second period of immigration of Muslim Albanians, United States Immigration and Naturalization figures list only 144 Albanians entering the United States between 1941 and 1960.[8] Again this is not broken down for religious affiliation, but in the Detroit area alone there are more than 144 Albanian Muslims who came during this time, not to mention those who settled in the growing New York and New Jersey communities. Rather, it is reasonable to estimate that there were several thousand Albanian Muslims who immigrated to America during the period from 1945 to 1960.

The third period, from 1962 to 1989, saw greater numbers than the second period, with immigrants coming principally from Albanian communities in the bordering republics of Yugoslavia. Again, officials figures list these people indiscriminantly as Yugoslavs. Further, there is immigration by way of Mexico that would not be registered at all. Tentatively, then, the Albanian immigrants of this period number in the tens of thousands, many of whom are Muslim, and many others of whom are Catholic.

Overall, if the estimate of 70,000 by the *Harvard Encyclopedia of American Ethnic Groups* (published in 1980, based on the 1970 census) is a conservative figure for the first two periods of immigration and most accurate for Orthodox Christian Albanians, it is possible that there are 150,000 people of Albanian descent in the United States of whom some 40,000 are Muslim. Thus it is understandable how such a relatively small immigrant group, and one that is dispersed across the American Northeast and Midwest, could be overlooked in surveys of Muslim groups in America. Further it is understandable how even an unusual Muslim institution like the Bektashi Tekke could be overlooked in a place like Detroit with its multiple Islamic centers. But with the history of their immigration fresh in mind, we now turn to organizational growth among Albanian Muslims in Michigan.

ORGANIZATIONAL GROWTH OF ALBANIAN MUSLIM IMMIGRANTS IN MICHIGAN

The first Albanian mosque and the Albanian Bektashi Tekke were both established in the Detroit area soon after World War II. At this time some of the Albanian Muslim immigrants had been in America up to forty years, but until World War II they had not planned on making America their permanent home. The chaos of the war followed by the Communist takeover in Albania made it clear to many of them, however, that their future was here. Concern then arose for the next generation and the continuity of Albanian cultural values and religious customs in a place where Albanians were like "a drop of water in an ocean." Muslim parents also feared the spread of atheist views among the young.[9]

To deal with these concerns, the Albanian American Moslem Society was founded in Detroit in August 1945.[10] Two years later, in August 1947, they held their first congress in the Southwestern Political Club in Detroit. The congress was attended by local Albanian Muslims as well as by delegates from the four affiliated branches: Warren, Ohio; Mansfield, Ohio, Buffalo-Rochester-Jamestown, New York; and East Pittsburgh, Pennsylvania. At this congress they proposed, discussed, modified, and accepted a constitution and planned the *Albanian Moslem Congress Review,* which was soon published as a ninety-two page booklet in Albanian and English. But as of then they had not found an Albanian Imam.

By August 1949, when the Albanian American Moslem Society held its Second Congress in the Leland Hotel in Detroit, however, they had secured an Albanian Imam from the Albanian community in Egypt. Further, the guests of honor at this gathering included the governor of Michigan, the mayor of Detroit, the president of the Detroit City Council, and the state chairman of the Democratic committee.[11] It is noteworthy that at only the Second Annual Congress of the Albanian Moslem Society, the top political notables of the state of Michigan were in attendance. Clearly this is not the work of people with only four years experience in organization.

Rather, the Albanian American Moslem Society drew heavily on the organizational experience of its members with Vatra ("the Hearth"), a pan-Albanian federation that was founded by Orthodox Christian Fan Noli and Muslim Faik Konitza in Boston in 1912 to try to save Albania from the territorial designs of its Balkan neighbors. As an immigrant organization, Vatra sent representatives and numerous telegrams to the Peace Conferences in Europe after World War I. Fan Noli also met with President Wilson to try to secure his support for Albania. At its height, Vatra had eighty branches across North America, and many Albanian immigrants learned to read through its newspaper *Dielli* (The Sun), which continues to be published.

The influence of Vatra on the Albanian American Moslem Society can be seen in its branch structure, its constitution, its recognition of the importance of a regular publication, and its proclivity for going to the top in seeking influence. The society further drew from the pan-Albanian aspect of Vatra in that it included Christian Albanian speakers at both its congresses. Indeed, Christian Albanians contributed funds toward securing a building for a mosque and later supporting the *tekke*. In like manner, Muslim Albanians have contributed to Christian Albanian churches and publications of the Orthodox Albanian archbishop, Fan Noli. Finally, the Albanian nationalism and emphasis on the Albanian language that was the glue of Vatra continues in both the mosque and the *tekke*.

In contrast, religious organization in the Balkans and the Middle East appear to have had little direct effect on the initial organization of the Albanian American Moslem Society. Before World War II, both Sunni Muslim and Bektashi organizations in the Balkans were essentially clerical hierarchies. But when the society was founded, it had no Imam or Baba; rather it elected its own leaders.[12]

The influence of other Muslim organizations in America on the Albanian American Moslem Society has been limited. The Albanians knew of the Dearborn Mosque and Hashemite Hall; indeed, it was the Lebanese Imam at the Dearborn Mosque, Imam Karoub, Sr., who was called on to bury the unfortunate Albanian Muslim who died in Michigan in the 1930s before he could return home to the Balkans. But on the whole, the Albanians noted the Arab character of that mosque and hall, and preferred to gather in their own homes or halls as Albanians to mark their holidays.

Later when the Albanians had their own regular Imam, there would be some interaction with other mosques at the level of the clergy. But before World War II, there were few Albanian Muslim clerics in America. One of the oldest Albanian Muslim communities, that of Waterbury, Connecticut, had Imam Tosun, a personally designated and informally educated leader. Various Bektashi dervishes had come to America: Dervish Kamber had come in 1916 to collect funds for a *tekke* back in Albania, and later an older Baba Kamber Fratari had come. But Dervish Kamber returned in 1920, and the Baba was old and sick and did not stay in America either.[13] There had been talk in the New York community of establishing a Bektashi *tekke* there in the 1930s, but it came to nothing. As Qani Adam Prespa, one of the early Albanian Muslim immigrants to Detroit described the religious situation of his people in the 1920s and the 1930s, "The coffeehouse was our church."

In 1950, the Albanian Moslem Society, with funds collected from Albanians, principally in the Detroit area—but also from Ohio, Buffalo and Jameston, New York; Waterbury, Connecticut; New York City; Pittsburgh; Philadelphia; and Toronto—rented a former church on the west side of Detroit and, with their newly arrived Imam, opened it as the first Albanian Mosque in America. Three years later a Bektashi cleric, Dervish Rexheb, came to the Detroit area and performed a memorial service in the home of an Albanian Muslim, Abbas Myrtezaj, which was attended by Albanian Muslims, many of whom were from Bektashi families. In October of that year, 1953, a group of fifteen[14] gathered in St. Andrew's Hall in Detroit and proposed setting up a *tekke* for the newly arrived dervish.

Traditionally *tekkes* are located outside cities, in quiet yet accessible places. In line with this, Qani Prespa located a farmhouse with 18 acres of land southwest of Detroit for $25,000. The founding members pooled their resources and purchased the farm. In 1954 with an Ashure ceremony attended by some 200 people, the *tekke* was officially opened.

Such a move was not without opposition. The Communist government of Albania was against it, and there was fear among Albanians in Detroit that if they supported the *tekke*, there would be retaliation against their relatives back in Albania. There was also fear that the presence of two Albanian Muslim institutions in the Detroit area would split the Albanian Muslim community.

What then is the relationship between the mosque and the *tekke*—what had it been back in Albania and what would it become in Michigan?

THE *TEKKE* AND THE MOSQUE:
SEPARATION AND CONTRASTIVE FUNCTION

Among those who founded the Albanian American Moslem Society in 1945 were people who characterized themselves simply as Albanian Muslims as well as those who had the added identity of coming from Bektashi families. In Albania, to come from a Bektashi family meant that some member of one's extended family had an affiliation with a Baba in a Bektashi *tekke*. But *tekkes* in Albania were never substitutes for mosques; they served different but complimentary functions. Thus Bektashi Babas and dervishes would attend the mosque on the major holidays. In some cases the Imam from the mosque was also an initiated member of the local *tekke*. In America then, to come from a Bektashi family meant that one's family in Albania visited a *tekke* during the year, and that in America one celebrated Ashure, with its ten-day mourning period, an Nevruz, the old Persian New Year and birthday of Ali.

The inclusion of both Bektashi Muslims and non-Bektashi Muslims in the early Albanian American Moslem Society in Detroit is reflected not only in membership lists, but also in articles in the 1947 review, and in the holidays included in its constitution. In particular, the articles in the 1947 review include several on Sufism, the Bektashis being one of the many Sufi or mystical orders in Islam. And the list of holidays in the constitution, also printed in the 1947 review, includes the Bektashi Matem as well as the traditional Sunni holidays of Ramadan, the Bajram of Fitr, Kurban Bajram, the Mevled (birthday of the Prophet). (Besides religious holidays, the list also includes national holidays of America and Albanian Independence Day.) Further, the constitution states specifically: "Being no division in Islam, the society is non-sectarian" (Article XIII).

With the arrival of the Albanian Imam in Detroit in 1949, however, the potential for differences between Bektashis and non-Bektashis surfaced. The Imam was from the city of Shkodra in northern Albania, where there were no Bektashis. Thus he was not familiar with the holiday of Nevruz, and wrote to Albanians in the Bektashi Kaygusuz Tekke in Egypt to learn about it. In contrast, most of the Albanian Muslim immigrants in America were from southern Albania where the Bektashis had been an important presence, and one well connected with the nationalist movement.[15] Despite these differences, the Albanian Moslem Society continued to be one group. Its quarterly in 1950 included a long article on the martyrdom of Hussein, signed by the new Imam.

The situation changed with the arrival of Dervish Rexheb in Detroit in 1953 and the decision by a group of Albanian Muslims of Bektashi background to found a Bektashi *tekke*. Controversy arose as to whether or not to support this initiative. The division however was not along Bektashi–non-Bektashi lines, but rather whether people thought a *tekke* should be established for the dervish or whether they feared that such an action would divide the Albanian Muslim community. There were non-Bektashis who favored founding a *tekke*. Instead of emphasizing religious difference, some saw it as an additional Albanian institution in the area and thus a strengthening of Albanian identity in America.

Indeed, a conspicuous feature of both the mosque and the *tekke* is their Albanian nationalism, evidenced in the omnipresence in both institutions of Albanian flags and representations of Skenderbeg (an Albanian national hero), in the importance accorded the Albanian language, and in the frequent reference to national sentiments at the public holiday celebrations. Building on these nationalist sentiments, the constitution of the Bektashi Tekke contrasts with the constitution of the Albanian Moslem Society in its even stronger emphasis on the Albanian language. For example, a requirement for the Baba, the main clerical leader, is that he be of the "Albanian race." Another article in the constitution of the *tekke* that may reflect the controversy surrounding the founding of a *tekke* in Michigan is the following: "If the spiritual leader (the Baba) permits himself to become involved in domestic or foreign politics, he will be dismissed from his position immediately" (Article XXIX). This has come to have the meaning that a Baba should not become involved in factional Albanian politics; initially though it was to counter attempts to discredit Dervish Rexheb that alleged he would favor one Albanian faction over another.

With time, and building on shared nationalism, overlapping membership, and the conciliatory nature of the Baba, the Albanian mosque and Bektashi Tekke have developed a working, cooperative relationship with a division of functions within the Albanian Muslim community. In particular, the mosque holds the regular weekly prayers, the prayers for Ramadan, and the celebration of the two main Sunni holidays (Eid al-Fitr and Eid al-Adha). Further, the Imam performs most marriages and funerals.

In contrast, the Bektashi Tekke holds the commemorations of Nevruz and Ashure, with its ten-day mourning period of Matem. It further holds private rituals for those who would become initiated members and sessions of *muhabbet* that follow the private rituals. On a few occasions, the Baba has also performed marriages when the family had an especially close relationship with him. In general though, the Imam performs marriages with the Baba blessing the couple beforehand if one or both come from a Bektashi family. The Baba has also officiated at funerals, particularly when the deceased is a *muhip*.

Weddings and funerals are a main function of the mosque and a minor one of the *tekke,* but the saying of personal prayers for people's particular needs is a main function of the Baba at the *tekke* and only a minor one at the mosque. People come to the *tekke* to ask the Baba to pray for matters of health, family, and work—that operations be successful, that depression be alleviated and nervousness calmed, that good spouses be found for their children, that children be born, and that new businesses flourish. They ask for prayers when their children begin college or enter the military and when they purchase a new house or car. They may ask for advice and consultation when there are marital problems or legal disputes. In the early 1970s, for example, the Baba presided over the equitable dissolution of a restaurant partnership where both parties were Bektashi. Having heard both sides' contentions presented aloud outside under the tree by the *tekke,* the Baba then took each party separately inside and talked with him. After that he pronounced his decision, and all was settled.

In requesting prayer or consultation with the Baba, people who live nearby come to the *tekke* for a short time. Those who live farther away may either call on the telephone, write letters, or come and stay in the guest rooms of the *tekke* for several days. To accommodate this, the *tekke* has six guest rooms, and its large kitchen regularly serves from five to twenty people for meals.

Indeed, a major difference between the mosque and *tekke* is one of atmosphere and accommodation. The mosque has prayer rooms, meeting rooms, a library, and offices. People come there to pray, to meet with the Imam, or to hold meetings and gatherings. But the Imam goes home at night.

In contrast, the *tekke* has the private ritual room (the *meydan*), a large meeting room, and a library. But it also has the Baba's quarters, a large kitchen, guest rooms, and rooms where permanent residents of the *tekke* live. The Baba is always there. People come to request prayers, to hold meetings and gatherings, or just to sit and talk with each other and the Baba in the kitchen, over coffee in the salon, or outside under a large tree where there is a round wooden table surrounded by benches with a special place for the Baba in the center. The fields around the *tekke* contribute to the peaceful setting. People come to stay in this setting for varying periods of time; one Bektashi from New York even came to stay at the *tekke* while he was studying for medical exams.

In matters and manners of instruction, the mosque and *tekke* also differ. The mosque is to teach the Qur'an and hadith. Therefore there are regular classes for children at the mosque on religion, along with classes on the Albanian language. The Imam gives regular sermons, publishes a quarterly review, and has written many books on Islam in Albanian.

In contrast, the purpose of the *tekke* is to offer the possibility for spiritual growth in a community setting by coming closer to God through a relationship with the Baba. As might be expected, instruction is less didactic. The Baba gives no regular sermons. Twice a year he does talk briefly at the public holiday celebrations, and for two years there was a quarterly publication of the *tekke* on Bektashi holidays, instruction, and history. The Baba has also written two books. However, the main instruction at the *tekke* is in the sessions of *muhabbet,* where Bektashi poems are chanted and the Baba talks on Bektashi matters if they arise. There is also private interaction with the Baba as people request it. Yet the most profound instruction is indirect, through observation of the Baba and the way he lives.

The life-style of the Imam is that of many religious leaders in America. He wears his robe and turban during prayer time, but otherwise dresses in civilian garb. He receives a regular salary. People consider his opinion with special respect, but his family life is similar to other families.

The Baba lives a very different life. He moved into a Bektashi Tekke in southern Albania when he was only 16 years old. When he completed his studies at age 21, he took the vows to be a dervish. Since that time he has always worn his special dervish garb of *hirka, kemer,* and *taç,*[16] and except for four years in displaced persons' camps in Italy after World War II, he has always lived in *tekkes.* He would see it a sin to wear secular clothing. He also took a vow of celibacy in Albania. An Arab Muslim visitor once suggested that celibacy went against the Qu'ran's prescriptions to be fruitful and multiply. The Baba responded quickly by asking rhetorically if the questioner thought that the only children were those of the flesh. The Baba considers all who come to the *tekke* his children.

Further, as the Baba has no private family to support, he receives no salary nor does he have any possessions. His dedication to God and his community is obvious, and he is much revered. People seek him out for prayers, but they also seek his company for his quick wit and nonjudgmental nature. He is especially appreciated by teenagers who do not always find such suspension of judgment in their immigrant parents.

THE *TEKKE* AND THE MOSQUE: MEMBERSHIP, LEADERSHIP, AND CONTINUITY

Finally there is the question of the continuity of the Albanian Mosque and Bektashi Tekke in Michigan. With attendance at holiday gatherings steady and real estate secure, both the mosque and the *tekke* appear hardy. Indeed, in 1990, the *tekke* completed a $200,000 addition including new quarters for the Baba, a larger kitchen, and more guest rooms. Nonetheless continuity remains an issue for the community in terms of changing membership and leadership.

Earlier, the membership of the mosque and the *tekke* was described as made up of immigrants who came to America at different times in the twentieth century. The membership of both can also be described as made up of social networks reinforced by family relationships, regional groupings, political groupings, and visiting patterns. Albania itself is not a large country, and many of the immigrants are related. People speak in offhand manner of relationships like the "wife of the uncle of my second cousin."

In line with the intertwined and frequent contact of its members, neither the mosque nor the *tekke* has a regular newsletter. There seems to be no need, with the calling and visiting that take place. Recently though there has been the added use of the radio for announcement of the times of lunar-based holiday celebrations along with occasional announcements in national Albanian papers. Still, despite the large size of the Detroit metropolitan area, communication among the Albanian Muslims of the mosque and the *tekke* resembles that of a much smaller town. Young people sometimes speak with longing for the more spread-out and less interactive Albanian Muslim community of the New York area, where they think they would be freer to seek their own identity.

A threat to this tight community, and one that affects the mosque and the *tekke* members is the possibility that children may marry outside the Albanian Muslim community. The matter of marriage has always been a concern for Albanian Muslims in America. Recall that the first wave of Albanian Muslim immigrants to Michigan were men who often remained unmarried. In the second wave, some had wives back in Albania who couldn't get out after the Communist takeover. Others, often young soldiers from World War II, sought brides in Turkey, Greece, or even England. The Turkish brides, to a lesser extent the Greek ones, and one of the English brides were accepted and participated in the *tekke* community.[17] As for the third wave of Albanian Muslim immigration, they often came as families or sent for brides from Yugoslavia.

Still there has been intermarriage in America. A few Albanian

Muslim men have married Lebanese Muslim women, and in the Detroit area one Albanian Muslim woman married an Albanian Christian man. But as might be expected, it is mostly the Albanian Muslim men who are allowed to date and who then marry American women. These couples tend to be lost to both mosque and *tekke*. And this either leaves Albanian Muslim women unmarried, for in general they are not allowed to date, or attempts are made to find husbands for them in Albanian Muslim communities in Yugoslavia or Turkey. In either case, these women tend to stay affiliated with the mosque and the *tekke*.

Another way of looking at changing membership, here only of the *tekke*, is to focus on the "inner members," the *muhiban*.[18] These people go through a private initiation, and have special responsibilities to the *tekke*. There were seventeen initiates in the 1950s, thirty in the 1960s, twenty-nine in the 1970s, and forty-three in the 1980s. Thus the numbers have continued to grow. Of these, the number of men has always greatly exceded the number of women, such that of the total number of initiated members, ninety-two have been men, twenty-seven women.[19]

But there are other patterns apparent in this inner membership. Most of those who seek the private initiation were born in the Balkans. Only two have been American born. Thus the *tekke*, at least in its inner membership, is still serving as an immigrant organization. Further, there is a high percentage of inner members who live in places such as New Jersey, Chicago, Toronto, or even Australia. Here it appears that the inner membership serves a branch function of keeping special contact with an organization that is far from home.

Inclusion of Bektashis living in cities other than Detroit is attested to not just in inner membership, but also in sponsorship of public holidays. The custom for each of the major Bektashi holidays, that is for Nevruz and Ashure, is to have several people underwrite the cost of the full lamb meal. This is considerable because 300 to 500 people attend these gatherings. In 1989, Ashure was sponsored by several couples from Waterbury, Connecticut, and one couple from Hackensack, New Jersey; in 1990 Ashure was sponsored by four people from Chicago and one from Michigan.

Interestingly, at its outset the mosque had a branch organization. However, as more Albanian mosques are built in places like Chicago, Waterbury, Connecticut, and New York, the Detroit Mosque is becoming more a local organization, whereas the *tekke*, which was originally more local, is becoming more national and international. This reflects not only the prestige of the Baba, but also the lack of other qualified Bektashi leaders.

Turning from questions of membership to leadership, the structure of lay leadership of the mosque and *tekke* is similar. Both have lay commissions, governed by constitutions, that along with the Imam or Baba direct the institution. These commissions are elected, but a person who is on the commission is generally on it for life. New members are brought in when an older member dies or moves away. Therefore the commissions until recently were composed largely of people from the first wave of immigration. These early leaders are now passing on, and people from the second and third waves of immigration are coming in. Not surprisingly, both commissions are entirely male although the mosque also has a female commission. The *tekke* has no formal female structure, but there is a sort of informal group of women in charge of the non-meat aspects of meals at holidays and other such tasks. The Baba's sister, who lives in one of the *tekke* apartments, is a central person in this informal group.

As for changing clerical leadership, the mosque and *tekke* have each had only one clerical leader: Imam Vehbi Ismail for the mosque, and Baba Rexheb for the *tekke*. Both these leaders are getting old, and the question of succession has arisen. Most likely the mosque will turn to the Albanian Muslim community in Kosovo, Turkey, or Egypt, where there are Imams and where Imam Vehbi and other members have contacts. The question of who will succeed the Baba is more precarious.

Earlier in the 1960s there were some likely candidates. Dervish Bajram, who was younger than Baba Rexheb, was the natural choice as successor, and in preparation for this, he was also initiated as a Baba. Unfortunately he died of a heart attack in 1973. Another, Dervish Lutfi, also died; and a third, Dervish Bektash, went back to Turkey. The potential source of a Baba would be the Muslim Albanian communities in Yugoslavia, the Albanian community in Cairo, that in Turkey, or the Bektashi community in America. But in none of these places are men currently receiving the training for this. Baba Rexheb was born in 1901, and his age and health are matters of great concern. Indeed, the very construction on *tekke* grounds of the *turbe* where the Baba will be buried when he dies can be seen as a hedge against the precariousness of succession. It has long been the Bektashi custom that the founder of a *tekke* be buried by that *tekke*. But as a result of the Baba being buried there, the ground will become holy and could never be sold. (People have already begun praying there.)

A possible new source of future Bektashi Babas is Albania itself. With the recent political thawing of Eastern Europe, there is hope that Albania will become more open. And there is word that Bektashi *muhib*, *ashiks*, and even a Bektashi Baba can still be found there. Hence people talk of the possibility of finding successors to the leadership of the *tekke* in Albania and even of reestablishing *tekkes* and mosques there. This reflects the particularly close ties to the homeland of the immigrant Albanians here as well as their children. Just what this potential opening of travel and exchange would mean for Albanian Muslim institutions in America is not known. It is interesting to speculate as to whether there will be a sizeable influx of Albanian Muslim immigrants as a result of thawing in Eastern Europe.

It is also interesting to speculate whether an institution like the Bektashi Tekke, with its private inner membership and its outward ethnic solidarity, can continue to flourish in America. On the surface it may appear to Americans that affiliation with the order resembles membership in a group such as the Masons or a Scottish-American Association, and as such is acceptable. Albanian American Bektashis are loathe to correct such an impression. Thus difficulties in the American context are not likely to come from direct collision with more common American organizations. Rather, difficulties of the *tekke* in the American context are more likely to come from a general weakening of ethnic ties, from religious indifference, or from an inability to find an acceptable Baba.

In a broader perspective however, throughout its 700 year history Bektashi *tekkes* have strengthened, declined, and strengthened again, as strong Babas have come and gone and come again. Thus, when personally questioned about the future of the *tekke* in America, Baba Rexheb has responded in Arabic:

"La yalim al-ghayibe illa Allah."
[Of the concealed, only God knows.]

NOTES

1.   Stavro Skendi, *Albania* (New York: Frederick Praeger, 1956), p. 285.

2. Stephan Thernstrom, ed., "Albanians," *Harvard Encyclopedia of American Ethnic Groups* (Cambridge, Mass.: Harvard University Press, 1980).

3. Dennis L. Nagi, *The Albanian-American Odyssey: A Pilot Study of the Albanian Community of Boston, Massachusetts* (New York: AMS Press, 1989).

4. Constantine Demo, "The Albanians in America: The First Arrivals" (Boston: [n.p.] 1960), p. 7.

5. Corroboration of Orhan Ali's presence in America in 1909 is found in Luarasi, Kristo. *Kalendari Kombiar 1909* (Sofia, Bulgaria: Mbrothësija, 1910), p. 151.

6. The date of Muslim Albanians' immigration is from Detroit immigrants themselves, corroborated by Albanians' testimony who stayed in Albania at this time but witnessed departures from their towns and by captions under pictures of Albanian families in America, collected unsystematically in the back of the *1952–1953 Yearbook of Vatra*, a sort of 'Who's Who' of Albanians in America at that time.

7. The Federal Writers' Project of the Works Progress Administration of Massachusetts, *The Albanian Struggle in the Old World and New* (Boston: The Writer, Inc., 1939), p. 5.

8. Nagi, *The Albanian-American Odyssey*, p. 5.

9. *Albanian Moslem Congress Review: Rivista e Kongresit Mysiman Shqiptar* (Detroit: [n.p.] August 1947), p. 5.

10. These concerns were voiced by founding members of the Albanian American Moslem Society who included Osman Gurra, Qamil Floqi, Feyzi Vavlla, Ameli Goskova, Riza Vokopi, Ali Orhan, Beqir Vlora, Riza Duncka, Nurri Mborja, Abas Berati, Banush Qyteza, Ahmet Ramo, Ferida Floqi, Mema Orhan, and Fatime Gurra (ibid., p. 6).

11. These persons were G. Mennen Williams, governor of Michigan; Eugene Van Antwerp, mayor of Detroit; George Edwards, president of the Detroit City Council; and Hicks Griffiths, state chairman of the Democratic committee. *Jeta Muslimane Shqiptare* [The Albanian Moslem Life, quarterly organ of the Albanian American Moslem Society] 1, no. 1, (October 1949): 33.

12. After World War II, there continued to be a few Muslim religious leaders in Albania, but they were under the control of the state. In the 1960s, Albania declared itself to be an atheist state.

Outside Albania, since the 1970s there has been interaction between the Sunni Imam and Muslim religious leaders in Yugoslavia. And there has always been communication between Baba and Bektashi leaders in Yugoslavia and Turkey, resulting most recently, in 1990, in the visit to the Michigan *tekke* by Dr. Bedri Noyan of Turkey, who is a Dede Baba, which is the highest position in Bektashi hierarchy.

13.   Xhevat Kallajxhi, *Bektashizmi dhe Teqeja Shqiptare n'Amerikë* (Detroit: Teqe, 1964), p. 1.

14.   The founders of the Albanian Bektashi Tekke include Gani Mosho, Jashar Petrusha, Banush Qyteza, Abas Myrtezaj, Nevrus Selfo, Surja Gorica, Dule Këlcyra, Muhammed Zagari, Qemal Roshanji, Qani Prespa, Haki Kozeli, Resul Shkembi, Selman Zagari, Xhafer Demiri, and Zenel Polaska.

15.   In Albania ever since the Ottomans took power in the fifteenth century, there have been Sufi orders, including Kadiri, Rifai, Saadi, Tijani, and Bektashi. But the Bektashis attained special prominence in Albania in the nineteenth century. Leading Albanian nationalists like the Frasheris were Bektashi and promoted Bektashism. In turn, the Bektashis supported the Albanian language movement and the movement for independence. Indeed, Bektashi Tekkes became meeting places for Albanian nationalist leaders as well as storage places for illegal materials like writings in Albanian. Several Bektashi Babas and dervishes were imprisoned by the Ottoman authorities for these activities. The Bektashies grew so much that in the 1920s in Albania they held their own Congresses; and when Ataturk outlawed all Sufi orders in Turkey, the headquarters of the Bektashis was moved from Anatolia to Tirana.

16.   The *hirka* is a long, sleeveless vest, the *kemer* is a sash, and the *taç* is a headpiece. Part of the ceremony of initiation of a dervish is the bestowing of these garments. The *hirka* is to cover what is shameful and to be a sign of new life on the right way. The *kemer* is for patience and control of self. The *taç* is from the Prophet Muhammed, given him on his *miraç*, his miraculous trip from Jerusalem to heaven and back. Baba Rexheb notes that earlier in Albania some dervishes felt that if they took off these clothes, they would need to go through their vows again.

17.   Facilitating this acceptance was the tolerance that Bektashis have traditionally had for other religions. In all cases, the Christian brides developed personal relations with the Baba.

18.   The hierarchy and affiliation structure of Bektashi *tekkes* is as follows:

CLERICAL: Dede Baba (top position)
Halife (regional head)
Baba (head of a *tekke*)
dervish ("monk")
LAY: *muhip* (initiated, inner member)
ashik (people drawn by their love of the Baba but not initiaed)
FAMILY OF ANY OF THE PRECEDING.

19.   In contrast, in my experience with Albanian Bektashis in Yugoslavia, the number of male and female *muhip* were more equal.

Although men are more likely to become *muhip* in the Michigan *tekke*, the women participate to a greater extent in other aspects of the *tekke* ritual and life than they did in *tekkes* in Albania. Thus the fewer number or women becoming initiates is not at all an indication of lack of involvement of women in the *tekke*.

BIBLIOGRAPHY

Books

Federal Writers' Project. *The Albanian Struggle in the Old World and New* (compiled and written by members of the Federal Writers' Project of the Works progress Administration of Massachusetts, sponsored by The Albanian Historical Society of Massachusetts). Boston: The Writer, Inc., 1939; republished by AMS Press of New York, 1975.

Gawrych, George Walter. "Ottoman Administration and the Albanians 1908–1913." Unpublished diss., University of Michigan, 1980.

Kallajxhi, Xhevat. *Bektashizmi dhe Teqeja Shqiptare N'Amerikë* [Bektashiam and the Albanian Tekke in America]. Detroit: Teqe, 1964.

Luarasi, Kristo (presumed). *Ditërëfenjësi (Kalendari) Kombiar për 1898.* Sofia, Bulgaria: Mbrothësija, 1898. (This and the following by Luarasi are a sort of almanac common to this time in the Balkans, that include dates of religious holidays, articles on current events, on history and geography and a variety of subjects. They also often include a listing in the back of subscribers, organized by city of residence, and sometimes including the amount of money contributed.)

_____. (acknowledged by Luarasi). *Kalendari Kombiar 1902.* Sofia, Bulgaria: Mbrothësija, 1902.

_____. *Kalendari Kombiar 1903.* Sofia, Bulgaria: Mbrothësija, 1903.

_____. *Kalendari Kombiar 1909.* Sofia, Bulgaria: Mbrothësija, 1910.

_____. *Kalendari Kombiar 1914.* Sofia, Bulgaria: Mbrothësija, 1915.

Nagi, Dennis. *The Albanian-American Odyssey: A Pilot Study of the Albanian Community of Boston, Massachusetts.* New York: AMS Press, 1989.

Noli, Fan S. *Historia e Skënderbeut* [*The Story of Skenderbey*]. Boston: Federata Pan-Shqiptare Vatra, 1950.

Skendi, Stavro. *Albania.* New York: Frederick Praeger, 1956.

_____. *The Albanian National Awakening: 1878–1912.* Princeton, N.J.: Princeton University Press, 1967.

Booklets, Albums, and Periodicals

"Albanian Moslem Congress Review." *Rivista e Kongresit Mysliman Shqiptar* [*The Magazine of the Albanian Muslim Congress*] 1 (1947).

Demo, Constantine A. "The Albanians in America: The First Arrivals" (in English and Albanian). Boston: Fatbardhësia of Katundi, 1960.

"Jeta Muslimane Shqiptare" [The Albanian Moslem Life], *Albanian-English Religious Review* 1, no. 1 (October 1949).

————. *Albanian-English Religious Review* 1, no. 4 (October 1950).

Vatra. *Albumi Dyzetvjeçar në Amerikë: 1906–1946 i Hirësisë Tij Peshkop Fan S. Noli* [*The Album of the Forty Years in America of His Holiness Archbishop Fan S. Noli*]. Boston: Federata Vatra, 1948.

————. "Anniversary Album of Pan-Albanian Federation of America for the Years 1953–1954." Boston: Vatra, 1955.

————. "Golden Anniversary Celebration of Pan-Albanian Federation of America Vatra, Branch no. 33, Detroit, Michigan," in conjunction with the fiftieth anniversary of Albanian independence, Sunday, June 3, 1962, Detroit, Michigan. (No place or date of publication given, presumed either Boston or Detroit by Vatra.)

"Zëri Bektashizmes" ["The Voice of Bektashism"], 1, no. 2. Detroit: Komisionit të Teqes (not dated, but published around 1955).

CHAPTER 17

Voluntary Associations in the Old Turkish Community of Metropolitan Detroit

Barbara Bilgé

Most of metropolitan Detroit's Turkish- and Kurdish-speaking Ottoman Sunni Muslim immigrants came to the United States before World War I and clustered in the Detroit area afterwards. For convenience, this group will be referred to as Detroit's old Turkish community. Although its members represented different linguistic groups, language played little part in their self-definition until the first decade after the creation of the Turkish Republic in the heartland of the defunct Ottoman Empire in 1923. The primary focus of their identity was their religion; only later were nationalistic identities predicated upon language internalized. Moreover, they usually presented themselves to outsiders at "Turks." That was how Americans, unaware of the salience of their religious unity and of their subsequent nationalist factions, defined them.

The following description and analysis of metropolitan Detroit's old Turkish community's voluntary organizations empirically assesses the roles they played in the adaptation of the group to the larger society. Adaptation refers in part to the socioeconomic status and political clout the group achieved in the city. It also involves the community members' changing perceptions of their social surroundings, their identities, and their relationship to their homeland over time. Inevitably adaptation raises issues of "the quality of life," which must be appraised according to the values of the community itself.

DATA COLLECTION

Data were gathered primarily by means of ethnographic interviews conducted from 1974 to the present with most surviving immigrant members of Detroit's old Turkish community and their locally residing descendants. A few respondents' American-born wives participated in the interviews and contributed much valuable information. Seventeen full and three partial interviews were completed. Nine persons provided additional information over an extended time period and became my key informants as well as my friends. They included two men and one woman who had held offices or been leading figures in the community's two charitable organizations.

Participant observation involved frequent socializing with key informants. Spontaneous conversations brought out many interesting facts about how the two organizations were run and gave insight into their significance in the lives of the members. One organization was closed in 1968, and the other continued to exist only as a funeral association until about 1980. I went to the final celebration of the former at its restaurant-coffeehouse in 1968, an event which first aroused my curiosity about the community. Preliminary interviews were carried out in two successive coffeehouses of the latter. I made several trips to the cemeteries where community members are buried and interviewed the manager-owner of one. She described the Muslim graveside services she had witnessed as a child, when her parents had operated the facility. I also attended the funerals of persons who died while I was doing this research. Only one of the founding members of Detroit's old Turkish community is still alive.

Inspection of a few hundred photographs and various written documents gave vivid testimony to the past activities of the two charitable societies. The documents consisted of books issued from the office of the Kızılay, or Red Crescent, in Ankara, Turkey, acknowledging the members' monthly donations; letters treating the purchase of cemetery plots; deeds; a typed list of contributors to Turkish earthquake victims in 1938; and a few articles from U.S. and Turkish newspapers. Minutes and treasurers' reports of both associations were nowhere to be found, although I was told they were made. Especially valuable was a collection of old photographs and papers kindly given to me by their inheritor, a post-

World War II Turkish immigrant not related to the original owner, who had been a long time leader of one organization. I could not interview him as he was terminally ill when I began my research.[1]

OTTOMAN SUNNI EMIGRATION AND ITS SOCIAL CONTEXT: 1860–1923

Emigration from the Ottoman Empire was negligible until the last quarter of the nineteenth century.[2] After 1860, aggressive encroachment of European business interests drastically altered the distribution of jobs, goods, and services throughout the empire.[3] To exert more direct control over Ottoman domain, European governments clandestinely fomented and abetted secessionist movements led by emergent nationalist cadres among its Christian minorities. Competition among European nations for the spoils of the empire retarded its ultimate demise.[4]

The empire's European-assisted modernization projects produced development in some regions and underdevelopment in others. From the 1870s on, groups of Armenian, Kurdish, and Turkish men from impoverished eastern Anatolian villages migrated seasonally to do hard manual labor in the developing zones of western Anatolia. The wages they earned supplemented the precarious subsistence their families were able to eke out in the countryside.[5] Scores of Arab men, mostly Christians but including some Muslims, from hinterland villages on Mount Lebanon and, to a lesser extent, in remote parts of Syria, traveled annually after 1860 to what is now Iraq, northern Arabia, Jordan, Palestine, and Egypt to buy and sell tobacco, handicrafts, and sundry items. Their profits allowed them to hold onto their village land, which did not provide adequate crops for their subsistence, and to purchase the food-stuffs they required in local market towns.[6] Thus, many Ottoman ethnic groups had established occupations away from home and forged their own internal migration routes and destinations before they finally emigrated from the empire.

The overwhelming majority of Ottoman subjects who came to the Americas from 1860 to 1923 were Christian Armenians from eastern Anatolia and the aforementioned Arabs from Lebanon-Syria.[7] Ottoman Sunni Muslims who crossed the Atlantic Ocean came primarily from the empire's politically turbulent Balkan and eastern Anatolian provinces. Arabic-speaking Muslims from

Lebanon-Syria were a numerical minority among their religious compatriots in the United States until the late 1930s, well after the empire had vanished.[8] The other Ottoman emigrants spoke many mutually unintelligible languages, although most could speak some Turkish, the standard language of the empire, in addition to their natal tongues.[9]

From the 1890s to 1923, eastern Anatolia was ravaged by Armenian uprisings and virulent reprisals on the part of the local Turkish and Kurdish-speaking Muslims, who constituted a numerical majority (65–70 percent) in both town and countryside.[10] Some Armenians emigrated voluntarily, but countless numbers were driven from the empire in all directions.[11] Groups of Muslim men also left this zone of turmoil, partly to evade the draft, partly to earn money elsewhere. They intended to return eventually with their riches, after the central government effectively quelled the rebellions and they were too old for military conscription. Then they would buy some land, hire others to cultivate it, marry a pretty bride or two, have lots of children, and live like pashas. Turks and Kurds who migrated to the United States from eastern Anatolia proceeded in steps. They first left their villages to find employment in nearby towns, then moved west to larger cities, and finally reached Istanbul. Along the way they worked as janitors in hospitals, gardeners in the villas of notables, construction workers, stokers, longshoremen, and porters. Until the mid-1890s Armenians monopolized jobs at the Istanbul docks. After the outbreak of Armenian insurrections in the east, Kurds edged them out of the Istanbul porters' guild.[12] Tales circulated among the Muslim working classes of Istanbul about a legendary land across the ocean where jobs were plentiful and the city streets were paved with gold. Only the boldest of Muslim men, however, ventured to leave their native country for this alien if promising Christian land, and those generally were men with few prospects of improving their lot at home.

From 1893 to 1914, the Balkan peninsula was convulsed by a multitude of nationalist independence struggles. The rural population was predominantly Greek Orthodox Christian (74–80 percent) but was divided into many contentious language groupings.[13] The Muslim minority included Albanians, Serbian-speaking Bosnians, and Turks. By the turn of the century Albanians of all faiths constructed a national identity centered on language, territory, and their pre-Islamic and pre-Christian heritage.[14] Thus, many Albanian-speaking Sunnis no longer regarded themselves as Ottoman subjects and shunned Balkan Turks and Bosnians, who still cohered on the basis of religion and Ottoman identity. Balkan Muslim emigrés went directly from their villages to the nearest ports to sail for America without intervening urban work experience.

Many Turkish and Kurdish migrants left Ottoman domain illegally, without a passport, with a forged passport, with an internal travel permit, or with no papers at all.[15] They hopped on mail boats and small commercial craft that eventually deposited them in Marseilles. There they encountered Ottoman Muslims who offered those whose money had run out living quarters and meals on credit and helped them find work. From their earnings, the beneficiaries paid off their debts and saved money for their trans-Atlantic passage. Some lingered in Marseilles over a year before embarking for the United States.

OTTOMAN SUNNI IMMIGRANTS IN THE UNITED STATES

Of the 22,089 self-identified Turks admitted to the United States, 1900–1925, 20,652 (93.1 percent) were male, and 1,433 (6.9 percent) were female. Peak immigration years were 1904–1908 (9,889 admitted), 1910 (1,283), and 1912–1914 (6,044). However, these figures do not accurately reflect the numbers of Turks and Kurds who entered the United States during this period. First, Kurds are not listed at all in United States immigration records; they were lumped with the other groups from "Turkey in Asia" by immigration authorities. Second, American newspapers of the day consistently portrayed Turks as fanatical Muslims, bloodthirsty slayers of innocent Christians,[16] and for this reason, many Ottoman Sunni migrants identified themselves to immigration officials as "Turkish Armenians," or "Serbs." From 1923 to 1941, Turks from former Ottoman areas under a British mandate (such as the island of Cyprus) were admitted to the United States under the British quota. After the establishment of the Republic of Turkey in 1923, its government discouraged emigration of its citizens. Its population had been decimated by the social and military upheavals attending the disintegration of the Ottoman Empire. Thus, only a trickle of emigrants from Turkey came to the United States from

1923 to 1941. Restrictive United States immigration policy was an additional constraining factor. Most of the post-World War I Turkish immigrants were married couples and families who planned to settle permanently in the United States.

The vast majority of the Ottoman Sunni immigrants were unskilled, illiterate sons of peasant families, 14–44 years of age. A few were artisans and traders from provincial Anatolian towns. Most were unmarried, but a few left wives and children behind. They could speak no English. Ports of entry included Providence, Rhode Island; Portland, Maine; and New York City. Upon arrival, the men were welcomed by their locally residing countrymen, who gave them shelter and food and helped them get work. They cut lumber in the forests of Maine, dug ditches in the factory towns of New England and the Great Lakes, and traveled west to work in the mines of Colorado and Wyoming and to lay tracks for the railroad companies. Some signed contracts to work on the Panama Canal and never were heard from again.

After World War I, an Armenian researcher[17] found settlements of Ottoman Muslims from Turkey, Palestine, Syria, Macedonia, and Albania in several U.S. cities, but he does not mention Detroit as one of them. He reports that a Turkish-language newspaper, *Sedai Vatar* [*The Call of the Fatherland*], was published in New York. He describes a visit to a Turkish cafe on Chicago's north side, where the patrons were singing love songs to the accompaniment of a small band and quaffing quantities of beer on a Sunday afternoon, during the peak of Prohibition. Chicago Turks, he notes, were divided into Balkan, Turkish (Anatolia), and Kurdish groups, each with its own social center in a coffeehouse, which usually was located in a building with rooms for lodging, a restaurant, a pool hall, and sometimes an attached gambling den and "vice resort." A few years later, another investigator[18] claimed that the Highland Park (a municipality surrounded by Detroit) Muslim community of 7,000–8,000 was the largest colony of Muslims in the country, and that nearly all of them were employees of the Ford Motor Company. Indeed, the burgeoning auto industry, with its associated foundries and tool-and-die shops, lured Ottoman Sunni Muslims as well as countless others to the Motor City. By the mid-1930s, the community had swelled to 10,000, according to one estimate.[19] My informants' estimates varied from 2,000–10,000.

THE METROPOLITAN DETROIT SUNNI
MUSLIM COMMUNITY

Detroit's first Ottoman Sunni, a Turk from a village near the Anatolian town of Elaziğ, arrived in 1903. A future leader in the community, he secured a job in a barber shop owned by a Greek immigrant in the city's Greektown district. By 1914, Detroit boasted 4,000–5,000 Ottoman Sunni Muslims. An Arabic-speaking Imam, Hussein Karoub (1895–1973), arrived with his family in 1912 to lead the prayers of the community. Until after World War II, Balkan and Anatolian Turks constituted about 45 percent of metropolitan Detroit's Sunnis, and another 45 percent were Kurdish speaking by birth. Some of the latter did not learn Turkish until they began their migrations to western Anatolia as teenagers. Although the two languages are mutually unintelligible, they share a limited Arabic lexicon of Islamic terms and a few Persian expressions. The remaining 10 percent of Detroit's Ottoman Sunnis were Arabic or Serbian speakers. The latter in the 1930s numbered only about 30 "Muslim Yugoslavs from Bosnia. . . . Their associates are Mohammedans, particularly Turks, the bond of religion apparently being stronger than the bonds of race or language."[20] Metropolitan Detroit's Sunni Muslims, even the Arabs among them, did not socialize with the Arabic-speaking Shi'a Muslims from south Lebanon who came to Detroit during the interwar years. Islam's major sectarian rift was sustained in Detroit.

Most of the Turks and Kurds toiled on the assembly lines of the automobile plants, welding, stoking furnaces, or performing custodial tasks when fully employed. During the depression of the 1930s, some lost their jobs, but instead of accepting welfare, they peddled peanuts, watermelon slices, and cigarettes provided to them by the handful of Turkish grocers and restaurant owners in Greektown. During the late 1930s, many regained their jobs in industry. None of the laborers became rich, but some achieved comfortable, albeit modest, middle-class income levels. During the 1950s and 1960s the workers retired, living simply but with dignity on small pensions and social security checks. Most of them never went home, even for a visit. Balkan Turkish immigrants had no homeland after World War I, and they lost contact with their overseas relatives. Anatolian Muslims feared permanent detainment in Turkey, even if they went there to fetch a bride.

A dozen or so Turkish men opened small businesses—grocery stores, cafes, coffeehouses, and pool halls. A few of them subsequently bought hotels and apartment houses and invested in real estate and the stock market, becoming affluent by middle age. Most of the community's businessmen were married to Turkish, Albanian, or Arabic-speaking women, some of whom served customers in their husbands' grocery stores, cooked food in the coffeehouses and restaurants, and did the bookkeeping for the family enterprise. Only three were white-collar workers.

Partly because of their dream of returning to their homeland to establish families of procreation, partly because of their misgivings about the purity of American women, who moved so freely among strange men in public places, 95 percent of the men immigrants never married. However, they maintained contact with relatives in the old country, forwarding money to them regularly, primarily to retain their rights to a fair share of the family land should they return. The remittances of the Anatolian men continued until they died.

Of the 5 percent of the men who married, only 25 percent had Muslim wives. All but two of these men wed in the old country and immigrated to the United States with their spouses. All but two of these marriages were arranged by the parents of the bride and groom. One marriage contracted in the United States by immigrant parents for their children followed some traditional Turkish customs, but also included some of American derivation.[21] Several couples consisted of one Albanian-speaking spouse and one Turkish-speaking spouse who were unable to communicate with one another in words until they both had learned English (the husband, from American coworkers; the wife, from American neighbors). However, both spouses knew their respective tasks in marriage, and each found companionship mainly with others of their own sex inside and outside of the community.[22] Most couples lacked relatives in this country and formed nuclear family households. There were no Kurdish women in the community.

The sixty–seventy Turks and Kurds who took American brides hoped to enjoy lasting conjugal relationships. They realized they would have to make some concessions to American norms regarding women's behavior, but some proved more flexible than others. Their American wives had urban, working-class parents, or parents who owned small farms in Michigan or Ohio. Many were second-generation Irish, German, Polish, Hungarian, or Jewish Americans who were not particularly interested in their respective ethnic heritages. Courtship followed the American pattern of dating. The educational level of the women exceeded that of their husbands in all cases. All the women were literate; most were high school graduates, and a few had attended classes at local business colleges. Most had worked before marriage, usually as waitresses, factory workers, or secretaries. Unlike their Muslim counterparts in the community, they did not continue to work after marriage. Half the mixed couples married too late in life to have children, and 33 percent of them divorced after a few years because they could not overcome their cultural differences. Couples with children did not divorce. Some marriages were described as very happy. Others persisted despite trying intercultural clashes between husband and wife, because both were committed to the permanence of the marital bond, and they loved their children. American-born wives made little attempt to learn Turkish or Kurdish. Only English was spoken at home. One American wife converted to Islam, but none of the others did, although they learned about and appreciated Islam and did not try to persuade their husbands to accept their own faiths. These families celebrated Islamic holidays at the local Sunni mosque, and Christmas and Easter at home for the benefit of their children, as did the community's unmixed Muslim couples. Encouraged by their American wives, a few Turks and Kurds joined American men's clubs, such as the Masons. Participation in such clubs offered these men a secondary network of fellowship and an arena for the social expression of their acquired American identity. American wives pressured their husbands to become naturalized U.S. citizens.

Most of the children of both the mixed and unmixed couples Americanized rapidly. They all attended public schools and made friends mainly with American children. The experience of Islam, a stigmatized and unfamiliar religion in the United States, differed for the community's boys and girls. Generally, the less restrictive and insistent the father that his children observe the tenets of his religion to the letter, the more tolerant they were of his faith and cultural traditions. The more domineering the father, the more alienated his children became from his religion and ethnic customs. As fathers constrained their daughters much more than their sons, girls were more likely to rebel against Islam than boys in adulthood. Girls came to associate Islam with loss of personal freedom. Many of the offspring of both mixed and unmixed couples married Americans, often of Roman Catholic background, in which faith their children (the third generation) have been socialized.

A few families produced an ethnic second generation. One son of a Kurdish man with an American wife—the previously mentioned convert to Islam— became interested in his Middle Eastern heritage and wed a Turkish woman who was visiting Detroit with her father in the 1950s. His children identify as Muslim Americans. His brother, however, married an Italian American, Roman Catholic woman and has no curiosity about his Kurdish origins. His children have adopted their mother's faith. One Turkish family, however, has managed to preserve its ethnicity over four generations by fetching brides from Turkey for its sons. They have adapted their traditions to life in the United States rather than abandoned them.

This community of Sunni Muslims rapidly evaporated in the 1960s and 1970s through attrition as its never-wed members died and through assimilation of most of its descendants into the Anglo American mainstream.

THE VOLUNTARY ORGANIZATIONS

Detroit's old Turkish community was more an ethnic fragment than a "subsociety,"[23] because of its disparate sex ratio. The organizations its members created reflected its predominantly male-only composition.

A "First Aid" Association—The Housing Cooperative

With the opening of the Ford Highland Park plant in 1907, Turks and Kurds were among the hundreds of workers hired. They gathered in nearby neighborhoods. One group of men rented a large house in Highland Park, sublet rooms to their countrymen, and employed a full-time cook. In 1914, a teenage Turk from Macedonia prepared meals for everyone; learning a trade in this capacity, he later opened a little restaurant of his own. Each boarder chipped in a few dollars every month. This money paid the rent, the cost of laundering the bedding, meals, and the cook's salary. Two men shared each bed in day and night shifts.

The ethnic boarding house served as a refuge from a strange and often unfriendly external world. There the men could relax in their spare time, play *tavla* (backgammon) or cards, listen to Turkish music on record, reminisce about the old country, have letters written to overseas relatives, and have letters from kinfolk back home read aloud by the few literate persons among them. This household endured until Ford closed its operation in Highland Park and opened the Rouge plant in 1924. The men then dispersed, some boarding with American families, but most taking flats in apartment houses and dining at restaurants owned by their entrepreneurial compatriots. The egalitarian arrangement of the cooperative was superceded by a patron-client structure as an income gap between the few property owners and the unskilled factory workers emerged.

Similar housing arrangements are described in a 1914 report published by the Massachusetts Commission on Immigration. Thirty-five cooperatives sheltering more than 300 men were investigated. Twenty-three were run by Greeks; nine by Armenians; and three by Turks. Only three households, all Greek, included a woman, the sister or wife of the manager. She did the cleaning and cooking. The report notes that Greeks usually took their meals at restaurants, but Turkish men prepared their own meals—probably to guarantee that Islamic dietary rules were followed in a land where lard was a basic cooking ingredient in so many dishes. Furthermore, unlike Armenians and Greeks, Turks did not bring their wives to America, according to the report, because of their "religious attitudes" toward women. The study laments the "forlorn" state of men without families and comments upon their isolation from the outside world. Without normal social relationships and working long hours for low wages, the text continues, the men are vulnerable to every temptation, and "abnormal vice" rages among them. In the Worcester Turkish colony of some 400 men conditions were very overcrowded; there was not one Turkish woman.

Shared housekeeping by single, unrelated males was characteristic of the three groups just mentioned. Unattached male immigrants of other nationalities, specifically Poles, Lithuanians, and Italians, preferred to lodge with married friends. Thus, the Ottoman Muslim cooperative in Highland Park was not an isolated phenomenon, but a recurring type of arrangement that met the needs of many ethnically distinctive, Eastern Mediterranean and Middle Eastern unwed men of village origin. They came to the United States to work hard and save money in order to return home as wealthy men. These objectives mandated a frugal life in this country.

The all-male housing cooperative was imported by Ottoman immigrants from the old country. A 1909 article in *Scribner's Magazine*[24] describes similarly doleful living conditions among the boatmen of Istanbul, many of whom were long-term, temporary migrants working far from their natal villages. They visited home every two or three years during their period of employment in the Ottoman capital and retired to their villages when they were too old and weak to continue their jobs.

The Coffeehouse

Detroit's first Turkish coffeehouse was opened in 1924 on the second floor of a building in Greektown. During the 1920s and 1930s, a half dozen Turkish and Kurdish coffeehouses flourished in metropolitan Detroit, which was dotted with the coffeehouses of many other ethnic groups as well. The coffeehouse is a Middle Eastern institution of long standing, first appearing in fifteenth century Ottoman cities. In the United States, owners of ethnic coffeehouses rarely are interested in expanding their clientele beyond their countrymen to increase their profits. The general public is not really welcome. The establishment functions primarily as a clubhouse where a group of male friends, usually from the same village, can engage in frequent, primarily social interaction and recreational activities apart from women. Most Detroit Turks and Kurds patronized all of the Turkish coffeehouses at one time or another and were not loyal to any particular one. This pattern underscored the scattered regional origins of the immigrants and their initial bonding as Ottoman Sunni Muslims. Husbands of American wives went to the coffeehouses far less often than the men married to immigrant Muslim women, and the bachelors spent nearly every evening there.

Detroit Ottoman Muslims used their coffeehouses not only as clubhouses, but also as mailing addresses, informal employment agencies where men working in different factories could inform their unemployed friends about job openings at their plants, meeting sites where the business of the funeral and charitable organizations was discharged, and places where religious and national holidays were celebrated by the community as a whole. They were public places where vital community activities took place.

Benevolent Societies

The Funeral Associations The two funeral associations formed by members of the community were affiliated with its two rival charitable societies. In 1920, Sait Mahcit, a Sudanese member of Detroit's Sunni community, initiated a Detroit chapter of Kızılay (described later) and simultaneously purchased some 300 grave plots in Roselawn Cemetery for the burial of local Muslim immigrants who might die before returning to their homeland. A duplicate of a deed for 538 graves was sent by the manager of this cemetery to Mehmet Malik, secretary of the Kızılay, on his request, in 1929. Subsequently, the Kızılay bought over 200 more lots in three other cemeteries. In 1938, the newly organized Türkiye Çocuk Esirgeme Kurumu (Turkish Orphans Association) purchased a block of 100 graves in a fifth cemetery.

The purpose of both associations was to assure the members of a proper Muslim burial in the United States. The men paid annual dues of $2.00 to belong in the 1920s. Inflation drove the fee up to $12.00 in the 1970s. The associations contracted with the cemeteries to obtain tents, chairs, and the like, and with funeral directors who agreed to bury the corpse without embalming it within twenty-four hours of the death. Imam Karoub (and later his successor) was called in to officiate at the funeral services and was invited to the memorial dinners held forty days, and then one year, after the burial. All costs were met by each association's treasury, which depended upon the members' dues and contributions.

Families did not join either funeral association, but instead took pride in paying all funeral costs themselves when one of their kinsmen died. However, American wives of Kızılay members frequently cooked and served the memorial feasts of bachelors at the society's coffeehouse. On the other hand, immigrant Muslim wives did not prepare or partake of the memorial meals in the coffeehouses, but often cooked and shared the food for memorial celebrations held in one of their homes.

One woman, the Turkish wife of the son of the first president of the Turkish Orphans' Association (see later), arranged the funerals and memorial dinners of the association's deceased, never-married men after her father-in-law died in the early 1960s. She also supervised the financial affairs of several of the aging bachelors, dealing with various public agencies and local banks on their behalf. Her role as counselor to these men, none of whom was her kinsman, violates traditional Middle Eastern codes of honor and shame and of seclusion of women from males outside the family circle. Yet she served as culture broker between members of the ethnic community and the larger society without losing face or besmirching her family's good reputation. Several factors contributed to this. First, her marriage linked her to the family that dominated the Orphan's Association and its funeral society. Second, she was past menopause when she took up these "public" activities. Third, bilingual and well educated, she had the skills an ethnic culture broker needs that her husband did not possess. Therefore, he was pleased to delegate these tasks to his capable wife, who acted as his representative after he inherited his father's coffeehouse and leadership in the ethnic organization his father had founded.

Not surprisingly, the funeral associations endured longer than their linked charitable organizations. Each association functioned as a surrogate family for its unmarried male members, who had no kin in the United States to take responsibility for their funerals. Yet many of the never-married men failed to join a funeral association. If they passed away in the United States, they simply were buried at public expense in the county where they died.

Charitable Societies   The activities and functions of the three charitable associations the community formed reflected its members' aspirations and their factional conflicts, which flourished from 1928 to 1938 and then subsided. The Detroit chapter of Kızılay, or Red Crescent, belonged to the official Ottoman branch of the international League of Red Cross Societies. It became an overseas chapter of the Turkish Kızılay after the establishment of the Republic in 1923.[25]

The Ottoman Kızılay, which convened in Geneva, Switzerland, in 1921, named Detroit its headquarters for the U.S. branch of the Turkish Red Crescent. Detroit was to direct branches located in the tristate area embracing southern Michigan, northern Indiana, and adjoining Illinois. In 1920, twelve Highland Park Sunni Muslims had contributed $25.00 or more to become Türk Kızılay American chapter founders through the fund-raising efforts of the aforementioned Sait Mahcit, its first president. The local membership soon swelled to almost 1,000 persons. They resided in greater Detroit and Pontiac, Michigan, as well as in Windsor, Canada. They conducted their business in a coffeehouse at the edge of Detroit's Greektown. A subsidiary of the Detroit chapter was opened in the mid-1920s in Whiting, Indiana, to accommodate Turkish and Kurdish immigrants in Chicago, Illinois, and Hammond and Gary, Indiana. Men affiliated with this branch worked in the steel mills of that region.

In 1922, active members were required to make monthly donations of $2.00 and attend an annual general meeting. Contributors of $25.00 per month would be added to the list of founders. Members could be expelled for being three months in arrears without cause, missing five consecutive general meetings without reasonable excuse, disrupting the society or not showing it due respect, using the society to further political ends, or divulging the secrets of the society. By 1940, at the end of the Great Depression, the required monthly contribution for founders had dropped to $5.00, while that for active members was fixed at $1.00, and the number of consecutive general meetings a member could miss was reduced to three. The 1922 regulations provide for a board of directors consisting of a president, vice president, treasurer, and secretary, plus a committee of sixteen. A comptroller was added in 1946. No restrictions on the number of terms an incumbent could serve are stipulated. The general meeting was to be presided over by officers especially elected for the occasion. Other regulations treat the necessary quorum at general meetings, matters of income and expenditure, and the relationship of the Detroit chapter to branches under its direction, to the home office in Istanbul, and later, in Ankara, and to the Detroit Red Cross Society. From its inception this organization occupied a clearly defined position in a complex international hierarchy, was formal in structure, and operated under explicit guidelines. Moreover, official Ottoman, then Turkish, recognition of its overseas colony is implied.

Booklets containing regulations of the society were issued to Detroit chapter members from "Stambol" in 1922. The book was produced in a combination of Arabic and English script. New books dispatched in 1946 from Ankara were printed in the Latin alphabet, in which the Turkish language has been written since 1928, and pagination followed the Western model. The new printing was prompted by the desire of Kızılay members to change the name of their organization from *Turkish Red Crescent Society* to

Turkish Crescent Association, or *Türk Ay Cemiyeti. Red* was deleted because members of the association did not want to be suspected of Communist leanings in the early years of the Cold War. The society's seventh president, Mehmet Malik, testified before the U.S. Congress to assure the American government of the loyalty of Türk Ay members to the United States and of the apolitical, humanitarian objectives of the association.

The main purpose of Kızılay was "to unite the Mohemmedans to back the Turkish Red Crescent Society and through this society enable them to help one another" (1922 handbook, regulation #2). Rules 20 and 22 endorse maintenance of a funeral association:

20. In case of a sickness of a member who had faithfully fulfilled his duty toward the society and is in need of help, the society shall come to his assistance in every way possible, and shall go as far as the expense of his funeral.

22. The society shall, upon request, look after the interest of the member's will after his death, to see that it shall go to the rightful party or parties.

In addition to offering aid to needy local members, who included Turks, Kurds, and a few Arabs,[26] all bonded by Sunni Islam, the society sent money to disaster victims in Turkey. In 1924, for example, $25,000 was mailed to Ankara to assist Turkish children orphaned during the War of Independence against the Greeks, who invaded and occupied southern Anatolia in 1919 but were routed by Ataturk's victorious army in 1922.

During the 1920s, national allegiances came to supercede Islamic brotherhood among Detroit's Ottoman Sunni Muslims. The men followed events in their homeland closely, gleaning information from articles in U.S. newspapers and from letters sent by relatives in the old country. Both Turkish- and Kurdish-speaking Detroiters felt a great surge of pride in 1923 with international recognition of the new republic in their shrunken homeland. Together they acquired a new national identity: Turkish. Even the Turkish-speaking members of the community had not felt a specifically "Turkish" identity heretofore. Prior to 1923, Turkish national consciousness was nurtured mainly among the tiny avante garde of Ottoman intellectuals, bureaucrats, and military officers who eventually launched the Republic.[27] However, when an uprising led by Kurdish tribesmen against the secularization of government in Turkey erupted along its Syrian border in 1928 and rapidly crystallized into a Kurdish nationalist movement,[28] the Detroit area Sunni community split into hostile political factions. "Detroit Kurds incorporated *Hoyboon* on February 6, 1929, to aid women and children of Kurds who participate in the struggle for the independence of Kurdistan, financed by the membership dues and donations, etc., thirty years existence (i.e., for the next 30 years)."[29] Most, but not all Turks from whom they solicited contributions were appalled and "would have nothing to do with it," in the words of one elderly Turkish informant. The Kurds and their Turkish sympathizers "took the Kızılay with them" and moved their headquarters to a new coffeehouse a few blocks away.[30] Turks opposed to the Kurdish cause allowed their membership in Kızılay to lapse and boycotted its coffeehouse, although Hoyboon was a separate society, with its own officers, independent of the Turkish Red Crescent.

The Turkish nationalist faction founded Türkiye Çocuk Esirgeme Kurumu, or Turkish Orphans' Association, in 1936. It was led by Nuri Ahmed Yardımcı, Detroit's first Ottoman Sunni immigrant who, by the 1920s, had become a wealthy property owner. This association was granted a license as a nonprofit, charitable, tax-exempt body by the Security and Exchange Commission of the state of Michigan. From 1936 to 1957, some 700 members gathered in Mr. Yardımcı's wood-paneled coffeehouse,[31] just around the corner from Kızılay headquarters, to socialize and organize philanthropic projects. They also created their own funeral association. Over the years the association sent close to $100,000 in aid to Turkey.

Conflict between the two factions diminished gradually after 1938, when Ataturk suppressed the Kurdish rebels. Turks and Kurds in metropolitan Detroit once against intermingled, frequented both coffeehouses, and contributed generously to the charitable projects of both organizations. Hoyboon simply faded away. Nevertheless, the two funeral associations remained separate, although members of each attended the death rituals of members of the other.

The structure of Kızılay was highly formalized, and that of Türkiey Çocuk Esirgeme Kurumu and Hoyboon were less so. Yet the meetings of all three societies were lively and expressive. No agenda was prepared, and strict procedure was not followed. During any fund-raising endeavor, each man jumped up to proclaim that amount of his donation and slapped his money or check on the table before him. The few women contributors behaved in a similar manner. Men often delivered spontaneous speeches, each outshouting his predecessor on some occasions. Women rarely made speeches. Entertainment was provided by local Turkish musicians, spiced up by a hired belly dancer. Such meetings served as a stage upon which members could display their worthiness, loyalty to country of origin and Islam, and conviviality. The charitable societies promoted community cohesion by sponsoring celebrations of Islam's two major holidays, Şeker Bayram (which concludes Ramadan, the month of fasting) and Kurban Bayram (which commemorates the sacrifice of Abraham), as well as Turkish Independence Day (Cumhuriyet Bayram), the Fourth of July, and Labor Day.

After World War II, *Türk Ay Cemiyeti* ventured cautiously into "public relations". Its members hosted many Detroit area dignitaries—mayors, aspiring politicians, and presidents of a few major corporations (General Electric, for instance)—at its annual Cumhuriyet dinner. The Orphans' Association channeled all its energy into its projects in Elazığ. The Yardımcı family visited Elazığ and other parts of Turkey in 1963 and were the subject of a front-page story in *Hurriyet*, a prominent Turkey newspaper.

In 1957, Mr. Yardımcı moved his Turkish Orphans' Association coffeehouse to more modest quarters. Upon his death in 1965, his son shifted the association's coffeehouse to an even smaller building. Both establishments were located in Greektown.[32] In 1972, the Orphans' Association transferred its remaining funds, except for the funeral association account, to the treasury of the Turkish-American Cultural Association of Michigan, which was formed that year by post-World War II immigrant couples from Turkey. The younger Yardımcı and his able wife operated their tiny coffeehouse for seven–ten surviving bachelors every Sunday until 1979, when they sold it. The last funeral arranged under their auspices transpired in 1979.

In 1953, Türk Ay Cemiyeti purchased a modest, three-story building in the south end of Dearborn, at 3048 Salina, in the midst of a growing Arab neighborhood. The second and third floors had rooms for eight tenants, whose rent payments defrayed the expenses of building upkeep. Downstairs was a coffeehouse-restaurant with a dozen or so tables and a tiny kitchen at the rear. By 1969 the active membership had fallen below twenty; utility costs became prohibitive. The building was sold in 1969, and the Detroit chapter of Türk Ay Cemiyeti was dissolved. Proceeds from the sale and funds remaining in the treasury were forwarded to the Kızılay office in Ankara. Uprooted boarders had to find rooms elsewhere in the metropolitan area. Money left in the funeral association account was divided among the surviving never-married men.

Cultural Organizations

Orchestras A few small bands were organized by musicians within the community. They played Turkish music with traditional instruments—the *zurna* (a wooden clarinet), *ud* (a lute), *saz* (a three-stringed violin), *kemençe* (a miniature three-stringed violin found along the Black Sea Coast of Anatolia), *tambur* (a tiny guitar), and others. Some men also played American songs with Western instruments.

Dervish Orders Turks belonging to at least two Sufi orders, brotherhoods of Muslim mystics, have practiced their unique rituals of spiritual union with God in metropolitan Detroit. A group of *mevlavi*, or Whirling Dervishes, immigrated to Detroit before World War I; for years they rented a room in Greektown for their ceremonies. A few Turkish Bektashi dervishes joined a largely Albanian Bektashi community, which established itself in the farmland near Taylor, Michigan, about 1952. The *Mevlavi* Turks were an integral part of Detroit's old Turkish community, but the Bektashi Turks, whose primary allegiance is to their heterodox order, never merged into the community of their compatriots.[33]

CONCLUSION

Detroit's old Turkish community lacked substantial numbers of families and widely spread webs of kinship; such as did function were activated primarily to facilitate the migration process for only a small proportion of the immigrants. Their scattered regional origins and unbalanced sex ratio, however, fostered solidarity on the basis of principles other than kinship or place of birth. Ethnicity derived from religious heritage initially brought Detroit area

Ottoman Sunni Muslims together. Their stigmatized position and lack of skills proved fertile ground for the spontaneous development of mutual aid associations. The importance of religion to the migrants and their inability or unwillingness to retire in their homeland prompted the funeral association, through which a proper Muslim burial could be guaranteed. Their wish to preserve cultural traditions, including Islamic dietary observances, and their ethnic distinctiveness despite their changing ethnic identities, motivated their formation of charitable organizations for the benefit of their compatriots in the old country. The charitable societies became a way for them to show their prosperity to family and friends overseas. In fact most of the migrants did not become rich in this land, and they were reluctant to return "unsuccessful" to Turkey. Yet they had little desire to Americanize any more than necessary to survive in their adopted nation. Many never became American citizens. The types of voluntary association they established not only reflected their preference for insulation against outsiders, but also actively served to thwart their acculturation and assimilation into the American mainstream.

The immigrants' small second generation did not perpetuate their parents' ethnic organizations. Most were busy becoming 100 percent American. Metropolitan Detroit's new Turkish community did not carry on the Turkish Crescent Association or the Turkish Orphans' Association. The newcomers arrived in the 1950s and 1960s as university students. Most earned degrees in engineering and medicine. They soon brought their spouses over and then settled permanently in this country to establish families upon completion of their studies. They are descendants of Turkey's urban and small-town educated elites. Thus, the social class origins of the members of metropolitan Detroit's old and new Turkish communities differ sharply. Differences in the sex ratio, educational attainment, range of occupations, and income levels mark the two communities. Each community has become structurally integrated in different adaptive niches in the United States: urban working class versus affluent, suburban, professional class. Moreover, half a century separated the time of each group's arrival; the United States itself had changed profoundly during those years. The needs and interests of the old timers and newcomers have been dissimilar. The latter have no need for mutual aid societies or funeral associations, and their charitable activities are minimal compared to those of their predecessors. The new community boasts a cultural association with a suburban center, by means of which they preserve and demonstrate to their suburban American peers their rich cultural heritage derived from the achievement of Ottoman civilization and Ataturk's creation of the thoroughly modern Republic of Turkey.

The study of ethnic voluntary associations in any nation illuminates its minority-majority relations, with different ethnic groups having differential access to power, wealth, and prestige in different nations. In comparisons of the voluntary organizations of the same group in different nations—for instance, of Turks in Germany versus Turks in the United States—and of different groups in the same nation—such as various Arab groups versus Turks in the United States—several factors promote or impede maintenance of ethnic boundaries over generations, ethnic transformations within firm boundaries, merging of minority groups, and assimilation of immigrant communities and their descendants into national mainstreams. The scenarios are varied, and each case must be analyzed in terms of how particular conditions in the settlement location affect the segment of the donor society from which the immigrants are derived, taking into account the immigrants' values and aspirations.

NOTES

This chapter was first presented as a paper at the Muslims of America Conference at the University of Massachusetts at Amherst, April 15–16, 1988.

1. I am deeply grateful to the entire Ziya Ahmed (Yardımcı) family, Enver Hally, Hıdır Al-Bay, Süleyman Khalil, Ferid Ali, and Ömer Aksu for the information they contributed toward this research, and to Dr. Stewart-Robinson, professor of Turkish at The University of Michigan, for translating bits of old documents written in Arabic script from Turkish into English.

2. Kemal H. Karpat, "The Ottoman Emigration to America, 1860–1914," *International Journal of Middle Eastern Studies* 17 (1985): 180–181.

3. Ibid., pp. 176–177; Donald Quataert, *Social Disintegration and Popular Resistance in the Ottoman Empire, 1881–1908: Reactions to European Economic Penetration* (New York: New York University Press, 1983), pp. 4–12.

4. C. Keyder, "The Dissolution of the Asiatic Mode of Production," *Economy and Society* 5 (1976): 178–196.

5. Quataert, *Social Disintegration and Popular Resistance*, p. 100.

6. Alixa Naff, *Becoming American: The Early Arab Immigrant Experience* (Carbondale: Southern Illinois University Press, 1985), p. 89.

7. Karpat, "The Ottoman Emigration to America," p. 175.

8. Nijibe Saliba, "Emigration from Syria," in *Arabs in the New World: Studies on Arab-American Communities*, ed. Sameer Y. Abraham and Nabeel Abraham (Detroit: Wayne State University, Center for Urban Studies, 1983), p. 38, and Naff, *Becoming American*, pp. 84–85, 90.

9. Ottoman Sunni Muslims' first-learned languages were many, and most of them are mutually unintelligible: Turkish and Tatar (Turkic branches of the Ural-Altaic language family); Arabic (Semitic language family); Kurdish (on the Iranian ranch of the Indo-European language family); Albanian (a unique branch of Indo-European); Serbian (a Slavic branch of Indo-European); Georgian and Circassian (unrelated languages spoken mainly in different regions of the Caucasus Mountains); plus a few others.

10. James Kay Sutherland, *The Adventures of an Armenian Boy* (Ann Arbor, Mich.: The Ann Arbor Press, 1964), pp. 2, 20; Stephen Duguid, "The Politics of Unity: Hamidian Policy in Eastern Anatolia," *Middle Eastern Studies* 9 (1973): 139–155; Gwynne Dyer, "Turkish 'Falsifiers' and Armenian 'Deceivers': Historiography and the Armenian Massacres," *Middle Eastern Studies* 12 (1976): 99–107; Stanford J. Shaw and Ezel K. Shaw, *History of the Ottoman Empire and Modern Turkey*, vol. 2. *Reform, Revolution, and Republic: The Rise of Modern Turkey, 1808–1975* (New York: Cambridge University Press, 1977); Justin McCarthy, "The Anatolian Armenians, 1912–1922," *Boğaçigi University Publications* (1984): 17–25.

11. Karpat, "The Ottoman Emigration to America," p. 175.

12. Quataert, *Social Disintegration and Popular Resistance*, pp. 98–99.

13. See, for instance, L. S. Stavrianos, *The Balkans Since 1453*, 3d ed. (New York: Holt, Rinehart and Winston, 1958); and Dimitrije Djordjevic and Stephen Fischer-Galati, *The Balkan Revolutionary Tradition* (New York: Columbia University Press, 1981).

14. S. Skendi, "Beginnings of Albanian Nationalist Trends in Culture and Education (1878–1912)," *Journal of Central European Affairs* 12 (1953): 356–367; and Skendi, "Beginnings of Albanian Nationalist and Autonomous Trends: The Albanian League: 1878–1881," *American Slavic and East European Review* 12 (1953): 219–232.

15. Karpat, "The Ottoman Emigration to America," p. 181. My informants statements also confirmed this.

16.   American prejudice against Turks was strong during the first three decades of the twentieth century. For example, 110 Pacific Coast businessmen and public school teachers ranked Turks the lowest of some 23 named ethnic groups on a 7 point scale of social distance devised by Bogardus. See E. S. Bogardus, *Immigration and Race Attitudes* (New York: D. C. Health and Company, 1928). In another study, 100 Princeton University undergraduate students, selecting words from a list supplied by the researchers, described Turks as "cruel, sly, quarrelsome, revengeful, conservative, and superstitious." None of the respondents had ever met or seen a Turk. See Daniel Katz and Kenneth W. Braly, "Racial Stereotypes of 100 College Students," *Journal of Abnormal and Social Psychology* 28 (1933): 280–290; and Daniel Katz and Kenneth W. Braly, "Racial Prejudice and Racial Stereotypes," *Journal of Abnormal and Social Psychology* 30 (1935): 175–193. American opinions of Turks apparently were derived from newspaper portrayals of the incorrigible and terrible Turk during the period (1890s–1921) when the Ottoman government expelled its Christian Armenian subjects from its eastern provinces, where many were active in a secessionist movement. The American and European press presented a one-sided view of these tragic events and sometimes deliberately falsified stories as well. See Sidney Whitman, *Turkish Memories* (New York: Charles Scribner's Sons, 1914), pp. 16–21, 23, 24, 29, 54–55, and 77. See also Roderic H. Davidson, "The Image of Turkey in the West, in Historical Perspective, *The Turkish Studies Association Bulletin* 5 (1981): 1–6.

17.   M. M. Aijian, "Mohammedans in the United States," *The Moslem World* 10 (1920): 30–35.

18.   Mary Caroline Holmes, "Islam in America," *The Moslem World* 26 (1926): 262–266.

19.   G. H. Bousquet, "Moslem Religious Influences in the United States," *The Moslem World* 25 (1935): 40–44.

20.   Lois Rankin, "Detroit Nationality Groups," *Michigan History Magazine,* 23 (1939): 165.

21.   A Greek grocer who had emigrated from Rhodes initiated the marriage process in 1938. He was acquainted with the families of both bride and groom. The groom's father owned a large coffeehouse, which was headquarters for one of the community's two major charitable societies, in Greektown, near the gobetween's grocery store. The bride's family and the gobetween's family had been neighbors on Rhodes, and he kept contact with them after they immigrated to a southwestern Pennsylvania town in 1931. The Greek introduced the two Turkish families to one another himself, and parents of the bride and groom negotiated the marriage contract with his generous assistance. Later a traditional engagement party was held in the bride's parents' home. The groom's par-

ents gave the bride's family expensive gifts, which were displayed alongside her hastily assembled trousseau. A few months later the couple obtained a civil marriage license at the Wayne County courthouse in Detroit. That afternoon, a most unconventional *nikâh*, or Muslim marriage rite, was performed by Imam Kharoud in the presence of the white-gowned bride and formally attired groom in the latter's father's coffee-house before several hundred guests. A reception followed in which the newlyweds danced stiffly to Western popular music while the guests sat at tables, chatted, and ate. The couple departed that evening for a brief honeymoon at a resort just 20 miles north of Detroit. They carefully preserved the bloodstained sheet of their wedding night and presented it to the groom's parents as validation of the bride's purity. The couple moved into the groom's father's house upon their return to Detroit.

22.   Albanian men with Turkish wives did not belong to Turkish-Kurdish voluntary associations; instead they joined Albanian societies, and they frequented Albanian coffeehouses. Their Turkish wives, who socialized with the Turkish wives of the Turkish men, went to some of the holiday celebrations sponsored by Turkiye Ay Cemiyeti. Their husbands sometimes accompanied them. Albanian wives of Turkish men evidently were more isolated from their own ethnic organizations and rarely attended the mixed social events given by the Turkish-Kurdish organizations.

23.   Milton M. Gordon, *Assimilation in American Life* (New York: Oxford University Press, 1964), p. 39.

24.   Quoted in Quataert, *Social Disintegration and Popular Resistance,* pp. 100, 178.

25.   See John Lawton, "Red Crescent: Symbol of Mercy," *ARAMCO World Magazine* 28, no. 2 (1977): 6, for a brief history of the International Red Cross and affiliated Red Crescent Societies. The Ottoman government joined the assembly of participating countries in 1877, becoming its twenty-second member nation. In 1876 the Ottomans notified Central Red Cross headquarters in Switzerland that, out of respect for the religious convictions of their troops, it had decided to adopt a red crescent instead of a red cross as its symbol.

26.   Among the twelve original founders of Kızılay was an Arab doctor.

27.   For two interpretations of the origins of the Turkish republic, see Lord Kinross, *Ataturk: A Biography of Mustafa Kemal, Father of Modern Turkey* (New York: William Morrow and Company, 1965); and Bernard Lewis, *The Emergence of Modern Turkey,* 2d ed. (London: Oxford University Press, 1968). For information on the social backgrounds of Turkish nationalists in the late Ottoman Empire, consult Ernest Edmonson Ramsaur, Jr., *The Young Turks: Prelude to the Revolution of*

1908 (Princeton, N.J.: Princeton University Press, 1957), pp. 1–7, 14. See Ziya Gökalp, *Turkish Nationalism and Western Civilization,* trans. and ed. Nıyazı Berkes (New York: Columbia University Press, 1959), for a prominent Turkish social philosopher's ideas about the content of Turkishness in the first two decades of the twentieth century.

28.   Lord Kinross, *Ataturk: A Biography of Mustafa Kemal,* pp. 451–459; Joane Nagel, "The Conditions of Ethnic Separatism: The Kurds in Turkey, Iran and Iraq, *Ethnicity* 7 (1980): 279–297.

29.   The only tangible evidence for Hoyboon's existence is a scrap of paper with the date, statement of purpose, and list of officers. It was among the personal documents of Mr. Mehmet Malik that I received in 1986. Informants spoke of fundraising for the Kurdish rebels and of the rift it caused within the community.

30.   At 705 East Lafayette Boulevard.

31.   At 742 Antoine Street in Greektown.

32.   At 577 Lafayette Boulevard and on Beaubien Street, respectively.

33.   J. K. Birge, *The Bektashi Order of Dervishes* (London: Luzac, 1937), gives a history of the order and describes its theology. See also Bernard Lewis, *Istanbul and the Civilization of the Ottoman Empire* (Norman: University of Oklahoma Press, 1963), pp. 155–157; and Frances Trix, "The Asure Ceremony of the Bektashi Tekke of Taylor, Michigan" (M.A. thesis, The University of Michigan, 1972).

CHAPTER 18

Elderly Muslim Immigrants: Needs and Challenges

Fariyal Ross-Sheriff

Recent efforts to study the growth of Islam in North America are beginning to take into account ways in which Muslims, who are facing assimilation, deal with issues of religious and cultural identity. Little attention has been paid thus far to the specific problems faced by the Muslim elderly in the assimilation process. This significant proportion of the growing Muslim population faces adjustment and adaptation problems that are also prevalent among elderly populations from other religious and ethnic groups in the United States (Chan 1988, Gelfand 1989, and Kiefer et al. 1985). Because of a lack of linguistic and cultural preparation, elderly immigrants frequently find themselves marginalized and passive as they cope with the difficult and complex process of adjustment to a totally new and often lonely environment.

This chapter describes issues that arise in the lives of members of the Muslim immigrant elderly community in America. The research is based on an ethnographic study carried out in one metropolitan area in the United States of first-generation elderly Ismaili immigrants from South Asia and South Asian Muslims relocating to the United States from Africa. The information was gathered in two stages. First, direct observations were made and small group discussions were held with key leaders within the community who are close to the elderly immigrants. Second, small group discussions were held with forty elderly people between the ages of 55 and 85 years, with more emphasis on the older ages. Issues addressed in the small group discussions relate to health, social, and

nal needs and other problems faced by elderly Muslims in
ited States. Because of the focus on problems confronting
elderly people, findings related to the contribution made by elderly
relatives to their families and community are not exhaustive. The
study is a part of a larger ongoing work on the lives of elderly
immigrant Muslims in America.

The Ismaili Muslim immigrants of South Asian ancestry, regardless of their country of origin—India, Pakistan, Bangladesh,
Burma, Kenya, Tanzania, or Uganda—share common religious
practices and South Asian cultural background. Having once experienced the resettlement process from Asia to Africa and having
learned to function within the larger African culture, Ismailis may
be better able to cope with American society than some other
Muslim immigrants. There are more similarities than differences
among Ismailis, regardless of their country of origin, because the
established institutions of the Ismaili communities worldwide provide familiar social structures. Despite this, however, elderly, Ismailis like other elderly Muslim immigrants in the United States, are
likely to experience stress in the process of adapting to life in this
country because of their feelings of isolation as members of a small
minority ethnic and religious group in this country.

SOCIETAL EXPECTATIONS OF ELDERLY MUSLIMS

In 1935 the United States government put into effect the Social
Security Act, mandating 65 years as the age at which workers
become eligible for full retirement benefits. Since that time, 65 has
come to be seen as the moment of transition from middle to old
age. This association continues, despite the fact that many workers
are retiring earlier even though there have been improvements in
social security benefits, increases in life expectancy, and national
policies to encourage later retirement. Age 65 signals in the minds
of most Americans the beginning of a new stage in life with related
life changes. In the dominant American culture, relatively abrupt
changes in life-style, roles, and responsibilities usually occur at the
time that the youngest child leaves home and at the time of retirement.

This quick transition from productivity to "old age" contrasts
sharply with the situation many elderly Muslims have been accus-
tomed to in their home countries.

In areas such as Bangladesh, India, Pakistan, Kenya, Tanzania, and Uganda, the changes are much more gradual (Osaka 1988). When children begin their own families, they typically stay either in the parents' household or live in the neighborhood. Most continue to carry out their responsibilities within the family businesses or households as long as their physical and mental health permits. People continue to work, but their tasks change as they age. People generally continue working in their respective positions as long as they are able, men in their family businesses or other work places and women in their homes, although their tasks change as they age. For them, aging is a part of a life-cycle continuum, with expectations based on health, physical and mental status, family resources, and position within the society. One elderly person in the study group echoed the sentiment of several as follows: "My father worked in our shop as long as he lived. Toward the late part of his life when he was getting weak, he came to the shop for about two to three hours a day. My mother and my grandmother worked around the house and took care of the young ones as long as they lived. Here in America once you get old you have no place and no work."

The elderly Muslims included in the current study are first-generation immigrants who, after age 50, joined their adult children in the United States. Once in the United States, most have not worked outside their homes or family businesses, and continue in a supportive role to their adult children or extended family members. Only those who identified themselves as elderly were included in the study, and the ways in which they determined this identification varied. Some saw it in terms of the time at which they first became grandparents rather than in terms of chronological age as such. Others, especially those who have worked outside the home, followed the more common American pattern of identifying old age with retirement. Most of the participants in the study are over 60 years of age, not in the paid labor force, and dependent on their adult children.

The effort to redirect their energies into adapting not only to a new country but to new roles within the family context presents special problems and pressures to elderly Muslim immigrants. Many of their adult children, aware of their ethnic minority status in the United States, feel the need to assume American ideas and standards. They in turn expect their elderly parents to adapt and to learn to accept the norms of American society, including those related to their status as senior citizens in their families and in the larger society.

PROBLEMS ADAPTING TO LIFE IN THE UNITED STATES

Old age in American society increasingly is being viewed as a period of continued psychological growth during which elderly people *must* adapt to new roles, discover creative outlets for leisure time, and prepare for the end of life (Newman and Newman 1985). With normal changes in biological and physiological functioning, the body's ability to recover from stressful events declines significantly, affecting personal and family lives as well as health status. In accordance with their South Asian Muslim cultural backgrounds and traditional expectations, the elderly Muslim immigrants in this study consider their roles as grandparents, positions as family "heads" of household, their spiritual growth and personal fulfillment, and ultimately preparation for death as important aspects of this stage of life. However, many depend on their adult children for social, economic, and emotional support. Like many if not all elderly people, their primary desire is to feel needed by their families; what is feared most is complete dependence. Their change of status from independent to dependent reverses the traditional roles and creates stresses for most elderly immigrants and their families with economic and other forms of dependency only increasing their problems.

Stereotypic images of Islam and Muslims also make adaptation to life in the United States difficult. Immigrant Muslims from South Asian backgrounds share a number of cultural characteristics with other Asian Americans whose experiences are more fully documented. One critical factor that differentiates elderly Muslim immigrants from other Asian immigrants is the negative portrayal of Muslims in the mass media. Turbulence in the Middle East and upheavals in Iran and Iraq have created stereotypical images of Muslims as fanatics. In contrast, Asians of Hindu, Buddhist, and Confucian religious backgrounds are considered peaceful and even a "model" minority. Immigrant Muslims therefore are likely to experience discrimination and related problems. Several elderly immigrants included in the current study expressed this problem as follows: "A few years ago some of our young people acted like they did not want to be identified as Muslims. We understand it now. We are proud to be Muslims, but Americans think that Muslims are terrorists. With the eyes of the world focused on Iraq and the Middle East, we Muslims feel harassed. We are peaceful people."

In the modern Western mode of thinking, science and religion, the natural and the supernatural, and mind and body often tend to be viewed dichotomously. Muslim immigrants, on the contrary, typically order and understand their world holistically, in indivisible terms. This difference in basic orientation, along with the stresses resulting from the immigration process and the recognition that life for the elderly in the United States inevitably involves a subordinate status, leads to problems that are especially severe for Muslim immigrant elderly who have health and economic concerns and whose dependence on adult children or grandchildren is enhanced because of language and cultural barriers.

Significant cultural values cherished by South Asian Muslim elderly such as family kin responsibilities, obligations, and filial piety, hierarchical order in carrying out responsibilities, sensitivity to the feelings of others, respect, loyalty, and right conduct tend to clash with those of Americans (Meemeduma 1987, AmaraSingham 1980, Wheeler 1979). Although group needs are emphasized over individual needs and behavior is regulated and governed accordingly, they expect their children and grandchildren to exhibit this same sensitivity and to reciprocate by anticipating and meeting their needs. They value harmonious relationships and go to great effort to avoid antagonisms that result in hard feelings. Therefore they often are concerned about differences in world-view as is evident in the following observations: "Here in America, people care mainly about getting ahead, work day and night to get more, more, more. . . . [They] focus on themselves . . . children are busy with school, parents are busy with work . . . all are doing very well; but it is not like home. We respected our elders, we took into consideration our family when we made our decisions. Our family and family prestige came before our individual achievements. I don't know what this world has come to! There is little balance in life here." Moreover, a code of conduct—*adab*—is clearly defined for all age groups and for all relationships in South Asian society (Metcalf 1984). Group pressures are applied to elicit appropriate behavior. Disciplinary techniques invoking shame and guilt and "saving face" lead toward conformity to the code. For example, inappropriate behavior of an individual may bring shame or loss of respect not just for the individual but for the whole family and the religious community, just as success results in achievement not only for the individual but for the whole family and the larger units.

Within the American context in the educational system at schools or in the social system among neighborhood peers, however, Muslim children sometimes develop attitudes and behaviors that are interpreted as insensitive and reflect a code of conduct that offends their grandparents. For example, in the American educational system in which independence, individuality, and competition are highly valued and encouraged, teenage grandchildren of elderly Muslim immigrants learn to be competitive and self-reliant. Under the influence of peers they learn to enjoy popular music and dance. Differences in the world-view of elderly immigrants and their grandchildren create conflicts within their families; for example, when members of the younger generation choose to be with their friends rather than participate in family activities or do household chores. Many expect to go to school dances or out on dates, activities that may be considered normal and harmless within the context of American society, but are inappropriate according to the traditional Muslim code of behavior. These changes in the conduct of their children and the new customs of their grandchildren are viewed by elderly immigrants as disrespectful. Thus the changes in the world-view of their children and patterns of social interactions of grandchildren, especially adolescent women, create tensions and stress for elderly relatives in the household.

Roles and Intergenerational Conflicts

In traditional Muslim societies, old age automatically affords a person respect and social position. However, this is often not the case in the United States. As a result, a large proportion of the elderly immigrants studied lack culturally appropriate coping skills for dealing with day-to-day American life. They find it difficult to accept that their children and grandchildren have adopted many of the values and traditions of the new culture and have rejected some of the old ways. They not only have trouble accepting the changes, but to avoid "losing face" with their age peers they try to pressure their children and grandchildren to conform to "old" ways. As a result, there is lack of cohesion within the family, often leading to open conflict. One elderly person described the feelings of several in the group as follows: "We can't stand it; we can't bear it. Sometimes the situation seems unbearable. We have to keep relying on Allah. Thanks to Allah!"

Elderly immigrants perceive these changes in behavior and practices arising from acculturation to the new society as a diminution of their role and function within the family unit. Some of them find new functions through activities within the family or community. For example, a few elderly immigrants in the sample have taken English classes and served as volunteers in social welfare programs. Some have participated in their local community programs by offering an occasional cooking or sewing class. Most participate in social activities organized by the Ismaili Muslim community and thus have begun to find a meaningful role or function. But those who feel that they are not valuable contributing members of the family or society often experience loneliness, isolation, confusion, frustration, boredom, and depression. These emotional responses negatively affect interactions with their family members.

Language Barriers

An inability to speak the language of the host nation prevents elderly immigrants from making social and professional contacts and adds to the loss of status they feel within their own families (Gozdziak 1988). Young family members begin to question their knowledge and authority, and they are no longer considered teachers or consulted for advice. The importance of and need for language skill is well understood within the mainstream society, and most states offer programs for teaching English as a second language to immigrants and refugees. These programs, however, are designed for younger people with few, if any, aimed at helping elderly immigrants learn the new language.

The majority of elderly Muslim immigrants, especially women over age 65, have limited English skills. Even those who have acquired enough English to manage day-to-day living situations report that they have great difficulty when they have to deal with such American systems as medical care, social services, or recreation. What may seem routine to most older Americans appears complex and confusing to elderly immigrants with limited language skills and little experience with the American systems. The group whose members reported having the most difficulty coping included those immigrants from rural areas in the originating countries, specifically from India and Pakistan, who have had no formal education. They avoid situations in the United States that would put them in awkward positions and place them at a loss. As a result, they see themselves as having limited control over their own lives and as a burden to their families. Those from urban areas, specifically those who are proficient in the English language, are better able to take control of their life situation and therefore are less dependent.

Almost all the elderly immigrants in the study sample who do not speak English fluently expressed interest in learning English or in improving their English language skills. They reported that they think the ability to communicate in English would make them more self-sufficient. The preferred setting for English language classes is the social hall at the mosque.

Dependence

Consistent with tradition, the Muslim elderly believe that it is the family's place to look after them. Most of the elderly in the current study became immigrants because they moved with their children, but few anticipated how difficult life would be in the United States. Some were ambivalent about the move and were unprepared for it. Once in the United States, the newly unemployed have not only lost the financial independence they may have enjoyed in their homeland, becoming financially dependent on their children, but also have come to rely on their children for social, emotional, and personal needs. The fear of dependency was best described by one elderly immigrant: "The one thing that I pray about is 'Oh, Allah protect me from being a burden on anyone, not even my children. You are the only one on whom I rely and seek reliance. . . . Please take me away before I become a burden to my children because of ill health.'"

For many Muslim elderly, contact with the host society is made through their children. In their countries of origin they lived in neighborhoods or communities where they had well-established networks to meet their emotional, personal, and social needs. In contrast, their living environments in the United States lack comparable support networks, making it difficult to meet even basic needs. The burden of carrying out tasks such as shopping for personal effects, visiting friends, going to the mosque, meeting health needs through interaction (communication and interpretation) with physicians and health care institutions and so forth in most cases falls on immediate family members, increasing elderly immigrants' feelings of dependency on adult children.

Elderly Muslims in the sample recognize that mosques in the United States serve not only as places of worship, but also as places for social gathering where they meet others who have similar problems and concerns and who also share their interests. "I look forward to Friday prayers. After a week of being cooped up in the house, I feel elated on Fridays . . . liberated from the bonds of this world," said one elderly immigrant. A large proportion of elderly immigrants in the sample depend on transportation organized by their religious community to the mosque or on their children when such an option is not available, adding yet again to their feelings of dependency.

Health and Mental Status

The need to rely on others experienced by Muslim elderly immigrants is exacerbated if they have physical health problems. The majority have chronic health conditions such as back pain, arthritis, hypertension, high cholesterol, and diabetes. Most do not have health insurance, but are able to obtain health care on a fee for service basis. Some describe difficulty in gaining access to the health care system; for example: "I have health insurance with a Health Maintenance Organization (HMO). But, half the time I have a difficult time obtaining a ride to go to the HMO, or I simply cannot get an appointment with the clinic." The few elderly in the study with severe health problems reported feeling depressed and particularly burdensome to their adult children. The elderly immigrants said that physical health issues were the most difficult problems they have to face. Yet very few expressed frustration or anger, most sharing the feeling that it is important to "Thank Allah for His bounty!"

Some describe what may be interpreted as mental health concerns. For example, several reported feeling depressed, literally translated into English as having "heart burns." The "heart burns" are manifest as stomach pains, headaches, and other physical ailments. Few, however, recognize the problems as mental health related. Adding to their worry is the anxiety that if their health deteriorates, their families might not be able to take care of them and might send them to live in "old folk homes." As a kind of reassurance to themselves, however, they continue to insist that, "Our children take care of their elders; they don't put elders in old folk homes."

A large number of elderly Muslim immigrants are unwilling to accept help for their mental health problems from social services. Indeed, like their families, they are neither able to accept that they have mental health problems, nor are they aware of appropriate city, county, or state social service agencies. In her survey of Asian Americans, Tsukahira (1988) stresses the importance of making the families of the Asian elderly aware of services for which they are eligible. Many families are more likely to provide necessary care at home than to institutionalize their elderly relatives if they know that there are social services to which they can turn (Kim and Kim, in press).

Socialization and Social Isolation

Most older Muslims socialize exclusively with others from their country of origin, with whom they share cultural and religious backgrounds. The majority of those interviewed are Ismailis, and in their countries of origin, especially in Africa, socialized with Ismailis as well as non-Ismailis. They were exposed to non-Ismailis through business or neighborhood contacts. Their Muslim as well as non-Muslim friends respected their Muslim culture and traditions. For personal and cultural reasons, many of these elderly immigrants have neither established ties with other Americans nor participated in established programs for U.S. citizens. Even though they indicate that their American neighbors and acquaintances are generally friendly, few have developed strong social ties or personal friendships with non-Muslim or non-Asian Americans. Reciprocal perceptions about cultural differences and the belief that other Americans have insufficient time or interest to develop personal friendships have resulted in feelings that other Americans do not understand or accept them. In turn, the elderly immigrants are unwilling to discuss personal or family problems with outsiders because this is a sphere of private life that is not easily shared outside the family boundaries (Ross-Sheriff and Nanji 1991). A few who could articulate reasons for their difficulty stated, "We have experienced racial differences, but not racial tensions. Even though the other Americans are polite, they don't understand Islam. . . . The moment we say we are Muslims, it will evoke a different response, not because they don't know Islam. It is because they have prejudices against Muslims. They don't act negatively against the Hindus or Buddhists." One articulate elderly member described this negative response: "It is not a social or a cultural phenomena. It is a definite negative political response that creates a feeling of frustration, a sense of helplessness that even if we explain who we are, it won't make a difference." In addition, many elderly are unlikely to use formal services and programs such as the day care centers for elderly since these programs are not culturally familiar nor enjoyable to them.

The elderly reported that one of the most serious problems they confront is the lack of opportunity to participate in religious or ethnic community activities. Places of worship are one arena where they could restore contact with their past, find people with similar backgrounds, and reestablish the social support networks they enjoyed in their countries of origin. All the study group members expressed interest in social activities organized by the community and indicated that they enjoy and appreciate such programs and would attend any future events. One elderly woman stated: "Sometimes I feel trapped. There is no place to go. But, my heart feels light and free when I go to the mosque or to these community organized functions."

For those who do not have frequent access to religious centers, the telephone serves as a medium of communication. Many elderly immigrants spend a great deal of time on the telephone. The problems with language, lack of access to public transportation, and lack of automobiles and driving skills make phone communication ideal for them. The telephone does not, however, replace the warmth of face-to-face contact and interaction.

Housing

Elderly Muslim immigrants prefer to live with adult children and their spouses. Otherwise if they are physically able and have available housing, most live within a reasonable traveling distance from the immediate family. Unfortunately, some immigrant Muslims studied were able to find housing only in the poorer neighborhoods, with limited access to resources and social services. In such neighborhoods, newly arrived elderly immigrants are often afraid;

many in the study expressed concern about violence, substance abuse, and other social ills to which they have been exposed through television and other media.

Most elderly immigrants value the idea of the extended family living together in harmony. Although few of those interviewed explicitly stated their difficulties, it was clear in several cases that harmonious extended family life is difficult because of differences in needs of the elderly immigrants and their adult children. In the culture of origin the extended family is highly valued; in the United States, however, the nuclear family is preferred and the elderly immigrants perceive themselves as a burden on this smaller unit. A discussion of family life with interviewees suggested that many have often encountered conflict in maintaining the extended family in an environment that does not seem to validate it. Adult children and their spouses generally have jobs outside their homes and demanding schedules. In contrast, the elderly immigrants have more personal time at their disposal, and consequently a greater need for attention from adult children and grandchildren. Conflicting expectations from all the members of the family—elderly relatives, adult children, and grandchildren (especially the adolescents)—often results in stress and are a source of perceived emotional neglect or abuse in some families. In a few extreme cases elderly immigrants feel really unwanted.

Some elderly people with spouses are able to establish separate households. Others cope by moving between the homes of adult children, living with each only part of the year to spread the "burden" among the children. Thus, some whose children are dispersed in different parts of the United States do not have one permanent residence and move periodically to wherever their children have settled. Hardly any live in situations such as homes for the aged. A few families manage to resolve their problems through collaborative arrangements where elderly share living quarters near mosques, and family members share responsibilities for finances, health care, and other tasks to meet the needs of their aged parents.

ELDERLY AS RESOURCES AND ROLE OF RELIGION

Although elderly Muslim immigrants generally appear to depend on their adult children, families and communities, often creating stress both for themselves and for those family members who attempt to maintain them in their homes, this image of the elderly is incomplete. Most elderly immigrants are not seen by their families as a burden. Indeed, some provide more help than they receive, and many more are capable of doing so if opportunities can be identified and facilitated. Not all the elderly immigrants studied have poor health or are economically dependent. Many perform valuable functions such as providing child care, household help, and emotional support, as well as teaching family and cultural traditions. Under these circumstances, the relative absence of conflict within the family seems to depend more on personality, openness, flexibility, and level of adaptation to life in the United States for the elderly immigrants as well as for their adult children.

One major finding of the study is that religion plays a significant role in the lives of the Muslim elderly immigrants. Religion provides an overall sense of order and meaning and serves as a significant source of comfort during times of personal and social distortion as a result of migration. A majority, men as well as women, participate in prayers every Friday, some every morning and evening. Those few who only nominally adhered to religion in their country of origin appear to have rediscovered religion during the process of adaptation to life in the United States. It offers a way of reducing the feelings of alienation experienced in times of uncertainty. Religious organizations for Muslims thus can play a significant role in either developing social service programs or working closely with social welfare agencies in addressing the needs of elderly immigrants.

MUSLIM COMMUNITY RESPONSE

Like other Muslim communities, the Ismailis have established support programs to serve elderly members and their families. The programs vary in nature and include services such as transportation to the prayer hall, ethnic entertainment, celebration of religious festivals, and emergency support during times of crisis (Ross-Sheriff and Nanji 1991). Such programs are highly valued by all elderly members of the community, and it is clear from conversations that more programs would be very welcome.

The religious community thus provides a haven of familiarity and safety for elderly immigrants in an otherwise difficult world. Within this community language and cultural barriers are temporarily forgotten. However, these programs are run by grass-roots leaders who are not professionally trained social workers, are not knowledgeable about the entitlement of residents, and do not have skills to deal with mental health problems. Collaborative arrangements between the grass-roots leaders in the religious community and social service agencies can greatly enhance the existing support programs as well as fulfill the need for socialization and cultural continuity. Grass-roots leaders within the ethnic or religious communities are in an ideal situation to articulate the needs of elderly Muslim immigrants and bring them to the attention of the appropriate public social service agencies in the host society.

A program based on a partnership between formal networks (public and private social service agencies) and informal support networks that meets the needs of elderly immigrants and that also provides help to family members who are responsible for their elderly relatives would be most effective. Ultimately, such a program would be aimed at empowering the elderly immigrants either within the extended or nuclear family structure or individually to take control of their own situations (Chunn, Dunston, and Ross-Sheriff 1983). Training for empowerment and some level of self-dependency would make the program comprehensive (Kim and Kim, in press). Muslim community leadership can facilitate access to health, income maintenance, and other technical services from public and private social services agencies. Additional services specific to ethnic or religious communities that are unavailable within the public sector can be planned by ethnic or religious organizations. Family members, friends, neighbors, and elderly relatives can be taught to interact flexibly and humanely to meet each other's crises and day-to-day emotional needs.

REFERENCES

AmaraSinghan, L. (1980). "Making Friends in a New Culture: South Asian Women in Boston, Massachusetts." In *Uprooting and Development: Dilemmas of Coping with Modernization*, ed. G. Coehlo and P. Ahmed, pp. 417–444. New York: Plenum.

Chan, F. (1988). "To Be Old and Asian: An Unsettled Life in America." *Aging* 358: 14–15.

Chunn, J., P. Dunston, and F. Ross-Sheriff. (1983). *Mental Health and People of Color*. Washington, D.C.: Howard University Press.

Davis, K. (1988). "Retirement as a Dubious Paradise—Another Point of View." In *Issues in Contemporary Retirement,* ed. R. Ricardo-Campbell and E. Lazear, pp. 191–203. Stanford, Calif.: Hoover Institution Press.

Gelfand, D. E. (1989). "Immigration, Aging, and Intergenerational Relationships." *The Gerontologist* 29, no. 3: 366–371.

Gozdziak, E. (1988). "Distant Roots." *Aging* 359: 3–7.

Hooyman, N., and H. Kiyak. (1991). *Social Gerontology: A Multidisciplinary Perspective,* 2d ed. Boston: Allyn and Bacon.

Kiefer, C. W., et. al. (1985). "Adjustment Problems of Korean American Elderly." *The Gerontologist* 25, no. 5: 477–482.

Kim, P., and J. Kim. (In press). "Korean-American Elderly: Policy, Program, and Practice Implications." In *Social Work Practice with Asian Americans,* ed. S. Furuto, R. Biswas, D. Chung, K. Murase, and F. Ross-Sheriff.

Markides, K., and C. Mindel. (1987). *Aging and Ethnicity.* Newbury Park, Calif.: Sage Publications.

Metcalf, B. (1984). "Introduction." In *Moral Conduct and Authority: The Place of Adab in South Asian Society,* ed. B. Metalf, pp. 1–20. Berkeley, Calif.: University of California Press.

Newman, B. M., and P. R. Newman. (1985). *Development Through Life: A Psychological Approach.* Homewood, Ill.: Dorsey Press.

Osako, M. M. (1988). " 'Downward Mobility' as a Form of Phased Retirement in Japan." *Ageing International* 15, no. 2: 19–22.

Ricardo-Campbell, R., and E. Lazear, eds. (1988). *Issues in Contemporary Retirement.* Stanford, Calif.: Hoover Institution Press.

Ross-Sheriff, F., and A. Nanji (1991). "Islamic Identity, Family and Community: The Case of the Nizari Ismaili Community." In *Muslim Families in North America,* ed. E. Waugh, S. Abu-Laban, and R. Qureshi, pp. 101–118. Edmonton, Alberta: University of Calgary Press.

Tsukahira, Y. (1988). "Reaching out to Families of the Asian Elderly." *Aging* 358: 11–13.

Wheeler, T., ed. (1979). *The Immigrant Experience.* New York: Penguin Books.

CHAPTER 19

The Yemenis of Delano: A Profile of a Rural Islamic Community

Jonathan Friedlander

This chapter traces the history of the small community of Yemeni Muslims settled in the agricultural town of Delano, California, and its environs. The narrative is based on continuing field research and photographic study carried out since 1980.[1] The focus is on the process of change experienced by Yemeni agricultural workers and increasingly by their families as they have made the transition from sojourners to settlers. The context of Yemeni immigration and the characteristics of the developing community—occupation and work, health, leisure, politics, and religious issues—are highlighted. The challenges of maintaining a Yemeni identity are explored by examining the opposing forces of preservation and assimilation.

The town of Delano lies in the southern San Joaquin Valley some 150 miles north of Los Angeles. The relatively short, scenic drive on Interstate 5 takes the rider past rolling hills that turn golden yellow in summer. The highway quickly ascends to an elevation of 5,000 feet, passing Fort Tejon and its preserved turn of the century army encampment—the final destination of the U.S. Camel Corps and its camel master Hajj Ali. "Hi Jolly," as he is known in the annals of the West, was perhaps the first Muslim to set eyes on California's San Joaquin Valley. The fields, spanning some four hundred miles northward to the Sacramento Valley, have changed considerably since the days of Hajj Ali, most notably from the mechanical-intensive cultivation of grain to the labor-intensive cultivation of fruit and vegetables. This historic transformation

423

brought with it a dependence on native and immigrant labor, including, most recently, villagers from Yemen.

The interstate highway soon bifurcates to California 99, once the main thruway and conduit to Yemeni migration to Delano. For more than a century agricultural work has brought both indigenous and foreign populations to the area: Native Americans who were forced to work on the ranches; Asians—Chinese, Japanese, and Filipinos; Europeans from the Ellis Island period; Oakies fleeing the Dust Bowl and Great Depression; and continuing waves of workers from Mexico, adding to the large number of hispanics employed in farming. Yemenis entered the picture in 1957 when a dozen young men drove from Lodi and Stockton to the Delano area. They came from villages in mountainous central Yemen, from a verdant environment surrounded by a harsh desert terrain, a "paradise" as many workers would describe their ancestral homeland. Turbulent political conditions, a bare subsistence economy, and the prospects of finding work abroad brought thousands of Yemenis to New York and Northeastern and Midwestern cities. Following the lead of the pioneering workers several hundred Yemenis came westward to the open fields of the San Joaquin Valley. They were farmers, but nothing in Yemen prepared them for farm work in California. One of the workers recalls: "We (new immigrants) were fooled. We didn't know what (kind of) work our Yemeni friends were doing here. . . . I dressed up in a suit and necktie and a nice pair of shoes and walked in (amid a group of Yemeni coworkers) and everyone started laughing. They asked me if I was going to work in the White House."

In Delano the first Yemeni immigrants met Yugoslavs and Italian immigrants who had come to the Valley some fifty years earlier. Now successful and wealthy growers, the South Europeans introduced and nurtured the table grape industry, making it second to none (at the onset of the project, billboards on the approaches to town proclaimed GRAPES, OUR CLAIM TO FAME). Filipino labor contractors and crew foremen were influential in hiring decisions in the early days. The Yemenis also encountered Japanese involved in agricultural work who have since ascended the economic scale and entered the urban professional class. Other groups arrived on the scene, including Hindu, Sikh, and Persian farmworkers and landowners. Today, the signs read DELANO, AN INTERNATIONAL COMMUNITY WORKING TOGETHER, a pronouncement that at once

FIGURE 19.1. Yemeni pruning crew, vineyards, Delano (photo by Ron Kelley).

reveals the changing ethnic composition of Delano and its self-image. Mirroring the rise in Arab immigration to the United States, the population of Yemenis increased gradually in the 1960s as the growers found them to be industrious and reliable workers and thus were willing to sponsor their long journey from the former Yemen Arab Republic and even from Marxist South Yemen. In this period most workers lived in exclusively Yemeni or ethnically mixed camps. Others shared apartments in towns in close proximity to the fields. A leading Yemeni foreman estimated in 1973 there were some 10,000 Yemeni workers in the Central Valley, with more than half the Yemeni population working in the Delano area.

By the mid-1970s the ranks of Yemeni workers dwindled as many left for better paying jobs in the automobile industries, sometimes doubling their salaries. Over the course of the decade and thereafter the size of the Yemeni population in the Central Valley decreased further as numerous workers completed their sojourn and returned permanently to Yemen. From a practical standpoint, the cost of air travel to the United States and a spiraling inflation in Yemen made working in neighboring Saudi Arabia a more attractive prospect. The numbers of Yemenis also shrank due

FIGURE 19.2. Grape harvest, Delano vineyards (photo by Ron Kelley).

FIGURE 19.3. Yemeni and Hispanic workers harvesting plums, Shafter
(photo by Ron Kelley).

FIGURE 19.4. Asparagus harvest, winter, Richgrove area (photo by Ron Kelley).

to difficulties in obtaining immigrant visas. Presently the Yemeni population in the Central Valley is approximately 1,000 and growing slowly, as many settled Yemenis have brought their families to America.

Farming remains the traditional occupation practiced in Delano, Porterville, Richgrove, and other locations in the southern San Joaquin Valley. Although table grapes continue to be the predominant cash crop (more than a dozen varieties are cultivated) the Yemeni and hispanic crews are also engaged in picking plums, pears, apricots, cherries, melons, asparagus, and other fruit and vegetables. The routines of farm work are invariably linked to agricultural cycles—the preparation of the vineyards in spring and harvesting the grape bounty in summer and fall. The type of work in the vineyards—picking, packaging, stacking, and supervision—commands its own pay scale, ranging from piecemeal work plus minimum wage to the $50,000 plus annual salaries earned by a few veteran Yemeni foremen. In the winter hiatus many workers collect unemployment or seek work on winter crops in the Imperial Valley further to the south, near Mexico. Some even travel to Arizona. "You work six months out of the year, so it's not a regular job," complained one Yemeni worker. "Two months in Delano, another month in asparagus. Couple of months in different areas. Travel just like Gypsies." In the past, and to some extent even today, the goal of the Yemeni workers has been to stay in California for approximately five years and send their hard-earned wages to Yemen. A great majority have succeeded in meeting this objective, yet in the process they have suffered from prolonged separation from families, isolation, and stress. As one worker remarked: "You get to miss your family. Some of them stay here two, three, four years or more. They get depressed and somebody comes up with the wrong advice: 'Why don't you have a couple of beers? Maybe that'll make you feel better.'" Other ethnic groups continue to experience severe hardships. A front-page *Los Angeles Times* article, serialized in the local San Joaquin newspapers, reported on September 29, 1991, that "squalor and poverty have again become common for farm workers in California."

Conversely, the accumulated investment in vineyards has brought considerable profit to the family-owned businesses and corporate farmers in the Delano area, whose assets are an integral part of the diversified and powerful economy of the region propelled by cotton, cattle, petroleum and chemicals, farm machinery, and high-technology industries. Still, the business of agriculture is both risky and expensive. At any hint of summer rain the growers hurriedly try to protect their best grapes with colored plastic sheets that cover the vineyards like environmental art. The losses due to droughts, frosts, and pests can also be colossal, for the growers and workers alike (the 1991 freeze that destroyed the orange crop also resulted in the loss of thousands of jobs). Human error exacerbates acts of nature. One summer a large part of the prized grape crop was destroyed by mistake when the temperature controls in a huge cold-storage facility were set too high. The annual company picnic was canceled that year.

Health issues remain a subject of concern for the Yemenis and other farm workers, and a point of contention with the growers. The intensive physical labor involved in farming has resulted in back injuries, broken arms and ankles, and accidents caused by falling from tress, all requiring hospitalization and follow-up care. Injuries leading to workers' compensation suits, however, frequently have been dismissed by the courts, which have been influenced by the pro-agribusiness stances of the Republican governors

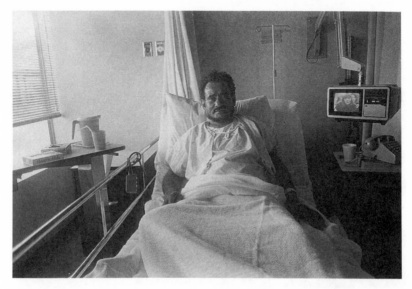

FIGURE 19.5. Injured Yemeni farmworker at a Delano hospital (photo by Ron Kelley).

of California. Respiratory and neurological damage attributed to exposure to pesticides is an even more serious issue.

"We have the problem with a lot of people with the spray. Chemicals in the field. A lot of people sneezing, tears in their eyes, a lot of allergies," remarked one Yemeni worker who served as the Delano representative to the Arab-American Anti-Discrimination Committee. "I have that too from the field. Now if I go to see any worker in the field, I can't breathe very good. I never had the problem before. My eyes and my nose and my chest. I think it's when I pulled leaves. When they spray chemicals to the trees, that's when I have that. I've been sick and too many doctors not helping me any good. We have one old man, he had to leave the country because of that. We fight his case for four months. We lost. He applied for social security benefits." The high incidence of cancer in neighboring McFarland was blamed on intensive use of pesticides over many years (a Yemeni associate of one of the companies absurdly attributed the cause of the cancer to chemicals sprayed on drywells in Mexico). Although soil and other sampling did not reveal any traces of toxins, the fear of cancer is ever present. The recent death of a young adolescent after eight years of fighting her

FIGURE 19.6. Delano vineyards (photo by Ron Kelley).

FIGURE 19.7. Delano vineyards (photo by Ron Kelley).

FIGURE 19.8. Yemeni store, Bakersfield (photo by Ron Kelley).

cancer bought back talk of the grape boycott that was carried out effectively in the 1970s.

The arrival of women and children from Yemen signified the end of the sojourning phase of the migration. Many workers pooled their resources to purchase small businesses to sustain their livelihood. Currently there are more than 300 Yemeni-owned supermarts and convenience stores in hamlets, towns and cities along Highway 99—in Pixlie, Bakersfield, Merced, Modesto, Stockton, and Fresno, as well as in Oakland, the site of the largest concentration of Yemenis in California. Driving along country roads which intersect endless stretches of vineyards, fruit orchards, cotton fields, and almond and pistachio groves, one may come across a small store stacked with cold soft drinks, beer, and other food items, including a variety of dried chili peppers catering to the tastes of the predominant hispanic clientele. It would not be unlikely to find a young Yemeni woman in a sparkling laced purple dress behind the cashier's counter with her children looking shyly at the customers while their father stocks merchandise in the storage room. Yemeni-owned stores often are located in a marginal part of town, where the Yemeni families would compete with Hispanics and Sikh immigrants for business.

Yemeni women helping their spouses or other family members

FIGURE 19.9. Yemeni store, Indio (photo by Ron Kelley).

remain in the minority, however, and most are isolated in their homes and depend to a great degree on their adolescent children for contacts with the outside world. Increasingly, the families have begun to face disciplinary problems with their growing children. The absence of grandparents involved in the raising of children is compounded by complaints from the Yemeni men that mothers' discipline is too lax. In one extreme case generational conflict exploded in the sensationalized killing of a Yemeni teenager who defied her family. The murderer, who happened to be her cousin, escaped to Yemen. His action is still justified by the family and other Yemenis.

Despite existing tensions Yemenis enjoy the fruit of their labor. At heart they have remained country folk, preferring the pace and setting of the rural sector to the bewildering urban centers (some workers have lived in Delano for more than three decades without having visited the relatively near Los Angeles metropolitan area). Leisure time is spent attending country fairs, harvest festivals, or going on communal outings to the footslopes of the nearby Tehachapis mountains. Company picnics usually are held in early November, where hundreds of workers, supervisors, administrators,

FIGURE 19.10. Shriners from Anaheim, California, and Yemeni onlookers at National Date Festival Parade, Indio (photo by Ron Kelley).

and the owners and their families turn out for a gigantic barbeque complete with a band performing popular Mexican tunes and a rendition of "Ya Mustapha" for the Yemenis. The long-term lease of a Yemeni Association hall in Delano has provided a focal point for informal gatherings, meetings, and passing time playing cards. Social visits remain the primary vehicle for maintaining cohesion among the closely linked Yemeni families scattered throughout the Delano area.

Although Yemenis are not politically active in Delano, they hold strong political convictions about a variety of subjects that affect their lives. The killing of Nagi Daifullah, a Yemeni worker who supported the United Farmworkers Union (UFW), still stirs debate among Yemenis more than a decade after his death. This period had witnessed the waning influence of the UFW, an organization that the majority of North Yemeni workers labeled communist. The reunification with Marxist South Yemen and the demise of communism in the Soviet Union and Eastern Europe were interpreted by many Yemenis as a vindication of their stance vis-à-vis the Soviet Union. The closure of the American Civil Liberty Union field office has dealt yet another blow to the activist agenda in Kern County. As one of the ACLU supporters lamented in a January 14, 1992, *Los Angeles Times* article: "If folks do not harbor outright hostility toward the 'liberal' group, it seems they are simply too busy raising cotton or pumping oil to pay it much heed . . . maybe someday when the pendulum swings to the left a little bit, we can try again." The Yemenis of Delano have traditionally managed to resolve their disputes internally and their foremen have acted as effective liaisons in dealing with work-related grievances. Nevertheless, their lives are inexorably intertwined in the national debate brought forth by the environmentally derived Big Green proposition, pesticide and other health-related issues, including the spraying of Malathion to eradicate the Mediterranean fruitfly in rural and urban areas. On the grand scale, the great issues surrounding the allocation of water and the representation of the large but invisible agricultural work force in central California continue to keep the politics of agriculture in the forefront.

Yemenis are more likely to discuss their own national politics. The ongoing democratization efforts in Yemen and the economic consequences of the expulsion of Yemeni workers from Saudi Arabia, fueling the long-standing bickering with the Saudis over ancient borders, are topics of interest that are supplemented by reports from individuals who have visited Yemen. The discourse on Yemeni and Middle Eastern politics is usually conducted in the abstract, but the dialogue between the Yemenis and representatives of their political institutions—the Consulate General of Yemen in San Francisco and the Union of Yemeni Immigrants—has been regular although infrequent. The importance of the Delano community in the eyes of Yemeni officials has been demonstrated by the visit of the Yemeni ambassador to the United States on the occasion of the twenty-five year celebration of Yemeni independence, an event attended by the city manager of Delano, other functionaires, and some 500 workers. More recently, several Yemeni foremen from the Delano area were invited to meet with Yemeni president Ali Abdullah Salah during his visit to San Francisco.

Contacts with American political institutions are rare as Yemenis express mixed feelings about U.S. foreign policy in the Middle East and the government's behavior toward Arabs and Muslims. The high-profile support accorded by Yemen to Saddam Hussein during the Gulf war has put many Yemenis on the defen-

sive. A biased American perception of Arabs and Muslims perpetu-
ated by the national media has worsened matters. During the
"Hostage Crisis" some Yemenis were mistaken for Iranians and
harassed by Americans. It is hoped that the increased level of daily
interaction between Yemenis and the general population of Delano
will lead to greater tolerance. The recent coverage of the Ramadan
fast in the Delano and Bakersfield papers may be one step in the
process of gaining a better understanding of the Yemenis, Arabs,
and Muslims residing in rural California.

The increased religiosity of the Yemeni community in Delano
can be correlated to particular settlement phases in the San Joaquin
Valley. The sojourning phase, accentuated by dislocation and a
distancing from the homeland, has led some Yemenis to stray from
Islam. As one farm worker recalls: "In Yemen, in your villages, you
heard the mosque's prayer five times a day. You're not doing heavy
work. You're speaking your language. There is no beer. There is no
dance. There is no things to do like here. And you see a lot of
people praying every day in their culture. But when they come
here . . . they start to forget about praying and like Americans
start drinking beer and dancing and those things." The arrival of
women and children from Yemen as well as family elders brought
an infusion of conservative attitudes and a rekindled interest in
Islam. The measure of Yemeni religiosity is revealed by examining
several indicators, beginning with the five pillars of faith.

PRAYER (SALAT)

Although most observant Yemenis pray at home, until five years
ago individual and communal praying took place in the various
labor camps. In the exclusively Yemeni camps makeshift mosques
served as focal points for the five required daily prayers. As cleanli-
ness is a requisite to prayer, religiously observant workers would
normally perform only early morning and evening prayers, before
and after their grueling work in the muddy or dusty vineyards.
Foremen and other workers with access to vehicles would sometimes return to their homes or to the camp for midday prayers and
respite. During the heyday of the workcamps an Imam, whose
qualifications depended mainly on the quality of his voice and
knowledge of the Qur'an, would lead the collective prayer. The
same criterion applies to the Imam who presently leads prayer at

FIGURE 19.11. Mosque, Yemeni work camp, Porterville (photo by Ron Kelley).

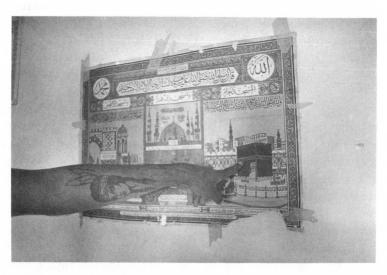

FIGURE 19.12. Tattooed Yemeni farmworkers pointing at a poster of the sacred Ka'ba (Black Stone) in Mecca, Porterville work camp (photo by Ron Kelley).

the Yemeni Association Hall. The Yemenis usually attend the Bakersfield mosque if they desire to consult a formally trained Imam.

FASTING (SAUM)

Like praying, the fast of Ramadan, which requires Muslims to abstain from eating for a month during the daylight hours, engages the Yemenis of Delano in varying degrees. For the workers in the field the fast is particularly harsh. More tolerant working conditions enable Yemeni storeowners to be stricter in their observance of Ramadan. The breaking of the fast in the sojourning phase occurred in the main dining hall of the predominantly Yemeni work camps. At present, the conclusion of the daily fast is marked by an evening meal attended by family members and friends. Specially prepared dishes readied with sweet fruit, particularly dates, are among the favorites. The end of Ramadan, marked by the sighting of the new moon, is celebrated by early morning prayer performed by Yemenis at their own center, or in the company of compatriots and other Muslims in the Bakersfield mosque.

FIGURE 19.13. Sheep sacrifice, 'Id al-Fitr celebration, Delano work camp (photo by Ron Kelley).

PILGRIMAGE (HAJJ)

The sacred duty of every Muslim to perform the pilgrimage to Mecca is especially profound for Yemeni workers whose extended stay in the United States has delayed the fulfillment of this holy ritual. The costly journey to the Arabian peninsula (a luxury often reserved for family visits) is always emotional and eventful. One prominent Yemeni foreman had to return from Saudi Arabia to attend an urgent company meeting that required his participation in an important decision regarding the grape harvest (the foreman rationalized his inability to participate in the hajj as an act of God's retribution for his past misconduct). To the chagrin of his family, when the same foreman made the hajj the following year thousands of pilgrims were trapped and perished when the ventilation system in an underground causeway failed. Upon his safe return from Mecca, the foreman, as is true of all who complete the pilgrimage, earned the coveted title of Hajj.

CHARITY (ZAKAT)

The prescription for a righteous Muslim life includes giving a tithe to help the needy or assist with charitable causes. As a closely knit community the Yemenis have felt obligated to assist newly arrived family members in the struggle and burden of initial adjustment, as well as others in need, such as relatives with ailments requiring hospitalization and intensive care. Because of these family responsibilities, contributions to the founding or maintenance of religious and educational institutions have been minimal; the Yemenis have not yet attained the financial means to sustain an Islamic center of their own.

PROFESSION OF FAITH (SHAHADA)

Almost without exception the Yemenis are professed believers in the omnipotent power and wisdom of God. This world-view is affirmed in the commonly told anecdote of the greedy city-folk who fenced off their newly purchased orange groves to guard against minimal shrinkage of crop and were the only ones in the Delano area to totally lose their investment to the freeze. On the other hand, the temptations of our secular society have also plant-

FIGURE 19.14. Barracks interior, Delano work camp. The Qur'anic verse taped to the wall reads "If God helps you no one can overcome you" (Sura 3:160) (photo by Ron Kelley).

ed some doubts in the heart of the believers. As one member of the community put it: "God, he knows I pray, but nobody see me. God, he know. Nobody see me, but God see me, I pray. I don't know which to believe, Christianity or Muslim or Buddha. I don't know. Because nobody prove it. Nobody went to heaven and come back. You see, how do you know we have heaven? Nobody knows. Can you prove it?"

Other religious issues affect the immigrants' daily lives and decision making. In the realm of work, the Yemenis have had to compromise their position on the sale of alcohol: "Some people start selling liquor and beer and stuff like that in here. Lots of them. When you buy a grocery store with alcohol in it, then your business goes to alcohol. If you discontinue selling alcohol, you're

FIGURE 19.15. Delano Harvest Festival (photo by Ron Kelley).

FIGURE 19.16. Yemeni and his American wife, Indio Date Festival
parade (photo by Ron Kelley).

out of business. If you give it up, you're giving up $200–$300,000 for nothing. You've lost." They have also had to come to terms with the consumption of beer: "When you try it, it's just like that potato chip commercial. You know 'you can't just eat one'." You have to try it and then you get used to it and there you go, you slide from the top of the mountain all the way down." Likewise, in the matter of finances they have had to distinguish between the prohibition on interest as it applies in their dealings with coreligionists and with secular banking institutions. Similar dilemmas extend to other spheres of Yemeni and Muslim life, most notably in the matters of intermarriage, education, and identity.

As the early phase of sojourning was characterized by the nearly complete absence of Yemeni women in the Delano area, some men married Hispanic women and raised families that now include adult children. The marriages have not been without their problems, especially for the offspring. In one case, a favorite daughter married a hispanic man against her father's wishes that she wed a Muslim. The father disowned his daughter, accusing her of disloyalty and betraying his expectations. This tragedy also estranged the daughter from her Catholic Mexican American mother, who sided with her Yemeni husband. Another case of exogamous marriage also involves a Yemeni man and his Hispanic wife who raised a family in Delano. The man also has a spouse and children in Yemen. In a melancholy tone he now laments how he has been deprived of getting to know his teenage Yemeni daughter. As for his American-born daughter, he says, "I can't teach her to speak Arabic. It's very difficult for me because I'm the only one. If I talk to her once, she forgets what I tell her. She's watching TV and hanging around with kids like her, talking with her mother and grandparents in English. She doesn't know anything else, only English." With the arrival of Yemeni women and their children, the prospects for endogenous marriages in the future generation have increased. Conversely, as Yemeni children interact and fraternize regularly with the predominantly hispanic school population in Delano, the incidence of intermarriage is bound to rise and confront the Yemenis of Delano in the same way that it has challenged earlier generations of Muslim immigrants.

The potential for strengthening the social network of disparate Yemeni families and individuals exists in the environment of the Yemeni Association hall, which affords Yemenis a place to assem-

FIGURE 19.17. Funeral, Delano (photo by Ron Kelley).

ble and practice Islam as a congregation. A good number of workers conveniently meet at the hall for regular Friday prayer, especially during the off-season. The hall also functions as a gathering
place for card games and male conversation carried out over the
strong aromas of coffee and cigarettes. Yet, unlike the urban
Yemeni communities of Hamtramack, Michigan, or Lackawanna,
New York, the Yemenis of Delano have not been able to institute
educational programs at the hall to formally teach their children
the Arabic language and about Islam. Perhaps the physical isolation and economic fragmentation of this rural community have
made centralizing common efforts difficult. Until such time as the
Yemenis can mobilize their resources and resolve, Arabic and Islamic education in Delano will be carried out in the informal
domain of homes.

The establishment of a mosque center in Bakersfield some 30
miles to the south may provide yet another point of linkage. Unlike
the exclusively Yemeni-Arab community of Delano, the Bakersfield
mosque encompasses the multiplicity of nations and ethnic groups
that constitute the mostly immigrant Islamic community in the
southern San Joaquin Valley—Egyptians, Palestinians, Iraqis,
Pakistanis, and a growing number of Yemenis who own stores and

FIGURE 19.18. English lessons at night school, Delano (photo by Ron Kelley).

FIGURE 19.19. Yemenis swearing allegiance at ceremony for American citizenship, Bakersfield (photo by Ron Kelley).

reside in the city. A further indication of the growing importance of this metropolitan area is evident in the dedication of a section in a local cemetery for Islamic burials. Although only a few Delano Yemenis attend mosque services in Bakersfield at present, might it be possible that increased contacts between the Bakersfield and Delano communities will lead at a future date to the merging or even blending of Yemeni identity within the multiethnic Islamic milieu represented at the Bakersfield mosque? Will the next generation of Yemenis succumb to the powerful influence of assimilation and acculturation into the Hispanic and Anglo mainstream? Or, will they be able to maintain their unique ethnic characteristics as Yemenis and as the first nation to embrace Islam fourteen centuries ago? Further research could yield interesting answers to these questions, especially at this pivotal stage of the history of the Yemeni community, which after thirty years of immigration has just begun to settle in Delano.

NOTE

1.   See *Sojourners and Settlers: The Yemeni Immigrant Experience*, ed. J. Friedlander (Salt Lake City: University of Utah Press, 1988). The cited interviews were conducted by Ron Kelley and appeared in the section entitled "The Workers Speak," pp. 99–119. All the photographs were taken by Ron Kelley.

CHAPTER 20

Secular Immigrants: Religiosity and Ethnicity Among Iranian Muslims in Los Angeles

Georges Sabagh and Mehdi Bozorgmehr

When the religion of an immigrant group is different from that of a receiving country, it is generally assumed that religion reinforces ethnicity. In recent years, popular magazines and a number of studies have emphasized the religious aspects of the ethnicity of Muslims who migrated in large numbers to Western Europe and North America. Thus, in 1990, an American weekly magazine had one news item on "Islam in America: Can Muslims Blend Here Without Succumbing to Secularism?" and another on "Islam's Brave New World: Why Europe's Growing Moslem Minority Seems to Resist Assimilation."[1] In a study of Muslims in Detroit's Southend, Abraham, Abraham, and Aswad show that "against a world of economic uncertainty, Islam has served as a unifying force in the life of the three Arab nationality groups which inhabit the Southend" in Detroit.[2] In another study of Muslim families in North America, Barazangi[3] states that "the youth in these families vary in their interests, place of education, and understanding of Islam. Yet they all seem to have developed a strong attachment to their 'Muslim' or ethnic identity."

The objective of this chapter is to challenge the assumption that ethnicity and religiosity are necessarily related, even for Muslims. Secular immigrants could be just as ethnic as religious immigrants, and the basis of their ethnic identity need not be their religion. This hypothesis, however, is only true under certain con-

445

ditions that need to be specified. First and foremost, migration should be selective of those who are least religious or most secular in the country of origin. The implication of this condition is that we need to assess the religiosity of immigrants before migration. Unfortunately, this is seldom done in studies of immigrants. Second, migration should also be selective of those of high social class origin. Third, immigrants should not have their own ethnic places of worship or religious bodies.[4] When all or some of these conditions are met, religion cannot be expected to sustain ethnicity. This is a complex problem, however, and we agree with Alba that the link between religion and ethnicity "deserves further study."[5] Before we turn to a test of our hypothesis with survey data on Iranians in Los Angeles, we shall briefly summarize the findings from studies of religiosity and ethnicity among immigrants.

RELATIONSHIP BETWEEN RELIGIOSITY AND ETHNICITY

There is an extensive literature on the relationship between religious observance and ethnicity.[6] The most prominent generalization in this literature pertains to changes in religiosity or ethnicity between immigrant generations.[7] Hansen's generalization that "what the son wishes to forget the grandson wishes to remember" implies a highly ethnic first generation. If we add religion as an element in the analysis, as Will Herberg[9] does in his classic study of Protestant-Catholic-Jew, the first generation is not only very ethnic but also very religious. Thus, describing the "new unity" among Irish and Italian immigrants, Herberg states that "the immigrant church was the primary expression of this unity."[10] Greeley[11] agrees that the ethnic church enhances the ethnic cohesion and identity of immigrants. What happens when there are no ethnic churches? Because Muslims are not required to attend mosque for prayers, the experience of Muslims in North America should be instructive. Unfortunately, there are only a few studies of the religiosity of Muslims in the United States, and, with two notable exceptions, most of them pertain to the Southend enclave in Detroit.[12] Furthermore, only one or two studies address systematically the issue of the relationship between religiosity and ethnicity. Nevertheless, we shall briefly discuss some of the findings of these studies.

In one of the earliest sociological studies of Muslims in the United States, Elkholy[13] presents an extensive analysis of the impact of religiosity on assimilation among Arab Muslims in Toledo and Detroit. Interestingly, his data show that a sizeable minority of the first generation did not observe some of the Muslim religious practices.[14] His conclusion that high religiosity among Muslims is not an obstacle to assimilation suggests that there is a relatively weak relationship between ethnicity and religiosity. On the other hand, later studies of working-class Arab immigrants in Detroit's Southend indicate that, in an Arab-Muslim enclave, the mosque may take on many of the functions of the ethnic church and thus reenforce Arab ethnic identity.[15]

A marked increase in the immigration of Muslims from non-Arab countries in the 1970s[16] led Haddad and Loomis to include non-Arab Muslim immigrants (mostly Pakistanis) in their study.[17] As in Elkholy's sample, there is a noticeable minority of Muslims who are nonobservant or who attend the mosque only on high holidays.[18] The latter are known as "Eid Muslims." Paradoxically, even though Pakistanis have a high socioeconomic status, they are also the most religious.

Studies of first-generation immigrants or those with a focus on immigrant generations suggest the following generalizations or hypotheses about the religiosity of immigrants:

1. A religio-ethnic immigrant population is not homogeneous as is often assumed and may include a large proportion of secularists.[19] Studies asserting that immigrants are highly religious are often based on the experience of earlier immigrant waves, many of whom were rural in origin and had low socioeconomic status. Thus, we hypothesize that immigrants who are predominantly secular have an urban origin and a high social class background.

2. Religious behavior in the country of immigration may reflect religious behavior in the country of origin. On the basis of a recent survey of Koreans in Chicago, Hurh and Kim[20] show that Koreans affiliated with a Christian church in Korea are more likely to be involved in church activities in the United States than those who were not. Also, in a study of Moroccan Muslims in Montreal, Canada, one of the reasons given for nonobservance in Canada was nonobservance in Morocco.[21]

3. Levels of religiosity may not be related to levels of ethnicity so that secular immigrants could be either highly ethnic or not. Hurh and Kim show that there is a weak association between

church participation and assimilation or, conversely, ethnic attachment among Koreans in Chicago.

As indicated earlier, the central objective of this chapter is to analyze the association between religiosity and ethnicity among Muslims in the United States and the factors that affect this relationship. Survey data for Iranian Muslim immigrants in Los Angeles will be used for this analysis. As part of the argument, we shall document the urban and high social class origins, as well as the exile status of these immigrants, all of which tend to reduce religiosity.

IRANIAN MUSLIMS IN LOS ANGELES

Coming from a country where Muslims represented about 98 percent of the population, Iranian Muslims now find themselves a minority in Los Angeles alongside other Iranian ethno-religious minorities (e.g., Christian Armenians, Baha'is, and Jews). But Iranian Muslims also find themselves in a metropolitan area that contains Muslim immigrants from other countries, including Lebanon, Egypt, and Pakistan.[22] Thus, Iranian Muslims have, at least, three choices in forming their ethnic identity: (1) emphasizing ethnic or national (Iranian) rather than religious (Muslim) elements; (2) conversely, stressing religious (Muslim) rather than ethnic facets; and (3) reenforcing both ethnic and religious components. On the other hand, Iranian Muslims may not retain their ethno-religiosity and become oriented toward Anglo-American culture and society.

The dominant pattern of ethno-religiosity among Iranian Muslims depends on various factors. First, if Iranian Muslims were to associate mainly with other Iranians, their choice would demonstrate an Iranian ethnicity. There are sociocultural bonds and barriers that facilitate or impede this process. The Persian language and cultural heritage fosters interaction between Iranian Muslims and other Iranians. This tendency is counterbalanced, however, by the fact that non-Muslim Iranians were already minorities in Iran and had a developed and separate ethno-religious identity even before migrating to the United States.[23]

Second, if Iranian Muslims were observant Muslims, and associated with other observant Muslims, that choice would stress the religious side of their ethnic identity. But because many Iranian Muslims were exiles from a country with a Muslim political regime, the religious aspect of their identity cannot be salient. Furthermore, there is a linguistic barrier between Iranian and non-Iranian Muslims, except possibly Afghans. Therefore, if Iranian Muslims were to associate with other Muslims they would have to speak English. In addition, Iranians are predominantly Shi'is, whereas other Muslim immigrants in Los Angeles are mainly Sunnis.

Third, Iranian Muslims may stress their Iranian Muslim ethnicity by associating mainly with other Iranian Muslims, thus becoming a minority within a minority. Iranian Muslim ethnicity would be reinforced by Persian language and culture and common religions, but weakened by low religious observance. It could also be weakened by the perception of being discriminated against as Iranian Muslims, thus leading to a rejection of this identity.

METHODOLOGY OF THE STUDY

The survey of Iranians in Los Angeles was based on probability samples of Armenians, Baha'is, Jews, and Muslims. Because Iranian Muslims are the focus of this chapter, only the sampling procedure for this subgroup will be described. Considering that ours was the first large-scale survey of Iranians in the United States, and Iran has no tradition of surveys, we decided to meet influential members of various Iranian ethno-religious subgroups to inform them of the study and gain their cooperation. There were no exclusively Iranian Muslim organizations in Los Angeles that might furnish lists of members or affiliates. This by itself is an indicator of the secularism of Iranian Muslims: they do not belong to any religious organizations. Unlike the Armenian, Baha'i, and Jewish samples, which relied on both community lists and telephone directories, the Muslim sample had to be drawn wholly from the white pages of telephone directories. This procedure excluded from the sampling frame persons with unlisted telephone numbers. We selected a random sample of two hundred pages from each of the eight regional telephone directories of Los Angeles County. Iranian coders checked off obvious Persian names on each page, thus creating a list of certain Persian names. When in doubt about a name, coders indicated it as uncertain, thus generating a separate list of uncertain names. Iranian names were identified in

the uncertain list with the aid of a master list of Iranian surnames
from the 1979 Immigration and Naturalization Service Alien Registration List. These names were added to the certain list. The list
of 1,758 names thus generated became the main sampling frame
for the study. Each name was then assigned a unique identification
number. A computer-generated list of random numbers reordered
the names to break up the alphabetical sequence of each list, and
preventing the possibility of excluding individuals whose surnames
begin with letters at the end of the English alphabet. A random
sample of respondents were first contacted by a letter that explained the nature of the study and asked for their cooperation.
Iranian interviewers interviewed respondents in person in a random sequence until the desired number of interviews were completed. The number was fixed a priori at 200 for Muslims strictly
based on budgetary considerations, and 201 (197 Shi'is and 4
Sunni Muslims) were interviewed in person. Interviewing for the
whole study took six and a half months from late August 1987 to
early March 1988.[24]

We limited interviews to heads of households for budgetary
reasons. Therefore, respondents tend to be older than a sample of
randomly selected adults from their households, and also tend to
be predominantly men. Indeed, the median age of respondents is
about 40 years and 86.6 percent of them are men. Also, almost all
respondents are nonstudents. Our analysis is based on data for
heads of households, irrespective of age, sex and marital status.
Whenever possible, data on spouses, obtained from heads of
households, are also included.

RELIGIOSITY AND ETHNIC IDENTITY

Because the survey included four religious groups (Christian Armenians, Baha'is, Jews, and Muslims), each with its own norms of
religious observance, it was impossible to devise detailed and comparable measures to capture the religious behavior and religiosity
of all these four groups in the same questionnaire. It would have
required questions on daily prayers, on fasting, and other specific
religious practices for Muslims that, of course, could not be asked
of non-Muslims. Furthermore, because the religious background of
the respondents sampled from the telephone directories was initially unknown we had no way of knowing which questionnaire to

use in advance. Screening the respondents for their religious background may have alarmed them, resulting in possible suspicion about the motivation of the study. This was particularly a problem in studying Iranians in light of the Islamic revolution in Iran and their concern over religious identification. Indeed, we encountered problems during the pretest of our questionnaire when we asked the respondents "what is your religion?" Several, mostly Muslim, respondents answered that they had none and avoided the question. Subsequently, we rephrased the question in the final version of the questionnaire to "In what religion were you raised?" Even then, some Muslims complained that there were too many references to religion in the questionnaire. We detected conversions through additional questions. Under these circumstances, we devised a general question on the level of observance of "religious ceremonial and ritual practices." We asked this question about both the present and Iran, since religious observations could have been higher in Iran. Because 21.8 percent of respondents were married to non-Muslims, the analysis of religious observance was limited to respondents married to Muslims.[25]

As documented in Table 20.1, 12.0 percent of respondents and 17.9 percent of their spouses stated that, "during the last few years in Iran," they observed Muslim religious practices "always or often." A much higher percent stated that they "never" observed these practices (54.7 and 48.2, respectively). These figures indicate very low levels of religiosity for the respondents in Iran. Considering the high educational and occupational achievement of the respondents, their low level of religious practice in Iran is not unusual.

In the United States, only 4.3 percent of respondents and 9.0 percent of their Muslim spouses "always or often" observed their religious practices. By contrast, 76.1 percent of the former and 67.0 percent of the latter never practiced Islamic duties such as daily prayers, fasting, and so forth.[26] When there was a discrepancy in the reported level of religious observance between Iran and the United States,[27] we asked the respondents to give us their reasons for this discrepancy. Of the one-quarter who stated that they are less religious now, most gave such reasons as "lack of time," "facilities too far in the United State," and "negative impact of religion in Iran." The last refers to the way Islam is currently interpreted in Iran.

TABLE 20.1.

Degree of Religious Observance in the United States and Iran, Muslim Respondents and Spouses of Iranian Sample, Los Angeles 1987–1988, and Behavioral Scale of Religious Activities, Sample of Muslims, United States, 1983–1984 (percent distribution)

| | Los Angeles Iranian Muslims | | | | |
| | Respondents with Muslim spouses | | | | |
Levels of Religious Observance	Iran	U.S.	Musilm Spouse* Iran	Muslim Spouse* U.S.	U.S. Muslims**
Frequency of Observance					
Always	2.6	1.7	6.3	3.6	—
Often	9.4	2.6	11.6	5.4	—
Occasionally	33.3	19.7	33.9	24.0	—
Never	54.7	76.1	48.2	67.0	—
Religious Activity Scale					
Very active	—	—	—	—	25.0
Somewhat active	—	—	—	—	28.0
A little active	—	—	—	—	23.0
Not very active	—	—	—	—	24.0
Total	100.0	100.0	100.0	100.0	100.0
Sample size	117	117	112	112	320

* It should be noted that 21.8 percent of heads of household are married to non-Muslims.

** Source: Yvonne Y. Haddad and Adair T. Lummis, Islamic Values in the United States. New York: Oxford University Press, 1987, p. 167. About two-thirds of the sample includes persons born in the United States. Lebanese constitute one-third of the sample and Pakistanis one-fourth.

To the subjective and open-ended question on ethnic self-identity—"what do you consider yourself to be *primarily?*"—only 27 percent of respondents stated Iranian Muslim, whereas 67 percent reported Iranian. The remaining 6 percent gave various other responses including "Iranian Turkish," "Muslim," and "American." Only 2 out of 117 respondents identified themselves as Muslims. The experience of discrimination and the perception that Americans are prejudiced against Iranian Muslims contribute to the respondents' reluctance to identify themselves as Iranian Muslims or as Muslims. Discrimination and prejudice are common problems confronting immigrant groups, but the "Iranian Hostage Crisis" and the continuing U.S.-Iran conflicts and tensions probably has singled out Iranians more so than other immigrant groups in the United States. About a third of the respondents who were in the United States during the hostage crisis reported a personal experience of discrimination, mostly verbal abuses and discrimination at the university, on the job, or in business. By the time of the survey in 1987–1988, however, only 14 percent of the respondents reported similar experiences. Nevertheless, they still feel that non-Iranians are prejudiced toward Iranians, and more specifically toward Iranian Muslims. About 55 percent of respondents stated that Iranian Muslims experience at least some prejudice from non-Iranians.

Partly because of perceived discrimination, Iranian Muslims consider national identity more important than ethno-religious identity.[28] This might explain, in part, why the findings on the religious observance of Iranian Muslim immigrants are different from results of other studies of the first-generation immigrant groups in America. For example, as shown in Table 20.1, there was a much higher level of religious observance (25 percent very observant) among the Arab and non-Arab immigrants studied by Haddad.

It should also be noted that hardly any Iranian Muslims in the sample belonged to religious organizations. Although 29 percent of respondents indicated that they were most active in one organization, only 3 percent stated that it is a religious organization. Also, only 8 percent preferred to belong to Iranian Muslim organizations. In prerevolutionary Iran, participation in voluntary organizations was not an integral aspect of social life, partly because of the regime's fear of organized oppositional activity. Therefore, only 20 percent of Muslim respondents belonged to an organization and less than 3 percent belonged to religious organizations in Iran. The very low participation rate of Muslims in religious organizations in Iran and in the United States is understandable in light of their secularism, and the fact that Islam is not an organized religion.

Although the roots of secularism and nationalism in Iran can be traced at least to the nineteenth century, culminating in the

Constitutional Revolution of 1905,[29] two important and more recent historical processes account for the secularism and nationalism of upper-class Muslims in Iran before the revolution of 1978–1979. The modernization of Iran under Reza Shah, which was continued under his son, Mohammad Reza Shah, resulted in a deliberative effort toward secularization of Iranian society. The Pahlavi Shahs advocated nationalism, and emphasized the pre-Islamic Iranian grandeur.[30] Many educated Iranians identified with ancient Persian civilization as a source of nationalism against the Western encroachment. As direct beneficiaries of the modernization process, the urban upper-class Muslims also identified with secular Iranian culture.

URBAN ORIGIN AND SOCIAL CLASS ORIGIN

We hypothesized that immigrants who are secular would also be of urban and high socioeconomic status origins. Because we established that Iranian Muslims immigrants are highly secular, we expect, that they would also share these traits.

Iranian Muslims in Los Angeles are almost entirely of urban origin. Furthermore, about 85 percent resided an average of twenty years in Tehran before leaving Iran. This result is in sharp contrast to the fact that, in 1976, Tehran accounted for only 13 percent of Iran's population, and less than half of Tehran's residents were originally born in the capital. This marked selectivity in the urban origin of Iranian Muslims in Los Angeles is related to their high social class origin.

The high social class origin of the respondents is documented by their education, their occupations in Iran, and their fathers' occupations and education. Nearly 90 percent of respondents have a college education and over 48 percent have graduate degrees (Table 20.2), an extremely high rate for an immigrant group. Many respondents obtained these advanced degrees in the United States. Respondents' fathers also had a high educational achievement (29 percent were college educated) compared to other urban Iranian men (5 percent were college educated). But even if we compare the educational achievement of the respondents' fathers to those of the top occupations (professional, technical, administrative, and managerial workers) in urban Iran in 1976 (39 percent were college educated), their achievement remains impressive.[31] Respondents

TABLE 20.2.
Educational Level of Muslim Iranian Respondents and Their Fathers, Los Angeles, 1987–1988; and of Men, Urban Iran, 1976 (percent distribution)

Levels of Education	Iranian Muslims in Los Angeles		Urban Iran 1976*	
	Respondents**	Respondents'** Fathers	All Men	Men in Professional and Managerial Occupations*
Illiterate	0	4.3	39.6	4.4
Literate, but no schooling	0	14.5		
Highly literate, but no schooling	0	3.4 } 19.6	5.3	4.7
Religious school	0	1.7		
Elementary school or junior high school	.9 } 10.5	18.9 } 47.1	49.7	52.1
High school or trade school	9.6	28.2		
Some college or college graduate	41.3 } 89.6	18.8 } 29.2	5.4	28.4
Graduate degrees up to doctorate	29.8	4.4		5.0
Doctorate and post-doctorate degrees	18.5	6.0		5.4
Total	100.0	100.0	100.0	100.0
Sample Size	117	117	—	—

Source: Statistical Center of Iran, *National Census of Population and Housing November 1976*, 1981.

** With Muslim spouses.

455

had a substantially higher occupational status in Iran than did other urban Iranians as reported by the 1976 Iranian national census. Respondents' fathers also held top occupations in Iran.[32]

In the United States, Iranian Muslim immigrants have a very high occupational achievement.[33] Even in their first job in the United States, 52.4 percent held the top occupations of managers, executives, and professionals. Although they experienced some upward occupational mobility between their first job in the United States and their current job, their current high occupational achievement is even lower than it was in Iran. This finding is consistent with findings from other studies of other immigrant groups in general and exile or refugee groups in particular.[34]

Another distinctive feature of the Iranian Muslim sample is a very high level of self-employment (46.2 percent)[35] This rate is about five times the rate of self-employment of the native-born Anglos in Los Angeles. It is almost as high as the rate of self-employment of Koreans in Los Angeles, who are widely regarded as entrepreneurial prodigies.[36] Finally, many respondents in our sample have extensive investments in real estate, stocks, and bonds. Therefore, Iranian Muslims in Los Angeles have both human capital (education and occupation) and financial capital (wealth and assets).

The high social class origin of respondents suggests that they or their families benefited from the developmental policies of the Shah's regime. Because an Islamic revolution undermined their social and economic achievement, they had good reasons to turn further away from religion.

EXILE STATUS

The special case of Iranian Muslims fleeing a religious revolution is another factor contributing to their secularism. Many respondents are exiles,[37] shown indirectly by the fact that 64 percent of them came for the first time or returned to the United States to stay continuously during and after the Iranian revolution. In addition, many of those who were in the United States before the revolution and intended to return to Iran later changed their mind due to the revolution. Indeed, when questioned about "the most important reason" for leaving Iran, about a third of the respondents gave political or religious reasons that would qualify them as exiles.

Furthermore, over half of Iranian Muslims in the sample intend to stay in the United States now, as opposed to only one-third who intended to stay when they first arrived in the United States. Although 88 percent of respondents were legal residents or naturalized citizens, only 6 percent acquired residency as asylees, as compared to 23 percent through marriage, 36 percent through occupational preference, and 9 percent through investor's exemption. Thus, the findings in this and the previous section suggest that many of the respondents are high-status exiles who settled in the United States because of the Islamic revolution in Iran.

ETHNICITY OF SOCIAL AND ECONOMIC NETWORKS

Clearly Iranian Muslim immigrants are highly secular, but does it follow that they have a low level of ethnicity? The hypothesized lack of relationship between religiosity and ethnicity implies that these immigrants are not likely to be highly ethnic. The aim of this section is to assess the level of ethnicity of Iranian Muslims.

Ethnicity is a multidimensional concept, whose measurement requires various indicators. In this chapter, we focus on the following dimensions of ethnicity: (1) ethno-religious identities of persons (including relatives) with whom the respondents associate socially, and (2) ethno-religious characteristics of persons with whom the respondents have economic links (partners, employees, employers, supervisors, and coworkers).

An important finding of the study is that respondents associate more frequently with Iranian Muslims than with non-Muslim Iranians (Table 20.3). More than half of the respondents' and their spouses' close friends are mostly Iranian Muslims. However, the category of "mixed" close friends is fairly high (33 percent for the respondents and 34 percent for the spouses) and includes various combinations of Iranian and non-Iranian respondents.[38] Only a very small percentage of respondents and their spouses had American or European close friends exclusively. Clearly, a large proportion of respondents associate more with Iranian Muslims than with any other group.[39] This indicates a fairly high level of ethnicity of social ties. Another important finding is that hardly any Iranian Muslims associate with non-Iranian Muslims. This is partly due to the low level of religious observance of Iranian Muslims in Los Angeles as documented in Table 20.1.

TABLE 20.3.
Ethnicity of Informal Social Networks in the United States, Iranian Muslim Respondents
with Muslim Spouses, 1987–1988 (percent distribution)

Ethno-Religiosity of Persons	Respondent's Close Friends	Respondent's Wife's Close Friends	Respondent's Children's Close Friends	People at Parties, Weddings, and Other Celebrations Attended by Respondent
Iranian Muslims	57.3	60.0	12.9	60.0
Iranian non-Muslims	6.8	4.6	4.7	10.4
Iranian Muslims and non-Muslims	26.5	26.6	31.8	27.0
Non-Iranian Muslims	2.6	1.8	3.5	0.9
Muslims and Americans	5.1	5.5	43.5*	1.7
All Others	1.8	0.9	3.5	0
Total	100.0	100.0	100.0	100.0
Sample size	117	109	85	115

* The majority are Americans.

The findings on organizational membership are less clear-cut. Only 5 percent of respondents are most active in organizations whose members are Iranian Muslims. Even if we restrict the analysis to the one-third of respondents who are most active in organizations, only 17 percent associate with Iranian Muslims in organizations as compared to about 47 percent who interact with non-Iranian members.

Given the concentration of salaried Iranian Muslims in skilled occupations, it is not surprising to find that their coworkers, supervisors, and owners of workplaces are predominantly non-Iranians.[40] However, the findings on the self-employed Iranians are different. The respondents' partners and co-owners are, in the order of importance, close relatives (spouse, parents, children, and siblings) (37 percent), Iranian Muslims (32 percent), other Iranians (14 percent), and all other non-Iranians (14 percent). These findings show the importance of family among Iranians, especially as it concerns economic issues that require trust. They also indicate that Iranian Muslim ethnicity is strengthened in partnerships. But the data on workers and employees of Muslim Iranian-owned businesses show that over half are not Iranians, and less than one-third are Iranian Muslims or other Iranians. This result is consistent with the socioeconomic profile of our sample, which does not show many Iranians working as employees in Iranian businesses.

It is clear from the preceding presentation that, although Iranian Muslim respondents were secular in their religious observance, their level of ethnicity was substantially higher. The vast majority of their close friends, as well as the people at celebrations they were attending, were either Iranian coreligionists or other Iranians. Similarly their Muslim spouses were much more ethnic than religious. Self-employed Iranian Muslims are noticeably more ethnic in their economic ties than Iranian Muslim wage and salary workers.

RELIGIOSITY AND ETHNICITY

In spite of their relative homogeneity with respect to secularism and socioeconomic status, we need statistical tests of the strength and direction of the relationship between religious observance in the United States and the variables of ethnicity, ethnic identity, socioeconomic status, year of arrival, and religious observance in

TABLE 20.4.

Relationship Between Religious Observance in the United States and Religious Observance in Iran, Education in the United States, Year of Arrival, Ethnicity of Friends, Preferred Ethnicity of Organizational Members, and Self-Identity, Respondents with Muslim Spouses and Muslim Spouses, Los Angeles, 1987–1988 (percent and N = number)

Variables	Respondents with Muslim Spouses			Muslim Spouses		
	Non-observant in U.S.	Observant in U.S.	N	Non-observant in U.S.	Observant in U.S.	N
Religious Observance in Iran						
Never Observant	100.0	0	64**	94.4	5.6**	54
Observant	47.2	52.8	53**	40.4	59.6**	57
Education now						
BA or less	78.0	22.0	59	—	—	52
MA or higher	72.7	27.3	55	—	—	52
AA or less	—	—	—	61.5	38.5	52
BA or more	—	—	—	71.7	28.3	53

Year of Arrival						
Before 1979	71.7	28.3	60	61.8	38.2	55
1979 and after	80.7	19.3	57	71.9	28.1	5
Ethnicity of friends						
Muslim Iranians	73.1	26.9	67	65.6	34.4	64
All others	81.6	18.4	49	68.8	31.2	48
Preferred ethnicity of organizational members						
Muslim Iranians	67.6	32.4	34	NA	NA	—
All others	89.5	10.5	19	NA	NA	—
No preference	76.6	23.4	64	NA	NA	—
Self-identity						
Muslim or Iranian Muslim	70.7	29.3	41	NA	NA	—
Other	79.0	21.8	76	NA	NA	—

** Fisher's exact test significant at .01 level.
NA = not applicable or not available.

461

TABLE 20.5.

Relationship Between Religious Observance in Iran and Religious Observance in the United States, Controlling for Education in Iran and the United States, Year of Arrival, Ethnicity of Friends, and Preferred Ethnicity of Organizational Members, Respondents with Muslim Spouses, Los Angeles, 1987–1988 (percent and N = number)

Respondents with Muslim Spouses

Control Variables	Nonobservant in Iran			Observant in Iran		
	Non-observant in U.S.	Observant in U.S.	N	Observant in U.S.	Non-observant in U.S.	N
Education now						
BA or less	100.0	0	32	51.8	48.2	27**
MA or higher	100.0	0	30	40.0	60.0	25**
Education in Iran						
High school or less	100.0	0	34	52.2	47.8	23**
AA or higher	100.0	0	30	47.4	58.6	29**

Year of Arrival						
Before 1979	100.0	0	28	46.9	53.1	60**
1979 and after	100.0	0	36	47.6	52.4	57**
Ethnicity of friends						
Muslim Iranians	100.0	0	36	58.1	41.9	31**
All others	100.0	0	28	42.1	57.1	21**
Preferred ethnicity of organizational members						
Muslim Iranians	100.0	0	17	64.7	35.3	17**
All others	100.0	0	10	20.0	80.0	9 NS
No preference	100.0	0	38	57.7	42.3	26**

** Relationship between religious observance in Iran and in the United States statistically significant at .01 level within the categories of the control variables (Fisher's Exact test).

NS = not statistically significant at .01 level (Fisher's exact test).

TABLE 20.6.

Muslim Spouses' Relationship Between Religious Observance in Iran and Religious Observance in the United States, Controlling for Education in Iran and in the United States, and Year of Arrival, Muslim Spouses, Los Angeles, 1987–1988 (percent and N = number)

Control Variables	Nonobservant in Iran			Observant in Iran		
	Non-observant in U.S.	Observant in U.S.	N	Non-observant in U.S.	Observant in U.S.	N
Education now						
AA or higher	95.4	4.6	22	36.7	63.3	30**
BA or higher	92.9	7.1	28	45.8	54.2	24**
Education in Iran						
High school or less	97.1	2.9	34	39.5	60.5	43**
AA or higher	88.2	11.8	17	38.5	61.5	13**
Year of Arrival						
Before 1979	85.0	15.0	20	47.1	52.9	34**
1979 and after	100.0	0	34	30.4	69.6	23**
Ethnicity of friends						
Muslim Iranians	96.9	3.1	32	32.3	67.7	31**
All others	90.9	9.1	22	50.0	50.0	26**

** Relationship between religious observance in Iran and in the United States statistically significant at .01 level within the categories of the control variables (Fisher's exact test).

Iran. Because a number of studies of first-generation immigrants assert that religiosity and ethnicity are the hallmark of ethno-religiosity, one would expect a strong positive association between these dimensions among Iranian Muslims. As shown in Table 20.4, there is indeed a positive relationship between religiosity and three indictors of ethnicity (ethnicity of close friends, preferred ethnicity of organizational members, and ethnic identity), but this relationship is very weak and not statistically significant. This finding supports the hypothesis of weak or no association between secularism and ethnicity.

As might be expected, respondents and their Muslim spouses who arrived before the revolution of 1978–1979 are somewhat more religious than those who came after, but this relationship is also not statistically significant. The lack of any relationship between religious observance and education for respondents may be partly due to the fact that most of them were highly educated. Religious observance in Iran is the only variable closely and significantly related to religious observance in the United States. All or almost all of the respondents and their spouses who "never" observed religious practices also "never" observed them in Los Angeles. About half of those who were observant in Iran were also observant in Los Angeles.

To find out if any other variables account for the strong relationship between religious observance in Iran and Los Angeles, we need to control for the effects of ethnicity, education, and year of arrival. With one minor exception,[41] Tables 20.5 and 20.6 show that the statistically significant relationship between religious observance in Iran and the United States is not modified when we introduce the control variables. Because all or almost all respondents who were not observant in Iran were also nonobservant in Los Angeles, we have to examine religious observance in the United States for those respondents who were observant in Iran. For example, 46.7 percent of those who arrived before 1979 were also observant at the time of the survey compared to 52.7 percent of those who arrived after 1979. The slight difference between these two figures suggests that year of arrival does not account for the strong relationship between religiosity in Iran and in Los Angeles. Similarly, small or nonsignificant differences are observed for other control variables in Tables 20.5 and 20.6.

The analysis given in Tables 20.5 and 20.6 is based on three variables: religiosity in Iran, religiosity in the United States, and year of arrival. We need to go beyond this analysis and compare the net effects of all pertinent variables on religious observance at the time of the survey. Because the dependent variable of religious observance has only two categories (observance and nonobservance) a logit analysis was used. The independence variables are religious observance in Iran, highest level of education, year of arrival, ethnicity of close friends, and organizational preference. Multivariate analysis was carried out separately for respondents and their spouses. For both groups, religious observance in Iran is the only variable that had a statistically significant and positive effect on religious observance in the United States.

SUMMARY AND CONCLUSION

The data from the study of Iranian Muslims in Los Angeles indicate that the patterns of ethno-religiosity may be quite complex and may differ among the various spheres of the respondents' interaction with others. At the informal level of friendship or social occasions, about half of the respondents have social ties with Iranian coreligionists, thus maintaining an Iranian Muslim ethnicity.

Iranian Muslim ethnicity is reenforced by business ties among the self-employed who have mostly Iranian Muslim business associates. Unlike other immigrant entrepreneurs, such as Koreans, however, high status Iranian Muslims are much less likely to have coethnic workers. Nearly half of the respondents are self-employed, so it is clear that social and economic ties together tend to strengthen Iranian Muslim ethnicity. The other half are wage and salary earners who have mostly non-Iranian coworkers and supervisors.

The bivariate and multivariate statistical analyses clearly demonstrate that there is no relationship between ethnicity and religious observance among Iranian Muslims in Los Angeles. These are two separate aspects of their lives. The only variable that matters is premigration religious behavior.

The findings of this study are relevant not only for analyses of the religious behavior and ethnicity of Muslim immigrants in the United States, but also for research on other first-generation immigrants. It is clear that any study of religiosity and ethnicity of immigrants has to take into account not only the socioeconomic status of these immigrants, but also religious behavior in the country of origin. Higher status immigrants who were somewhat secular in their country of origin will probably continue to be secular in the United States or any other immigrant-receiving country. The same association could apply for those who were very observant in their country of origin.

What will happen to the religiosity and ethnicity of the second-generation immigrants? Will there be a "twilight" of Iranian Muslim ethnicity? There is no definitive answer to this problem from studies of the fate of ethnicity after the first generation.[42] In the study of Iranians in Los Angeles we asked about the ethnoreligiosity of the respondents' children's close friends as a way of anticipating what might happen to the second generation. As shown in Table 20.3, only 11.0 percent of the children's best friends were Muslim Iranians in contrast to comparable figures of 47.3 percent for the father and 46.9 percent for the mother.[43] This finding suggests that when immigrant parents are not religious, there may be a sharp drop in ethnicity between the first and second generations. In other words, if ethnicity is not reinforced by religiosity in the first generation, the second generation is much more likely to lose its ethnicity. Only the future and further research will tell if this is true.

NOTES

The research reported in this paper was made possible by grant #SES-8512007 from the National Science Foundation. We would like to acknowledge the invaluable assistance of Claudia Der-Martirosian.

1.   *U.S. News and World Report* (October 8, 1990), p. 14 and (August 6, 1990), p. 6.

2.   Sameer Y. Abraham, Nabeel Abraham, and Barbara C. Aswad, "The Southend: An Arab Muslim Working Class Community," in *Arabs in the New World*, ed. Sameer Y. Abraham and Nabeel Abraham Detroit: Wayne State University, 1982), p. 181.

3.   Nimat Hafez Barazangi, "Islamic Education in the United States and Canada: Conception and Practice of the Islamic Belief System," in *The Muslims of America*, ed. Yvonne Y. Haddad (New York: Oxford University Press, 1991), p. 186.

4.   This is implied by the statement that "except for the ethnic groups that are also religious bodies (such as Greeks and Jews), the evidence that religion sustains ethnicity is not convincing" in Richard D.

Alba, *Ethnic Identity: The Transformation of White America* (New Haven, Conn., and London: Yale University Press, 1990), p. 304.

5. Ibid., p. 304.

6. For a comprehensive review of this literature, see Wsevolod Isajiw, "Ethnic Identity Retention," in *Ethnic Identity and Equality: Varieties of Experience in a Canadian City,* ed. Raymond Breton, Wsevolod Isajiw, Warren E. Kalbach, and Jeffrey G. Reitz (Toronto: University of Toronto Press, 1990), pp. 34–49. See also J. Milton Yinger, "Ethnicity," *Annual Review of Sociology* 11 (1985): 151–180; and Andrew M. Greeley, "The Sociology of American Catholics," *Annual Review of Sociology* 5 (1979): 91–111.

7. The three-generations hypothesis has been tested and critically assessed in a number of studies of religio-ethnic groups in the United States, Canada, and Australia. See, for example, Harold J. Abramson, "The Religioethnic Factor and the American Experience: Another Look at the Three-Generation Hypothesis," *Ethnicity* 2 (1975): 163–177; Arnold Dashefsky, "And the Search Goes on: The Meaning of Religio-Ethnic Identity and Identification," *Sociological Analysis* 33 (1972): 239–245; Bernard Lazarewitz and Louis Rowitz, "The Three-Generations Hypothesis," *American Journal of Sociology* 69 (1964): 529–538; Gerhard Lenski, *The Religious Factor: A Sociological Study of Religious Impact upon Politics, Economics and Family Life* (New York: Doubleday and Co., 1961), pp. 16–22; Frank W. Lewins, "Religion and Ethnic Identity," in *Identity and Religion,* ed. Hans Mol (London: Sage Publishers, 1978), pp. 19–38; Hart M. Nelsen and David H. Allen, "Ethnicity, Americanization, and Religious Attendance," *American Journal of Sociology* 79 (1974): 906–922; Nicholas J. Russo, "Three Generations of Italians in New York City: Their Religious Acculturation," *International Migration Review* 3 (1969): 3–17; A. Scourby, "Three Generations of Greek Americans: A Study in Ethnicity," *International Migration Review* 14 (1980): 43–52; Stephen Sharot, "The Three-Generations Thesis and American Jews," *British Journal of Sociology* 24 (1973): 151–164; John Simpson, "Ethnic Groups and Church Attendance in the United States and Canada," in *Ethnicity,* ed. Andrew M. Greeley and Gregory Baum (New York: Seabury Press, 1977), p. 8.

Isajiw ("Ethnic Identity retention," pp. 49–91) has presented the most elaborate test of this hypothesis by using many indicators of ethnicity for German, Italian, Jewish, and Ukrainian minorities and the English majority in Canada. Unfortunately, religious observance or behavior is not included in his analysis. Several sociologists have challenged the theory of the revival of ethnicity in the third generation. They either argue that, for some European religio-ethnic groups, ethnicity is maintained throughout the three generations, or that there is a continuous loss of ethnicity over time or between generations particularly for white ethnics of European ancestry. For discussions of this point see, for example, Alba, *Ethnic Identity;* Stanley Lieberson and Mary C. Waters, *From Many Strands: Ethnic and Racial Groups in Contemporary America* (New York: Russell Sage Foundation, 1988); and Mary C. Waters, *Ethnic Options: Choosing Identities in America* (Berkeley and Los Angeles: University of California Press, 1990).

8. Marcus Lee Hansen, *The Problem of the Third Generation Immigrant* (Rock Island, Ill.: Augustana Historical Society, 1938), p. 9.

9. Will Herberg, *Protestant-Catholic-Jew: An Essay in American Religious Sociology* (Garden City, N.Y.: Doubleday and Company, 1955), Herberg argues that "the outstanding feature of the religious situation in America today is the pervasiveness of religious self-identification along the tripartite scheme of Protestant, Catholic, Jew" (p. 272). What makes this possible is the third generation's desire to recover its heritage that consists of the grandfathers' religion rather than the grandfathers' foreign language and culture.

10. Ibid., pp. 23–24.

11. Andrew M. Greeley, *The Denominational Society: A Sociological Approach to Religion in America* (Glenview, Ill.: Scott, Foresman, 1972).

12. These studies include: Abraham, Abraham, and Aswad, "The Southend"; Barbara C. Aswad, "The Southeast Dearborn Arab Community Struggles for Survival Against Urban 'Renewal'," in *Arab Speaking Communities in American Cities,* ed. Barbara C. Aswad (Staten Island, N.Y.: Center for Migration Studies, 1974), pp. 53–84; Yvonne Yazback Haddad and Adair T. Lummis, *Islamic Values in the United States: A Comparative Study* (New York and Oxford: Oxford University Press, 1987); Yvonne Yazbeck Haddad, ed. *The Muslims of America* (New York and Oxford: Oxford University Press, 1991); Abdo El Kholy, *The Arab Moslems in the United States: Religion and Assimilation* (New Haven, Conn.: College and University Press, 1966); Hasan A. Qader Yahya, "Factors Influencing the Satisfaction of Muslim Organizational Members in a University Town in the United States (Lansing, Michigan)," *Journal Institute of Muslim Minority Affairs* 9 (1988): 280–295; and Laurel D. Wiggle, "An Arab Muslim Community in Michigan" in *Arab Speaking Communities,* pp. 155–168. There are also a few studies of the impact of religiosity on ethnicity or assimilation among Arab Christians. See Philip Kayal, "Religion and Assimilation: Catholic 'Syrians' in America," *International Migration Review* 7 (1973): 409–426; Mary Sengstock, *Chaldean Americans: Changing Conceptions of Ethnic Identity* (Staten Island, N.Y.: Center for Migration Studies, 1982).

13. El Kholy's analysis is based on his 1959 survey of 211 Muslims

in Toledo, Ohio, and 211 Muslims in Detroit, Michigan. See El Kholy, *The Arab Moslems,* pp. 16 and 28. El Kholy devised the following four measures of religiosity: (1) religious beliefs, (2) norms of religious observance or behavior, (3) religious knowledge, and (4) religious observance.

14.   Thus, 59 percent of first-generation respondents in both cities "prayed at least once a week" and 49 percent were "fasting at least seven days during Ramadan." Many more, however, abstained from eating pork and drinking alcoholic beverages (El Kholy, ibid., p. 117).

15.   See Abraham, Abraham, and Aswad, "Southend."

16.   See Arif M. Ghayur, "Muslims in the United States: Settlers and Visitors," *The Annals* 454 (1981): 150–163.

17.   Immigrants make up two-thirds of their sample of 347 Muslims, and the remaining one-third are second-, third-, or fourth-generation Muslims. Among immigrants, 33 percent are from Syria or Lebanon, 29 percent from India or Pakistan, and the remaining 38 percent from other Muslim countries (Haddad and Lummis, *Islamic Values,* pp. 15 and 89).

18.   According to Haddad and Lummis, 24 percent of respondents rarely or never observed the following religious practices: fasting at Ramadan, reading the Qur'an, praying five times a day, attending the Friday prayer at a mosque or Islamic center, and inviting a Muslim to pray (ibid., p. 167). There are, however, substantial differences in religious observance among immigrants from Pakistan, Lebanon, and otehr Muslim countries (pp. 29 and 169).

19.   See, for example, Sharot, "The Three-Generation Thesis," pp. 151–164.

20.   Won Moo Hurh and Kwang Chung Kim, "Religious Participation of Korean Immigrants in the United States," *Journal for the Scientific Study of Religion* 29 (1990): 19–34.

21.   Mounir Gharbi, "L'immigration marocaine au Canada: juifs et musulmans," in *Le facteur religieux en Amerique du Nord,* ed. Jean Beranger and Pierre Guillaume (Talence, France: Maison des Sciences de l'Homme d'Aquitaine, 1982), p. 215.

22.   The diversity of the Muslim population of Los Angeles is described in a *Los Angeles Times* article, "L.A. Muslims Feel Push, Pull of Divided Loyalty" (July 3, 1985), p. V-1). This article indicates that the Muslim Shi'a are not only from Iran but also from Iraq, Lebanon, and Pakistan.

23.   See Mehdi Bozorgmehr, "Internal Ethnicity: Armenian, Bahai, Jewish, and Muslim Iranians in Los Angeles." Ph.D. diss. University of California, Los Angeles, 1991). Internal ethnicity refers to the presence of ethno-religious subgroups within an immigrant population. For example, immigrants from Iran to North America include Armenians, Baha'is,

Jews, and Muslims and immigrants from Egypt include Copts and Muslims. When studying immigrant populations, such as Iranians and Egyptians, characterized by internal ethnicity based on religion, it is assumed that religion is the most salient component of each subgroup's ethnicity.

24. For more details on the survey design, see Mehdi Bozorgmehr and Georges Sabagh, "Survey Research Among Middle Eastern Immigrant Groups in the United States: Iranians in Los Angeles," *Middle East Studies Association Bulletin* 23 (1989): 23–34.

25. Unlike Iranian Armenians, Baha'is, and Jews, intermarriage among Iranian Muslims was more common. This reflects the fact that a larger proportion of Muslim Iranians than the other three subgroups married in the United States. Despite a relatively more open outlook to marrying non-coreligionist Iranians, Muslim Iranians are at a disadvantage to marry other Iranians because of the minorities' preference to marry coreligionists.

26. It appears that the same secularism characterizes Muslim Iranians in other communities in the United States. Thus, according to Fischer and Abedi "a large proportion of Iranians in Houston are not particularly religious" (Michael M. Fischer and Mehdi Abedi, *Debating Muslims* [Madison: University of Wisconsin Press, 1990], p. 271). But, as suggested by Fischer and Abedi, even "secularized Muslims . . . have a need for Islamic ritual at crisis points" (p. 268).

27. The question of religiosity in the United States was asked *after* the question on religiosity in Iran. Consequently, the decline in religiosity between Iran and the United States could not be attributed to a survey effect.

28. It is interesting to note that the opposite is true for Iranian Jews, 78 percent of whom identified themselves as Jewish Iranian.

29. Mehrdad Amanat, "Prelude to Migration: Nationalism, Social Change, and Revolution in Contemporary Iran," in Ron Kelley and Jonathan Friedlander, eds., "Irangeles: Iranian Life and Culture in Los Angeles" (unpublished manuscript, 1991).

30. Nikki Keddie, *Roots of Revolution: An Interpretative History of Modern Iran* (New Haven, Conn.: Yale University Press, 1981).

31. The comparison with the 1976 census overestimates the educational and occupational achievement of men in urban Iran. Even this overestimate is much lower than the achievement of the respondents' fathers.

32. Since the mean age of respondents was 43 in 1987–1988, the occupations of their fathers refer to the economic conditions prevailing in Iran in the 1950s and the 1960s, when respondents were on average 16 years old. Even if we use the most recent Iranian census figure of 10 percent for men in managerial, executive, and professional occupations in

urban areas in 1976, this is much lower than the comparable 38.7 percent for respondents' fathers in the same occupations.

33.   The high status of Iranians in the United States is documented by Mehdi Bozorgmehr and Georges Sabagh, "High Status Immigrants: A Statistical Profile of Iranians in the United States," *Iranian Studies* 21 (1988): 5–36.

34.   For a discussion of these studies, see Georges Sabagh and Mehdi Bozorgmehr, "Are the Characteristics of Exiles Different from Immigrants? The Case of Iranians in Los Angeles," *Sociology and Social Research* 71 (1987): 77–84.

35.   Some of this self-employment reflects a tradition of entrepreneurship. In Iran, self-employment was reported by one-third of respondents, by about half of their fathers, and by nearly one-third (28 percent) of urban men in the 1976 census. It was not uncommon for salaried workers to be self-employed in a second job.

36.   See Ivan Light and Edna Bonacich, *Immigrant Entrepreneurs: Koreans in Los Angeles 1965–1982* (Berkeley: University of California Press, 1988); and Pyong Gap Min, "Some Positive Functions of Ethnic Business for an Immigrant Community: Koreans in Los Angeles" (Final Report Submitted to the National Science Foundation, 1989).

37.   Mehdi Bozorgmehr and Georges Sabagh, "Iranian Exiles and Immigrants in Los Angeles," in Asghar Fathi, ed., *Iranian Refugees and Exiles Since Khomeini* (Costa Mesa, Calif.: Mazda Publishers, 1991), pp. 121–144.

38.   The combinations given in Table 20.3 are as follows: Iranian Muslims and other Iranians (17 percent); Iranian Muslims, other Iranians, and Americans (13 percent); and Iranian Muslims and Americans (6 percent). Over 80 percent of respondents have as their best friends Iranian Muslims only or Iranian Muslims in combination with other groups.

39.   Survey data on language use indicate that, although the respondents are oriented toward Iranian ethnicity in their informal social ties, they are not so oriented in their relationships with coworkers or business partners. In speaking to their close friends, 81.3 percent use mostly Persian, but in their interaction with coworkers and business partners 67.8 percent speak mostly English. It may be noted that 90 percent of respondents stated that they know English well or very well.

40.   Thus, 57 percent of salaried respondents work in a place where at least 90 percent of workers are non-Iranians, 87 percent have supervisors who are all non-Iranians, and 89 percent work in enterprises owned by non-Iranians.

41.   The exception pertains to the nonsignificant relationship between religiosity in Iran and in the United States for the "all others"

category of the "preferred ethnicity of organizational members" control variable (Table 20.5). The sample size is too small, however, to conclude that there is an interaction between this control variable and religiosity in Iran in their effects on religiosity in the United States.

42.   Reference to some of these studies are given in note 8. On the basis of a study of American Catholics of European ancestry, Alba has prophesied the "twilight of ethnicity," leaving only what Gans has called symbolic ethnicity. See Richard D. Alba, "The Twilight of Ethnicity Among American Catholics of European Descent," *The Annals* 454 (1981); and Richard D. Alba, "The Twilight of Ethnicity Among Americans of European Ancestry: The Case of Italians," in Richard D. Alba, ed. *Ethnicity and Race in the U.S.A.* (Boston: Routledge and Kegan Paul, 1985), pp. 134–157. El Kholy in *Arab Muslims* reports a sharp increase in assimilation and a marked decrease in religiosity between the first and second generations.

43.   It should be noted that the information for children was provided by the respondent.

CHAPTER 21

Masjid ul-Mutkabir: The Portrait of an African American Orthodox Muslim Community

Christine Kolars

Dutchess County is located in the Hudson River Valley of New York state. It is home to two Muslim communities, one made up of a primarily immigrant population and the other based in the African American community. There are two separate Muslim masjids, the Mid-Hudson Islamic Association Masjid located in Wappinger Falls, which serves the immigrant Muslim community, and Masjid ul-Mutkabir in the city of Poughkeepsie,[1] which belongs to the African American community. Although the communities serve a population sharing the same geographical locale, they have distinct histories and maintain distinctly separate identities.[2]

THE MID-HUDSON ISLAMIC ASSOCIATION

The Mid-Hudson Islamic Association community is made up mainly of Indian, Pakistani, and Bangladeshi immigrants. The Imam of the Masjid is Indian, a recent immigrant to the Hudson Valley. He oversees the running of the masjid, which opened in its present location in 1990. The community underwrote the construction of the building, located in the town of Wappinger Falls, on several acres on a hill above Route 9, one of the major north-south thoroughfares in the Hudson Valley. Attendance at Friday Juma'a services is estimated by the Imam at an average of 150 people, although during Ramadan the masjid has had as many as

800 worshipers attending prayer services. Although the masjid caters to several groups of immigrants from all over the Muslim world, the Imam states, "We are each brothers, Pakistanis, Indians, Bangledeshis, Egyptians. No matter where you are from, we are all brothers, man and woman, we are not divided. It is bad to be divided."[3] The Imam said that there are no African Americans in his congregation, and he asserted that he was aware of the presence of Masjid ul-Mutkabir in Poughkeepsie.

The primary function of the Mid-Hudson Islamic Association is religious in nature, providing religious services throughout the year, as well as serving as a meeting place for the Muslims of the community. It fills another important role by giving support to families newly arrived in the United States or in the Hudson Valley. Because the majority of its membership has undergone similar experiences in adjusting to life in the United States, members have a common point of reference beyond their cultural and language ties. The masjid does not provide services available in other Muslim communities, such as a school for the children. However, when the issue of a Muslim school is suggested to the Imam, he replies hopefully, "En sha Allah, one day we will be able to build a school for the children on some of the acres we own around the masjid."

The apparent stability of the Mid-Hudson Islamic Association is demonstrated by its consistently large congregation, and it appears to have gained a growing sense of acceptance in the greater Hudson Valley ecumenical community as well. Gail Berger, executive director of the Dutchess County Interfaith Council, cites increasing interaction between the Islamic Association Muslims and other Poughkeepsie area religious groups.[4] Although they are not official members of the council, the interfaith directory lists several Muslim groups, and in the past Muslims have attended dialogue groups conducted by the council. In 1991, the Interfaith Council sponsored a tour of religious sites of worship for members of the local religious community. Approximately fifty people spent the day touring four sites, one of which was the Islamic Association Masjid. The group was escorted around the grounds and the building and refreshments were provided by the women of the masjid. Berger suggests that as a result of the tour there is greater empathy toward the Muslim community and that participation by non-Muslims in Muslim-sponsored activities will increase.

The Interfaith Council is hoping to include members of the

Muslim community in more of its activities and discussion groups. It is currently planning to hold a series of talks dealing with the relationships between Christianity, Judaism, and Islam in celebration of the council's twentieth anniversary. Although the council's interaction to this point has been primarily with the Islamic Association community, Berger reports that they hope to increase interaction between her group and the members of Masjid ul-Mutkabir, the African American Muslim group in Poughkeepsie. The council currently has a listing for the masjid, but they have had no real interaction with its members.

INTERMASJID RELATIONS

The fact that levels of participation differ between the respective Muslim communities and the Interfaith Council is indicative of their unique identities. Although the two communities share the same faith, a similar geographic setting, and have developed simultaneously over the last two decades, they occupy disparate spheres of mid-Hudson Valley society. Each group is internally focused, the African American Muslims of Masjid ul-Mutkabir interacting mainly with other members of the African-American community (both Muslims and non-Muslims), and the immigrant groups of the Islamic Association interacting mainly with each other.

The children may provide a way to project the respective futures of the communities. The children of Islamic Association families attend public school and are being raised as countless other first-generation children have been raised in the United States, as American children with strong home-based ethnic traditions. Seventeen-year-old Rashed Abdullah is the son of a couple who immigrated to the United States from Bangladesh. He has attended public school since kindergarten and says, "You don't have to pound a child with religions. I'm a Muslim, but I've gotten that at home. It's been good to go to the public schools."[5] Rashed appears to be typical of the future of immigrant-based Muslim communities such as the Islamic Association, well versed in his parent's traditional culture and religion, but also identifying strongly as an American.

In contrast, the children of Masjid ul-Mutkabir come from an American cultural tradition but are members of an undeniably marginalized portion of American society. Their parents are usually the first generation of Muslims in their families, instead of being the first generation of Americans. On the whole they have been raised according to a strict Muslim tradition, attending Juma'a services and Muslim schools, and have had this aspect of their identities particularly emphasized since infancy. The children of both Muslim communities have had to learn to adjust and to balance the two very prominent characteristics of their lives, Islam and American identity. Perhaps as a result of these two elements playing such crucial roles in the lives of both sets of children, the two communities will be able to enjoy more commonalities in the future and expand their respective bases of operation to include one another more fully.

There is a certain amount of interaction between the groups. Although the vast majority of the Muslims who worship at Masjid ul-Mutkabir are African American, a number of immigrant Muslims also attend Friday afternoon services. Any given Masjid ul-Mutkabir service might have several Pakistani men in attendance, and occasional members of the Mid-Hudson Islamic Association and other neighboring masjids. The communities cooperate on various projects and it is not unusual for a neighboring Muslim community to ask the members of Masjid ul-Mutkabir for help in locally based projects, such as the painting and renovation of local mosques and activity centers. When the new Islamic Association mosque was in its final stages of completion, for instance, a request was announced during Juma'a services at Masjid ul-Mutkabir for volunteers to go to the new mosque during the weekend to help finish painting the walls of the building. Any request is reciprocal in nature, and it is not unusual for leading members of the immigrant Muslim communities to attend social functions sponsored by the African American Muslim community.

It is important to note here that although there is some cooperation between the groups, it is not highly developed and there is no great overlap between membership or participation in the various communities. Significant barriers stand in the way of interaction, such as language skills and extremely different cultural traditions. However, differences between the Masjid ul-Mutkabir community and the surrounding immigrant communities are not only cultural in nature, there is also a wide disparity in the economic circumstances of the members of the two communities, which undoubtedly exacerbates the logistical distance between them.

Many of the members of the Islamic Association masjid are professionals and own houses in the middle-class suburbs surrounding Poughkeepsie. Their relative financial prosperity is reflected in the community's ability to buy land in the area and construct the new masjid building. In contrast, the members of Masjid ul-Mutkabir are less economically prosperous, the majority living in subsidized housing projects in downtown Poughkeepsie. The masjid operates on a shoestring budget, and has no permanent structure in which to base its operations. During the 1980s the masjid was located in a dilapidated rented building in downtown Poughkeepsie and in 1990 moved to its present site in another rented property on the Mall, a run-down pedestrian shopping area in downtown Poughkeepsie developed in an urban renewal project during the 1960s. The masjid operates on a "bootstrap" philosophy, one originally promoted in the Nation of Islam. Although the community does accept help from outside sources, such as volunteers in the school it runs, the vast majority of its resources come from members of the local community itself and their own fundraising efforts.

An appraisal of both the Mid-Hudson Islamic Association and the Masjid ul-Mutkabir communities would be undeniably interesting and important. However, this chapter will focus on the African American orthodox Muslim community of Masjid ul-Mutkabir. An understanding of this orthodox Muslim group is critical to the completion of the picture of Muslims in the United States, as this masjid is a member of the first truly indigenous American Muslim community, the African American orthodox Muslim community that evolved out of the Nation of Islam in the 1970s.

Masjid ul-Mutkabir was founded in Poughkeepsie, New York, in 1975–1976. Originally it was made up of members of the former Nation of Islam, a black nationalist movement based loosely on Muslim principles. The appearance of Masjid ul-Mutkabir marked a turning point in the evolution of the Poughkeepsie branch of the Nation of Islam; from a black nationalist political movement employing a proto-Islamic framework emphasizing racial separation it turned into a strictly religious community working toward the empowerment of the African American community under the auspices of Sunni Islam. Masjid ul-Mutkabir underwent this transition because of major structural and ideological changes occurring in the upper levels of the NOI. Although the Masjid ul-Mutkabir community now practices a standard Sunni version of Islam, its roots are undeniably in the Nation of Islam, and certain characteristics of the community can be traced to its early history. It is important therefore, to examine briefly the history of the Nation of Islam and its transition to orthodox Islam.

THE NATION OF ISLAM

The Lost-Found Nation of Islam, founded by Master Wali Farrad in 1930, was the first major group indigenous to the United States. Its doctrine incorporated elements of Islam, Christianity, and black nationalism in a manner that would prove remarkably successful in ensuring the future of the movement and would pave the way for the subsequent acceptance of orthodox Islam by thousands of African Americans. Elijah Muhammed, one of Farrad's original followers, became leader of the organization when Farrad disappeared in 1934. He declared Farrad as Allah (God) and himself as Allah's prophet on earth, and he shortened the name of the group to the Nation of Islam.

Elijah Muhammed instituted a doctrine of strict discipline and self-sufficiency as well as religious values upon his followers in an effort to create a cohesive and united community. He insisted that the people of the Nation of Islam remain within strict moral boundaries and work to further the causes of the movement. He also promoted a belief in black power and black rights. The movement embodied the ideas of nationalism and separatism by calling for the unity of African Americans as well as demanding separate lands for them. Malcolm X was an important member of the NOI until he converted to orthodox Islam, making the hajj to Mecca in 1964 and changing his name to el-Hajj Malik el-Shabazz in recognition of his orthodox identity. Malcolm Shabazz, as he came to be known, continued to be an adamant supporter of black nationalism, although he tempered his views to accord with those of orthodox Islam, which espouses racial equality. Malcolm Shabazz was assassinated in 1964, but the religious path he had chosen was not lost on Elijah Muhammed's son Warith Deen, who took over the leadership of the NOI after Elijah's death in 1975.

Beginning in 1976, Warith Deen Muhammed instituted some of the most radical changes the group had seen in its relatively short history. He changed its name from the Nation of Islam first to the World Community of al-Islam in the West and then four years later to the American Muslim Mission. This change was important to the message the newly orthodox movement was trying to convey. The use of the term *nation* had been indicative of the separatist nationalist goals adopted by the group; when Warith Deen Muhammed changed the name to incorporate the term *mission*, it reflected the more inclusionary orientation of the orthodox movement as well as the intent that the group would seek out and accept converts from all parts of American society. The group's main focus shifted from black nationalism to orthodox Muslim doctrine, and subsequently the dogma shifted away from ideas of racial separation promoted by Elijah Muhammed. The de-emphasis of the issue of race brought the new group closer to the beliefs of orthodox Islam, which calls for religion to be void of racism and discrimination.

In 1986 Warith Deen Muhammed resigned as the head of the American Muslim Mission and officially disbanded the organization. His motivation behind this move was to further unify the African American Muslim community with the international Muslim community. According to Warith Deen Muhammed the departmentalized structure of the group was not in accordance with the Muslim concept of *Umma,* which emphasizes the notion of a universal Muslim community. The dissolution of the American Muslim Mission has to some extent produced the effects initially hoped for by Warith Deen Muhammed. Imam Shamsideen of Masjid ul-Mutkabir in Poughkeepsie states, "So what this did, by him resigning and disbanding the American Muslim Mission, was to ease tensions all around. It went from being a divided community to being a bigger and more effective international community. That's why Muslims can come here [Masjid ul-Mutkabir] from wherever they happen to be from and it's no big deal."[6] In distinction to the focus on African American solidarity of the 1970s the community now emphasizes Muslim solidarity.

The Poughkeepsie branch of the NOI had been headed by Minister Mark X, and it was he who led the group through the transition from proto-Islam to Islam, after 1976 adopting the name Subir al-Hajji. In 1979 Marshall Shamsideen joined the Masjid and began to take a powerful role in the leadership of the community. Currently he leads the Muslim community, working as the Imam of the masjid and as the primary teacher of the Sister Clara Muhammed School, which is run under the auspices of the masjid.

MASJID UL-MUTKABIR

Masjid ul-Mutkabir is headquartered in a rented building in downtown Poughkeepsie. Membership is small, with twenty to thirty families who are active in the community on a regular basis. These families are African American, and a number of the older members were members of the NOI until 1975 when they espoused orthodoxy as a result of the transition. It is interesting to note that the use of the term older can be misleading, because the movement from Nation of Islam ideology to orthodoxy has been so recent, the oldest members of this community in their forties. Adult members of the community for the most part are married and have children, and family life is strongly emphasized by the society and its Imam. Abstinence from premarital sex, alcohol, and drugs are also crucial elements in the doctrine of the community, and these topics are addressed on a regular basis in the *khutba* (sermon) at Juma'a (Friday) worship services. Because the adult members of the community have converted from Christianity to Islam, they have had to adopt an Arabic first name or choose to retain their name from before the conversion, although many combine the two. The community's children all have Arabic first names, such as Nitara, Fatima, and Kasib.

Islam plays an integral role in the lives of the members of Masjid ul-Mutkabir. In contrast to Muslims who were born into the religion in cultures where it predominates, African American Muslims for the most part have had to make the choice to reject their religion of birth and to become Muslims because of specific characteristics found in Islam that they feel are essential to their lives. Imam Shamsideen encourages members to perform the five daily prayers, but is adamant in his belief that the sincere piety of the believer is the crucial element to his or her success as a Muslim. "In Islam," he states, "a person is just as worthy if he or she says only one Sura devoutly and sincerely as if he or she recites a third of the Qur'an without paying attention to its message. The main point is that you believe in your heart of hearts that Allah is the one and only Creator."[7]

Children are also taught to respect their elders and to always be polite. For instance, on my first visit to the Masjid, I was greeted warmly by Imam Shamsideen and introduced to the children, who were taking their morning break from class before the beginning of Juma'a services. When one small boy failed to greet me in the manner which Imam Shamsideen deemed proper, he gently suggested to the boy that for him to be a gentleman he would have to do a better job in greeting me. After several attempts, the child satisfied the Imam. The episode demonstrated the children's sense of respect for their elders and the positive manner in which the Imam's criticism was delivered. It also exemplified one of the basic rules at Masjid ul-Mutkabir: always treat others with respect no matter how they treat you.

Although some African American Muslim groups hold their primary meeting on Sunday, the Poughkeepsie community does not (although they often hold social activities on that day). The principal meeting conducted at the masjid takes place on Friday afternoons, the traditional day of prayer for Muslims all over the world. The prayer service typically begins at 1 P.M. and lasts about an hour. There are usually twenty to thirty people at worship services, although this number varies greatly from week to week. The majority of worshipers are men, and the operation of the school is suspended during this time so that the children can also participate in the worship service. Very few women attend services, the primary purpose for their presence being the supervision of the children during prayers; the older students are also responsible for the discipline of the younger ones. The men take their place in the front of the room in neat rows facing the Imam. The children are then seated behind the men, with the women next to the children. The service begins with the worshipers listening attentively to several prayers being said by the Imam in Arabic, and then the congregation relaxes to listen to the *khutba* delivered by the Imam or whichever male member of the community the Imam has chosen to perform this service. The *khutba* usually lasts twenty minutes and is topical in nature, dealing with the religious season, the duties of followers, or like issues. The ritual Friday prayers are performed following the *khutba*.

At the end of the service the women collect their small children and leave, the children resume their academic activities, and the men gather in a circle on the floor in the middle of the room to discuss Muslim community business. It is at this time that requests for assistance are made by members of the masjid or by visiting Muslims. Upcoming community activities are also discussed and current events in the local community are reviewed. Following the men's meeting, members of the community are invited to remain at the masjid and receive instruction in the Arabic language from Imam Shamsideen, along with the school children. Anyone in the community is welcome to attend the lessons, and participation varies from week to week. During the Juma'a services there is always a lesson from the Qur'an read in Arabic by Imam Shamsideen, although very few of the members of the community actually speak or understand Arabic. The Arabic lessons conducted by the Imam are an effort to increase participation in the masjid and to help worshipers understand the Qur'an in its original form. The few Arab immigrant Muslims who attend services obviously do understand, and they often participate directly in this portion of the service by reading or translating the verses.

THE ROLE OF ISLAM IN PERSONAL IDENTITY

The Imam and other community members point to Islam as a key element in determining the manner in which they conduct their lives. Sister Lisa, a young woman who converted to Islam in 1987 after marrying a Muslim, states, "I'm happy being a Muslim. It's given me an answer to my questions. Now I have a reason for doing things in a certain way."[8] Lisa regularly supervises the children of the community during Juma'a services, although she avoids taking a disciplinary role. One Friday she quietly tells a small girl not to pull her skirt up above her knees, reminding her that "you know how to act when you wear a skirt; you shouldn't let your skirt go so high."[9] Sister Lisa's role minding the children during Juma'a services is typical of the responsibilities assigned to women at the masjid. Even though few women attend Juma'a services, they are encouraged to participate in community-based activities such as fund-raising dinners, lectures on religion given by visiting Muslims, and social get-togethers such as dances held for the community's members.

The interpretation of Islam adopted by the Masjid ul-Mutkabir community has a great effect on male-female relations within the group. Although the doctrine encourages women to devote themselves to the raising of their children, it also supports their education and stresses their participation as often as possible in community activities. Mohammed Rashid, the parent of one of the children attending the Muslim school asserts, "The Qur'an says that we must educate women. That's the only way we can have a strong community. You see, our daughters are being taught here in the [Sister Clara Muhammad] School; they even want to go to college."[10]

Although this mixture of encouragement to be both mother and community activist may seem contradictory, the movement interprets these as two dimensions of the woman's primary role as a teacher of children. This role is considered intrinsic to the community's existence and is viewed as perhaps the most important task in the structure of the African American Muslim community as it is in immigrant-based communities. Mrs. Rashida Abdullah of the Mid-Hudson Islamic Association states, "I'm building the biggest thing in the world. If I can make my children good all around . . . then I'm helping the world, not just myself."[11] Mrs. Abdullah also sees no apparent conflict between her role as a wife and mother and that of a woman living in the United States of the 1990s. "I don't go out and work . . . staying in is alright with me. As a Muslim woman, if you can find it at home, find it at home. . . . It's okay for women to work outside the home if you can maintain everything, but if you have to do it, don't let one side go down the drain in order to fix the other one."[12] When queried regarding who makes decisions in his own family, Imam Shamsideen echoes Mrs. Abdullah's sentiments. "I'm the head of the family. My wife takes care of our children. That's her duty. But if a decision needs to be made, I consult my wife. We are together, we can't make decisions without talking to the other person."[13]

The identity and role of women in the African American and immigrant Muslim communities of Dutchess County is undeniably different from the image of the "liberated" American woman of the 1970s and 1980s. However, the group's emphasis on women's education and their participation in community activities indicates the primacy of the concern the community shows for the well-being of its female members. Mrs. Abdullah decisively sums up her position within the Muslim community. "Being a Muslim woman, I feel I am very protected by my religion. It stops me from doing lots of things. I can't do this because of my religion, and I can't do that because of my religion. I do not cover my head and I do not cover my whole body, but I definitely have covered my mind so that nothing can touch me in this world; I am totally converted. . . . I am automatically protected. . . . I feel very strong, I feel very good about it."[14]

The members of Masjid ul-Mutkabir have made a sincere effort to construct their own new Muslim identity, rejecting their Christian origins. Although they maintain contact with the African American community through their extended families, their main organized contact is through other African American masjids. An interesting dialectic exists in the relationship of community members with non-Muslims. Although the Muslims of Masjid ul-Mutkabir are devoutly religious and claim to have completely rejected their Christian upbringing, they maintain contact with their non-Muslim family members despite religious differences. A frequent topic of Friday *khutba* is the rejection of Christian beliefs, and the resistance of American Christian culture. At Christmas time the Imam concentrates his message on the continuation and support of Muslim identity; he states that he recognizes it can be difficult to resist singing the Christmas carols the majority of African American Muslims were raised with, but emphasizes that this rejection is crucial to the true Muslim identity. Another frequent topic of the *khutbas* is the Christian concept of the Trinity and how illogical this notion is. Imam Shamsideen stresses that if there is to be only one true God, then it is impossible to reconcile the Trinity with this idea. He also questions the Christian belief that Jesus Christ was the son of God. He reminds those in attendance that Islam recognizes Jesus as a prophet in a long line of prophets, but rejects once again the idea that Christ could be of divine origin.

As this documentation suggests, perhaps the most consistent and dominant message of the Friday *khutbas* is the importance of maintaining a strong Muslim identity. The proximity of the masjid to New York City, which has a large African American population, means that the Poughkeepsie Muslims have a wider base of African American Muslim support than adherents in many other regions of the country. On a trip to New York in December 1991, for example, Warith Deen Muhammed visited the Hudson Valley and addressed an audience of some 3,000 Muslims in the Poughkeepsie, New York, Civic Center, the majority of whom traveled from around the tristate area to attend.[15] Although he resigned as the leader of the American Muslim Mission, he continues to play a highly instrumental role in the African American Muslim community. He acts as its main advisor and symbolic, if not official leader. His appearance in Poughkeepsie was indicative of the powerful leadership role he continues to play, and his presence at community functions elicits strong response from followers. The majority of Muslims present at the Civic Center were from the African American Muslim community, although some immigrant Muslims were in attendance.

Imam Shamsideen is the primary leader of the Masjid ul-Mutkabir community, organizing social activities, teaching and administering the school, and overseeing all the forms of religious worship that take place at the masjid. Shamsideen holds the community together and ensures its effectiveness as a forum for all types of social action. He also works full time as a mental health counselor in the Poughkeepsie area in addition to his duties at the masjid.

An extremely modest man, Shamsideen ascribes his success to the strength of his faith. When questioned about his leadership role, he responds that it is a role he has taken on more as a moral obligation than a social honor. He believes that one should not seek out leadership positions but rather should accept them dutifully if nominated and appointed to such positions; by way of example he cites the reluctance of the Prophet Muhammed to begin preaching the message of Allah.

Imam Shamsideen plays a key part in the lives of the members of the community, in particular influencing the children who attend the Sister Clara Muhammed School run by the masjid. He acts as a role model in terms of both social and religious behavior and is always prepared to provide an explanation for why a child is obliged to carry out a chore. He believes his role is to listen and respond to the children's questions, and he is committed to their development as caring and thinking adults. The school is perhaps the most concrete method the Masjid ul-Mutkabir community has to ensure its long-term survival and expansion.

THE SISTER CLARA MUHAMMED SCHOOL

The Sister Clara Muhammed School in Poughkeepsie was founded in 1987 by Imam Shamsideen and the parents of the Masjid ul-

Mutkabir community. It is run as an uncertified home-study program and comes under the jurisdiction of the Poughkeepsie school district and is subject to review by its board.[16] The school is designed to serve the children of the Poughkeepsie Muslim community, but its primary efforts are directed toward African American children. The vast majority of the students are Muslim, although non-Muslim children have been enrolled by their parents because of the strict discipline and solid set of values promoted in the school. Imam Shamsideen states, "[In public school] there's more being learned than what's written on the board; whoever is putting it on the board sends off a message to you, and if he doesn't look like you, it sends a message to you. . . . This is one of the things we do in school studies: 'Where were *we*?' We look at the contributions of African Americans in every part of American life."[17]

The underlying premise of the importance of African American education comes out of a long tradition of emphasis on education in the black Muslim community. This concept was originally crystallized in the form of the Universities of Islam run by the Nation of Islam. The first University of Islam was founded in the 1930s by the founder of the Nation of Islam, Wali Farrad. The original university was in reality an elementary and secondary school designed to teach the children of the NOI in an effort to achieve a higher standard of living for the members and a greater effectiveness on the part of the movement. Elijah Muhammed expanded the role of the University of Islam, and by 1972 fourteen universities were in operation with a standard curriculum consisting of science, reading, mathematics, history, art, and Arabic.[18] (After Elijah Muhammed's death, Warith Deen Muhammed renamed the schools after his mother, Sister Clara Muhammed, who had taken a great interest in education during her lifetime.) Not only did these schools teach the standard American curriculum, but they played a key role in the black power movement, emphasizing through their curriculum the heritage and history of people of African descent in the United States. This helped create an institutional basis for the emphasis on self-awareness and self-help by the Nation of Islam, one that continues to be dominant in the orthodox African American Muslim community.

The founding of the Sister Clara Muhammed School in Poughkeepsie and its subsequent popularity serve as proof of the continuing perceived need for special interest schools within the African

American community. Imam Shamsideen states, "The main reason for having the kids out of public school . . . is because in public school they're not teaching in the name of God. . . . Education and all we do are to support our faith, that Allah is God, and that Muhammed is his messenger."[19]

The Sister Clara Muhammed School is officially classified as a home-study program, although it does not function precisely in the manner this rubric implies. The enrollment figures for the school vary from year to year, averaging approximately fifteen students, ranging from 3 to 16 years of age. All the students are African American including one non-Muslim child who was enrolled during the 1989–90 school year. Many are related to one another, either as siblings or cousins. In an era of increased disintegration of family networks, this community is thriving by reinforcing the traditional Muslim emphasis on the importance of solid extended family structures.

The school's operation depends on the good will and volunteer services of parents and community members who act as teachers and chaperones for the children. A Muslim woman in the nearby town of Hyde Park sews the green uniforms that the children are required to wear to school. The text books are borrowed from the Poughkeepsie school system. Extra-academic subjects such as arts and crafts are covered when a teacher and supplies become available. In the 1989–90 school year two volunteers from the Poughkeepsie community helped with art projects, and other volunteers taught classes in which they had expertise. Parents pay a monthly tuition fee for their children, although scholarships are available for the needy. The school budget is small and the facilities and resources of the school reflect this element of financial instability. The school continues to function because of the tuition payments, but also because of the donations of both money and material goods, such as desks and chairs, from members of the community at large and other supporters in the Poughkeepsie area.

Imam Shamsideen, who has no official teaching certification, is the primary teacher of the school and is responsible for teaching all subjects. He has been required to review the educational material at the same time as he has been learning how to teach. His lack of qualifications is not contrary to state regulations as the Sister Clara Muhammed program is not certified and therefore is not required to have certified teachers. The school operates as an amalgamation of many children removed from public school on religious grounds to be taught at home. In this case the children have been assembled as a group by their parents and religious leaders to facilitate teaching and create a cohesive community of young Muslims. The children must cover a required amount of material specified by the Poughkeepsie School Board, and they undergo standardized testing along with public school students.

Until 1990 the Sister Clara Muhammed School was run in the two rooms of the run-down building which the Masjid leased as a headquarters in downtown Poughkeepsie. This space was structurally in questionable condition, and classroom equipment had to be moved at the end of each school day and on Fridays to provide room for community functions, such as prayer services. It had an exposed heater on the main wall of the central room which served as an adequate but not good source of heat. The building lacked any type of recreational facilities, forcing the children to walk to the corner store during recess, instead of going to a playground. In the spring of 1990, 8-year-old Fatima lamented, "I wish I were still in public school—they get to go outside for recess. We have to stay in this old building all the time."[20] Imam Shamsideen would try to take the children on as many outings to neighborhood parks and playgrounds as possible, but this of course was contingent on the number of children in school on a given day and the presence of a volunteer at the school to help with supervision.

The negative aspects of this logistical problem are countered by the fact that the students are not subjected to the violence and the presence of drugs frequently found in the public school system. The pupils themselves do not notice the absence of these destructive influences in their school because the majority attended public school for only a short period at a very young age. The children seemed surprisingly patient with the logistics of their situation, although understandably some complaints were voiced when it was time to rearrange the room.

In the spring of 1990, the Sister Clara Muhammed School moved temporarily to a Poughkeepsie community recreational center, which houses several community service programs and is located next to a subsidized housing complex where several of the students live with their families. This new facility was larger and in slightly better condition. Classes were held in the gymnasium of the center, a high-ceilinged room complete with bleachers and a highly polished floor. Imam Shamsideen separated the children into work groups in various corners of the room, depending on their level and the subject upon which they were working. Students were encouraged to work independently and given assistance when required. Because Imam Shamsideen worked for an anti-drug program based at the center, he had an office available for his use which at times served as a classroom.

In the five years since the founding of the school, students have been enrolled in the program for a variety of reasons, some religious and some stemming from individual needs of the child in question and the inadequacies of the public school system. Parents appear to have positive feelings about their children's progress. Subora Coleman, whose 7-year-old daughter Sahira has been in the school since its founding, states, "I've seen such growth. And she's learning to respect her family."[21] Although test scores have risen slowly, in 1989 they were still below the Poughkeepsie average. However, the scores and the students' academic performance continue to show consistent improvement.

Some parents in the neighboring Muslim communities remain skeptical of the necessity of a Muslim school. Rashida Abdullah, an immigrant from Bangladesh, whose three children have attended public school in the nearby town of Wappingers Falls, comments, "I am raising [my youngest son] as a Muslim child, but I don't see a reason to isolate him. He knows what is good and bad and as the time comes I expect him to take it [religion]."[22] Despite her own reluctance to involve her own children in a Muslim school, however, she acknowledges the special educational needs of the African American community. "I don't see it as necessary, taking kids out of school. But I understand that the public schools may not provide what African American children need."[23]

Her son Rashid is positive about his experience in the public schools. "I think that its good that we have a secular school system because it doesn't leave people of different religions out and make them the oddball. You don't have to pound a child with religion every hour of every day to get him to appreciate it or like it."[24] He also questions the kind of preparation the Sister Clara Muhammed School provides a child in terms of the "outside world."

> As you get older you have a hard time with your peers if you have been pulled out of [the system]. The kids in Poughkeepsie are

going to have a really tough time coping with their peers when they go to college, because the public and private schools have a really different way of looking at things than those kids will have seen. They're going to have it harder than if they had been in the public system and just taught religion at home. Being in the public system is a really big part of learning to cope with the people around you.[25]

Although this criticism has unquestionable merit, it is important to take into account the interactions of the Sister Clara Muhammed School students with non-Muslims outside the classroom. Because the families of the students are recent converts to Islam, the children all have a significant number of non-Muslim extended family members. In addition, they professed without exception to having friends outside the school and seemed unconcerned regarding their abilities to cope with the world outside the classroom. When asked about their plans for the future, the older children expressed interest in attending college, discussing it as an eventuality rather than a possibility. During the 1989–90 school year, only one student, Imam Shamsideen's tenth grade son Kasib, was of the age to begin considering the SAT exam. He had begun review for the test during the second half of the 1989–90 academic year, studying from a borrowed copy of a test preparatory book.

The activities as well as the curriculum of the Sister Clara Muhammed School in Poughkeepsie revolve around Islam, and an example from the Qur'an or Islamic history is applied to nearly every situation. The children are instructed in Arabic for forty-five minutes every day, and participate in the five daily prayers, three of which usually take place during the school day. At prayer time the children are encouraged to wrap up the activity on which they are working and to perform their ritual ablutions before the actual prayers. Imam Shamsideen then assembles the children in a straight line and leads them in prayer, the boys in the front row and the girls in the back. The smallest children join in the devotions, but their attention span is short which necessitates discipline from the Imam. If a female member is present, she inevitably assumes responsibility for the behavior of the smallest children.

There is also usually one period during the day dedicated to learning and reciting Suras from Qur'an. They recite these in Arabic as best they can and then discuss the meaning of the words in English. Although the children have daily instruction in Arabic, it is at a basic level. This instruction of Arabic is a unique feature of the Sister Clara Muhammed Schools; few other schools in the United States provide Arabic instruction at the secondary level, and these are primarily Muslim parochial schools. This opportunity is not always appreciated, however, by the students in the school; 13-year-old Nitara comments, "In public schools you can take Spanish or French, whatever you want. My friends are learning Spanish, and I want to learn it, too."[26] Imam Shamsideen counters this complaint, stating, "Arabic is the language of al-Islam, and something they need to learn. This way they can understand the Qur'an like it was originally. They're lucky to learn it so young."[27]

OTHER MUSLIM SOCIAL PROGRAMS

Since the beginning of the Nation of Islam, education has been seen as one of several critical tools to be used in the struggle of the community to establish a cohesive self-sufficient Muslim group. This over-arching goal of self-sufficiency, strongly stressed by Elijah Muhammed, continues to be significant today under Warith Deen Muhammed. Elijah Muhammed had hoped to establish the NOI as an economically self-sufficient unit by emphasizing notions of Muslim as well as African American solidarity. He had developed a five-point plan for the stability of the NOI.

1. Know thyself and be yourself. Islam makes a true Brother to [every other] Brother. . . . Recognize the necessity for unity. . . . This requires actions and deeds, not words and lip service.
2. Pool your resources, physically as well as financially.
3. Stop wanton criticism of everything that is black-owned and black-operated.
4. Keep in mind—*Jealousy destroys from within.*
5. Observe the operations of the white man. He is successful. He makes no excuses for his failures. He works hard—in a collective manner. You do the same.[28]

Although this original doctrine of the Nation of Islam has since been abandoned by orthodox African American Muslims under the leadership of Warith Deen, distinct traces of its crucial elements are visible in the Masjid ul-Mutkabir community's efforts toward social and economic development.

The Masjid ul-Mutkabir community strives to remain financially solvent and to this end stresses to its members the importance of the patronage of Muslim-owned businesses. Community
members are informed through the masjid leadership of services
offered by the local Muslim community, and the *Muslim Green
Pages,* a comprehensive national listing compiled and produced by
Muslims and advertising services offered to and owned by Muslims, is available for purchase through the masjid. The masjid also
works in conjunction with several social service programs operated in the Hudson Valley by members of its own community as
well as by African American Muslim communities in neighboring
counties. The three main programs in which members of the masjid are involved are run under a rehabilitative community help
program called Baitul Nasr (House of Help). They are the Innovative Therapeutic Program, which counsels clients on drug abuse;
the Violent Behavior Awareness Program, which seeks to provide
clients with alternatives to violent behavior; and the Mother WIT
(Women in Transition) Program, which provides shelter and resources for women and children in need. Baitul Nasr is also extremely active in helping former offenders orient themselves to life
outside the correctional facility. Subsequently, because the characteristics of those seeking help from Baitul Nasr are not mutually
exclusive, the programs have overlapping client populations.

BAITUL NASR

Baitul Nasr is run by Abdul-Qaadir Islam, the Muslim "chaplain"
of Greenhaven Maximum Security Prison in Greenhaven, New
York. It began as a counseling service for offenders within the
prison. The prison has two masjids for prisoners' worship. These
communal spaces consist of several rooms each and are well
equipped with books, religious paraphernalia, and even VCRs for
viewing religious programs. Muslim prisoners are allowed certain
privileges connected with their participation in the masjids, such as
being allowed to attend Juma'a services on Fridays and religious
programs sponsored by the masjid. The Baitul Nasr program begins counseling prisoners while they are still incarcerated, teaching
them job interview skills and placing them in hypothetical situations through role playing to help them prepare for situations they
might encounter on the "outside."

This type of rehabilitative support has been offered consistently throughout the history of the Nation of Islam and the Sunni African American Muslim community. The Nation of Islam accepted many prisoners and former offenders into its movement. Recruiters for the NOI were active within the prison system and many prisoners embraced the doctrine of Elijah Muhammed while inside. Malcolm X is probably the most famous of those who converted while in prison. The movement did not originally run programs specifically for prisoners, but rather depended on its strict doctrine to rehabilitate members. Subsequently, incarcerated members of the NOI had a reputation for being model prisoners. Warith Deen Muhammed saw the value of the rehabilitation of offenders and believed that the emphasis on rehabilitative effort is consistent with Muslim belief regarding sin. "This religion says that man is not a natural sinner—the natural impulse in man is the impulse towards excellence," he asserts. "I have the freedom to make choices outside my own interest and outside my own dignity. So if I make choices outside of that, charge it to my judgment and not to my nature."[29] This sentiment is echoed by Najee'ullah Shahid, in an essay on the Violent Behavior Awareness Program in the Baitul Nasr newsletter: "We view violence from the point of view that most violent acts occur within some situational crisis. To teach people to adequately handle these crises, we draw on the insights from various social sciences, where we find Consistency with the universal teachings of Al-Islam."[30]

Once offenders are released from prison, they are welcomed as members into Masjid ul-Mutkabir if they so choose. Brother Yusuf Muhammed, assistant director and program coordinator of Baitul Nasr, states, "Having a support group is essential to the person coming out of prison. . . . Although the initial stage of release is intimidating, with the right guidance, and the help of God, I've been instrumental in assisting brothers to stand firm on the outside and begin to take the necessary steps to reconstruct their family life, and promote dignity in themselves and their community."[31] Imam Shamsideen says that although not all Muslim former offenders remain in the religion, those who do tend to play an active role in the community.[32]

The Innovative Therapeutic Program (ITP) works to help both former offenders and other members of the local community break the cycle of drug dependency and addresses the problem as one based in negative attitudes acquired through social learning experiences. Abdullah Salahuddin, who works in the ITP at Baitul Nasr, asserts,

> People do not get addicted to drugs as such, rather they become addicted to the false feelings of worth and competence drug use induces. . . . We believe that in order to counter the influence of the drug subculture, and shape a new vision of a better and lasting future, the Individual must be given a POSITIVE SELF CONCEPT which will provide him or her with an opportunity to develop and become useful to the community.[33]

The ITP attempts to serve a dual purpose, breaking people of their dependency to drugs while helping them to maintain a clean lifestyle once the dependency is broken.

Even though the Baitul Nasr's main interaction with the incarcerated community is through the Greenhaven facility, which is a men's facility, female former offenders are also welcomed into the community and take part in the Innovative Therapeutic Program and other programs run by Baitul Nasr. Other women, both Muslim and non-Muslim, also use the services. The Mother WIT Program was developed in 1988–1989 and opened in the spring of 1990. Yusuf Muhammed describes the goals of the program as, "temporary emergency housing for women and small children, [which] will also include drug and alcohol counseling, a crisis intervention team for immediate support and counseling, as well as a referral service to further help and direct women in restoring their lives and situation to normalcy."[34] The Mother WIT Program works in conjunction with other Dutchess County social service programs, referring clients to both privately and municipally run agencies, such as the Grace Smith House for battered women.

CONCLUSION

The programs run by Baitul Nasr provide a cohesive example of the efforts of the African American Sunni Muslim community to make social services available to its members, as well as members of the Poughkeepsie community at large. Baitul Nasr operates with the help and support of the local municipal government, both suggesting to community leaders areas of concern that they feel should be addressed by the local government and working to fill the gaps left by the inevitable inadequacy of government-run welfare programs. For example, the Mother WIT Program was able to purchase the house in which it is located from the city at a reduced price because of its community-oriented function. Letters of support from Dutchess County executive Lucille Patterson, mayor of Poughkeepsie Robert Bleakly, and city manager William Theyson, have also been received by Baitul Nasr with regard to its efforts to improve the quality of life of the residents of downtown Poughkeepsie. Patterson writes, "There is a need in our communities for additional housing and support services on behalf of those who struggle to lead productive, constructive lives, but who so far have failed. I write to commend you for your goal of providing both housing and desperately needed support services."[35]

The dialectic of the interaction between Baitul Nasr and the Poughkeepsie municipal government with the retention of its Muslim identity serves as an analogy for the role played by the Masjid ul-Mutkabir in the Poughkeepsie community. The Muslims of the community are intent on maintaining and strengthening their Muslim identities while increasing their self-confidence and multiplying their strategies for self-help. African American Muslim community participation is increasing through the delivery of social programs and its growing acceptance by government officials and other religious community members. At the same time efforts made through activities such as the Sister Clara Muhammed School are helping to expand the community's inner base of support. The future of the masjid will be assured if its members can continue to augment their support within the local community while remaining true to their orthodox belief system and values.

NOTES

1.   Poughkeepsie is a town of 30,000 people, situated on the east bank of the Hudson River. It is located about 100 miles north of New York City, and is the major city in a heavily inhabited area. Its population in 1988 was 73 percent Anglo, 26 percent African American, and 1 percent other. Although it is located in wealthy Dutchess County, which ranks in the top 20 percent of all counties in the United States in terms of wealth and where the per capital income was $12,299 in 1988, the city of Poughkeepsie figure was considerably lower at $11,234. The economic contrast between the town and the surrounding area is further indicated by the fact that 17.3 percent of Poughkeepsie residents were living below the poverty line in 1979, whereas only 7.3 percent of Dutchess County

residents were. The city of Poughkeepsie is the only area in the county with a poverty rate above 15 percent, which stands in sharp contrast to neighboring Wappingers Falls, which has a poverty rate under 5 percent (sources: "Comparing Appalachian Counties with the Nation's," *Appalachia* 19, nos. 2–4, [Spring 1986]; and, *Cities and Counties Index,* 1988.)

2. Unless otherwise noted, the research presented in this chapter is based primarily on field work conducted in 1989–90 by the author in the Masjid ul-Mutkabir community. Participant observation was the predominant research method employed, accompanied by interviews with members of both the Mid-Hudson Islamic Association and the Masjid ul-Mutkabir communities.

3. Personal correspondence, January 1992.

4. Ibid.

5. Interviews with Rashed Abdullah, Wappingers Falls, N.Y., April 8, 1990.

6. Interview with Imam Marshall Shamsideen, Poughkeepsie, N.Y., February 22, 1990.

7. Interview with Marshall Shamsideen, November 18, 1989.

8. Interview with Lisa Rashid, November 18, 1989.

9. Ibid.

10. Interview with Mohammed Rashid, December 8, 1989.

11. Interview with Rashida Abdullah, Wappingers Falls, N.Y., April 15, 1990.

12. Ibid.

13. Interview with Marshall Shamsideen, January 28, 1990.

14. Interview with Rashida Abdullah, April 8, 1990.

15. Personal correspondence, January 1992.

16. Kathleen Norton, "Sister Clara Muhammed School," *The Poughkeepsie Journal* (October 30, 1988), pp. 1E–2E.

17. Interview with Marshall Shamsideen, December 15, 1989.

18. C. Eric Lincoln, *The Black Muslims in America* (Boston: Beacon Press, 1973), p. 131.

19. Interview with Marshall Shamsideen, February 22, 1990.

20. Interview with Fatima Rashid, Poughkeepsie, N.Y., March 5, 1990.

21. Norton, "Sister Clara Muhammed School."

22. Interview with Rashida Abdullah, April 8, 1990.

23. Ibid.

24. Interview with Rashid Abdullah, Wappingers Falls, N.Y., April 8, 1990.

25. Ibid.

26. Interview with Nitara Rashid, Poughkeepsie, N.Y., March 5, 1990.

27.   Interview with Marshall Shamsideen, December 22, 1989.

28.   The honorable Elijah Muhammed, as cited in Lincoln, *The Black Muslims in America*, pp. 95–96.

29.   W. D. Muhammed, as quoted in Ayesha Muhammed, ed., *Focus on al-Islam: Interviews with W. Deen Muhammed* (Chicago: Zakat Publications, 1988), p. 41.

30.   "Violent Behavior Awareness: An Innovative Approach to Dealing with Violence," Najee'ullah Shahid, Phase Two Fund Raiser program (Poughkeepsie, N.Y.: Baitul Nasr Inc., 1989).

31.   Yusuf Akbar, *The Voice of Help: Baitul Nasr Newsletter* 1, no. 4 (November–December, 1989).

32.   Personal interview with Marshall Shamsideen, December 18, 1989.

33.   Countering the Influence of the Drug Subculture," Abdullah Y. Salahuddin, Phase Two Fund Raiser program.

34.   "Action Plan," ibid.

35.   Letter from Lucille Patterson, county executive, to the Friends of Baitul Nasr, April 14, 1989.

CHAPTER 22

Attitudes of Immigrant Women and Men in the Dearborn Area Toward Women's Employment and Welfare

Barbara Aswad

It is often said that married women in the Southend of Dearborn, Michigan, cannot get jobs because they lack the skills for an industrial society, including knowledge of English. This is true to some extent, but most of them differ little from their husbands in this respect. The removal of production processes from the household historically has made it difficult for women to combine childbearing and domestic functions with employment. In the Southend of Dearborn, the site of this research, the male dominated nature of the auto industry makes this reality acute.

A number of other factors also affect the current employment position of women who have migrated primarily from villages into this Muslim working-class neighborhood. The first is what I call the "rich peasant mentality" of their husbands, a carryover from class realities in the Middle East. Among the several characteristics of this attitude, which will be described later, is an emphasis on female modesty. The second factor is the new acceptance of welfare brought about both by the combined auto recession of the early 1980s, which resulted in up to 40 percent unemployment in the community, and by economic pressures caused by the presence of many new immigrants. Finally, the reality of coming to an alien culture has increased the emphasis on Islamic modesty and segregation, particularly insofar as American culture seems to encourage dating and permit premarital sexual relations as part of the process of mate selection. Traditional Arab concern over female virginity before marriage requires greater vigilance and often leads to the promotion of early marriages, with the result that educational opportunities for girls are lessened. This also further limits employment opportunities. The recent trend to reassert traditional Islamic values in the Middle East has carried over to immigrants and has added to these attitudes. The increased religiosity in the community is due both to the infusion of immigrants and to the attempts to assume a position of solidarity in the face of the antagonism felt in the United States in general and in Dearborn in particular against Arabs and Islam.

Before considering in greater detail the particular circumstances of these immigrant women it is helpful to consider the general context in which they live. The Southend of Dearborn has been a depot for Lebanese, Yemeni, and Palestinian Muslims. The community had its roots in Highland Park, a city within the metropolitan area of Detroit where immigrants had gone to work for the original Ford Motor Plant in the early part of the century. A Sunni mosque was built in 1919 in Highland Park under the direction of Imam Hussein Karoub, but it soon closed. The Shi'a, organized under Imam Buzzy, met in the New Orleans Hall in Highland Park. When Ford moved its plant to Dearborn in the late 1920s, most of the Arab community followed. The Sunni congregation built a mosque in 1938 and the Shi'i Hashemite Hall was founded in 1940 in Dearborn.[1] The Arabs were a small part of the larger immigrant community, which was primarily Eastern European and Italian until the 1960s, when increased numbers of Arabs migrated to the area and the Europeans began to move out. The population of the area is now approximately 6,000, 75 percent of whom are Arab. They form a community where people live close to each other, and know and share each other's business. It contains a dozen coffeehouses, a mosque, and numerous stores and businesses. There were some stormy periods for the community when the city was determined to destroy it,[2] but it remains today as a lively center for immigrants and a home for up to three generations of Arabs.

The earliest immigrants were the south Lebanese, mainly Shi'a. They were joined after 1948 by Palestinian Muslims and in the 1960s by Yemeni Muslims from villages that surrounded Sana or from the region near Ib on the border of what was then the Yemen

Arab Republic and the Democratic Union of the Yemeni Republic. A low-income region, it has been regarded as the "other side of the tracks" for many in Dearborn. More recently, due to such factors as the expansion of the Arab community numerically and geographically and the political turmoil and wars in the Middle East, there has been tension between the two sections of Dearborn and various instances of cultural misunderstanding and racism. The Southend Arab community expanded north; most of the immigrants entered the new sister community, which now has fifty-six bustling Arab shops including bakeries, restaurants, dress shops, insurance and doctors offices in a six-block section of Warren Avenue. As a result of the wars in south Lebanon and Beirut, people have come from Middle Eastern towns and villages such as Tibnine and Bint Jbail in Lebanon and the Palestinian village of Beit Hanina.[3] Many of these recent immigrants from Lebanon have skills and higher levels of education.

In the larger metropolitan Detroit area there are approximately 200,000 persons of Arab background. Of that number, approximately 70,000 are Muslims. Dearborn, located on the western side of Detroit, is the center of the Muslim community; Muslims compose 18,000 or about 20 percent of that city's population. Much of the expansion of the second and third generations of this community has continued westward to other suburbs such as Dearborn Heights and Westland. In contrast, the Lebanese Christian Catholic communities expanded to the eastern suburbs, with most of the mainly Lebanese and Palestinian Christian Orthodox and Iraqi Chaldeans moving to the northern suburbs.

There is a great deal of diversity even with the Detroit area Arab Muslim population, reflected in terms of country of origin, class and occupation, rural or urban generation, religious sect, and political affiliation. Numerous upper-class professionals live in the more affluent suburbs. This population has arrived since the 1960s. Class is a barrier to interaction between the Dearborn community and these professionals, although religious activities and Middle East crises have brought some members together sporadically. Distance between communities might be seen as a further barrier, although members of the upper classes often travel long distances to visit each other.

There are five mosques or Islamic centers in the Dearborn region attended by Arab Muslims, three Shi'a and two Sunni. The largest is the Islamic Center in Detroit just outside Dearborn on Joy Road. Called the Jami', it was built in 1963 and has served primarily the early Lebanese Shi'a community and their descendants, who are the majority in the area. A second Lebanese Shi'a center is the Islamic Institute, which is referred to as the Majma'. The congregation was formed in 1980 and moved into a building in 1985 in the midst of the growing Warren Avenue community of recent and older immigrants. It is considered more orthodox than the Islamic Center. The smaller Islamic Council of America, called the Majlis, opened in 1989 in a renovated storefront. Also part of the Warren Avenue community, it is even more conservative than the Majma'. One indicator of that conservatism is the modesty of women's dress.[4] Differences in political persuasion, because they are related to religion in Lebanon, are also reflected to some extent in the mosques and centers.

One of the two Sunni mosques is that located on Dix Road. Started originally by the Lebanese, it took on characteristics of the assimilated second-generation Lebanese. It now primarily serves the Yemeni population and strongly resembles Middle Eastern mosques in both its architectural style and its customs. The other Sunni community, which was displaced by the Yemenis, is the more more liberal Lebanese congregation, organized as the Beka'a Center in Dearborn.

There are other mosques in the Detroit area, but they are not primarily Arab. Some Arab professionals send their children to a suburban mosque in Auburn Hills, which is mainly Pakistani but with other ethnic groups represented. An Islamic school is being built in the western suburb of Canton, located between Detroit and Ann Arbor. It is financed primarily by upper class Egyptians and Pakistanis from the Detroit area as well as by some professionals from Ann Arbor. There are now plans to build another Islamic school in the Dearborn area. This is being financed primarily by members of the Islamic Institute. Funds were coming from the Khoi foundation in Iraq, but because of the Gulf War these have been delayed and progress in building the school has been slowed considerably. This interest in building specifically Islamic schools reflects the desire to provide an educational experience for Muslim children in which there is some segregation of sexes, no influence of dating and alcohol, and a strict discipline.

This, then, is the general environment in which the present

study of immigrant Muslim Arab women in Dearborn is set. Its main focus is village women, most of whom have not worked outside of the home or had much of any educational training, who know very little English, and who have come to the area in the last twenty years or so.

Several studies of women and work in the Middle East are relevant to an understanding of the situation of these Michigan immigrants. Janet Abu-Lughod, writing thirty years ago about migration from rural Egyptian villages to Cairo, discovered a decrease in the activities of women once they came to the city, including a reduced work load, reduced social life, and confinement to the neighborhood. She contrasted this with the circumstances of their husbands, whose work typically took them outside the neighborhood and brought them into association with a variety of men.[5] More recent studies in Yemen and Lebanon have emphasized the importance of the urban neighborhood for working-class women and women who have migrated from the countryside.[6] Studies done in lower income areas of Cairo have found that for women to work is considered degrading for husbands and threatening to their masculinity,[7] and that men blame working women for social problems such as juvenile delinquency and place more restrictions on them.[8] Andrea Rugh working in Cairo discovered that among the elements determining the response of husbands to the employment of their wives are such things as the degree of protection of the work place, how public is the display of family need, the status of the work, the amount earned, and how much employment interferes with the woman's housework.[9] Also relevant for understanding immigrant Muslim women in Detroit is G. Mirdel's study of Turkish women accompanying their husbands to Denmark. She reports that many of these women depend more on their husbands after having been taken from a structured role; they feel alone and isolated, with the additional stress of raising children in a different country.[10]

It is important to observe that patrilineal societies in general guard female sexuality and behavior more than matrilineal kinship systems to assure pure line of descent. Furthermore, with the class system of agrarian states it becomes a function of the political systems found in such societies as India, precommunity China, classical Greece and Rome.[11]

Because this study will focus on the section of the community that is of peasant background, let us return to the concept of the "rich peasant" mentality, and why it has materialized in the United States. A rich peasant is generally defined as one who manages a medium amount of land and has a surplus; neither he nor his family members do physical labor themselves on the land. Instead he hires poorer peasants who have little land or sharecroppers who have none. Increasingly they have begun to use machinery in the Middle East. Because they have a surplus, they serve as middlemen in the flow of trade and capital to poorer rural peasants in areas such as Lebanon and Yemen. Rich peasants generally have very large extended kin groupings, which they use in a corporate political and economic fashion. In a study of Middle East villages I found that they are more highly patrilineal, are more endogamous, and have higher rates of polygamy and first-cousin marriage on the father's side than middle or poor peasants.[12] Middle peasants, on the other hand, generally till their own plots with family labor, are more bilateral and less patrilineal, less polygamous, and have smaller extended families than rich peasants.[13] Poor peasants and sharecroppers with no land usually have nuclear families, are mobile, have a very limited sense of patrilineality, are monogamous and marry outside of their kin unit. They work primarily for richer peasants and large landowners, and their major alignment is to their patrons rather than extended kin.

The rich peasant male attitude towards agriculture and other manual labor in the Middle East is to avoid it at all costs. I clearly remember one of the first conversations I had with some of these men in which I asked them how many weeks they worked a year. At first they rather proudly said, "None". When I protested that that was impossible, they reconsidered and answered, "Well O.K., about eight." My initial response was that I was never going to get a straight answer, but as I sat there month after month and saw no male movement I realized that they were not lying. Although occasionally they carried out some important political, managerial, and curing functions, they certainly did no physical labor. Many were overweight and there were numerous heart attacks among men in their forties. Leisure was definitely considered a reward.

Second only to their denegration of labor for themselves was their desire not to have their wives or daughters seen in the fields laboring with men and for other persons. The symbolism of power and control over their women greatly affects men's status and honor. Many times I was told that their wives "didn't have to work," even though the wives of course were working very hard processing food, washing clothes, and caring for children. Along with the pride rich peasants seem to feel in not having wives and daughters employed is the fact that women can have more time to produce and care for as many children as possible. However, their definition of work clearly is employment outside the home. Women generally agree with this definition, and also look down on agricultural work.[14]

It is critical to note that the middle peasants in the area have always emulated rich peasant behavior and, in the unlikely case that they obtained the wealth, followed the rich peasant customs and morals. When a government reform project provided land to peasants, the poorer peasants emulated middle and rich peasant styles. They increased the number of their children, continued to put their children to work, and tried to rent tractors and workers to reduce their own load. The important point for this study is that they tried to restrict their wives from working. These strategies worked for only one generation, because they had many children and no additional land from the government. Most were soon back to their previous positions if not worse, with the exception of a few who had gotten access to credit as individuals and who were primarily responsible for the ruin of the others. The successful few totally imitated the rich peasants, and their wives and children did not work in the fields.[15]

Early studies of Arab Americans in the Dearborn community, although excellent in their discussion of the dynamics of assimilation between different generations, were conducted through interviews only with men. Questions were not asked about the attitudes of men toward women working, and little attention was paid to female employment patterns or the lack of them.[16] More recent works have provided much of this missing data. In an extensive study on childbearing practices among forty-one immigrant women from the Dearborn community, for example, E. Alldredge found that none of the women worked outside the home. She notes that with men out of the house at work or in the coffeehouse women seem to increase their decision-making power at home, although deferring to the power of their husbands in public roles such as employment and banking. Alldredge links the lack of female employment to modesty and the continuation of traditional attitudes, although she cites a change in women's attitudes toward their daughters in relation to their sons and concludes that a more egalitarian male-female approach may be developing in the community.[17]

Various studies of early immigrant women in the United States report on the particular circumstances of their manual labor, especially in their work in family stores and clothing factories and serving as peddlers or petty salespersons. S. Haddad in her study of Syrian Americans in Chicago reports that the early immigrant women helped their husbands by baking and selling, and that this put them in a good position in the family business later when the men were successful.[18] Alexa Naff reports cases of exploitation of daughters who sometimes gave up or delayed marriage and family by working to help support or educate their brothers. Doumato tells of a woman who had been indentured to owners of a New York garment factory at age 12 to pay for her passage to America,[19] most probably not an isolated case. Early employment for women usually kept them in or near the home or in factories where they could be working together. The issue of modesty has been of very great concern for women working in the auto industry, where they are forced to be in close proximity with men who are not relatives.[20] Neither the Lebanese nor the Yemeni women in this study were prepared in any way by their village life in the Middle East for life in an area influenced by the male-dominated auto industry.

This, then, is the general background of the immigrants coming to the Dearborn community. The women in this survey of Dearborn moved into a working-class community composed primarily of unskilled auto workers and their families. The vast majority have come from middle peasant backgrounds. In the United States their husbands earn salaries unheard of in the villages of Yemen and Lebanon. The women have been hindered in gaining employment in the United States and thereby hindered in gaining control over resources by the attitudes both of the auto companies and their husbands. The men could not initially adopt the leisure habits of the rich peasants for themselves because of the nature of their unskilled wage labor jobs, but they could attain a degree of such status through restricting the employment of their wives. In addition, heads of patrilineages have built political bases similar to those in the Middle East. It should be added that, although individual wage labor jobs make patrilineal corporate kin units less viable than joint rural land ownership, urban shop ownership is more amenable to this, and we do find some persons living in a leisurely fashion in the suburbs when successful. Like the early store-owning immigrants, the Detroit Iraqi Chaldean population has monopolized the "Mom and Pop" stores of Detroit, and many women worked under the protection of their male relatives for little pay and sometimes under dangerous conditions. The recent Lebanese immigrants on Warren Avenue have also opened shops and practically monopolize the gas stations in the region, but most have not acquired enough wealth to become leisurely.

In this study of the attitudes of forty married women about employment and their understanding of the attitudes of their husbands toward women working, Yemeni and Lebanese women were analyzed separately. Earlier Yemeni immigrants were almost entirely men with a pattern of recurrent migration. The women therefore represent a recent migration. All of the Yemeni women in the survey have come from villages and small towns, have neither education nor job experience, and have few relatives in this country. They do not drive and seldom venture from the Southend. Only one is employed and she teaches English to the others. All are from middle peasant background or have only recently been urbanized. The few who are from the "rich peasant" class live in the middle-class city of Southfield, 15 miles away, and feel rather isolated. Most Yemeni women have come only in the last 15 years, and most are fairly young and have few family members here compared with the large number that the Lebanese indicate that they have.

A good half of the Yemeni women express a strong desire to work and to learn English to be able to do so. None except the teacher has ever been to school, and only half say that their husbands would be strongly opposed to their working here. The other half indicate that their husbands would not mind at all and would welcome the money. Of those who would welcome work, half are on welfare. Eighty percent feel that their husbands would be strongly opposed to their working in local factories, and they themselves are not eager to work there either. None has ever been to the bank, and all say that their husbands control the money in the house. They feel that they are losing control of their patrilineal assets in Yemen as well because of their migration. All say that their husbands make the major decisions in the household.

The majority of these women indicate that their husbands rely on religious authorities as a means of controlling them. Half describe themselves as not religious at all and nearly half as very religious. Few attend the local mosque, and because of the low rate of literacy few read the Koran. Although there is a small women's group, they are not as active as Lebanese women in their mosques. Yemeni women veil when they do attend the mosque, but seldom do so in the community, which they view as their village. In Yemen they veiled when they went to town, but do not do so here when they leave the Southend, which is seldom. Their dress continues to be that of the village.

In the extended family of the Middle East mothering is not the exclusive occupation for working-class families; they combine various jobs such as processing food, sewing, and raising poultry. This is true only to a minimal extent for the Dearborn immigrants, with the result that there is a great sense of boredom among these Yemeni women. With their work confined to household chores and raising children, they spend a great deal of time watching TV and videos. They are pretty much restricted to the Southend of the city and express the need for more kinds of activity. Most of the Dearborn Yemenis now live in nuclear families; and although they say that they miss their mothers and sisters, they feel some relief at being freed from kinship pressures and particularly the presence of their mothers-in-law. The neighborhood has replaced their kin and they exchange many services and visits.

Men of the Yemeni community generally are not active in local or national politics, but remain primarily involved in political matters in Yemen. Women are not politically involved in politics either here or in the Middle East. Half indicate that they are not concerned about Middle East politics, although they know that their husbands are and express concern about their husband's anxieties. Only 10 percent of the women belong to any local Arab American group. Women do, however, take advantage of the resources of the local Arab Community Center for Economic and Social Services (ACCESS). The fact that several hundred Arab women from the local community have signed up for English courses given at ACCESS is indicative of several things: (1) they want to improve their skills, (2) they want to get out of the house to relieve their boredom, (3) it is an activity that their husbands consider legitimate, partly because it is in the immediate community, and (4) as welfare recipients they may take classes that improve their ability to be part of the workplace.

What of the attitudes of these Yemeni women toward their daughters? Some 60 percent said that they would permit their daughters to work, but only with other women. They also want them to get a good education, but they are concerned about dating in the high schools. A number discussed the possibility of sending their teenagers back to Yemen until they marry, especially their daughters. All Yemeni women want their children to marry Muslims, and 90 percent want them to marry Yemenis. These mothers are in a difficult situation. To avoid the possibility of any kind of scandal some of them feel pressured to cut off their daughters' education and arrange for them to be married at a young age. The resistance of daughters to this as well as to other attempts at family control are among the primary problems brought to the Family Counseling Center of ACCESS. Of the sixty major cases that came to the center during its first year, nearly half concerned mothers having problems with the discipline of daughters; other issues concerned problems between mothers and sons, between fathers and sons, and between fathers and daughters. This also reflects the fact that 80 percent of the clients were women.

The Lebanese in the Dearborn area have had different migration patterns from the Yemenis and can be characterized as a four-generation established community with significant kin connections[21] as well as more varied work experience before migrating. Some have been employed as teachers in urban areas, although others (at least 60 percent of the sample) have little or no education. One illiterate woman was brought here as a second wife for a widower thirty years her senior who already had eight children. All, however, indicate that they do want education. About a third are currently employed in jobs such as cooks, custodians, aids at the local community center, babysitters and teachers. In contrast with the Yemenis, the great majority indicate that husbands and wives control the family money jointly. Lebanese women also share more in decision-making processes in general; this is particularly true for those who were employed outside the home in Lebanon.

When asked whether women should work outside the home in this country, most responded affirmatively and expressed a desire to do so. They reject the rich peasant women's attitudes, very likely related to the reality that as homemakers in America they have considerably less to do than the peasant homemaker in Lebanon.[22] Answers to the question of how their husbands would react to the idea of their working ranged from strongly opposed to not at all. Those whose husbands would not be opposed included women who do work and, like the Yemeni, those who are receiving or have received some form of welfare. All the Lebanese indicated that it would be permissible for their daughters to work. But they would prefer that their daughters work in stores or traditional female jobs. Few said that it must be with all women, and some 20 percent said that they would approve of unskilled auto factory work.

Lebanese women are more active in religious organizations than Yemeni women, and none in this study said that they are not religious at all. Many wear religious dress, and there are frequent arguments on such matters as the degree to which one's hair should be allowed to show. Much of this has to do with the involvement of religion as a political issue in the Middle East.[23] It is clear, however, that religion does not have as negative an effect on women's work among the Lebanese as among the Yemenis, even though the Lebanese see themselves as more religious. Lebanese women are also more involved in both local and international political groups than Yemeni women, due both to the war in Lebanon and local problems. Lebanese men are also highly involved politically. Some 70 percent of the women indicate that they have been active in political affairs. The political involvement of second-generation Arab women also influences the new arrivals; it is also sometimes the case that to be too American in political attitudes or activities is perceived as being disloyal to one's heritage.[24]

Taking the Yemenis and the Lebanese groups together, then, one can see that the women believe their husbands to be still influenced by the "rich peasant" ideology and by the extreme importance of female modesty and that such an attitude does limit women's participation in employment, particularly in the auto factories of Detroit. This seems to be stronger among the Yemenis than the Lebanese, and less so for women who already work or have worked. Religious attitudes are different between the two communities and tend to limit the Yemeni women more. Women's own attitudes show that the vast majority want to be employed and, under the right circumstances, would allow their daughters to be employed. Although they may not prefer factory work, about a fifth of the Lebanese would allow their daughters to work at the Ford plant. However, some women have experienced a need for more security for their daughters in an alien environment and may themselves limit their daughters' potential by removing them from school, pressuring them into early marriages, or restricting their movement and opportunities for mobility and involvement by constant vigilance. There are numerous informal reports of girls and boys sneaking off in cars when they are supposed to be "in the library." Those who are ready for a college education often are encouraged to attend a local university or college so they can live at home. At the university, the girl's brothers generally assume the surveillance duties so that it becomes a place of very limited freedom.

The other issue with clear economic ramifications for Arab immigrant families, in addition to that of employment for women, is the question of welfare and attitudes toward it. Current high unemployment rates have forced some men not only to accept the idea of employment on the part of their wives, but in some cases to accept the reality of being on welfare. Unfortunately it seems clear from a comparison of my study of Dearborn Arabs in 1971 and this more recent study that the numbers of Arabs on welfare is markedly increasing[25] due both to high rates of unemployment and the influx of new refugees. We may also have more accurate information now because the community center is staffed by Arabic speaking social workers and secretaries. Among the younger generation are numerous feminists who choose to speak out on social issues and bring this kind of information to light.

Many women feel that it is difficult for them and their husbands to accept welfare. This feeling seems to be strongest among both unemployed women and unemployed men. Many women in the community mentioned the high cost of health insurance as a major reason for going on welfare; health insurance is paid for recipients. Men in the community are frequently heard complaining that "America is a country for women." They indicate that welfare, custody, and divorce favor women here. Although Michigan allows two-parent households to receive welfare, traditionally it has been easier or more beneficial to get welfare through separation or divorce and by establishing two residences. Michigan also allows welfare to supplement very low earnings. There may also be some cheating, such as putting the wife on welfare while the man continues to work above the low limit, maintaining the family unity. There is evidence that welfare has helped widowed, divorced, and abused women to gain some independence. The female-headed household has a basis for support, but is still viewed with suspicion or as an unfortunate situation.

There is also disagreement over welfare among others in the community. Some, especially second-generation Arabs who are surviving financially, think that there is cheating and look down on those whom they feel are trying to get "a free ride," saying that the early generations had more of the work ethic. One mentioned that he thinks they feel America owes them something because it supported Israel's invasion of south Lebanon and destroyed their homeland. Preliminary analysis of a study of Arab women and men welfare clients in both the Southend and Warren Avenue communities[26] indicates that welfare causes some shift in gender relations. Most feel it makes women feel more independent and strengthens their role in the family, and they conclude it is generally a good thing for women. Some add that it helps the woman keep the family together. This is particularly true for women who have few skills or little education. Others disagree. One young Lebanese wife whose family had escaped the war noted that welfare is only a bandage. "It does not help because when you work you are free and independent, but when you are on welfare you are still dependent." She said that rather than aiding women, welfare encourages the feelings of depression among many in the community over their lives as refugees who have suffered and lost so much in Lebanon and now find little employment here. Another said she feels that people "become dependent on easy money, and it's bad for the soul" and that "men will lose their independence."

Men feel more embarrassed than women about welfare assistance; both Lebanese and Yemeni women feel it is risky for the man's role as husband, although that was stated more often by Lebanese women. A widow in her fifties from south Lebanon and the mother of five children said that her husband did not want her to work, and when she went on welfare before he died he was shamed. She, however, feels that welfare gives her a sense of independence and has been happy to be on it. She added that it might make a husband "think twice" in his treatment of his wife and felt it is very good for women generally. Her children are embarrassed that she is receiving welfare, but she is not. In a situation in which the husband and wife are separated, almost all of the Lebanese women think the woman will control the welfare money, but three-quarters of the Yemeni women think the husband will. When men are unemployed they are usually more agreeable both to women working and to receiving welfare.

As with other ethnic groups, welfare for these Arab families is often used to supplement low incomes while allowing the family to remain intact. It may, however, also discourage women from seeking employment. With welfare a woman can contribute to the family income without leaving the home or the area, an important factor for the honor of the husband and in terms of her ability to raise children. For those totally dependent upon it welfare can be extremely important, but most feel that the amount of money is actually so small that it does not really give one a sense of independence at all. On the other hand, it also serves as a means of encouraging women to learn English and Arabic, since in Michigan to register for welfare necessitates going to school, working, or taking job training. English- or Arabic-language classes are the option most satisfactory to women and their husbands, partially because they are offered in the community. A new job retraining program offered through ACCESS may also involve increased numbers of women, although lack of English and low educational levels continue to handicap both men and women.

CONCLUSIONS

It appears that numerous issues have operated against women's employment in the Dearborn area. Among these are lack of skills and education; fewer piecemeal or part-time jobs than in the Middle East; the "rich peasant" mentality of husbands from villages with its emphasis on increased female modesty and a restricted environment; increasing Islamic values operating in a host country that does not seem to value premarital chastity; restrictions (including, sometimes, educational) placed by some mothers on their daughters even though theoretically they accept the idea of employment and education for them; and restrictions of the male-dominant auto industry in contrast to family-run businesses. Differences were found between Lebanese and Yemeni attitudes due to the background of immigrants, community, and work experiences, whereby the Lebanese presented more liberal attitudes. It appears that now there may be increasing basis for gender role changes as higher unemployment leads to growing acceptance of welfare. This in turn provides unskilled women with ways of making a contribution to the family income without leaving the home, generally adds to their power in the family, and with more language and job training programs may allow them to attain marketable skills.

NOTES

1. The bulk of this study was conducted in 1984 with the assistance of a sabbatical leave from Wayne State University and a contract with the Arab Community Center for Economic and Social Services (ACCESS) in Dearborn. The author would like to thank Anisa Nasar, Zana Shouchair and Aliya Zeidan for their assistance. An earlier version, "How the 'Rich Peasant Mentality' and Welfare Affect Immigrant Arab Women and Employment Patterns in Michigan" was published in 1991 as Working Paper #1 by the Von Grunebaum Center for Near Eastern Studies, UCLA, 1991. Some of the statistical figures have been presented in a lengthier article, "Yemeni and Lebanese Muslim Immigrant Women in Southeast Dearborn, Michigan" in *Muslim Families in America*, ed. E. Waugh, S. Abu-Laban, and R. Qureshi (Edmonton: University of Alberta Press, 1991), pp. 258–281.

2. See B. Aswad, "The Lebanese Muslim Community in Dearborn, Michigan," in *The Lebanese in the World: A Century of Lebanese Emigration*, ed. A. Hourani and N. Shehadi (London: Tauris Press, 1992).

3. See B. Aswad, "The Southeast Dearborn Arab Community Struggles for Survival Against Urban Renewal," in *Arabic Speaking Communities in American Cities*, ed. B. Aswad (Staten Island, N.Y.: Center for Migration Studies, 1974), pp. 53–83.

4. B. Aswad, "The Expanding Lebanese Muslim Community."

4. A recent study by Linda Walbridge of the history and religious differences of these Shi'a centers indicates that the degree of modesty as exhibited by women's dress is a much debated fact and reflects their degree of conservatism. "Shi'i Islam in an American Community" (Ph.D. diss., Wayne State University, 1991).

5. Janet Abu-Lughod, "Migrant Adjustment to City Life: The Egyptian Case," *American Journal of Sociology* 67 (1961): 22–32.

6. See S. Joseph, "Women and the Neighborhood Street in Borj Hammoud, Lebanon," in *Women in the Muslim World*, ed. L. Beck and N. Keddie (Cambridge, Mass.: Harvard University Press, 1978), pp. 541–

558; S. Dorsky, *Women of 'Amran* (Salt Lake City: University of Utah Press, 1986); C. Myntti, "Yemen Workers Abroad: The Impact on Women," *MERIP Report* 124 (1984): 11–16.

7. A. Rugh, "Women and Work: Strategies and Choices in a Lower Class Quarter of Cairo," in *Women and the Family in the Middle East*, ed. E. Fernea (Austin: University of Texas Press, 1985), p. 279.

8. S. Mohsen, "New Images, Old Reflections: Working Middle East Women in Egypt," in *Women and the Family in the Middle East*, pp. 56–71.

9. Rugh, "Women and Work," p. 279.

10. G. Mirdel, "Stress and Distress in Migration: Turkish Women in Denmark," in Women in Migration, *International Migration Review* 18, no. 4 (1982): 984–1003.

11. M. Martin and B. Voorhies, *Female of the Species* (New York: Columbia University Press, 1975), pp. 296–300. See also *Men and Women in Society*, ed. C. O. O'Kelly and L. Carney (Belmont, Calif.: Wadsworth, 1986), pp. 97, 237. Antoun and others have written extensively on how the legitimate conjugal relationship is guarded in Middle Eastern villages through child bethrothal, virginity tests, arranged marriages and elopment involving cases of honor. "On the Modesty of Women in Arab Muslim Villages," *American Anthropologist* 70 (1968): 671–697. Keddie recently discusses how the use of the veil in Muslim societies is linked with socioeconomic and class and political opinions. "The Past and Present of Women in the Muslim World," *Journal of World History* 1: 1990 77–108.

12. B. Aswad, *Property Control and Social Strategies: Settlers on a Middle Eastern Plain.* Anthropological Papers, No. 44 (Ann Arbor: University of Michigan Press, 1971), pp. 27–80.

13. E. Peters, "Aspects of Rank and Status Among Muslims in a Lebanese Village," in *Mediterranean Countrymen*, ed. J. Pitt-Rivers (Paris: Mouton, 1963), pp. 27–80. An early study by Peters in a Lebanese Shi'a village demonstrates the more bilateral relations, that is relations through both mother's and father's descent groups, of middle peasants in marriage and landholding patterns.

14. Changes in the villages have occurred with boys going off to school in the cities, getting urban jobs and often marrying urban girls, stranding their female cousins in the village. Their sisters and cousins, not allowed to follow the same path, have begun to be apprehensive about their futures. Fathers have been concerned, but have kept the girls in the village and away from urban areas. Although there are elementary schools in the village, few girls have attended and none have gone beyond that because it means leaving home.

15.   B. Aswad, "Family Size and Access to Resources: A Case Study from the Middle East, in *And The Poor Have Children,* ed. K. Michaelson, *Monthly Review Press,* 1981, pp. 89–105.

16.   See A. Wasfi, "Dearborn Arab Moslem Community (Ph.D. diss., Michigan State University, 1984); A. Elkholy, *The Arab Moslems in the United States* (New Haven, Conn.: College and University Press, 1983); N. Abraham, "The Yemeni Immigrant Community of Detroit: Background, Emigration and Community Life", in *Arabs in the New World,* ed. S. Abraham and N. Abraham (Detroit: Wayne State University Center for Urban Studies, 1983); H. al-Yami, "A Study of an Ethnic Group: The Yemeni Community in the South End, Dearborn, Michigan" (M.A. thesis, Michigan State University, 1984).

17.   E. Alldredge, "Childbearing Practices in the Homes of Arab Immigrants: A Study of Persistence" (Ph.D. diss., Michigan State University, 1984), pp. 197–203. Alldredge says that 71 percent of the women studied felt that their daughters should have the same educational opportunities as their sons.

18.   S. Haddad, "The Women's Role in Socialization of Syrian-Americans in Chicago," in *The Arab-Americans, Studies in Assimilation,* ed. Elaine Hagopian and Add Paden (Wilmette, Ill.: Medina University Press International, 1969), p. 92.

19.   E. Doumato, "Celebrating Tradition in Rhode Island," in *Taking Root,* vol. 2, ed. Eric Hoogland (Washington, D.C.: Arab American Anti-Discrimination Committee, 1985), p. 13.

20.   A. Naff, *Becoming American: The Early Arab Immigrant Experience* (Carbondale: Southern Illinois University Press, 1985), pp. 175, 274–276; G. Orfelea, *Before the Flames* (Austin: University of Texas Press, 1988), pp. 76–79.

21.   B. Aswad, in Waugh, 1991, pp. 256–81.

22.   This finding contrasts with Alldrege's survey, according to which most Lebanese women did not want to work.

23.   N. Keddie, "The Past and Present of Women," has shown the vast differences and attitudes ascribed to the use of the veil and religious dress in many religions of the Islamic world.

24.   See L. Cainkar, who has discovered the same phenomenon among immigrant Palestinians. *Coping with Tradition, Change and Alienation: The Lives of Palestinian Women in the U.S.* Ph.D. Dissertation, Northwestern University, 1988.

25.   When Wasfi wrote in 1964, he found one person on AFDC (Aid to Families with Dependent Children) in his sample. In 1971 I found 13 percent of the general population on welfare; of the 1,033 Arabs who visited the Family Counseling Center in 1986, 70 percent earned less than

$10,000 and 40 percent had some form of financial assistance. Nearly 20 percent of the clients were on AFDC.

26.   This study was conducted by the author on fifty-five men and women through a grant from the Center for Urban, Labor and Metropolitan Affairs, Wayne State University, 1989–1990. Most of the Yemeni in this sample grew up in village homes, as was true of those in her first sample, although most Lebanese did not.

BIBLIOGRAPHY

Abraham, Sameer Y., Nabeel Abraham, and Barbara C. Aswad. "The Southend: An Arab Muslim Working Class Community." In *Arabs in the New World*, ed. Sameer Y. Abraham and Nabeel Abraham. Detroit, Michigan: Wayne State University, 1982.

Abraham, Nabeel. "The Yemeni Immigrant Community of Detroit: Background, Emigration and Community Life." In *Arabs in the New World*, ed. S. Abraham and N. Abraham. Detroit: Wayne State University Center for Urban Studies, 1983.

Abramson, Harold J. "The Religioethnic Factor and the American Experience: Another Look at the Three-Generations Hypothesis." *Ethnicity* 2 (1975): 163–177.

Abu-Lughod, Janet. "Migrant Adjustment to City Life: The Egyptian Case." In *The American Journal of Sociology* 67 (1961): 22–32.

Ahearn, Charlie. "Lakim Gets Busy Dropping Science." *The City Sun* 6, no. 17 (April 26, 1989), p. 13.

Aijian, M. M. "Mohammedans in the United States." *The Moslem World*, 10 (1920): 30–35.

Akbar, Na'im. *Visions for Black Men*. Nashville: Winston-Derek, 1991.

Alba, Richard D. The Twilight of Ethnicity Among Americans of European Ancestry: The Case of Italians." In Richard D. Alba, ed. *Ethnicity and Race in the U.S.A.* Boston: Routledge and Kegan Paul, 1985.

_____. "The Twilight of Ethnicity Among American Catholics of European Descent." *The Annals* 454 (1981).

_____. *Ethnic Identity: The Transformation of White America*. New Haven, Conn., and London: Yale University Press, 1990.

Alldredge, E. "Childbearing Practices in the Homes of Arab Immigrants: A Study of Persistence." Ph.d. Dissertation, Michigan State University, 1984.

Ansari, Abdolmaboud. *Iranian Immigrants in the United States: A Case Study of Dual Marginality*. Millwood, N.Y.: Associated Faculty Press, 1988.

Ansari, Zafar Ishaq. "Aspects of Black Muslim Theology." *Studia Islamica* 53 (Spring 1981): 137–176.

Antoun, Richard. "On the Modesty of Women in Arab Muslim Villages." *American Anthropologist* 70 (1968): 671–697.

521

Armanat, Mehrdad. "Prelude to Migration: Nationalism, Social Change, and Revolution in Contemporary Iran." In Ron Kelley and Jonathan Friedlander, eds., "Irangeles: Iranian Life and Culture in Los Angeles." Unpublished manuscript, 1991.

Ashabranner, Brent. *An Ancient Heritage—The Arab-American Minority.* New York: Harper Collins Publishers, 1991.

Assagioli, Robert. *The Act of Will.* Baltimore: Penguin Books, 1974.

Aswad, Barbara C. "The Southeast Dearborn Arab Community Struggles for Survival Against Urban 'Renewal'." In *Arab Speaking Community in American Cities,* ed. Barbara C. Aswad, pp. 53–84. Staten Island, N.Y.: Center for Migration Studies, 1974.

———. "The Southeast Dearborn Arab Community Struggles for Survival Against Urban Renewal." In *Arabic Speaking Communities in American Cities,* ed. Barbard Aswad, pp. 53–83. Staten Island: Center for Migration Studies, 1974.

———. *Property Control and Social Strategies: Settlers on a Middle Eastern Plain.* Anthropological Papers, No. 44. Ann Arbor: University of Michigan, 1971.

———. "The Expanding Lebanese Muslim Community in Dearborn, Michigan." In *A Century of Lebanese Emigration,* ed. A. Hourani and N. Shehadi. London: Tauris Press, 1992.

Austin, Allan D. *African Muslims in Antebellum America.* New York: Garland Publishing, 1974.

Ayoub, Mahmoud. *Redemptive Suffering in Islam. A Study of the Devotional Aspects of 'Ashura' in Twelver Shi'ism.* The Hague: Mouton Publishers, 1978.

Azim Nanji. "The Nizari Ismaeli Muslim Community in North America: Background and Development." *The American Ismaeli,* n.d. Special Edition.

Barclay, Harold. "The Muslim Experience in Canada." In *Religion and Ethnicity in Canada,* ed. Harold Coward and Leslie Kamamura, pp. 101–113. Waterloo, Ont.: Wilfred Laurier University Press, 1978.

Béliveau, Jules. "Un infidèle chez les musulmens de Montréal." *La Presse* (April 4, 1987).

Berger, Peter, and Thomas Luckman. *The Social Construction of Reality.* Garden City, N.Y.: Doubleday Books, 1966.

Beynon, Erdmann D. "The Voodoo Cult Among Negro Migrants in Detroit." *The American Journal of Sociology* 43, no. 6 (May 1938).

Birge, J. K. *The Bektashi Order of Dervishes.* London: Luzac, 1937.

Blyden, Edward W. *Christianity, Islam and the Negro Race.* Edinburgh: Edinburgh University Press, 1967.

Booker, Simeon. *Black Man's America.* Englewood Cliffs, N.J.: Prentice-Hall, 1964.

Borgadus, E. S. *Immigration and Race Attitudes*. New York: D. C. Health and Company, 1928.

Bousquet, G. H. "Moslem Religious Influences in the United States," *The Moslem World*, 25 (1935): 40–44.

Bozorgmehr, Mehdi. "Internal Ethnicity: Armenian, Bahaia, Jewish, and Muslim Iranians in Los Angeles." Doctoral dissertation, University of California, Los Angeles, 1991.

_____ and Georges Sabagh, "High Status Immigrants: A Statistical Profile of Iranians in the United States." *Iranian Studies* 21 (1988): 5–36.

_____ and Georges Sabagh. "Survey Research Among Middle Eastern Immigrant Groups in the United States: Iranians in Los Angeles." *Middle East Studies Association Bulletin* 23 (1989): 23–34.

_____ and Georges Sabagh. "Iranian Exiles and Immigrants in Los Angeles." In Asghar Fathi, ed., *Iranian Refugees and Exiles Since Khomeini*, pp. 121–144. Costa Mesa, Calif.: Mazda Publishers, 1991.

Breitman, George. *The Last Year of Malcolm X: the Evolution of a Revolutionary*. New York: Schocken Books, 1967.

_____, ed. *By Any Means Necessary: Speeches, Interviews, and a Letter by Malcolm X*. New York: Pathfinder, 1970.

al-Bukhari. *Sahih* [Muhammad ibn Isma'il], vol. 8, p. 18. Beirut: Dar Ihya' al-Turath al-'Arabi, 1958.

Chambers, Bradford, ed. *Chronicles of Negro Protest*. New York: Parents' Magazine Press, 1968.

Chittick, William C. *The Sufi Path of Love*. New York: State University of New York Press, 1983.

_____. "Ibn 'Arabi and His School." In S. H. Nasr, *Islamic Spirituality: Manifestations*. New York: Crossroads Press, 1991.

Cushmeer, Bernard. *This Is the One: Messenger Muhammad. We Need Not Look for Another.* Phoenix: Truth Publications, 1971.

Dashefsky, Arnold. "And the Search Goes On: The Meaning of Religio-Ethnic Identity and Identification." *Sociological Analysis* 33 (1972): 239–245.

Davidson, Roderic H. "The Image of Turkey in the West, in Historical Perspective." *The Turkish Studies Association Bulletin* 5 (1981): 1–6.

Davis, George A. and O. Fred Donaldson. *Blacks in the United States: A Geographic Perspective*. Boston: Houghton Mifflin, 1975.

De Bono, Edward. *Lateral Thinking*. New York: Harper and Row, 1970.

Demo, Constantine A. *The Albanians in America: The First Arrivals*. Boston: Fatbardhesia of Katundi, 1960.

Djordjevic, Dimitrije and Stephen Fischer-Galati. *The Balkan Revolutionary Tradition*. New York: Columbia University Press, 1981.

Dorsky, S. *Women of 'Amran*. Salt Lake City: University of Utah Press, 1986.

Doyle, Ann. "Mosque Determined to be Rebuilt from Ashes." *Patriot Ledger* (May 12, 1990).

Doyle, Bertram. *The Etiquette of Race Relations in the South: A Study in Social Control.* Chicago: University of Chicago Press, 1937.

Duiguid, Stephen. "The Politics of Unity: Hamidian Policy in Eastern Anatolia." *Middle Eastern Studies* 9 (1973): 139–155.

Dyer, Gwynne. "Turkish 'Falsifiers' and Armenian 'Deceivers': Historiography and the Armenian Massacres." *Middle Eastern Studies* 12 (1976): 99–107.

Elkholy, A. *The Arab Moslems in the United States.* New Haven, Conn.: College and University Press, 1983.

Ernst, Carl. *Words of Ecstasy in Sufism.* Albany: State University of new York Press, 1985.

Esposito, John. *Islam, The Straight Path.* New York: Oxford University Press, 1988.

Essien-Udom, E. E. *Black Nationalism.* Chicago: The University of Chicago Press, 1962.

Farid al-Deen, Muhammad ibn Ibrahim. *Tadhkirat al-Awliya 'Memoirs of the Saints' of Muhammad ibn Ibrahim Farid al-Deen,* trans. Reynold Nicholson. London: Luzac, 1905–1907.

Farrakhan, Louis. *Warning to the Government of America.* Chicago: Honorable Elijah Muhammad Educational Foundation, 1983.

Federal Writers' Project. *The Albanian Struggle in the Old World and New.* Boston: The Writer, Inc., 1939; New York: AMS Press, 1975.

Fisher, Maxine. *The Indians of New York City: A Study of Immigrants From India.* New York: Heritage Publishers, 1980.

Fischer, Michael M., and Mehdi Abedi. *Debating Muslims.* Madison: University of Wisconsin Press, 1990.

Foucault, Michel. *Discipline and Punish: The Birth of the Prison.* Harmondsworth: Penguin Books, 1979.

Gardell, Mattias. "Religios nationalism och nationalistisk religion: Om den senaste utvecklingen inom politisk islam i det svarta USA." *Svensk Religionshistorisk Arsskrift,* no. 3 (1988).

Garvey, Marcus, *Philosophy and Opinions II, The Philosophy and Opinions by Marcus Garvey. Or, Africa for the Africans,* ed. Amy Garvey. Dover, Mass.: The Majority Press, 1986.

Gawrych, George Walter. "Ottoman Administration and the Albanians 1908–1913." Unpublished dissertation, University of Michigan, 1980.

Ghalwash, Ahmad. *The Religion of Islam.* Supreme Council for Islamic Affairs, 1966.

Gharbi, Mounir. "L'immigration marocaine au Canada: Juifs et musulmans." In *Le facteur religieux en Amerique du Nord,* ed. Jean Beranger and Pierre Guillaume. Talence, France: Maison des Sciences de l'Homme d'Aquitaine, 1982.

Ghayur, Arif M. "Muslims in the United States: Settlers and Visitors." *The Annals* 454 (1981): 150–163.

Gokalp, Ziya. *Turkish Nationalism and Western Civilization*, trans. and ed. Niyazi Berkes. New York: Columbia University Press, 1959.

Gordon, Milton M. *Assimilation in American Life*. New York: Oxford University Press, 1964.

Gottesman, Lois. *Islam in America: A Background Report*. American Jewish Committee, Institute of Human Relations, 1979.

Graham, William. *Divine Word and Prophetic Word in Early Islam*. The Hague: Mouton and Co., 1977.

Greeley, Andrew M. *The Denominational Society: A Sociological Approach to Religion in America*. Glenview, Ill.: Scott, Forsman, 1972.

———. "The Sociology of American Catholics." *Annual Review of Sociology* 5 (1979): 91–111.

Gumperz, John. *Discource Strategies*. Cambridge: Cambridge University Press, 1982.

Haddad, S. "The Women's Role in Socialization of Syrian-Americans in Chicago." In *The Arab-Americans, Studies in Assimilation*, ed. Elaine Hagopian and Add Paden, p. 92. Wilmette, Ill.: Medina University Press International, 1969.

Haddad, Yvonne. "The Impact of the Islamic Revolution in Iran on the Syrian Muslims of Montreal." In Earle Waugh et al., eds., *The Muslim Community in North America*, pp. 165–181. Edmonton: University of Alberta Press, 1983.

———, ed. *The Muslims of America*. New York: Oxford University Press, 1991.

——— and Adair T. Lummis. *Islamic Values in the United States: A Comparative Study*. New York and Oxford: Oxford University Press, 1991.

Hammad, Ahmad Zaki. *Islamic Law*. Indianapolis: American Trust Publications, 1992.

Hamdani, Daood Hasan. "Muslims and Christian Life in Canada" in *Journal Institute of Muslim Minority Affairs* 1, no. 1 (1979): 51–59.

Hansen, Marcus Lee. *The Problem of the Third Generation Immigrant*. Rock Island, Ill.: Augustana Historical Society, 1938.

al Haq, Anwar. *The Faith Movement of Maulana Ilyas*. London: Allen and Unwin, 1972.

Herbert, Will. *Protestant-Catholic-Jew: An Essay in American Religious Sociology*. Garden City, N.Y.: Doubleday and Company, 1955.

Hill, Robert A., ed. *The Marcus Garvey and Universal Negro Improvement Association Papers*. Berkeley: University of California Press, 1983.

Holmes, Mary Caroline. "Islam in America." *The Moslem World*, 26 (1926): 262–266.

Hornsby, Alton, Jr. *Chronology of African-American History: Significant Events and People from 1619 to the Present.* Detroit: Gale Research, 1991.

al-Hujwiri, Ali ibn Uthman al-Julaibi. *Kashif al-Mahjub*, trans. Reynold Nicholson. Leiden: Brill, 1911; reprint ed., London: Luzac, 1936, 1959, 1967; Lahore: Islamic Book Foundation, 1976.

Hurh, Won Moo, and Kwang Chung Kim. "Religious Participation of Korean Immigrants in the United States." *Journal for the Scientific Study of Religion* 29 (1990): 19–34.

Husain, Asad, and Asifa Husain. "Islam and Non-Muslim Society, A Case Study of Islam in the United States of America." Paper read in the Muslim Community Development Conference, Chicago, March 1978.

Ibn Arabi. *Tarjuman al-Ashwaq*, trans. and ed. R. Nicholson. London: Theosophical Publishing House, 1911.

Ibn Hisham, Abd al-Malik. *The Life of Muhammad: A Translation of Ibn Ishaq's Sirat Rasul Allah*, trans. Alfred Guillaume. New York: Oxford University Press, 1955.

Ibn Kathir, Isma'il. *Tafsir al-Quran al-'Azim*. Beirut: Dar al-Andalus, 1983.

Isajiw, Wsevolod. "Ethnic Identity Retention." in *Ethnic Identity and Equality Varieties of Experience in a Canadian City*, ed. Raymond Breton, Wsevolod Isajiw, Warren E. Kalbach, and Jeffrey G. Reitz, pp. 34–49. Toronto: University of Toronto Press, 1990.

Izutsu, T. *A Comparative Study of the Key Philosophical Concepts in Sufism and Taoism*. Tokyo: Keio Institute of Cultural and Linguistic Studies, 1966.

al-Jilani, Abd Al-Qadir. *Futuh al-Ghaib*, trans. Aftab al-Deen Ahmad. Lahore: Sh. Muhammad Ashraf, 1972, 1967.

Joseph, Suad. "Women and the Neighborhood Street in Borj Hammoud, Lebanon." In *Women in the Muslim World*, ed. L. Beck and N. Keddie, pp. 541–558. Cambridge, Mass.: Harvard University Press, 1978.

Kallajxhi, Xhevat. *Bektashizmi dhe Teqeja Shqiptare N'Amerike*. Detroit: Teqe, 1964.

Kareem, Yahya A. "Take Not the Unbelievers for Friends." *Al-Jihadul Akbar* (Spring 1400 A.H.; 1980): 13–14, 23–26.

Karon, Bertram. *The Negro Personality*. New York: Springer, 1958.

Karpat, Kemal H. "The Ottoman Emigration to America, 1860–1914." *International Journal of Middle Eastern Studies* 17 (1985): 180–181.

Katz, Daniel, and Kenneth W. Braly. "Racial Stereotypes of 100 College Students." *Journal of Abnormal and Social Psychology*, 28 (1933): 280–290.

———. "Racial Prejudice and Racial Stereotypes." *Journal of Abnormal and Social Psychology* 30 (1935): 175–193.

Katz, Steve. "The 'Conservative' Character of Mysticism." In Steven Katz, ed., *Mysticism and Religious Traditions*, pp. 3–61. New York: Oxford, 1983.

Kayal, Philip. "Religion and Assimilation; Catholic 'Syrians' in America." *International Migration Review* 7 (1973): 409–426.

———. *Roots of Revolution: An Interpretative History of Modern Iran.* New Haven, Conn.: Yale University Press, 1981.

———. *An Islamic Response to Imperialism.* Berkeley and Los Angeles: University of California Press, 1983.

Kelley, Ron. "The Workers Speak." *Sojourners and Settlers: The Yemeni Immigrant Experience*, ed. J. Friedlander. Salt Lake City: University of Utah Press, 1988.

Keyder, C. "The Dissolution of the Asiatic Mode of Production." *Economy and Society* 5 (1976): 178–196.

Latham, Frank B. *The Dred Scott Decision, March 6, 1857: Slavery and the Supreme Court's "Self-Inflicted Wound".* New York: Franklin Watts, 1968.

Lawton, John. "Red Crescent: Symbol of Mercy." *ARAMCO World Magazine* 28, no. 2 (1977): 6.

Lenski, Gerhard. *The Religious Factor: A Sociological Study of Religious Impact upon Politics, Economics and Family Life.* New York: Doubleday and Co., 1961.

Lewins, Frank W. "Religion and Ethnic Identity." In *Identity and Religion*, ed. Hans Mol. London: Sage Publishers, 1978.

Lewis, Bernard. *The Emergence of Modern Turkey*, 2d ed. London: Oxford University Press.

———. *Istanbul and the Civilization of the Ottoman Empire.* Norman: University of Oklahoma Press, 1963.

Lieberson, Stanley, and Mary C. Water. *From Many Strands: Ethnic and Racial Groups in Contemporary America.* New York: Russell Sage Foundation, 1988.

Light, Ivan, and Edna Bonacich. *Immigrant Entrepreneurs: Koreans in Los Angeles 1965–1982.* Berkeley: University of California Press, 1988.

Lincoln, Eric C. *The Black Muslims in America.* Boston: Beacon Press, 1961.

———. "The American Muslim Mission in the Context of American Social History." In *The Muslim Community in North America*, ed. Earle Waugh, Baha Abu-Laban, and Regula Quereshi. Edmonton: The University of Alberta Press, 1983.

———. "The American Muslim Mission in the Context of American Social History." *African American Religious Studies*, ed. G. Wilmore. Durham, N.C.: Duke University Press, 1989.

Lord Kinross. *Ataturk: A Biography of Mustafa Kemal, Father of Modern Turkey*. New York: William Morrow and Company, 1965.

Luarisi, Kristo. *Diterefenjesi (Kalendari) Kombiar per 1898*. Sofia, Bulgaria: Mbrothesija, 1898.

———. *Kalendari Kombiar 1902*. Sofia, Bulgaria: Mbrothesija, 1902.

———. *Kalendari Kombiar 1909*. Sofia, Bulgaria: Mbrothesija, 1909.

———. *Kalendari Kombiar 1914*. Sofia, Bulgaria: Mbrothesija, 1914.

Lynch, Hollis. *Edward Wilmot Blyden. Pan-Negro Patriot*. London: Oxford University Press, 1967.

Mahaiyaddeen, Bawa. *Asma' ul-Husna. The 99 Beautiful Names of Allah*. Philadelphia: Fellowship Press, 1979.

Malcolm X. "God's Judgement of White America." In *The End of White World Supremacy*, ed. B. Karim. New York: Seaver Books, 1971.

Mamiya, Lawrence H. "From Black Muslim to Bilalian. The Evolution of a Movement." *Journal for the Scientific Study of Religion* 2, no. 6 (June 1982).

———. "Minister Louis Farrakhan and the Final Call: Schism in the Muslim Movement." *The Muslim Community in North America*, ed. Earle Waugh, Baha Abu-Laban, and Regula Quereshi. Edmonton: University of Alberta Press, 1983.

M. Martin and B. Voorhies. *Female of the Species*, pp. 296–300. New York: Columbia University Press, 1975.

Maudoodi, Abul Ala. *The Islamic Law and Constitution*. Karachi: Jamaat-e-Islami Publications, 1955.

Min, Pyong Gap. "Some Positive Functions of Ethnic Business for an Immigrant Community: Koreans in Los Angeles." Final report submitted to the National Science Foundation, 1989.

Mirdel, G. "Stress and Distress in Migration: Turkish Women in Denmark." In Women in Migration, *International Migration Review* 18, no. 4 (1982): 984–1003.

Morris, James. "Situating Islamic Mysticism: Between Written Traditions and Popular Spirituality." In Robert Herrera, ed., *Mystics of the Book: Themes and Typologies*. New York: Peter Lang Publishing, 1992.

Moses, Wilson J. *The Golden Age of Black Nationalism*. New York and Oxford: Oxford University Press, 1978.

Muhaiyaddeedn, Bawa. *God. His Prophets and His Children*. Philadelphia: Fellowship Press, 1978.

———. *Sheikh and Disciple*. Philadelphia: Fellowship Press, 1983.

———. *Islam and World Peace*. Philadelphia: Fellowship Press, 1987.

Muhajir, Ali Musa Raza. *The Tenets of Islam*. Lahore: Sh. Muhammad Ashraf, 1969.

Muhammad, Abdul-Rauf. *Bilal Ibn Rabah*. Indianapolis: American Trust Publications, 1977.

Muhammad, Akbar. "Muslims in the United States." In *The Islamic Impact*, ed. Yvonne Yazbeck Haddad et al. Syracuse, N.Y.: Syracuse University Press, 1984.

Muhammad, Ayesha, ed. *Focus on al-Islam: Interviews with W. Deen Muhammad*. Chicago: Zakat Publications, 1988.

Muhammad, Elijah. *Message to the Blackman*. Chicago: Muhammad's Temple No. 2, 1965.

_____. *The Fall of America*. Chicago: Muhammad's Temple of Islam No. 2, 1973.

_____. *The Flag of Islam*. Chicago: Muhammad's Temple of Islam No. 2, 1974.

_____. *Our Saviour Has Arrived*. Chicago: Muhammad's Temple of Islam No. 2, 1974.

Muhammad, Tynetta. *The Comer by Night*. Chicago: Honorable Elijah Muhammad Educational Foundation, 1986.

Muhammad, Warith D. (Wallace, Warithuddin). *Challenges That Face Man Today*. Chicago: W. D. Muhammad Publications, 1985.

_____. *Focus on Al-Islam*. Chicago: Zakat Publications, 1988.

Myntti, C. "Yemen Workers Abroad: The Impact on Women." *MERIP Report* 124 (1984): 11–16.

Naff, Alixa. *Becoming American: The Early Arab Immigrant Experience*. Carbondale: Southern Illinois University Press, 1985.

Nagel, Joane. "The Conditions of Ethnic Separatism: The Kurds in Turkey, Iran and Iraq." *Ethnicity* 7 (1980): 279–297.

Nagi, Dennis. *The Albanian-American Odyssey: A Pilot Study of the Albanian Community of Boston, Massachusetts*. New York: AMS Press, 1989.

Nasr, Seyyed Hossein. *Three Muslim Sages*. Delmar, N.Y.: Caravan, 1976.

_____. *Sufi Essays*. New York: Schocken Books, 1977.

_____. *Islamic Spirituality: Foundations*. New York: Crossroads Press, 1989.

Nelsen, Hart M., and David H. Allen. "Ethnicity, Americanization, and Religious Attendance," *American Journal of Sociology* 79 (1974): 906–922.

Noli, Fan S. *Historia e Skenderbeut*. Boston: Federata Pan-Shqiptare Vatra, 1950.

Nu'man, Imam Muhammad. *What Every American Should Know About Islam and the Muslims*. Jersey City, N.J.: New Mind Publications, 1985.

O'Reilly, Kenneth. "The Only Good Panther." *Racial Matters: The F.B.I.'s Secret Files on Black America. 1960–1972*. New York: The Free Press, 1989.

Orfelea, G. *Before the Flames*. Austin: University of Texas Press, 1988.

Oschinsky, Lawrence. "Islam in Chicago: Being a Study of the Acculturation of a Muslim Palestinian Community in That City." Ph.D. diss., University of Chiacgo, 1952.

Ottley, Roi. *New World A-Coming*, pp. 56. Reprint of 1943 ed., New York: Arno Press and The New York Times, 1968.

Pélchat, Martin. "Pèlerinage à la mosquée, angle St. Laurent-Maisonneuve." *Le Matin M* (March 10, 1987).

Perry, Bruce, ed. *Malcolm X: The Last Speeches*. New York: Pathfinder, 1989.

Peters, E. "Aspects of Rank and Status Among Muslims in a Lebanese Village." In *Mediterranean Countrymen*, ed. J. Pitt-Rivers, pp. 27–80. Paris: Mouton, 1963.

Quataert, Donald. *Social Disintegration and Popular Resistance in the Ottoman Empire, 1881–1908: Reactions to European Economic Penetration*. New York: New York University Press, 1983.

al-Qushayri, al-Nisaburi, Muslim ibn al-Hajjaj ibn Muslim. *Sahih Muslim*, trans. Abdul Hamid Siddiqi. India: Academy of Islamic Research and Publications, n.d.

Raboteau, Albert J. *Slave Religion*. Oxford: Oxford University Press, 1978.

Rahman, Fazlur. *Major Themes of the Quran*. Chicago: Bibliotheca Islamica, 1980.

Ramsauer, Ernest Edmonson, Jr. *The Young Turks: Prelude to the Revolution of 1908*. Princeton, N.J.: Princeton University Press, 1957.

Rankin, Lois. "Detroit Nationality Groups." *Michigan History Magazine* 23 (1939): 165.

Rauf, Muhammad Andrea. "Islam and Islamic Institutions in North America." *Impact* 6–77 (April 9–22, 1976).

Redkey, Edwin S. *Black Exodus*. New Haven, Conn., and London: Yale University Press, 1969.

Roby, Jeff. "The Rainbow in 1984: The Jackson-Farrakhan Alliance." *The Honorable Louis Farrakhan: A Minister for Progress*. New York: New Alliance Productions, 1987.

Rugh, Andrea. "Women and Work: Strategies and Choices in a Lower Class Quarter of Cairo." In *Women and the Family in the Middle East*, ed. E. Fernea, p. 279. Austin: University of Texas Press, 1985.

Russo, Nicholas J. "Three Generations of Italians in New York City: Their Religious Acculturation." *International Migration Review* 3 (1969): 3–17.

Sabagh, Georges, and Mehdi Bozorgmehr. "Are the Characteristics of Exiles Different from Immigrants? The Case of Iranians in Los Angeles." *Sociology and Social Research* 71 (1987): 77–84.

Sachedina, Abdulaziz. *Islamic Messianism: The Idea of the Mahdi in Twelver Shi'ism.* Albany: State University of New York Press, 1981.

Sachedina, Abdulaziz. *The Just Ruler in Shi'ite Islam: The Comprehensive Authority of the Jurist in Imamite Jurisprudence.* New York: Oxford University Press, 1988.

Saliba, Najibe. "Emigration from Syria." in *Arabs in the New World: Studies on Arab-American Communities,* ed. Sameer Y. Abraham and Nabeel Abraham. Detroit: Wayne State University, Center for Urban Studies, 1983.

Schimmel, AnnMarie. *Mystical Dimensions of Islam.* Chapel Hill: University of North Carolina Press, 1975.

_____. *As Through A Veil, Mystical Poetry in Islam.* New York: Columbia University Press, 1982.

Sengstock, Mary. *Chaldean Americans: Changing Conception of Ethnic Identity.* Staten Island, N.Y.: Center for Migration Studies, 1982.

Shaheen, Ghazala, and Cecilia Gonzales. "Clothing Practices of Pakistani Women Residing in Canada." *Canadian Ethnic Studies* 13, no. 3 (1981).

Sharif, Sidney R. *The African American (Bilalian) Image in Crisis.* Jersey City, N.J.: New Mind Productions, 1985.

Sharot, Stephen. "The Three-Generatios Thesis and American Jews." *British Journal of Sociology* 24 (1973): 151–164.

Shaw, Stanford J., and Ezel K. Shaw. *History of the Ottoman Empire and Modern Turkey,* Vol. 2. *Reform, Revolution, and Republic: The Rise of Modern Turkey, 1808–1975.* New York: Cambridge University Press, 1977.

Shiek Daoud Ahmed Faisal. *Islam the True Faith: The Religion of Humanity.* New York: Author, 1965.

Siddiqi, Amir Hasan. *Origins and Development of Islamic Institutions.* Karachi: Jamiyat al-Fallah, 1962.

Silberman, Charles E. *Criminal Violence, Criminal Justice.* New York: Vintage Books, 1978.

Simpson, John. "Ethnic Groups and Church Attendance in the United States and Canada." In *Ethnicity,* ed. Andrew W. Greeley and Gregory Baum. New York: Seabury Press, 1977.

Skendi, S. "Begginings of Albanian Nationalist and Autonomous Trends: The Albanian League: 1878–1881." *American Slavic and East European Review* 12 (1953): 219–232.

_____. "Beginnings of Albanian Nationalist Trends in Culture and Education (1878–1912)." *Journal of Central European Affairs* 12 (1953): 356–367.

Skendi, Stavro. *Albania.* New York: Frederick Praeger, 1956.

————. *The Albanian National Awakening: 1878–1912.* Princeton, N.J.: Princeton University Press, 1967.

Smitherman, Geneva. *Talkin' and Testifyin':* *The Language of Black America.* Boston: Houghton Mifflin, 1977.

al-Suhrawardi, Umar ibn Muhammad. ʿAwarif al-Maʾarif, trans. H. Wilberforce. Lahore: Sh. Muhammad Ashraf, 1973.

Sutherland, James Kay. *The Adventures of an Armenian Boy.* Ann Arbor, Mich.: The Ann Arbor Press, 1964.

al-Tahir, Abdul Jalil. "The Arab Community in Chicago Area, A Comparative Study of the Christian-Syrians and the Muslim-Palestinians." Ph.D. dissertation, University of Chicago, 1947.

Talmon, Yonina. "Millenarianism," *International Encyclopedia of the Social Sciences.* New York: Crowell, Collier and Macmillan, 1968.

Trix, Frances. "The Asure Ceremony of the Bektashi Tekke of Taylor, Michigan." M.A. thesis, The University of Michigan, 1972.

Vatra. *Albumi Dyzetviecar ne Amerike: 1906–1946 i Hiresise Tij Peshkop Fan S. Noli.* Boston: Federata Vatra, 1948.

————. "Anniversary Album of Pan-Albanian Federation of America for the Years 1953–1954." Boston: Vatra, 1955.

Vehbi, Imam Ismail, ed. "Jeta Muslimane Shqiptare." *Albanian-English Religious Review* 1, no. 1 (October, 1949).

————, ed. "Jeta Muslimane Shqiptare," *Albanian-English Religious Review* 1, no. 4 (October, 1950).

Walbridge, Linda. "Shi'i Islam in an American Community." Ph.D. dissertation, Wayne State University, 1991.

Wasfi, A. "Dearborn Arab Moslem Community." Ph.D. dissertation, Michigan State University, 1984.

Water, Mary C. *Ethnic Options: Choosing Identities in America.* Berkely and Los Angeles: University of California Press, 1990.

Watt, W. Montgomery. *Muhammad at Medina.* New York: Oxford University Press, 1956.

Waugh, Earle. "The Imam in the New World: Models and Modifications." In *Transitions and Transformations in the History of Religion,* ed. F. E. Reynolds and S. N. Ludwig, pp. 125–149. Leiden: E. J. Brill, 1980.

————. "Muslim Leadership and the Shaping of the Ummah: Classical Traditon and Religious Tension in the North American Setting." In Earle Waugh et al., eds., *The Muslim Community in North America.* Edmonton: University of Alberta Press, 1983.

————. *The Munshidin of Egypt: Their World and Their Song.* Columbia: University of South Carolina Press, 1988.

————, Baha Abu-Laban, and Regula Qureshi. *Muslim Families in North America.* Edmonton: University of Alberta Press, 1991.

Webb, Gisela. "The Human/Angelic Relation in the Philosophies of Suhrawardi and Ibn 'Arabi." Ph.D. Disseration, Temple University, 1989.

Whitman, Sidney. *Turkish Memories*. New York: Charles Scribner's Sons, 1914.

Wiggle, Laura D. "An Arab Muslim Community in Mighigan." In *Arab Speaking Communities in American Cities*, ed. Barbara C. Aswad, pp. 155–168. Staten Island, N.Y.: Center for Migration Studies, 1974.

Williams, Raymond. *Religions of Immigrants from India and Pakistan*. New York: Cambridge University Press, 1988.

Yahya, Hasan A. Qader. "Factors Influencing the Satisfaction of Muslim Organizational Members in a University Town in the United States (Lansing, Michigan)." In *Arab Speaking Communities in Amerian Cities*, ed. Barbara C. Aswad, pp. 155–168. Staten Island, N.Y.: Center for Migration Studies, 1974.

al-Yami, H. "A Study of an Ethnic Group: The Yemeni Community in the South End, Dearborn, Michigan." M.A. thesis, Michigan State University, 1984.

Yinger, J. Milton. "Ethnicity." *Annual Review of Sociology* 11 (1985): 151–180.

Zaheer Uddin. "Did '80s Teach Us Anything? An Overview of Islam in North America." *The Message International* 13, no. 8 (January 1990).

INDEX

535